# GRUBER'S
## COMPLETE
# PSAT/
# NMSQT*
## GUIDE 2011

*PSAT and NMSQT are registered trademarks of the College Entrance Examination Board
and National Merit Scholarship Corporation. Neither the College Entrance Examination
Board nor NMSC are associated with this book, nor do they endorse it.

## GARY R. GRUBER, PhD

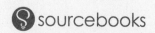

Published by Sourcebooks, Inc.
P.O. Box 4410, Naperville, Illinois 60567-4410
(630) 961-3900
Fax: (630) 961-2168
www.sourcebooks.com

Library of Congress Cataloging-in-Publication Data is on file with the publisher.

Printed and bound in the United States of America.
DR 10 9 8 7 6 5 4 3 2 1

# Recent and Forthcoming Study Aids from Dr. Gary Gruber Include:

*Gruber's Complete SAT Guide 2011*

*Gruber's SAT 2400*

*Gruber's Complete SAT Math Workbook*

*Gruber's Complete SAT Reading Workbook*

*Gruber's Complete SAT Writing Workbook*

*Gruber's SAT Word Master*

*Gruber's Complete ACT Guide 2010*

*Gruber's Essential Guide to Test Taking: Grades 6–9*

*Gruber's Essential Guide to Test Taking: Grades 3–5*

www.sourcebooks.com

www.drgarygruber.com

# Welcome to *Gruber's Complete PSAT/NMSQT Guide 2011*

The PSAT is great practice for the SAT, which contains the same type of questions. You can also compete for a National Merit Scholarship if you get really good scores on the PSAT. In fact, there is a unique test in this book that will tell you if you have a good chance of qualifying for the scholarship! But—please—make sure that after you take the PSAT, you get your exam back with your answers. You can obtain the test about two months after you take it. Once you get the test back, you can go over the test and make sure you used the strategies and other material in this book. If you're taking the SAT in the next year after you have taken the PSAT, get *Gruber's Complete SAT Guide* for complete preparation for the SAT. Having already read through my PSAT book, and then using my Complete SAT Guide, you'll reinforce all the strategies and skills and be completely prepared for the SAT.

What I want to do for you is get you to look at problems and questions and know exactly how to extract something important from them that leads you to the next step and then to the answer—without any panic or brain-racking. The material in this book should help you develop a passion for problem solving so that you will find the test interesting, as if you were looking at interesting puzzles rather than trying to figure out the answer to problems you couldn't care less about. After you learn and use the material in this book, the hard problems should become a lot easier and the less difficult problems should become really easy.

# Important Note About This Book and Its Author

This book is the most up-to-date and complete book on the current PSAT. EVERY EXAM is patterned after the PSAT, and *all* the strategies and techniques deal with the PSAT. The PSAT incorporates all the Gruber Critical-Thinking Strategies.

This book was written by Dr. Gary Gruber, the leading authority on standard tests such as the SAT, PSAT, and ACT, who knows more than anyone else in the test-prep market exactly what is being tested for in the PSAT. In fact, the procedures to answer the PSAT questions rely more heavily on the Gruber Critical-Thinking Strategies than ever before, and this is the only book that has the exact thinking strategies you need to use to maximize your PSAT score. Gruber's SAT books are used more than any other books by the nation's school districts and are proven to get the highest documented school district SAT scores.

Dr. Gruber has published more than 35 books with major publishers on test-taking and critical-thinking methods, with over 7 million copies sold. He has also authored over 1,000 articles on his work in scholarly journals and nationally syndicated newspapers, has appeared on numerous television and radio shows, and has been interviewed in hundreds of magazines and newspapers. He has developed major programs for school districts and for city and state educational agencies for improving and restructuring curriculum, increasing learning ability and test scores, increasing motivation and developing a "passion" for learning and problem solving, and decreasing the student dropout rate. For example, PBS (Public Broadcasting System) chose Dr. Gruber to train the nation's teachers on how to prepare students for the PSAT and SAT through a national satellite teleconference and videotape. His results have been lauded by people throughout the country from all walks of life.

Dr. Gruber is recognized nationally as the leading expert on standardized tests. It is said that no one in the nation is better at assessing the thinking patterns of *how* a person answers questions and providing the mechanism to improve the faulty thinking approaches. SAT score improvements by students using Dr. Gruber's techniques have been the highest in the nation.

Gruber's unique methods have been and are being used by the Public Broadcasting Service (PBS), by the nation's learning centers, by international encyclopedias, by school districts throughout the country, in homes and workplaces across the nation, and by a host of other entities.

His goal and mission is to get people's potential realized and the nation impassioned with learning and problem solving so that they don't merely try to get a "fast" uncritical answer, but actually enjoy and look forward to solving the problem and learning.

For more information on Gruber courses and additional Gruber products, visit: www.drgarygruber.com.

**Important:** Many books do not reflect the current PSAT questions. Don't practice with questions that misrepresent the actual questions on the PSAT. For example, the math questions created by the test makers are oriented to allow someone to solve many problems without a calculator as fast as with one, and some faster without a calculator. This book reflects the PSAT more accurately than any other commercial book, and the strategies contained in it are exactly those needed for taking the PSAT. It is said that only Dr. Gruber has the expertise and ability to reflect the exam far more closely than any competitor! Don't trust your future with less than the best material.

# The Author Has Something Important to Tell You About How to Raise Your PSAT Score

## What Are Critical-Thinking Skills?

First of all, I believe that intelligence can be taught. Intelligence, simply defined, is the aptitude or ability to reason things out. I am convinced that *you can learn* to *think logically* and figure things out better and faster, *particularly in regard to PSAT Math and Verbal problems.* But someone must give you the tools. Let us call these tools *strategies.* And that's what Critical-Thinking Skills are all about—*strategies.*

## Learn the Strategies to Get More Points

The Critical-Thinking Skills (beginning on page 41) will sharpen your reasoning ability so that you can increase your score dramatically on each part of the PSAT.

These Critical-Thinking Skills—5 General Strategies, 19 Math Strategies, and 13 Verbal Strategies—course right through this book. The Explanatory Answers for the 3 Practice Tests in the book direct you to those strategies that may be used to answer specific types of PSAT questions. We can readily prove that the strategies in Part 3 of this book are usable for more than 90 percent of the questions that will appear on the PSAT. *Each additional correct answer gives you approximately 1 point.* It is obvious, then, that your *learning* and *using* the 32 easy-to-understand strategies in this book will very likely raise your PSAT score substantially.

## Are the Practice Tests in This Book Like an Actual PSAT?

If you compare any one of the 3 Practice Tests in this book with an actual PSAT, you will find the book test very much like the *actual* test in regard to *format, question types,* and *level of difficulty.* Compare our book tests with any one of the official PSAT tests.

## Building Your Vocabulary Can Make a Big Difference on Your Test

Although antonyms no longer appear on the PSAT, Vocabulary will still be tested, especially in Sentence Completions and Reading Comprehension. This book includes three vital sections to build your vocabulary:

1. The Vocabulary Strategies, p. 105
2. The Hot Prefixes and Roots, p. 108
3. The Most Important/Frequently Used PSAT Words, p. 116

## Study the Hot Prefixes and Roots

We have developed a list of hot roots and prefixes that can help you determine the meaning of more than 110,000 words. Learning all of them will increase your vocabulary immensely.

## Study the Most Important/Frequently Used PSAT/SAT Words

We have developed a list of the most frequently used words and their opposites related to specific categories for easy memorization. Study these words.

## Study the Mini-Math Refresher

If you believe you are weak in the basic math skills area, study the Mini-Math Refresher. The material in this section is keyed to the Complete Math Refresher section for more complete instruction.

## Take the 101 Most Important Math Questions Test

To determine weak basic math skills areas, take the 101 Most Important Math Questions Test and look at the solutions to the questions. The questions are keyed to the Complete Math Refresher so you can further brush up on your weak areas by referring to those pages in the Complete Math Refresher part for those questions you missed.

## The Explanatory Answers to Questions Are Keyed to Specific Strategies and Basic Skills

The Explanatory Answers in this book are far from skimpy—so unlike those of other PSAT books. Our detailed answers will direct you to the strategy that will help you arrive at a correct answer quickly. In addition, the Math solutions in the book refer directly to the Math Refresher section, particularly useful in case your Math skills are rusty.

## Lift That PSAT Score

By using the material in this book—that is, by taking the tests, learning the specific strategies, refreshing your basic skills, etc., as described above—you should increase your PSAT score substantially.

**—Gary Gruber**

# Contents

**INTRODUCTION**        xiii

I.      Important Facts About the PSAT / xiv

II.     The Inside Track on How PSAT Questions Are Developed and How They Vary from Test to Test / xxi

III.    What Are Critical-Thinking Skills? / xxii

IV.    Strategies for Women / xxiv

V.      Multi-Level Approaches to the Solution of Problems / xxv

VI.    A Four-Hour Study Program for the PSAT / xxviii

VII.   Longer-Range Study Program and Helpful Steps for Using This Book / xxix

VIII.  Format of the PSAT / xxx

## PART 1

## DO YOU HAVE A GOOD CHANCE OF WINNING A NATIONAL MERIT SCHOLARSHIP?     1

Critical Reading / 2

Math / 4

Writing Skills / 5

Answers / 6

Scoring / 7

Explanatory Answers for the National Merit Scholarship Diagnostic Test / 8

## PART 2

## THE 101 MOST IMPORTANT MATH QUESTIONS YOU NEED TO KNOW HOW TO SOLVE     13

101 Math Questions Answer Sheet / 14

101 Math Questions Test / 16

101 Math Questions: Answers, Diagnosis, Solutions, Generalizations, Rules / 27

101 Math Questions: Answers / 28

Basic Skills Math Diagnosis / 30

Solutions, Generalizations, Rules / 31

## PART 3

## STRATEGY SECTION
41

5 General Strategies / 42

32 Easy-to-Learn Strategies / 44

How to Learn the Strategies / 44

Important Note on the Allowed Use of Calculators on the PSAT / 44

Important Note on Math Questions on the PSAT / 45

The Grid-Type Math Question / 45

Practice with Grids / 47

Answers / 48

Use of a Calculator in the Grid-Type Question / 49

19 Math Strategies / 51

Critical Reading Strategies / 80

4 Sentence Completion Strategies / 81

Introduction to Passage Reading / 87

Summary / 94

6 Reading Comprehension Strategies / 95

3 Vocabulary Strategies / 105

Hot Prefixes and Roots / 108

Words Commonly Mistaken for Each Other / 113

The Most Important/Frequently Used PSAT Words and Their Opposites / 116

## PART 4

## MINI-MATH REFRESHER
119

Algebra and Arithmetic / 120

Geometry / 123

## PART 5

## COMPLETE PSAT MATH REFRESHER
129

**Session 1—Fractions, Decimals, Percentages, Deviations, Ratios and Proportions, Variations, and Comparison of Fractions / 131**

Fractions, Decimals, Percentages / 132

Deviations / 135

Ratios and Proportions / 136

Variations / 136

Comparison of Fractions / 137

Practice Test 1 / 140

Answer Key for Practice Test 1 / 149

Answers and Solutions for Practice Test 1 / 149

**Session 2—Rate Problems / 153**

Word Problem Setup / 154

Distance and Time / 156

Work / 157

Mixture / 157

Cost / 158

Practice Test 2 / 159

Answer Key for Practice Test 2 / 168

Answers and Solutions for Practice Test 2 / 168

**Session 3—Area, Perimeter, and Volume Problems / 178**

Area, Perimeter, and Volume / 179

Practice Test 3 / 187

Answer Key for Practice Test 3 / 196

Answers and Solutions for Practice Test 3 / 196

**Session 4—Algebra Problems / 202**

Algebraic Properties / 203

Fundamental Laws of Our Number System / 203

Algebraic Expressions / 204

Equations / 204

Algebra of Graphs / 206

Inequalities / 213

Exponents and Roots / 218

Practice Test 4 / 219

Answer Key for Practice Test 4 / 227

Answers and Solutions for Practice Test 4 / 227

**Session 5—Geometry Problems / 232**

Basic Definitions / 233

Triangles / 235

Properties of Triangles / 236

Four-Sided Figures / 239

Many-Sided Figures / 240

Circles / 240

Practice Test 5 / 243

Answer Key for Practice Test 5 / 251

Answers and Solutions for Practice Test 5 / 251

**Session 6—Miscellaneous Problems / 261**

Averages, Medians, and Modes / 262

Properties of Integers / 263

Approximations / 265

Combinations / 266

Probability / 267

The Absolute Value Sign / 267

Functions / 267

Practice Test 6 / 268

Answer Key for Practice Test 6 / 276

Answers and Solutions for Practice Test 6 / 276

**Session 7—Tables, Charts, and Graphs / 281**

Charts and Graphs / 282

Tables and Charts / 282

Graphs / 283

Bar Graphs / 283

Circle Graphs / 284

Line Graphs / 285

Practice Test 7 and Solutions / 286

**Session 8—Modern Math / 291**

Sets / 292

Relations / 293

Solution Sets / 293

Axioms / 294

Closed Sets / 294

Mathematical Symbols / 294

Practice Test 8 and Solutions / 295

<u>PART 6</u>

# THE PSAT WRITING SKILLS TEST 303

Types of Questions on the PSAT Writing Test / 304

Identifying Errors / 304

Sample Questions with Answers / 304

Improving Sentences / 307

Sample Questions with Answers / 307

Explanatory Answers / 309

Improving Paragraphs / 311

    Sentence Order / 311

    Diction / 313

    Sentence Relationship / 314

Irrelevancy / 315

Economy / 316

Clarity / 317

Paragraphing / 319

## PART 7

# A BRIEF REVIEW OF ENGLISH GRAMMAR      321

Frequent Grammatical Problems / 322

Correct Usage: Choosing the Right Word / 330

## PART 8

# THREE PSAT PRACTICE TESTS      335

Five Important Reasons for Taking These Practice Tests / 336

10 Tips for Taking the Practice Tests / 337

Answer Sheet for Practice Test 1 / 339

**PSAT Practice Test 1 / 342**

How Did You Do on This Test? / 370

Answer Key for Practice Test 1 / 371

PSAT Score Conversion Table / 375

PSAT/NMSQT Percentiles and Mean Scores / 376

National Merit Scholarship Selection Index Percentiles and Mean Score / 377

Explanatory Answers for PSAT Practice Test 1 / 378

What You Must Do Now to Raise Your PSAT Score / 399

Answer Sheet for Practice Test 2 / 401

**PSAT Practice Test 2 / 404**

How Did You Do on This Test? / 434

Answer Key for Practice Test 2 / 435

PSAT Score Conversion Table / 439

PSAT/NMSQT Percentiles and Mean Scores / 440

National Merit Scholarship Selection Index Percentiles and Mean Score / 441

Explanatory Answers for PSAT Practice Test 2 / 442

What You Must Do Now to Raise Your PSAT Score / 459

Answer Sheet for Practice Test 3 / 461

**PSAT Practice Test 3 / 464**

How Did You Do on This Test? / 492

Answer Key for Practice Test 3 / 493

PSAT Score Conversion Table / 497

PSAT/NMSQT Percentiles and Mean Scores / 498

National Merit Scholarship Selection Index Percentiles and Mean Score / 499

Explanatory Answers for PSAT Practice Test 3 / 500

What You Must Do Now to Raise Your PSAT Score / 518

# INTRODUCTION

# I. Important Facts About the PSAT

## What Is the PSAT and What Is It Used For?

The PSAT/NMSQT is a 2 hour and 10 minute test that measures important skills for college success. It has two purposes—practice for the upcoming SAT for college entrance and to possibly obtain a National Merit Scholarship, which would certainly look pretty good on your record! The PSAT/NMSQT is very much like the SAT, but it is shorter and does not contain a Writing Sample as on the SAT. The test measures the same skills and has the same format, directions, and question types as the SAT. The approximate score of the SAT can be obtained by multiplying the PSAT score by 10.

Approximately 3.5 million students take the PSAT/NMSQT each year. Eleventh graders constitute the largest group of test-takers, and the remainder of participants are in the 10th and lower grades.

## What's on the PSAT/NMSQT?

The Test contains Five Sections.

**Note that the test measures students' ability to reason with facts and concepts and not just measure their ability to recall them. The three areas tested are:**

<u>Critical Reading:</u> Two 25-minute sections—48 questions

13 Sentence Completions; 35 Critical Reading questions

Abilities tested: Drawing inferences, synthesizing information;

<u>Math:</u> Two 25-minute sections—38 questions

28 multiple-choice questions; 10 student-produced grid-in questions

Abilities tested: Number and number operations, algebra, functions, geometry, coordinate geometry, measurement, data analysis, statistics, and probability. No third-year math that may appear on SAT.

<u>Writing:</u> One 30-minute section—39 questions

14 Identifying Sentence Errors
20 Improving Sentences
5 Improving Paragraph questions

Abilities tested: Expression of ideas effectively in standard written English, recognizing faults in grammar and usage; and using language to express meaning.

# How Will the Test Be Scored?

There will be a range of three scores each from 20–80 for the Writing, Math, and Critical Reading sections.

# How Long Will the Test Be?

The total time of the test will be 2 hours and 10 minutes.

# What Verbal Background Must I Have?

The reading and vocabulary level is at the 10th- to 12th-grade level, but strategies presented in this book will help you even if you are at a lower grade level.

# What Math Background Must I Have?

The Math part will test first- and second-year algebra (Algebra I and II) and geometry. However, if you use common sense, rely on just a handful of geometrical formulas, and learn the strategies and thinking skills presented in this book, you don't need to take a full course in geometry or memorize all the theorems. If you have not taken algebra, you should still be able to answer many of the math questions using the strategies presented in this book.

# Is Guessing Advisable?

Although there is a small penalty for wrong answers (¼ point for 5-choice questions), in the long run, you *break even* if you guess *or* leave the answer blank. For a full explanation of why, see p. 43, Strategy 3. So it really will not affect your score in the long run if you guess or leave answers out. And, if you can eliminate an incorrect choice, it is imperative that you do not leave the answer blank.

# Can I Use a Calculator on the Math Portion of the Test?

Students can use a four-function, scientific, or graphing calculator. While it is possible to solve every question without the use of a calculator, it is recommended that you use a calculator if you don't immediately see a faster way to solve the problem without a calculator.

# Should I Take an Administered Actual PSAT for Practice?

Yes, but only if you will learn from your mistakes by seeing what strategies you should have used on your exam. Taking the PSAT merely for its own sake is a waste of time and may in fact reinforce bad methods and habits. Note that the PSAT is released to students usually in January.

# Can I Get Back the PSAT with My Answers and the Correct Ones After I Take It? How Can I Make Use of This?

The PSAT is disclosed after the student takes it. Very few people take advantage of this fact or use the disclosed PSAT to see what mistakes they've made and what strategies they could have used on the questions.

## Should I Use Scrap Paper to Write on and to Do Calculations?

Always use your test booklet (not your answer sheet) to draw on. Many of my strategies expect you to label diagrams, draw and extend lines, circle important words and sentences, etc., so feel free to write anything in your booklet. The booklets aren't graded—just the answer sheets are (see General Strategy 4, page 43).

## Should I Be Familiar with the Directions to the Various Items on the PSAT Before Taking the PSAT?

Make sure you are completely familiar with the directions to each of the item types on the PSAT—the directions for answering the Sentence Completions, the Reading, the Writing, the Regular Math, and especially the Grid-Type (see General Strategy 2, page 42).

## What Should a Student Bring to the Exam on the Test Date?

You should bring a few sharpened #2 pencils with erasers, and also your ID.

Bring a calculator to the test, but be aware that every math question on the PSAT can be solved without a calculator; in many questions, it's actually easier not to use one.

Acceptable calculators: Graphing calculators, scientific calculators, and four-function calculators (the last is not recommended) are all permitted during testing. If you have a calculator with characters that are one inch or higher, or if your calculator has a raised display that might be visible to other test takers, you will be seated at the discretion of the test supervisor.

Unacceptable calculators: Laptops or portable/handheld computers; calculators that have a QWERTY keyboard, make noise, use an electrical outlet, or have a paper tape; electronic writing pads or stylus-driven devices; pocket organizers; and cell phone calculators will not be allowed during the test.

## How Should a Student Pace Himself/Herself on the Exam? How Much Time Should One Spend on Each Question?

Calculate the time allowed for the particular section. For example, 25 minutes. Divide by the number of questions. For example, 20. That gives you an average of spending 1¼ minutes per question in this example. However, the first set of questions within an item type in a section is easier, so spend less than a minute on the first set of questions and perhaps more than a minute on the last set. With the reading passages you should give yourself only about 30 seconds a question and spend the extra time on the reading passages. Also, more difficult reading questions may take more time.

## How Is the Exam Scored? Are Some Questions Worth More Points?

Each question is worth the same number of points. After getting a raw score—the number of questions right minus a penalty for wrong answers—this is equated to a "scaled" score from 20 to 80 in each of the Critical Reading, Math, and Writing sections. A scaled score of 50 in each part is considered average.

## It's 3 Days Until the PSAT; What Can a Student Do to Prepare?

Make sure you are completely familiar with the structure of the test (page xxx), the basic math skills needed (pages 119–127), and the basic verbal skills, such as prefixes and roots (pages 108–112). Take one practice test and refresh your understanding of the strategies used to answer the questions (see page xxviii for the Four-Hour Study Program).

## What Is the Most Challenging Type of Question on the Exam and How Does One Attack It?

Many questions on the test, especially at the end of a section, can be challenging. You should always attack challenging questions by using a specific strategy or strategies and common sense.

## What Should a Student Do to Prepare on Friday Night? Cram? Watch TV? Relax?

On Friday night, I would just refresh my knowledge of the structure of the test, some strategies, and refresh some basic skills (verbal or math). You want to do this to keep the thinking going so that it is continual right up to the exam. Don't overdo it; just do enough so that it's somewhat continuous—this will also relieve some anxiety, so that you won't feel you are forgetting things before the exam.

## The Test Is Given in One Booklet. Can a Student Skip Between Sections?

No—you cannot skip between the sections. You have to work on the section until the time is called. If you get caught skipping sections or going back to earlier sections, then you risk being asked to leave the exam.

## Should a Student Answer All Easy Questions First and Save Difficult Ones for Last?

The easy questions usually appear at the beginning of the section, the middle difficulty ones in the middle, and the hard ones toward the end. So I would answer the questions as they are presented to you, and if you find you are spending more than 30 seconds on a question and not getting anywhere, go to the next question. You may, however, find that the more difficult questions toward the end are actually easy for you because you have learned the strategies in this book.

## What Is the Recommended Course of Study for Those Retaking the Exam?

Get a copy of the exam that you took. Try to learn from your mistakes by seeing what strategies you could have used to get questions right. Certainly learn the specific strategies for taking your next exam.

## What Are the Most Crucial Strategies for Students?

All specific Verbal (Critical Reading) and Math Strategies are crucial, including the general test-taking strategies (described on pages 41–107), guessing, writing and drawing in your test booklet, and being familiar with question-type directions. The key Reading Strategy is to know the four general types of questions that are asked in reading—main idea, inference, specific details, and tone or mood. In math, it's the translations strategy—verbal to math, drawing of lines, etc. Also make sure you know the math basic skills cold (see pages 119–127 for these rules—*make sure you know them*).

## How Does the Gruber Preparation Method Differ from Other Programs and PSAT Books?

Many other PSAT programs try to use "quick fix" methods or subscribe to memorization. So-called quick fix methods can be detrimental to effective preparation because the PSAT people constantly change questions to prevent "gimmick" approaches. Rote memorization methods do not enable you to answer a variety of questions that appear on the PSAT. With more than thirty years of experience writing preparation books for the SAT, PSAT, ACT, and many other exams, Dr. Gruber has developed and honed the Critical-Thinking Skills and Strategies that are based on all standardized tests' construction. So, while his method immediately improves your performance on the PSAT, it also provides you with the confidence to tackle problems in all areas of study for the rest of your life. He remarkably enables you to be able to, without panic, look at a problem or question, extract something curious or useful from the problem, and lead you to the next step and finally to a solution, without rushing into a wrong answer or getting lured into a wrong choice. It has been said that test taking through his methodology becomes enjoyable rather than a pain.

# A Table of What's on the PSAT

| Math | |
|---|---|
| Time | 50 min. (two 25-min. sections) |
| Content | Multiple-Choice Items<br>Student-Produced Responses<br>Measuring:<br>Number and Operations<br>Algebra I and Functions<br>Geometry and Measurement; Statistics,<br>Probability, and Data Analysis |
| Score | 20–80 |
| **Critical Reading** | |
| Time | 50 min. (two 25-min. sections) |
| Content | Sentence Completion<br>Critical Reading: Short and Long<br>Reading Passages, with one Double<br>Long Passage and one Double Short<br>Passage |
| Score | 20–80 |
| **Writing** | |
| Time | 30 min. (one section) |
| Content | Multiple-Choice: Identifying Errors<br>Improving Sentences and Paragraphs<br>Measuring: Grammar, Usage, Word Choice |
| Score | 20–80 |

# A Table of What's on the SAT

| **Math** | |
| --- | --- |
| Time | 70 min. (two 25-min. sections, one 20-min. section) |
| Content | Multiple-Choice Items<br>Student-Produced Responses<br>Measuring:<br>Number and Operations<br>Algebra I, II, and Functions<br>Geometry, Statistics,<br>Probability, and Data Analysis |
| Score | M 200–800 |

| **Critical Reading** | |
| --- | --- |
| Time | 70 min. (two 25-min. sections, one 20-min. section) |
| Content | Sentence Completion<br>Critical Reading: Short and<br>Long Reading Passages with<br>one Double Long Passage and<br>one Double Short Passage |
| Score | CR 200–800 |

| **Writing** | |
| --- | --- |
| Time | 60 min. (25 min. essay, 35 min. multiple-choice in two sections) |
| Content | Multiple-Choice: Identifying Errors<br>Improving Sentences and Paragraphs<br>and Student-Written Essay; Effectively<br>Communicate a Viewpoint, Defining and<br>Supporting a Position |
| Score | W 200–800<br>Essay Subscore: 0–12<br>Multiple-Choice Subscore: 20–80 |

*Note:* There is an experimental section that does not count toward your SAT score. This section can contain any of the SAT item types (writing [multiple-choice], critical reading, or math) and can appear in any part of the test. Do not try to outguess the test maker by trying to figure out which of the sections is experimental on the actual test (believe me, you won't be able to)—treat every section as if it counts toward your SAT score.

# II. The Inside Track on How PSAT Questions Are Developed and How They Vary from Test to Test

When a question is developed, it is based on a set of criteria and guidelines. Knowing how these guidelines work should demystify the test-making process and convince you why the strategies in this book are so critical to getting a high score.

Inherent in the PSAT questions are Critical-Thinking Skills, which present strategies that enable you to solve a question by the quickest method with the least amount of panic and brain-racking, and describe an elegance and excitement in problem solving. Adhering to and using the strategies (which the test makers use to develop the questions) will let you sail through the PSAT. This is summed up in the following statement:

*Show me the solution to a problem, and I'll solve that problem. Show me a Gruber strategy for solving the problem, and I'll solve hundreds of problems.*

—Gary Gruber

Here's a sample of a set of guidelines presented for making up a PSAT-type question in the Math area:

The test maker is to make up a hard math problem in the regular math multiple-choice area, which involves

(A) algebra
(B) two or more equations
(C) two or more ways to solve: one way being standard substitution, the other faster way using the *strategy* of merely *adding* or *subtracting* equations.*

Previous examples given to test maker for reference:

1.  If $x + y = 3$, $y + z = 4$, and $z + x = 5$, find the value of $x + y + z$.

    (A) 4
    (B) 5
    (C) 6
    (D) 7
    (E) 8

**Solution:** *Add* equations and get $2x + 2y + 2z = 12$; divide both sides of the equation by 2 and we get $x + y + z = 6$. (Answer C)

2.  If $2x + y = 8$ and $x + 2y = 4$, find the value of $x - y$.

    (A) 3
    (B) 4
    (C) 5
    (D) 6
    (E) 7

**Solution:** *Subtract* equations and get $x - y = 4$. (Answer B)

*Here's an example from a recent test.*

If $y - x = 5$ and $2y + z = 11$, find the value of $x + y + z$.

    (A) 3
    (B) 6
    (C) 8
    (D) 16
    (E) 55

**Solution:** *Subtract* equation $y - x = 5$ from $2y + z = 11$. We get $2y - y + z - (-x) = 11 - 5$. So, $y + z + x = 6$. (Choice B)

* *Note:* See Math Strategy #13 on p. 68

# III. What Are Critical-Thinking Skills?

Critical-Thinking Skills, a current buzz phrase, are generic skills for the creative and most effective way of solving a problem or evaluating a situation. The most effective way of solving a problem is to extract some piece of information or observe something curious from the problem, then use one or more of the specific strategies or Critical-Thinking Skills (together with basic skills or information you already know) to get to the next step in the problem. This next step will catapult you toward a solution with further use of the specific strategies or thinking skills.

---

1. EXTRACT OR OBSERVE SOMETHING CURIOUS
2. USE SPECIFIC STRATEGIES TOGETHER WITH BASIC SKILLS

---

These specific strategies will enable you to "process" think rather than just be concerned with the end result, the latter which usually gets you into a fast, rushed, and wrong answer. The Gruber strategies have been shown to make one more comfortable with problem solving and make the process enjoyable. The skills will last a lifetime, and you will develop a passion for problem solving. These Critical-Thinking Skills show that conventional "drill and practice" is a waste of time unless the practice is based on these generic thinking skills.

Here's a simple example of how these Critical-Thinking Skills can be used in a math problem:

---

Which is greater, $7\frac{1}{7} \times 8\frac{1}{8} \times 6\frac{1}{6}$ or $8\frac{1}{8} \times 6\frac{1}{6} \times 7$?

---

**Long and tedious way:** Multiply $7\frac{1}{7} \times 8\frac{1}{8} \times 6\frac{1}{6}$ and compare it with $8\frac{1}{8} \times 6\frac{1}{6} \times 7$.

**Error in doing the problem the "long way":** You don't have to *calculate;* you just have to *compare,* so you need a *strategy* for *comparing* two quantities.

**Critical-Thinking Way:**  1.   *Observe:* There is a common $8\frac{1}{8}$ and $6\frac{1}{6}$

2.   *Use Strategy:* Since both $8\frac{1}{8}$ and $6\frac{1}{6}$ are just weighting factors, like the same quantities on both sides of a balance scale, just *cancel* them from both multiplied quantities above.

3.   You are then left comparing $7\frac{1}{7}$ with 7, so the first quantity, $7\frac{1}{7}$, is greater. Thus $7\frac{1}{7} \times 8\frac{1}{8} \times 6\frac{1}{6}$ is greater than $8\frac{1}{8} \times 6\frac{1}{6} \times 7$.

Here's a simple example of how Critical-Thinking Skills can be used for a Verbal problem:

If you see a word such as DELUDE in a sentence or in a reading passage, you can assume that the word DELUDE is negative and probably means "taking away from something" or "distracting," since the prefix DE means "away from" and thus has a negative connotation. Although you may not get the exact meaning of the word (in this case the meaning is to "deceive" or "mislead"), you can see how the word may be used in the context of the sentence it appears in, and thus get the flavor or feeling of the sentence, paragraph, or sentence completion. I have researched and developed a prefix and root list (present in this book) that can let you make use of this context strategy.

Notice that the Critical-Thinking approach gives you a fail-safe and exact way to the solution without superficially trying to solve the problem or merely guessing at it. This book contains all the Critical-Thinking Strategies you need to know for the PSAT test.

**Dr. Gruber has researched hundreds of PSAT tests (thousands of PSAT questions) and documented 37 Critical-Thinking Strategies (all found in this book) coursing through every test. These strategies can be used for any Math, Critical Reading, or Writing Skills problem.**

**In short, you can learn how to solve a specific problem and thus find how to answer that specific problem, or you can learn a powerful strategy that will enable you to answer hundreds of problems.**

# IV. Strategies for Women

These are questions that women found significantly more difficult than men, because women tend to rely on a more intuitive approach. However, *after* learning the strategies in this book, women scored just as high as men on these sections.

## Critical Reading

### Sentence Completion

Choose the word or set of words that when inserted in the sentence best fits the meaning of the sentence as a whole.

1. The most ____ means of transportation in the world is the bicycle; indeed, no powered vehicle requires less energy to move as much mass over the same distance.

   (A) grandiose
   (B) infallible
   (C) efficient
   (D) engrossing
   (E) unstable

2. The artistry of cellist Yo Yo Ma is essentially ____; the melodic line rises ____, imbued with feeling and totally lacking in apparent calculation.

   (A) carefree / stiffly
   (B) reserved / involuntarily
   (C) lyrical / passionately
   (D) detached / carefully
   (E) deliberate / methodically

## Math

1. Carol has twice as many books as Beverly has. After Carol gives Beverly 5 books, she still has 10 more books than Beverly has. How many books did Carol have originally?

   (A) 20   (B) 25   (C) 30   (D) 35   (E) 40

2. 
$$\begin{array}{r} 5\,\Delta\,2 \\ \times \qquad 9 \\ \hline 5,2\,\square\,2 \end{array}$$

   In the correctly computed multiplication problem above, if $\Delta$ and $\square$ are different digits, then $\Delta =$

   (A) 1   (B) 5   (C) 6   (D) 7   (E) 8

3. If $s$ equals $\frac{1}{2}$ percent of $t$, what percent of $s$ is $t$ ?

   (A) 2%  (B) 200%  (C) 2,000%  (D) 20,000%
   (E) 200,000%

*Answers, Strategy, and Page in Book for Questions:*

| ANSWER | STRATEGY | PAGE |
|---|---|---|
| **Verbal** | | |
| 1. C | Sentence Completion 1 | 81 |
| 2. C | Sentence Completion 2, 4 | 82, 85 |
| | | |
| **Math** | | |
| 1. E | Math 2 | 52 |
| 2. E | Math 8 | 62 |
| 3. D | Math 2 and 7 | 52, 61 |

# V. Multi-Level Approaches to the Solution of Problems

How a student answers a question is more important than the answer given by the student. For example, the student may have randomly guessed, the student may have used a rote and unimaginative method for solution, or the student may have used a very creative method. It seems that one should judge the student by the *way* he or she answers the question and not just by the answer to the question.

Example:

> **Question: Without using a calculator, which is greater:**
> **355 × 356 or 354 × 357?**

*Case 1:* **Rote Memory Approach** (a completely mechanical approach not realizing the fact that there may be a faster method that takes into account patterns or connections of the numbers in the question): The student multiplies 355 × 356, gets 126,380, and then multiplies 354 × 357 and gets 126,378.

*Case 2:* **Observer's Rote Approach** (an approach that makes use of a mathematical strategy that can be memorized and tried for various problems): The student does the following:
Divide both quantities by 354:
He or she then gets 355 × 356/354 compared with 354 × 357/354.
He or she then divides these quantities by 356 and then gets 355/354 compared with 357/356.
Now he or she realizes that 355/354 = 1 and 1/354; 357/356 = 1 and 1/356.
He or she then reasons that since the left side 1 and 1/354 is greater than the right side, 1 and 1/356, the left side of the original quantities, 355 × 356, is greater than the right side of the original quantities, 354 × 357.

*Case 3:* **The Pattern Seeker's Method** (most mathematically creative method—an approach in which the student looks for a pattern or sequence in the numbers and then is astute enough to represent the pattern or sequence in more general algebraic language to see the pattern or sequence more clearly):
Look for a pattern. Represent 355 × 356 and 354 × 357 by symbols.
Let $x = 354$.
Then $355 = x + 1, 356 = x + 2, 357 = x + 3$.
So $355 \times 356 = (x + 1)(x + 2)$ and $354 \times 357 = x(x + 3)$.
Multiplying the factors we get
$355 \times 356 = (x \text{ times } x) + 3x + 2$ and $354 \times 357 = (x \text{ times } x) + 3x$.
The difference: $355 \times 356 - 354 \times 357 = (x \text{ times } x) + 3x + 2$ minus $(x \text{ times } x)$ minus $3x$, which is just 2.
So 355 × 356 is greater than 354 × 357 by 2.

*Note:* You could have also represented 355 by $x$. Then $356 = x + 1$; $354 = x - 1$; $357 = x + 2$. We would then get $355 \times 356 = (x)(x + 1)$ and $354 \times 357 = (x - 1)(x + 2)$. Then we would use the method above to compare the quantities.
—OR—
You could have written 354 as $a$ and 357 as $b$. Then $355 = a + 1$ and $356 = b - 1$. So $355 \times 356 = (a + 1)(b - 1)$ and $354 \times 357 = ab$. Let's see what $(355 \times 356) - (354 \times 357)$ is. This is the same as $(a + 1)(b - 1) - ab$, which is $(ab + b - a - 1) - ab$, which is in turn $b - a - 1$. Since $b - a - 1 = 357 - 354 - 1 = 2$, the quantity $355 \times 356 - 354 \times 357 = 2$, so 355 × 356 is greater than 354 × 357 by 2.

*Case 4:* **The Astute Observer's Approach** (simplest approach—an approach that attempts to figure out a connection between the numbers and uses that connection to figure out the solution):

$355 \times 356 = (354 + 1) \times 356 = (354 \times 356) + 356$ and
$354 \times 357 = 354 \times (356 + 1) = (354 \times 356) + 354$
One can see that the difference is just 2.

*Case 5:* **The Observer's Common Relation Approach** (this is the approach that people use when they want to connect two items to a third to see how the two items are related):

$355 \times 356$ is greater than $354 \times 356$ by 356.
$354 \times 357$ is greater than $354 \times 356$ by 354.
So this means that $355 \times 356$ is greater than $354 \times 357$.

*Case 6:* **Scientific, Creative, and Observational Generalization Method** (a highly creative method and the most scientific method, as it spots a critical and curious aspect of the sums being equal and provides for a generalization to other problems of that nature):

Represent $354 = a$, $357 = b$, $355 = c$, and $356 = d$
We have now that (1) $a + b = c + d$
$\qquad\qquad\qquad$ (2) $|b - a| > |d - c|$
We want to prove: $ab < dc$
Proof:
Square inequality (2): $(b - a)^2 > (d - c)^2$
Therefore: (3) $b^2 - 2ab + a^2 > d^2 - 2dc + c^2$
Multiply (3) by $(-1)$ and this reverses the inequality sign:
$-(b^2 - 2ab + a^2) < -(d^2 - 2dc + c^2)$
or
(4) $-b^2 + 2ab - a^2 < -d^2 + 2dc - c^2$
Now square (1): $(a + b) = (c + d)$ and we get:
(5) $a^2 + 2ab + b^2 = c^2 + 2dc + d^2$
Add inequality (4) to equality (5) and we get:
$4ab < 4dc$
Divide by 4 and we get:
**$ab < dc$**
The generalization is that for any positive numbers $a$, $b$, $c$, $d$ when $|b - a| > |d - c|$ and $a + b = c + d$, then $ab < dc$.
This also generalizes in a geometrical setting where for two rectangles whose perimeters are the same ($2a + 2b = 2c + 2d$), the rectangle whose absolute difference in sides $|d - c|$ is <u>least</u> has the <u>greatest</u> area.

*Case 7:* **Geometric and Visual Approach\*:** (this is the approach used by visual people or people who have a curious geometric bent and possess "out-of-the-box" insights):

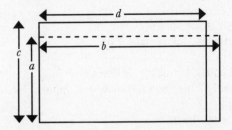

Where $a = 354$, $b = 357$, $c = 355$, and $d = 356$, we have two rectangles where the first one's length is $d$ and width is $c$, and the second one's length is $b$ (dotted line) and width is $a$.

Now the area of the first rectangle ($dc$) is equal to the area of the second ($ab$) minus the area of the rectangular slab, which is $(b - d)\, a$ plus the area of the rectangular slab $(c - a)d$. So we get: $cd = ab - (b - d)a + (c - a)d$. Since $b - d = c - a$, we get $cd = ab - (c - a)\, a + (c - a)d = ab + (d - a)(c - a)$.
Since $d > a$ and $c > a$, $cd > ab$. So $355 \times 356 > 354 \times 357$.

*\*This method of solution was developed by and sent to the author from Dr. Eric Cornell, a Nobel Laureate in Physics.*

*Note:* Many people have thought that by multiplying units digits from one quantity and comparing that with the multiplication of the units digits from the other quantity, they'd get the answer. For example, they would multiply $5 \times 6 = 30$ from $355 \times 356$ then multiply $4 \times 7 = 28$ from $354 \times 357$ and then say that $355 \times 356$ is greater than $354 \times 357$ because $5 \times 6 > 4 \times 7$. They would be lucky. That works if the sum of units digits of the first quantity is the same as or greater than the sum of units digits of the second quantity. However, if we want to compare something like $354 \times 356 = 126{,}024$ with $352 \times 359 = 126{,}368$, that initial method would not work.

# VI. A Four-Hour Study Program for the PSAT

For those who have only a few hours to spend in PSAT preparation, I have worked a *minimum* study program to get you by. It tells you what basic Math skills you need to know, what vocabulary practice you need, and the most important strategies you need from the 37 in this book.

## General

Study General Strategies, pages 42–43.

## Critical Reading

Study the following Verbal Strategies beginning on page 80 (first 2 questions):

Sentence Completion Strategies 1 and 2, pages 81–83
Vocabulary Strategies 1, 2, and 3, pages 105–107
Reading Comprehension Strategies 1 and 2, pages 95–99

## Math

Study the Mini-Math Refresher beginning on page 119.
Study the following Math Strategies beginning on page 51* (first 2 questions for each strategy):

Strategy 2, page 52
Strategy 4, page 57
Strategy 8, page 62
Strategy 12, page 67
Strategy 13, page 68
Strategy 14, page 70
Strategy 17, page 74
Strategy 18, page 75

If you have time, take Practice Test 1 starting on page 342. Do all sections. Check your answers with the explanatory answers starting on page 378, and look again at the strategies and basic skills that apply to the questions you missed.

## Writing

Look through the material in Part 6—The PSAT Writing Skills Test starting on page 303.

*Make sure you read pages 44–50 before you study Math Strategies.

# VII. Longer-Range Study Program and Helpful Steps for Using This Book

1. Learn the 5 General Strategies for test taking on pages 42–43.
2. Take the PSAT Practice Test 1 on page 342 and score yourself according to the instructions.
3. For those problems or questions that you answered incorrectly or were uncertain of, see the explanatory answers, beginning on page 378, and make sure that you learn the strategies keyed to the questions, beginning on page 41. For complete strategy development, it is a good idea to study *all* the strategies starting with the Math strategies beginning on page 51, and learn how to do all the problems within each strategy.
4. If you are weak in basic Math skills, take the 101 Most Important Math Questions test on page 13 and follow the directions for diagnosis.
5. To see if you are making use of the strategies you've learned, you should take the National Merit Scholarship test on page 1 and read the explanatory answers.

## For Vocabulary Building

6. Learn the Hot Prefixes and Roots beginning on page 108. This will significantly build your vocabulary.
7. Study the Vocabulary Strategies beginning on page 105.
8. Study the Most Important/Frequently Used SAT Words and Their Opposites beginning on page 116.

## For Math-Area Basic Skills Help

9. For the basic Math skills keyed to the questions, study the Complete PSAT Math Refresher beginning on page 129, or for quicker review, look at the Mini-Math Refresher, beginning on page 119.

## For Writing Help

10. Look through Part 6—The PSAT Writing Skills Test beginning on page 303. You may also wish to refresh your grammar ability by looking through the Brief Review of English Grammar starting on page 321.

## Now

11. Take the remaining two practice PSAT tests beginning on page 404, score yourself, and go over your answers with the explanatory answers. Always refer to the associated strategies and basic skills for questions you answered incorrectly or were not sure how to do.

# VIII. Format of the PSAT

Total Time for CRITICAL READING: 50 minutes—48 questions

Total Time for MATH: 50 minutes—38 questions

Total Time for WRITING: 30 minutes—39 questions

| 5 Sections of the PSAT | Number of Questions | Number of Minutes |
|---|---|---|
| **Section 1: CRITICAL READING** | **24** | **25 Minutes** |
| Sentence Completions (4 single blank; 4 double blank) | 8 | |
| Reading: Double Short Passages (130 words each) | 4 | |
| Reading: Long Passage (650–850 words) | 12 | |
| **OR** | | |
| Sentence Completions (3 single blank; 5 double blank) | 8 | |
| Reading: Short Passage (60–125 words) | 2 | |
| Reading: Short Passage (60–125 words) | 2 | |
| Reading: Double Passage (350–450 words each) | 12 | |
| **Section 2: MATH** | **20** | **25 Minutes** |
| Regular Math—5 choices | 20 | |
| **Section 3: CRITICAL READING** | **24** | **25 Minutes** |
| Sentence Completions (3 single blank; 2 double blank) or (2 single blank; 3 double blank) | 5 | |
| Reading: Short Passage (60–125 words) | 2 | |
| Reading: Short Passage (60–125 words) | 2 | |
| Reading: Double Passage (250–400 words each) or Double Passage (350–450 words each) | 6 9 | |
| Reading Passage (400–550 words) or Reading Passage (350–500 words each) | 9 6 | |
| **OR** | | |
| Sentence Completions (3 single blank; 2 double blank) | 5 | |
| Reading: Double Short Passages (130 words each) | 4 | |
| Reading Passage (400–600 words) | 5 | |
| Reading Long Passage (650–850 words) | 10 | |

| 5 Sections of the PSAT | Number of Questions | Number of Minutes |
|---|---|---|
| **Section 4: MATH** | **18** | **25** |
| Regular Math—5 choices | 8 | |
| Student-Produced ("grid type") | 10 | |
| **Section 5: WRITING (Multiple-Choice)** | **39** | **30** |
| Improving Sentences | 20 | |
| Identifying Sentence Errors | 14 | |
| Improving Paragraphs | 4 | |

TOTAL MINUTES = 130 (2 hrs 10 min.)

# PART 1

# DO YOU HAVE A GOOD CHANCE OF WINNING A NATIONAL MERIT SCHOLARSHIP?

## Take This 22-Question Diagnostic Test to Find Out

The National Merit Scholarship is a mark of distinction for high-performing college-bound students. Winners can apply the scholarship to any accredited U.S. college; semifinalists and commended students also get a boost on their college applications, having been nationally recognized as among the brightest in their state. In order to qualify, you'll need a top score on the PSAT.

These very difficult PSAT questions were tested on students who received a National Merit Scholarship, and their scores were tabulated. These same questions were tested on students who scored very high on the PSAT but did not receive a National Merit Scholarship; their scores were also tabulated. If you can match the scores of former scholarship winners on this test, you have an excellent chance of qualifying for the National Merit Scholarship.

# Critical Reading

Allow 8 minutes for this part.

## Sentence Completions

Fill in the blank(s) with the appropriate choice:

1. The crude animated effects _____ projected images from seventeenth-century lantern slides have now been recognized as _____ of modern film animation.

   (A) complemented by...antecedents
   (B) forestalled by...harbingers
   (C) depicted in...derivatives
   (D) featured in...replicas
   (E) afforded by...forerunners

2. For Nancy, anything she had done or seen previously was now loathsomely boring; repetition, therefore, was _____ to her.

   (A) solace
   (B) anathema
   (C) hyperbole
   (D) duplicity
   (E) ecstasy

3. Although some readers admired the critic's consistently _____ reviews, most were put off by her unrelentingly _____ denunciations.

   (A) conciliatory...sarcastic
   (B) bombastic...euphemistic
   (C) staid...insufferable
   (D) vitriolic...caustic
   (E) clandestine...pallid

4. By focusing on Hopkins' _____ nature, this discerning study succeeds in _____ the prevailing stereotype of comedians as irrepressibly garrulous.

   (A) affluent...corrupting
   (B) talkative...neglecting
   (C) taciturn...rebutting
   (D) amiable...displacing
   (E) hilarious...dedicating

## Reading Comprehension

**Questions 5–8 are based on the following passages.**

### Passage 1

Once, the word "genius" was reserved for people of towering intellect or unimaginable ability. Genius was rare and almost magical. Nowadays, one reads about makeup artists and magazine editors who are "geniuses."
5 This same inflation can be seen in the use of the word "visionary," a term once reserved for geniuses who altered the course of history. I read the other day that a real estate developer who is converting some industrial building in Brooklyn to residential use is a "great visionary." (Not
10 just a visionary, mind you, but a *great* one.) If this guy is a "great visionary," what does that make the likes of Darwin and Freud?

### Passage 2

I know beyond any reasonable doubt that my best friend Madison is a genius, and I can't help but feel smugly
15 pleased that nobody searching for the common, everyday, Einstein-style genius would ever recognize that fact. Madison's genius is not the flashy sort destined to move mountains or invent computer chips, but it is genius nonetheless. Without seeming insincere or manipulative,
20 Madison can effortlessly locate the precise compliment that will soften the hard-eyed stare of a teacher intent on enforcing an arbitrary school rule. With a single quip, she can melt away the tension from any gathering. The geniuses among us may be few and far between, but
25 Madison is definitely one of them.

5. The first two sentences of Passage 1 serve primarily to

   (A) explain a difficult concept in popular terms
   (B) provide a humorous introduction to the discussion
   (C) highlight a common misconception
   (D) suggest a course of action that should be undertaken
   (E) establish the context for the subsequent discussion

**6.** Which statement best expresses the relationship between the two passages?

    (A) Passage 1 mocks someone who is lauded in Passage 2.

    (B) Passage 1 offers a scholarly analysis of a situation that is trivialized by the author of Passage 2.

    (C) Passage 2 describes someone by using a term that the author of Passage 1 would challenge.

    (D) Passage 2 discusses a historical figure noted in Passage 1.

    (E) Both Passage 1 and Passage 2 use irony to advance their arguments.

**7.** The author of Passage 1 would most likely insist that the characterization of Madison in Passage 2 is

    (A) unflattering

    (B) perceptive

    (C) calculated

    (D) overstated

    (E) uninspired

**8.** Which statement best characterizes the attitudes toward genius in the two passages?

    (A) Passage 1 attacks the idea that geniuses are commonplace, while Passage 2 presents several examples challenging that notion.

    (B) Passage 1 notes that true geniuses are unappreciated by most people, while Passage 2 questions that sentiment.

    (C) Passage 1 laments the scarcity of geniuses in contemporary society, while Passage 2 observes that geniuses are all around us.

    (D) Passage 1 indicates that true geniuses are exceptional, while Passage 2 assumes that genius is possible in everyday life.

    (E) Passage 1 contends that the true geniuses are well known, while Passage 2 argues that some geniuses are never discovered.

# Math

Allow 10 minutes for this part.

**Answer the following questions:**

1. $z = x - y + 4$
   $z = y - w - 3$
   $z = w - x + 5$

   Based on the systems of equations above, what is the value of $z$?

   (A) 2
   (B) 3
   (C) 4
   (D) 6
   (E) 12

2. If $x$ and $y$ are two different integers and the product of $35xy$ is the square of an integer, which of the following could be equal to $xy$?

   (A) 5
   (B) 70
   (C) 105
   (D) 140
   (E) 350

3. $xy = x + y$

   If $y > 2$, what are all the possible values of $x$ that satisfy the equation above?

   (A) $x < 0$
   (B) $0 < x < 1$
   (C) $0 < x < 2$
   (D) $1 < x < 2$
   (E) $x < 2$

4.

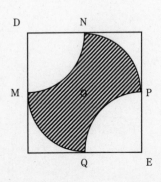

The figure above shows a square with side of length 6. The center of the square is $O$, and $M$, $N$, $P$, and $Q$ are the midpoints of the sides. If the arcs shown have centers at $D$, $O$, and $E$, what is the area of the shaded region?

(A) 18
(B) $6\pi$
(C) $9\pi - 9$
(D) $9 - \dfrac{9\pi}{4}$
(E) $36 - 6\pi$

Each of the remaining 4 questions requires you to solve the problem and write out your answer:

5. If $90n + 23p = 4523$, and $n$ and $p$ are both positive integers, what is one possible value of $n + p$?

6. At a certain hospital, 89 children were born in the month of June. If more children were born on June 15 than on any other day in the 30-day month, what is the *least* number of children that could have been born on the 15th of June?

7.

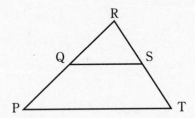

In the figure above, $Q$ is the midpoint of $PR$ and $S$ is the midpoint of $RT$. The area of trapezoid $PQST$ is what fraction of the area of the triangle $PRT$?

8. The average (arithmetic mean) of the test scores of a class of $p$ students is 70, and the average of the test scores of a class of $n$ students is 92. When the scores of both classes are combined, the average score is 86. What is the value of $\dfrac{p}{n}$ ?

# Writing Skills

Allow 5 minutes for this part.

The following 3 sentences test your ability to recognize grammar or usage errors. Each sentence contains either a <u>single</u> error (A, B, C, or D) or no error at all (E):

1. Vanessa had a tendency <u>of changing</u> her mind
                   A

   often, <u>so often</u> in fact that her friends <u>gave up</u>
        B                           C

   <u>expecting</u> her to <u>show up</u> at their parties. <u>No error</u>
     C           D                    E

2. In the middle of the eighteenth century, American

   surveyors <u>such as</u> George Washington created
            A

   maps that were <u>much more accurate</u> than
                 B

   <u>previous mapmakers</u> <u>because of</u> dramatic
          C          D

   improvements in surveying techniques. <u>No error</u>
                                     E

3. <u>Until</u> the train stopped at the station, neither the
     A

   engineer nor the conductor <u>were</u> aware <u>that one</u>
                      B         C

   of the passengers <u>had become</u> ill. <u>No error</u>
              D       E

For the following 3 questions, correctly identify the phrasing that best replaces the underlined portion of the sentence; if there is no correction, select choice A:

4. The new medical school is accepting applications from around the <u>world, there will be</u> 200 places in the entering class.

   (A) world, there will be
   (B) world, it will have
   (C) world, and there would be
   (D) world; with
   (E) world for the

5. The struggling theater may have to shut down soon because most of the money has been spent and <u>there is an insufficiency of new income coming in</u> to pay expenses.

   (A) there is an insufficiency of new income coming in
   (B) insufficient new income coming
   (C) an insufficiency of income
   (D) its income is insufficient there
   (E) its income is insufficient

6. Dr. Seuss, whose 44 books have sold more than 500 million copies, <u>have made him</u> probably the best-selling children's author in history.

   (A) have made him
   (B) making him
   (C) and was thereby
   (D) is
   (E) are

# Answers

## Critical Reading

**1.** E

**2.** B

**3.** D

**4.** C

**5.** E

**6.** C

**7.** D

**8.** D

## Math

**1.** A

**2.** D

**3.** D

**4.** A

**5.** 51, 118, or 185

**6.** 4

**7.** $\frac{3}{4}$

**8.** $\frac{3}{8}$

## Writing Skills

**1.** A

**2.** C

**3.** B

**4.** E

**5.** E

**6.** D

# Scoring

| | Your Score | Scholarship Winners |
|---|---|---|
| **Critical Reading** | | |
| Questions 1–4: | _____ | at least 3 |
| Questions 5–8: | _____ | at least 3 |
| **Math** | | |
| Questions 1–8: | _____ | at least 6 |
| **Writing Skills** | | |
| Questions 1–6: | _____ | at least 5 |
| Total | _____/22 | at least 17/22 |

# Explanatory Answers for the National Merit Scholarship Diagnostic Test

## Critical Reading

1. Choice E is correct. Notice that we're talking about the past ("seventeenth century") in the present ("modern") context. Choices A, C, and D use terms that describe the present in terms of the past—an old thing cannot be a "replica" of a new thing. The first half of Choice B suggests that the lantern images forestall (or halt) the animation, which makes no sense.

2. Choice B is correct. Start by using **Sentence Completion Strategy 4: Pay Close Attention to the Key Words.** The word "therefore" indicates that the second part of the sentence will be the *result* of the first part. Notice that the first part of the sentence shows that Nancy did not want to do something she did before. So repetition (doing something she did before) would be something she would be against. Choices A and E would mean that she enjoyed repetition. Now use **Vocabulary Strategy 1: Use Prefixes and Roots.** *An-* of anathema could mean "against"; *hyper-* means "extremely" and *dupl-* means "double." Even without knowing the exact definition of anathema (something detested or cursed), you can see that Choice B makes the most sense.

3. Choice D is correct. Use **Sentence Completion Strategy 3: Complete the Sentence in Your Own Words.** What kind of reviews do critics write? Harsh, brutal, scathing…a long list of negative words. Now try **Vocabulary Strategy 2: Pay Attention to the Feeling of the Word.** "Conciliatory" feels positive, while you probably know "sarcastic" is negative. "Bombastic" could sound destructive (it actually means pompous), but "euphemistic" does not. Neither "staid" nor "clandestine" fit what we're looking for. However, "vitriolic" and "caustic" both sound harsh.

4. Choice C is correct. Start with the second set of words: verbs connecting "study" to "stereotype." Studies don't corrupt or dedicate, so Choices A and E are incorrect. The remaining choices—neglecting, rebutting, and displacing—are all negative, meaning the study somehow disagrees with the stereotype. Even if you don't know the definition of "garrulous," think about how you'd stereotype comedians: loud, funny, talkative, offensive, etc. "Talkative" does not disagree with this list, so Choice B is incorrect. Try **Vocabulary Strategy 1: Use Roots, Prefixes, and Suffixes.** *Ami-* means "love," so *amiable* means loveable or friendly; many comics seem friendly, so this isn't the best choice. If you play an instrument, you might recognize *tacit* as "silent." Silent definitely disagrees with the comic stereotype, making Choice C the clear choice.

5. Choice E is correct. Note that the first two sentences set the tone and context for the rest of the passage by describing what "genius" means.

6. Choice C is correct. The author of Passage 1 considers "genius" to be very specific and associates "genius" with people like Einstein and Freud. The author of Passage 2 associates the term "genius" with someone not of the stature of Einstein or Freud, but an "everyday" person. The contention of Author 2 would most likely be challenged by Author 1, especially because of what Author 1 says toward the end of the first passage.

7. Choice D is correct. As in Question 6, Author 1 would insist that the claim that Madison is a genius is overstated. Choices A and E are incorrect because Author 1 considers "genius" a term of high praise. Choice B is incorrect because Author 1 *disagrees* with Author 2's definition. Choice C does not apply to this situation.

8. Choice D is correct. See lines 2–3 and 15–16. Choice A is incorrect because Author 2 presents only 1 non-traditional genius, not "several examples." Choice B is incorrect because the authors do not disagree in their appreciation of true genius. Choices C and E are both incorrect because Author 1 never makes these claims.

# Math

1. Choice A is correct. Don't try to solve the equations by substitution! Use **Strategy 13: Add Equations**.

$$z = x - y \qquad + 4$$
$$+z = \qquad y - w - 3$$
$$+z = -x \qquad + w + 5$$
$$\overline{\phantom{xxxxxxxxxxxxxxxxxxxxxxxxxxxxxx}}$$
$$3z = (x - x) + (y - y) + (w - w) + (4 - 3 + 5)$$
$$3z = 6$$
$$z = 2$$

2. Choice D is correct. Use **Strategy 2: Translate Words into Mathematical Expressions**.

$35xy = n^2$

Now use **Strategy 8: Start with Choice E and Work Backward**.

(E) $xy = 350$

For Choice E to be true, $\sqrt{35\,(350)}$ must be an integer.

$$\sqrt{35\,(350)} = \sqrt{35\,(35)\,(10)} = \sqrt{35\,(35)}\sqrt{10} = 35\sqrt{10}$$

Since $35\sqrt{10}$ is not an integer, Choice E is incorrect.

Next try Choice D.

(D) $xy = 140$

For Choice D to be true, $\sqrt{35\,(140)}$ must be an integer.

$$\sqrt{35\,(140)} = \sqrt{35\,(70)\,(2)} = \sqrt{35\,(35)\,(2)\,(2)} =$$
$$\sqrt{35\,(35)}\sqrt{2\,(2)} = 35(2) = 70$$

Since 70 is an integer, Choice D is correct.

3. Choice D is correct. Use **Strategy 12: Factor to Make Simpler**.

We want to get $x$ in terms of $y$:

$$xy = x + y$$
$$xy - x = y$$
$$x(y - 1) = y$$
$$x = \frac{y}{y-1}$$

Use **Strategy 6:  Know How to Work with Inequalities**.

Since $y > 2$, you can see that when $y$ is just about 2, $x$ is just about $\dfrac{2}{2-1}$, or about 2.

When $y$ is extremely large, like 1,000,000, $x$ is about $\dfrac{1,000,000}{1,000,000 - 1}$, or about 1.

So it is safe to say that the range of $x$ can be represented as $1 < x < 2$.

4. Choice A is correct.

Use **Strategy 14: Draw and Label Lines and Arcs to Get More Information**.

Draw lines MP and NQ to split the shape into four quadrants.

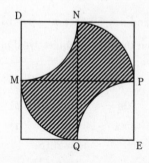

Use **Strategy 3: Subtract Knowns from Knowns to Get Unknowns**.

Because the outer shape is a square and $M$, $N$, $P$, and $Q$ are midpoints of its sides, all of the arcs have the same radius, $r$, which is also the length of each quadrant square.

Area of shade in top-right or bottom-left quadrant:

$$\frac{Area\ of\ circle}{4}$$

Area of shade in top-left or bottom-right quadrant:

Area of quadrant $- \dfrac{Area\ of\ circle}{4}$

Given: Sides of the outer square $= 6$

$$r = 3$$

Top-left quadrant: $(3)(3) - \dfrac{\pi(3^2)}{4} = 9 - \dfrac{9\pi}{4}$

Top-right quadrant: $\dfrac{\pi(3^2)}{4} = \dfrac{9\pi}{4}$

Bottom-left quadrant: $\dfrac{\pi(3^2)}{4} = \dfrac{9\pi}{4}$

Bottom-right quadrant: $(3)(3) - \dfrac{\pi(3^2)}{4} = 9 - \dfrac{9\pi}{4}$

Therefore, total area of shade:

$$\left(9 - \frac{9\pi}{4}\right) + \left(\frac{9\pi}{4}\right) + \left(\frac{9\pi}{4}\right) + \left(9 - \frac{9\pi}{4}\right) = 9 + 9 = 18$$

**5. 51, 118, or 185.**

**Use Strategy 17: Use Given Information Effectively.**

On one side of the equation you have $23\underline{p}$; on the other side $45\underline{23}$. You can use this to your advantage.

$$90n + 23p = 4523$$
$$90n = 4523 - 23p$$
$$90n = 4500 + 23 - 23p$$
$$90n = 4500 + 23(1 - p)$$

At this point, since you only need one answer, the easiest route is to plug in $p = 1$ and solve for $n$:

$$90n = 4500 + 23(1 - 1) = 4500 + 0 = 4500$$
$$n = \frac{4500}{90} = 50$$

If $p = 1$ and $n = 50$, then $n + p = 51$.

To explain the other options, we'll need a bit more calculation:

$$90n = 4500 + 23(1 - p)$$
$$90n - 4500 = 23(1 - p)$$
$$4500 - 90n = 23(p - 1)$$
$$90(50 - n) = 23(p - 1)$$
$$50 - n = \frac{23(p - 1)}{90}$$

Since $n$ is an integer, $50 - n$ will always be an integer; therefore $\dfrac{23(p - 1)}{90}$ must also be an integer.

The only way this is possible is if $p - 1 = 0, 90,$ 180, 270, etc. Note that we are actually limited to 0, 90, or 180, because if $p - 1$ is 270 (or any larger multiple of 90), $n$ would be negative, which is not true.

If $p - 1 = 90$
$50 - n = 23$
$n = 50 - 23 = 27$
$n + p = 27 + 91 = 118$

If $p - 1 = 180$
$50 - n = 46$
$n = 50 - 46 = 4$
$n + p = 4 + 181 = 185$

**6. 4.**

**Use Strategy 17: Know What to Do First in the Question.** Since you are asked for the lowest number, start by trying 1. But that would be impossible, since you'd have no children born any other day.

So try 2. Since there are 29 other days in June, the greatest number of children born on other days would be $1 \times 29$. Since $29 + 2$ is less than 89, that's also incorrect.

So try 3. The greatest number of children born on other days would be $2 \times 29$ or 58, which again leaves us short of 89.

So try 4. The greatest number of children born would be $3 \times 29 = 87$, and since $87 + 4 > 89$, this scenario fits.

**7. $\dfrac{3}{4}$**

**Use Strategy 3: Subtract Knowns from Knowns to Get Unknowns.**

To find the ratio:

$$\frac{A_{PQST}}{A_{PRT}}$$

First, substitute known quantities for the area of the trapezoid:

$$A_{PQST} = A_{PRT} - A_{QRS}$$
$$\frac{A_{PQST}}{A_{PRT}} = \frac{A_{PRT} - A_{QRS}}{A_{PRT}}$$

Now find the area of $\triangle QRS$ and $\triangle PRT$

**Use Strategy 14: Draw Lines and Label Sides.**

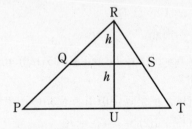

Draw $RU$ perpendicular to $PT$.

$$A_{PRT} = \frac{(h + h)(PT)}{2} = \frac{2h(PT)}{2} = h(PT)$$
$$A_{QRS} = \frac{h(QS)}{2}$$

$\triangle QRS$ is similar to $\triangle PRT$ because $\dfrac{RQ}{RP} = \dfrac{RS}{RT}$ and angle $R$ is common to both triangles.

From similar triangles, we know that $\dfrac{QS}{PT} = \dfrac{h}{h + h}$
$= \dfrac{1}{2}$

So $QS = \dfrac{PT}{2}$

Thus, $A_{QRS} = \dfrac{h\left(\dfrac{PT}{2}\right)}{2} = \dfrac{h\,(PT)}{4}$

Now plug in these values to the initial ratio:

$$\dfrac{A_{PQST}}{A_{PRT}} = \dfrac{A_{PRT} - A_{QRS}}{A_{PRT}} = \dfrac{h\,(PT) - \dfrac{h\,(PT)}{4}}{h\,(PT)}$$

$$= \dfrac{h\,(PT)\left(1 - \dfrac{1}{4}\right)}{h\,(PT)} = 1 - \dfrac{1}{4} = \dfrac{3}{4}$$

8. $\dfrac{3}{8}$.

Use **Strategy 5: Know How to Evaluate Averages**.

Write the average of the class of $p$ students as:

$$\dfrac{a + b + c + \ldots}{p} = 70$$

Now write the average of the class of $n$ students as:

$$\dfrac{A + B + C + \ldots}{n} = 92$$

To get rid of the fractions, multiply both equations by the denominators:

$a + b + c + \ldots = 70p$
$A + B + C + \ldots = 92n$

The average of the scores when both classes are combined is

$$\dfrac{a + b + c + \ldots + A + B + C + \ldots}{p + n} = 86$$

Plug in the known values of $a + b + c + \ldots$ and $A + B + C + \ldots$

$$\dfrac{70p + 92n}{p + n} = 86$$

$70p + 92n = 86(p + n) = 86p + 86n$
$92n - 86n = 86p - 70p$

$6n = 16p$
$\dfrac{p}{n} = \dfrac{6}{16} = \dfrac{3}{8}$

# Writing Skills

1. Choice A is correct. One has a tendency *to do something*, not a tendency of doing something. Thus, "of changing" should be "to change."

2. Choice C is correct. As written, the sentence compares the accuracy of *maps* to the accuracy of *mapmakers*. In reality, maps were created that were more accurate than maps of previous mapmakers. You need to substitute language that makes an apples-to-apples comparison, such as "those of previous mapmakers" or the possessive "previous mapmakers'."

3. Choice B is correct. You might have noticed both "engineer" and "conductor" in the subject and therefore assumed the verb should be plural. However, because this is a "neither...nor" statement, the subject is singular; for the sake of subject-verb agreement, "were" should be changed to "was." If it stated "the engineer *and* the conductor," then the plural *were* would be correct.

4. Choice E is correct. Choices A and B create compound sentences without the necessary conjunction. Choice D is incorrect because a prepositional phrase cannot stand alone after a semicolon. Choice C transitions properly, but the verb "would be" is in the wrong tense (past-perfect instead of the future "will be"). Choice E makes the sentence concise and to the point.

5. Choice E is correct. You want to make the sentence concise, consistent, and clear. Choice A is too cluttered. For consistency, the underlined section should be in passive voice, eliminating Choice B. Choice C needs a verb for clarity. In Choice D, the use of both "its" and "there" is repetitive. Choice E is concise, consistent, and clear.

6. Choice D is correct. Dr. Seuss is the subject of this sentence, meaning the verb should be third-person singular. "Whose 44 books have sold more than 500 million copies" is just a parenthetical clause; you can ignore it while answering the question. Choice A applies to the *books*, not Dr. Seuss. (You wouldn't say Dr. Seuss <u>have made him</u>...). Choice E is plural instead of singular. Choices B and C treat the underlined portion as the start of a new idea. Choice D correctly inserts the third-person singular "is": *Dr. Seuss <u>is</u> probably the best-selling children's author in history.*

## PART 2

# THE 101 MOST IMPORTANT MATH QUESTIONS YOU NEED TO KNOW HOW TO SOLVE

Take This Test to Determine Your Basic
(as Contrasted with Strategy) Math Weaknesses
(Diagnosis and Corrective Measures Follow Test)

# 101 Math Questions
# Answer Sheet

A. Fractions
1.
2.
3.
4.
5.

B. Even–Odd Relationships
6.
7.
8.
9.
10.
11.
12.

C. Factors
13.
14.
15.
16.
17.
18.
19.
20.
21.

D. Exponents
22.
23.
24.
25.
26.
27.
28.
29.
30.
31.
32.

E. Percentages
33.
34.
35.

F. Equations
36.
37.
38.
39.
40.

G. Angles
41.
42.
43.
44.

## H. Parallel Lines

**45.**
**46.**
**47.**
**48.**
**49.**
**50.**
**51.**

## I. Triangles

**52.**
**53.**
**54.**
**55.**
**56.**
**57.**
**58.**
**59.**
**60.**
**61.**
**62.**
**63.**
**64.**
**65.**

## J. Circles

**66.**
**67.**
**68.**
**69.**
**70.**

## K. Other Figures

**71.**
**72.**
**73.**
**74.**
**75.**
**76.**
**77.**
**78.**
**79.**
**80.**

## L. Number Lines

**81.**
**82.**

## M. Coordinates

**83.**
**84.**
**85.**
**86.**

## N. Inequalities

**87.**
**88.**
**89.**
**90.**
**91.**
**92.**

## O. Averages

**93.**
**94.**

## P. Shortcuts

**95.**
**96.**
**97.**
**98.**
**99.**
**100.**
**101.**

# 101 Math Questions
# Test

Following are the 101 most important math questions you should know how to solve. After you take the test, check to see whether your answers are the same as those described, and whether or not you answered the question in the way described. After a solution, there is usually (where appropriate) a rule or generalization of the math concept just used in the solution to the particular problem. Make sure that you understand this generalization or rule, as it will apply to many other questions. Remember that these are the most important basic math questions you need to know how to solve. Make sure that you understand *all of them* before taking any standardized math test such as the PSAT.

DO NOT GUESS AT ANY ANSWER! LEAVE ANSWER BLANK IF YOU DON'T KNOW HOW TO SOLVE.

## A. Fractions

1. $\dfrac{\frac{a}{b}}{c} =$

   (A) $\dfrac{ab}{c}$

   (B) $\dfrac{ac}{b}$

   (C) $\dfrac{a}{bc}$

   (D) $abc$

   (E) None of these.

2. $\dfrac{1}{\frac{1}{y}} =$

   (A) $y$
   (B) $y^2$
   (C) $\dfrac{1}{y}$
   (D) infinity
   (E) None of these.

3. $\dfrac{\frac{a}{b}}{c} =$

   (A) $\dfrac{a}{bc}$

   (B) $\dfrac{ac}{b}$

   (C) $\dfrac{ab}{c}$

   (D) $abc$
   (E) None of these.

4. $\dfrac{1}{\frac{x}{y}} =$

   (A) $xy$

   (B) $\dfrac{x}{y}$

   (C) $\dfrac{y}{x}$

   (D) $\left(\dfrac{x}{y}\right)^2$

   (E) None of these.

5. $\dfrac{\frac{a}{b}}{\frac{b}{a}} =$

   (A) $\dfrac{b^2}{a^2}$

   (B) $\dfrac{a^2}{b^2}$

   (C) 1

   (D) $\dfrac{a}{b}$

   (E) None of these.

## B. Even−Odd Relationships

6. ODD INTEGER × ODD INTEGER =

   (A) odd integer only
   (B) even integer only
   (C) even or odd integer

**7.** ODD INTEGER + or − ODD INTEGER =

(A) odd integer only
(B) even integer only
(C) even or odd integer

**8.** EVEN INTEGER × EVEN INTEGER =

(A) odd integer only
(B) even integer only
(C) even or odd integer

**9.** EVEN INTEGER + or − EVEN INTEGER =

(A) odd integer only
(B) even integer only
(C) even or odd integer

**10.** (ODD INTEGER)$^{\text{ODD POWER}}$ =

(A) odd integer only
(B) even integer only
(C) even or odd integer

**11.** (EVEN INTEGER)$^{\text{EVEN POWER}}$ =

(A) odd integer only
(B) even integer only
(C) even or odd integer

**12.** (EVEN INTEGER)$^{\text{ODD POWER}}$ =

(A) odd integer only
(B) even integer only
(C) even or odd integer

## C. Factors

**13.** $(x + 3)(x + 2) =$

(A) $x^2 + 5x + 6$
(B) $x^2 + 6x + 5$
(C) $x^2 + x + 6$
(D) $2x + 5$
(E) None of these.

**14.** $(x + 3)(x - 2) =$

(A) $x^2 - x + 6$
(B) $x^2 + x + 5$
(C) $x^2 + x - 6$
(D) $2x + 1$
(E) None of these.

**15.** $(x - 3)(y - 2) =$

(A) $xy - 5y + 6$
(B) $xy - 2x - 3y + 6$
(C) $x + y + 6$
(D) $xy - 3y + 2x + 6$
(E) None of these.

**16.** $(a + b)(b + c) =$

(A) $ab + b^2 + bc$
(B) $a + b^2 + c$
(C) $a^2 + b^2 + ca$
(D) $ab + b^2 + ac + bc$
(E) None of these.

**17.** $(a + b)(a - b) =$

(A) $a^2 + 2ba - b^2$
(B) $a^2 - 2ba - b^2$
(C) $a^2 - b^2$
(D) 0
(E) None of these.

**18.** $(a + b)^2 =$

(A) $a^2 + 2ab + b^2$
(B) $a^2 + b^2$
(C) $a^2 + b^2 + ab$
(D) $2a + 2b$
(E) None of these.

**19.** $-(a - b) =$

(A) $a - b$
(B) $-a - b$
(C) $a + b$
(D) $b - a$
(E) None of these.

**20.** $a(b + c) =$

(A) $ab + ac$
(B) $ab + c$
(C) $abc$
(D) $ab + bc$
(E) None of these.

**21.** $- a(b - c) =$

(A) $ab - ac$
(B) $- ab - ac$
(C) $ac - ab$
(D) $ab + ac$
(E) None of these.

## D. Exponents

**22.** $10^5 =$

(A) 1000
(B) 10,000
(C) 100,000
(D) 1,000,000
(E) None of these.

**23.** $107076.5 = 1.070765 \times$

(A) $10^4$
(B) $10^5$
(C) $10^6$
(D) $10^7$
(E) None of these.

**24.** $a^2 \times a^5 =$

(A) $a^{10}$
(B) $a^7$
(C) $a^3$
(D) $(2a)^{10}$
(E) None of these.

**25.** $(ab)^7 =$

(A) $ab^7$
(B) $a^7b$
(C) $a^7b^7$
(D) $a^{14}b^{14}$
(E) None of these.

**26.** $\left(\dfrac{a}{c}\right)^8 =$

(A) $\dfrac{a^8}{c^8}$

(B) $\dfrac{a^8}{c}$

(C) $\dfrac{a}{c^8}$

(D) $\dfrac{a^7}{c}$

(E) None of these.

**27.** $a^4 \times b^4 =$

(A) $(ab)^4$
(B) $(ab)^8$
(C) $(ab)^{16}$
(D) $(ab)^{12}$
(E) None of these.

**28.** $a^{-3} \times b^5 =$

(A) $\dfrac{b^5}{a^3}$

(B) $(ab)^2$
(C) $(ab)^{-15}$

(D) $\dfrac{a^3}{b^5}$

(E) None of these.

**29.** $(a^3)^5 =$

(A) $a^8$
(B) $a^2$
(C) $a^{15}$
(D) $a^{243}$
(E) None of these.

**30.** $2a^{-3} =$

(A) $\dfrac{2}{a^3}$

(B) $2a^3$

(C) $2^3\sqrt{a}$
(D) $a^{-6}$
(E) None of these.

**31.** $2a^m \times \dfrac{1}{3}a^{-n} =$

(A) $\dfrac{2}{3}a^{m+n}$

(B) $\dfrac{2}{3}\dfrac{a^m}{a^n}$

(C) $\dfrac{2}{3}a^{-mn}$

(D) $-\dfrac{2}{3}a^{-mn}$

(E) None of these.

**32.** $3^2 + 3^{-2} + 4^1 + 6^0 =$

(A) $8\dfrac{1}{9}$

(B) $12\dfrac{1}{9}$

(C) $13\dfrac{1}{9}$

(D) $14\dfrac{1}{9}$

(E) None of these.

# E. Percentages

**33.** 15% of 200 =

(A) 3
(B) 30
(C) 300
(D) 3,000
(E) None of these.

**34.** What is 3% of 5?

(A) $\frac{5}{3}\%$

(B) 15

(C) $\frac{3}{20}$

(D) $\frac{3}{5}$

(E) None of these.

**35.** What percent of 3 is 6?

(A) 50
(B) 20
(C) 200
(D) $\frac{1}{2}$
(E) None of these.

# F. Equations

**36.** If $y^2 = 16$, $y =$

(A) + 4 only
(B) − 4 only
(C) + or − 4
(D) + or − 8
(E) None of these.

**37.** If $x − y = 10$, $y =$

(A) $x − 10$
(B) $10 + x$
(C) $10 − x$
(D) 10
(E) None of these.

**38.** What is the value of $x$ if $x + 4y = 7$ and $x − 4y = 8$?

(A) 15

(B) $\frac{15}{2}$

(C) 7

(D) $\frac{7}{2}$

(E) None of these.

**39.** What is the value of $x$ and $y$ if $x − 2y = 2$ and $2x + y = 4$?

(A) $x = 2, y = 0$
(B) $x = 0, y = − 2$
(C) $x = − 1, y = 2$
(D) $x = 0, y = 2$
(E) None of these.

**40.** If $\frac{x}{5} = \frac{7}{12}$, $x =$

(A) $\frac{35}{12}$

(B) $\frac{12}{35}$

(C) $\frac{7}{60}$

(D) $\frac{60}{7}$

(E) None of these.

# G. Angles (Vertical, Supplementary)

Questions 41−42 refer to the diagram below:

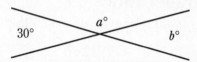

**41.** $a =$

(A) 30
(B) 150
(C) 45
(D) 90
(E) None of these.

**42.** $b =$

(A) 30
(B) 150
(C) 45
(D) 90
(E) None of these.

Question 43 refers to the diagram below:

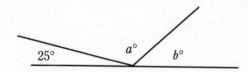

**43.** $a + b =$

(A) 155
(B) 165
(C) 180
(D) 145
(E) None of these.

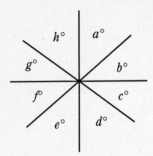

**44.** What is the value of $a + b + c + d + e + f + g + h$ in the diagram above?

(A) 180
(B) 240
(C) 360
(D) 540
(E) None of these.

## H. Parallel Lines

Questions 45−51 refer to the diagram below:

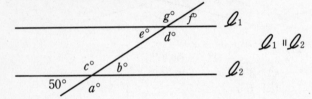

$\ell_1 \parallel \ell_2$

**45.** $a =$

(A) 50
(B) 130
(C) 100
(D) 40
(E) None of these.

**46.** $b =$

(A) 50
(B) 130
(C) 100
(D) 40
(E) None of these.

**47.** $c =$

(A) 50
(B) 130
(C) 100
(D) 40
(E) None of these.

**48.** $d =$

(A) 50
(B) 130
(C) 100
(D) 40
(E) None of these.

**49.** $e =$

(A) 50
(B) 130
(C) 100
(D) 40
(E) None of these.

**50.** $f =$

(A) 50
(B) 130
(C) 100
(D) 40
(E) None of these.

**51.** $g =$

(A) 50
(B) 130
(C) 100
(D) 40
(E) None of these.

## I. Triangles

**52.**

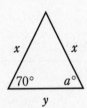

(Note: Figure is not drawn to scale.)

$a =$

(A) 70
(B) 40
(C) $\frac{xy}{70}$
(D) Cannot be determined.
(E) None of these.

**53.**

(Note: Figure is not drawn to scale.)

$x =$

(A) 3
(B) $\frac{50}{3}$
(C) $3\sqrt{2}$
(D) Cannot be determined.
(E) None of these.

**54.**

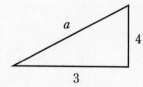

(Note: Figure is not drawn to scale.)

Which is a possible value for *a*?

(A) 1
(B) 6
(C) 10
(D) 7
(E) None of these.

**55.**

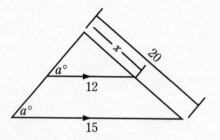

(Note: Figure is not drawn to scale.)

In the triangle above, *x* =

(A) 12
(B) 16
(C) 15
(D) 10
(E) None of these.

**56.**

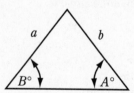

In the triangle above, if B > A, then

(A) *b = a*
(B) *b > a*
(C) *b < a*
(D) A relation between *b* and *a* cannot be
     determined.
(E) None of these.

**57.**

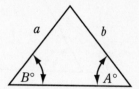

In the triangle above, if *b < a,* then

(A) B > A
(B) B = A
(C) B < A
(D) A relation between B and A cannot be
     determined.
(E) None of these.

**58.**

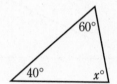

In the triangle above, *x* =

(A) 100
(B) 80
(C) 90
(D) 45
(E) None of these.

**59.**

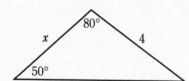

(Note: Figure is not drawn to scale.)

In the triangle above, *x* =

(A) $4\sqrt{2}$
(B) 8
(C) 4
(D) a number between 1 and 4
(E) None of these.

**60.**

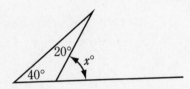

In the diagram above, $x =$

(A) 40
(B) 20
(C) 60
(D) 80
(E) None of these.

**61.**

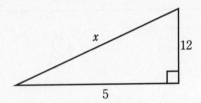

(Note: Figure is not drawn to scale.)

In the right triangle above as shown, $x =$

(A) 17
(B) 13
(C) 15
(D) $12\sqrt{2}$
(E) None of these.

Questions 62–63 refer to the diagram below:

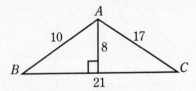

(Note: Figure is not drawn to scale.)

**62.** The perimeter of the triangle $ABC$ is

(A) 16
(B) 48
(C) 168
(D) 84
(E) None of these.

**63.** The area of triangle $ABC$ is

(A) 170
(B) 85
(C) 168
(D) 84
(E) None of these.

Questions 64–65 refer to the diagram below:

**64.** The area of the triangle is

(A) 6
(B) 7
(C) 12
(D) any number between 5 and 7
(E) None of these.

**65.** The perimeter of the triangle is

(A) 7
(B) 12
(C) 15
(D) any number between 7 and 12
(E) None of these.

## J. Circles

Questions 66–67 refer to the diagram below:

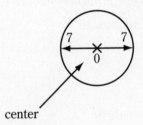

center

**66.** The area of the circle is

(A) 49
(B) $49\pi$
(C) $14\pi$
(D) $196\pi$
(E) None of these.

**67.** The circumference of the circle is

(A) $14\pi$
(B) $7\pi$
(C) $49\pi$
(D) 14
(E) None of these.

**68.**

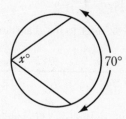

In the diagram above, $x =$

(A) 70
(B) 35
(C) 90
(D) a number that cannot be determined
(E) None of these.

**69.**

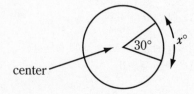

In the diagram above, $x =$

(A) 30
(B) 60
(C) 90
(D) a number that cannot be determined
(E) None of these.

**70.**

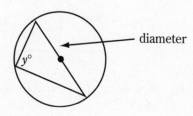

In the diagram above, $y =$

(A) 145
(B) 60
(C) 90
(D) a number that cannot be determined
(E) None of these.

# K. Other Figures

Questions 71–72 refer to the diagram below:

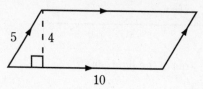

**71.** The area of the figure is

(A) 15
(B) 20
(C) 40
(D) 50
(E) None of these.

**72.** The perimeter of the figure is

(A) 15
(B) 30
(C) 40
(D) 50
(E) None of these.

Questions 73–75 refer to the figure below:

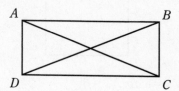

*ABCD* is a rectangle

**73.** What is *BC* if *AD* = 6?

(A) 4
(B) 6
(C) 8
(D) 10
(E) 12

**74.** What is *DC* if *AB* = 8?

(A) 4
(B) 6
(C) 8
(D) 10
(E) 12

**75.** What is *DB* if *AC* = 10?

(A) 4
(B) 6
(C) 8
(D) 10
(E) 12

Questions 76–77 refer to the diagram below:

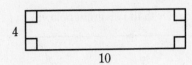

**76.** The area of the figure is

(A) 14
(B) 40
(C) 80
(D) 28
(E) None of these.

**77.** The perimeter of the figure is

(A) 14
(B) 28
(C) 36
(D) 40
(E) None of these.

Questions 78–79 refer to the figure below:

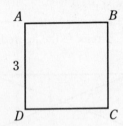

$ABCD$ is a square; $AC = 3$

**78.** What is the area of the square?

(A) 9
(B) 12
(C) 16
(D) 20
(E) None of these.

**79.** What is the perimeter of the square?

(A) 9
(B) 12
(C) 16
(D) 20
(E) None of these.

**80.** The volume of the rectangular solid below is

(A) 48
(B) 64
(C) 128
(D) 72
(E) None of these.

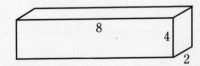

## L. Number Lines

Questions 81–82 refer to the diagram below:

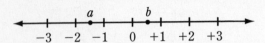

**81.** Which defines the range in values of $b$ best?

(A) $1 > b > -2$
(B) $2 > b > 0$
(C) $1 > b > 0$
(D) $3 > b > -3$
(E) $b > 0$

**82.** Which defines the range in values of $a$ best?

(A) $a > -2$
(B) $-1 > a > -2$
(C) $0 > a > -2$
(D) $-1 > a$
(E) $0 > a > -3$

## M. Coordinates

Questions 83–85 refer to the diagram below:

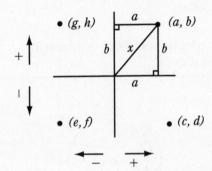

**83.** How many of the variables $a, b, c, d, e, f, g, h$ are positive?

(A) 1
(B) 2
(C) 3
(D) 4
(E) 5

**84.** How many of the variables $a, b, c, d, e, f, g, h$ are negative?

(A) 1
(B) 2
(C) 3
(D) 4
(E) 5

**85.** If $a = 3$, $b = 4$, what is $x$?

    (A) 3
    (B) 4
    (C) 5
    (D) 6
    (E) None of these.

**86.**

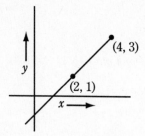

What is the slope of the line above?

    (A) −1
    (B) 0
    (C) +1
    (D) +2
    (E) +3

# N. Inequalities

*Note:* Any variable can be positive or negative or 0.

**87.** If $x > y$, then $4x > 4y$

    (A) always
    (B) sometimes
    (C) never

**88.** If $x + y > z$, then $y > z - x$

    (A) always
    (B) sometimes
    (C) never

**89.** If $-4 < -x$, then $+4 > +x$

    (A) always
    (B) sometimes
    (C) never

**90.** If $m > n$, where $q$ is any number, then $qm > qn$

    (A) always
    (B) sometimes
    (C) never

**91.** If $x > y$ and $p > q$, then $x + p > y + q$

    (A) always
    (B) sometimes
    (C) never

**92.** If $x > y$ and $p > q$, then $xp > qy$

    (A) always
    (B) sometimes
    (C) never

# O. Averages

**93.** What is the average of 30, 40, and 80?

    (A) 150
    (B) 75
    (C) 50
    (D) 45
    (E) None of these.

**94.** What is the average speed in mph of a car traveling 40 miles in 4 hours?

    (A) 160
    (B) 10
    (C) 120
    (D) 30
    (E) None of these.

# P. Shortcuts

**95.** Which is greater? *Don't calculate a common denominator!*

$$\frac{7}{16} \text{ or } \frac{3}{7}$$

    (A) $\frac{7}{16}$

    (B) $\frac{3}{7}$

    (C) They are equal.
    (D) A relationship cannot be determined.

**96.** Add: $\frac{7}{12} + \frac{3}{5}$:

    (A) $1\frac{11}{60}$

    (B) $1\frac{13}{60}$

    (C) $1\frac{15}{60}$

    (D) $\frac{10}{17}$

    (E) None of these.

**97.** Subtract: $\frac{7}{12} - \frac{3}{5}$:

    (A) $-\frac{1}{60}$

    (B) $-\frac{3}{60}$

    (C) $-1\frac{11}{60}$

    (D) $\frac{4}{7}$

    (E) None of these.

**98.** $\dfrac{4}{250} =$

    (A) .016
    (B) .04
    (C) .004
    (D) .025
    (E) None of these.

*Note: Do not divide 250 into 4 in the above question!*

**99.** What is $c$ if

$$200 = \frac{a+b+c}{2} \text{ and } 80 = \frac{a+b}{3}?$$

    (A) 160
    (B) 140
    (C) 120
    (D) 100
    (E) None of these.

**100.** What is the value of $95 \times 75 - 95 \times 74$? (*Don't multiply* $95 \times 75$ *or* $95 \times 74!$)

    (A) 65
    (B) 75
    (C) 85
    (D) 95
    (E) None of these.

**101.** Find the value of

$$\frac{140 \times 15}{5 \times 7} \quad (\textit{Don't multiply } 140 \times 15!)$$

    (A) 20
    (B) 40
    (C) 60
    (D) 90
    (E) None of these.

# 101 Math Questions:
## Answers, Diagnosis, Solutions, Generalizations, Rules

# 101 Math Questions:
# Answers

## A. Fractions
1. B
2. A
3. A
4. C
5. B

## B. Even−Odd Relationships
6. A
7. B
8. B
9. B
10. A
11. B
12. B

## C. Factors
13. A
14. C
15. B
16. D
17. C
18. A
19. D
20. A
21. C

## D. Exponents
22. C
23. B
24. B
25. C
26. A
27. A
28. A
29. C
30. A
31. B
32. D

## E. Percentages
33. B
34. C
35. C

## F. Equations
36. C
37. A
38. B
39. A
40. A

## G. Angles
41. B
42. A
43. A
44. C

## H. Parallel Lines
45. B
46. A
47. B
48. B
49. A
50. A
51. B

## I. Triangles
52. A
53. A
54. B
55. B
56. B
57. C
58. B
59. C
60. C
61. B
62. B
63. D
64. A
65. B

## J. Circles

66. B
67. A
68. B
69. A
70. C

## K. Other Figures

71. C
72. B
73. B
74. C
75. D
76. B
77. B
78. A
79. B
80. B

## L. Number Lines

81. C
82. B

## M. Coordinates

83. D
84. D
85. C
86. C

## N. Inequalities

87. A
88. A
89. A
90. B
91. A
92. B

## O. Averages

93. C
94. B

## P. Shortcuts

95. A
96. A
97. A
98. A
99. A
100. D
101. C

# Basic Skills Math Diagnosis

| Math area | Total questions | *If you got any of the answers to the following questions wrong, study answers to those questions. | Page in text for review | Complete Math Refresher: Refer to the sections of the Math Refresher (Part 5, starting on page 129) shown here for a refresher on the applicable rules. |
|---|---|---|---|---|
| A. Fractions | 5 | 1–5 | 31 | 101–112, 123–128 |
| B. Even-Odd Relationships | 7 | 6–12 | 31 | 603–611 |
| C. Factors | 9 | 13–21 | 31–32 | 409 |
| D. Exponents | 11 | 22–32 | 32 | 429–430 |
| E. Percentages | 3 | 33–35 | 33 | 106, 107, 114 |
| F. Equations | 5 | 36–40 | 33 | 406–409 |
| G. Angles | 4 | 41–44 | 33–34 | 500–503 |
| H. Parallel Lines | 7 | 45–51 | 34 | 504 |
| I. Triangles | 14 | 52–65 | 34–36 | 505–516, 306–308 |
| J. Circles | 5 | 66–70 | 36–37 | 524–529, 310–311 |
| K. Other Figures | 10 | 71–80 | 37–38 | 517–523, 303–305, 309, 312–316 |
| L. Number Lines | 2 | 81–82 | 38 | 410a |
| M. Coordinates | 4 | 83–86 | 38 | 410b–418 |
| N. Inequalities | 6 | 87–92 | 39 | 419–428 |
| O. Averages | 2 | 93–94 | 39 | 601 |
| P. Shortcuts | 7 | 95–101 | 39–40 | 128, 609 |

*Answer sheet is on pages 28–29.

# Solutions, Generalizations, Rules

## A. Fractions

**1. (B)**

$$\frac{\frac{a}{b}}{c} = a \times \frac{c}{b} = \boxed{\frac{ac}{b}}$$

*Alternate way:*

$$\frac{a}{\frac{b}{c}} = \frac{a}{\frac{b}{c}} \times \frac{c}{c} = \frac{ac}{\frac{b}{\not c} \times \not c} = \boxed{\frac{ac}{b}}$$

**2. (A)**

$$\frac{1}{\frac{1}{y}} = 1 \times \frac{y}{1} = y$$

INVERT TO MULTIPLY

**3. (A)**

$$\frac{\frac{a}{b}}{c} = \frac{a}{b} \times \frac{b}{b} = \boxed{\frac{a}{cb}}$$

**4. (C)**

$$\frac{1}{\frac{x}{y}} = 1 \times \frac{y}{x} = \boxed{\frac{y}{x}}$$

INVERT TO MULTIPLY

**5. (B)**

$$\frac{\frac{a}{b}}{\frac{b}{a}} = \frac{a}{b} \times \frac{a}{b} = \boxed{\frac{a^2}{b^2}}$$

INVERT TO MULTIPLY

*Alternate way:*

$$\frac{\frac{a}{b}}{\frac{b}{a}} = \frac{\frac{a}{b} \times a}{\frac{b}{a} \times a} = \frac{\frac{a^2}{b}}{\frac{b}{a}a} = \frac{\frac{a^2}{b}}{b} = \frac{\frac{a^2}{b} \times b}{b \times b} = \boxed{\frac{a^2}{b^2}}$$

## B. Even−Odd Relationships

**6. (A)** ODD × ODD = $\boxed{\text{ODD}}$

$3 \times 3 = 9; 5 \times 5 = 25$

**7. (B)** ODD + or − ODD = $\boxed{\text{EVEN}}$

$5 + 3 = 8$
$5 - 3 = 2$

**8. (B)** EVEN × EVEN = $\boxed{\text{EVEN}}$

$2 \times 2 = 4; 4 \times 2 = 8$

**9. (B)** EVEN + or − EVEN = $\boxed{\text{EVEN}}$

$6 + 2 = 8; 10 - 4 = 6$

**10. (A)** $(\text{ODD})^{\text{ODD}}$ = $\boxed{\text{ODD}}$

$3^3 = 3 \times 3 \times 3 = 27$ (odd)

$1^{27} = 1 = $ odd

**11. (B)** $(\text{EVEN})^{\text{EVEN}}$ = $\boxed{\text{EVEN}}$

$2^2 = 4$ (even); $4^2 = 16$ (even)

**12. (B)** $(\text{EVEN})^{\text{ODD}}$ = $\boxed{\text{EVEN}}$

$2^3 = 2 \times 2 \times 2 = 8$ (even)
$4^1 = 4$ (even)

## C. Factors

**13. (A)** $(x + 3)(x + 2) = x^2 \ldots$

$(x + 3)(x + 2) = x^2 + 3x + 2x \ldots$

$(x + 3)(x + 2) = x^2 + 3x + 2x + 6$

$(x + 3)(x + 2) = \boxed{x^2 + 5x + 6}$

**14. (C)** $(x + 3)(x - 2) = x^2 \ldots$

$(x + 3)(x - 2) = x^2 - 2x + 3x \ldots$

$(x + 3)(x - 2) = x^2 - 2x + 3x - 6$

$(x + 3)(x - 2) = \boxed{x^2 + x - 6}$

15. (B) $(x - 3)(y - 2) = xy \ldots$

$(x - 3)(y - 2) = xy - 2x - 3y \ldots$

$(x - 3)(y - 2) = \boxed{xy - 2x - 3y + 6}$

16. (D) $(a + b)(b + c) = ab \ldots$

$(a + b)(b + c) = ab + ac + b^2 \ldots$

$(a + b)(b + c) = \boxed{ab + ac + b^2 + bc}$

17. (C) $(a + b)(a - b) =$

$(a + b)(a - b) = a^2$

$(a + b)(a - b) = a^2 - ab + ba \ldots$

$(a + b)(a - b) = a^2 - ab + ba - b^2$

$(a + b)(a - b) = a^2 - ab + ba - b^2$

$\boxed{(a + b)(a - b) = a^2 - b^2}$   MEMORIZE

18. (A) $(a + b)^2 = (a + b)(a + b)$

$(a + b)(a + b) = a^2 \ldots$

$(a + b)(a + b) = a^2 + ab + ba \ldots$

$(a + b)(a + b) = a^2 + ab + ba + b^2$

$\boxed{(a + b)^2 = a^2 + 2ab + b^2}$   MEMORIZE

19. (D) $- (a - b) = - a - (- b)$

$- (a - b) = - a + b$

$\boxed{-(a - b) = b - a}$   MEMORIZE

20. (A) $a(b + c) =$

$a(b + c) = \boxed{ab + ac}$

21. (C) $- a(b - c) =$

$- a(b - c) = - ab - a(-c)$

$= - ab + ac = \boxed{ca - ab}$

## D. Exponents

22. (C) $10^5 = 100000$

5 zeroes

23. (B) $107076.5 = 1\,0\,7\,0\,7\,0\,.\,5$

$\phantom{107076.5 = }5\ 4\ 3\ \ 2\ 1$

$= 1.070765 \times \boxed{10^5}$

24. (B) ADD EXPONENTS

$a^2 \times a^5 = \boxed{a^7}\ a^m \times a^n = a^{m + n}$

25. (C) $(ab)^7 = \boxed{a^7 b^7}$

$(ab)^m = a^m b^m$

26. (A)

$\left(\dfrac{a}{c}\right)^8 = \boxed{\dfrac{a^8}{c^8}}; \left(\dfrac{a}{c}\right)^m = \dfrac{a^m}{c^m}$

27. (A) $a^4 \times b^4 = \boxed{(ab)^4}; a^m \times b^m = (ab)^m$

28. (A)

$a^{-3} \times b^5 = \boxed{\dfrac{b^5}{a^3}}$

$a^{-m} \times b^n = \dfrac{b^n}{a^m}$

29. (C) $(a^3)^5 = \boxed{a^{15}}\ (a^m)^n = a^{mn}$

MULTIPLY
EXPONENTS

30. (A)

$2a^{-3} = \boxed{\dfrac{2}{a^3}}$

$ax^{-b} = \dfrac{a}{x^b}$

Since $a^{-n} = \dfrac{1}{a^n}$

31. (B)

$2a^m \times \dfrac{1}{3} a^{-n} = \dfrac{2}{3} a^m a^{-n}$

$= \dfrac{2}{3} a^{m-n} \text{ or } \boxed{\dfrac{2\,a^m}{3\,a^n}}$

32. (D) $3^2 = 3 \times 3 = 9$

$3^{-2} = \dfrac{1}{3^2} = \dfrac{1}{9}$

$4^1 = 4$

$6^0 = 1$ (any number to 0 power = 1)

$3^2 + 3^{-2} + 4^1 + 6^0 = 9 + \dfrac{1}{9} + 4 + 1 = \boxed{14\dfrac{1}{9}}$

# E. Percentages

Translate is → =
  of → × (times)
  percent (%) → $\dfrac{}{100}$
  what → $x$ (or $y$, etc.)

**33.** (B) 15%  of 200 =
↓↓  ↓ ↓ ↓
$15\dfrac{}{100} \times 200 =$

$\dfrac{15}{100} \times 200 =$

$\dfrac{15}{1\cancel{00}} \times 2\cancel{00} = \boxed{30}$

---

**34.** (C) What is 3% of 5?
↓ ↓ ↓↓  ↓↓
$x = 3\dfrac{}{100} \times 5$

$x = \dfrac{3}{100} \times 5$

$x = \dfrac{15}{100} = \boxed{\dfrac{3}{20}}$

---

**35.** (C) What percent of  3  is  6?
↓    ↓   ↓   ↓   ↓  ↓
$x$  $\dfrac{}{100}$  ×  3  =  6

$\dfrac{x}{100} \times 3 = 6$

$\dfrac{3x}{100} = 6$

$3x = 600$

$x = \boxed{200}$

# F. Equations

**36.** (C) $y^2 = 16$

$\sqrt{y^2} = \pm\sqrt{16}$

$y = \boxed{\pm 4}$

Note: $\sqrt{y}$ means the *positive* square root of $y$. That is, the positive number that when multiplied by itself will give you the value of $y$.

$(\sqrt{y}) \times (\sqrt{y}) = y$

---

**37.** (A) $x - y = 10$
Add $y$:
$x - y + y = 10 + y$
$x = 10 + y$
Subtract 10:
$x - 10 = 10 - 10 + y$
$\boxed{x - 10 = y}$

---

**38.** (B) Add equations:
$$x + 4y = 7$$
$$x - 4y = 8$$
$$\overline{2x + \cancel{4y} - \cancel{4y} = 15}$$
$2x = 15$

$\boxed{x = \dfrac{15}{2}}$

---

**39.** (A) $x - 2y = 2$  ⬜1
$2x + y = 4$  ⬜2
Multiply ⬜1 by 2:
$2(x - 2y) = 2(2)$
We get:
$2x - 4y = 4$
Subtract ⬜2 from ⬜3:

$2x - 4y = 4$  ⬜3
$-\ (2x + y = 4)$  ⬜2
$\overline{\quad 0 - 5y = 0\quad}$

$\boxed{y = 0}$  ⬜4

Substitute: ⬜4 into either ⬜1 or ⬜2:
In ⬜1:
$x - y = 2$
$x - 2(0) = 2$
$\boxed{x = 2}$

---

**40.** (A) $\dfrac{x}{5} = \dfrac{7}{12}$, $x =$

Cross-multiply $x$:

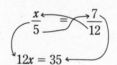

$12x = 35$

Divide by 12:

$\dfrac{12x}{12} = \dfrac{35}{12}$

$\boxed{x = \dfrac{35}{12} = 2\dfrac{11}{12}}$

# G. Angles

This diagram refers to questions 41–42.

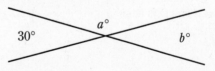

**41.** (B) $a°$ and $30°$ are supplementary angles (they add up to $180°$).

So $a + 30 = 180$; $a = \boxed{150}$.

42. (A) $b°$ and 30° are *vertical* angles (vertical angles are equal).

So $b = \boxed{30}$.

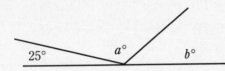

43. (A) $a°$, $b°$ and 25° make up a *straight* angle which is 180°.

$a + b + 25 = 180$

$a + b = 180 - 25$

$a + b = \boxed{155}$

44. (C) The sum of the angles in the diagram is $\boxed{360°}$, the number of degrees around the circumference of a circle.

## H. Parallel Lines

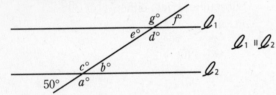

$\ell_1 \parallel \ell_2$

45. (B) $a + 50 = 180$

$a = \boxed{130}$

46. (A) $\boxed{b = 50}$ (vertical angles)

47. (B) $c = a$ (vertical angles)

$= \boxed{130}$

48. (B) $d = c$ (alternate interior angles are equal)

$= \boxed{130}$

49. (A) $e = b$ (alternate interior angles)

$= \boxed{50}$

50. (A) $f = e$ (vertical angles)

$= \boxed{50}$

51. (B) $g = d$ (vertical angles)

$= \boxed{130}$

## I. Triangles

52. (A)

(Note: Figure is not drawn to scale.)

If two sides are equal, base angles are equal. Thus $a = \boxed{70°}$.

53. (A)

(Note: Figure is not drawn to scale.)

If base angles are equal, then sides are equal, so $\boxed{x = 3}$.

54. (B)

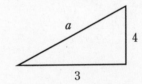

(Note: Figure is not drawn to scale.)

The sum of two sides must be *greater* than the third side. Try choices:

(A) $1 + 3 \not> 4$: (A) is not possible

(B) $3 + 4 > 6; 6 + 3 > 4; 4 + 6 > 3$ ...O.K.

(C) $3 + 4 \not> 10$. (C) is not possible

(D) $4 + 3 = 7$. (D) is not possible

55. (B) Using similar triangles, write a *proportion*.

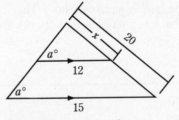

(Note: Figure is not drawn to scale.)

$\dfrac{x}{20} = \dfrac{12}{15}$

$15x = 12 \times 20$

$x = \dfrac{12 \times 20}{15}$

$x = \dfrac{\overset{4}{\cancel{12}} \times \overset{4}{\cancel{20}}}{\underset{5}{\cancel{15}}} = \boxed{16}$

In general:

$$\frac{m}{n} = \frac{q}{p} = \frac{r}{r+s}$$

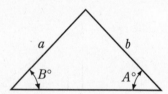

(Note: Figure is not drawn to scale.)

---

**56.** (B) The greater angle lies opposite the greater side and vice versa.

If $B > A$, $\boxed{b > a}$

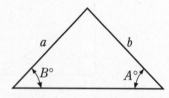

---

**57.** (C) The greater side lies opposite the greater angle and vice versa.

If $b < a$ then $\boxed{B < A}$

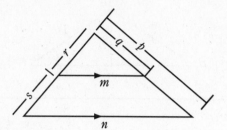

---

**58.** (B) Sum of angles of triangle = 180°.

So $40 + 60 + x = 180$.

$100 + x = 180$

$\boxed{x = 80}$

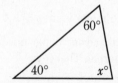

---

**59.** (C)

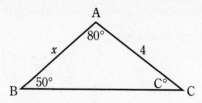

(Note: Figure is not drawn to scale.)

First calculate ∡ $C$. Call it $y$.

$80 + 50 + y = 180$ (Sum of ∡'s = 180°)

$y = 50$

Since ∡ $C = y = 50$ and ∡ $B = 50$, side $AB =$ side $AC$.

$AB = \boxed{x = 4}$

---

**60.** (C) $x° = 20° + 40°$ (sum of *remote* interior angles = exterior angle).

$\boxed{x = 60}$

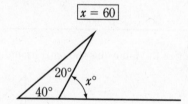

In general,

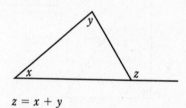

$z = x + y$

---

**61.** (B)

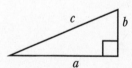

In right $\Delta$, $a^2 + b^2 = c^2$
So for

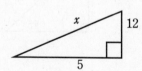

$5^2 + 12^2 = x^2$

$25 + 144 = x^2$

$169 = x^2$

$\sqrt{169} = x$

$\boxed{13} = x$

*Note:* Specific right triangles you should memorize; use multiples to generate other triangles.

Example of multiple:

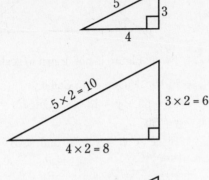

Memorize the following standard triangles:

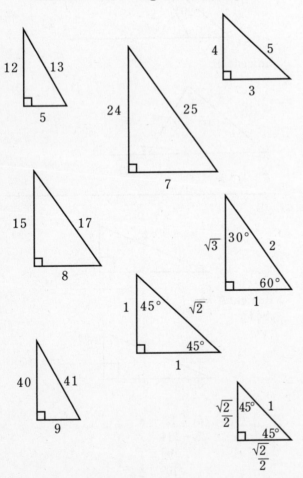

**62.** (B) Perimeter = sum of sides

$10 + 17 + 21 = \boxed{48}$

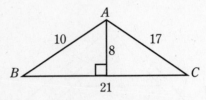

**63.** (D)

Area of $\Delta = \frac{1}{2}\,hb$

Area of $\Delta = \frac{1}{2}\,(8)(21) = \boxed{84}$

**64.** (A) Area of any triangle $= \frac{1}{2}$ base $\times$ height

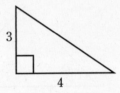

Here 4 is base and 3 is height. So area $= \frac{1}{2}\,(4 \times 3)$

$= \frac{1}{2}\,(12) = \boxed{6}$.

**65.** (B)

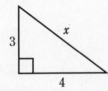

To find perimeter, we need to find the sum of the sides. The sum of the sides is $3 + 4 + x$.

We need to find x. From the solution in Question 61, we should realize that we have a 3-4-5 right triangle, so $x = 5$.

The perimeter is then $3 + 4 + 5 = \boxed{12}$.

Note that you could have found $x$ by using the Pythagorean Theorem:

$3^2 + 4^2 = x^2; 9 + 16 = x^2; 25 = x^2; \sqrt{25} = x; 5 = x.$

# J. Circles

**66.** (B) Area $= \pi r^2 = \pi(7)^2$

$= \boxed{49\pi}$

**67.** (A) Circumference $= 2\pi r = 2\pi(7)$
$$= \boxed{14\pi}$$

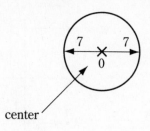

center

---

**68.** (B) Inscribed angle $= \frac{1}{2}$ arc

$$x° = \frac{1}{2}\, 70°$$

$$= \boxed{35°}$$

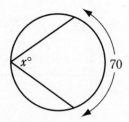

---

**69.** (A) Central angle $=$ arc

$$\boxed{30°} = x°$$

*Note:* The *total* number of degrees around the circumference is $360°$. So a central angle of $30°$ like the one above, cuts $\frac{30}{360} = \frac{1}{12}$ the circumference.

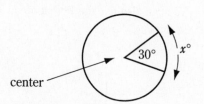

center

---

**70.** (C) The diameter cuts a $180°$ arc on circle, so an inscribed angle $y = \frac{1}{2}$ arc $= \frac{1}{2}\,(180°) = \boxed{90°}$.
Here is a good thing to remember:

Any inscribed angle whose triangle base is a diameter is $90°$.

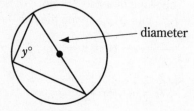

diameter

---

# K. Other Figures

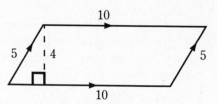

**71.** (C) Area of parallelogram $=$ base $\times$ height $= (10)(4) = \boxed{40}$

**72.** (B) Perimeter $=$ sum of sides $=$
$5 + 5 + 10 + 10 = \boxed{30}$

---

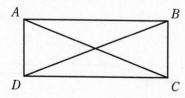

*ABCD* is a rectangle

**73.** (B) In a rectangle (as in a parallelogram) opposite sides are equal.
So $AD = BC = \boxed{6}$.

---

**74.** (C) In a rectangle (as in a parallelogram) opposite sides are equal.
So $DC = AB = \boxed{8}$.

---

**75.** (D) In a rectangle (but not in a parallelogram) the diagonals are equal.
So $DB = AC = \boxed{10}$.

---

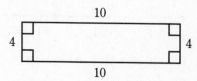

**76.** (B) Area of rectangle $=$ length $\times$ width $= 4 \times 10 = \boxed{40}$.

---

**77.** (B) Perimeter $=$ sum of sides $=$
$4 + 4 + 10 + 10 = \boxed{28}$.

---

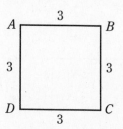

**78.** (A) Area of square with side $x$ is $x^2$. (All sides of a square are equal.) So length = width. Since $x = 3$, $x^2 = \boxed{9}$.

---

**79.** (B) Perimeter of square is the sum of all sides of square. Since all sides are equal, if one side is $x$, perimeter = $4x$.

$x = 3$, so $4x = \boxed{12}$.

---

**80.** (B) VOLUME OF RECTANGULAR SOLID shown below = $a \times b \times c$

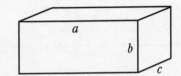

So for:

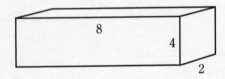

$a = 8, b = 4, c = 2$

and $a \times b \times c = 8 \times 4 \times 2 = \boxed{64}$.

Note: VOLUME OF CUBE shown below = $a \times a \times a = a^3$

## L.  Number Lines

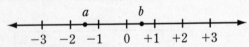

**81.** (C) $b$ is between 0 and $+1$
so $\boxed{1 > b > 0}$.

**82.** (B) $a$ is between $-2$ and $-1$
so $\boxed{-1 > a > -2}$.

## M. Coordinates

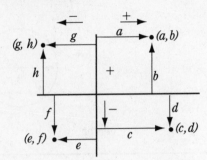

Horizontal right = $+$
Horizontal left  = $-$
Vertical up      = $+$
Vertical down    = $-$

**83.** (D) $a,b,c,h$ positive (4 letters)

**84.** (D) $d,e,f,g$ negative (4 letters)

---

**85.** (C)

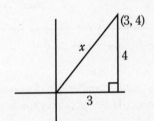

Remember 3-4-5 right triangle. $\boxed{x = 5}$

You can also use the Pythagorean Theorem:

$3^2 + 4^2 = x^2$; $9 + 16 = x^2$; $x^2 = 25$; $\boxed{x = 5}$

**86.** (C)

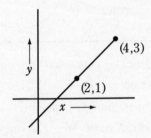

The slope of a line $y = mx + b$ is $m$. If two points $(x_1, y_1)$ and $(x_2, y_2)$ are on the line then the slope is

$\dfrac{y_2 - y_1}{x_2 - x_1} = m$. Here $x_1 = 2, y_1 = 1, x_2 = 4, y_2 = 3$

So $\dfrac{y_2 - y_1}{x_2 - x_1} = \dfrac{3 - 1}{4 - 2} = 1$.

# N. Inequalities

**87.** (A) You can multiply an inequality by a positive number and retain the same inequality:

$x > y$

$\boxed{4x > 4y}$   $\boxed{\text{ALWAYS}}$

**88.** (A) You can subtract the same number from both sides of an inequality and retain the same inequality:

$$x + y > z$$
$$x + y - x > z - x$$

$\boxed{y > z - x}$   $\boxed{\text{ALWAYS}}$

**89.** (A) If you multiply an inequality by a minus sign, you *reverse* the original inequality sign:

$$-4 < -x$$
$$-(-4 < -x)$$

$\boxed{+4 > +x}$   $\boxed{\text{ALWAYS}}$

**90.** (B) If $m > n$,

$qm > qn$ if $q$ is *positive*

$qm < qn$ if $q$ is *negative*

$qm = qn$ if $q$ is *zero*

So, $\boxed{qm > qn}$   $\boxed{\text{SOMETIMES}}$

**91.** (A) You can always add inequality relations:

$$x > y$$
$$+ p > q$$
$$\overline{x + p > y + q}$$   $\boxed{\text{ALWAYS}}$

**92.** (B) You can't always multiply inequality relations to get the same inequality relation. For example:

$$3 > 2 \qquad\qquad 3 > 2$$
$$\times -2 > -3 \qquad\qquad \times 2 > 1$$
$$\overline{-6 \ngtr -6} \qquad\qquad \overline{6 > 2}$$

However, if $x, y, p, q$ are positive, then if $x > y$ and $p > q$, $xp > yq$.

# O. Averages

**93.** (C) Average of $30 + 40 + 80 =$

$$\frac{30 + 40 + 80}{3} = \boxed{50}$$

Average of $x + y + z + t + \ldots = \dfrac{x + y + z + t + \ldots}{\text{number of terms}}$

**94.** (B) Average speed $\dfrac{\text{TOTAL DISTANCE}}{\text{TOTAL TIME}}$

Distance = 40 miles, Time = 4 hours

Average speed $= \dfrac{40 \text{ miles}}{4 \text{ hours}} = \boxed{10 \text{ miles per hour}}$

# P. Shortcuts

**95.** Don't get a common denominator if you can do something more easily:

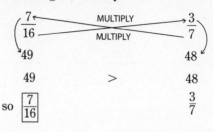

$$49 \qquad\qquad > \qquad\qquad 48$$

so $\boxed{\dfrac{7}{16}}$ $\qquad\qquad\qquad \dfrac{3}{7}$

**96.** (A)

$$\frac{7}{12} \underset{\text{MULTIPLY}}{\overset{\text{MULTIPLY}}{+}} \frac{3}{5} = \frac{7 \times 5 + 3 \times 12}{12 \times 5}$$

$$= \frac{35 + 36}{60}$$

$$= \frac{71}{60} = \boxed{1\frac{11}{60}}$$

**97.** (A)

$$\frac{7}{12} \underset{\text{MULTIPLY}}{\overset{\text{MULTIPLY}}{-}} \frac{3}{5} = \frac{7 \times 5 - 3 \times 12}{12 \times 5}$$

$$= \frac{35 - 36}{60}$$

$$= \boxed{-\frac{1}{60}}$$

**98.** (A) Don't divide by 250! Multiply both numerator and denominator by 4:

$$\frac{4}{250} \times \frac{4}{4} = \frac{16}{1,000} = \boxed{0.016}$$

**99.** (A) Get rid of denominators!

$$200 = \frac{a + b + c}{2} \qquad\qquad ①$$

Multiply ① by 2:

$$200 \times 2 = a + b + c \qquad\qquad ②$$

$$80 = \frac{a + b}{3} \qquad\qquad ③$$

Multiply ③ by 3:

$$80 \times 3 = a + b \qquad\qquad ④$$

Now subtract ④ from ②:

$$200 \times 2 - 80 \times 3 = a + b + c - (a + b)$$
$$= \cancel{a} + \cancel{b} + c - \cancel{a} - \cancel{b}$$
$$400 - 240 = c$$
$$\boxed{160} = c$$

**100.** (D) Don't multiply $95 \times 75$ or $95 \times 74$ !

Factor *common* 95:

$$95 \times 75 - 95 \times 74 =$$
$$= 95 \ (75 - 74)$$
$$= 95(1)$$
$$= \boxed{95}$$

**101.** (C) $\dfrac{140 \times 15}{5 \times 7}$

Don't multiply $140 \times 15$ if you can first *reduce*.

$$\dfrac{\overset{20}{\cancel{140}} \times 15}{\underset{1}{5 \times \cancel{7}}} = \dfrac{20 \times 15}{5}$$

Further reduce:

$$\dfrac{20 \times \overset{3}{\cancel{15}}}{\underset{1}{\cancel{5}}} = \boxed{60}$$

# PART 3

# STRATEGY
# SECTION

## Using Critical-Thinking Skills to Score High on the PSAT

# 5 General Strategies

## General Strategies for Taking the PSAT Examination

Before studying the 32 specific strategies for the Math and Critical Reading questions, you will find it useful to review the following 5 General Strategies for taking the PSAT examination.

## Strategy 1:

DON'T RUSH INTO GETTING AN ANSWER WITHOUT THINKING. BE CAREFUL IF YOUR ANSWER COMES TOO EASILY, ESPECIALLY IF THE QUESTION IS TOWARD THE END OF THE SECTION.

### Beware of Choice A If You Get the Answer Fast or Without Really Thinking

Everybody panics when they take an exam like the PSAT. And what happens is that they rush into getting answers. That's OK, except that you have to think carefully. If a problem looks too easy, beware! And, especially beware of the Choice A answer. It's usually a "lure" choice for those who rush into getting an answer without critically thinking about it. Here's an example:

Below is a picture of a digital clock. The clock shows that the time is 6:06. Consider all the times on the clock where the hour digit is the same as the minute digit like in the clock shown below. Another such "double" time would be 8:08 or 9:09. What is the smallest time period between any two such doubles?

(A) 61 minutes
(B) 60 minutes
(C) 58 minutes
(D) 50 minutes
(E) 49 minutes

**6:06**

Did you subtract 7:07 from 8:08 and get 1 hour and 1 minute (61 minutes)? If you did you probably chose Choice A: the *lure choice*. Think—do you really believe that the test maker would give you such an easy question? The fact that you figured it out so easily and saw that Choice A was your answer should make you think twice. The thing you have to realize is that there is another possibility: 12:12 to 1:01 gives 49 minutes, and so Choice E is correct.

*So, in summary, if you get the answer fast and without doing much thinking, and it's a Choice A answer, think again. You may have fallen for the Choice A lure.*

NOTE: Choice A is often a "lure choice" for those who quickly get an answer without doing any real thinking. However, you should certainly realize that Choice A answers can occur, especially if there is no "lure choice."

## Strategy 2:

KNOW AND LEARN THE DIRECTIONS TO THE QUESTION TYPES BEFORE YOU TAKE THE ACTUAL TEST.

### Never Spend Time Reading Directions During the Test or Doing Sample Questions That Don't Count

All SATs are standardized. For example, all the Regular Math questions have the same directions from test to test as do the Sentence Completions, etc. So it's a good idea to learn these sets of directions and familiarize yourself with their types of questions early in the game before you take your actual PSAT.

Here's an example of a set of PSAT directions, together with an accompanying example for the Sentence Completion type of questions.

*For each question in this section, select the best answer from among the choices given and fill in the corresponding oval on the answer sheet.*

---

Each sentence below has one or two blanks, each blank indicating that something has been omitted. Beneath the sentence are five words or sets of words labeled A through E. Choose the word or set of words that, when inserted in the sentence, best fits the meaning of the sentence as a whole.

Example:

Hoping to _____ the dispute, negotiators proposed a compromise that they felt would be _____ to both labor and management.

   (A)  enforce...useful
   (B)  end...divisive
   (C)  overcome...unattractive
   (D)  extend...satisfactory
   (E)  resolve...acceptable

---

If on your actual test you spend time reading these directions and/or answering the sample question, you will waste valuable time.

As you go through this book, you will become familiar with all the question types so that you won't have to read their directions on the actual test.

# Strategy 3:

IT MAY BE WISER NOT TO LEAVE AN ANSWER BLANK.

## *The Penalty for Guessing Is Much Smaller Than You Might Expect*

On the PSAT you lose a percentage of points if you guess and get the wrong answer. Of course, you should always try to eliminate choices. You'll find that, after going through this book, you'll have a better chance of eliminating wrong answers, However, if you cannot eliminate any choice in a question and have no idea of how to arrive at an answer, you might want to pick any answer and go on to the next question.

There are two reasons for this:

1. You don't want to risk mismarking a future answer by leaving a previous answer blank.
2. Even though there is a penalty for guessing, the penalty is much smaller than you might expect, and

this way you have at least a chance of getting the question right. Suppose, for example, that you have a five-choice question:

---

From a probablistic point of view, it is very likely that you would get one question right and four wrong (you have a 1 in 5 chance of getting a five-choice question right) if you randomly guess at the answers. Since $\frac{1}{4}$ point is taken off for each wrong five-choice question, you've gotten $1 - \frac{1}{4} \times 4 = 0$ points, because you've gotten 1 question right and 4 wrong. Thus you break even. So the moral is whether you randomly guess at questions you're not sure of at all or whether you leave those question answers blank, it doesn't make a difference in the long run!

---

# Strategy 4:

WRITE AS MUCH AS YOU WANT IN YOUR TEST BOOKLET.

## *Test Booklets Aren't Graded—So Use Them as You Would Scrap Paper*

Many students are afraid to mark up their test booklets. But, the booklets are not graded! Make any marks you want. In fact, some of the strategies demand that you extend or draw lines in geometry questions or label diagrams, or circle incorrect answers, etc. That's why when I see computer programs that show only the questions on a screen and prevent the student from marking a diagram or circling an answer, I realize that such programs prevent the student from using many powerful strategies. *So write all you want on your test booklet—use your test paper as you would scrap paper.*

# Strategy 5:

USE YOUR OWN CODING SYSTEM TO TELL YOU WHICH QUESTIONS TO RETURN TO.

## *If You Have Extra Time after Completing a Test Section, You'll Know Exactly Which Questions Need More Attention*

When you are sure that you have answered a question correctly, mark your question paper with ✓. For questions you are not sure of but for which you have eliminated some of the choices, use **?**. For questions that you're not sure of at all or for which you have not been able to eliminate any choices, use **??**. This will give you a bird's-eye view of what questions you should return to, if you have time left after completing a particular test section.

# 32 Easy-to-Learn Strategies

## 19 Math Strategies + 13 Verbal (Critical Reading) Strategies

Critical thinking is the ability to think clearly in order to solve problems and answer questions of all types—SAT questions, for example, both Math and Verbal!

Educators who are deeply involved in research on Critical-Thinking Skills tell us that such skills are straightforward, practical, teachable, and learnable.

The 19 Math Strategies and 13 Verbal Strategies in this section are Critical-Thinking Skills. These strategies have the potential to raise your PSAT scores dramatically, approximately 5 points to 30 points in each of the Critical Reading and Math parts of the test. Since each correct PSAT question gives you an additional 1 point on average, it is reasonable to assume that if you can learn and then use these valuable PSAT strategies, you can boost your PSAT scores phenomenally!

**BE SURE TO LEARN AND USE THE STRATEGIES THAT FOLLOW!**

## How to Learn the Strategies

1. For each strategy, look at the heading describing the strategy.

2. Try to answer the first example without looking at the EXPLANATORY ANSWER.

3. Then look at the EXPLANATORY ANSWER and if you got the right answer, see if the method described would enable you to solve the question in a better way with a faster approach.

4. Then try each of the next EXAMPLES without looking at the EXPLANATORY ANSWERS.

5. Use the same procedure as in (3) for each of the EXAMPLES.

The MATH STRATEGIES start on page 51, and the VERBAL STRATEGIES start on page 80. However, before you start the Math Strategies, it would be wise for you to look at the *Important Note on the Allowed Use of Calculators on the PSAT* following; the *Important Note on Math Questions on the PSAT*, page 45; *The Grid-Type Math Question*, page 45; and *Use of a Calculator in the Grid-Type Question*, page 49.

## Important Note on the Allowed Use of Calculators on the PSAT

Although the use of calculators on the PSAT will be allowed, using a calculator may be sometimes more tedious, when in fact you can use another problem-solving method or shortcut. So you must be selective on when and when not to use a calculator on the test.

Here's an example of when a calculator should *not* be used:

$$\frac{2}{5} \times \frac{5}{6} \times \frac{6}{7} \times \frac{7}{8} \times \frac{8}{9} \times \frac{9}{10} \times \frac{10}{11} =$$

(A) $\frac{9}{11}$  (B) $\frac{2}{11}$  (C) $\frac{11}{36}$  (D) $\frac{10}{21}$  (E) $\frac{244}{360}$

Here the use of a calculator may take some time. However, if you use the strategy of canceling numerators and denominators (Math Strategy 1 on page 51) as shown:

*Cancel numerators/denominators:*

$$\frac{2}{\cancel{5}} \times \frac{\cancel{5}}{\cancel{6}} \times \frac{\cancel{6}}{\cancel{7}} \times \frac{\cancel{7}}{\cancel{8}} \times \frac{\cancel{8}}{\cancel{9}} \times \frac{\cancel{9}}{\cancel{10}} \times \frac{\cancel{10}}{11} = \frac{2}{11}$$

You can see that the answer comes easily as $\frac{2}{11}$.

Later I will show you an example in the *grid-type* question where the use of a calculator will also take you a longer time to solve a problem than without the calculator. Here's an example where using a calculator may get you the solution *as fast as* using a strategy without the calculator:

25 percent of 16 is equivalent to $\frac{1}{2}$ of what number?

(A) 2    (B) 4    (C) 8    (D) 16    (E) 32

Using a calculator, you'd use Math Strategy 2 (page 52) (translating *of* to *times* and *is* to *equals*), first calculating 25 percent of 16 to get **4**. Then you'd say 4 = half of what number and you'd find that number to be **8**.

Without using a calculator, you'd still use Math Strategy 2 (the translation strategy), but you could write 25 percent as $\frac{1}{4}$, so you'd figure out that $\frac{1}{4} \times 16$ was (**4**). Then you'd call the number you want to find $x$, and say 4 $= \frac{1}{2}(x)$. You'd find $x = $ **8**.

Note that both methods, with and without a calculator, are about equally efficient; however, the technique in the second method can be used for many more problems and hones more thinking skills.

# Important Note on Math Questions on the PSAT

There are two types of math questions on the PSAT.

1. The Regular Math (total of 28 counted questions), which has five choices. The strategies for these start on page 51.

2. The "Grid-Type" Math Question (total of 10 counted questions) is described below.

   *Note:* The grid-type questions can be solved using the Regular Math Strategies.

# The Grid-Type Math Question

There will be 10 questions on the PSAT where you will have to "grid" in your answer rather than choose from a set of five choices. Here are the directions to the "grid-type" question. Make sure that you understand these directions completely before you answer any of the grid-type questions.

**Directions:** For Student-Produced Response questions 1–15, use the grids at the bottom of the answer sheet page on which you have answered questions 1–8.

Each of the remaining 10 questions requires you to solve the problem and enter your answer by marking the circles in the special grid, as shown in the examples below. You may use any available space for scratchwork.

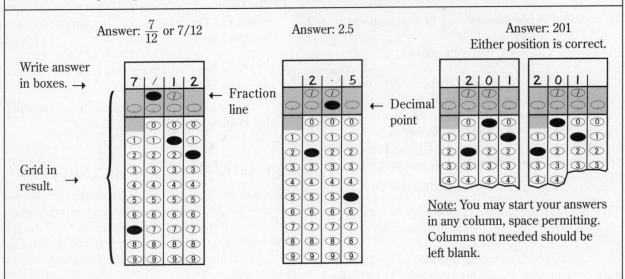

Answer: $\frac{7}{12}$ or 7/12

Answer: 2.5

Answer: 201
Either position is correct.

Write answer in boxes. →

← Fraction line

← Decimal point

Grid in result. →

Note: You may start your answers in any column, space permitting. Columns not needed should be left blank.

- Mark no more than one oval in any column.

- Because the answer sheet will be machine-scored, **you will receive credit only if the ovals are filled in correctly.**

- Although not required, it is suggested that you write your answer in the boxes at the top of the columns to help you fill in the ovals accurately.

- Some problems may have more than one correct answer. In such cases, grid only one answer.

- No question has a negative answer.

- **Mixed numbers** such as $2\frac{1}{2}$ must be gridded as 2.5 or 5/2. (If [2 1/2 grid] is gridded, it will be interpreted as $\frac{21}{2}$, not $2\frac{1}{2}$.)

- <u>Decimal Accuracy:</u> If you obtain a decimal answer, **enter the most accurate value the grid will accommodate.** For example, if you obtain an answer such as 0.6666 ... , you should record the result as .666 or .667. **Less accurate values such as .66 or .67 are not acceptable.**

Acceptable ways to grid $\frac{2}{3}$ = .6666 ...

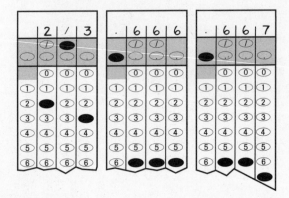

# Practice with Grids

According to the directions on the previous page, grid the following values in the grids 1–15:

317     4.2     .5     $\frac{1}{12}$     2474

$3\frac{1}{2}$     $\frac{57}{3}$     0     .346     $4\frac{3}{4}$

39     1     $\frac{3}{8}$     45.3     $8\frac{1}{7}$

# Answers

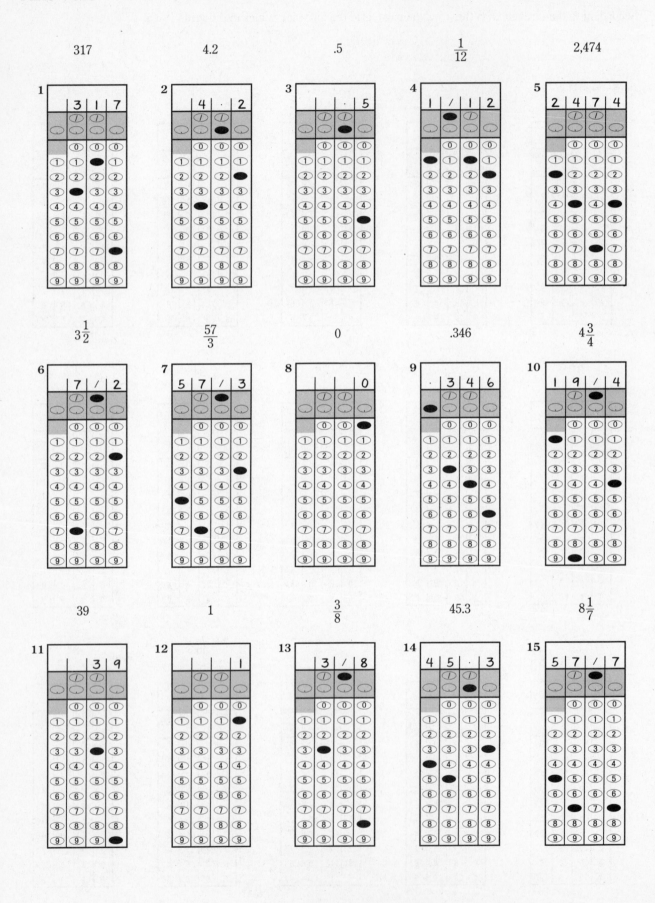

# Use of a Calculator in the Grid-Type Question

In the following example, you can either use a calculator or not. However, the use of a calculator will require a different gridding.

EXAMPLE:

If $\frac{2}{7} < x < \frac{3}{7}$ find one value of $x$.

SOLUTION *WITHOUT* A CALCULATOR:

Get some value between $\frac{2}{7}$ and $\frac{3}{7}$. Write $\frac{2}{7} = \frac{4}{14}$ and $\frac{3}{7} = \frac{6}{14}$

So we have $\frac{4}{14} < x < \frac{6}{14}$ and $x$ can be $\frac{5}{14}$.

The grid will look like:

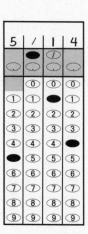

SOLUTION *WITH* A CALCULATOR:

Calculate on calculator:

$\frac{3}{7} = .4285714\ ...$

$\frac{2}{7} = .2857142\ ...$

So $.2857142 < x < .4285714$.

You could have the grid as follows:

all the way to:

# 19 Math Strategies

## Using Critical-Thinking Skills in Math Questions

MATH STRATEGY 1

---

### Cancel Quantities to Make the Problem Simpler

---

Cancel numbers or expressions that appear on both sides of an equation; cancel same numerators and denominators. But make sure that you don't divide by 0 in what you're doing! You will save precious time by using this strategy. You won't have to make any long calculations.

EXAMPLE 1

If $P \times \frac{11}{14} = \frac{11}{14} \times \frac{8}{9}$, then $P =$

(A) $\frac{8}{9}$

(B) $\frac{9}{8}$

(C) 8
(D) 11
(E) 14

Choice A is correct. Do not multiply $\frac{11}{14} \times \frac{8}{9}$!

Cancel the common $\frac{11}{14}$:

$P \times \frac{11}{14} = \frac{11}{14} \times \frac{8}{9}$, then $P =$

$P = \frac{8}{9}$ (*Answer*)

**Note:** You can cancel the $\frac{11}{14}$ because you are *dividing* both sides by the same nonzero number. Suppose you had a problem like the following:

If $R \times a = a \frac{4}{5}$ , then $R =$

(A) $\frac{2}{3}$

(B) $\frac{4}{5}$

(C) 1

(D) $\frac{5}{4}$

(E) Cannot be determined.

What do you think the answer is? It's not Choice A! It is Choice E because you cannot cancel the "*a*" because

*a* may be 0 and you cannot divide by 0. So if $a = 0$, $R$ can be *any* number.

EXAMPLE 2

$\frac{2}{5} \times \frac{5}{6} \times \frac{6}{7} \times \frac{7}{8} \times \frac{8}{9} \times \frac{9}{10} \times \frac{10}{11} =$

(A) $\frac{9}{11}$

(B) $\frac{2}{11}$

(C) $\frac{11}{36}$

(D) $\frac{10}{21}$

(E) $\frac{244}{360}$

Choice B is correct.

Cancel numerators/denominators:

$\frac{2}{\cancel{5}} \times \frac{\cancel{5}}{\cancel{6}} \times \frac{\cancel{6}}{7} \times \frac{7}{\cancel{8}} \times \frac{\cancel{8}}{\cancel{9}} \times \frac{\cancel{9}}{\cancel{10}} \times \frac{\cancel{10}}{11} = \frac{2}{11}$

EXAMPLE 3

If $a + b > a - b$, which must follow?

(A) $a < 0$
(B) $b < 0$
(C) $a > b$
(D) $b > a$
(E) $b > 0$

Choice E is correct.

$a + b > a - b$

Cancel common *a*'s:

$$\cancel{a} + b > \cancel{a} - b$$
$$b > -b$$
Add *b*: $\quad b + b > b - b$
$$2b > 0$$
$$b > 0$$

## Translate English Words into Mathematical Expressions

Many of the PSAT problems are word problems. Being able to translate word problems from English into mathematical expressions or equations will help you to score high on the test. The following table translates some commonly used words into their mathematical equivalents:

### TRANSLATION TABLE

| *Words* | *Math Way to Say It* |
|---|---|
| is, as, was, has, cost | = (equals) |
| of | × (times) |
| percent | /100 (the percent number over 100) |
| $x$ percent | $x/100$ |
| which, what | $x$ (or any other variable) |
| $x$ and $y$ | $x + y$ |
| the sum of $x$ and $y$ | $x + y$ |
| the difference between $x$ and $y$ | $x - y$ |
| $x$ more than $y$ | $x + y$ |
| $x$ less than $y$ | $y - x$ |
| the product of $x$ and $y$ | $xy$ |
| the square of $x$ | $x^2$ |
| $x$ is greater than $y$ | $x > y$ (or $y < x$) |
| $x$ is less than $y$ | $x < y$ (or $y > x$) |
| $y$ years ago | $-y$ |
| $y$ years from now | $+y$ |
| $c$ times as old as John | $c \times$ (John's age) |
| $x$ older than $y$ | $x + y$ |
| $x$ younger than $y$ | $y - x$ |
| the increase from $x$ to $y$ | $y - x$ |
| the decrease from $x$ to $y$ | $x - y$ |
| the percent increase from $x$ to $y$ ($y > x$) | $\left(\frac{y-x}{x}\right)100$ |
| the percent decrease from $x$ to $y$ ($y < x$) | $\left(\frac{x-y}{x}\right)100$ |
| the percent of increase | $\left(\frac{\text{amount of increase}}{\text{original amount}}\right) \times 100$ |
| the percent of decrease | $\left(\frac{\text{amount of decrease}}{\text{original amount}}\right) \times 100$ |
| $n$ percent greater than $x$ | $x + \left(\frac{n}{100}\right)x$ |
| $n$ percent less than $x$ | $x - \left(\frac{n}{100}\right)x$ |

By knowing this table, you will find word problems much easier to do.

# OPTIONAL QUIZ ON TRANSLATION TABLE

Take this quiz to see if you understand the translation table before attempting the problems in Strategy #2 that follow.

1.  **Mary is five years older than John** translates to:

    (A)  J = 5 + M
    (B)  M + J = 5
    (C)  M > 5 + J
    (D)  M = 5 + J
    (E)  None of these.

1.  (D) Translate: **Mary** to **M**; **John** to **J**; **is** to =; **older than** to +
    So **Mary is five years older than John** becomes:

    $$\begin{array}{ccccc} \downarrow & \downarrow\ \downarrow & & \downarrow & & \downarrow \\ M & = \ \ 5 & & + & & J \end{array}$$

2.  **3 percent of 5** translates to:

    (A)  3/5
    (B)  3/100 divided by 5
    (C)  (3/100) × 5
    (D)  3 × 100 × 5
    (E)  None of these.

    (C) percent or % = /100; of = ×; so

    **3% of 5** translates to:

    3/100 × 5

3.  **What percent of 3** translates to:

    (A)  $x(100) \times 3$
    (B)  $(x/100) \times 3$
    (C)  $(x/100)$ divided by 3
    (D)  $(3/100)x$
    (E)  None of these.

    (B) Translate: what to $x$; percent to /100. Thus

    **What percent of 3** becomes:

    $$\begin{array}{cccc} \downarrow & \downarrow & \downarrow & \downarrow \\ x & /100 & \times & 3 \end{array}$$

4.  **Six years ago, Sarah was 4 times as old as John was then** translates to:

    (A)  S − 6 = 4J
    (B)  6 − S = 4J
    (C)  6 − S = 4(J − 6)
    (D)  S − 6 = 4(J − 6)
    (E)  None of these.

    (D) **Six years ago, Sarah was** translates to S − 6 = **4 times as old as John is** would be 4J. However, **4 times as old as John *was then*** translates to 4(J − 6). Thus
    **Six years ago, Sarah was 4 times as old as John was then** translates to:
    S − 6 = 4 × (J − 6)

5.  **The percent increase from 5 to 10** is

    (A)  [(10 − 5)/5] × 100
    (B)  [(5 − 10)/5] × 100
    (C)  [(10 − 5)/10] × 100
    (D)  [(5 − 10)/10] × 100
    (E)  None of these.

    (A) Percent increase from $a$ to $b$ is [($b − a$) /$a$] × 100. So the percent increase from 5 to 10 would be [(10 − 5)/5] × 100.

6.  **Harry is older than John and John is older than Mary** translates to:

    (A)  H > J > M
    (B)  H > J < M
    (C)  H > M > J
    (D)  M > H > J
    (E)  None of these.

    (A) **Harry is older than John** translates to: H > J. **John is older than Mary** translates to J > M. So we have H > J and J > M which consolidated becomes: H > J > M.

7. **Even after Phil gives Sam 6 compact discs, he still has 16 more compact discs than Sam has** translates to:

(A)  P − 6 = 16 + S
(B)  P − 6 = 16 + S + 6
(C)  P + 6 = 16 + S + 6
(D)  P + 6 + 16 + S
(E)  None of these.

(B) (1) **Even after Phil gives Sam 6 compact discs** translates to:
P–6
(2) **He still has 16 more compact discs than Sam has** translates to:
= 16 + S + 6 since Sam has gotten 6 additional compact discs. Thus combining (1) and (2), we get: P − 6 = 16 + S + 6.

8. **q is 10% greater than p** translates to:

(A)  q = (10/100)q + p
(B)  q > (10/100)p
(C)  q = (10/100)p + p
(D)  q = (10/100) + p
(E)  None of these.

(C) (1) **q is** translates to **q =**
(2)  **10% greater than p** translates to
     **(10/100)p + p** so

          **q is 10% greater than p**

translates to:   ↓ ↓  ‾‾‾‾‾‾‾‾‾‾‾‾‾‾‾‾
          q = (10/100)p + p

9. **200 is what percent of 20** translates to:

(A)  200 = $x$ × 100 × 20
(B)  200 = ($x$/100) divided by 20
(C)  200 = ($x$/100) × 20
(D)  200 = $x$ × 20
(E)  None of these.

(C) Translate **is** to **=**; **what** to $x$; **percent** to **/100**, **of** to × so we get that:
**200 is what percent of 20** translates to:
200 =   $x$   /100  × 20

10. **The product of the sums of $x$ and $y$ and $y$ and $z$ is 5** translates to:

(A)  $xy + yz = 5$
(B)  $x + y + y + z = 5$
(C)  $(x + y)(yz) = 5$
(D)  $(x + y)(y + z) = 5$
(E)  None of these.

(D) The sum of $x$ and $y$ is $x + y$. The sum of $y + z$ is $y + z$. So the product of those sums is $(x + y)(y + z)$.

Thus **The product of the sums of $x$ and $y$ and $y$ and $z$ is 5** translates to:
$(x + y)(y + z) = 5$

EXAMPLE 1

Sarah is twice as old as John. Six years ago, Sarah was 4 times as old as John was then. How old is John now?

(A)  3
(B)  9
(C)  18
(D)  20
(E)  impossible to determine

Choice B is correct. Translate:
        Sarah is twice as old as John.
          ↓    ↓   ↓    ↓        ↓
          S  =  2  ×        J
                              S = 2J          $\boxed{1}$

Six years ago Sarah was 4 times as old as John was then
  ↓              ↓    ↓ ↓ ↓              ↓
 − 6            S = 4 ×              (J − 6)
      This becomes S − 6 = 4(J − 6)      $\boxed{2}$

Substituting $\boxed{1}$ into $\boxed{2}$:
          $2J − 6 = 4(J − 6)$
          $2J − 6 = 4J − 24$
             $18 = 2J$
              $9 = J$      *(Answer)*

## EXAMPLE 2

200 is what percent of 20?

(A) $\frac{1}{10}$

(B) 10

(C) 100

(D) 1,000

(E) 10,000

Choice D is correct. Translate:

$$\begin{array}{cccccc} 200 & \text{is} & \text{what} & \text{percent} & \text{of} & 20 \\ \downarrow & \downarrow & \downarrow & \downarrow & \downarrow & \downarrow \\ 200 & = & x & \overline{100} & \times & 20 \end{array}$$

$$200 = \frac{x}{100}(20)$$

Divide by 20: $10 = \frac{x}{100}$

Multiply by 100: $1,000 = x$ (*Answer*)

## EXAMPLE 3

John is now $m$ years old and Sally is 4 years older than John. Which represents Sally's age 6 years ago?

(A) $m + 10$

(B) $m - 10$

(C) $m - 2$

(D) $m - 4$

(E) $4m - 6$

Choice C is correct.

Translate:

John is now $m$ years old

$$\begin{array}{ccc} \downarrow & \downarrow & \downarrow \\ J & = & m \end{array}$$

Sally is 4 years older than John

$$\begin{array}{ccccc} \downarrow & \downarrow & \downarrow & \downarrow & \downarrow \\ S & = 4 & & + & J \end{array}$$

Sally's age 6 years ago =

$$\begin{array}{ccc} \downarrow & \downarrow & \\ S & - \quad 6 & = \end{array}$$

So we get: $\quad J = m$

$\qquad\qquad S = 4 + J$

and find: $\ S - 6 = 4 + J - 6$

$\qquad\qquad S - 6 = J - 2$ (substituting $m$ for $J$)

$\qquad\qquad S - 6 = m - 2$

## EXAMPLE 4

Phil has three times as many DVDs as Sam has. Even after Phil gives Sam 6 DVDs, he still has 16 more DVDs than Sam has. What was the original number of DVDs that Phil had?

(A) 20

(B) 24

(C) 28

(D) 33

(E) 42

Choice E is correct.

Translate:

Phil has three times as many DVDs as Sam has

$$\begin{array}{cccccc} \downarrow & \downarrow & \downarrow & \downarrow & & \downarrow \\ P & = & 3 & \times & & S \end{array}$$

Even after Phil gives Sam 6 DVDs, he still has 16

$$\begin{array}{cccccc} \downarrow & \downarrow & \underbrace{\qquad} & \downarrow & & \downarrow \ \downarrow \\ P & - & & 6 & & = \ 16 \end{array}$$

more DVDs than Sam has

$$\begin{array}{cc} \downarrow & \underbrace{\qquad} \\ + & S+6 \end{array}$$

Sam now has $S + 6$ DVDs because Phil gave Sam 6 DVDs. So we end up with the equations:

$P = 3S$

$P - 6 = 16 + S + 6$

Find $P$; get rid of $S$:

$$P = 3S; \qquad \frac{P}{3} = S$$

$$P - 6 = 16 + \frac{P}{3} + 6$$

$$P - 6 = \frac{48 + P + 18}{3}$$

$$3P = 18 = 48 + P + 18$$
$$2P = 84$$
$$P = 42$$

MATH STRATEGY 3

## Know How to Find Unknown Quantities (Areas, Lengths, Arc and Angle Measurements) from Known Quantities (the Whole Equals the Sum of Its Parts)

*When Asked to Find a Particular Area or Length, Instead of Trying to Calculate It Directly, Find It by Subtracting Two Other Areas or Lengths—a Method Based on the Fact That the Whole Minus a Part Equals the Remaining Part*

This strategy is very helpful in many types of geometry problems. A very important equation to remember is

The whole = the sum of its parts     $\boxed{1}$

Equation $\boxed{1}$ is often disguised in many forms, as seen in the following examples:

### EXAMPLE 1

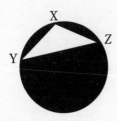

In the diagram above, $\triangle XYZ$ has been inscribed in a circle. If the circle encloses an area of 64, and the area of $\triangle XYZ$ is 15, then what is the area of the shaded region?

(A)  25
(B)  36
(C)  49
(D)  79
(E)  It cannot be determined from the information given.

Choice C is correct. Use equation $\boxed{1}$. Here, the whole refers to the area within the circle, and the parts refer to the areas of the shaded region and the triangle. Thus,

Area within circle =
Area of shaded region +
Area of $\triangle XYZ$

64 = Area of shaded region + 15

or Area of shaded region = 64 − 15 = 49 *(Answer)*

### EXAMPLE 2

In the diagram below, $\overline{AE}$ is a straight line, and F is a point on $\overline{AE}$. Find an expression for $m \sphericalangle DFE$.

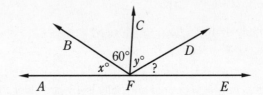

(A)  $x + y - 60$
(B)  $x + y + 60$
(C)  $90 - x - y$
(D)  $120 - x - y$
(E)  $180 - x - y$

Choice D is correct. Use equation $\boxed{1}$. Here, the whole refers to the straight angle, $\sphericalangle AFE$, and its parts refer to $\sphericalangle AFB$, $\sphericalangle BFC$, $\sphericalangle CFD$, and $\sphericalangle DFE$. Thus,

$$m \sphericalangle AFE = m \sphericalangle AFB + m \sphericalangle BFC +$$
$$m \sphericalangle CFD + m \sphericalangle DFE$$
$$180 = x + 60 + y + m \sphericalangle DFE$$
or
$$m \sphericalangle DFE = 180 - x - 60 - y$$
$$m \sphericalangle DFE = 120 - x - y \ (Answer)$$

### EXAMPLE 3

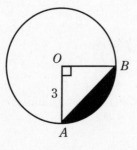

In the figure above, $O$ is the center of the circle. Triangle $AOB$ has side 3 and angle $AOB = 90°$. What is the area of the shaded region?

(A) $9\left(\dfrac{\pi}{4}-\dfrac{1}{2}\right)$

(B) $9\left(\dfrac{\pi}{2}-1\right)$

(C) $9(\pi-1)$

(D) $9\left(\dfrac{\pi}{4}-\dfrac{1}{4}\right)$

(E) Cannot be determined.

EXPLANATORY ANSWER

Choice A is correct.

<u>Subtract knowns from knowns:</u>

Area of shaded region = area of quarter circle $AOB$ − area of triangle $AOB$

Area of quarter circle $AOB = \dfrac{\pi(3)^2}{4}$

Area of triangle $AOB = \dfrac{3\times 3}{2}$ (since $OB = 3$ and

area of a triangle $= \dfrac{1}{2}$ base $\times$ height)

Thus, area of shaded region $= \dfrac{9\pi}{4} - \dfrac{9}{2} = 9\left(\dfrac{\pi}{4}-\dfrac{1}{2}\right)$.

MATH STRATEGY 4

---

## Remember Classic Expressions Such as
$$x^2 - y^2,\ x^2 + 2xy + y^2,\ x^2 - 2xy + y^2,\ \dfrac{x+y}{xy}$$

---

Memorize the following factorizations and expressions:

$x^2 - y^2 = (x + y)(x - y)$   Equation 1

$x^2 + 2xy + y^2 = (x + y)(x + y) = (x + y)^2$   Equation 2

$x^2 - 2xy + y^2 = (x - y)(x - y) = (x - y)^2$   Equation 3

$\dfrac{x+y}{xy} = \dfrac{1}{x} + \dfrac{1}{y}$   $x, y \neq 0$   Equation 4

$\dfrac{x-y}{xy} = \dfrac{1}{y} - \dfrac{1}{x}$   $x, y \neq 0$   Equation 4A

$xy + xz = x(y + z)$   Equation 5

$xy - xz = x(y - z)$   Equation 5A

EXAMPLE 1

If $(x + y) = 9$ and $xy = 14$, find $\dfrac{1}{x} + \dfrac{1}{y}$.

(Note: $x, y > 0$)

(A) $\dfrac{1}{9}$   (B) $\dfrac{2}{7}$   (C) $\dfrac{9}{14}$   (D) 5   (E) 9

Choice C is correct. We are given:

$$(x + y) = 9 \qquad \boxed{1}$$
$$xy = 14 \qquad \boxed{2}$$
$$x, y > 0 \qquad \boxed{3}$$

I hope that you did not solve $\boxed{2}$ for $x$ (or $y$), and then substitute it into $\boxed{1}$. If you did, you obtained a quadratic equation.

Here is the FAST method. Use Equation 4:

$$\dfrac{1}{x} + \dfrac{1}{y} = \dfrac{x+y}{xy} \qquad \boxed{4}$$

From $\boxed{1}$ and $\boxed{2}$, we find that $\boxed{4}$ becomes

$$\dfrac{1}{x} + \dfrac{1}{y} = \dfrac{9}{14} \ (\textit{Answer})$$

EXAMPLE 2

If $y + \dfrac{1}{y} = 9$, then $y^2 + \dfrac{1}{y^2} =$

(A) 76
(B) 77
(C) 78
(D) 79
(E) 81

Choice D is correct.

Square $\left(y + \dfrac{1}{y}\right)$

$$\left(y + \dfrac{1}{y}\right)2 = 81 = y^2 + \dfrac{1}{y^2} + 2 \qquad \text{(Equation 2)}$$

$$79 = y^2 + \dfrac{1}{y^2}$$

EXAMPLE 3

If $a - b = 4$ and $a + b = 7$, then $a^2 - b^2 =$

(A) $5\dfrac{1}{2}$

(B) 11

(C) 28

(D) 29

(E) 56

Choice C is correct.

Use $(a - b)(a + b) = a^2 - b^2$            (Equation 1)

$$a - b = 4$$
$$a + b = 7$$
$$(a - b)(a + b) = 28 = a^2 - b^2$$

#### EXAMPLE 4

If $(a + b)^2 = 20$ and $ab = -3$, then $a^2 + b^2 =$

(A)  14
(B)  20
(C)  26
(D)  32
(E)  38

Choice C is correct.

Use $(a + b)^2 = a^2 + 2ab + b^2 = 20$      (Use Equation 2)

$$ab = -3$$

So, $2ab = -6$

Substitute $2ab = -6$ in:

$$a^2 + 2ab + b^2 = 20$$

We get:

$$a^2 - 6 + b^2 = 20$$
$$a^2 + b^2 = 26$$

#### EXAMPLE 5

If $998 \times 1{,}002 > 10^6 - x$, $x$ could be

(A)  4 but not 3
(B)  4 but not 5
(C)  5 but not 4
(D)  3 but not 4
(E)  3, 4, or 5

Choice C is correct.

Use $(a + b)(a - b) = a^2 - b^2$            (Use Equation 1)

Write: $998 \times 1{,}002 = (1{,}000 - 2)(1{,}000 + 2) > 10^6 - x$
$$= 1{,}000^2 - 4 > 10^6 - x$$
$$= (10^3)^2 - 4 > 10^6 - x$$
$$= 10^6 - 4 > 10^6 - x$$

Multiply by $-1$; *reverse inequality sign:*

$$-1(-4 > -x)$$
$$+4 < +x$$

MATH STRATEGY **5**

---

# Know How to Manipulate Averages

Almost all problems involving averages can be solved by remembering that

$$\text{Average} = \frac{\text{Sum of the individual quantities or measurements}}{\text{Number of quantities or measurements}}$$

(*Note:* Average is also called Arithmetic Mean.)

#### EXAMPLE 1

The average height of three students is 68 inches. If two of the students have heights of 70 inches and 72 inches respectively, then what is the height (in inches) of the third student?

(A)  60
(B)  62
(C)  64
(D)  65
(E)  66

Choice B is correct. Recall that

$$\text{Average} = \frac{\text{Sum of the individual measurements}}{\text{Number of measurements}}$$

Let $x$ = height (in inches) of the third student. Thus,

$$68 = \frac{70 + 72 + x}{3}$$

Multiplying by 3,

$$204 = 70 + 72 + x$$
$$\text{or } 204 = 142 + x$$
$$\text{or } x = 62 \text{ inches } (Answer).$$

#### EXAMPLE 2

The average length of 6 objects is 25 cm. If 5 objects are each 20 cm in length, what is the length of the sixth object in cm?

(A)  55
(B)  50
(C)  45
(D)  40
(E)  35

EXAMPLE 3

Scores on five tests range from 0 to 100 inclusive. If Don gets 70 on the first test, 76 on the second, and 75 on the third, what is the minimum score Don may get on the fourth test to average 80 on all five tests?

(A)  76
(B)  79
(C)  82
(D)  89
(E)  99

EXPLANATORY ANSWERS FOR EXAMPLES 2–3

EXAMPLE 2

(B) *Use the formula:*

$$\text{Average} = \frac{\text{Sum of individual items}}{\text{Number of items}}$$

Now call the length of the sixth item, $x$. Then:

$$25 = \frac{20 + 20 + 20 + 20 + 20 + x}{6}$$

or $25 = \dfrac{20 \times 5 + x}{6}$

Multiply by 6:

$$25 \times 6 = 20 \times 5 + x$$
$$150 = 100 + x$$
$$50 = x$$

EXAMPLE 3

(B) *Use the formula:*

$$\text{Average} = \frac{\text{Sum of scores on tests}}{\text{Number of tests}}$$

Let $x$ be the score on the fourth test and $y$ be the score on the fifth test.

Then:

$$80 = \text{Average} = \frac{70 + 76 + 75 + x + y}{5}$$

The minimum score $x$ Don can get is the *lowest* score he can get. The higher the score $y$ is, the lower the score $x$ can be. The greatest value of $y$ can be 100. So:

$$80 = \frac{70 + 76 + 75 + x + 100}{5}$$
$$80 = \frac{321 + x}{5}$$

Multiply by 5:

$$400 = 321 + x$$
$$79 = x$$

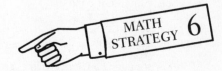

MATH STRATEGY 6

## Know How to Manipulate Inequalities

Most problems involving inequalities can be solved by remembering one of the following statements.

If $x > y$, then $x + z > y + z$    Statement 1

If $x > y$ and $w > z$, then $x + w > y + z$    Statement 2

If $w > 0$ and $x > y$, then $wx > wy$    Statement 3

If $w < 0$ and $x > y$, then $wx < wy$    Statement 4

If $x > y$ and $y > z$, then $x > z$    Statement 5

$x > y$ is the same as $y < x$    Statement 6

$a < x < b$ is the same as both
$a < x$ and $x < b$    Statement 7

If $x > y > 0$ and $w > z > 0$, then
$xw > yz$    Statement 8

If $x > 0$ and $z = x + y$, then $z > y$    Statement 9

Note that Statement 1 and Statement 2 are also true if all the ">" signs are changed to "<" signs

If $x > 0$, then
$$\begin{cases} x^n < 0 \text{ if } n \text{ is odd} & \text{Statement 10} \\ x^n > 0 \text{ if } n \text{ is even} & \text{Statement 11} \end{cases}$$

If $xy > 0$, then $x > 0$ and $y > 0$
or $x < 0$ and $y < 0$    Statement 12

If $xy < 0$, then $x > 0$ and $y < 0$
or $x < 0$ and $y > 0$    Statement 13

### EXAMPLE 1

If $0 < x < 1$, then which of the following must be true?

I. $2x < 2$
II. $x - 1 < 0$
III. $x^2 < x$

(A) I only
(B) II only
(C) I and II only
(D) II and III only
(E) I, II, and III

Choice E is correct. We are told that $0 < x < 1$. Using

$\boxed{\text{Statement 7}}$, we have

$$0 < x \qquad \boxed{1}$$
$$x < 1 \qquad \boxed{2}$$

For Item I, we multiply $\boxed{2}$ by 2.

See $\boxed{\text{Statement 3}}$

$$2x < 2$$

Thus, Item I is true.
For Item II, we add $-1$ to both sides of $\boxed{2}$.

See $\boxed{\text{Statement 1}}$ to get
$$x - 1 < 0$$

Thus Item II is true.
For Item III, we multiply $\boxed{2}$ by $x$.

See $\boxed{\text{Statement 3}}$ to get
$$x^2 < x$$

Thus, Item III is true.

All items are true, so Choice E is correct.

### EXAMPLE 2

Which combination of the following statements can be used to demonstrate that $x$ is positive?

I. $x > y$
II. $1 < y$

(A) I alone but not II
(B) II alone but not I
(C) I and II taken together but neither taken alone
(D) Both I alone and II alone
(E) Neither I nor II nor both

Choice C is correct. We want to know which of the following

$$x > y \qquad \boxed{1}$$
$$1 < y \qquad \boxed{2}$$

is enough information to conclude that

$$x > 0 \qquad \boxed{3}$$

$\boxed{1}$ alone is not enough to determine $\boxed{3}$ because $0 > x > y$ could be true. (Note: $x$ is greater than $y$, but they both could be negative.)

$\boxed{2}$ alone is not enough to determine $\boxed{3}$ because we don't know whether $x$ is greater than, less than, or equal to $y$.

However, if we use $\boxed{1}$ and $\boxed{2}$ together, we can compare the two:

$$1 < y \text{ is the same as } y > 1$$

Therefore, $x > y$ with $y > 1$ yields: $\boxed{\text{Statement 5}}$

$$x > 1 \qquad \boxed{4}$$

Since $1 > 0$ is always true, then from $\boxed{4}$

$$x > 0 \text{ is always true}$$

### EXAMPLE 3

What are all values of $x$ such that $(x - 7)(x + 3)$ is positive?

(A) $x > 7$
(B) $-7 < x < 3$
(C) $-3 < x < 7$
(D) $x > 7$ or $x < -3$
(E) $x > 3$ or $x < -7$

Choice D is correct.

$$(x - 7)(x + 3) > 0 \text{ when}$$
$$x - 7 > 0 \text{ and } x + 3 > 0 \qquad \boxed{1}$$
$$\text{or} \quad x - 7 < 0 \text{ and } x + 3 < 0 \qquad \boxed{2}$$

$\boxed{\text{Statement 12}}$

From $\boxed{1}$ we have $x > 7$ and $x > -3$ $\qquad \boxed{3}$
when $x > 7$ $\qquad \boxed{4}$
then $\boxed{3}$ and $\boxed{1}$ are always satisfied.
From $\boxed{2}$, we have $x < 7$ and $x < -3$ $\qquad \boxed{5}$
when $x < -3$ $\qquad \boxed{6}$
then $\boxed{5}$ and $\boxed{2}$ are always satisfied.
Thus, $\boxed{4}$ and $\boxed{6}$ together represent the entire solution.

### EXAMPLE 4

Janie is older than Tammy, but she is younger than Lori. Let $j$, $t$, and $l$ be the ages in years of Janie, Tammy, and Lori, respectively. Which of the following is true?

(A) $j < t < l$
(B) $t < j < l$
(C) $t < l < j$
(D) $l < j < t$
(E) $l < t < j$

Choice B is correct. **(First, use Strategy 2: Translate English words into mathematical expressions.)** Janie is older than Tammy but she is younger than Lori, translates to:

$$\text{Janie's age} > \text{Tammy's age} \qquad \boxed{1}$$
$$\text{Janie's age} < \text{Lorie's age} \qquad \boxed{2}$$
$$\textit{Given:} \quad \text{Janie's age} = j \qquad \boxed{3}$$
$$\text{Tammy's age} = t \qquad \boxed{4}$$
$$\text{Lori's age} = l \qquad \boxed{5}$$

Substituting $\boxed{3}$, $\boxed{4}$, and $\boxed{5}$ into $\boxed{1}$ and $\boxed{2}$, we get

$$j > t \qquad \boxed{6}$$
$$j < l \qquad \boxed{7}$$

Use $\boxed{\text{Statement 5}}$. Reversing $\boxed{6}$, we get

$$t < j \qquad \boxed{8}$$

Combining $\boxed{8}$ and $\boxed{7}$, we get

$$t < j < l$$

MATH STRATEGY 7

---

## Use Specific Numerical Examples to Prove or Disprove Your Guess

When you do not want to do a lot of algebra, or when you are unable to prove what you think is the answer, you may want to substitute numbers.

EXAMPLE 1

The sum of the cubes of any two consecutive positive integers is always

(A) an odd integer
(B) an even integer
(C) the cube of an integer
(D) the square of an integer
(E) the product of an integer and 3

Choice A is correct. Try specific numbers. Call consecutive positive integers 1 and 2.
Sum of cubes:

$$1^3 + 2^3 = 1 + 8 = 9$$

You have now eliminated choices B and C. You are left with choices A, D, and E.

Now try two other consecutive integers: 2 and 3

$$2^3 + 3^3 = 8 + 27 = 35$$

Choice A is acceptable. Choice D is false. Choice E is false.

Thus, Choice A is the only choice remaining.

EXAMPLE 2

John is now $m$ years old and Sally is 4 years older than John. Which represents Sally's age 6 years ago?

(A) $m + 10$
(B) $m - 10$
(C) $m - 2$
(D) $m - 4$
(E) $4m - 6$

Choice C is correct.

Try a specific number.

Let $m = 10$

John is 10 years old.
Sally is 4 years older than John, so Sally is 14 years old.
Sally's age 6 years ago was 8 years.

Now look for the choice that gives you 8 with $m = 10$.

(A) $m + 10 = 10 + 10 = 20$
(B) $m - 10 = 10 - 10 = 0$
(C) $m - 2 = 10 - 2 = 8$—that's the one

EXAMPLE 3

The sum of three consecutive even integers is $P$. Find the sum of the next three consecutive *odd* integers that follow the greatest of the three even integers.

(A) $P + 9$
(B) $P + 15$
(C) $P + 12$
(D) $P + 20$
(E) None of these.

Choice B is correct.

Try specific numbers.
Let the three consecutive even integers be 2, 4, 6.

$$\text{So, } 2 + 4 + 6 = P = 12.$$

The next three consecutive odd integers that follow 6 are:

$$7, 9, 11$$

So the sum of

$$7 + 9 + 11 = 27.$$

Now, where $P = 12$, look for a choice that gives you 27:

(A) $P + 9 = 12 + 9 = 21$—NO
(B) $P + 15 = 12 + 15 = 27$—YES

MATH STRATEGY 8

## When Each Choice Must Be Tested, Start with Choice E and Work Backward

If you must check each choice for the correct answer, start with Choice E and work backward. The reason for this is that the test maker of a question *in which each choice must be tested* often puts the correct answer as Choice D or E. In this way, the careless student must check all or most of the choices before finding the correct one. So if you're trying all the choices, start with the last choice, then the next to last choice, etc.

EXAMPLE 1

If $p$ is a positive integer, which *could* be an odd integer?

(A) $2p + 2$
(B) $p^3 - p$
(C) $p^2 + p$
(D) $p^2 - p$
(E) $7p - 3$

Choice E is correct. Start with Choice E first since you have to *test* out the choices.

*Method 1:* Try a number for $p$. Let $p = 1$. Then (starting with choice E)

$7p - 3 = 7(1) - 3 = 4$. 4 is even, so try another number for $p$ to see whether $7p - 3$ is odd. Let $p = 2$.

$7p - 3 = 7(2) - 3 = 11$. 11 is odd. Therefore, Choice E is correct.

*Method 2:* Look at Choice E. $7p$ could be even or odd, depending on what $p$ is. If $p$ is even, $7p$ is even. If $p$ is odd, $7p$ is odd. Accordingly, $7p - 3$ is either even or odd. Thus, Choice E is correct.

*Note:* By using either Method 1 or Method 2, it is not necessary to test the other choices.

EXAMPLE 2

If $y = x^2 + 3$, then for which value of $x$ is $y$ divisible by 7?

(A) 10
(B) 8
(C) 7
(D) 6
(E) 5

Choice E is correct. Since you must check all of the choices, start with Choice E:

$$y = 5^2 + 3 = 25 + 3 = 28$$
$$28 \text{ is divisible by 4 } (\textit{Answer})$$

If you had started with Choice A, you would have had to test four choices instead of one choice before finding the correct answer.

EXAMPLE 3

Which fraction is greater than $\frac{1}{2}$ ?

(A) $\frac{4}{9}$

(B) $\frac{17}{35}$

(C) $\frac{6}{13}$

(D) $\frac{12}{25}$

(E) $\frac{8}{15}$

Choice E is correct.

<u>Look at Choice E first.</u>

$$\text{Is } \frac{1}{2} > \frac{8}{15}?$$

Use the cross-multiplication method.

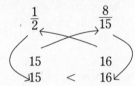

So, $\frac{1}{2} < \frac{8}{15}$

You also could have looked at Choice E and said $\frac{8}{16} = \frac{1}{2}$ and realized that $\frac{8}{15} > \frac{1}{2}$ because $\frac{8}{15}$ has a smaller denominator than $\frac{8}{16}$.

EXAMPLE 4

$$\begin{array}{r} 3 \ \# \ 2 \\ \times \quad 8 \\ \hline 28 \ \star \ 6 \end{array}$$

If # and ⋆ are different digits in the correctly calculated multiplication problem above, then # could be

(A) 1
(B) 2
(C) 3
(D) 4
(E) 6

Choice E is correct.

<u>Try Choice E first.</u>

9 and 6 are different numbers, so Choice E is correct.

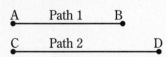

MATH STRATEGY 9

---

## Know How to Solve Problems Using the Formula R × T = D

Almost every problem involving motion can be solved using the formula

$$R \times T = D$$
or
rate × elapsed time = distance

EXAMPLE 1

The diagram below shows two paths: Path 1 is 10 miles long, and Path 2 is 12 miles long. If Person X runs along Path 1 at 5 miles per hour and Person Y runs along Path 2 at $y$ miles per hour, and if it takes exactly the same amount of time for both runners to run their whole path, then what is the value of $y$?

A   Path 1   B

C   Path 2   D

(A) 2

(B) $4\frac{1}{6}$

(C) 6

(D) 20

(E) 24

Choice C is correct. Let T = Time (in hours) for either runner to run the whole path.

Using R × T = D, for Person X, we have
(5 mi/hr)(T hours) = 10 miles
or   5T = 10 or       $\boxed{1}$
    T = 2

For Person Y, we have
($y$ mi/hr)(T hours) = 12 miles
     or     $y$T = 12
    Using $\boxed{1}$ $y$(2) = 12 or $y$ = 6

EXAMPLE 2

A car traveling at 50 miles per hour for two hours travels the same distance as a car traveling at 20 miles per hour for $x$ hours. What is $x$?

(A) $\dfrac{4}{5}$

(B) $\dfrac{5}{4}$

(C) 5

(D) 2

(E) $\dfrac{1}{2}$

Choice C is correct.

Use $R \times T = D$. Call distance both cars travel, $D$ (since distance is same for both cars).

So we get:

$$50 \times 2 = D \; (= 100) \quad \boxed{1}$$
$$20 \times x = D \; (= 100) \quad \boxed{2}$$

Solving $\boxed{2}$ you can see that $x = 5$.

EXAMPLE 3

John walks at a rate of 4 miles per hour. Sally walks at a rate of 5 miles per hour. If John and Sally both start at the same starting point, how many miles is one person from the other after $T$ hours of walking? (*Note:* Both are walking on the same road in the same direction.)

(A) $\dfrac{t}{2}$

(B) $t$

(C) $2t$

(D) $\dfrac{4}{5}t$

(E) $\dfrac{5}{4}t$

Choice B is correct.

Draw a diagram:

John (4 mph)

Sally (5 mph)

Let $D_J$ be distance that John walks in $t$ hours.
Let $D_S$ be distance that Sally walks in $t$ hours.
Then, using $R \times T = D$,

for John: $4 \times t = D_J$
for Sally: $5 \times t = D_S$

The distance between Sally and John after $T$ hours of walking is:

$$D_S - D_J = 5t - 4t = t$$

## Know How to Use Units of Time, Distance, Area, or Volume to Find or Check Your Answer

By knowing what the units in your answer must be, you will often have an easier time finding or checking your answer. A very helpful thing to do is to treat the units of time or space as variables (like "*x*" or "*y*"). Thus, you should substitute, multiply, or divide these units as if they were ordinary variables. The following examples illustrate this idea.

---

### EXAMPLE 1

What is the distance in miles covered by a car that traveled at 50 miles per hour for 5 hours?

(A)  10
(B)  45
(C)  55
(D)  200
(E)  250

Choice E is correct. Although this is an easy "R × T = D" problem, it illustrates this strategy very well.

Recall that

$$\text{rate} \times \text{time} = \text{distance}$$
$$(50 \text{ mi./hr.})(5 \text{ hours}) = \text{distance}$$

Notice that when I substituted into R × T = D, *I kept the units of rate and time* (miles/hour and hours). Now I will *treat these units as if they were ordinary variables.* Thus,

$$\text{distance} = (50 \text{ mi./hr.})(5 \text{ hours})$$

I have canceled the variable "hour(s)" from the numerator and denominator of the right side of the equation. Hence,

$$\text{distance} = 250 \text{ miles}$$

The distance has units of "miles" as I would expect. In fact, if the units in my answer had been "miles/hour" or "hours," then I would have been in error.

Thus, *the general procedure* for problems using this strategy is:

Step 1. <u>Keep the units given in the question.</u>

Step 2. <u>Treat the units as ordinary variables.</u>

Step 3. <u>Make sure the answer has units that you would expect.</u>

---

### EXAMPLE 2

How many inches is equivalent to 2 yards, 2 feet, and 7 inches?

(A)  11
(B)  37
(C)  55
(D)  81
(E)  103

Choice E is correct.
Remember that

$$1 \text{ yard} = 3 \text{ feet} \qquad \boxed{1}$$
$$1 \text{ foot} = 12 \text{ inches} \qquad \boxed{2}$$

Treat the units of length as variables! Divide $\boxed{1}$ by 1 yard, and $\boxed{2}$ by 1 foot, to get

$$1 = \frac{3 \text{ feet}}{1 \text{ yard}} \qquad \boxed{3}$$

$$1 = \frac{12 \text{ inches}}{1 \text{ foot}} \qquad \boxed{4}$$

We can multiply any expression by 1 and get the same value. Thus, 2 yards + 2 feet + 7 inches =

$$(2 \text{ yards})(1)(1) + (2 \text{ feet})(1) + 7 \text{ inches} \qquad \boxed{5}$$

Substituting $\boxed{3}$ and $\boxed{4}$ into $\boxed{5}$, 2 yards + 2 feet + 7 inches

$$= 2 \text{ yards}\left(\frac{3 \text{ feet}}{\text{yard}}\right)\left(\frac{12 \text{ inches}}{\text{foot}}\right) + 2 \text{ feet}\left(\frac{12 \text{ inches}}{\text{foot}}\right) + 7 \text{ inches}$$

$$= 72 \text{ inches} + 24 \text{ inches} + 7 \text{ inches}$$

$$= 103 \text{ inches}$$

Notice that the answer is in "inches" as I expected. If the answer had come out in "yards" or "feet," then I would have been in error.

EXAMPLE 3

A car wash cleans $x$ cars per hour, for $y$ hours at $z$ dollars per car. How much money in *cents* did the car wash receive?

(A) $\dfrac{xy}{100z}$

(B) $\dfrac{xyz}{100}$

(C) $100xyz$

(D) $\dfrac{100x}{yz}$

(E) $\dfrac{yz}{100x}$

Choice C is correct.

Use units: $\left(\dfrac{x \text{ cars}}{\text{hour}}\right)(y \text{ hours})\left(\dfrac{z \text{ dollars}}{\text{car}}\right) = xyz$ dollars $\boxed{1}$

Multiply $\boxed{1}$ by 100. We get $100xyz$ cents.

MATH STRATEGY 11

---

## Use New Definitions and Functions Carefully

Some SAT questions use new symbols, functions, or definitions that were created in the question. At first glance, these questions may seem difficult because you are not familiar with the new symbol, function, or definition. *However, most of these questions can be solved through simple substitution or application of a simple definition.*

EXAMPLE 1

If the symbol $\phi$ is defined by the equation

$$a \phi b = a - b - ab$$

for all $a$ and $b$, then $\left(-\dfrac{1}{3}\right) \phi (-3) =$

(A) $\dfrac{5}{3}$

(B) $\dfrac{11}{3}$

(C) $-\dfrac{13}{3}$

(D) $-4$

(E) $-5$

Choice A is correct. All that is required is substitution:

$$a \phi b = a - b - ab$$
$$\left(-\dfrac{1}{3}\right) \phi (-3)$$

Substitute $-\dfrac{1}{3}$ for $a$ and

$-3$ for $b$ in $a - b - ab$:

$$\left(-\dfrac{1}{3}\right) \phi (-3) = -\dfrac{1}{3} - (-3) - \left(-\dfrac{1}{3}\right)(-3)$$

$$= -\dfrac{1}{3} + 3 - 1$$

$$= 2 - \dfrac{1}{3}$$

$$= \dfrac{5}{3} \text{ (Answer)}$$

EXAMPLE 2

Let $\boxed{x} = \begin{cases} \dfrac{5}{2}(x+1) & \text{if } x \text{ is an odd integer} \\ \dfrac{5}{2}x & \text{if } x \text{ is an even integer} \end{cases}$

Find $\boxed{2y}$, where $y$ is an integer.

(A) $\dfrac{5}{2}y$  (B) $5y$  (C) $\dfrac{5}{2}y + 1$

(D) $5y + \dfrac{5}{2}$  (E) $5y + 5$

Choice B is correct. All we have to do is to substitute $2y$ into the definition of $\boxed{x}$. In order to know which definition of $\boxed{x}$ to use, we want to know if $2y$ is even. Since $y$ is an integer, then $2y$ is an even integer. Thus,

$$\boxed{2y} = \dfrac{5}{2}(2y)$$

or

$$\boxed{2y} = 5y \text{ (Answer)}$$

EXAMPLE 3

The symbol 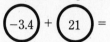 is defined as the greatest integer less than or equal to $x$.

$$\left(-3.4\right) + \left(21\right) =$$

(A)  16
(B)  16.6
(C)  17
(D)  17.6
(E)  18

Choice C is correct.

$\left(-3.4\right)$ is defined as the *greatest integer less than or equal to* −3.4. This is −4, since −4 < −3.4.

$\left(21\right)$ is defined as the *greatest integer less than or equal to* 21. That is just 21, since 21 = 21.

Thus, −4 + 21 = 17

MATH
STRATEGY 12

## Try Not to Make Tedious Calculations Since There Is Usually an Easier Way

In many of the examples given in these strategies, it has been explicitly stated that one should not calculate complicated quantities. In some of the examples, we have demonstrated a fast and a slow way of solving the same problem. On the actual exam, if you find that your solution to a problem involves a tedious and complicated method, then you are probably doing the problem in a long, hard way.* Almost always there will be an easier way.

EXAMPLE 1

If $y^8 = 4$ and $y^7 = \dfrac{3}{x}$,

what is the value of $y$ in terms of $x$?

(A)  $\dfrac{4x}{3}$

(B)  $\dfrac{3x}{4}$

(C)  $\dfrac{4}{x}$

(D)  $\dfrac{x}{4}$

(E)  $\dfrac{12}{x}$

Choice A is correct.

Don't solve for the *value* of $y$ first, by finding $y = 4^{\frac{1}{8}}$. Just divide the two equations:

(Step 1)  $y^8 = 4$

(Step 2)  $y^7 = \dfrac{3}{x}$

(Step 3)  $\dfrac{y^8}{y^7} = \dfrac{4}{\frac{3}{x}}$

(Step 4)  $y = 4 \times \dfrac{x}{3}$

(Step 5)  $y = \dfrac{4x}{3}$  *(Answer)*

EXAMPLE 2

If $(a^2 + a)^3 = (a + 1)^3 x$, where $a + 1 \neq 0$, then $x =$

(A)  $a$
(B)  $a^2$
(C)  $a^3$

(D)  $\dfrac{a + 1}{a}$

(E)  $\dfrac{a}{a + 1}$

Choice C is correct.

Isolate $x$ first:

$$x = \frac{(a^2 + a)^3}{(a + 1)^3}$$

Now use the fact that $\left(\dfrac{x^3}{y^3}\right) = \left(\dfrac{x}{y}\right)^3$:

$$\frac{(a^2 + a)^3}{(a + 1)^3} = \left(\frac{a^2 + a}{a + 1}\right)^3$$

Now <u>factor</u> $a^2 + a = a\,(a + 1)$

* Many times, you can DIVIDE, MULTIPLY, ADD, SUBTRACT, or FACTOR to simplify.

So:

$$\left(\frac{a^2 + a}{a + 1}\right)^3 = \left[\frac{a(a + 1)}{a + 1}\right]^3$$
$$= \left[\frac{a\cancel{(a + 1)}}{\cancel{a + 1}}\right]^3$$
$$= a^3$$

EXAMPLE 3

If $\frac{p + 1}{r + 1} = 1$ and $p$, $r$ are nonzero, and $p$ is not equal to $-1$, and $r$ *is* not equal to $-1$, then

(A)  $2 > p/r > 1$ always
(B)  $p/r < 1$ always
(C)  $p/r = 1$ always
(D)  $p/r$ can be greater than 2
(E)  $p/r = 2$ always

Choice C is correct.

Get rid of the fraction. <u>Multiply</u> both sides of the equation

$$\frac{p + 1}{r + 1} = 1 \; by \; r + 1!$$
$$\left(\frac{p + 1}{r + 1}\right)\cancel{r + 1} = r + 1$$
$$p + 1 = r + 1$$

Cancel the 1's:
$$p = r$$

So:
$$\frac{p}{r} = 1$$

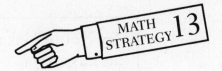

## Know How to Find Unknown Expressions by Adding, Subtracting, Multiplying, or Dividing Equations or Expressions

When you want to calculate composite quantities like $x + 3y$ or $m - n$, often you can do it by adding, subtracting, multiplying, or dividing the right equations or expressions.

EXAMPLE 1

If $4x + 5y = 10$ and $x + 3y = 8$,
then $\frac{5x + 8y}{3} =$

(A)  18
(B)  15
(C)  12
(D)  9
(E)  6

Choice E is correct. Don't solve for $x$, then for $y$.

Try to get the quantity $\frac{5x + 8y}{3}$ by adding or subtracting the equations. In this case, <u>add</u> equations.

$$\begin{array}{r} 4x + 5y = 10 \\ + \; x + 3y = 8 \\ \hline 5x + 8y = 18 \end{array}$$

Now divide by 3:

$$\frac{5x + 8y}{3} = \frac{18}{3} = 6 \; (\textit{Answer})$$

EXAMPLE 2

If $x + 2y = 4$, then $5x + 10y - 8 =$

(A)  10
(B)  12
(C)  $-10$
(D)  $-12$
(E)  0

Choice B is correct.

<u>Multiply</u> $x + 2y = 4$ by 5 to get:
$$5x + 10y = 20$$

Now subtract 8:
$$5x + 10y - 8 = 20 - 8$$
$$= 12$$

EXAMPLE 3

If $\frac{m}{n} = \frac{3}{8}$ and $\frac{m}{q} = \frac{4}{7}$, then $\frac{n}{q} =$

(A) $\frac{12}{15}$

(B) $\frac{12}{56}$

(C) $\frac{56}{12}$

(D) $\frac{32}{21}$

(E) $\frac{21}{32}$

Choice D is correct.

First get rid of fractions!

Cross-multiply $\frac{m}{n} = \frac{3}{8}$ to get $8m = 3n$.　　$\boxed{1}$

Now cross-multiply $\frac{m}{q} = \frac{4}{7}$ to get $7m = 4q$.　　$\boxed{2}$

Now divide equations $\boxed{1}$ and $\boxed{2}$:

$$\frac{8m}{7m} = \frac{3n}{4q} \qquad \boxed{3}$$

The $m$'s cancel and we get:

$$\frac{8}{7} = \frac{3n}{4q} \qquad \boxed{4}$$

Multiply Equation $\boxed{4}$ by 4 and divide by 3 to get

$$\frac{8 \times 4}{7 \times 3} = \frac{n}{q}.$$

Thus　　　　　　　$\frac{n}{q} = \frac{32}{21}.$

EXAMPLE 4

If $\dfrac{a + b + c + d}{4} = 20$

And $\dfrac{b + c + d}{3} = 10$

Then $a =$

(A) 50
(B) 60
(C) 70
(D) 80
(E) 90

Choice A is correct.

We have

$$\frac{a + b + c + d}{4} = 20 \qquad \boxed{1}$$

$$\frac{b + c + d}{3} = 10 \qquad \boxed{2}$$

Multiply Equation $\boxed{1}$ by 4:

We get: $a + b + c + d = 80$　　$\boxed{3}$

Now multiply equation $\boxed{2}$ by 3:

We get: $b + c + d = 30$　　$\boxed{4}$

Now subtract Equation $\boxed{4}$ from Equation $\boxed{3}$:

$$\begin{aligned} a + b + c + d &= 80 \qquad \boxed{3}\\ -\,(b + c + d &= 30) \qquad \boxed{4} \end{aligned}$$

We get  $a = 50$.

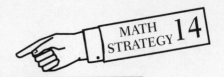

Draw or Extend Lines in a Diagram to Make a Problem Easier; Label Unknown Quantities

EXAMPLE 1

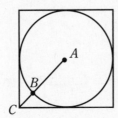

The circle with center $A$ and radius $AB$ is inscribed in the square above. $AB$ is extended to $C$. What is the ratio of $AB$ to $AC$?

(A)  $\sqrt{2}$

(B)  $\dfrac{\sqrt{2}}{4}$

(C)  $\dfrac{\sqrt{2}-1}{2}$

(D)  $\dfrac{\sqrt{2}}{2}$

(E)  None of these.

Choice D is correct. Always draw or extend lines to get more information. Also label unknown lengths, angles, or arcs with letters.

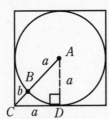

Label $AB = a$ and $BC = b$.
Draw perpendicular $AD$. Note it is just the radius, $a$. $CD$ also $= a$, because each side of the square is length $2a$ (the diameter) and $CD$ is $\frac{1}{2}$ the side of the square.

$$\text{We want to find } \frac{AB}{AC} = \frac{a}{a+b}$$

Now $\triangle ADC$ is an isosceles right triangle so $AD = CD = a$.

By the Pythagorean Theorem,
$a^2 + a^2 = (a+b)^2$ where $a+b$ is hypotenuse of right triangle.

We get: $2a^2 = (a+b)^2$
Divide by $(a+b)^2$:

$$\frac{2a^2}{(a+b)^2} = 1$$

Divide by 2:

$$\frac{a^2}{(a+b)^2} = \frac{1}{2}$$

Take square roots of both sides:

$$\frac{a}{(a+b)} = \frac{1}{\sqrt{2}} =$$

$$= \frac{1}{\sqrt{2}}\left(\frac{\sqrt{2}}{\sqrt{2}}\right)$$

$$= \frac{\sqrt{2}}{2} \quad (\textit{Answer})$$

EXAMPLE 2

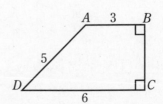

What is the perimeter of the above figure if $B$ and $C$ are right angles?

(A)  14
(B)  16
(C)  18
(D)  20
(E)  Cannot be determined.

Choice C is correct.

Draw perpendicular $AE$. Label side $BC = h$. You can see that $AE = h$.

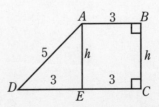

*ABCE* is a rectangle, so *CE* = 3. This makes *ED* = 3 since the whole *DC* = 6.

Now use the Pythagorean Theorem for triangle *AED:*

$$h^2 + 3^2 = 5^2$$
$$h^2 = 5^2 - 3^2$$
$$h^2 = 25 - 9$$
$$h^2 = 16$$
$$h = 4$$

So the perimeter is 3 + *h* + 6 + 5 = 3 + 4 + 6 + 5 = 18 (*Answer*)

EXAMPLE 3

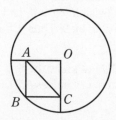

In the figure above, *O* is the center of a circle with a radius of 6, and *AOCB* is a square. If point *B* is on the circumference of the circle, the length of *AC* =

(A)  6 $\sqrt{2}$
(B)  3 $\sqrt{2}$
(C)  3
(D)  6
(E)  6 $\sqrt{3}$

Choice D is correct.

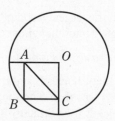

This is tricky if not impossible if you don't draw *OB*. <u>So draw *OB*</u>:

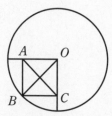

Since *AOCB* is a square, *OB* = *AC;* and since *OB* = radius 6, *AC* = 6.

EXAMPLE 4

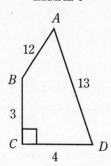

(Note: Figure is not drawn to scale.)

The area of the above figure *ABCD*

(A)  is 36
(B)  is 108
(C)  is 156
(D)  is 1,872
(E)  Cannot be determined.

Choice A is correct.

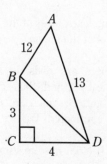

Draw *BD*. *BCD* is a 3-4-5 right triangle, so *BD* = 5. Now remember that a 5-12-13 triangle is also a right triangle, so angle *ABD* is a right angle. The area of triangle *BCD* is (3 × 4)/2 = 6 and the area of triangle *BAD* is (5 × 12)/2 = 30, so the total area is 36.

MATH STRATEGY 15

## Know How to Eliminate Certain Choices

Instead of working out a lot of algebra, you may be able to eliminate several of the choices at first glance. In this way you can save yourself a lot of work. The key is to remember to use pieces of the given information to eliminate several of the choices at once.

### EXAMPLE 1

The sum of the digits of a three-digit number is 15. If this number is not divisible by 2 but is divisible by 5, which of the following is the number?

(A)  384
(B)  465
(C)  635
(D)  681
(E)  780

Choice B is correct. Use pieces of the given information to eliminate several of the choices.

Which numbers are divisible by 2? Choices A and E are divisible by 2 and, thus, can be eliminated. Of Choices B, C, and D, which are *not* divisible by 5? Choice D can be eliminated. We are left with Choices B and C.

Only Choice B (465) has the sum of its digits equal to 15. Thus, 465 is the only number that satisfies all the pieces of the given information.

If you learn to use this method well, you can save loads of time.

### EXAMPLE 2

Which of the following numbers is divisible by 5 and 9, but not by 2?

(A)  625
(B)  639
(C)  650
(D)  655
(E)  675

Choice E is correct. Clearly, a number is divisible by 5 if, and only if, its last digit is either 0 or 5. A number is also divisible by 2 if, and only if, its last digit is divisible by 2. *Certain choices are easily eliminated.* Thus we can *eliminate* Choices B and C.

*Method 1:* To eliminate some more choices, remember that a number is divisible by 9 if, and only if, the sum of its digits is divisible by 9. Thus, Choice E is the only correct answer.

*Method 2:* If you did not know the test for divisibility by 9, divide the numbers in Choices A, D, and E by 9 to find the answer.

### EXAMPLE 3

If the last digit and the first digit are interchanged in each of the numbers below, which will result in the number with the *largest* value?

(A)  5,243
(B)  4,352
(C)  4,235
(D)  2,534
(E)  2,345

Choice E is correct.

The numbers with the largest last digit will become the largest numbers after interchanging. ⬚1

*Certain choices are easily eliminated.*

Using ⬚1, we see that Choices B and E each end in 5. All others end in digits less than 5 and may be eliminated. Starting with Choice E (See Strategy 8).
Choice E, 2,345, becomes 5,342. ⬚2
Choice B, 4,235, becomes 5,234. ⬚3
⬚2 is larger than ⬚3.

MATH STRATEGY 16

## Watch Out for Questions That Seem Very Easy But That Can Be Tricky—Beware of Choice A as a "Lure Choice"

When questions appear to be solved very easily, think again! Watch out especially for the "lure" Choice A.

### EXAMPLE 1*

$$6{:}06$$

The diagram above shows a 12-hour digital clock whose hour digit is the same as the minutes digit. Consider each time when the same number appears for both the hour and the minutes as a "double time" situation. What is the shortest elapsed time period between the appearance of one double time and an immediately succeeding double time?

(A) 61 minutes
(B) 60 minutes
(C) 58 minutes
(D) 50 minutes
(E) 49 minutes

Choice E is correct. Did you think that just by subtracting something like 8:08 from 9:09 you would get the answer (1 hour and 1 minute = 61 minutes)? That's Choice A, which is wrong. So beware, because your answer came too easily for a test like the PSAT. You must realize that there is another possibility of double time occurrence—12:12 and 1:01, whose difference is 49 minutes. This is Choice E, the correct answer.

### EXAMPLE 2

The letters $d$ and $m$ are integral digits in a certain number system. If $0 \leq d \leq m$, how many different possible values are there for $d$?

(A) $m$
(B) $m - 1$
(C) $m - 2$
(D) $m + 1$
(E) $m + 2$

Choice D is correct. Did you think that the answer was $m$? Do not be careless! The list $1, 2, 3, \ldots, m$ contains $m$ elements. If 0 is included in the list, then there are $m + 1$ elements. Hence, if $0 \leq d \leq m$ where $d$ is integral, then $d$ can have $m + 1$ different values.

### EXAMPLE 3

There are some flags hanging in a horizontal row. Starting at one end of the row, the U.S. flag is 25th. Starting at the other end of the row, the U.S. flag is 13th. How many flags are in the row?

(A) 36
(B) 37
(C) 38
(D) 39
(E) 40

Choice B is correct. **The obvious may be tricky!**

*Method 1: Given:*

The U.S. flag is 25th from one end. $\boxed{1}$

The U.S. flag is 13th from the other end. $\boxed{2}$

At first glance it may appear that adding $\boxed{1}$ and $\boxed{2}$, $25 + 13 = 38$, will be the correct answer. This is WRONG!

The U.S. flag is being counted twice: Once as the 25th and again as the 13th from the other end. The correct answer is

$$25 + 13 - 1 = 37.$$

*Method 2:*

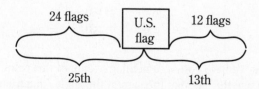

$$24 + 12 + \text{U.S. flag} = 36 + \text{U.S. flag} = 37$$

*Note:* This problem also appears in Strategy 1 of the 5 General Strategies on page 42.

## Use the Given Information Effectively (and Ignore Irrelevant Information)

You should always use first the piece of information that tells you the most, or gives you a useful idea, or that brings you closest to the answer.

EXAMPLE 1

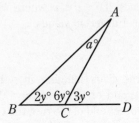

(Note: Figure is not drawn to scale.)

In the figure above, side *BC* of triangle *ABC* is extended to *D*. What is the value of *a*?

(A) 15
(B) 17
(C) 20
(D) 24
(E) 30

Choice C is correct.

Use the piece of information that will give you something definite. You might have first thought of using the fact that the sum of the angles of a triangle = 180°. However, that will give you

$$a + 2y + 6y = 180$$

That's not very useful. However, if you use the fact that the sum of the angles in a straight angle is 180 we get:

$$6y + 3y = 180$$
$$\text{and we get } 9y = 180$$
$$y = 20$$

Now we have gotten something useful. At this point, we can use the fact that the sum of the angles in a triangle is 180.

$$a + 2y + 6y = 180$$

Substituting 20 for *y,* we get

$$a + 2(20) + 6(20) = 180$$
$$a = 20 \quad (Answer)$$

EXAMPLE 2

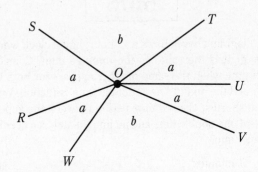

(Note: Figure is not drawn to scale.)

Which of the above angles has a degree measure that can be determined?

(A)  ∠*WOS*
(B)  ∠*SOU*
(C)  ∠*WOT*
(D)  ∠*ROV*
(E)  ∠*WOV*

Choice C is correct.

Use information that will get you something useful.

$$4a + 2b = 360 \text{ (sum of all angles = 360°)}$$

Divide by 2 to simplify:

$$2a + b = 180$$

Now try all the choices. You could work backward from Choice E, but we'll start with Choice A:

(A)  ∠*WOS* = 2*a*—You know that 2*a* + *b* = 180 but don't know the value of 2*a*.
(B)  ∠*SOU* = *b* + *a*—You know 2*a* + *b* = 180 but don't know the value of *b* + *a*.
(C)  ∠*WOT* = b + 2*a*—You know that 2*a* + *b* = 180, so you know the value of *b* + 2*a*.

Choice C is correct.

EXAMPLE 3

If $xry = 0$, $yst = 0$, and $rxt = 1$, then which must be 0?

(A) $r$
(B) $s$
(C) $t$
(D) $x$
(E) $y$

Choice E is correct.

<u>Use information that will give you something to work with.</u>

$rxt = 1$ tells you that $r \neq 0$, $x \neq 0$, and $t \neq 0$. So if $xry = 0$ then $y$ must be 0.

EXAMPLE 4

On a street with 25 houses, 10 houses have *fewer than 6 rooms,* 10 houses have *more than 7 rooms,* and 4 houses have *more than 8 rooms.* What is the total number of houses on the street that are either 6-, 7-, or 8-room houses?

(A) 5
(B) 9
(C) 11
(D) 14
(E) 15

Choice C is correct.

There are three possible situations:

(a) Houses that have *fewer than 6 rooms* (call the number $a$)
(b) Houses that have *6, 7, or 8 rooms* (call the number $b$)
(c) Houses that have *more than 8 rooms* (call the number $c$)

$a + b + c$ must total **25** (given). $\boxed{1}$

$a$ is **10** (given). $\boxed{2}$

$c$ is **4** (given). $\boxed{3}$

Substituting $\boxed{2}$ and $\boxed{3}$ in $\boxed{1}$ we get $10 + b + 4 = 25$. $b$ must therefore be **11**.

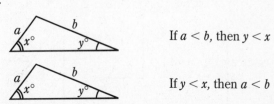

MATH STRATEGY 18

# Know and Use Facts about Triangles

By remembering these facts about triangles, you can often save yourself a lot of time and trouble.

I.

If $a = b$, then $x = y$

The base angles of an isosceles triangle are equal.

If $x = y$, then $a = b$

If the base angles of a triangle are equal, the triangle is isosceles.

II.

$\ell$ is a straight line.
Then, $x = y + z$

The measure of an exterior angle is equal to the sum of the measures of the remote interior angles.

III.

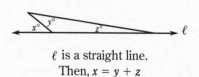

If $a < b$, then $y < x$

If $y < x$, then $a < b$

In a triangle, the greatest angle lies opposite the greatest side.

IV.

Similar Triangles

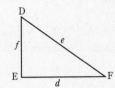

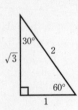

If △ABC ~ △DEF, then

$$m \sphericalangle A = m \sphericalangle D$$
$$m \sphericalangle B = m \sphericalangle E$$
$$m \sphericalangle C = m \sphericalangle F$$

and $\dfrac{a}{d} = \dfrac{b}{e} = \dfrac{c}{f}$

V.

$$m \sphericalangle A + m \sphericalangle B + m \sphericalangle C = 180°$$

The sum of the interior angles of a triangle is 180 degrees.

VI.

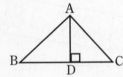

Area of $\triangle ABC = \dfrac{AD \times BC}{2}$

The area of a triangle is one-half the product of the altitude to a side and the side.

*Note:* If $m \sphericalangle A = 90°$,

Area also $= \dfrac{AB \times AC}{2}$

VII.

In a right triangle,
$c^2 = a^2 + b^2$
and $x° + y° = 90°$

VIII. Memorize the following standard triangles:

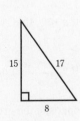

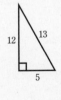

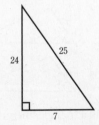

**EXAMPLE 1**

In the diagram below, what is the value of *x*?

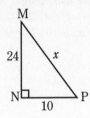

(A)  20
(B)  25
(C)  26
(D)  45
(E)  48

Choice C is correct.

*Method 1:* Use VII above. Then,

$$x^2 = 24^2 + 10^2$$
$$= 576 + 100$$
$$= 676$$

Thus, $x = 26$ (*Answer*)

*Method 2:* Look at VIII in left column. Notice that △MNP is similar to one of the standard triangles:

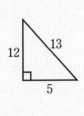

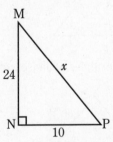

This is true because

$$\frac{12}{24} = \frac{5}{10} \text{ (Look at IV).}$$

Hence, $\dfrac{12}{24} = \dfrac{13}{x}$ or $x = 26$ (*Answer*)

EXAMPLE 2

If Masonville is 50 kilometers due north of Adamston and Elvira is 120 kilometers due east of Adamston, then the minimum distance between Masonville and Elvira is

(A)  125 kilometers
(B)  130 kilometers
(C)  145 kilometers
(D)  160 kilometers
(E)  170 kilometers

Choice B is correct. *Draw a diagram first.*

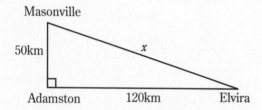

The given information translates into the diagram above. Note Statement VIII on p. 76. The triangle above is a multiple of the special 5, 12, 13 right triangle.

$$50 = 10(5)$$
$$120 = 10(12)$$
$$\text{Thus, } x = 10(13) = 130 \text{ km}$$

(*Note:* The Pythagorean Theorem could also have been used: $50^2 + 120^2 = x^2$.)

EXAMPLE 3

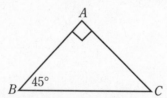

(Note: Figure is not drawn to scale.)

The triangle above has side $BC = 10$, angle $B = 45°$, and angle $A = 90°$. The area of the triangle

(A)  is 15
(B)  is 20
(C)  is 25
(D)  is 30
(E)  Cannot be determined.

Choice C is correct.

First find angle C using V.

$$90° + 45° + m \sphericalangle C = 180°$$

So $m \sphericalangle C = 45°$.
Using I, we find $AB = AC$,
since $m \sphericalangle B = m \sphericalangle C = 45°$.
Since our right triangle $ABC$ has $BC = 10$, using statement VIII (the right triangle $\frac{\sqrt{2}}{2}, \frac{\sqrt{2}}{2}, 1$), multiply by 10 to get a right triangle:

$$\frac{10\sqrt{2}}{2}, \frac{10\sqrt{2}}{2}, 10$$

Thus side $AB = \frac{10\sqrt{2}}{2} = 5\sqrt{2}$

side $AC = \frac{10\sqrt{2}}{2} = 5\sqrt{2}$

Now the area of triangle $ABC$, according to VI is

$$\frac{5\sqrt{2} \times 5\sqrt{2}}{2} = \frac{25 \times 2}{2} = 25$$

EXAMPLE 4

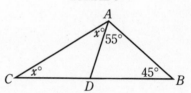

In the figure above what is the value of $x$?

(A)  30
(B)  40
(C)  50
(D)  80
(E)  100

Choice B is correct.

Remember triangle facts. Use Statement II.

$\angle ADB$ is an exterior angle of $\angle ACD$, so

$$m\angle ADB = x + x = 2x \qquad \boxed{1}$$

In $\angle ADB$, the sum of its angles = 180 (Statement V), so

$$m\angle ADB + 55 + 45 = 180$$
or $\qquad\qquad m\angle ADB + 100 = 180$
or $\qquad\qquad\qquad m\angle ADB = 80 \qquad \boxed{2}$

Equating $\boxed{1}$ and $\boxed{2}$ we have

$$2x = 80$$
$$x = 40 \ (\textit{Answer})$$

MATH STRATEGY 19

---

## When Calculating Answers, Never Multiply and/or Do Long Division If Reducing Can Be Done First

---

*Note:* On the PSAT exam, because calculators are permitted, you may do the following problems with a calculator also. But it would be wise for you to see the other approach too—how the problem can be solved *without* the use of a calculator.

### EXAMPLE 1

If $w = \dfrac{81 \times 150}{45 \times 40}$, then $w =$

(A) 3

(B) $6\frac{3}{4}$

(C) $7\frac{1}{4}$

(D) 9

(E) $20\frac{1}{4}$

*Do not multiply in this case.* $\quad 81 \times 150$ and $45 \times 40$ to get

$$\frac{12,150}{1,800}$$

Factor first

$$\frac{\overbrace{9 \times 9}^{81} \times \overbrace{15 \times 10}^{150}}{\underbrace{9 \times 5}_{45} \times \underbrace{4 \times 10}_{40}}$$

Then cancel like factors in numerator and denominator

$$\frac{\cancel{9} \times 9 \times 15 \times \cancel{10}}{\cancel{9} \times 5 \times 4 \times \cancel{10}}$$

Reduce further

$$\frac{9 \times \cancel{5} \times 3}{\cancel{5} \times 4}$$

Then simplify

$$\frac{27}{4} = 6\frac{3}{4} \; \text{(Answer)}$$

Thus, Choice B is correct.

### EXAMPLE 2

$$\frac{4^2 + 4^2 + 4^2}{3^3 + 3^3 + 3^3} =$$

(A) $\dfrac{16}{27}$

(B) $\dfrac{8}{9}$

(C) $\dfrac{4}{3}$

(D) $\dfrac{64}{27}$

(E) $\dfrac{512}{81}$

Choice A is correct.

$$\frac{4^2 + 4^2 + 4^2}{3^3 + 3^3 + 3^3} =$$

Factor and reduce: $\quad \dfrac{\cancel{3}(4^2)}{\cancel{3}(3^3)} =$

$$\frac{16}{27}$$

### EXAMPLE 3

If $6 \times 7 \times 8 \times 9 = \dfrac{12 \times 14 \times 18}{x}$, then $x =$

(A) $\dfrac{1}{2}$

(B) 1

(C) 4

(D) 8

(E) 12

Choice B is correct.

*Given:* $6 \times 7 \times 8 \times 9 = \dfrac{12 \times 14 \times 18}{x}$ $\quad \boxed{1}$

so that $x = \dfrac{12 \times 14 \times 18}{6 \times 7 \times 8 \times 9}$ $\quad \boxed{2}$

Do *not* multiply the numbers out in the numerator and denominator of $\boxed{2}$! It is too much work! Rewrite $\boxed{2}$.

<u>Factor and reduce:</u>
$x =$

$$\frac{12 \times 14 \times 18}{6 \times 7 \times 8 \times 9} = \frac{2 \times \cancel{6} \times 2 \times \cancel{7} \times 2 \times \cancel{9}}{\cancel{6} \times \cancel{7} \times 8 \times \cancel{9}}$$

$$= \frac{2 \times 2 \times 2}{8} = \frac{\cancel{8}}{\cancel{8}} = 1 \qquad \textit{(Answer)}$$

EXAMPLE 4

Find the value of $\dfrac{y^2 - 7y + 10}{y - 2}$ rounded to the nearest whole number if $y = 8.000001$.

(A) 2
(B) 3
(C) 5
(D) 6
(E) 16

Choice B is correct.

*Given:* $\dfrac{y^2 - 7y + 10}{y - 2}$ $\qquad \boxed{1}$

Factor and reduce:

Factor the numerator of $\boxed{1}$. We get

$$\frac{(y - 5)\,\cancel{(y - 2)}}{\cancel{y - 2}} = y - 5 \qquad \boxed{2}$$

Substitute 8.000001 in $\boxed{2}$. We have

$$8.000001 - 5 =$$
$$3.000001 \approx 3$$

# Critical Reading Strategies

## Using Critical-Thinking Skills in
## Verbal Questions

# 4 Sentence Completion Strategies

> For a Sentence with Only One Blank, Fill the Blank with Each Choice to See the Best Fit*

Before you decide which is the best choice, fill the blank with each of the five answer choices to see which word will fit best into the sentence as a whole.

### EXAMPLE 1

He believed that while there is serious unemployment in our auto industry, we should not _____ foreign cars.

(A) discuss
(B) regulate
(C) research
(D) import
(E) disallow

#### EXPLANATORY ANSWER

Choice D is correct. The word "import" means to bring in from another country or place. The sentence now makes good sense. The competition resulting from importation of foreign cars reduces the demand for American-made cars. This throws many American auto workers out of jobs.

### EXAMPLE 2

His attempt to _____ his guilt was betrayed by the tremor of his hand as he picked up the paper.

(A) extenuate
(B) determine
(C) conceal
(D) intensify
(E) display

#### EXPLANATORY ANSWER

Choice C is correct. The word "conceal" means to keep secret or to hide. The sentence now makes good sense. The nervousness caused by his guilty conscience is shown by the shaking of his hand. He is thus prevented in his attempt to hide his guilt.

### EXAMPLE 3

Legal _____ initiated by the government necessitate that manufacturers use _____ in choosing food additives.

(A) entanglements...knowledge
(B) devices...intensification
(C) talents...decretion
(D) proclivities...moderation
(E) restraints...caution

#### EXPLANATORY ANSWER

Choice E is correct. Although this is a two-blank question, we should use Sentence Completion Strategy 1. Try the words in each of the choices in the blanks in the sentence.

Another possibility is Choice A. But the point of the sentence evidently is that government prohibitions of certain food additives necessitate care by manufacturers in choosing food additives that are permitted. Thus Choice A is not as good as Choice E.

---

*Strategy 1 is considered the Master Strategy for *one-blank* Sentence Completion questions because it can be used effectively to answer every *one-blank* Sentence Completion question. However, it is important that you learn all of the other Sentence Completion Strategies because they can be used to double-check your answers.

SENT. COMPL.
STRATEGY 2

## For a Sentence with Two Blanks, Begin by Eliminating the Initial Words That Don't Make Sense in the Sentence*

This strategy consists of 2 steps.

**Step 1.** Find out which "first words" of the choices make sense in the first blank of the sentence. Don't consider the second word of each pair yet. *Eliminate those choices that contain "first words" that don't make sense in the sentence.*

**Step 2.** Now consider the *remaining* choices by filling in the pair of words for each choice.

### EXAMPLE 1

The salesmen in that clothing store are so _____ that it is impossible to even look at a garment without being _____ by their efforts to convince you to purchase.

(A) offensive…considerate
(B) persistent…harassed
(C) extensive…induced
(D) immune…aided
(E) intriguing…evaluated

### EXPLANATORY ANSWER

Choice B is correct.

#### STEP 1 [ELIMINATION]

We have eliminated Choice (C) extensive…induced because saying salesmen who are "extensive" does not make sense here. We have eliminated Choice (D) immune…aided because salesmen who are "immune" does not make sense here.

#### STEP 2 [REMAINING CHOICES]

This leaves us with these remaining choices to be considered. Choice (A) offensive…considerate. The sentence *does not* make sense. Choice (B) persistent…harassed. The sentence *does* make sense. Choice (E) intriguing…evaluated. The sentence *does not* make sense.

### EXAMPLE 2

Television in our society is watched so _____ that intellectuals who detest the "tube" are _____ .

(A) reluctantly…offended
(B) stealthily…ashamed
(C) frequently…revolted
(D) intensely…exultant
(E) noisily…amazed

### EXPLANATORY ANSWER

Choice C is correct. We have eliminated Choice A because television is not watched reluctantly in our society. We have eliminated Choice B because television is not watched stealthily in our society. We have eliminated Choice E because it is not common for the viewer to watch television noisily. This leaves us with these remaining choices to be considered. Choice D—intensely…exultant. The sentence does *not* make sense. Choice C— frequently… revolted. The sentence *does* make sense.

### EXAMPLE 3

In view of the company's _____ claims that its scalp treatment would grow hair on bald heads, the newspaper _____ its advertising.

(A) unproved…banned
(B) interesting…canceled
(C) unreasonable…welcomed
(D) innocent…settled
(E) immune…questioned

### EXPLANATORY ANSWER

Choice A is correct. The first step is to examine the first words of each choice. We eliminate Choice (D) innocent…and Choice (E) immune…because "claims" are not innocent or immune. Now we go on to the remaining choices. When you fill in the two blanks of Choice B and of Choice C, the sentence does *not* make sense. So these two choices are also incorrect. Filling in the two blanks of Choice A makes the sentence meaningful.

*Strategy 2 is considered the Master Strategy for *two-blank* Sentence Completion questions because it can be used effectively to answer every *two-blank* Sentence Completion question. However, it is important to learn all of the other Sentence Completion Strategies because they can be used to double-check your answers.

Sometimes you can try the "second word" in the choices and see that only one choice's second word fits in the second blank in the sentence. That choice is the correct one and there is no need to try the choice's first words in the first blank of the sentence.

### EXAMPLE 4

The antithesis of an ideal Olympic athlete, the champion diver was _____ rather than gracious, and unscrupulous rather than _____.

(A) skillful...trustworthy
(B) rowdy...deceitful
(C) urbane...resolute
(D) surly...honorable
(E) egotistical...artificial

### EXPLANATORY ANSWER

Choice D is correct. Even if you don't know what the word "antithesis" is, because the prefix "anti" means against, it is a *negative* sounding word. Since "gracious" is a positive sounding word, the word in the first blank must be *negative*. Similarly, because of the word *and*, the word in the second blank must be *positive*, parallel with the word "gracious" in the sentence. the only word that fits is "honorable," Choice D. Note that "trustworthy" in Choice A would not really apply to a champion diver.

## Try to Complete the Sentence in Your Own Words before Looking at the Choices

This strategy often works well, especially with one-blank sentences. You may be able to fill in the blank with a word of your own that makes good sense. Then look at the answer choices to see whether any of the choices has the same meaning as your own word.

### EXAMPLE 1

Many buildings with historical significance are now being _____ instead of being torn down.

(A) built
(B) forgotten
(C) destroyed
(D) praised
(E) repaired

#### EXPLANATORY ANSWER

Choice E is correct. The key words "instead of" constitute an *opposite indicator.* The words give us a good clue—we should fill the blank with an antonym (opposite) for "torn down." If you used the strategy of trying to complete the sentence *before* looking at the five choices, you might have come up with any of the following appropriate words:

remodeled
reconstructed
remade
renovated

These words all mean the same as the correct Choice E word, "repaired."

### EXAMPLE 2

Wishing to _____ the upset passenger who found a nail in his steak, the flight attendant offered him a complimentary bottle of champagne.

(A) appease
(B) berate
(C) disregard
(D) reinstate
(E) acknowledge

#### EXPLANATORY ANSWER

Choice A is correct. Since the passenger was upset, the flight attendant wished to do something to make him feel better. If you used the strategy of trying to complete the sentence *before* looking at the five choices, you might have come up with the following words that would have the meaning of "to make someone feel better":

pacify
soothe
satisfy
conciliate
relieve

These words all mean the same as the Choice A word, "appease."

### EXAMPLE 3

Just as the person who is kind brings happiness to others, so does he bring _____ to himself.

(A) wisdom
(B) guidance
(C) satisfaction
(D) stinginess
(E) insecurity

#### EXPLANATORY ANSWER

Choice C is correct. You must look for a word that balances with "happiness." Here are some of the words:

joy
goodness
satisfaction
enjoyment

All these words can be linked to Choice C.

SENT. COMPL.
STRATEGY 4

---

## Pay Close Attention to the Key Words in the Sentence

---

A key word may indicate what is happening in the sentence. Here are some examples of key words and what these words may indicate.

| Key Word | Indicating |
|---|---|
| although<br>however<br>in spite of<br>rather than<br>nevertheless<br>on the other hand<br>but | OPPOSITION |

| Key Word | Indicating |
|---|---|
| moreover<br>besides<br>additionally<br>furthermore<br>in fact | SUPPORT |

| Key Word | Indicating |
|---|---|
| therefore<br>consequently<br>accordingly<br>because<br>when<br>so | RESULT |

There are many other words—in addition to these—that can act as key words to help you considerably in getting the right answer. A key word frequently appears in the sentence. Watch for it!

EXAMPLE 1

Richard Wagner was frequently intolerant; moreover, his strange behavior caused most of his acquaintances to _____ the composer whenever possible.

(A) contradict
(B) interrogate
(C) shun
(D) revere
(E) tolerate

EXPLANATORY ANSWER

Choice C is correct. The word "moreover" is a *support indicator* in this sentence. As we try each choice word in the blank, we find that "shun" (avoid) is the only logical word that fits. You might have selected Choice A ("contradict"), but very few would seek to contradict Wagner because most of his acquaintances tried to avoid him.

EXAMPLE 2

Until we are able to improve substantially the _____ status of the underprivileged in our country, a substantial _____ in our crime rate is remote.

(A) burdensome…harmony
(B) beneficial…gloom
(C) financial…reduction
(D) remarkable…puzzle
(E) questionable…disappointment

EXPLANATORY ANSWER

Choice C is correct. The word "Until" is a *result indicator.* As we try the first word of each choice in the first blank, we find that "burdensome," "financial," and "questionable" all make sense up until the second part of the sentence except "beneficial" and "remarkable." We therefore eliminate Choices B and D. Now let us try both words in Choices A, C, and E. We then find that we can eliminate Choices A and E as not making sense in the entire sentence. This leaves us with the correct Choice C, which *does* bring out the result of what is stated in the first part of the sentence.

EXAMPLE 3

All of the efforts of the teachers will bring about no _____ changes in the scores of the students because the books and other _____ educational materials are not available.

(A)  impartial…worthwhile
(B)  unique…reflected
(C)  spiritual…inspiring
(D)  marked…necessary
(E)  effective…interrupted

EXPLANATORY ANSWER

Choice D is correct. First see **Sentence Strategy 2.** Let us first eliminate Choices (A) impartial…and (C) spiritual…because we do not speak of "impartial" or "spiritual" changes. Now note that we have a *result* situation here as indicated by the presence of the conjunction "because" in the sentence. Choices B and E do not make sense because "unique" changes have nothing to do with "reflected" educational materials, and "effective" changes have nothing to do with "interrupted" educational materials. Choices B and E certainly do not meet the *result* requirement. Choice D is the only correct choice because it makes sense to say that there will be no "marked" changes in the scores because the books and other "necessary" educational materials are not available.

For two-blank sentences, look for contrasts or opposition in the two parts of the sentence—then look for opposite relationships in the choices.

EXAMPLE 4

In spite of the _____ of his presentation, many people were _____ with the speaker's concepts and ideas.

(A)  interest…enthralled
(B)  power…taken
(C)  intensity…shocked
(D)  greatness…gratified
(E)  strength…bored

EXPLANATORY ANSWER

Choice E is correct. The words in *spite of* at the beginning of the sentence tell you that the two blanks have an *opposite* flavor. Watch for opposites in the choices:

(A)  interest…enthralled—NOT OPPOSITE
(B)  power…taken—NOT OPPOSITE
(C)  intensity…shocked—NOT OPPOSITE
(D)  greatness…gratified—NOT OPPOSITE
(E)  strength…bored—OPPOSITE

# Introduction to Passage Reading

Before getting into the detailed strategies, I want to say that the most important way to really understand what you're reading is to **get involved** with the passage—as if a friend of yours were reading the passage to you and you had to be interested so you wouldn't slight your friend. When you see the passage on paper it is also a good idea to **underline** important parts of the passage—which we'll also go over later in one of the strategies.

So many students ask, How do I answer reading comprehension questions? How do I read the passage effectively? Do I look at the questions before reading the passage? Do I underline things in the passage? Do I have to memorize details and dates? How do I get interested and involved in the passage?

All these are good questions. They will be answered carefully and in the right sequence.

## What Reading Comprehension Questions Ask

First of all it is important to know that most reading comprehension questions ask about one of four things:

For example, following are some typical question stems.

> 1. the MAIN IDEA of the passage
> 2. INFORMATION SPECIFICALLY MENTIONED in the passage
> 3. INFORMATION IMPLIED (not directly stated) in the passage
> 4. the TONE or MOOD of the passage

Each lets you immediately know which of the above four things is being asked about.

1. It can be inferred from the passage that…(IMPLIED INFORMATION)

2. According to the author…(MAIN IDEA)

3. The passage is primarily concerned with…(MAIN IDEA)

4. The author's statement that…(SPECIFIC INFORMATION)

5. Which of the following describes the mood of the passage? (TONE or MOOD)

6. The author implies that…(IMPLIED INFORMATION)

7. The use of paper is described in lines 14–16… (SPECIFIC INFORMATION)

8. The main purpose of the passage…(MAIN IDEA)

9. The author's tone is best described as…(TONE or MOOD)

10. One could easily see the author as…(IMPLIED INFORMATION)

## Getting Involved with the Passage

Now, let's first put aside the burning question, Should I read the questions first, before reading the passage? The answer is NO! If you have in mind the four main question types given above, you will not likely be in for any big surprises. Many questions, when you get to them, will be reassuringly familiar in the way they're framed and in their intent. You can best answer them by reading the passage first, allowing yourself to become involved with it.

To give you an idea of what I mean, look over the following passage. When you have finished, I'll show you how you might read it so as to get involved with it and with the author's intent.

### Introductory Passage 1

We should also know that "greed" has little to do with the environmental crisis. The two main causes are population pressures, especially the pressures of large metropolitan populations, and the desire—a highly commendable one—to bring a decent living at the lowest possible cost to the largest possible number of people.

The environmental crisis is the result of success—success in cutting down the mortality of infants (which has given us the population explosion), success in raising farm output sufficiently to prevent mass famine (which has given us contamination by pesticides and chemical fertilizers), success in getting the people out of the tenements of the 19th-century cities and into the greenery and privacy of the single-family home in the suburbs (which has given us urban sprawl and traffic jams). The environmental crisis, in other words, is largely the result of doing too much of the right sort of thing.

To overcome the problems that success always creates, one must build on it. But where to start? Cleaning up the environment requires determined, sustained effort with clear targets and deadlines. It requires, above all, concentration of effort. Up to now we have tried to do a little bit of everything—and tried to do it in the headlines—when what we ought to do first is draw up a list of priorities.

# Breakdown and Underlining of Passage

Before going over the passage with you, I want to suggest some underlining you might want to make and to show what different parts of the passage refer to.

We should also know that "greed" has little to do with the environmental crisis. The two main causes are <u>population pressures,</u> especially the pressures of large metropolitan populations, and the <u>desire</u>—a highly commendable one—<u>to bring a decent living at the lowest possible cost</u> to the largest possible number of people.

    *Sets stage.*

The <u>environmental crisis is the result of success</u>—success in cutting down the mortality of infants (which has given us the population explosion), success in raising farm output sufficiently to prevent mass famine (which has given us contamination by pesticides and chemical fertilizers), success in getting the people out of the tenements of the 19th-century cities and into the greenery and privacy of the single-family home in the suburbs (which has given us urban sprawl and traffic jams). The environmental crisis, in other words, is largely the result of doing <u>too much of the right sort of thing.</u>

    *This should interest and surprise you.*

    *Examples of success.*

    *Summary of the success examples.*

To overcome the problems that success always creates, <u>one must build on it</u>. But where to start? Cleaning up the environment requires determined, <u>sustained effort with clear targets and deadlines</u>. It requires above all, <u>concentration of effort</u>. Up to now we have tried to do a little bit of everything—and tried to do it in the headlines—when what we ought to do first is <u>draw up a list of priorities.</u>

    *Solutions.*

    *We should also know that "greed" has little to do with the environmental crisis.*

Now I'll go over the passage with you, showing you what might go through your mind as you read. This will let you see how to get involved with the passage, and how this involvement facilitates answering the questions that follow the passage. In many cases, you'll actually be able to anticipate the questions. Of course, when you are preparing for the SAT, you'll have to develop this skill so that you do it rapidly and almost automatically.

Let's look at the first sentence:

Immediately you should say to yourself, "So something else must be involved with the environmental crisis." Read on:

*The two main causes are population pressures, especially the pressures of large metropolitan populations, and the desire—a highly commendable one—to bring a decent living at the lowest possible cost to the largest possible number of people.*

Now you can say to yourself, "Oh, so population pressures and the desire to help the people in the community caused the environmental crisis." You should also get a feeling that the author is not really against these causes of the environmental crisis, and that he or she believes that the crisis is in part a side effect of worthwhile efforts and enterprises. Read on:

*The environmental crisis is the result of success—success in cutting down the mortality of infants (which has given us the population explosion), success in raising farm output sufficiently to prevent mass famine (which has given us contamination by pesticides and chemical fertilizers), success in getting the people out of the tenements of the 19th-century city and into the greenery and privacy of the single-family home in the suburbs (which has given us urban sprawl and traffic jams).*

Now you should say to yourself, "It seems that for every positive thing that the author mentions, there is a negative occurrence that leads to the environmental crisis."

Now read the last sentence of this paragraph:

*The environmental crisis, in other words, is largely the result of doing too much of the right sort of thing.*

Now you can say to yourself, "Gee, we wanted to do the right thing, but we created something bad. It looks like you can't have your cake and eat it, too!"

Now you should anticipate that in the next and final paragraph, the author will discuss what may be done to reduce the bad effects that come from the good. Look at the first sentence of the third paragraph:

*To overcome the problem that success always creates, one must build on it.*

Now you can say to yourself, "Well, how?" In fact, in the next sentence the author asks the very question you just asked: *But where to start?* Read on to find out the author's answer.

*Cleaning up the environment requires determined, sustained effort with clear targets and deadlines. It requires, above all, concentration of effort.*

So now you can say to yourself, "Oh, so that's what we need—definite goals, deadlines for reaching those goals, and genuine effort to achieve the goals."

The author then discusses what you may have already thought about:

*Up to now we have tried to do a little bit of everything...*

What the author is saying (and you should realize this) is that up to now, we haven't concentrated on one particular problem at a time. We used "buckshot instead of bullets." Read on:

*—and tried to do it in the headlines—when what we ought to do first is to draw up a list of priorities.*

So you can now see that, in the author's opinion, making a list of priorities and working on them one at a time, with a target in mind, may get us out of the environmental crisis and still preserve our quality of life.

## How to Answer Reading Comprehension Questions Most Effectively

Before we start to answer the questions, let me tell you the best and most effective way of answering passage questions. You should read the question and proceed to look at the choices in the order of Choice A, Choice B, etc. If a choice (such as Choice A) doesn't give you the definite feeling that it is correct, don't try to analyze it further. Go on to Choice B. Again, if that choice (Choice B) doesn't make you feel that it's the right one, and you really have to think carefully about the choice, go on to Choice C and the rest of the choices and choose the best one.

Suppose you have gone through all five choices, and you don't know which one is correct, or you don't see any one that stands out as obviously being correct. Then quickly guess or leave the question blank if you wish and go on to the next question. You can go back after you have answered the other questions relating to the passage. But remember, when you return to the questions you weren't sure of, don't spend too much time on them. Try to forge ahead on the test.

Let's proceed to answer the questions now. Look at the first question:

1. This passage assumes the desirability of

   (A) using atomic energy to conserve fuel
   (B) living in comfortable family lifestyles
   (C) settling disputes peacefully
   (D) combating cancer and heart disease with energetic research
   (E) having greater government involvement in people's daily lives

Look at Choice A That doesn't seem correct. Now look at Choice B. Do you remember that the author claimed that the environmental crisis is the result of the successful attempt to get people out of their tenements into a better environment? We can only feel that the author *assumes* this desirability of *living in comfortable family lifestyles* (Choice B) since the author uses the word *success* in describing the transition from living in tenements to living in single-family homes. Therefore, Choice B is correct. You don't need to analyze or even consider the other choices, since we have zeroed in on Choice B.

Let's look at Question 2:

2. According to this passage, one early step in any effort to improve the environment would be to

(A) return to the exclusive use of natural fertilizers
(B) put a high tax on profiteering industries
(C) ban the use of automobiles in the cities
(D) study successful efforts in other countries
(E) set up a timetable for corrective actions

Again let's go through the choices in the order Choice A, Choice B, etc., until we come up with the right choice. Choices A, B, C, and D seem unlikely to be correct. So look at Choice E. We remember that the author said that we should establish clear targets and deadlines to improve the environment. That makes Choice E look like the correct answer.

Let's look at Question 3:

3. The passage indicates that the conditions which led to overcrowded roads also brought about

(A) more attractive living conditions for many people
(B) a healthier younger generation
(C) greater occupational opportunities
(D) the population explosion
(E) greater concentration of population pressures

Here we would go back to the part of the passage that discussed overcrowded roads. This is where (second paragraph) the author says that urban sprawl and traffic jams are one result of success in getting people out of tenements to single-family homes. So you can see that Choice A is correct. Again, there is no need to consider other choices, since you should be fairly comfortable with Choice A.

Let's look at Question 4:

4. It could logically be assumed that the author of this passage would support legislation to

(A) ban the use of all pesticides
(B) prevent the use of automobiles in the cities
(C) build additional conventional power plants immediately
(D) organize an agency to coordinate efforts to cope with environmental problems
(E) restrict the press coverage of protests led by environmental groups

This is the type of question that asks you to determine what the author would feel about something else, when you already know something about the author's sentiments on one particular subject.

Choices A, B, and C do not seem correct. But look at Choice D. The author said that the way to get out of the energy crisis is to set targets and deadlines in order to cope with specific problems. The author would therefore probably organize an agency to do this. Choice D is correct.

Let's look at another passage, and what I'm going to tell you is what would be going through my mind as I'm reading it. The more you can get involved with the passage in an "active" and not "passive" way, the faster you'll read it, and the more you'll get out of it.

## Introductory Passage 2

Some scraps of evidence bear out those who hold a very high opinion of the average level of culture among the Athenians of the great age. The funeral speech of Pericles is the most famous indication from Athenian literature that its level was indeed high. Pericles was, however, a politician, and he may have been flattering his audience. We know that thousands of Athenians sat hour after hour in the theater listening to the plays of the great Greek dramatists. These plays, especially the tragedies, are at a very high intellectual level throughout. There are no letdowns, no concessions to the lowbrows or to the demands of "realism," such as the scene of the gravediggers in *Hamlet*. The music and dancing woven into these plays were almost certainly at an equally high level. Our opera—not Italian opera, not even Wagner, but the restrained, difficult opera of the 18th century—is probably the best modern parallel. The comparison is no doubt dangerous, but can you imagine almost the entire population of an American city (in suitable installments, of course) sitting through performances of Mozart's *Don Giovanni* or Gluck's *Orpheus?* Perhaps the Athenian masses went to these plays because of a lack of other amusements. They could at least understand something of what went on, since the subjects were part of their folklore. For the American people, the subjects of grand opera are not part of their folklore.

Let's start reading the passage:

*Some scraps of evidence bear out those who hold a very high opinion of the average level of culture among the Athenians of the great age.*

Now this tells you that the author is going to talk about the culture of the Athenians. Thus the stage is set. Go on reading now:

*The funeral speech of Pericles is the most famous indication from Athenian literature that its level was indeed high.*

At this point you should say to yourself: "That's interesting, and there was an example of the high level of culture."

Read on:

*Pericles was, however, a politician, and he may have been flattering his audience.*

Now you can say, "So that's why those people were so attentive in listening—they were being flattered."

Read on:

*We know that thousands of Athenians sat hour after hour in the theater listening to the plays of the great Greek dramatists. These plays, especially the tragedies, are at a very high intellectual level throughout. There are no letdowns, no concessions to the lowbrows or to the demands of "realism"... .*

At this point you should say to yourself, "That's strange—it could not have been just flattery that kept them listening hour after hour. How did they do it?" You can almost anticipate that the author will now give examples and contrast what he is saying to our plays and our audiences.

Read on:

*The music and dancing woven into these plays were almost certainly at an equally high level. Our opera, not Italian opera...is probably the best modern parallel. The comparison is no doubt dangerous, but can you imagine almost the entire population of an American city...sitting through performances of ...*

Your feeling at this point should be, "No, I cannot imagine that. Why is that so?" So you should certainly be interested to find out.

Read on:

*Perhaps the Athenian masses went to these plays because of a lack of other amusements. They could at least understand something of what went on, since the subjects were part of their folklore.*

Now you can say, "So that's why those people were able to listen hour after hour—the material was all part of their folklore!"

Read on:

*For the American people, the subjects...are not part of their folklore.*

Now you can conclude, "So that's why the Americans cannot sit through these plays and perhaps cannot understand them—they were not part of their folklore!"

Here are the questions that follow the passage:

1. The author seems to question the sincerity of

   (A) politicians
   (B) playwrights
   (C) opera goers
   (D) "low brows"
   (E) gravediggers

2. The author implies that the average American

   (A) enjoys *Hamlet*
   (B) loves folklore
   (C) does not understand grand opera
   (D) seeks a high cultural level
   (E) lacks entertainment

3. The author's attitude toward Greek plays is one of

   (A) qualified approval
   (B) grudging admiration
   (C) studied indifference
   (D) partial hostility
   (E) great respect

4. The author suggests that Greek plays

   (A) made great demands upon their actors
   (B) flattered their audiences
   (C) were written for a limited audience
   (D) were dominated by music and dancing
   (E) stimulated their audiences

Let's try to answer them.

Question 1:  Remember the statement about Pericles? This statement was almost unrelated to the passage since it was not discussed or referred to again. And here we have a question about it. Usually, if you see something that you think is irrelevant in a passage you may be pretty sure that a question will be based on that irrelevancy. It is apparent that the author seems to question the sincerity of politicians (*not* playwrights) since Pericles was a politician. Therefore Choice A is correct.

Question 2:  We know that it was implied that the average American does not understand grand opera. Therefore Choice C is correct.

Question 3:  From the passage, we see that the author is very positive about the Greek plays. Thus the author must have great respect for the plays. Note that the author may not have respect for Pericles, but Pericles was not a playwright; he was a politician. Therefore Choice E (not Choice A) is correct.

Question 4:  It is certainly true that the author suggests that the Greek plays stimulated their audiences. They didn't necessarily flatter their audiences—there was only one indication of flattery, and that was by Pericles, who was not a playwright, but a politician. Therefore Choice E (not Choice B) is correct.

## Example of Underlinings

Some scraps of evidence bear out those who hold a very high ← *sets stage*
opinion of the average level of culture among the Athenians of
the great age. The funeral speech of Pericles is the most famous
indication from Athenian literature that its level was indeed
high. Pericles was, however, <u>a politician</u>, and he may have <u>been</u> ← *example*
<u>flattering his audience.</u> We know that thousands of Athenians
sat hour after hour in the theater listening to the plays of the
great Greek dramatists. These plays, especially the tragedies,
are <u>at a very high intellectual</u> level throughout. There are no ← *qualification*
letdowns, no concessions to the lowbrows or to the demands
of "realism," such as the scene of the gravediggers in *Hamlet*. ← *further*
The music and dancing woven into these plays were almost *examples*
certainly at an equally high level. <u>Our opera</u>—not Italian opera, ✓
not even Wagner, but the restrained, difficult opera of the 18th
century—<u>is probably the best modern parallel.</u> The comparison ← *comparison*
is no doubt dangerous, but can you imagine almost the entire
population of an American city (in suitable installments, of
course) sitting through performances of Mozart's *Don Giovanni*
or Gluck's *Orpheus?* <u>Perhaps the Athenian masses went to</u>
<u>these plays because of a lack of other amusements.</u> They could
at least understand something of what went on, since <u>the</u> ← *explanation*
<u>subjects were part of their folklore. For the American people,</u> *of previous*
<u>the subjects of grand opera are not part of their folklore.</u> *statements*

Now the whole purpose of analyzing this passage the way I did was to show you that if you get involved and interested in the passage, you will not only anticipate many of the questions, but when you answer them you can zero in on the right question choice without having to necessarily analyze or eliminate the wrong choices first. That's a great time-saver on a standardized test such as the PSAT.

Now here's a short passage from which four questions were derived. Let's see if you can answer them after you've read the passage.

## Introductory Passage 3

Sometimes the meaning of glowing water is ominous. Off the Pacific Coast of North America, it may mean that the sea is filled with a minute plant that contains a poison of strange and terrible virulence. About four days after this
5 minute plant comes to alter the coastal plankton, some of the fishes and shellfish in the vicinity become toxic. This is because in their normal feeding, they have strained the poisonous plankton out of the water.

1. Fish and shellfish become toxic when they

    (A) swim in poisonous water
    (B) feed on poisonous plants
    (C) change their feeding habits
    (D) give off a strange glow
    (E) take strychnine into their systems

2. One can most reasonably conclude that plankton are

    (A) minute organisms
    (B) mussels
    (C) poisonous fish
    (D) shellfish
    (E) fluids

3. In the context of the passage, the word "virulence" in line 4 means

    (A) strangeness
    (B) color
    (C) calamity
    (D) potency
    (E) powerful odor

4. The paragraph preceding this one most probably discussed

    (A) phenomena of the Pacific coastline
    (B) poisons that affect man
    (C) the culture of the early Indians
    (D) characteristics of plankton
    (E) phenomena of the sea

EXPLANATORY ANSWERS

1. Choice B is correct. See the last three sentences. Fish become toxic when they feed on poisonous plants. Don't be fooled by using the first sentence, which seemingly leads to Choice A.

2. Choice A is correct. Since we are talking about *minute* plants (second sentence), it is reasonable to assume that plankton are *minute* organisms.

3. Choice D is correct. We understand that the poison is very strong and toxic. Thus it is "potent," virulent.

4. Choice E is correct. Since the second and not the first sentence was about the Pacific Coast, the paragraph preceding this one probably didn't discuss the phenomena of the Pacific coastline. It would have, if the first sentence—the sentence that links the ideas in the preceding paragraph—were about the Pacific coastline. Now, since we are talking about glowing water being ominous (first sentence), the paragraph preceding the passage is probably about the sea or the phenomena of the sea.

# Summary

So in summary:

1. Make sure that you get involved with the passage. You may even want to select first the passage that interests you most. For example, if you're interested in science, you may want to choose the science passage first. Just make sure that you make some notation so that you don't mismark your answer sheet by putting the answers in the wrong answer boxes.

2. Pay attention to material that seems unrelated in the passage—there will probably be a question or two based on that material.

3. Pay attention to the mood created in the passage or the tone of the passage. Here again, especially if the mood is striking, there will probably be a question relating to mood.

4. Don't waste valuable time looking at the questions before reading the passage.

5. When attempting to answer the questions (after reading the passage) it is sometimes wise to try to figure out the answer before going through the choices. This will enable you to zero in on the correct answer without wasting time with all of the choices.

6. You may want to underline any information in the passages involving dates, specific names, etc., on your test to have as ready reference when you come to the questions.

7. Always try to see the overall attempt of the author of the passage or try to get the main gist of why the passage was being written. Try to get involved by asking yourself if you agree or disagree with the author, etc.

**Next, the 6 Reading Comprehension Strategies.**

## About the Double-Reading Passages

On your PSAT you will be given a "double passage" (two separate passages) with 6–12 questions. You will also be given a "double paragraph" (two separate paragraphs) with about 4 questions. Some of the questions will be based on *only* the first passage, some will be based on *only* the second passage, and some will be based on *both* passages. Although you may want to read both passages first, then answer all the questions, some of you may find it less anxious to **read the first passage, then answer those questions relating to the first passage, then read the second passage and answer those questions relating to the second passage, then finally answer the remaining questions relating to both the passages.** By using this approach, since you are reading one passage at a time, the time you would have spent on the second passage could be spent on answering the first set of questions relating to the first passage. This is in case you would have run out of time by reading both passages. The other advantage of this approach is that you do not have to keep both passages in mind at all times when answering the questions. That is, the only time you have to be aware of the content of both passages is when answering only those few questions related to both passages.

# 6 Reading Comprehension Strategies

This section of Reading Comprehension Strategies includes several passages. These passages, though somewhat shorter than the passages that appear on the actual PSAT and in the 3 PSAT Practice Tests in this book, illustrate the general nature of the "real" PSAT reading passages.

Each of the 6 Reading Comprehension Strategies that follow is accompanied by at least two different passages followed by questions and explanatory answers in order to explain how the strategy is used.

READ. COMP. STRATEGY 1

---

**As You Read Each Question, Determine the Type: Main Idea, Detecting Details, Inference, Tone/Mood**

---

Here are the 4 major abilities tested in Reading Comprehension questions:

1. **Main Idea.** Selection of the main thought of a passage; ability to judge the general significance of a passage; ability to select the best title of a passage.

2. **Detecting Details.** Ability to understand the writer's explicit statements; to get the literal meaning of what is written; to identify details.

3. **Inferential Reasoning.** Ability to weave together the ideas of a passage and to see their relationships; to draw correct inferences; to go beyond literal interpretation to the implications of the statements.

4. **Tone/Mood.** Ability to determine from the passage the tone or mood that is dominant in the passage—humorous, serious, sad, mysterious, etc.

EXAMPLE 1

The fight crowd is a beast that lurks in the darkness behind the fringe of white light shed over the first six rows by the incandescents atop the ring, and is not to be trusted with pop bottles or other hardware.

5 People who go to prize fights are sadistic.

When two prominent pugilists are scheduled to pummel one another in public on a summer's evening, men and women file into the stadium in the guise of human beings, and thereafter become a part of a gray thing that squats in 10 the dark until, at the conclusion of the bloodletting, they may be seen leaving the arena in the same guise they wore when they entered.

As a rule, the mob that gathers to see men fight is unjust, vindictive, swept by intense, unreasoning hatreds, 15 proud of its swift recognition of what it believes to be sportsmanship. It is quick to greet the purely phony move of the boxer who extends his gloves to his rival who has slipped or been pushed to the floor, and to reward this stimulating but still baloney gesture with a pattering of 20 hands which indicates the following: "You are a good sport. We recognize that you are a good sport, and we know a sporting gesture when we see one. Therefore we are all good sports, too. Hurrah for us!"

The same crowd doesn't see the same boxer stick his 25 thumb in his opponent's eye or try to cut him with the laces of his glove, butt him or dig him a low one when the referee isn't in a position to see. It roots consistently for the smaller man, and never for a moment considers the desperate psychological dilemma of the larger of the two. It howls 30 with glee at a good finisher making his kill. The Roman hordes were more civilized. Their gladiators asked them

whether the final blow should be administered or not. The main attraction at the modern prize fight is the spectacle of a man clubbing a helpless and vanquished opponent into
35 complete insensibility. The referee who stops a bout to save a slugged and punch-drunken man from the final ignominy is hissed by the assembled sportsmen.

### QUESTIONS

1. The tone of the passage is chiefly

   (A) disgusted
   (B) jovial
   (C) matter-of-fact
   (D) satiric
   (E) devil-may-care

2. Which group of words from the passage best indicates the author's opinion?

   (A) "referee," "opponent," "finisher"
   (B) "gladiators," "slugged," "sporting gesture"
   (C) "stimulating," "hissing," "pattering"
   (D) "beast," "lurks," "gray thing"
   (E) "dilemma," "hordes," "spectacle"

3. Apparently, the author believes that boxing crowds find the referee both

   (A) gentlemanly and boring
   (B) entertaining and essential
   (C) blind and careless
   (D) humorous and threatening
   (E) necessary and bothersome

### EXPLANATORY ANSWERS

1. Choice A is correct. The author is obviously much offended (disgusted) by the inhuman attitude of the crowd watching the boxing match. For example, see these lines:

   Line 1: "The fight crowd is a beast."
   Line 5: "People who go to prize fights are sadistic."
   Lines 13–14: "…the mob that gathers to see men fight is unjust, vindictive, swept by intense…hatreds."
   Lines 30–31: "The Roman hordes were more civilized."

   To answer this question, you must be able to determine the tone that is dominant in the passage. Accordingly, this is a TONE/MOOD type of question.

2. Choice D is correct. The author's opinion is clearly one of disgust and discouragement because of the behavior of the fight crowd. Accordingly, you would expect the author to use words that were condemnatory, like "beast," and gloom-filled words like "lurks" and "gray thing." To answer this ques-

tion, you must see relationships between words and feelings. So, we have here an INFERENTIAL REASONING question-type.

3. Choice E is correct. Lines 24–27 show that the referee is *necessary:* "The same crowd doesn't see the same boxer stick his thumb in his opponent's eye…when the referee isn't in a position to see." Lines 35–37 show that the referee is bothersome: "The referee who stops a bout…is hissed by the assembled sportsmen." To answer this question, the student must have the ability to understand the writer's specific statements. Accordingly, this is a DETECTING DETAILS type of question.

### EXAMPLE 2

Mist continues to obscure the horizon, but above us the sky is suddenly awash with lavender light. At once the geese respond. Now, as well as their cries, a beating roar rolls across the water as if five thousand housewives have taken
5 it into their heads to shake out blankets all at one time. Ten thousand housewives. It keeps up—the invisible rhythmic beating of all those goose wings—for what seems a long time. Even Lonnie is held motionless with suspense.

Then the geese begin to rise. One, two, three
10 hundred—then a thousand at a time—in long horizontal lines that unfurl like pennants across the sky. The horizon actually darkens as they pass. It goes on and on like that, flock after flock; for three or four minutes, each new contingent announcing its ascent with an accelerating roar of
15 cries and wingbeats. Then gradually the intervals between flights become longer. I think the spectacle is over, until yet another flock lifts up, following the others in a gradual turn toward the northeastern quadrant of the refuge.

Finally the sun emerges from the mist; the mist itself
20 thins a little, uncovering the black line of willows on the other side of the wildlife preserve. I remember to close my mouth—which has been open for some time—and inadvertently shut two or three mosquitoes inside. Only a few straggling geese oar their way across the sun's red
25 surface. Lonnie wears an exasperated, proprietary expression, as if he had produced and directed the show himself and had just received a bad review. "It would have been better with more light," he says; "I can't always guarantee just when they'll start moving." I assure him I thought it
30 was a fantastic sight. "Well," he rumbles, "I guess it wasn't too bad."

### QUESTIONS

1. In the descriptive phrase "shake out blankets all at one time" (line 5), the author is appealing chiefly to the reader's

   (A) background
   (B) sight
   (C) emotions
   (D) thoughts
   (E) hearing

2. The mood created by the author is one of

(A) tranquility
(B) excitement
(C) sadness
(D) bewilderment
(E) unconcern

3. The main idea expressed by the author about the geese is that they

(A) are spectacular to watch
(B) are unpredictable
(C) disturb the environment
(D) produce a lot of noise
(E) fly in large flocks

4. Judging from the passage, the reader can conclude that

(A) the speaker dislikes nature's inconveniences
(B) the geese's timing is predictable
(C) Lonnie has had the experience before
(D) both observers are hunters
(E) the author and Lonnie are the same person

### EXPLANATORY ANSWERS

1. Choice E is correct. See lines 3–5: "…a beating roar rolls across the water…shake out blankets all at one time." The author, with these words, is no doubt appealing to the reader's hearing. To answer this question, the reader has to identify those words dealing with sound and noise. Therefore, we have here a DETECTING DETAILS type of question. It is also an INFERENTIAL REASONING question-type in that the "sound" words such as "beating" and "roar" lead the reader to infer that the author is appealing to the auditory (hearing) sense.

2. Choice B is correct. Excitement courses right through this passage. Here are examples:
   Lines 6–7: "…the invisible rhythmic beating of all those goose wings."
   Line 8: "Even Lonnie is held motionless with suspense."
   Lines 9–10: "Then the geese begin to rise…a thousand at a time."
   Lines 12–15: "…flock after flock…roar of cries and wingbeats."

   To answer this question, you must determine the dominant tone in this passage. Therefore, we have here a TONE/MOOD question type.

3. Choice A is correct. The word "spectacular" means *dramatic, thrilling, impressive*. There is considerable action expressed throughout the passage. Sometimes there is a lull—then the action begins again. See lines 16–17: "I think the spectacle is over, until yet another flock lifts up, following the others." To answer this question, you must have the ability to judge the general significance of the passage. Accordingly, we have here a MAIN IDEA type of question.

4. Choice C is correct. See lines 25–29: "Lonnie wears an exasperated, proprietary expression…when they'll start moving." To answer this question, you must be able to draw a correct inference. Therefore, we have here an INFERENTIAL REASONING type of question.

READ. COMP. STRATEGY 2

## Underline the Key Parts of the Reading Passage*

The underlinings will help you to answer questions. Reason: Practically every question will ask you to detect

a)   the main idea

*or*

b)   information that is specifically mentioned in the passage

*or*

c)   information that is implied (not directly stated) in the passage

*or*

d)   the tone or mood of the passage

If you find out quickly what the question is aiming for, you will more easily arrive at the correct answer by referring to your underlinings in the passage.

### EXAMPLE 1

That one citizen is as good as another is a favorite American axiom, supposed to express the very essence of our Constitution and way of life. But just what do we mean when we utter that platitude? One surgeon is not as good
5  as another. One plumber is not as good as another. We soon become aware of this when we require the attention of either. Yet in political and economic matters we appear to have reached a point where knowledge and specialized training count for very little. A newspaper reporter is sent
10 out on the street to collect the views of various passers-by on such a question as "Should the United States defend El Salvador?" The answer of the barfly who doesn't even know where the country is located, or that it is a country, is quoted in the next edition just as solemnly as that of
15 the college teacher of history. With the basic tenets of democracy—that all men are born free and equal and are entitled to life, liberty, and the pursuit of happiness—no decent American can possibly take issue. But that the opinion of one citizen on a technical subject is just as
20 authoritative as that of another is manifestly absurd. And to accept the opinions of all comers as having the same value is surely to encourage a cult of mediocrity.

### QUESTIONS

1.  Which phrase best expresses the main idea of this passage?

   (A)  the myth of equality
   (B)  a distinction about equality
   (C)  the essence of the Constitution
   (D)  a technical subject
   (E)  knowledge and specialized training

2.  The author most probably included the example of the question on El Salvador (lines 11–12) in order to

   (A)  move the reader to rage
   (B)  show that he is opposed to opinion sampling
   (C)  show that he has thoroughly researched his project
   (D)  explain the kind of opinion sampling he objects to
   (E)  provide a humorous but temporary diversion from his main point

3.  The author would be most likely to agree that

   (A)  some men are born to be masters; others are born to be servants
   (B)  the Constitution has little relevance for today's world
   (C)  one should never express an opinion on a specialized subject unless he is an expert in that subject
   (D)  every opinion should be treated equally
   (E)  all opinions should not be given equal weight

### EXPLANATORY ANSWERS

1.  Choice B is correct. See lines 1–7: "That one citizen...attention of either." These lines indicate that there is quite a distinction about equality when we are dealing with all the American people.

---

* Strategy 2 is considered the Master Reading Comprehension Strategy because it can be used effectively in every Reading Comprehension question. However, it is important that you learn the other Reading Comprehension Strategies because they can often be used to double-check your answers.

2. Choice D is correct. See lines 9–15: "A newspaper reporter...college teacher of history." These lines show that the author probably included the example of the question of El Salvador in order to explain the kind of opinion sampling he objects to.

3. Choice E is correct. See lines 18–22: "But that the opinion...to encourage a cult of mediocrity." Accordingly, the author would be most likely to agree that all opinions should *not* be given equal weight.

## EXAMPLE 2

She walked along the river until a policeman stopped her. It was one o'clock, he said. Not the best time to be walking alone by the side of a half-frozen river. He smiled at her, then offered to walk her home. It was the first day of the
5 new year, 1946, eight and a half months after the British tanks had rumbled into Bergen-Belsen.

That February, my mother turned twenty-six. It was difficult for strangers to believe that she had ever been a concentration camp inmate. Her face was smooth and
10 round. She wore lipstick and applied mascara to her large dark eyes. She dressed fashionably. But when she looked into the mirror in the mornings before leaving for work, my mother saw a shell, a mannequin who moved and spoke but who bore only a superficial resemblance to her real self.
15 The people closest to her had vanished. She had no proof that they were truly dead. No eyewitnesses had survived to vouch for her husband's death. There was no one living who had seen her parents die. The lack of confirmation haunted her. At night before she went to sleep and during the day as
20 she stood pinning dresses she wondered if, by some chance, her parents had gotten past the Germans or had crawled out of the mass grave into which they had been shot and were living, old and helpless, somewhere in Poland. What if only one of them had died? What if they had survived and had
25 died of cold or hunger after she had been liberated, while she was in Celle* dancing with British officers? She did not talk to anyone about these things. No one, she thought, wanted to hear them. She woke up in the mornings, went to work, bought groceries, went to the Jewish
30 Community Center and to the housing office like a robot.

*Celle is a small town in Germany.

1. The policeman stopped the author's mother from walking along the river because

   (A) the river was dangerous
   (B) it was the wrong time of day
   (C) it was still wartime
   (D) it was so cold
   (E) she looked suspicious

2. The author states that his mother thought about her parents when she

   (A) walked along the river
   (B) thought about death
   (C) danced with officers
   (D) arose in the morning
   (E) was at work

3. When the author mentions his mother's dancing with the British officers, he implies that his mother

   (A) compared her dancing to the suffering of her parents
   (B) had clearly put her troubles behind her
   (C) felt it was her duty to dance with them
   (D) felt guilty about dancing
   (E) regained the self-confidence she once had

### EXPLANATORY ANSWERS

1. Choice B is correct. See lines 1–4: "She walked along...offered to walk her home." The policeman's telling her that it was not the best time to be walking alone indicates clearly that "it was the wrong time of day."

2. Choice E is correct. Refer to lines 19–26: "...during the day...dancing with British officers."

3. Choice D is correct. See lines 24–26: "What if they had survived...dancing with British officers?"

# Look Back at the Passage When in Doubt

Sometimes while you are answering a question, you are not quite sure whether you have chosen the correct answer. Often, the underlinings that you have made in the reading passage will help you to determine whether a certain choice is the only correct choice.

### EXAMPLE 1

A critic of politics finds himself driven to deprecate the power of words, while using them copiously in warning against their influence. It is indeed in politics that their influence is most dangerous, so that one is almost tempted to wish
5 that they did not exist, and that society might be managed silently, by instinct, habit and ocular perception, without this supervening Babel of reports, arguments and slogans.

### QUESTION

1. Which statement is true according to the passage?

   (A) Critics of politics are often driven to take desperate measures.
   (B) Words, when used by politicians, have the greatest capacity for harm.
   (C) Politicians talk more than other people.
   (D) Society would be better managed if mutes were in charge.
   (E) Reports and slogans are not to be trusted.

### EXPLANATORY ANSWER

1. Choice B is correct. An important part that you might have underlined is in the second sentence: "It is indeed in politics that their influence is most dangerous...."

### EXAMPLE 2

All museum adepts are familiar with examples of *ostrakoi*, the oystershells used in balloting. As a matter of fact, these "oystershells" are usually shards of pottery, conveniently glazed to enable the voter to express his wishes in writing.
5 In the Agora, a great number of these have come to light, bearing the thrilling name, Themistocles. Into rival jars were dropped the ballots for or against his banishment. On account of the huge vote taken on that memorable date, it was to be expected that many ostrakoi would be found,
10 but the interest of this collection is that a number of these ballots are inscribed in an *identical* handwriting. There is nothing mysterious about it! The Boss was on the job, then as now. He prepared these ballots and voters cast them—no doubt for the consideration of an obol or two. The *ballot box*
15 *was stuffed.*
   How is the glory of the American boss diminished! A vile imitation, he. His methods as old as Time!

### QUESTION

1. The title that best expresses the ideas of this passage is

   (A) An Odd Method of Voting
   (B) Themistocles, an Early Dictator
   (C) Democracy in the Past
   (D) Political Trickery—Past and Present
   (E) The Diminishing American Politician

### EXPLANATORY ANSWER

1. Choice D is correct. An important idea that you might have underlined is expressed in lines 12–13: "The Boss was on the job, then as now."

### EXAMPLE 3

But the weather predictions which an almanac always contains are, we believe, mostly wasted on the farmer. He can take a squint at the moon before turning in. He can "smell" snow or tell if the wind is shifting dangerously east.
5 He can register forebodingly an extra twinge in a rheumatic shoulder. With any of these to go by, he can be reasonably sure of tomorrow's weather. He can return the almanac to the nail behind the door and put a last stick of wood in the stove. For an almanac, a zero night or a morning's drifted
10 road—none of these has changed much since Poor Richard wrote his stuff and barns were built along the Delaware.

### QUESTION

1. The author implies that, in predicting weather, there is considerable value in

   (A) reading the almanac
   (B) placing the last stick of wood in the stove
   (C) sleeping with one eye on the moon
   (D) keeping an almanac behind the door
   (E) noting rheumatic pains

### EXPLANATORY ANSWER

1. Choice E is correct. Important ideas that you might have underlined are the following
   Lines 2–3: "He can take a squint at the moon."
   Lines 3–4: "He can 'smell' snow..."

   Lines 5–6: "He can register forebodingly an extra twinge in a rheumatic shoulder."
These underlinings will reveal that, in predicting weather, the text in lines 5–6 gives you the correct answer.

READ. COMP. 4
STRATEGY

---

## Get the Meanings of "Tough" Words by Using the Context Method

Suppose you don't know the meaning of a certain word in a passage. Then try to determine the meaning of that word from the context—that is, from the words that are close in position to that word whose meaning you don't know. Knowing the meanings of difficult words in the passage will help you to better understand the passage as a whole.

EXAMPLE 1

Like all insects, it wears its skeleton on the outside—a marvelous chemical compound called chitin which sheathes the whole of its body. This flexible armor is tremendously tough, light and shatterproof, and resistant to alkali and
5 acid compounds which would eat the clothing, flesh and bones of man. To it are attached muscles so arranged around catapult-like hind legs as to enable the hopper to hop, if so diminutive a term can describe so prodigious a leap as ten or twelve feet—about 150 times the length of
10 the one-inch or so long insect. The equivalent feat for a man would be a casual jump, from a standing position, over the Washington Monument.

QUESTIONS

1. The word "sheathes" (line 2) means

   (A) strips
   (B) provides
   (C) exposes
   (D) encases
   (E) excites

2. The word "prodigious" (line 8) means

   (A) productive
   (B) frightening
   (C) criminal
   (D) enjoyable
   (E) enormous

EXPLANATORY ANSWERS

1. Choice D is correct. The words in line 1: "it wears a skeleton on the outside" gives us the idea that "sheathes" probably means "covers" or "encases."

2. Choice E is correct. See the surrounding words in lines 7–10 "enable the hopper to hop...so prodigious a leap as ten or twelve feet—about 150 times the length of the one-inch or so long insect." We may easily imply that the word "prodigious" means "great in size"; "enormous."

EXAMPLE 2

Since the days when the thirteen colonies, each so jealous of its sovereignty, got together to fight the British soldiers, the American people have exhibited a tendency—a genius to maintain widely divergent viewpoints in normal times,
5 but to unite and agree in times of stress. One reason the federal system has survived is that it has demonstrated this same tendency. Most of the time the three coequal divisions of the general government tend to compete. In crises they tend to cooperate. And not only during war. A singular
10 instance of cooperation took place in the opening days of the first administration of Franklin D. Roosevelt, when the harmonious efforts of Executive and Legislature to arrest the havoc of depression brought the term *rubber-stamp Congress* into the headlines. On the other hand, when in
15 1937 Roosevelt attempted to bend the judiciary to the will of the executive by "packing" the Supreme Court, Congress rebelled. This frequently proved flexibility—this capacity of both people and government to shift from competition to cooperation and back again as circumstances warrant—
20 suggests that the federal system will be found equal to the very real dangers of the present world situation.

QUESTIONS

1. The word "havoc" (line 13) means

   (A) possession
   (B) benefit
   (C) destruction
   (D) symptom
   (E) enjoyment

2. The word "divergent" (line 4) means

   (A) interesting
   (B) discussed
   (C) flexible
   (D) differing
   (E) appreciated

EXPLANATORY ANSWERS

1. Choice C is correct. The prepositional phrase "of depression," which modifies "havoc," should indicate that this word has an unfavorable meaning. The only choice that has an unfavorable meaning is Choice C—"destruction."

2. Choice D is correct. See lines 3–5: "…the American people…widely divergent viewpoints…but to unite and agree in times of stress." The word "but" in this sentence is an *opposite* indicator. We may, therefore, assume that a "divergent viewpoint" is a "differing" one from the idea expressed in the words "to unite and agree in times of stress."

READ. COMP. STRATEGY 5

# Circle Transitional Words in the Passage

There are certain transitional words—also called "bridge" or "key" words—that will help you to discover logical connections in a reading passage. *Circling* these transitional words will help you to get a better understanding of the passage.

Here are examples of commonly used transitional words and what these words may indicate.

| Transitional Word | Indicating |
|---|---|
| although<br>however<br>in spite of<br>rather than<br>nevertheless<br>on the other hand<br>but | OPPOSITION |
| *Key Word* | *Indicating* |
| moreover<br>besides<br>additionally<br>furthermore<br>in fact | SUPPORT |
| *Key Word* | *Indicating* |
| therefore<br>consequently<br>accordingly<br>because<br>when<br>so | RESULT |

EXAMPLE 1

Somewhere between 1860 and 1890, the dominant emphasis in American literature was radically changed. But it is obvious that this change was not necessarily a matter of conscious concern to all writers. In fact, many writers
5 may seem to have been actually unaware of the shifting emphasis. Moreover, it is not possible to trace the steady march of the realistic emphasis from its first feeble notes to its dominant trumpet-note of unquestioned leadership. The
progress of realism is to change the figure to that of a small
10 stream, receiving accessions from its tributaries at unequal points along its course, its progress now and then balked by the sand bars of opposition or the diffusing marshes of error and compromise. Again, it is apparent that any attempt to classify rigidly, as romanticists or realists, the writers of
15 this period is doomed to failure, since it is not by virtue of the writer's conscious espousal of the romantic or realistic creed that he does much of his best work, but by virtue of that writer's sincere surrender to the atmosphere of the subject.

QUESTIONS

1. The title that best expresses the ideas of this passage is

(A) Classifying American Writers
(B) Leaders in American Fiction
(C) The Sincerity of Writers
(D) The Values of Realism
(E) The Rise of Realism

2. Which characteristic of writers does the author praise?

(A) their ability to compromise
(B) their allegiance to a "school"
(C) their opposition to change
(D) their awareness of literary trends
(E) their intellectual honesty

EXPLANATORY ANSWERS

1. Choice E is correct. Note some of the transitional words that will help you to interpret the passage: "but" (line 2); "in fact" (line 4); "moreover" (line 5); "again" (line 13). A better understanding of

the passage should indicate to you that the main idea (title)—"The Rise of Realism"—is emphasized throughout the passage.

2. Choice E is correct. See lines 15–19: "...since it is not by virtue of...but by virtue of the writer's sincere...of the subject." The transitional word "but" helps us to arrive at the correct answer, which is "their intellectual honesty."

### EXAMPLE 2

A humorous remark or situation is, furthermore, always a pleasure. We can go back to it and laugh at it again and again. One does not tire of the *Pickwick Papers,* or of the humor of Mark Twain, any more than the child tires of a
5 nursery tale which he knows by heart. Humor is a feeling and feelings can be revived. But wit, being an intellectual and not an emotional impression, suffers by repetition. A witticism is really an item of knowledge. Wit, again, is distinctly a gregarious quality; whereas humor may abide in
10 the breast of a hermit. Those who live by themselves almost always have a dry humor. Wit is a city, humor a country, product. Wit is the accomplishment of persons who are busy with ideas; it is the fruit of intellectual cultivation and abounds in coffeehouses, in salons, and in literary clubs.
15 But humor is the gift of those who are concerned with persons rather than ideas, and it flourishes chiefly in the middle and lower classes.

### QUESTION

1. It is probable that the paragraph preceding this one discussed the

    (A) *Pickwick Papers*
    (B) characteristics of literature
    (C) characteristics of human nature
    (D) characteristics of humor
    (E) nature of human feelings

### EXPLANATORY ANSWER

1. Choice D is correct. See lines 1–2: "A humorous remark or situation is, furthermore, always a pleasure." The transitional word "furthermore" means "in addition." We may, therefore, assume that something dealing with humor has been discussed in the previous paragraph.

READ. COMP. STRATEGY 6

## Increase Your Vocabulary to Boost Your Reading Comprehension Score

1. You can increase your vocabulary tremendously by learning Latin and Greek roots, prefixes, and suffixes. Knowing the meanings of difficult words will thereby help you to understand a passage better.

    Sixty percent of all the words in our English language are derived from Latin and Greek. By learning certain Latin and Greek roots, prefixes, and suffixes, you will be able to understand the meanings of over 110,000 additional English words. See "Hot Prefixes and Roots" beginning on page 108.

2. Read through the vocabulary strategies beginning on page 105.
3. Learn the Most Important/Frequently Used PSAT Words beginning on page 116.

    There are other steps—in addition to the three steps explained above—to increase your vocabulary. Here they are:

4. Read as widely as possible—novels, nonfiction, newspapers, magazines.
5. Listen to people who speak well. Many TV programs have very fine speakers. You can pick up many new words listening to such programs.
6. Get into the habit of using the dictionary often. Why not carry a pocket-size dictionary with you?
7. Play word games—crossword puzzles will really build up your vocabulary.

## EXAMPLE 1

Acting, like much writing, is probably a compensation for and release from the strain of some profound maladjustment of the psyche. The actor lives most intensely by proxy. He has to be somebody else to be himself. But it is
5 all done openly and for our delight. The dangerous man, the enemy of nonattachment or any other wise way of life, is the born actor who has never found his way into the Theater, who never uses a stage door, who does not take a call and then wipe the paint off his face. It is the intrusion
10 of this temperament into political life, in which at this day it most emphatically does not belong, that works half the mischief in the world. In every country you may see them rise, the actors who will not use the Theater, and always they bring down disaster from the angry gods who like to
15 see mountebanks in their proper place.

### QUESTIONS

1. The meaning of "maladjustment" (line 2) is a

   (A) replacement of one thing for another
   (B) profitable experience in business
   (C) consideration for the feelings of others
   (D) disregard of advice offered by other
   (E) poor relationship with one's environment

2. The meaning of "psyche" (line 3) is

   (A) person
   (B) mind
   (C) personality
   (D) psychology
   (E) physique

3. The meaning of "intrusion" (line 9) is

   (A) entering without being welcome
   (B) acceptance after considering the facts
   (C) interest that has developed after a period of time
   (D) fear as the result of imagination
   (E) refusing to obey a command

4. The meaning of "mountebanks" (line 15) is

   (A) mountain climbers
   (B) cashiers
   (C) high peaks
   (D) fakers
   (E) mortals

### EXPLANATORY ANSWERS

1. Choice E is correct. The prefix "mal" means bad. Obviously a maladjustment is a bad adjustment—that is, a poor relationship with one's environment.

2. Choice B is correct. The root "psyche" means the mind functioning as the center of thought, feeling, and behavior.

3. Choice A is correct. The prefix "in" means "into" in this case. The root "trud, trus" means "pushing into"—or entering without being welcome.

4. Choice D is correct. The root "mont" means "to climb." The root "banc" means a "bench." A mountebank means literally "one who climbs on a bench." The actual meaning of mountebank is a quack (faker) who sells useless medicines from a platform in a public place.

## EXAMPLE 2

The American Museum of Natural History has long portrayed various aspects of man. Primitive cultures have been shown through habitat groups and displays of man's tools, utensils, and art. In more recent years, there has been a
5 tendency to delineate man's place in nature, displaying his destructive and constructive activities on the earth he inhabits. Now, for the first time, the Museum has taken man apart, enlarged the delicate mechanisms that make him run, and examined him as a biological phenomenon.
10 In the new Hall of the Biology of Man, Museum technicians have created a series of displays that are instructive to a degree never before achieved in an exhibit hall. Using new techniques and new materials, they have been able to produce movement as well as form and color. It is a human
15 belief that beauty is only skin deep. But nature has proved to be a master designer, not only in the matter of man's bilateral symmetry but also in the marvelous packaging job that has arranged all man's organs and systems within his skin-covered case. When these are taken out of the
20 case, greatly enlarged and given color, they reveal form and design that give the lie to that old saw. Visitors will be surprised to discover that man's insides, too, are beautiful.

### QUESTIONS

1. The meaning of "bilateral" (line 17) is

   (A) biological
   (B) two-sided
   (C) natural
   (D) harmonious
   (E) technical

2. The meaning of "symmetry" (line 17) is

   (A) simplicity
   (B) obstinacy
   (C) sincerity
   (D) appearance
   (E) proportion

### EXPLANATORY ANSWERS

1. Choice B is correct. The prefix "bi" means "two." The root "latus" means "side." Therefore, "bilateral" means "two-sided."

2. Choice E is correct. The prefix "sym" means "together." The root "metr" means "measure." The word "symmetry," therefore, means "proportion," "harmonious relation of parts," "balance."

# 3 Vocabulary Strategies

## Introduction

Although **antonyms** (opposites of words) are not on the PSAT, it is still important for you to know vocabulary and the strategies to figure out the meanings of words, since there are many questions involving difficult words in all the sections on the Verbal part of the PSAT, that is, the **Sentence Completions** and **Critical Reading Parts.**

VOCABULARY STRATEGY 1

## Use Roots, Prefixes, and Suffixes to Get the Meanings of Words

You can increase your vocabulary tremendously by learning Latin and Greek roots, prefixes, and suffixes. Sixty percent of all the words in our English language are derived from Latin and Greek. By learning certain Latin and Greek roots, prefixes, and suffixes, you will be able to understand the meanings of more than 110,000 additional English words. See "Hot Prefixes and Roots" beginning on page 108.

### EXAMPLE 1

Opposite of PROFICIENT:

(A) antiseptic
(B) unwilling
(C) inconsiderate
(D) neglectful
(E) awkward

#### EXPLANATORY ANSWER

Choice E is correct. The prefix PRO means *forward, for the purpose of.* The root FIC means *to make* or *to do.* Therefore, PROFICIENT literally means *doing something in a forward way.* The definition of *proficient* is *skillful, adept, capable.* The antonym of *proficient* is, accordingly, *awkward, incapable.*

### EXAMPLE 2

Opposite of DELUDE:

(A) include
(B) guide
(C) reply
(D) upgrade
(E) welcome

#### EXPLANATORY ANSWER

Choice B is correct. The prefix DE means *downward, against.* The root LUD means *to play* (a game). Therefore, DELUDE literally means *to play a game against.* The definition of *delude* is *to deceive, to mislead.* The antonym of *delude* is, accordingly, to *guide.*

### EXAMPLE 3

Opposite of LAUDATORY:

(A) vacating
(B) satisfactory
(C) revoking
(D) faultfinding
(E) silent

#### EXPLANATORY ANSWER

Choice D is correct. The root LAUD means *praise.* The suffix ORY means a *tendency toward.* Therefore, LAUDATORY means having a *tendency toward praising someone.* The definition of *laudatory* is *praising.* The antonym of laudatory is, accordingly, *faultfinding.*

EXAMPLE 4

Opposite of SUBSTANTIATE:

(A) reveal
(B) intimidate
(C) disprove
(D) integrate
(E) assist

EXPLANATORY ANSWER

Choice C is correct. The prefix SUB means *under.* The root STA means *to stand.* The suffix ATE is a verb form indicating *the act of.* Therefore, SUBSTANTIATE literally means *to perform the act of standing under.* The definition of *substantiate* is *to support* with proof or evidence. The antonym is, accordingly, *disprove.*

VOCABULARY
STRATEGY 2

---

## Pay Attention to the Sound or Feeling of the Word—Whether Positive or Negative, Harsh or Mild, Big or Little, Etc.

If the word sounds harsh or terrible, such as "obstreperous," the meaning probably is something harsh or terrible. If you're looking for a word opposite in meaning to "obstreperous," look for a word or words that have a softer sound, such as "pleasantly quiet or docile." The sense of "obstreperous" can also seem to be negative—so if you're looking for a synonym, look for a negative word. If you're looking for an opposite (antonym), look for a positive word.

EXAMPLE 1

Opposite of BELLIGERENCY:

(A) pain
(B) silence
(C) homeliness
(D) elegance
(E) peace

EXPLANATORY ANSWER

Choice E is correct. The word BELLIGERENCY imparts a tone of forcefulness or confusion and means warlike. The opposite would be calmness or peacefulness. The closest choices are choice B or E, with E a little closer to the opposite in tone for the capitalized word. Of course, if you knew the root BELLI means "war," you could see the opposite as (E) peace.

EXAMPLE 2

Opposite of DEGRADE:

(A) startle
(B) elevate
(C) encircle
(D) replace
(E) assemble

EXPLANATORY ANSWER

Choice B is correct. Here you can think of the DE in DEGRADE as a prefix that is negative (bad) and means *down,* and in fact DEGRADE does mean to debase or lower. So you should look for an opposite that would be

a word with a *positive* (good) meaning. The best word from the choices is (B) elevate.

EXAMPLE 3

Opposite of OBFUSCATION:

(A) illumination
(B) irritation
(C) conviction
(D) minor offense
(E) stable environment

EXPLANATORY ANSWER

Choice A is correct. The prefix OB is usually negative, as in obstacle or obliterate, and in fact OBFUSCATE means darken or obscure. So since we are looking for an opposite, you would look for a *positive* word. Choices A and E are positive, and you should go for the more positive of the two, which is Choice A.

EXAMPLE 4

Opposite of MUNIFICENCE:

(A) disloyalty
(B) stinginess
(C) dispersion
(D) simplicity
(E) vehemence

EXPLANATORY ANSWER

Choice B is correct because MUNIFICENCE means generosity. Many of the words ending in ENCE, like

OPULENCE, EFFERVESCENCE, LUMINESCENCE, QUINTESSENCE, etc., represent or describe something big or bright. So the opposite of one of these words would denote something small or dark.

You can associate the prefix MUNI with MONEY, as in "municipal bonds," so the word MUNIFICENCE must deal with money and in a big way. The opposite deals with money in a small way. Choice B fits the bill.

VOCABULARY STRATEGY 3

## Use Word Associations to Determine Word Meanings and Their Opposites

Looking at the root or part of any capitalized word may suggest an association with another word that looks similar and whose meaning you know. This new word's meaning may give you a clue as to the meaning of the original word or the opposite in meaning to the original word if you need an opposite. For example, *extricate* reminds us of the word "extract," the opposite of which is "to put together."

### EXAMPLE 1

Opposite of STASIS:

(A) stoppage
(B) reduction
(C) depletion
(D) fluctuation
(E) completion

#### EXPLANATORY ANSWER

Choice D is correct. Think of STATIC or STATIONARY. The opposite would be moving or fluctuating since STASIS means stopping or retarding movement.

### EXAMPLE 2

Opposite of APPEASE:

(A) criticize
(B) analyze
(C) correct
(D) incense
(E) develop

#### EXPLANATORY ANSWER

Choice D is correct. Appease means to placate. Think of PEACE in APPEASE. The opposite would be violent or *incense*.

### EXAMPLE 3

Opposite of COMMISERATION:

(A) undeserved reward
(B) lack of sympathy
(C) unexpected success
(D) absence of talent
(E) inexplicable danger

#### EXPLANATORY ANSWER

Choice B is correct. Think of MISERY in the word COMMISERATION. Commiseration means the sharing of misery. Choice B is the only appropriate choice.

# Hot Prefixes and Roots

Here is a list of the most important prefixes and roots that impart a certain meaning or feeling. They can be instant clues to the meanings of more than 110,000 words.

## PREFIXES THAT MEAN *TO*, *WITH*, *BETWEEN*, OR *AMONG*

| PREFIX | MEANING | EXAMPLES |
|---|---|---|
| ad, ac, af, an, ap, ap, as, at | to, toward | adapt—to fit into<br>adhere—to stick to<br>attract—to draw near |
| com, con, co, col | with, together | combine—to bring together<br>contact—to touch together<br>collect—to bring together<br>co-worker—one who works together with another worker |
| in, il, ir, im | into | inject—to put into<br>impose—to force into<br>illustrate—to put into example<br>irritate—to put into discomfort |
| inter | between, among | international—among nations<br>interact—to act among the people |
| pro | forward, going ahead | proceed—to go forward<br>promote—to move forward |

## PREFIXES THAT MEAN *BAD*

| PREFIX | MEANING | EXAMPLES |
|---|---|---|
| mal | wrong, bad | malady—illness<br>malevolent—bad<br>malfunction—bad functioning |
| mis | wrong, badly | mistreat—to treat badly<br>mistake—to get wrong |

# PREFIXES THAT MEAN *AWAY FROM*, *NOT*, OR *AGAINST*

| PREFIX | MEANING | EXAMPLES |
|---|---|---|
| ab | away from | absent—not to be present, away<br>abscond—to run away |
| de, dis | away from, down,<br>the opposite of, apart, not | depart—to go away from<br>decline—to turn down<br>dislike—not to like<br>dishonest—not honest<br>distant—apart |
| ex, e, ef | out, from | exit—to go out<br>eject—to throw out<br>efface—to rub out, erase |
| in, il, ir, im | not | inactive—not active<br>impossible—not possible<br>ill-mannered—not mannered<br>irreversible—not reversible |
| non | not | nonsense—no sense<br>nonstop—having no stops |
| un | not | unhelpful—not helpful<br>uninterested—not interested |
| anti | against | anti-freeze—a substance used<br>to prevent freezing<br>anti-social—refers to someone<br>who's not social |
| ob | against, in front of | obstacle—something that<br>stands in the way of<br>obstinate—inflexible |

## PREFIXES THAT DENOTE DISTANCE

| PREFIX | MEANING | EXAMPLES |
|---|---|---|
| circum | around | circumscribe—to write or inscribe in a circle<br>circumspect—to watch around or be very careful |
| equ, equi | equal, the same | equalize—to make equal<br>equitable—fair, equal |
| post | after | postpone—to do after<br>postmortem—after death |
| pre | before | preview—a viewing that goes before another viewing<br>prehistorical—before written history |
| trans | across | transcontinental—across the continent<br>transit—act of going across |
| re | back, again | retell—to tell again<br>recall—to call back, to remember |
| sub | under | subordinate—under something else<br>subconcious—under the conscious |
| super | over, above | superimpose—to put something over something else<br>superstar—a star greater than other stars |
| un, uni | one | unity—oneness<br>unanimous—sharing one view<br>unidirectional—having one direction |

# ROOTS

| ROOT | MEANING | EXAMPLES |
|---|---|---|
| cap, capt, cept, ceive | to take, to hold | captive—one who is held<br>receive—to take<br>capable—to be able to take hold of things<br>concept—an idea or thought held in mind |
| cred | to believe | credible—believable<br>credit—belief, trust |
| curr, curs, cours | to run | current—now in progress, running<br>cursor—a moveable indicator<br>recourse—to run for aid |
| dic, dict | to say | indicate—to say by demonstrating<br>diction—verbal saying |
| duc, duct | to lead | induce—to lead to action<br>aqueduct—a pipe or waterway that leads water somewhere |
| fac, fic, fect, fy | to make, to do | facile—easy to do<br>fiction—something that has been made up<br>satisfy—to make happy<br>affect—to make a change in |
| jec, ject | to throw | project—to put forward<br>trajectory—a path of an object that has been thrown |
| mit, mis | to send | admit—to send in<br>missile—something that gets sent through the air |

| ROOT | MEANING | EXAMPLES |
| --- | --- | --- |
| pon, pos | to place | transpose—to place across<br>compose—to put into place<br>many parts<br>deposit—to place in something |
| scrib, script | to write | describe—to write or tell about<br>scripture—a written tablet |
| spec, spic | to look | specimen—an example to look at<br>inspect—to look over |
| ten, tain | to hold | maintain—to hold up or keep<br>retentive—holding |
| ven, vent | to come | advent—a coming<br>convene—to come together |

# Words Commonly Mistaken for Each Other

Review the following lists of words quickly, and use a pencil to mark the pairs that you have trouble remembering. This way, you'll be able to focus your attention on these on subsequent reviews.

AGGRAVATE/IRRITATE
—to make worse
—to annoy

ALLUSION/ILLUSION
—reference
—error in vision

ARBITER/ARBITRARY
—a supposedly unprejudiced judge
—prejudiced

ASCENT/ASSENT
—upward movement
—agreement; to agree

ASCETIC/AESTHETIC
—self-denying
—pertaining to the beautiful

AVERSE/ADVERSE
—disciplined
—opposed

BAN/BANE
—prohibit
—woe

CANVAS/CANVASS
—coarse cloth
—examine; solicit

CAPITAL/CAPITOL
—excellent; chief town; money; punishable by death or life imprisonment
—state house

CENSURE/CENSOR
—find fault
—purge or remove offensive passages

COMPLACENT/COMPLAISANT
—self-satisfied; smug
—kindly; submissive

COMPLEMENT/COMPLIMENT
—that which completes
—praise

CONSUL/COUNCIL/COUNSEL
—diplomatic representative
—group of advisors —advice

CONTEMPTIBLE/CONTEMPTUOUS
—despicable
—scornful

CONTINUAL/CONTINUOUS
—occurring in steady, but not unbroken, order
—occurring without interruption

COSMOPOLITAN/METROPOLITAN
—sophisticated
—pertaining to the city

| | |
|---|---|
| CREDIBLE/CREDITABLE | —believable<br>—worthy of praise |
| DEMURE/DEMUR | —pretending modesty<br>—hesitate; raise objection |
| DEPRECATE/DEPRECIATE | —disapprove regretfully<br>—undervalue |
| DISCREET/DISCRETE | —judicious; prudent<br>—separate |
| DISINTERESTED/UNINTERESTED | —unprejudiced<br>—not interested |
| DIVERS/DIVERSE | —several<br>—varied |
| ELICIT/ILLICIT | —extract<br>—unlawful |
| EMEND/AMEND | —correct a text or manuscript<br>—improve by making slight changes |
| EMINENT/IMMINENT | —high in rank<br>—threatening; at hand |
| EQUABLE/EQUITABLE | —even-tempered<br>—just |
| EXULT/EXALT | —rejoice<br>—raise; praise highly |
| FORMALLY/FORMERLY | —in a formal manner<br>—at a previous time |
| GOURMET/GOURMAND | —lover of good food<br>—glutton |
| GORILLA/GUERRILLA | —large ape<br>—mercenary |
| HAIL/HALE | —frozen pellets; to call; originate<br>—strong, healthy |
| HEALTHY/HEALTHFUL | —possessing health<br>—bringing about health |
| IMPLY/INFER | —indicate or suggest<br>—draw a conclusion from |
| INCREDIBLE/INCREDULOUS | —unbelievable<br>—unbelieving |
| INDIGENT/INDIGENOUS | —poor<br>—native |
| INGENIUS/INGENUOUS | —skillful; clever; resourceful<br>—frank; naïve |

| | |
|---|---|
| INTERNMENT/INTERMENT | —imprisonment<br>—burial |
| MAIZE/MAZE | —corn<br>—confusing network |
| MARTIAL/MARITAL | —warlike<br>—pertaining to marriage |
| MENDACIOUS/MERITORIOUS | —lying<br>—possessing merit; praiseworthy |
| PERSONAL/PERSONABLE | —private<br>—attractive |
| PERSPICACIOUS/PERSPICUOUS | —shrewd; acute<br>—clear; lucid |
| PRACTICAL/PRACTICABLE | —sensible; useful<br>—timely; capable of being accomplished |
| PRODIGAL/PRODIGIOUS | —wastefully lavish<br>—extraordinarily large |
| PROPHECY/PROPHESY | —prediction<br>—to predict |
| PROVIDED/PROVIDING | —on condition that<br>—furnishing; giving |
| REGAL/REGALE | —royal<br>—entertain lavishly |
| RESPECTFULLY/RESPECTIVELY | —with respect<br>—in the order already suggested |
| SANCTION/SANCTITY | —authorize<br>—holiness |
| SOCIAL/SOCIABLE | —pertaining to human society<br>—companionable; friendly |
| STATUE/STATURE | —piece of sculpture<br>—height |
| URBAN/URBANE | —pertaining to the city<br>—polished; suave |
| VENAL/VENIAL | —corrupt, mercenary<br>—pardonable |

# The Most Important/Frequently Used PSAT Words and Their Opposites

Following is a list of popular PSAT words and their opposites. *Note:* These words fit into specific categories, and it may be a little easier memorizing the meaning of these important words knowing what category they fit into.

| POSITIVE | NEGATIVE | POSITIVE | NEGATIVE |
|----------|----------|----------|----------|
| TO PRAISE | TO BELITTLE | TO CALM OR MAKE BETTER | TO MAKE WORSE OR RUFFLE |
| acclaim | admonish | abate | alienate |
| applaud | assail | accede | antagonize |
| commend | berate | accommodate | contradict |
| eulogize | calumniate | allay | dispute |
| exalt | castigate | ameliorate | fend off |
| extol | censure | appease | embitter |
| flatter | chastise | assuage | estrange |
| hail | chide | comply | incense |
| laud | decry | concede | infuriate |
| panegyrize | denigrate | conciliate | nettle |
| resound | denounce | gratify | oppugn |
| tout | disparage | mitigate | oppose |
| | excoriate | mollify | rebuff |
| | execrate | pacify | repel |
| | flay | palliate | repulse |
| | lambaste | placate | snub |
| | malign | propitiate | |
| | reprimand | quell | |
| | reproach | satiate | |
| | scold | | |
| | upbraid | | |
| | vilify | | |

| POSITIVE | NEGATIVE | POSITIVE | NEGATIVE |
|---|---|---|---|
| PLEASANT | UNPLEASANT | YIELDING | NOT YIELDING |
| affable | callous | accommodating | adamant |
| amiable | cantankerous | amenable | determinate |
| agreeable | captious | compliant | immutable |
| captivating | churlish | deferential | indomitable |
| congenial | contentious | docile | inflexible |
| cordial | gruff | flexible | intractable |
| courteous | irascible | hospitable | intransigent |
| decorous | ireful | inclined | recalcitrant |
| engaging | obstinate | malleable | relentless |
| gracious | ornery | obliging | resolute |
| obliging | peevish | pliant | steadfast |
| sportive | perverse | submissive | tenacious |
| unblemished | petulant | subservient | |
| undefiled | querulous | tractable | |
| | testy | | |
| | vexing | | |
| | wayward | | |

| POSITIVE | NEGATIVE | POSITIVE | NEGATIVE |
|---|---|---|---|
| GENEROUS | CHEAP | COURAGEOUS | TIMID |
| altruistic | frugal | audacious | diffident |
| beneficent | miserly | dauntless | indisposed |
| benevolent | niggardly | gallant | laconic |
| charitable | paltry | intrepid | reserved |
| effusive | parsimonious | stalwart | reticent |
| hospitable | penurious | undaunted | subdued |
| humanitarian | provident | valiant | timorous |
| magnanimous | skinflinty | valorous | |
| munificent | spartan | | |
| philanthropic | tight-fisted | | |
| | thrifty | | |

| POSITIVE | NEGATIVE | POSITIVE | NEGATIVE |
|---|---|---|---|
| ABUNDANT OR RICH | SCARCE OR POOR | LIVELY | BLEAK |
| affluent | dearth | brisk | dejected |
| bounteous | deficit | dynamic | forlorn |
| copious | destitute | ebullient | lackluster |
| luxuriant | exiguous | exhilaration | lugubrious |
| multifarious | impecunious | exuberant | melancholy |
| multitudinous | impoverished | inspiring | muted |
| myriad | indigent | provocative | prostrate |
| opulent | insolvent | scintillating | somber |
| pecunious | meager | stimulating | tenebrous |
| plenteous | paltry | titillating | |
| plentiful | paucity | | |
| plethoric | penurious | | |
| profuse | scanty | | |
| prosperous | scarcity | | |
| superabundant | sparse | | |
| teeming | | | |
| wealthy | | | |

| POSITIVE | NEGATIVE | POSITIVE | NEGATIVE |
| --- | --- | --- | --- |
| CAREFUL | CARELESS | HUMBLE | HAUGHTY |
| chary | culpable | demure | affected |
| circumspect | felonious | diffident | aristocratic |
| conscientious | indifferent | indisposed | arrogant |
| discreet | insouciant | introverted | audacious |
| exacting | lackadaisical | laconic | authoritarian |
| fastidious | lax | plebian | autocratic |
| gingerly | negligent | reluctant | condescending |
| heedful | perfunctory | restrained | disdainful |
| judicious | rash | reticent | egotistical |
| meticulous | remiss | subdued | flagrant |
| provident | reprehensible | subservient | flippant |
| prudent | temerarious | taciturn | imperious |
| punctilious | | timid | impertinent |
| scrupulous | | timorous | impudent |
| scrutiny | | unassuming | insolent |
| wary | | unostentatious | ostentatious |
| | | unpretentious | pompous |
| | | | proud |
| | | | supercilious |
| | | | vainglorious |

*Note:* In many cases you can put a prefix "im" or "un" in front of the word and change its meaning to an opposite.

EXAMPLE: Pecunious. Opposite: Impecunious
Ostentatious. Opposite: Unostentatious

# PART 4

# MINI-MATH REFRESHER

## The Most Important Basic Math Rules and Concepts You Need to Know

Make sure that you understand each of the following math rules and concepts. It is a good idea to memorize them all. Refer to the section of the Math Refresher (Part 5 starting on page 129) shown in parentheses, e.g., (409), for a complete explanation of each.

# Algebra and Arithmetic

**(409)**
$$a(b + c) = ab + ac$$

*Example:*
$$5(4 + 5) = 5(4) + 5(5)$$
$$= 20 + 25$$
$$= 45$$

**(409)**
$$(a + b)(c + d) = ac + ad + bc + bd$$

*Example:*
$$(2 + 3)(4 - 6) = (2)(4) + (2)(-6)$$
$$+ (3)(4) + (3)(-6)$$
$$= 8 - 12 + 12 - 18$$
$$= -10$$

**(409)**
$$(a + b)^2 = a^2 + 2ab + b^2$$

**(409)**
$$(a - b)^2 = a^2 - 2ab + b^2$$

**(409)**
$$(a + b)(a - b) = a^2 - b^2$$

**(409)**
$$-(a - b) = b - a$$

**(429)**
$$a^2 = (a)(a)$$

*Example:*
$$2^2 = (2)(2) = 4$$
$$a^3 = (a)(a)(a), \text{ etc.}$$

**(429)**
$$\frac{a^x}{a^y} = a^{x-y}$$

*Examples:*
$$\frac{a^3}{a^2} = a^{3-2} = a;$$
$$\frac{2^3}{2^2} = 2^{3-2} = 2$$

**(429)**
$$a^x a^y = a^{x+y}$$

*Examples:*
$$a^2 \times a^3 = a^5;$$
$$2^2 \times 2^3 = 2^5 = 32$$

**(429)**
$$a^0 = 1$$
$$10^0 = 1$$
$$10^1 = 10$$
$$10^2 = 100$$
$$10^3 = 1,000, \text{ etc.}$$

*Example:*
$$8.6 \times 10^4 = 8.6\underset{1\ 2\ 3\ 4}{000}.0$$

**(429)**
$$(a^x)y = a^{xy}$$

*Examples:*
$$(a^3)^5 = a^{15}; (2^3)^5 = 2^{15}$$

**(429)**
$$(ab)^x = a^x b^x$$

*Examples:*
$$(2 \times 3)^3 = 2^3 \times 3^3; (ab)^2 = a^2 b^2$$

**(430)**

If $y^2 = x$ then $y = \pm\sqrt{x}$

*Example*:

If $y^2 = 4$,

then $y = \pm\sqrt{4} = \pm 2$

**(429)**

$a^{-y} = \dfrac{1}{a^y}$

*Example*: $2^{-3} = \dfrac{1}{2^3} = \dfrac{1}{8}$

**(107)**

Percentage

$x\% = \dfrac{x}{100}$

*Example*:

$5\% = \dfrac{5}{100}$

## Percentage Problems

**(107)**

*Examples*:

(1) What percent of 5 is 2?

$\dfrac{x}{100} \quad\quad \times\ 5\ =\ 2$

or

$\left(\dfrac{x}{100}\right)(5) = 2$

$\dfrac{5x}{100} = 2$

$5x = 200$

$x = 40$

Answer = 40%

**(107)**

RULE:  "What" becomes $x$

"Percent" becomes $\dfrac{1}{100}$

"of" becomes $\times$ (times)

"is" becomes $=$ (equals)

**(107)**

(2) 6 is what percent of 24?

$6\ =\ \dfrac{x}{100} \quad\quad \times\ 24$

$6 = \dfrac{24x}{100}$

$600 = 24x$

$100 = 4x$ (dividing both sides by 6)

$25 = x$

Answer = 25%

# Equations

**(409)**

*Example*: $x^2 - 2x + 1 = 0$. Solve for $x$.

*Procedure*:

*Factor*: $(x-1)(x-1) = 0$

$$x - 1 = 0$$

$$x = 1$$

**(407)**

*Example*: $x + y = 1$; $x - y = 2$. Solve for $x$ and $y$.

*Procedure*:

Add equations:

$$x + y = 1$$
$$\underline{x - y = 2}$$
$$2x + 0 = 3$$

Therefore $2x = 3$ and $x = \dfrac{3}{2}$

Substitute $x = \dfrac{3}{2}$ back into one of the equations:

$$x + y = 1$$

$$\dfrac{3}{2} + y = 1$$

$$y = -\dfrac{1}{2}$$

# Equalities

**(402)**

$$a + b = c \qquad\qquad 3 + 4 = 7$$
$$\underline{+\quad\ d = d} \qquad\qquad \underline{+\quad\ 2 = 2}$$
$$a + b + d = c + d \qquad 3 + 4 + 2 = 7 + 2$$

# Inequalities

$>$ means greater than, $<$ means less than, $\geq$ means greater than or equal to, etc.

**(419–425)**

$$b > c \qquad\quad 4 > 3 \qquad\quad 4 > 3$$
$$\underline{d > e} \qquad\quad \underline{7 > 6} \qquad\quad \underline{-6 > -7}$$
$$b + d > c + e \quad 11 > 9 \qquad -2 > -4$$

---

$$5 > 4 \qquad\quad -5 < -4$$
$$(6)\,5 > 4\,(6) \quad -(-5) > -(-4) \qquad \text{(reversing inequality)}$$

Thus

$$30 > 24 \qquad 5 > 4$$

---

If $\ -2 < x < +2$ $\qquad\qquad a > b > 0$

then $+2 > -x > -2$ $\qquad$ Thus $a^2 > b^2$

# Geometry

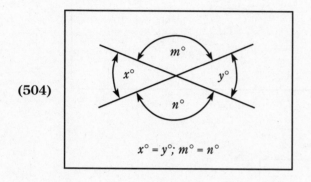

**(504)**

$x° = y°;\ m° = n°$

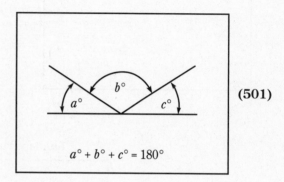

**(501)**

$a° + b° + c° = 180°$

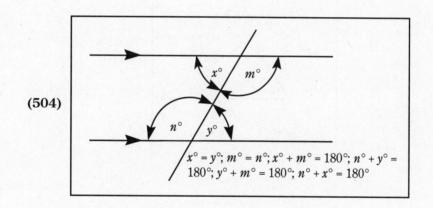

**(504)**

$x° = y°;\ m° = n°;\ x° + m° = 180°;\ n° + y° =$ $180°;\ y° + m° = 180°;\ n° + x° = 180°$

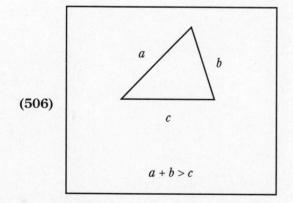

**(506)**

$a + b > c$

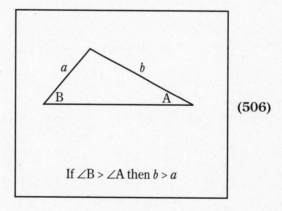

**(506)**

If $\angle B > \angle A$ then $b > a$

**(507)**

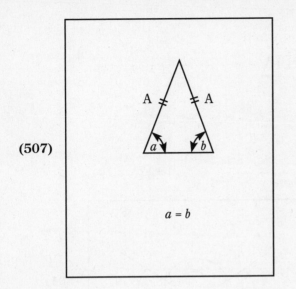

$a = b$

**(501)**

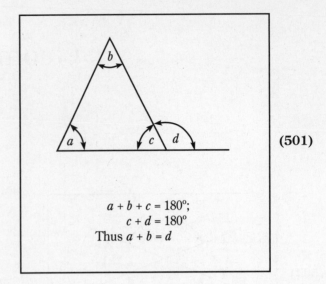

$a + b + c = 180°;$
$c + d = 180°$
Thus $a + b = d$

### Similar Triangles

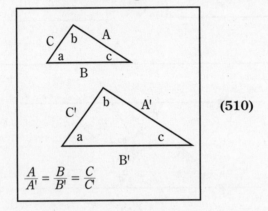

**(510)**

$$\frac{A}{A'} = \frac{B}{B'} = \frac{C}{C'}$$

# Areas & Perimeters

**(304)**

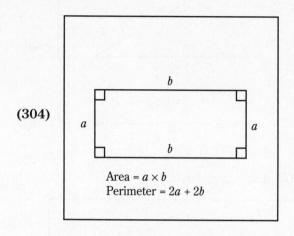

Area = $a \times b$
Perimeter = $2a + 2b$

**(306)**

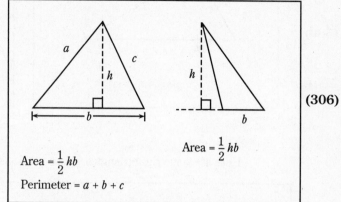

Area = $\frac{1}{2} hb$
Perimeter = $a + b + c$

Area = $\frac{1}{2} hb$

**(310)**

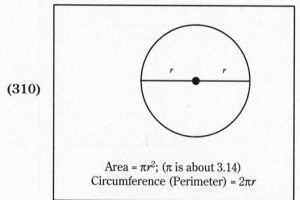

Area = $\pi r^2$; ($\pi$ is about 3.14)
Circumference (Perimeter) = $2\pi r$

**(305)**

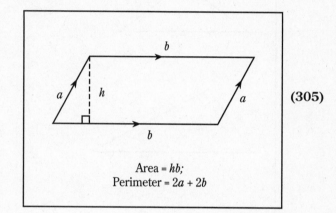

Area = $hb$;
Perimeter = $2a + 2b$

# More on Circles

**(526–527)**

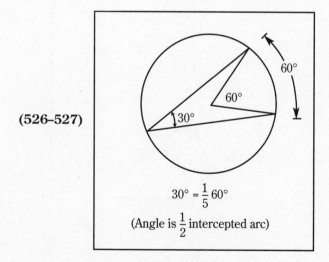

$30° = \frac{1}{5} 60°$
(Angle is $\frac{1}{2}$ intercepted arc)

**(527)**

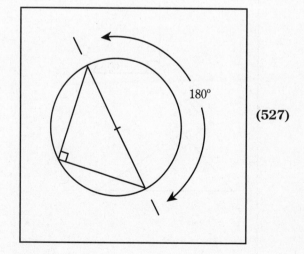

**(509)**

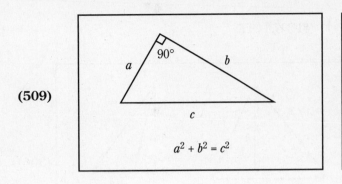

**(509)**

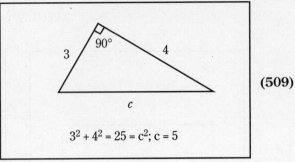

Here are some right triangles whose relationship of sides you should memorize:

**(509)**

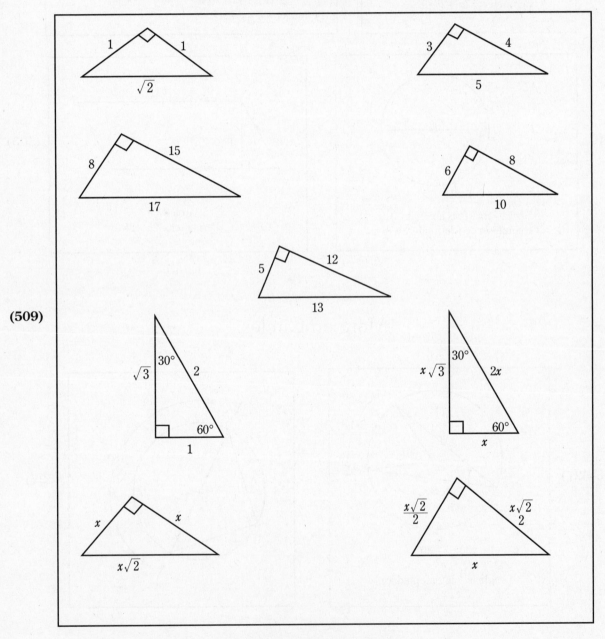

# Coordinate Geometry

**(410)**

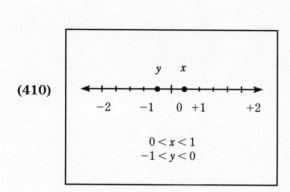

$$0 < x < 1$$
$$-1 < y < 0$$

**(410–411)**

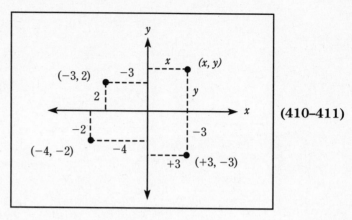

**(411)**

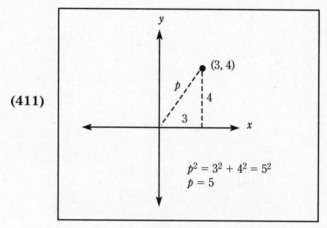

$$p^2 = 3^2 + 4^2 = 5^2$$
$$p = 5$$

**(416)**

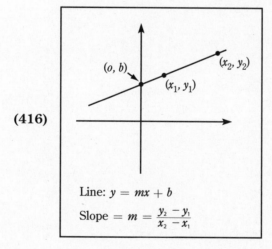

Line: $y = mx + b$

Slope $= m = \dfrac{y_2 - y_1}{x_2 - x_1}$

# PART 5

# COMPLETE PSAT MATH REFRESHER

There are many PSAT exam takers whose Math background is not quite up to par—probably because their basic Math skills are "rusty" or because they never did do well in their Math classes. For these Math-troubled students, this Math Refresher section will be "manna from heaven." The pages that follow constitute a complete basic Math course that will help students greatly in preparing for the Math part of the PSAT.

This Math Refresher offers the following:

1. a systematic review of every Math area covered by the questions in the Math part of the PSAT

*and*

2. short review tests throughout the Refresher to check whether the student has grasped the Math principles that he or she has just studied.

The review tests will also provide students with valuable reinforcement so that they will remember how to go about solving math problems they would otherwise have difficulty with on the actual PSAT.

Each of the 8 "Sessions" in this Math Refresher has a review test ("Practice Test"). Almost every review test has 50 questions followed by 50 detailed solutions. All of the solutions for the 8 review tests include a number (or numbers) in parentheses *after each solution*. The number refers to a specific instructional section where the rules and principles involved in the question are explained simply and clearly.

There is another very important purpose that this Math Refresher serves. You will find, after every solution in the Math sections of the 3 PSAT Practice Tests in this book, a key to the mathematical principles of this Math Refresher. For example, a solution may direct you to Math Refresher 202, which deals with Distance and Time problems. If you happen to be weak in this mathematical operation, the 202 Math Refresher explanation will immediately clarify for you how to do Distance and Time problems. In other words, for those who are weak in any phase of Basic Math, this invaluable keying system will help you get the right answer to your PSAT Math question—and thereby add approximately 1 point to your PSAT score.

# MATH REFRESHER*
# SESSION 1

# Fractions, Decimals, Percentages, Deviations, Ratios and Proportions, Variations, and Comparison of Fractions

## Fractions, Decimals, Percentages

These problems involve the ability to perform numerical operations quickly and correctly. It is essential that you learn the arithmetical procedures outlined in this section.

**101.** Four different ways to write "$a$ divided by $b$" are $a \div b$, $\frac{a}{b}$, $a : b$, $b \overline{)a}$.

**Example:** 7 divided by 15 is $7 \div 15 = \frac{7}{15} = 7 : 15 = 15 \overline{)7}$.

**102.** The numerator of a fraction is the upper number and the denominator is the lower number.

**Example:** In the fraction $\frac{8}{13}$, the numerator is 8 and the denominator is 13.

**103.** Moving a decimal point one place to the right multiplies the value of a number by 10, whereas moving the decimal point one place to the left divides a number by 10. Likewise, moving a decimal point two places to the right multiplies the value of a number by 100, whereas moving the decimal point two places to the left divides a number by 100.

**Example:**  $24.35 \times 10 = 243.5$ (decimal point moved to *right*)
$24.35 \div 10 = 2.435$ (decimal point moved to *left*)

**104.** To change a fraction to a decimal, divide the numerator of the fraction by its denominator.

**Example:** Express $\frac{5}{6}$ as a decimal. We divide 5 by 6, obtaining 0.83.

$$\frac{5}{6} = 5 \div 6 = 0.833 \dots$$

**105.** To convert a decimal to a fraction, delete the decimal point and divide by whatever unit of 10 the number of decimal places represents.

**Example:** Convert 0.83 to a fraction. First, delete the decimal point. Second, two decimal places represent hundredths, so divide 83 by 100: $\frac{83}{100}$.

$$0.83 = \frac{83}{100}$$

**106.** To change a fraction to a percent, find its decimal form, multiply by 100, and add a percent sign.

**Example:** Express $\frac{3}{8}$ as a percent. To convert $\frac{3}{8}$ to a decimal, divide 3 by 8, which gives us 0.375. Multiplying 0.375 by 100 gives us 37.5%.

$$\frac{3}{8} = 3 \div 38 = .375$$

$$.375 \times 100 = 37.5\%$$

**107.** To change a percent to a fraction, drop the percent sign and divide the number by 100.

**Example:** Express 17% as a fraction. Dropping the % sign gives us 17, and dividing by 100 gives as $\frac{17}{100}$.

**108.** To *reduce* a fraction, divide the numerator and denominator by the largest number that divides them both evenly.

**Example:** Reduce $\frac{10}{15}$. Dividing both the numerator and denominator by 5 gives us $\frac{2}{3}$.

**Example:** Reduce $\frac{12}{36}$. The largest number that goes into both 12 and 36 is 12. Reducing

the fraction, we have $\dfrac{\overset{1}{\cancel{12}}}{\underset{3}{\cancel{36}}} = \frac{1}{3}$.

*Note:* In both examples, the reduced fraction is exactly equal to the original fraction:

$$\frac{2}{3} = \frac{10}{15} \text{ and } \frac{12}{36} = \frac{1}{3}.$$

**109.** To add fractions with like denominators, add the numerators of the fractions, keeping the same denominator.

**Example:** $\frac{1}{7} + \frac{2}{7} + \frac{3}{7} + \frac{6}{7}$.

**110.** To add fractions with different denominators, you must first change all of the fractions to *equivalent fractions* with the same denominators.

**STEP 1.** Find the *lowest (or least) common denominator,* the smallest number divisible by all of the denominators.

**Example:** If the fractions to be added are $\frac{1}{3}$, $\frac{1}{4}$, and $\frac{5}{6}$, then the lowest common denominator is 12, because 12 is the smallest number that is divisible by 3, 4, and 6.

**STEP 2.** Convert all of the fractions to *equivalent fractions,* each having the lowest common denominator as its denominator. To do this, multiply the numerator of each fraction by the number of times that its denominator goes into the lowest common denominator. The product of this multiplication will be the *new numerator.* The denominator of the equivalent fractions will be the lowest common denominator. (See Step 1 above.)

**Example:** The lowest common denominator of $\frac{1}{3}$, $\frac{1}{4}$, and $\frac{5}{6}$ is 12. Thus, $\frac{1}{3} = \frac{4}{12}$, because 12 divided by 3 is 4, and 4 times 1= 4. $\frac{1}{4} = \frac{3}{12}$, because 12 divided by 4 is 3, and 3 times 1 = 3. $\frac{5}{6} = \frac{10}{12}$ because 12 divided by 6 is 2, and 2 times 5 = 10.

**STEP 3.** Now add all of the equivalent fractions by adding the numerators.

**Example:** $\frac{4}{12} + \frac{3}{12} + \frac{10}{12} = \frac{17}{12}$

**STEP 4.** Reduce the fraction if possible, as shown in Section 108.

**Example:** Add $\frac{4}{5}$, $\frac{2}{3}$ and $\frac{8}{15}$. The lowest common denominator is 15 because 15 is the smallest number that is divisible by 5, 3, and 15. Then, $\frac{4}{5}$ is equivalent to $\frac{12}{15}$; $\frac{2}{3}$ is equivalent to $\frac{10}{15}$; and $\frac{8}{15}$ remains as $\frac{8}{15}$. Adding these numbers gives us $\frac{12}{15} + \frac{10}{15} + \frac{8}{15} = \frac{30}{15}$. Both 30 and 15 are divisible by 15, giving us $\frac{2}{1}$, or 2.

**111.** To *multiply fractions,* follow this procedure:

**STEP 1.** To find the numerator of the product, multiply all the numerators of the fractions being multiplied.

**STEP 2.** To find the denominator of the answer, multiply all of the denominators of the fractions being multiplied.

**STEP 3.** Reduce the product.

**Example:** $\frac{5}{7} \times \frac{2}{15} = \frac{5 \times 2}{7 \times 15} = \frac{10}{105}$. Reduce by dividing both the numerator and denominator by 5, the common factor. $\frac{10}{105} = \frac{2}{21}$.

**112.** To *divide fractions,* follow this procedure:

**STEP 1.** Invert the divisor. That is, switch the positions of the numerator and denominator in the fraction you are dividing *by.*

**STEP 2.** Replace the division sign with a multiplication sign.

**STEP 3.** Carry out the multiplication indicated.

**STEP 4.** Reduce the product.

**Example:** Find $\frac{3}{4} \div \frac{7}{8}$. Inverting $\frac{7}{8}$, the divisor, gives us $\frac{8}{7}$. Replacing the division sign with a multiplication sign gives us $\frac{3}{4} \times \frac{8}{7}$. Carrying out the multiplication gives us $\frac{3}{4} \times \frac{8}{7} = \frac{24}{28}$. The fraction $\frac{24}{28}$ may then be reduced to $\frac{6}{7}$ by dividing both the numerator and the denominator by 4.

**113.** To multiply decimals, follow this procedure:

**STEP 1.** Disregard the decimal point. Multiply the factors (the numbers being multiplied) as if they were whole numbers.

**STEP 2.** In each factor, count the number of digits to the *right* of the decimal point. Find the total number of these digits in all the factors. In the product start at the right and count to the left this (total) number of places. Put the decimal point there.

**Example:** Multiply 3.8 × 4.01. First, multiply 38 and 401, getting 15,238. There is a total of 3 digits to the right of the decimal points in the factors. Thus, the decimal point in the product is placed 3 units to the left of the digit farthest to the right (8).

$$3.8 \times 4.01 = 15.238$$

**Example:** 0.025 × 3.6. First, multiply 25 × 36, getting 900. In the factors, there is a total of 4 digits to the right of the decimal points; therefore, in the product, we place the decimal point 4 units to the left of the digit farthest to the right in 900. However, there are only 3 digits in the product, so we add a 0 to the left of the 9, getting 0900. This makes it possible to place the decimal point correctly, thus: .0900. From this example, we can make up the rule that in the product we add as many zeros as are needed to provide the proper number of digits to the left of the digit farthest to the right.

**114.** To find a percent of a given quantity:

**STEP 1.** Replace the word "of" with a multiplication sign.

**STEP 2.** Convert the percent to a decimal: drop the percent sign and divide the number by 100. This is done by moving the decimal point two places to the left, adding zeros where necessary.

**Examples:** 30% = 0.30.   2.1% = 0.021.   78% = 0.78.

**STEP 3.** Multiply the given quantity by the decimal.

**Example:** Find 30% of 200.

30% of 200 = 30% × 200 = 0.30 × 200 = 60.00

# Deviations

Estimation problems arise when dealing with approximations, that is, numbers that are not mathematically precise. The error, or *deviation*, in an approximation is a measure of the closeness of that approximation.

**115.** *Absolute error,* or *absolute deviation,* is the difference between the estimated value and the real value (or between the approximate value and the exact value).

> **Example:** If the actual value of a measurement is 60.2 and we estimate it as 60, then the absolute deviation (absolute error) is 60.2 − 60 = 0.2.

**116.** *Fractional error,* or *fractional deviation,* is the ratio of the absolute error to the exact value of the quantity being measured.

> **Example:** If the exact value is 60.2 and the estimated value is 60, then the fractional error is
>
> $$\frac{60.2-60}{60.2} = \frac{0.2}{60.2} = \frac{1}{301}.$$

**117.** *Percent error,* or *percent deviation,* is the fractional error expressed as a percent. (See Section 106 for the method of converting fractions to percents.)

**118.** Many business problems, including the calculation of loss, profit, interest, and so forth, are treated as deviation problems. Generally, these problems concern the difference between the original value of a quantity and some new value after taxes, after interest, etc. The following chart shows the relationship between business and estimation problems.

| Business Problems | Estimation Problems |
|---|---|
| original value | = exact value |
| new value | = approximate value |
| net profit<br>net loss<br>net interest } | = absolute error |
| fractional profit<br>fractional loss<br>fractional interest } | = fractional error |
| percent profit<br>percent loss<br>percent interest } | = percent error |

> **Example:** An item that originally cost $50 is resold for $56. Thus the *net profit* is $56 − $50 = $6. The *fractional profit* is $\frac{\$56-\$50}{\$50} = \frac{\$6}{\$50} = \frac{3}{25}$. The *percent profit* is equal to the percent equivalent of $\frac{3}{25}$, which is 12%.

**119.** When there are two or more *consecutive changes in value,* remember that the new value of the first change becomes the original value of the second; consequently, successive fractional or percent changes may not be added directly.

> **Example:** Suppose that a $100 item is reduced by 10% and then by 20%. The first reduction puts the price at $90 (10% of $100 = $10; $100 − $10 = $90). Then, reducing the $90 (the new original value) by 20% gives us $72 (20% of $90 = $18; $90 − $18 = $72). Therefore, it is *not* correct to simply add 10% and 20% and then take 30% of $100.

# Ratios and Proportions

**120.** A proportion is an equation stating that two ratios are equal. For example, $3 : 2 = 9 : x$ and $7 : 4 = a : 15$ are proportions. To solve a proportion:

**STEP 1.** First change the ratios to fractions. To do this, remember that $a : b$ is the same as $\frac{a}{b}$, or $1 : 2$ is equivalent to $\frac{1}{2}$, or $7 : 4 = a : 15$ is the same as $\frac{7}{4} = \frac{a}{15}$.

**STEP 2.** Now cross-multiply. That is, multiply the numerator of the first fraction by the denominator of the second fraction. Also multiply the denominator of the first fraction by the numerator of the second fraction. Set the first product equal to the second. This rule is sometimes stated as "The product of the means equals the product of the extremes."

> **Example:** When cross-multiplying in the equation $\frac{3}{2} = \frac{9}{y}$, we get $3 \times y = 2 \times 9$, or $3y = 18$
>
> When we cross-multiply in the equation $\frac{a}{2} = \frac{4}{8}$, we get $8a = 8$.

**STEP 3.** Solve the resulting equation. This is done algebraically.

> **Example:** Solve for $a$ in the proportion $7 : a = 6 : 18$.
>
> Change the ratios to the fractional relation $\frac{7}{a} = \frac{6}{18}$. Cross-multiply: $7 \times 18 = 6 \times a$, or $126 = 6a$.
>
> Solving for $a$ gives us $a = 21$.

**121.** In solving proportions that have units of measurement (feet, seconds, miles, etc.), each ratio must have the same units. For example, if we have the ratio 5 inches : 3 feet, we must convert the 3 feet to 36 inches and then set up the ratio 5 inches : 36 inches, or 5 : 36. We might wish to convert inches to feet. Noting that 1 inch $= \frac{1}{12}$ foot, we get 5 inches : 3 feet $= 5\left(\frac{1}{12}\right)$ feet : 3 feet $= \frac{5}{12}$ feet : 3 feet.

> **Example:** On a blueprint, a rectangle measures 6 inches in width and 9 inches in length. If the actual width of the rectangle is 16 inches, how many feet are there in the length?
>
> *Solution:* We set up the proportions, 6 inches : 9 inches = 16 inches : $x$ feet. Since $x$ feet is equal to $12x$ inches, we substitute this value in the proportion. Thus, 6 inches : 9 inches = 16 inches : $12x$ inches. Since all of the units are now the same, we may work with the numbers alone. In fractional terms we have $\frac{6}{9} = \frac{16}{12x}$. Cross-multiplication gives us $72x = 144$, and solving for $x$ gives us $x = 2$. The rectangle is 2 feet long.

# Variations

**122.** In a variation problem, you are given a relationship between certain variables. The problem is to determine the change in one variable when one or more of the other variables changes.

## Direct Variation (Direct Proportion)

If $x$ varies directly with $y$, this means that $x/y = k$ (or $x = ky$) where $k$ is a constant.

> **Example:** If the cost of a piece of glass varies directly with the area of the glass and a piece of glass of 5 square feet cost $20, then how much does a piece of glass of 15 square feet cost?

Represent the cost of the glass as $c$ and the area of the piece of glass as $A$. Then we have $c/A = k$

Now since we are given that a piece of glass of 5 square feet cost $20, we can write 20/5 = k and we find k = 4

Let's say a piece of glass of 15 square feet cost $x, then we can write

x/15 = k. But we found k = 4, so x/15 = 4 and x = 60, $60 is then the answer.

## Inverse Variation (Inverse Proportion)

If x varies inversely with y, this means that $xy = k$ where k is a constant.

> **Example:** If a varies inversely with b and when a = 5, b = 6, then what is b when a = 10?

We have $ab = k$. Since a = 5 and b = 6, $5 \times 6 = k = 30$. So if a = 10, $10 \times b = k = 30$ and b = 3.

## Other Variations

> **Example:** In the formula A = bh, if b doubles and h triples, what happens to the value of A?

**STEP 1.** Express the new values of the variables in terms of their original values, i.e., $b' = 2b$ and $h' = 3h$.

**STEP 2.** Substitute these values in the formula and solve for the desired variable: $A' = b'h' = (2b)(3h) = 6bh$.

**STEP 3.** Express this answer in terms of the original value of the variable, *i.e.,* since the new value of A is 6bh, and the old value of A was bh, we can express this as $A_{new} = 6A_{old}$. The new value of the variable is expressed with a prime mark and the old value of the variable is left as it was. In this problem the new value of A would be expressed as A' and the old value as A. $A' = 6A$.

> **Example:** If $V = e^3$ and e is doubled, what happens to the value of V?

> *Solution:* Replace e with 2e. The new value of V is $(2e)^3$. Since this is a new value, V becomes V'. Thus $V' = (2e)^3$, or $8e^3$. Remember, from the original statement of the problem, that $V = e^3$. Using this, we may substitute V for $e^3$ found in the equation $V' = 8e^3$. The new equation is $V' = 8V$. Therefore, the new value of V is 8 times the old value.

# Comparison of Fractions

In fraction comparison problems, you are given two or more fractions and are asked to arrange them in increasing or decreasing order, or to select the larger or the smaller. The following rules and suggestions will be very helpful in determining which of two fractions is greater.

**123.** If fractions A and B have the same denominators, and A has a larger numerator, then fraction A is larger. (We are assuming here, and for the rest of this Refresher Session, that numerators and denominators are positive.)

> **Example:** $\frac{56}{271}$ is greater than $\frac{53}{271}$ because the numerator of the first fraction is greater than the numerator of the second.

**124.** If fractions A and B have the same numerator, and A has a larger denominator, then fraction A is smaller.

> **Example:** $\frac{37}{256}$ is smaller than $\frac{37}{254}$.

**125.** If fraction A has a larger numerator and a smaller denominator than fraction B, then fraction A is larger than B.

**Example:** $\frac{6}{11}$ is larger than $\frac{4}{13}$. (If this does not seem obvious, compare both fractions with $\frac{6}{13}$.)

**126.** Another method is to convert all of the fractions to equivalent fractions. To do this follow these steps:

**STEP 1.** First find the *lowest common denominator* of the fractions. This is the smallest number that is divisible by all of the denominators of the original fractions. See Section 108 for the method of finding lowest common denominators.

**STEP 2.** The fraction with the greatest numerator is the largest fraction.

**127.** Still another method is the *conversion to approximating decimals.*

**Example:** To compare $\frac{5}{9}$ and $\frac{7}{11}$, we might express both as decimals to a few places of accuracy: $\frac{5}{9}$ is approximately equal to 0.555, while $\frac{7}{11}$ is approximately equal to 0.636, so $\frac{7}{11}$ is obviously greater. To express a fraction as a decimal, divide the numerator by the denominator.

**128.** If all of the fractions being compared are very close in value to some easy-to-work-with number, such as $\frac{1}{2}$ or 5, you may subtract this number from each of the fractions without changing this order.

**Example:** To compare $\frac{151}{75}$ with $\frac{328}{163}$ we notice that both of these fractions are approximately equal to 2. If we subtract 2 (that is $\frac{150}{75}$ and $\frac{326}{163}$, respectively) from each, we get $\frac{1}{75}$ and $\frac{2}{163}$, respectively. Since $\frac{1}{75}$ (or $\frac{2}{150}$) exceeds $\frac{2}{163}$, we see that $\frac{151}{75}$ must also exceed $\frac{328}{163}$.

An alternative method of comparing fractions is to change the fractions to their decimal equivalents and then compare the decimals. (See Section 104.) The student would weigh the relative amount of work and difficulty involved in each method when he faces each problem.

## Quick Way of Comparing Fractions

*Example:* Which is greater, $\frac{3}{8}$ or $\frac{7}{18}$?

*Procedure:*

$$\frac{3}{8} \xleftarrow{\text{MULTIPLY}} \quad \xrightarrow{\text{MULTIPLY}} \frac{7}{18}$$

*Multiply* the 18 by the 3. We get 54. Put the 54 on the *left* side.

54

Now *multiply* the 8 by the 7. We get 56. Put the 56 on the *right* side.

54                                    56

Since 56 > 54 and 56 is on the *right* side, the fraction $\frac{7}{18}$ (which was also originally on the *right* side) is *greater* than the fraction $\frac{3}{8}$ (which was originally on the *left* side).

*Example:* If $y > x$, which is greater, $\frac{1}{x}$ or $\frac{1}{y}$ ? (*x* and *y* are positive numbers).

*Procedure:*

$$\frac{1}{x} \xleftarrow{\text{MULTIPLY}} \qquad \xrightarrow{\text{MULTIPLY}} \frac{1}{y}$$

*Multiply y* by 1. We get *y.* Put *y* on the left:

$$y$$

*Multiply x* by 1. We get *x.* Put *x* on the right side:

$$y \qquad\qquad\qquad x$$

Since $y > x$ (given), $\frac{1}{x}$ (which was originally on the left) is greater than $\frac{1}{y}$ (which was originally on the right).

*Example:* Which is greater?

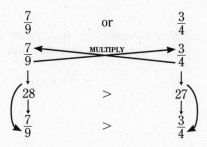

$$\frac{7}{9} \qquad \text{or} \qquad \frac{3}{4}$$

# Practice Test 1

## Fractions, Decimals, Percentages, Deviations, Ratios and Proportions, Variations, and Comparison of Fractions

Correct answers and solutions follow each test.

1. Which of the following answers is the sum of the following numbers:

$$2\frac{1}{2}, \frac{21}{4}, 3.350, \frac{1}{8}?$$

*2.5, 5.25, 3.350, .125*

(A) 8.225
(B) 9.825
(C) 10.825
(D) 11.225
(E) 12.350

2. A chemist was preparing a solution that should have included 35 milligrams of a chemical. If she actually used 36.4 milligrams, what was her percentage error (to the nearest 0.01%)?

(A) 0.04%
(B) 0.05%
(C) 1.40%
(D) 3.85%
(E) 4.00%

$R = \dfrac{P}{B} = \dfrac{36.4}{35} = 1.04$

3. A retailer buys a radio from the wholesaler for $75.00. He then marks up the price by $\frac{1}{3}$ and sells it at a discount of 20%. What was his profit on the radio (to the nearest cent)?

(A) $5.00
(B) $6.67
(C) $7.50
(D) $10.00
(E) $13.33

$75.00

$\begin{array}{r} 100 \\ -\ 20 \\ \hline 80 \end{array}$

4. On a blueprint, $\frac{1}{4}$ inch represents 1 foot. If a window is supposed to be 56 inches wide, how wide would its representation on the blueprint be?

(A) $1\frac{1}{6}$ inches

(B) $4\frac{2}{3}$ inches

(C) $9\frac{1}{3}$ inches

(D) 14 inches

(E) $18\frac{2}{3}$ inches

$\frac{1}{4} = 1$

$\begin{array}{r} 14 \\ 4\overline{)56} \\ 16^b \end{array}$

5. If the radius of a circle is increased by 50%, what will be the percent increase in the circumference of the circle? (Circumference = $2\pi r$)

(A) 25%
(B) 50%
(C) 100%
(D) 150%
(E) 225%

$2\pi r$

6.

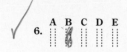

6. Which of the following fractions is the greatest?

? (A) $\frac{403}{134}$   3.007

(B) $\frac{79}{26}$   3.038

(C) $\frac{527}{176}$   2.99

(D) $\frac{221}{73}$   3.027

(E) $\frac{99}{34}$   2.91T

7. A store usually sells a certain item at a 40% profit. One week the store has a sale, during which the item is sold for 10% less than the usual price. During the sale, what is the percent profit the store makes on each of these items?

(A) 4%             40%

(B) 14%

(C) 26%

(D) 30%

(E) 36%

8. What is 0.05 percent of 6.5?

(A) 0.00325     $P = \frac{B}{R} = \frac{6.5}{.05}$      $\boxed{P = B \times R}$

(B) 0.013

(C) 0.325

(D) 1.30     $6\frac{3}{4} + 6\frac{3}{4} = 12\frac{6}{4} = 13\frac{1}{2}$

(E) 130.0

9.

9. What is the value of $\dfrac{3\frac{1}{2} + 3\frac{1}{4} + 3\frac{1}{4} + 3\frac{1}{2}}{4\frac{1}{2}}$?

(A) $1\frac{1}{2}$

(B) $2\frac{1}{4}$

(C) 3

(D) $3\frac{1}{4}$

(E) $3\frac{3}{8}$

10.

10. If 8 men can chop down 28 trees in one day, how many trees can 20 men chop down in one day?

$8 = 28$

(A) 28 trees

(B) 160 trees

(C) 70 trees

(D) 100 trees     $\frac{8}{28} = \frac{20}{X}$

(E) 80 trees

$X = 70$

**11.** A B C D E

11. What is the product of the following fractions: $\frac{3}{100}, \frac{15}{49}, \frac{7}{9}$?

(A) $\frac{215}{44,100}$

(B) $\frac{1}{140}$

(C) $\frac{1}{196}$

(D) $\frac{25}{158}$

(E) $\frac{3}{427}$

**12.** A B C D E

12. In reading a thermometer, Mr. Downs mistakenly observed a temperature of 72° instead of 77°. What was his percentage error (to the nearest hundredth of a percent)?

(A) 6.49%
(B) 6.50%
(C) 6.64%
(D) 6.94%
(E) 6.95%

**13.** A B C D E

13. A businessman buys 1,440 dozen pens at $2.50 a dozen and then sells them at a price of 25¢ apiece. What is his total profit on the lot of pens?

(A) $60.00
(B) $72.00
(C) $720.00
(D) $874.00
(E) $8740.00

**14.** A B C D E

14. On a map, 1 inch represents 1,000 miles. If the area of a country is actually 16 million square miles, what is the area of the country's representation on the map?

(A) 4 square inches
(B) 16 square inches
(C) 4,000 square inches
(D) 16,000 square inches
(E) 4,000,000 square inches

**15.** A B C D E

15. The formula for the volume of a cone is $V = \frac{1}{3} \pi r^2 h$. If the radius ($r$) is doubled and the height ($h$) is divided by 3, what will be the ratio of the new volume to the original volume?

(A) 2 : 3
(B) 3 : 2
(C) 4 : 3
(D) 3 : 4
(E) None of these.

**16.** A B C D E

16. Which of the following fractions has the smallest value?

(A) $\frac{34.7}{163}$

(B) $\frac{125}{501}$

(C) $\frac{173}{700}$

(D) $\frac{10.9}{42.7}$

(E) $\frac{907}{3,715}$

**17.** A B C D E

**17.** Mr. Cutler usually makes a 45% profit on every radio he sells. During a sale, he reduces his margin of profit to 40%, while his sales increase by 10%. What is the ratio of his new total profit to the original profit?

(A) 1 : 1
(B) 9 : 8
(C) 9 : 10
(D) 11 : 10
(E) 44 : 45

**18.** A B C D E

**18.** What is 1.3 percent of 0.26?

(A) 0.00338
(B) 0.00500
(C) 0.200
(D) 0.338
(E) 0.500

**19.** A B C D E

**19.** What is the average of the following numbers: $3.2, \frac{47}{12}, \frac{10}{3}$?

(A) 3.55

(B) $\frac{10}{3}$

(C) $\frac{103}{30}$

(D) $\frac{209}{60}$

(E) $\frac{1,254}{120}$

**20.** A B C D E

**20.** If it takes 16 faucets 10 hours to fill 8 tubs, how long will it take 12 faucets to fill 9 tubs?

(A) 10 hours
(B) 12 hours
(C) 13 hours
(D) 14 hours
(E) 15 hours

**21.** A B C D E

**21.** If the 8% tax on a sale amounts to 96¢, what is the final price (tax included) of the item?

(A) $1.20
(B) $2.16
(C) $6.36
(D) $12.00
(E) $12.96

**22.** A B C D E

**22.** In a certain class, 40% of the students are girls, and 20% of the girls wear glasses. What percent of the children in the class are girls who wear glasses?

(A) 6%
(B) 8%
(C) 20%
(D) 60%
(E) 80%

**23.** A B C D E

**23.** What is 1.2% of 0.5?

(A) 0.0006
(B) 0.006
(C) 0.06
(D) 0.6
(E) 6.0

**24.** A B C D E

**24.** Which of the following quantities is the largest?

(A) $\dfrac{275}{369}$

(B) $\dfrac{134}{179}$

(C) $\dfrac{107}{144}$

(D) $\dfrac{355}{476}$

(E) $\dfrac{265}{352}$

**25.** A B C D E

**25.** If the length of a rectangle is increased by 120%, and its width is decreased by 20%, what happens to the area of the rectangle?

(A) It decreases by 4%.
(B) It remains the same.
(C) It increases by 24%.
(D) It increases by 76%.
(E) It increases by 100%.

**26.** A B C D E

**26.** A merchant buys an old carpet for $25.00. He spends $15.00 to have it restored to good condition and then sells the rug for $50.00. What is the percent profit on his total investment?

(A) 20%
(B) 25%
(C) 40%
(D) $66\dfrac{2}{3}$%
(E) 100%

**27.** A B C D E

**27.** Of the following sets of fractions, which one is arranged in *decreasing* order?

(A) $\dfrac{5}{9}, \dfrac{7}{11}, \dfrac{3}{5}, \dfrac{2}{3}, \dfrac{10}{13}$

(B) $\dfrac{2}{3}, \dfrac{3}{5}, \dfrac{7}{11}, \dfrac{5}{9}, \dfrac{10}{13}$

(C) $\dfrac{3}{5}, \dfrac{5}{9}, \dfrac{7}{11}, \dfrac{10}{13}, \dfrac{2}{3}$

(D) $\dfrac{10}{13}, \dfrac{2}{3}, \dfrac{7}{11}, \dfrac{3}{5}, \dfrac{5}{9}$

(E) None of these.

**28.** A B C D E

**28.** If the diameter of a circle doubles, the circumference of the larger circle is how many times the circumference of the original circle? (Circumference $= \pi d$)

(A) $\pi$
(B) $2\pi$
(C) 1
(D) 2
(E) 4

**29.** A B C D E

**29.** The scale on a set of plans is $1 : 8$. If a man reads a certain measurement on the plans as 5.6″, instead of 6.0″, what will be the resulting approximate percent error on the fullsize model?

(A) 6.7%
(B) 7.1%
(C) 12.5%
(D) 53.6%
(E) 56.8%

**30.**  A B C D E

**30.** A salesman bought 2 dozen television sets at $300 each. He sold two-thirds of them at a 25% profit but was forced to take a 30% loss on the rest. What was his total profit (or loss) on the television sets?

(A) a loss of $200
(B) a loss of $15
(C) no profit or loss
(D) a gain of $20
(E) a gain of $480

**31.**  A B C D E

**31.** The sum of $\frac{1}{2}$, $\frac{1}{3}$, $\frac{1}{8}$, and $\frac{1}{15}$ is:

(A) $\frac{9}{8}$

(B) $\frac{16}{15}$

(C) $\frac{41}{40}$

(D) $\frac{65}{64}$

(E) $\frac{121}{120}$

**32.**  A B C D E

**32.** What is $\frac{2}{3}$% of 90?

(A) 0.006
(B) 0.06
(C) 0.6
(D) 6.0
(E) 60

**33.**  A B C D E

**33.** A man borrows $360. If he pays it back in 12 monthly installments of $31.50, what is his interest rate?

(A) 1.5%
(B) 4.5%
(C) 10%
(D) 5%
(E) 7.5%

**34.**  A B C D E

**34.** A merchant marks a certain lamp up 30% above original cost. Then he gives a customer a 15% discount. If the final selling price of the lamp was $86.19, what was the original cost?

(A) $66.30
(B) $73.26
(C) $78.00
(D) $99.12
(E) $101.40

**35.**  A B C D E

**35.** In a certain recipe, $2\frac{1}{4}$ cups of flour are called for to make a cake that serves 6. If Mrs. Jenkins wants to use the same recipe to make a cake for 8, how many cups of flour must she use?

(A) $2\frac{1}{3}$ cups

(B) $2\frac{3}{4}$ cups

(C) 3 cups

(D) $3\frac{3}{8}$ cups

(E) 4 cups

**36.**

A B C D E

**36.** If 10 men can survive for 24 days on 15 cans of rations, how many cans will be needed for 8 men to survive for 36 days?

(A) 15 cans
(B) 16 cans
(C) 17 cans
(D) 18 cans
(E) 19 cans

**37.**

A B C D E

**37.** If, on a map, $\frac{1}{2}$ inch represents 1 mile, how long is a border whose representation is $1\frac{1}{15}$ feet long?

(A) $2\frac{1}{30}$ miles

(B) $5\frac{1}{15}$ miles

(C) $12\frac{4}{5}$ miles

(D) $25\frac{3}{5}$ miles

(E) $51\frac{1}{5}$ miles

**38.**

A B C D E

**38.** In the formula $e = hf$, if $e$ is doubled and $f$ is halved, what happens to the value of $h$?

(A) $h$ remains the same.
(B) $h$ is doubled.
(C) $h$ is divided by 4.
(D) $h$ is multiplied by 4.
(E) $h$ is halved.

**39.**

A B C D E

**39.** Which of the following expresses the ratio of 3 inches to 2 yards?

(A) $3 : 2$
(B) $3 : 9$
(C) $3 : 12$
(D) $3 : 24$
(E) $3 : 72$

**40.**

A B C D E

**40.** If it takes Mark twice as long to earn $6.00 as it takes Carl to earn $4.00, what is the ratio of Mark's pay per hour to Carl's pay per hour?

(A) $2 : 1$
(B) $3 : 1$
(C) $3 : 2$
(D) $3 : 4$
(E) $4 : 3$

**41.**

A B C D E

**41.** What is the lowest common denominator of the following set of fractions:

$\frac{1}{6}, \frac{13}{27}, \frac{4}{5}, \frac{3}{10}, \frac{2}{15}$ ?

(A) 27
(B) 54
(C) 135
(D) 270
(E) None of these.

**42.** A B C D E

42. The average grade on a certain examination was 85. Ralph, on the same examination, scored 90. What was Ralph's *percent* deviation from the average score (to the nearest tenth of a percent)?

(A) 5.0%
(B) 5.4%
(C) 5.5%
(D) 5.8%
(E) 5.9%

**43.** A B C D E

43. Successive discounts of 20% and 12% are equivalent to a single discount of:

(A) 16.0%
(B) 29.6%
(C) 31.4%
(D) 32.0%
(E) 33.7%

**44.** A B C D E

44. On a blueprint of a park, 1 foot represents $\frac{1}{2}$ mile. If an error of $\frac{1}{2}$ inch is made in reading the blueprint, what will be the corresponding error on the actual park?

(A) 110 feet
(B) 220 feet
(C) 330 feet
(D) 440 feet
(E) None of these.

**45.** A B C D E

45. If the two sides of a rectangle change in such a manner that the rectangle's area remains constant, and one side increases by 25%, what must happen to the other side?

(A) It decreases by 20%
(B) It decreases by 25%
(C) It decreases by $33\frac{1}{3}$%
(D) It decreases by 50%
(E) None of these.

**46.** A B C D E

46. Which of the following fractions has the smallest value?

(A) $\frac{6043}{2071}$

(B) $\frac{4290}{1463}$

(C) $\frac{5,107}{1,772}$

(D) $\frac{8935}{2963}$

(E) $\frac{8016}{2631}$

**47.** A B C D E

47. A certain company increased its prices by 30% during 2003. Then, in 2004, it was forced to cut back its prices by 20%. What was the net change in price?

(A) −4%
(B) −2%
(C) +2%
(D) +4%
(E) 0%

**48.**  **48.** What is 0.04%, expressed as a fraction?

(A) $\frac{2}{5}$

(B) $\frac{1}{25}$

(C) $\frac{4}{25}$

(D) $\frac{1}{250}$

(E) $\frac{1}{2,500}$

**49.**  **49.** What is the value of the fraction

$$\frac{16 + 12 + 88 + 34 + 66 + 21 + 79 + 11 + 89}{25}?$$

(A) 15.04
(B) 15.44
(C) 16.24
(D) 16.64
(E) None of these.

**50.**  **50.** If coconuts are twice as expensive as bananas, and bananas are one-third as expensive as grapefruits, what is the ratio of the price of one coconut to one grapefruit?

(A) 2 : 3
(B) 3 : 2
(C) 6 : 1
(D) 1 : 6
(E) None of these.

# Answer Key for Practice Test 1

| | | | |
|---|---|---|---|
| **1.** D | **14.** B | **27.** D | **39.** E |
| **2.** E | **15.** C | **28.** D | **40.** D |
| **3.** A | **16.** A | **29.** A | **41.** D |
| **4.** A | **17.** E | **30.** E | **42.** E |
| **5.** B | **18.** A | **31.** C | **43.** B |
| **6.** B | **19.** D | **32.** C | **44.** A |
| **7.** C | **20.** E | **33.** D | **45.** A |
| **8.** A | **21.** E | **34.** C | **46.** C |
| **9.** C | **22.** B | **35.** C | **47.** D |
| **10.** C | **23.** B | **36.** D | **48.** E |
| **11.** B | **24.** E | **37.** D | **49.** D |
| **12.** A | **25.** D | **38.** D | **50.** A |
| **13.** C | **26.** B | | |

# Answers and Solutions for Practice Test 1

1. Choice D is correct. First, convert the fractions to decimals, as the final answer must be expressed in decimals: $2.500 + 5.250 + 3.350 + 0.125 = 11.225$. (104, 109)

2. Choice E is correct. This is an estimation problem. Note that the correct value was 35, not 36.4. Thus the *real* value is 35 mg and the *estimated* value is 36.4 mg. Thus, percent error is equal to $(36.4\ 35) \div 35$, or 0.04, expressed as a percent, which is 4%. (117)

3. Choice A is correct. This is a business problem. First, the retailer marks up the wholesale price by $\frac{1}{3}$, so the marked-up price equals $75 $(1 + \frac{1}{3})$, or $100; then it is reduced 20% from the $100 price, leaving a final price of $80. Thus, the net profit on the radio was $5.00. (118)

4. Choice A is correct. Here we have a proportion problem: length on blueprint: actual length $\frac{1}{4}$ inch; 1 foot. The second ratio is the same as 1 : 48 because 1 foot = 12 inches. In the problem the actual length is 56 inches, so that if the length on the blueprint equals $x$, we have the proportion $x : 56 = 1 : 48$; $\frac{x}{56} = \frac{1}{4}$; $48x = 56$; so $x = \frac{56}{48}$, or $1\frac{1}{6}$ inches. (120)

5. Choice B is correct. Since $C = 2\pi r$ (where $r$ is the radius of the circle, and $C$ is its circumference), the new value of $r$, $r'$, is $(1.5)\ r$ since $r$ is increased by 50%. Using this value of $r'$, we get the new $C$, $C' = 2\pi r' = 2\pi\ (1.5)\ r\ (1.5)\ 2\pi r$. Remembering that $C = 2\pi r$, we get that $C' = (1.5)\ C$. Since the new circumference is 1.5 times the original, there is an increase of 50%. (122)

6. Choice B is correct. In this numerical comparison problem, it is helpful to realize that all of these fractions are approximately equal to 3. If we subtract 3 from each of the fractions, we get $\frac{1}{134}$, $\frac{1}{26}$, $\frac{-1}{176}$, $\frac{2}{73}$, and $\frac{-3}{34}$, respectively. Clearly, the greatest of these is $\frac{1}{26}$ and is therefore the greatest of the five given fractions. Another method of solving this type of numerical comparison problem is to convert the fractions to decimals by dividing the numerator by the denominator. (127, 128)

7. Choice C is correct. This is another business problem, this time asking for percentage profit. Let the original price be $P$. Then the marked-up price will be $1.4(P)$. Ten percent is taken off this price, to yield a final price of $(0.90)(1.40)(P)$, or $(1.26)(P)$. Thus, the fractional increase was 0.26, so the percent increase was 26%. (118)

8. Choice A is correct. Remember that the phrase "percent of" may be replaced by a multiplication sign. Thus, $0.05\% \times 6.5 = 0.0005 \times 6.5$, so the answer is 0.00325. (114)

9. Choice C is correct. First, add the fractions in the numerator to obtain $13\frac{1}{2}$. Then divide $13\frac{1}{2}$ by $4\frac{1}{2}$. If you cannot see immediately that the answer is 3, you can convert the halves to decimals and divide, or you can express the fractions in terms of their common denominator, thus: $13\frac{1}{2} = \frac{27}{2}$; $4\frac{1}{2} = \frac{9}{2}$; $\frac{27}{2} \div \frac{9}{2} = \frac{27}{2} \times \frac{2}{9} = \frac{54}{18} = 3$. (110, 112)

10. Choice C is correct. This is a proportion problem. If $x$ is the number of men needed to chop down = 20 trees, then we form the proportion: 8 men : 28 trees 20 men : $x$ trees, or $\frac{8}{28} = \frac{20}{x}$. Solving for $x$, we get $x = x = \frac{(28)(20)}{8}$, or $x = 70$. (120)

11. Choice B is correct. $\frac{3}{100} \times \frac{15}{49} \times \frac{7}{9} = \frac{3 \times 15 \times 7}{100 \times 49 \times 9}$. Canceling 7 out of the numerator and denominator gives us $\frac{3 \times 15}{100 \times 7 \times 9}$. Canceling 5 out of the numerator and denominator gives us $\frac{3 \times 3}{20 \times 7 \times 9}$. Finally, canceling 9 out of both numerator and denominator gives us $\frac{1}{20 \times 7}$, or $\frac{1}{140}$. (111)

12. Choice A is correct. Percent error = (absolute error) ÷ (correct measurement) = $5 \div 77 = 0.0649$ (approximately) $\times 100 = 6.49\%$. (117)

13. Choice C is correct. Profit on each dozen pens = selling price − cost = 12(25¢) − $2.50 = $3.00 − $2.50 = 50¢, profit per dozen. Total profit = profit per dozen × number of dozens = 50¢ × 1440 = $720.00.

(118)

14. Choice B is correct. If 1 inch represents 1,000 miles, then 1 square inch represents 1,000 miles squared, or 1,000,000 square miles. Thus, the area would be represented by 16 squares of this size, or 16 square inches. (120)

15. Choice C is correct. Let $V'$ equal the new volume. Then if $r' = 2r$ is the new radius, and $h' = \frac{h}{3}$ is the new height, $V' = \frac{1}{3}\pi(r')^2(h') = \frac{1}{3}\pi(2r)^2\left(\frac{h}{3}\right) = \frac{4}{9}\pi r^2 h = \frac{4}{3}V$, so the ratio $V' : V$ is equal to 4 : 3. (122)

16. Choice A is correct. All of these fractions are approximately equal to $\frac{1}{4}$. Thus, by subtracting $\frac{1}{4}$ from each one we get remainders of, respectively, $\frac{-6.05}{163}, \frac{-0.25}{501}, \frac{-2}{700}, +\frac{0.225}{42.7}$, and $\frac{-21.75}{3715}$. The first of these is the smallest. That is because of all of the negative fractions, it has the largest value without its sign. Therefore, it is the most negative and, consequently, the smallest so that $\frac{34.7}{163}$ is the desired answer. (123−128)

17. Choice E is correct. Let $N$ = the original cost of a radio. Then, original profit = 45% × $N$. New profit = 40% × 110% $N$ = 44% × $N$. Thus, the ratio of new profit to original profit is 44 : 45. (118)

18. Choice A is correct.
1.3% × 0.26 = 0.013 × 0.26 = 0.00338. (114)

19. Choice D is correct. Average = $\frac{1}{3}\left(3.2 + \frac{47}{12} + \frac{10}{3}\right)$. The decimal $3.2 = \frac{320}{100} = \frac{16}{5}$, and the lowest common denominator of the three fractions is 60, then $\frac{16}{5} = \frac{192}{60}, \frac{47}{12} = \frac{235}{60}$ and $\frac{10}{3} = \frac{200}{60}$. Then, $\frac{1}{3}\left(\frac{192}{60} + \frac{235}{60} + \frac{200}{60}\right) = \frac{1}{3}\left(\frac{627}{60}\right) = \frac{209}{60}$.

(101, 105, 109)

20. Choice E is correct. If it takes 16 faucets 10 hours to fill 8 tubs, then it takes 1 faucet 160 hours to fill 8 tubs (16 faucets : 1 faucet = $x$ hours : 10 hours; $\frac{16}{1} = \frac{x}{10}$; $x = 160$). If it takes 1 faucet 160 hours to fill 8 tubs, then (dividing by 8) it takes 1 faucet 20 hours to fill 1 tub. If it takes 1 faucet 20 hours to fill 1 tub, then it takes 1 faucet 180 hours (9 × 20 hours) to fill 9 tubs. If it takes 1 faucet 180 hours to fill 9 tubs, then it takes 12 faucets $\frac{180}{12}$ or 15 hours to fill 9 tubs.

(120)

21. Choice E is correct. Let $P$ be the original price. Then $0.08P = 96¢$, so that $8P = \$96$, or $P = \$12$. Adding the tax, which equals 96¢, we obtain our final price of $12.96. (118)

22. Choice B is correct. The number of girls who wear glasses is 20% of 40% of the children in the class. Thus, the indicated operation is multiplication; 20% × 40% = 0.20 × 0.40 = 0.08 = 8%. (114)

23. Choice B is correct. 1.2% × 0.5 = 0.012 × 0.5 = 0.006. (114)

24. Choice E is correct. Here, we can use $\frac{3}{4}$ as an approximate value for all the fractions. Subtracting $\frac{3}{4}$ from each, we get remainders of: $\frac{-1.75}{369}, \frac{-0.25}{179}, \frac{-1.00}{144}, \frac{-2.00}{476}$, and $\frac{+1.00}{352}$. Clearly, the last of these is the greatest (it is the only positive one), so $\frac{256}{352}$ is the fraction that is the largest. This problem may also be solved by converting the fractions to decimals. (104, 123, 127)

25. Choice D is correct. Area = length × width. The new area will be equal to the new length (2.20 times the old length) times the new width (0.80 times the old width), giving a product of 1.76 times the original area, an increase of 76%. (122)

26. Choice B is correct. Total cost to merchant = $25.00 + $15.00 = $40.00.

Profit = selling price − cost = $50 − $40 = $10. Percent profit = profit ÷ cost = $10 ÷ $40 = 25%. (118)

27. Choice D is correct. We can convert the fractions to decimals or to fractions with a lowest common denominator. Inspection will show that all sets of fractions contain the same members; therefore, if we convert one set to decimals or find the lowest common denominator for one set, we can use our results for all sets. Converting a fraction to a decimal involves only one operation, a single division, whereas converting to the lowest common denominator involves a multiplication, which must be followed by a division and a multiplication to change each fraction to one with the lowest common denominator. Thus, conversion to decimals is often the simpler method: $\frac{10}{13} = 0.769; \frac{2}{3} = 0.666; \frac{7}{11} = 0.636; \frac{3}{5} = 0.600; \frac{5}{9} = 0.555$. (104)

However, in this case there is an even simpler method. Convert two of the fractions to equivalent fractions: $\frac{3}{5} = \frac{6}{10}$ and $\frac{2}{3} = \frac{8}{12}$. We now have $\frac{5}{9}$,

$\frac{6}{10}$, $\frac{7}{11}$, $\frac{8}{12}$, and $\frac{10}{13}$. Remember this rule: When the numerator and denominator of a fraction are both positive, adding 1 to both will bring the value of the fraction closer to 1. (For example, $\frac{3}{4} = \frac{2+1}{3+1}$, so $\frac{3}{4}$ is closer to 1 than $\frac{2}{3}$ and is therefore the greater fraction.) Thus we see that $\frac{5}{9}$ is less than $\frac{6}{10}$, which is less than $\frac{7}{11}$, which is less than $\frac{8}{12}$, which is less than $\frac{9}{13}$. $\frac{9}{13}$ is obviously less than $\frac{10}{13}$, so $\frac{10}{13}$ must be the greatest fraction. Thus, in decreasing order the fractions are $\frac{10}{13}$, $\frac{2}{3}$, $\frac{7}{11}$, $\frac{3}{5}$, and $\frac{5}{9}$. This method is a great time-saver once you become accustomed to it.

28. Choice D is correct. The formula governing this situation is $C = \pi d$, where $C$ = circumference, and $d$ = diameter. Thus, if the new diameter is $d' = 2d$, then the new circumference is $C' = \pi d' = 2\pi d = 2C$. Thus, the new, larger circle has a circumference of twice that of the original circle. (122)

29. Choice A is correct. The most important feature of this problem is recognizing that the scale does not affect percent (or fractional) error, since it simply results in multiplying the numerator and denominator of a fraction by the same factor. Thus, we need only calculate the original percent error. Although it would not be incorrect to calculate the full-scale percent error, it would be time-consuming and might result in unnecessary errors. Absolute error = 0.4″. Actual measurement = 6.0″. Therefore, percent error = (absolute error ÷ actual measurement) × 100% = $\frac{0.4}{6.0}$ × 100%, which equals 6.7% (approximately). (117)

30. Choice E is correct. Total cost = number of sets × cost of each = 24 × \$300 = \$7200.

    Revenue = (number sold at 25% profit price at 25% profit) + (number sold at 30% loss × price at 30% loss)

    = (16 × \$375) + (8 × \$210) = \$6000 + \$1680 = \$7680.

    Profit = revenue − cost = \$7680 − \$7200 = \$480. (118)

31. Choice C is correct. $\frac{1}{2} + \frac{1}{3} + \frac{1}{8} + \frac{1}{15} = \frac{60}{120} + \frac{40}{120} + \frac{15}{120} + \frac{8}{120} = \frac{123}{120} = \frac{41}{40}$. (110)

32. Choice C is correct. $\frac{2}{3}\% \times 90 = \frac{2}{300} \times 90 = \frac{180}{300} = \frac{6}{10} = 0.6$. (114)

33. Choice D is correct. If the man makes 12 payments of \$31.50, he pays back a total of \$378.00. Since the loan is for \$360.00, his net interest is \$18.00. Therefore, his rate of interest is $\frac{\$18.00}{\$360.00}$, which can be reduced to 0.05, or 5%. (118)

34. Choice C is correct. Final selling price = 85% × 130% × cost = $110\frac{1}{2}$ × cost. Thus, \$86.19 = 1.105C, where C = cost. C = \$86.19 ÷ 1.105 = \$78.00 (exactly). (118)

35. Choice C is correct. If $x$ is the amount of flour needed for 8 people, then we can set up the proportion $2\frac{1}{4}$ cups : 6 people = $x$ : 8 people. Solving for $x$ gives us $x = \frac{8}{6} \times 2\frac{1}{4}$ or $\frac{8}{6} \times \frac{9}{4} = 3$. (120)

36. Choice D is correct. If 10 men can survive for 24 days on 15 cans, then 1 man can survive for 240 days on 15 cans. If 1 man can survive for 240 days on 15 cans, then 1 man can survive for $\frac{240}{15}$ or 16 days on 1 can. If 1 man can survive for 16 days on 1 can, then 8 men can survive for $\frac{16}{8}$ or 2 days on 1 can. If 8 men can survive for 2 days on 1 can, then for 36 days 8 men need $\frac{36}{2}$ or 18 cans to survive. (120)

37. Choice D is correct. $1\frac{1}{15}$ feet = $12\frac{4}{5}$ inches. Thus, we have the proportion: $\frac{1}{2}$ inch : 1 mile = 12.8 inches : $x$. Solving for $x$, we have $x$ = 25.6 miles = $25\frac{3}{5}$ miles. (120)

38. Choice D is correct. If $e = hf$, then $h = \frac{e}{f}$. If $e$ is doubled and $f$ is halved, then the new value of $h$, $h' = \left(\frac{2e}{\frac{1}{2}f}\right)$. Multiplying the numerator and denominator by 2 gives us $h' = \frac{4e}{f}$. Since $h = \frac{e}{f}$ and $h' = \frac{4e}{f}$ we see that $h' = 4h$. This is the same as saying that $h$ is multiplied by 4. (122)

39. Choice E is correct. 3 inches : 2 yards = 3 inches : 72 inches = 3 : 72. (121)

40. Choice D is correct. If Carl and Mark work for the same length of time, then Carl will earn \$8.00 for every \$6.00 Mark earns (since in the time Mark can earn one \$6.00 wage, Carl can earn *two* \$4.00 wages). Thus, their hourly wage rates are in the ratio \$6.00 (Mark) : \$8.00 (Carl) = 3 : 4. (120)

**41.** Choice D is correct. The lowest common denominator is the smallest number that is divisible by all of the denominators. Thus we are looking for the smallest number that is divisible by 6, 27, 5, 10, and 15. The smallest number that is divisible by 6 and 27 is 54. The smallest number that is divisible by 54 and 5 is 270. Since 270 is divisible by 10 and 15 also, it is the lowest common denominator.    (110, 126)

**42.** Choice E is correct.

Percent deviation $= \dfrac{\text{absolute deviation}}{\text{average score}} \times 100\%$.

Absolute deviation = Ralph's score − average score
$= 90 - 85 = 5$.

Percent deviation $= \dfrac{5}{85} \times 100\% = 500\% \div 85 = 5.88\%$ (approximately).

5.88% is closer to 5.9% than to 5.8%, so 5.9% is correct.    (117)

**43.** Choice B is correct. If we discount 20% and then 12%, we are, in effect, taking 88% of 80% of the original price. Since "of" represents multiplication, when we deal with percent we can multiply 88% × 80% = 70.4%. This is a deduction of 29.6% from the original price.    (119, 114)

**44.** Choice A is correct.

This is a simple proportion: $\dfrac{1 \text{ foot}}{\frac{1}{2} \text{ mile}} = \dfrac{\frac{1}{2} \text{ inch}}{x}$. Our first step must be to convert all these measurements to one unit. The most logical unit is the one our answer will take—feet. Thus, $\dfrac{1 \text{ ft.}}{2,640 \text{ ft.}} = \dfrac{\frac{1}{24} \text{ ft.}}{x}$. (1 mile equals 5,280 feet.) Solving for $x$, we find $x = \dfrac{2,640}{24}$ feet = 110 feet.    (120, 121)

**45.** Choice A is correct. Let the two original sides of the rectangle be $a$ and $b$, and the new sides be $a'$ and $b'$. We know that $a' = 1.25a = \dfrac{5a}{4}$, and that $ab = (a')(b') = \dfrac{5a(b')}{4}$. Therefore, $b' = \left(\dfrac{4}{5}\right)b$, a decrease of $\dfrac{1}{5}$, or 20%.    (122)

**46.** Choice C is correct. The first thing to notice is that these fractions are all approximately equal to 3. Thus, it will aid our comparison if we subtract 3 from each of the numbers and compare the remainders instead. The five remainders are: $\dfrac{-170}{2,071}$, $\dfrac{-99}{1,463}$, $\dfrac{-209}{1,772}$, $\dfrac{+46}{2,963}$, and $\dfrac{+123}{2,631}$, respectively. We must find the smallest of these remainders, which is obviously the third one (the fourth and fifth are positive, and the other two are greater than $\dfrac{-1}{10}$). Thus, the third choice, $\dfrac{5,107}{1,772}$, is the smallest one.    (123–128)

**47.** Choice D is correct. Let's say that the price was $100 during 2003. 30% of $100 = $30 so the new price in 2003 was $130. In 2004, the company cut back its prices 20% so the new price in 2004 = $130

$- \left(\dfrac{20}{100}\right)\$130 =$

$\$130 - \left(\dfrac{1}{5}\right)\$130 =$

$\$130 - \$26 = \$104$.
The net change is $104 − $100 = $4.
$4/$100 = 4% increase    (118)

**48.** Choice E is correct. $0.04\% = \dfrac{0.04}{100} = \dfrac{4}{10,000} = \dfrac{1}{2,500}$.    (107)

**49.** Choice D is correct. Before adding you should examine the numbers to be added. They form pairs, like this: 16 + (12 + 88) + (34 + 66) + (21 + 79) + (11 + 89), which equals 16 + 100 + 100 + 100 + 100 = 416. Dividing 416 by 25, we obtain $16\dfrac{16}{25}$, which equals 16.64.    (112)

**50.** Choice A is correct. We can set up a proportion as follows:

$\dfrac{1 \text{ coconut}}{1 \text{ banana}} = \dfrac{2}{1}$, $\dfrac{1 \text{ banana}}{1 \text{ grapefruit}} = \dfrac{1}{3}$, so by multiplying the two equations together $\left(\dfrac{1 \text{ coconut}}{1 \text{ banana}} \times \dfrac{1 \text{ banana}}{1 \text{ grapefruit}}\right.$ and $\left.\dfrac{2}{1} \times \dfrac{1}{3}\right)$ and canceling the bananas and the 1's in the numerators and denominators, we get: $\dfrac{1 \text{ coconut}}{1 \text{ grapefruit}} = \dfrac{2}{3}$.    (120)

# MATH REFRESHER
# SESSION 2

# Rate Problems:
# Distance and Time, Work,
# Mixture, and Cost

## Word Problem Setup

**200.** Some problems require translation of words into algebraic expressions or equations. For example: 8 more than 7 times a number is 22. Find the number. Let $n$ = the number. We have

$$7n + 8 = 22 \qquad\qquad 7n = 14 \qquad\qquad n = 2$$

Another example: There are 3 times as many boys as girls in a class. What is the ratio of boys to the total number of students? Let $n$ = number of girls. Then

$$3n = \text{number of boys}$$
$$4n = \text{Total number of students}$$

$$\frac{\text{number of boys}}{\text{Total students}} = \frac{3n}{4n} = \frac{3}{4}$$

**201.** Rate problems concern a special type of relationship that is very common: rate × input = output. This results from the definition of rate as *the ratio between output and input*. In these problems, input may represent any type of "investment," but the most frequent quantities used as inputs are time, work, and money. Output is usually distance traveled, work done, or money spent.

Note that the word *per*, as used in rates, signifies a ratio. Thus a rate of 25 miles per hour signifies the ratio between an output of 25 miles and an input of 1 hour.

Frequently, the word *per* will be represented by the fraction sign, thus $\frac{25\,\text{miles}}{1\,\text{hour}}$.

> **Example:** Peter can walk a mile in 10 minutes. He can travel a mile on his bicycle in 2 minutes. How far away is his uncle's house if Peter can walk there and bicycle back in 1 hour exactly?

To solve a rate problem such as the one above, follow these steps:

**STEP 1.** Determine the names of the quantities that represent input, output, and rate in the problem you are doing. In the example, Peter's input is *time*, and his output is *distance*. His rate will be *distance per unit of time*, which is commonly called *speed*.

**STEP 2.** Write down the fundamental relationship in terms of the quantities mentioned, making each the heading of a column. In the example, set up the table like this:

$$\text{speed} \times \text{time} = \text{distance}$$

**STEP 3.** Directly below the name of each quantity, write the unit of measurement in terms of the answer you want. Your choice of unit should be the most convenient one, but remember, once you have chosen a unit, you must convert all quantities to that unit.

We must select a unit of time. Since a *minute* was the unit used in the problem, it is the most logical choice. Similarly, we will choose a *mile* for our unit of distance. *Speed* (which is the ratio of distance to time) will therefore be expressed in *miles per minute*, usually abbreviated as mi/min. Thus, our chart now looks like this:

**speed   ×   time   =   distance**

| mi/min | minutes | miles |
|--------|---------|-------|

**STEP 4.**  The problem will mention various situations in which some quantity of input is used to get a certain quantity of output. Represent each of these situations on a different line of the table, leaving blanks for unknown quantities.

In the sample problem, four situations are mentioned: Peter can walk a mile in 10 minutes; he can bicycle a mile in 2 minutes; he walks to his uncle's house; and he bicycles home. On the diagram, with the appropriate boxes filled, the problem will look like this:

**speed   ×   time   =   distance**

|              | mi/min | minutes | miles |
|--------------|--------|---------|-------|
| 1. walking   |        | 10      | 1     |
| 2. bicycling |        | 2       | 1     |
| 3. walking   |        |         |       |
| 4. bicycling |        |         |       |

**STEP 5.**  From the chart and from the relationship at the top of the chart, quantities for filling some of the empty spaces may become obvious. Fill in these values directly.

In the example, on the first line of the chart, we see that the walking speed times 10 equals 1.

Thus, the walking *speed* is 0.1 mi/min (mi/min × 10 = 1 mi; mi/min = $\frac{1\,\text{mi}}{10\,\text{min}} = 0.1$).

Similarly, on the second we see that the bicycle speed equals 0.5 mi/min. Furthermore, his walking speed shown on line 3 will be 0.1, the same speed as on line 1; and his bicycling speed shown on line 4 will equal the speed (0.5) shown on line 2. Adding this information to our table, we get:

**speed   ×   time   =   distance**

|              | mi/min | minutes | miles |
|--------------|--------|---------|-------|
| 1. walking   | 0.1    | 10      | 1     |
| 2. bicycling | 0.5    | 2       | 1     |
| 3. walking   | 0.1    |         |       |
| 4. bicycling | 0.5    |         |       |

**STEP 6.**  Next, fill in the blanks with algebraic expressions to represent the quantities indicated, being careful to take advantage of simple relationships stated in the problem or appearing in the chart.

Continuing the example, we represent the time spent traveling shown on line 3 by $x$. According to the fundamental relationship, the distance traveled on this trip must be (0.1) $x$. Similarly, if $y$ represents the time shown on line 4, the distance traveled is (0.5) $y$. Thus our chart now looks like this:

**speed × time = distance**

|            | mi/min | minutes | miles     |
|------------|--------|---------|-----------|
| 1. walking | 0.1    | 10      | 1         |
| 2. bicycling | 0.5  | 2       | 1         |
| 3. walking | 0.1    | $x$     | $(0.1)\,x$ |
| 4. bicycling | 0.5  | $y$     | $(0.5)\,y$ |

**STEP 7.** Now, from the statement of the problem, you should be able to set up enough equations to solve for all the unknowns. In the example, there are two facts that we have not used yet. First, since Peter is going to his uncle's house and back, it is assumed that the distances covered on the two trips are equal. Thus we get the equation: $(0.1)\,x = (0.5)\,y$. We are told that the total time to and from his uncle's house is one hour. Since we are using minutes as our unit of time, we convert the one hour to 60 minutes. Thus we get the equation: $x + y = 60$. Solving these two equations ($0.1x = 0.5y$ and $x + y = 60$) algebraically, we find that $x = 50$ and $y = 10$. (See Section 407 for the solution of simultaneous equations.)

**STEP 8.** Now that you have all the information necessary, you can calculate the answer required. In the sample problem we are required to determine the distance to the uncle's house, which is $(0.1)\,x$ or $(0.5)\,y$. Using $x = 50$ or $y = 10$ gives us the distance as 5 miles.

Now that we have shown the fundamental steps in solving a rate problem, we shall discuss various types of rate problems.

## Distance and Time

**202.** In *distance and time problems* the fundamental relationship that we use is *speed × time = distance*. Speed is the rate, time is the input, and distance is the output. The example in Section 201 was this type of problem.

> **Example:** In a sports car race, David gives Kenny a head start of 10 miles. David's car goes 80 miles per hour and Kenny's car goes 60 miles per hour. How long should it take David to catch up to Kenny if they both leave their starting marks at the same time?

**STEP 1.** Here the fundamental quantities are *speed*, *time*, and *distance*.

**STEP 2.** The fundamental relationship is speed × time = distance. Write this at the top of the chart.

**STEP 3.** The unit for *distance* in this problem will be a *mile*. The unit for *speed* will be *miles per hour*. Since the speed is in miles per hour, our *time* will be in *hours*. Now our chart looks like this:

**speed × time = distance**

| mi/hr | hours | miles |
|-------|-------|-------|

**STEP 4.** The problem offers us certain information that we can add to the chart. First we must make two horizontal rows, one for Kenny and one for David. We know that Kenny's speed is 60 miles per hour and that David's speed is 80 miles per hour.

**STEP 5.** In this case, none of the information in the chart can be used to calculate other information in the chart.

**STEP 6.** Now we must use algebraic expressions to represent the unknowns. We know that both Kenny and David travel for the same amount of time, but we do not know for how much time, so we will place an $x$ in the space for each boy's time. Now from the relationship of speed × time = distance, we can calculate Kenny's distance as $60x$ and David's distance as $80x$. Now the chart looks like this:

$$\textbf{speed} \quad \times \quad \textbf{time} \quad = \quad \textbf{distance}$$

| | mi/hr | hours | miles |
|---|---|---|---|
| **Kenny** | 60 | $x$ | $60x$ |
| **David** | 80 | $x$ | $80x$ |

**STEP 7.** From the statement of the problem we know that David gave Kenny a 10-mile head start. In other words, David's distance is 10 more miles than Kenny's distance. This can be stated algebraically as $60x + 10 = 80x$. That is, Kenny's distance + 10 miles = David's distance.

Solving for $x$ gives us $x = \frac{1}{2}$.

**STEP 8.** The question asks how much time is required for David to catch up to Kenny. If we look at the chart, we see that this time is $x$, and $x$ has already been calculated as $\frac{1}{2}$ so the answer is $\frac{1}{2}$ hour.

# Work

**203.** In *work problems* the input is time and output is the amount of work done. The rate is the work per unit of time.

**Example:** Jack can chop down 20 trees in 1 hour, whereas it takes Ted $1\frac{1}{2}$ hours to chop down 18 trees. If the two of them work together, how long will it take them to chop down 48 trees?

*Solution:* By the end of Step 5 your chart should look like this:

$$\textbf{rate} \quad \times \quad \textbf{time} \quad = \quad \textbf{work}$$

| | trees/hr. | hours | trees |
|---|---|---|---|
| **1. Jack** | 20 | 1 | 20 |
| **2. Ted** | 12 | $1\frac{1}{2}$ | 18 |
| **3. Jack** | 20 | | |
| **4. Ted** | 12 | | |

In Step 6, we represent the time that it takes Jack by $x$ in line 3. Since we have the relationship that rate × time = work, we see that in line 3 the work is $20x$. Since the two boys work together (therefore, for the same amount of time), the time in line 4 must be $x$, and the work must be $12x$. Now, in Step 7, we see that the total work is 48 trees. From lines 3 and 4, then, $20x + 12x = 48$. Solving for $x$ gives us $x = 1\frac{1}{2}$. We are asked to find the number of hours needed by the boys to chop down the 48 trees together, and we see that this time is $x$, or $1\frac{1}{2}$ hours.

# Mixture

**204.** In *mixture problems* you are given a percent or a fractional composition of a substance, and you are asked questions about the weights and compositions of the substances. The basic relationship here is that the percentage of a certain substance in a mixture × the amount of the mixture = the amount of substance.

Note that it is often better to change percents to decimals because it makes it easier to avoid errors.

**Example:** A chemist has two quarts of 25% acid solution and one quart of 40% acid solution. If he mixes these, what will be the concentration of the mixture?

*Solution:* Let $x$ = concentration of the mixture. At the end of Step 6, our table will look like this:

|  | rate $\times$ | amount of sol $=$ | amount of acid |
|---|---|---|---|
|  | $\dfrac{\text{qt (acid)}}{\text{qt (sol)}}$ | qts (sol) | qts (acid) |
| 25%, solution | 0.25 | 2 | 0.50 |
| 40% solution | 0.40 | 1 | 0.40 |
| mixture | $x$ | 3 | $3x$ |

We now have one additional bit of information: The amount of acid in the mixture must be equal to the total amount of acid in each of the two parts, so $3x = 0.50 + 0.40$. Therefore $x$ is equal to 0.30, which is the same as a 30% concentration of the acid in the mixture.

# Cost

**205.** In *cost problems* the rate is the *price per item*, the input is the *number of items*, and the output is the *value* of the items considered. When you are dealing with dollars and cents, you must be very careful to use the decimal point correctly.

**Example:** Jim has $3.00 in nickels and dimes in his pocket. If he has twice as many nickels as he has dimes, how many coins does he have altogether?

*Solution:* After Step 6, our chart should look like this (where $c$ is the number of dimes Jim has):

|  | rate $\times$ | number $=$ | value |
|---|---|---|---|
|  | cents/coin | coins | cents |
| nickels | 5 | $2c$ | $10c$ |
| dimes | 10 | $c$ | $10c$ |

Now we recall the additional bit of information that the total value of the nickels and dimes is $3.00, or 300 cents. Thus, $5(2c) + 10c = 300$; $20c = 300$; so $c = 15$, the number of dimes. Jim has twice as many nickels, so $2c = 30$.

The total number of coins is $c + 2c = 3c = 45$.

The following table will serve as review for this Refresher Section.

| TYPE OF PROBLEM | FUNDAMENTAL RELATIONSHIP |
|---|---|
| distance | speed $\times$ time $=$ distance |
| work | rate $\times$ time $=$ work done |
| mixture | concentration $\times$ amount of solution $=$ amount of ingredient |
| cost | rate $\times$ number of items $=$ value |

# Practice Test 2

## Rate Problems: Distance and Time, Work, Mixture, and Cost

Correct answers and solutions follow each test.

**1.** A B C D E

1. A man rowed 3 miles upstream in 90 minutes. If the river flowed with a current of 2 miles per hour, how long did the man's return trip take?

   (A) 20 minutes
   (B) 30 minutes
   (C) 45 minutes
   (D) 60 minutes
   (E) 80 minutes

**2.** A B C D E

2. Charles can do a job in 1 hour, Bill can do the same job in 2 hours, and Bob can do the job in 3 hours. How long does it take them to do the job working together?

   (A) $\frac{6}{11}$ hours

   (B) $\frac{1}{2}$ hour

   (C) 6 hours

   (D) $\frac{1}{3}$ hours

   (E) $\frac{1}{6}$ hours

**3.** A B C D E

3. Mr. Smith had $2,000 to invest. He invested part of it at 5% per year and the remainder at 4% per year. After one year, his investment grew to $2,095. How much of the original investment was at the 5% rate?

   (A) $500
   (B) $750
   (C) $1,000
   (D) $1,250
   (E) $1,500

**4.** A B C D E

4. A man walks down the road for half an hour at an average speed of 3 miles per hour. He waits 10 minutes for a bus, which brings him back to his starting point at 3:15. If the man began his walk at 2:25 the same afternoon, what was the average speed of the bus?

   (A) 1.5 miles per hour
   (B) 3 miles per hour
   (C) 4.5 miles per hour
   (D) 6 miles per hour
   (E) 9 miles per hour

**5.** A B C D E

5. Faucet A lets water flow into a 5-gallon tub at a rate of 1.5 gallons per minute. Faucet B lets water flow into the same tub at a rate of 1.0 gallons per minute. Faucet A runs alone for 100 seconds; then the two of them together finish filling up the tub. How long does the whole operation take?

   (A) 120 seconds
   (B) 150 seconds
   (C) 160 seconds
   (D) 180 seconds
   (E) 190 seconds

A B C D E

**6.** Coffee A normally costs 75¢ per pound. It is mixed with Coffee B, which normally costs 80¢ per pound, to form a mixture that costs 78¢ per pound. If there are 10 pounds of the mix, how many pounds of Coffee A were used in the mix?

(A) 3
(B) 4
(C) 4.5
(D) 5
(E) 6

A B C D E

**7.** If a man can run $p$ miles in $x$ minutes, how long will it take him to run $q$ miles at the same rate?

(A) $\frac{pq}{x}$ minutes

(B) $\frac{px}{q}$ minutes

(C) $\frac{q}{px}$ minutes

(D) $\frac{qx}{p}$ minutes

(E) $\frac{x}{pq}$ minutes

A B C D E

**8.** A train went 300 miles from City $X$ to City $Y$ at an average rate of 80 mph. At what speed did it travel on the way back if its average speed for the whole trip was 100 mph?

(A) 120 mph

(B) 125 mph

(C) $133\frac{1}{3}$ mph

(D) $137\frac{1}{2}$ mph

(E) 150 mph

A B C D E

**9.** A man spent exactly $2.50 on 3¢, 6¢, and 10¢ stamps. If he bought ten 3¢ stamps and twice as many 6¢ stamps as 10¢ stamps, how many 10¢ stamps did he buy?

(A) 5
(B) 10
(C) 12
(D) 15
(E) 20

A B C D E

**10.** If 6 workers can complete 9 identical jobs in 3 days, how long will it take 4 workers to complete 10 such jobs?

(A) 3 days
(B) 4 days
(C) 5 days
(D) 6 days
(E) more than 6 days

A B C D E

**11.** A barge travels twice as fast when it is empty as when it is full. If it travels 20 miles north with a cargo, spends 20 minutes unloading, and returns to its original port empty, taking 8 hours to complete the entire trip, what is the speed of the barge when it is empty?

(A) less than 3 mph
(B) less than 4 mph but not less than 3 mph
(C) less than 6 mph but not less than 4 mph
(D) less than 8 mph but not less than 6 mph
(E) 8 mph or more

**12.** A B C D E

**12.** Bill can hammer 20 nails in 6 minutes. Jeff can do the same job in only 5 minutes. How long will it take them to finish if Bill hammers the first 5 nails, then Jeff hammers for 3 minutes, then Bill finishes the job?

(A) 4.6 minutes
(B) 5.0 minutes
(C) 5.4 minutes
(D) 5.8 minutes
(E) 6.0 minutes

**13.** A B C D E

**13.** Jack has two quarts of a 30% acid solution and three pints of a 20% solution. If he mixes them, what will be the concentration (to the nearest percent) of the resulting solution?

(A) 22%
(B) 23%
(C) 24%
(D) 25%
(E) 26%

**14.** A B C D E

**14.** Robert has 12 coins totaling $1.45. None of his coins is larger than a quarter. Which of the following *cannot* be the number of quarters he has?

(A) 1
(B) 2
(C) 3
(D) 4
(E) 5

**15.** A B C D E

**15.** Jim's allowance is $1.20 per week. Stan's is 25¢ per day. How long will they have to save, if they save both their allowances together, before they can get a model car set that costs $23.60?

(A) 6 weeks
(B) 8 weeks
(C) 10 weeks
(D) 13 weeks
(E) 16 weeks

**16.** A B C D E

**16.** Chuck can earn money at the following schedule: $2.00 for the first hour, $2.50 an hour for the next two hours, and $3.00 an hour after that. He also has the opportunity of taking a different job that pays $2.75 an hour. He wants to work until he has earned $15.00. Which of the following is true?

(A) The first job will take him longer by 15 minutes or more.
(B) The first job will take him longer by less than 15 minutes.
(C) The two jobs will take the same length of time.
(D) The second job will take him longer by 30 minutes or more.
(E) The second job will take him longer by less than 10 minutes.

**17.** A B C D E

**17.** If Robert can seal 40 envelopes in one minute, and Paul can do the same job in 80 seconds, how many minutes (to the nearest minute) will it take the two of them, working together, to seal 350 envelopes?

(A) 4 minutes
(B) 5 minutes
(C) 6 minutes
(D) 7 minutes
(E) 8 minutes

**18.** A B C D E

18. Towns A and B are 400 miles apart. If a train leaves A in the direction of B at 50 miles per hour, how long will it take before that train meets another train, going from B to A, at a speed of 30 miles per hour?

(A) 4 hours

(B) $4\frac{1}{3}$ hours

(C) 5 hours

(D) $5\frac{2}{3}$ hours

(E) $6\frac{2}{3}$ hours

**19.** A B C D E

19. A tub is shaped like a rectangular solid, with internal measurements of 2 feet × 2 feet × 5 feet. If two faucets, each with an output of 2 cubic feet of water per minute, pour water into the tub simultaneously, how many minutes does it take to fill the tub completely?

(A) less than 3 minutes
(B) less than 4 minutes, but not less than 3
(C) less than 5 minutes, but not less than 4
(D) less than 6 minutes, but not less than 5
(E) 6 minutes or more

**20.** A B C D E

20. A 30% solution of barium chloride is mixed with 10 grams of water to form a 20% solution. How many grams of the original solution did we start with?

(A) 10
(B) 15
(C) 20
(D) 25
(E) 30

**21.** A B C D E

21. Mr. Adams had a coin collection including only nickels, dimes, and quarters. He had twice as many dimes as he had nickels, and half as many quarters as he had nickels. If the total face value of his collection was $300.00, how many quarters did the collection contain?

(A) 75
(B) 100
(C) 250
(D) 400
(E) 800

**22.** A B C D E

22. A storekeeper stocks a high-priced pen and a lower-priced model. If he sells the high-priced pens, which yield a profit of $1.20 per pen sold, he can sell 30 in a month. If he sells the lower-priced pens, making a profit of 15¢ per pen sold, he can sell 250 pens in a month. Which type of pen will yield more profit per month, and by how much?

(A) The cheaper pen will yield a greater profit, by $1.50.
(B) The more expensive pen will yield a greater profit, by $1.50.
(C) The cheaper pen will yield a greater profit, by 15¢.
(D) The more expensive pen will yield a greater profit, by 15¢.
(E) Both pens will yield exactly the same profit.

**23.** A B C D E

23. At a cost of $2.50 per square yard, what would be the price of carpeting a rectangular floor, 18' × 24'?

(A) $120
(B) $360
(C) $750
(D) $1,000
(E) $1,080

24. A B C D E    24. Tom and Bill agreed to race across a 50-foot pool and back again. They started together, but Tom finished 10 feet ahead of Bill. If their rates were constant, and Tom finished the race in 27 seconds, how long did Bill take to finish it?

(A) 28 seconds
(B) 30 seconds
(C) $33\frac{1}{3}$ seconds
(D) 35 seconds
(E) 37 seconds

25. A B C D E    25. If four men need $24.00 worth of food for a three-day camping trip, how much will two men need for a two-week trip?

(A) $12.00
(B) $24.00
(C) $28.00
(D) $42.00
(E) $56.00

26. A B C D E    26. A man walks 15 blocks to work every morning at a rate of 2 miles per hour. If there are 20 blocks in a mile, how long does it take him to walk to work?

(A) $12\frac{1}{2}$ minutes
(B) 15 minutes
(C) $22\frac{1}{2}$ minutes
(D) $37\frac{1}{2}$ minutes
(E) 45 minutes

27. A B C D E    27. A certain river has a current of 3 miles per hour. A boat takes twice as long to travel upstream between two points as it does to travel downstream between the same two points. What is the speed of the boat in still water?

(A) 3 miles per hour
(B) 6 miles per hour
(C) 9 miles per hour
(D) 12 miles per hour
(E) The speed cannot be determined from the given information.

28. A B C D E    28. Stan can run 10 miles per hour, whereas Jack can run only 8 miles per hour. If they start at the same time from the same point and run in opposite directions, how far apart (to the nearest mile) will they be after 10 minutes?

(A) 1 mile
(B) 2 miles
(C) 3 miles
(D) 4 miles
(E) 5 miles

29. A B C D E    29. Machine A can produce 40 bolts per minute, whereas Machine B can produce only 30 per minute. Machine A begins alone to make bolts, but it breaks down after $1\frac{1}{2}$ minutes, and Machine B must complete the job. If the job requires 300 bolts, how long does the whole operation take?

(A) $7\frac{1}{2}$ minutes
(B) 8 minutes
(C) $8\frac{1}{2}$ minutes
(D) 9 minutes
(E) $9\frac{1}{2}$ minutes

30.

A B C D E
30. ⁞⁞ ⁞⁞ ⁞⁞ ⁞⁞ ⁞⁞

**30.** Ten pints of 15% salt solution are mixed with 15 pints of 10% salt solution. What is the concentration of the resulting solution?

(A) 10%
(B) 12%
(C) 12.5%
(D) 13%
(E) 15%

31.

A B C D E
31. ⁞⁞ ⁞⁞ ⁞⁞ ⁞⁞ ⁞⁞

**31.** Jeff makes $5.00 every day, from which he must spend $3.00 for various expenses. Pete makes $10.00 a day but has to spend $7.00 each day for expenses. If the two of them save together, how long will it take before they can buy a $150 car?

(A) 10 days
(B) 15 days
(C) 30 days
(D) 50 days
(E) 75 days

32.

A B C D E
32. ⁞⁞ ⁞⁞ ⁞⁞ ⁞⁞ ⁞⁞

**32.** Two cities are 800 miles apart. At 3:00 P.M., Plane A leaves one city, traveling toward the other city at a speed of 600 miles per hour. At 4:00 the same afternoon, Plane B leaves the first city, traveling in the same direction at a rate of 800 miles per hour. Which of the following answers represents the actual result?

(A) Plane A arrives first, by an hour or more.
(B) Plane A arrives first, by less than an hour.
(C) The two planes arrive at exactly the same time.
(D) Plane A arrives after Plane B, by less than an hour.
(E) Plane A arrives after Plane B, by an hour or more.

33.

A B C D E
33. ⁞⁞ ⁞⁞ ⁞⁞ ⁞⁞ ⁞⁞

**33.** Peter has as many nickels as Charlie has dimes; Charlie has twice as many nickels as Peter has dimes. If together they have $2.50 in nickels and dimes, how many nickels does Peter have?

(A) 1 nickel
(B) 4 nickels
(C) 7 nickels
(D) 10 nickels
(E) The answer cannot be determined from the given information.

34.

A B C D E
34. ⁞⁞ ⁞⁞ ⁞⁞ ⁞⁞ ⁞⁞

**34.** A man can travel 120 miles in either of two ways. He can travel at a constant rate of 40 miles per hour, or he can travel halfway at 50 miles per hour, then slow down to 30 miles per hour for the second 60 miles. Which way is faster, and by how much?

(A) The constant rate is faster by 10 minutes or more.
(B) The constant rate is faster by less than 10 minutes.
(C) The two ways take exactly the same time.
(D) The constant rate is slower by less than 10 minutes.
(E) The constant rate is slower by 10 minutes or more.

35.

A B C D E
35. ⁞⁞ ⁞⁞ ⁞⁞ ⁞⁞ ⁞⁞

**35.** John walks 10 miles at an average rate of 2 miles per hour and returns on a bicycle at an average rate of 10 miles per hour. How long (to the nearest hour) does the entire trip take him?

(A) 3 hours
(B) 4 hours
(C) 5 hours
(D) 6 hours
(E) 7 hours

**36.** A B C D E

**36.** If a plane can travel $P$ miles in $Q$ hours, how long will it take to travel $R$ miles?

(A) $\dfrac{PQ}{R}$ hours

(B) $\dfrac{P}{QR}$ hours

(C) $\dfrac{QR}{P}$ hours

(D) $\dfrac{Q}{PR}$ hours

(E) $\dfrac{PR}{Q}$ hours

**37.** A B C D E

**37.** A boy can swim 75 feet in 12 seconds. What is his rate to the nearest mile per hour?

(A) 1 mph
(B) 2 mph
(C) 3 mph
(D) 4 mph
(E) 5 mph

**38.** A B C D E

**38.** How many pounds of a \$1.20-per-pound nut mixture must be mixed with two pounds of a 90¢-per-pound mixture to produce a mixture that sells for \$1.00 per pound?

(A) 0.5
(B) 1.0
(C) 1.5
(D) 2.0
(E) 2.5

**39.** A B C D E

**39.** A broken clock is set correctly at 12:00 noon. However, it registers only 20 minutes for each hour. In how many hours will it again register the correct time?

(A) 12
(B) 18
(C) 24
(D) 30
(E) 36

**40.** A B C D E

**40.** If a man travels $p$ hours at an average rate of $q$ miles per hour, and then $r$ hours at an average rate of $s$ miles per hour, what is his overall average rate of speed?

(A) $\dfrac{pq + rs}{p + r}$

(B) $\dfrac{q+s}{2}$

(C) $\dfrac{q+s}{p+r}$

(D) $\dfrac{p}{q} + \dfrac{r}{s}$

(E) $\dfrac{p}{s} + \dfrac{r}{q}$

**41.** A B C D E

**41.** If Walt can paint 25 feet of fence in an hour, and Joe can paint 35 feet in an hour, how many minutes will it take them to paint a 150-foot fence, if they work together?

(A) 150
(B) 200
(C) 240
(D) 480
(E) 500

42. **A B C D E**

42. If a man travels for a half hour at a rate of 20 miles per hour, and for another half hour at a rate of 30 miles per hour, what is his average speed?

(A) 24 miles per hour
(B) 25 miles per hour
(C) 26 miles per hour
(D) 26.5 miles per hour
(E) The answer cannot be determined from the given information.

43. **A B C D E**

43. New York is 3,000 miles from Los Angeles. Sol leaves New York aboard a plane heading toward Los Angeles at the same time that Robert leaves Los Angeles aboard a plane heading toward New York. If Sol is moving at 200 miles per hour and Robert is moving at 400 miles per hour, how soon will one plane pass the other?

(A) 2 hours
(B) $22\frac{1}{2}$ hours
(C) 5 hours
(D) 4 hours
(E) 12 hours

44. **A B C D E**

44. A man exchanged a dollar bill for change and received 7 coins, none of which were half dollars. How many of these coins were dimes?

(A) 0
(B) 1
(C) 4
(D) 5
(E) The answer cannot be determined from the information given.

45. **A B C D E**

45. A man adds two quarts of pure alcohol to a 30% solution of alcohol in water. If the new concentration is 40%, how many quarts of the original solution were there?

(A) 12
(B) 15
(C) 18
(D) 20
(E) 24

46. **A B C D E**

46. A certain power company charges 8¢ per kilowatt-hour for the first 1000 kilowatt-hours, and 6¢ per kilowatt-hour after that. If a man uses a 900-watt toaster for 5 hours, a 100-watt lamp for 25 hours, and a 5-watt clock for 400 hours, how much is he charged for the power he uses? (1 kilowatt = 1,000 watts)

(A) 56¢
(B) 64¢
(C) 72¢
(D) $560.00
(E) $720.00

47. **A B C D E**

47. At 30¢ per yard, what is the price of 96 inches of ribbon?

(A) 72¢
(B) 75¢
(C) 80¢
(D) 84¢
(E) 90¢

48.  A B C D E

**48.** A man travels for 6 hours at a rate of 50 miles per hour. His return trip takes him $7\frac{1}{2}$ hours. What is his average speed for the whole trip?

(A) 44.4 miles per hour
(B) 45.0 miles per hour
(C) 46.8 miles per hour
(D) 48.2 miles per hour
(E) 50.0 miles per hour

49.  A B C D E

**49.** Stanley puts $100 in the bank for two years at 5% interest compounded annually. At the end of the two years, what is his balance?

(A) $100.00
(B) $105.00
(C) $105.25
(D) $110.00
(E) $110.25

50.  A B C D E

**50.** A 12-gallon tub has a faucet that lets water in at a rate of 3 gallons per minute, and a drain that lets water out at a rate of 1.5 gallons per minute. If you start with 3 gallons of water in the tub, how long will it take to fill the tub completely?

(A) 3 minutes
(B) 4 minutes
(C) 6 minutes
(D) 7.5 minutes
(E) 8 minutes

# Answer Key for Practice Test 2

| | | | |
|---|---|---|---|
| 1. B | 14. A | 27. C | 39. B |
| 2. A | 15. B | 28. C | 40. A |
| 3. E | 16. B | 29. E | 41. A |
| 4. E | 17. B | 30. B | 42. B |
| 5. C | 18. C | 31. C | 43. C |
| 6. B | 19. D | 32. B | 44. E |
| 7. D | 20. C | 33. E | 45. A |
| 8. C | 21. D | 34. A | 46. C |
| 9. B | 22. A | 35. D | 47. C |
| 10. C | 23. A | 36. C | 48. A |
| 11. D | 24. B | 37. D | 49. E |
| 12. C | 25. E | 38. B | 50. C |
| 13. E | 26. C | | |

# Answers and Solutions for Practice Test 2

1. Choice B is correct. The fundamental relationship here is: rate × time = distance. The easiest units to work with are miles per hour for the rate, hours for time, and miles for distance. Note that the word *per* indicates division because when calculating a rate, we *divide* the number of miles (distance units) by the number of hours (time units).

We can set up our chart with the information given. We know that the upstream trip took $1\frac{1}{2}$ hours (90 minutes) and that the distance was 3 miles. Thus the upstream rate was 2 miles per hour. The downstream distance was also 3 miles, but we use $t$ for the time, which is unknown. Thus the downstream rate was $\frac{3}{t}$. Our chart looks like this:

**rate × time = distance**

| | mi/hr | hours | miles |
|---|---|---|---|
| upstream | 2 | $2\frac{1}{2}$ | 3 |
| downstream | $\frac{3}{t}$ | $t$ | 3 |

We use the rest of the information to solve for $t$. We know that the speed of the current is 2 miles per hour. We assume the boat to be in still water and assign it a speed, $s$; then the upstream (against the current) speed of the boat is $s - 2$ miles per hour. Since $s - 2 = 2$, $s = 4$.

Now the speed of the boat downstream (with the current) is $s + 2$, or 6 miles per hour. This is equal to $\frac{3}{t}$, and we get the equation $\frac{3}{t} = 6$, so $t = \frac{1}{2}$ hour.

We must be careful with our units because the answer must be in minutes. We can convert $\frac{1}{2}$ hour to 30 minutes to get the final answer.

(201, 202)

2. Choice A is correct.

**rate × time = work**

| | job/hr | hours | jobs |
|---|---|---|---|
| Charles | 1 | 1 | 1 |
| Bill | $\frac{1}{2}$ | 2 | 1 |
| Bob | $\frac{1}{3}$ | 3 | 1 |
| together | $r$ | $t$ | 1 |

Let $r$ = rate together and $t$ = time together.

Now, $r = 1 + \frac{1}{2} + \frac{1}{3} = \frac{11}{6}$ because *whenever two or more people are working together, their joint rate is the sum of their individual rates.* This is not necessarily true of the time or the work done. In this case, we know that $r \times t = 1$ and $r = \frac{11}{6}$, so $t = \frac{6}{11}$.

(201, 203)

3. Choice E is correct.

**rate × principal = interest**

| | \$/\$ | \$ | \$ |
|---|---|---|---|
| 5% | 0.05 | $x$ | $0.05x$ |
| 4% | 0.04 | $y$ | $0.04y$ |

Let $x$ = part of the \$2,000 invested at 5%. Let $y$ = part of \$2,000 invested at 4%. We know that since the whole \$2,000 was invested, $x + y$ must equal \$2,000. Furthermore, we know that the sum of the interests on both investments equaled \$95, so $0.05x + 0.04y = 95$. Since we have to solve only for $x$, we can express this as $0.01x + 0.04x + 0.04y = 95$. Then we factor out 0.04. Thus $0.01x + 0.04 (x + y) = 95$. Since we know that $x + y = 2,000$, we have $0.01x + 0.04 (2,000) = 95$; $0.01x + 80 = 95$, and $x = 1,500$. Thus, \$1,500 was invested at 5%.

(201, 205)

**4.** Choice E is correct.

rate × time = distance

|  | mi/min | min | miles |
|---|---|---|---|
| **walk** | $\frac{1}{20}$ | 30 | $a$ |
| **wait** | 0 | *1* | 0 |
| **bus** | $r$ | $t$ | $a$ |

Let $a$ = distance the man walks. Since the man walks at 3 miles per hour, he walks at $\frac{3\text{ mi}}{60\text{ min}}$ or $\frac{1\text{ mi}}{20\text{ min}}$. From this we can find $a = \frac{1\text{ mi}}{20\text{ min}} \times 30\text{ min} = 1\frac{1}{2}$ miles. The total time he spent was 50 minutes (the difference between 3:15 and 2:25), and 30 + 10 + $t$ = 50, so $t$ must be equal to 10 minutes. This reduces our problem to the simple equation $10r = 1\frac{1}{2}$ (where $r$ = rate of the bus), and, on solving, $r$ = 0.15 miles per minute. But the required answer is in miles per hour. In one hour, or 60 minutes, the bus can travel 60 times as far as the 0.15 miles it travels in one minute, so that the bus travels 60 × 0.15 = 9 miles per hour.

(201, 202)

**5.** Choice C is correct.

rate × time = water

|  | gal/min | min | gal |
|---|---|---|---|
| **A only** | 1.5 | $\frac{5}{3}$* | 2.5 |
| **B only** | 1.0 | 0 | 0 |
| **A and B** | 2.5 | $t$ | $x$ |

\* ($\frac{5}{3}$ min = 100 sec.)

Let $t$ = time faucets A and B run together.

Let $x$ = amount of water delivered when A and B run together.

We know that the total number of gallons is 5, and A alone delivers 2.5 gallons (1.5 gal/min × $\frac{5}{3}$ min = 2.5 gal), so $x$ equals 2.5. This leads us to the simple equation $2.5t = 2.5$, so $t$ = 1 minute, or 60 seconds.

Thus, the whole operation takes $\frac{5}{3}$ + $t$ minutes, or 100 + 60 seconds, totaling 160 seconds.

(201, 203)

**6.** Choice B is correct.

rate × amount = cost

|  | ¢/lb | lb | ¢ |
|---|---|---|---|
| **Coffee A** | 75 | $x$ | $75x$ |
| **Coffee B** | 80 | $y$ | $80y$ |
| **mix** | 78 | 10 | 780 |

Let $x$ = weight of Coffee A in the mix.

Let $y$ = weight of Coffee B in the mix.

We know that the weight of the mix is equal to the sum of the weights of its components. Thus, $x + y$ = 10. Similarly, the cost of the mix is equal to the sum of the costs of the components. Thus, $75x + 80y$ = 780. Solving these two equations simultaneously gives us $x$ = 4 and $y$ = 6, so 4 pounds of Coffee A were used.

(201, 204, 407)

**7.** Choice D is correct.

rate × time = distance

|  | mi/min | min | miles |
|---|---|---|---|
| **first run** | $r$ | $x$ | $p$ |
| **second run** | $r$ | $t$ | $q$ |

Let $r$ = rate of the man.

Let $t$ = time it takes him to run $q$ miles.

From the first line, we know that $rx = p$, then $r = \frac{p}{x}$. Substituting this in the second line, we get $\left(\frac{p}{x}\right) t = q$, so $t = q\left(\frac{x}{p}\right)$, or $\frac{qx}{p}$ minutes.

(201, 202)

**8.** Choice C is correct.

rate × time = distance

|  | mi/hr | hrs | miles |
|---|---|---|---|
| **X to Y** | 80 | $t$ | 300 |
| **Y to X** | $r$ | $s$ | 300 |
| **whole trip** | 100 | $s + t$ | 600 |

Let $t$ = time from city X to city Y.

Let $s$ = time from city Y to city X.

Let $r$ = rate of the train from Y to X.

We know that $80t = 300$, so $t = \frac{300}{80}$, or $\frac{15}{4}$. Also, $100(s + t) = 600$, so $s + t = 6$. This and the last equation lead us to the conclusion that $s = 6 - \frac{15}{4}$, or $\frac{9}{4}$. Now, from the middle line, we have $r\left(\frac{9}{4}\right) = 300$, so $r = \frac{400}{3}$, or $133\frac{1}{3}$ miles per hour.

(Note that the reason why we chose the equations in this particular order was that it is easiest to concentrate first on those with the most data already given.)　(201, 202)

9. Choice B is correct.

rate × number = cost

|  | ¢/stamp | stamps | ¢ |
|---|---|---|---|
| 3¢ stamps | 3 | 10 | 30 |
| 10¢ stamps | 10 | $x$ | $10x$ |
| 6¢ stamps | 6 | $2x$ | $12x$ |

Let $x$ = the number of 10¢ stamps bought.

We know that the total cost is 250¢, so $30 + 10x + 12x = 250$. This is the same as $22x = 220$, so $x = 10$. Therefore, he bought ten 10¢ stamps.　(201, 205)

10. Choice C is correct.

rate × time = work

|  | jb/day | days | jobs |
|---|---|---|---|
| 6 workers | $6r$ | 3 | 9 |
| 4 workers | $4r$ | $t$ | 10 |

Let $r$ = rate of one worker.

Let $t$ = time for 4 workers to do 10 jobs.

From the first line, we have $18r = 9$, so $r = \frac{1}{2}$.

Substituting this in the second line, $4r = 2$, so $2t = 10$. Therefore $t = 5$. The workers will take 5 days.　(201, 203)

11. Choice D is correct.

rate × time = distance

|  | mi/hr | hrs | miles |
|---|---|---|---|
| north | $r$ | $\frac{20}{r}$ | 20 |
| unload | 0 | $\frac{1}{3}$ | 0 |
| return | $2r$ | $\frac{10}{r}$ | 20 |

Let $r$ = loaded rate; then

$$2r = \text{empty rate}$$

Total time = $\frac{20}{r} + \frac{1}{3} + \frac{10}{r} = 8$ hours.

Multiplying by $3r$ on both sides, we get $90 = 23r$, so $r = 90 \div 23$, or about 3.9 miles per hour. However, the problem asks for the speed *when empty*, which is $2r$, or 7.8. This is less than 8 mph, but not less than 6 mph.

(201, 202)

12. Choice C is correct.

rate × time = work

|  | nl/min | min | nails |
|---|---|---|---|
| Bill | $r$ | 6 | 20 |
| Jeff | $s$ | 5 | 20 |
| Bill | $r$ | $\frac{5}{r}$ | 5 |
| Jeff | $s$ | 3 | $3s$ |
| Bill | $r$ | $\frac{x}{r}$ | $x$ |

Let $r$ = Bill's rate.

Let $s$ = Jeff's rate.

$x$ = number of nails left after Jeff takes his turn.

$6r = 20$, so $r = 3\frac{1}{3}$.

$5s = 20$, so $s = 4$.

Total work = $5 + 3s + x = 20 = 5 + 12 + x$, so $x = 3$. Thus $\frac{x}{r} = 0.9$.

Total time = $\frac{5}{r} + 3 + \frac{x}{r} = 1.5 + 3 + 0.9$

(201, 203)

13. Choice E is correct.

concentration × volume = amount of acid

|  | % acid | pts | pts |
|---|---|---|---|
| old sol | 30% | 4 | 1.2 |
|  | 20% | 3 | 0.6 |
| new sol | $x\%$ | 7 | 1.8 |

(2 qts = 4 pts)

Let $x\%$ = concentration of new solution.

4 pts of 30% + 3 pts of 20% = 7 pts of $x\%$

1.2 pts + 0.6 pt = 1.8 pts

$(x\%)(7) = 1.8$, so $x = 180 \div 7 = 25.7$ (approximately), which is closest to 26%. (201, 204)

**14.** Choice A is correct.

coin × number = total value

|  | ¢/coin | coins | cents |
|---|---|---|---|
| pennies | 1 | $p$ | $p$ |
| nickels | 5 | $n$ | $5n$ |
| dimes | 10 | $d$ | $10d$ |
| quarters | 25 | $q$ | $25q$ |

Let $p$ = number of pennies

$n$ = number of nickels

$d$ = number of dimes

$q$ = number of quarters

Total number of coins = $p + n + d + q = 12$.

Total value = $p + 5n + 10d + 25q = 145$.

Now, if $q = 1$, then $p + n + d = 11$, $p + 5n + 10d = 120$. But in this case, the greatest possible value of the other eleven coins would be the value of eleven dimes, or 110 cents, which falls short of the amount necessary to give a total of 145 cents for the twelve coins put together. Therefore, Robert cannot have only one quarter. (201, 205)

**15.** Choice B is correct.

rate × time = money

|  | ¢/wk | weeks | cents |
|---|---|---|---|
| Jim | 120 | $w$ | $120w$ |
| Stan | 175 | $w$ | $175w$ |
| together | 295 | $w$ | $295w$ |

(25¢/day = $1.75/week)

Let $w$ = the number of weeks they save.

Total money = $295w = 2,360$.

Therefore, $w = 2,360 \div 295 = 8$.

So, they must save for 8 weeks. (201, 205)

**16.** Choice B is correct.

rate × time = pay

|  | ¢/hr | hours | ¢ |
|---|---|---|---|
| first job | 200 | 1 | 200 |
|  | 250 | 2 | 500 |
|  | 300 | $x$ | $300x$ |
| second job | 275 | $y$ | $275y$ |

Let $x$ = hours at $3.00.

Let $y$ = hours at $2.75.

Total pay first job = $200 + 500 + 300x = 1,500$, so $x = 2\frac{2}{3}$.

Total time first job = $1 + 2 + 2\frac{2}{3} = 5\frac{2}{3}$.

Total pay second job = $275y = 1500$, so $y = 5\frac{5}{11}$.

Total time second job = $5\frac{5}{11}$.

$\frac{2}{3}$ hour = 40 minutes

$\frac{5}{11}$ hour = 27.2727 . . . minutes (less than $\frac{2}{3}$ hour).

Thus, the first job will take him longer by less than 15 minutes.

**17.** Choice B is correct.

rate × time = work

|  | envelopes/min | min | envelopes |
|---|---|---|---|
| Robert | 40 | $t$ | $40t$ |
| Paul | 30 | $t$ | $30t$ |
| both | 70 | $t$ | $70t$ |

Let $t$ = time to seal 350 envelopes.

Paul's rate is 30 envelopes/minute, as shown by the proportion:

$$\text{rate} = \frac{40 \text{ envelopes}}{80 \text{ seconds}} = \frac{30 \text{ envelopes}}{60 \text{ seconds}}$$

Total work = $70t = 350$, so $t = 5$ minutes. (201, 203)

**18.** Choice C is correct.

rate × time = distance

|  | mi/hr | hr | miles |
|---|---|---|---|
| A to B | 50 | $t$ | $50t$ |
| B to A | 30 | $t$ | $30t$ |

Let $t$ = time to meet.

Total distance traveled by two trains together equals $50t + 30t = 80t = 400$ miles, so $t = 5$ hrs. (201, 202)

**19. Choice D is correct.**

|  | rate × | time | = amount of water |
|---|---|---|---|
|  | cu. ft/m | min | cu. ft. |
| 2 faucets | 4 | $t$ | 20 |

Let $t$ = time to fill the tub.

Volume of tub = $2' \times 2' \times 5'$ = 20 cu. ft.

Rate = 2 × rate of each faucet = 2 × 2 cu. ft./min. = 4 cu. ft./min.

Therefore, $t$ = 5 minutes.  (201, 203)

**20. Choice C is correct.**

|  | concentration × | weight | = amount of barium chloride |
|---|---|---|---|
|  | % | grams | grams |
| original | 30% | $x$ | $0.30x$ |
| water | 0% | 10 | 0 |
| new | 20% | $10 + x$ | $0.30x$ |

Let $x$ = number of grams of original solution.

Total weight and amounts of barium chloride may be added by column.

$(20\%) \times (10 + x) = 0.30x$, so $10 + x = 1.50x$, $x = 20$.  (201, 204)

**21. Choice D is correct.**

|  | coin × | number | = value |
|---|---|---|---|
|  | ¢/coin | coins | cents |
| nickels | 5 | $n$ | $5n$ |
| dimes | 10 | $2n$ | $20n$ |
| quarters | 25 | $\frac{n}{2}$ | $\frac{25n}{2}$ |

Let $n$ = number of nickels.

Total value = $5n + 20n + \frac{25n}{2} = \left(37\frac{1}{2}\right)n$ = 30,000.

Thus, $n = 30{,}000 \div 37\frac{1}{2} = 800$.

The number of quarters is then $\frac{n}{2} = \frac{800}{2} = 400$.  (201, 205)

**22. Choice A is correct.**

|  | rate × | number | = profit |
|---|---|---|---|
|  | ¢/pen | pens | cents |
| high-price | 120 | 30 | 3600 |
| low-price | 15 | 250 | 3750 |

Subtracting 3,600¢ from 3,750¢, we get 150¢.

Thus, the cheaper pen yields a profit of 150¢, or $1.50, more per month than the more expensive one.  (201, 205)

**23. Choice A is correct.**

|  | price × | area | = cost |
|---|---|---|---|
|  | $/sq yd | sq yd | dollars |
|  | 2.50 | 48 | 120 |

Area must be expressed in square yards; $18' = 6$ yds, and $24' = 8$ yds, so $18' \times 24' = 6$ yds × 8 yds = 48 sq yds. The cost would then be $2.50 × 48 = $120.00.  (201, 205)

**24. Choice B is correct.**

|  | rate × | time | = distance |
|---|---|---|---|
|  | ft/sec | sec | feet |
| Tom | $r$ | 27 | 100 |
| Bill | $s$ | 27 | 90 |
| Bill | $s$ | $t$ | 100 |

Let $r$ = Tom's rate.

Let $s$ = Bill's rate.

Let $t$ = Bill's time to finish the race.

$27r = 100$, so $r = \frac{100}{27}$;

$27s = 90$, so $s = \frac{90}{27} = \frac{10}{3}$;

$st = 100$, and $s = \frac{10}{3}$, so $\frac{10t}{3} = 100$, thus $t = 30$.  (201, 202)

**25.** Choice E is correct. This is a rate problem in which the fundamental relationship is rate × time × number of men = cost. The rate is in dollars/man-days. Thus, our chart looks like this:

rate × time × number = cost

|         | $/man-days | days | men | $ |
|---------|------------|------|-----|-----|
| **1st trip** | $r$ | 3 | 4 | $12r$ |
| **2nd trip** | $r$ | 14 | 2 | $28r$ |

The cost of the first trip is $24, so $12r = 24$ and $r = 2$.

The cost of the second trip is $28r$, or $56.

(201, 205)

**26.** Choice C is correct.

rate × time = distance

| blocks/min. | min | blocks |
|-------------|-----|--------|
| $\frac{2}{3}$ | $t$ | 15 |

Let $t$ = time to walk to work.

2 miles/hr = 2 (20 blocks)/(60 min) = $\frac{2}{3}$ blocks/minute.

$t = 15 \div \frac{2}{3} = 22\frac{1}{2}$ minutes.　　(201, 202)

**27.** Choice C is correct.

rate × time = distance

|      | mi/hr | hrs | miles |
|------|-------|-----|-------|
| **down** | $r + 3$ | $h$ | $h(r + 3)$ |
| **up** | $r - 3$ | $2h$ | $2h(r - 3)$ |

Let $h$ = time to travel downstream.

Let $r$ = speed of the boat in still water.

Since the two trips cover the same distance, we can write the equation: $h(r + 3) = 2h(r - 3)$. Dividing by $h$, $r + 3 = 2r - 6$, so $r = 9$.　　(201, 202)

**28.** Choice C is correct. We could treat this as a regular distance problem and make up a table that would solve it, but there is an easier way here, if we consider the quantity representing the distance between the boys. This distance starts at zero and increases at the rate of 18 miles per hour. Thus, in 10 minutes, or $\frac{1}{6}$ hour, they will be 3 miles apart.

$(\frac{1}{6}$ hr $\times 18 \frac{\text{mi}}{\text{hr}} = 3$ mi$)$.　　(201, 202)

**29.** Choice E is correct.

rate × time = work

|   | bolts/min | min | bolts |
|---|-----------|-----|-------|
| **A** | 40 | $1\frac{1}{2}$ | 60 |
| **B** | 30 | $t$ | 240 |

Let $t$ = time B works.

Since A produces only 60 out of 300 that must be produced, B must produce 240; then, $30t = 240$, so $t = 8$.

Total time = $t + 1\frac{1}{2} = 8 + 1\frac{1}{2} = 9\frac{1}{2}$.　　(201, 203)

**30.** Choice B is correct.

concentration × volume = amount of salt

|        | % | pints | "pints" of salt* |
|--------|---|-------|------------------|
| **15%** | 15 | 10 | 1.5 |
| **10%** | 10 | 15 | 1.5 |
| **Total** | $x$ | 25 | 3.0 |

*One "pint" of salt actually represents a weight of salt equal to the weight of one pint of water.

Let $x$ = concentration of resulting solution.

$(x\%)(25) = 3.0$, so $x = 300 \div 25 = 12$.　　(201, 204)

**31.** Choice C is correct.

rate × time = pay (net)

|       | $/day | days | $ |
|-------|-------|------|-----|
| **Jeff** | 2 | $d$ | $2d$ |
| **Pete** | 3 | $d$ | $3d$ |
| **total** | 5 | $d$ | $5d$ |

(Net pay = pay − expenses.)

Let $d$ = the number of days it takes to save.

Total net pay = $150.00, so $150 = 5d$, thus $d = 30$.

Do not make the mistake of using 5 and 10 as the rates!　　(201, 205)

**32.** Choice B is correct.

rate $\times$ time = distance

|        | mi/hr | hours | miles |
|--------|-------|-------|-------|
| plane A | 600 | $h$ | 800 |
| plane B | 0 | 1 | 0 |
| plane B | 800 | $t$ | 800 |

Let $h$ = time for trip at 600 mph − waiting time before second flight.

Let $t$ = time for trip at 800 mph.

Plane A: $600h = 800$, so $h = \frac{800}{600} = 1\frac{1}{3}$ hours = 1 hour, 20 minutes.

Plane B: $800t = 800$, so $t = 1$.

Total time for plane A = 1 hour, 20 minutes.

Total time for plane B = 1 hour + 1 hour = 2 hours.

Thus, plane A arrives before plane B by 40 minutes (less than an hour). (201, 202)

**33.** Choice E is correct.

coin $\times$ number = value

|         | ¢/coin | coins | cents |
|---------|--------|-------|-------|
| Peter   | 5      | $n$   | $5n$  |
| Peter   | 10     | $d$   | $10d$ |
| Charlie | 5      | $2d$  | $10d$ |
| Charlie | 10     | $n$   | $10n$ |

Let $n$ = number of Peter's nickels.

Let $d$ = number of Peter's dimes.

Total value of coins = $5n + 10d + 10d + 10n = 15n + 20d$.

Thus, $15n + 20d = 250$. This has many different solutions, each of which is possible (e.g., $n = 2$, $d = 11$, or $n = 6$, $d = 8$, etc.). (201, 205)

**34.** Choice A is correct.

rate $\times$ time = distance

|               | mi/hr | hours | miles |
|---------------|-------|-------|-------|
| constant rate | 40    | $h$   | 120   |
| two rates     | 50    | $m$   | 60    |
|               | 30    | $n$   | 60    |

Let $h$ = time to travel 120 miles at the constant rate.

Let $m$ = time to travel 60 miles at 50 mi/hr.

Let $n$ = time to travel 60 miles at 30 mi/hr.

Forming the equations for $h$, $m$, and $n$, and solving, we get:

$$40h = 120; h = \frac{120}{40}; h = 3$$

$$50m = 60; m = \frac{60}{50}; m = 1.2$$

$$30n = 60; n = \frac{60}{30}; n = 2$$

Total time with constant rate = $h$ = 3 hours.

Total time with changing rate = $m + n = 3.2$ hours.

Thus, the constant rate is faster by 0.2 hours, or 12 minutes. (201, 202)

**35.** Choice D is correct.

rate $\times$ time = distance

|           | mi/hr | hours | miles |
|-----------|-------|-------|-------|
| walking   | 2     | $h$   | 10    |
| bicycling | 10    | $t$   | 10    |

Let $h$ = time to walk.

Let $t$ = time to bicycle.

Forming equations: $2h = 10$, so $h = 5$; and $10t = 10$, so $t = 1$.

Total time = $h + t = 5 + 1 = 6$. (201, 202)

**36.** Choice C is correct.

rate $\times$ time = distance

| mi/hr | hours | miles |
|-------|-------|-------|
| $x$   | $Q$   | $P$   |
| $x$   | $y$   | $R$   |

Let $x$ = rate of traveling $Q$ miles.

Let $y$ = time to travel $R$ miles.

$Qx = P$, so $x = \frac{P}{Q}$.

$xy = \left(\frac{P}{Q}\right) y = R$, so $y = \frac{RQ}{P}$ hours = time to travel $R$ miles. (201, 202)

**37.** Choice D is correct.

**rate × time = distance**

| mi/hr | hours | miles |
|---|---|---|
| $r$ | $\frac{1}{300}$ | $\frac{75}{5280}$ |

Let $r$ = rate of swimming.

75 feet = $75(\frac{1}{5,280}$ mile$) = \frac{75}{5,280}$ mile

12 seconds = $12(\frac{1}{3,600}$ hour$) = \frac{1}{300}$ hour

$r = \frac{75}{5,280} \div \frac{1}{300} = \frac{22,500}{5,280} = 4.3$ (approximately)

= 4 mi/hr (approximately). (201, 202)

**38.** Choice B is correct.

**price × amount = value**

| | ¢/lb | lbs. | cents |
|---|---|---|---|
| $1.20 nuts | 120 | $x$ | $20x$ |
| $0.90 | 90 | 2 | 180 |
| mixture | 100 | $x + 2$ | $180 + 120x$ |

Let $x$ = pounds of $1.20 mixture.

Total value of mixture = $100(x + 2) = 180 + 120x$. $100x + 200 = 180 + 120x$, so $x = 1$ pound.

(201, 204)

**39.** Choice B is correct.

**rate × time = loss**

| hr/hr | hrs | hrs |
|---|---|---|
| $\frac{2}{3}$ | $t$ | 12 |

(Loss is the amount by which the clock time differs from real time.)

Let $t =$ hours to register the correct time.

If the clock registers only 20 minutes each hour, it loses 40 minutes, or $\frac{2}{3}$ hour each hour. The clock will register the correct time only if it has lost some multiple of 12 hours. The first time this can occur is after it has lost 12 hours. $\left(\frac{2}{3}\right) t = 12$, so $t = 18$ hours. (201)

**40.** Choice A is correct.

**rate × time = distance**

| | mi/hr | hrs | miles |
|---|---|---|---|
| | $q$ | $p$ | $pq$ |
| | $s$ | $r$ | $rs$ |
| total | $x$ | $p + r$ | $pq + rs$ |

Let $x$ = average speed.

We may add times of travel at the two rates, and also add the distances. Then, $x(p + r) = pq + rs$; thus, $x = \frac{pq + r}{p + r}$. (201, 202)

**41.** Choice A is correct.

**rate × time = work**

| | ft/hr | hrs | feet |
|---|---|---|---|
| Joe | 35 | $x$ | $35x$ |
| Walt | 25 | $x$ | $25x$ |
| Both | 60 | $x$ | $60x$ |

Let $x$ = the time the job takes.

Since they are working together, we add their rates and the amount of work they do. Thus, $60x = 150$, so $x = 2.5$ (hours) = 150 minutes. (201, 203)

**42.** Choice B is correct.

**rate × time = distance**

| | mi/hr | hrs | miles |
|---|---|---|---|
| first $\frac{1}{2}$ hour | 20 | $\frac{1}{2}$ | 10 |
| second $\frac{1}{2}$ hour | 30 | $\frac{1}{2}$ | 15 |
| total | | $x$ | 1 | 25 |

Let $x$ = average speed.

We add the times and distances; then, using the rate formula, $(x)(1) = 25$, so $x = 25$ mi/hr. (201, 202)

**43.** Choice C is correct.

$$\text{rate} \times \text{time} = \text{distance}$$

|  | mi/hr | hours | miles |
|---|---|---|---|
| **Sol** | 200 | $t$ | $200t$ |
| **Robert** | 400 | $t$ | $400t$ |

Let $t$ = time from simultaneous departure to meeting.

Sol's time is equal to Robert's time because they leave at the same time and then they meet. Their combined distance is 3,000 miles, so $200t + 400t = 3{,}000$, or $t = 5$ hours. (201, 202)

**44.** Choice E is correct.

$$\text{coin} \times \text{number} = \text{value}$$

|  | ¢/coin | coins | ¢ |
|---|---|---|---|
| **pennies** | 1 | $P$ | $P$ |
| **nickels** | 5 | $n$ | $5n$ |
| **dimes** | 10 | $d$ | $10d$ |
| **quarters** | 25 | $q$ | $25q$ |

Let $p$ = number of pennies.
Let $n$ = number of nickels.
Let $d$ = number of dimes.
Let $q$ = number of quarters.

Adding the numbers of coins and their values, we get $p + n + d + q = 7$, and $p + 5n + 10d + 25q = 100$. These equations are satisfied by several values of $p$, $n$, $d$, and $q$. For example, $p = 0$, $n = 0$, $d = 5$, $q = 2$ satisfies the equation, as does $p = 0$, $n = 3$, $d = 1$, $q = 3$, and other combinations.

Thus, the number of dimes is not determined. (201, 205)

**45.** Choice A is correct.

$$\text{am't of} \qquad \text{amount of}$$
$$\text{concentration} \times \text{solution} = \text{alcohol}$$

|  | % | qts | qts |
|---|---|---|---|
| **pure alcohol** | 100% | 2 | 2 |
| **solution** | 30% | $x$ | $0.30x$ |
| **mixture** | 40% | $2 + x$ | $2 + 0.30x$ |

Let $x$ = qts of original solution

Amounts of solution and of alcohol may be added.

$(40\%)(2 + x) = 2 + 0.30x$; so $0.8 + 0.4x = 2.0 + 0.30x$; thus, $x = 12$. (201, 204)

**46.** Choice C is correct.

$$\text{rate} \times \text{time} = \text{cost}$$

|  | ¢/kwh | kwh | ¢ |
|---|---|---|---|
| **first 1000 kwh** | 8¢ | $t$ | $8t$ |

(time expressed in kilowatt-hours, or kwh)

Let $t$ = number of kwh.

This problem must be broken up into two different parts: (1) finding the total power or the total number of kilowatt-hours (kwh) used, and (2) calculating the charge for that amount. (1) Total power used, $t = (900w)(5 \text{ hr}) + (100w)(25 \text{ hr}) + (5w)(400 \text{ hr}) = (4{,}500 + 2{,}500 + 2{,}000)$ watt-hours = 9,000 watt-hours. One thousand watt-hours equals one kilowatt-hour. Thus, $t = 9$ kilowatt-hours, so that the charge is $(8¢)(9) = 72¢$. (201, 205)

**47.** Choice C is correct.

$$\text{rate} \times \text{amount} = \text{cost}$$

|  | ¢/in | in | ¢ |
|---|---|---|---|
| **1 yard** | $r$ | 36 | 30 |
| **96 inches** | $r$ | 96 | $96r$ |

Let $r$ = cost per inch of cloth.

From the table, $r \times 36 \text{ in} = 30¢$; $r = \dfrac{30¢}{36 \text{ in}} = \dfrac{5¢}{6 \text{ in}}$.

Thus, $96r = 96 \dfrac{5}{6} = 80¢$. (201, 205)

**48.** Choice A is correct.

$$\text{rate} \times \text{time} = \text{distance}$$

|  | mi/hr | hrs | miles |
|---|---|---|---|
| **trip** | 50 | 6 | 300 |
| **return** | $r$ | $7\frac{1}{2}$ | 300 |
| **total** | $s$ | $13\frac{1}{2}$ | 600 |

Let $r$ = rate for return.

Let $s$ = average overall rate.

$(13\frac{1}{2})(s) = 600$; thus, $s = 600 \div 13\frac{1}{2} = 44.4$ (approximately). (201, 202)

**49.** Choice E is correct.

|  | rate × | principal = | interest |
|---|---|---|---|
|  | %/year | $ | $/year |
| **first year** | 5 | 100 | 5 |
| **second year** | 5 | 105 | 5.25 |

Interest first year equals rate × principal = 5% × $100 = $5.

New principal = $105.00.

Interest second year = rate × new principal = 5% × $105 = $5.25.

Final principal = $105.00 + $5.25 = $110.25.

(201, 205)

**50.** Choice C is correct.

|  | rate × | time = | amount |
|---|---|---|---|
|  | gal/min | min | gallons |
| **in** | 3 | $x$ | $3x$ |
| **out** | $1\frac{1}{2}$ | $x$ | $1\frac{1}{2}x$ |
| **net** | $1\frac{1}{2}$ | $x$ | $1\frac{1}{2}x$ |

(Net = in − out.)

Let $x$ = time to fill the tub completely.

Since only 9 gallons are needed (there are already 3 in the tub), we have $1\frac{1}{2}x = 9$, so $x = 6$. (201)

# MATH REFRESHER
## SESSION 3

# Area, Perimeter, and
# Volume Problems

## Area, Perimeter, and Volume

**301.** *Formula Problems.* Here, you are given certain data about one or more geometric figures, and you are asked to supply some missing information. To solve this type of problem, follow this procedure:

**STEP 1.** If you are not given a diagram, draw your own; this may make the answer readily apparent or may suggest the best way to solve the problem. You should try to make your diagram as accurate as possible, but *do not waste time perfecting your diagram.*

**STEP 2.** Determine the formula that relates to the quantities involved in your problem. In many cases it will be helpful to set up tables containing the various data. (See Sections 303–316.)

**STEP 3.** Substitute the given information for the unknown quantities in your formulas to get the desired answer.

When doing volume, area, and perimeter problems, keep this hint in mind: Often the solutions to such problems can be expressed as the sum of the areas *or* volumes *or* perimeters of simpler figures. In such cases do not hesitate to break down your original figure into simpler parts.

---

**In doing problems involving the following figures, these approximations and facts will be useful:**

$\sqrt{2}$ is approximately 1.4.

$\sin 45° = \dfrac{\sqrt{2}}{2}$ which is approximately 0.71.

$\sqrt{3}$ is approximately 1.7.

$\sqrt{10}$ is approximately 3.16.

$\sin 60° = \dfrac{\sqrt{3}}{2}$ which is approximately 0.87.

$\pi$ is approximately $\dfrac{22}{7}$ or 3.14.

$\sin 30° = \dfrac{1}{2}$

**Example:** The following figure contains a square, a right triangle, and a semicircle. If *ED = CD* and the length of *CD* is 1 unit, find the area of the entire figure.

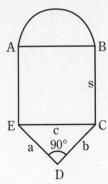

*Solution:* To calculate the area of the entire figure, we calculate the areas of the triangle, square, and semicircle and then add these together. In a right triangle, the area is $\frac{1}{2}ab$ where *a* and *b* are the sides of the triangle. In this case we will call side *ED, a* and side *CD, b. ED = CD* = 1, so the area of the triangle is $\frac{1}{2}$ (1)(1), or $\frac{1}{2}$.

The area of a square is $s^2$, where *s* is a side. We see that the side *EC* of the square is the hypotenuse of the right triangle. We can calculate this length by using the formula $c^2 = a^2 + b^2$ where *a = b* = 1; then we can see that $c = \sqrt{2}$. Thus, in this case, $s = \sqrt{2}$ so the area of the square is $(\sqrt{2})^2 = 2$.

*AB* is the diameter of the semicircle, so $\frac{1}{2}$ *AB* is the radius. Since all sides of a square are equal, $AB = \sqrt{2}$, and the radius is $\frac{1}{2}\sqrt{2}$. Further, the area of a semicircle is $\frac{1}{2}\pi r^2$ where *r* is the radius, so the area of this semicircle is $\frac{1}{2}\pi\left(\frac{1}{2}\sqrt{2}\right)^2 = \frac{1}{4}\pi$.

The total area of the whole figure is equal to the area of the triangle plus the area of the square plus the area of the semicircle $= \frac{1}{2} + 2 + \frac{1}{4}\pi = 2\frac{1}{2} + \frac{1}{4}\pi$.

**Example:** If water flows into a rectangular tank with dimensions of 12 inches, 18 inches, and 30 inches at the rate of 0.25 cubic feet per minute, how long will it take to fill the tank?

*Solution:* This problem is really a combination of a rate problem and a volume problem. First we must calculate the volume, and then we must substitute in a rate equation to get our final answer. The formula for the volume of a rectangular solid is *V = lwh* where *l, w,* and *h* are the length, width, and height, respectively. We must multiply the three dimensions of the tank to get the volume. However, if we look ahead to the second part of the problem, we see that we want the volume in cubic *feet;* therefore we convert 12 inches, 18 inches, and 30 inches to 1 foot, 1.5 feet, and 2.5 feet, respectively. Multiplying gives us a volume of 3.75 cubic feet. Now substituting in the equation: rate × time = volume, we get 0.25 × time = 3.75; time = $\frac{3.75}{0.25}$; thus, the time is 15 minutes.

**302.** *Comparison problems.* Here you are asked to identify the largest, or smallest, of a group of figures, or to place them in ascending or descending order of size. The following procedure is the most efficient one:

**STEP 1.** Always diagram each figure before you come to any conclusions. Whenever possible, try to include two or more of the figures in the same diagram, so that their relative sizes are most readily apparent.

**STEP 2.** If you have not already determined the correct answer, then (and only then) determine the size of the figures (as you would have done in Section 301) and compare the results.

(Note that even if Step 2 is necessary, Step 1 should eliminate most of the possible choices, leaving only a few formula calculations to be done.)

**Example:** Which of the following is the greatest in length?

(A) The perimeter of a square with a side of 4 inches.
(B) The perimeter of an isosceles right triangle whose equal sides are 8 inches each.
(C) The circumference of a circle with a diameter of $4\sqrt{2}$ inches.
(D) The perimeter of a pentagon whose sides are all equal to 3 inches.
(E) The perimeter of a semicircle with a radius of 5 inches.

*Solution:* Diagramming the five figures mentioned, we obtain the following illustration:

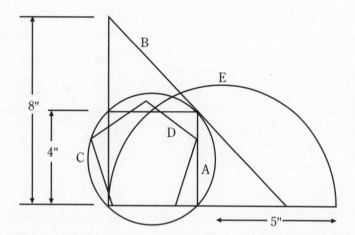

From the diagram, it is apparent that the square and the pentagon are both smaller than the circle. Further observation should show that the circle is smaller than the triangle. Thus we need only to see which is larger—the semicircle or the triangle. The perimeter of the semicircle is found by the formula: $P = 2r + \pi r$ (the sum of the diameter and the semicircular arc, where $r$ is the radius). Since $r$ in this case is 5 inches, the perimeter is approximately $10 + (3.14)5$, or 25.7 inches. The formula for the perimeter of a triangle is the sum of the sides. In this case, two of the sides are 8 inches and the third side can be found by using the relationship $c^2 = a^2 + b^2$, where $a$ and $b$ are the sides of a right triangle, and $c$ is the hypotenuse. Since in our problem $a = b = 8$ inches, $c = \sqrt{8^2 + 8^2} = \sqrt{128} = \sqrt{2(64)} = 8\sqrt{2}$, which is the third side of the triangle. The perimeter is $8 + 8 + 8\sqrt{2}$, which is $16 + 8\sqrt{2}$. This is approximately equal to $16 + 8(1.4)$ or 27.2, so the triangle is the largest of the figures.

---

### FORMULAS USED IN AREA, PERIMETER, AND VOLUME PROBLEMS

**It is important that you know as many of these formulas as possible. Problems using these formulas appear frequently on tests of all kinds. You should not need to refer to this table when you do problems. Learn these formulas before you go any further.**

---

**303.** *Square.* The area of a square is the square of one of its sides. Thus, if $A$ represents the area, and $s$ represents the length of a side, $A = s^2$. The area of a square is also one-half of the square of its diagonal and may be written as $A = \frac{1}{2}d^2$, where $d$ represents the length of a diagonal. The perimeter of a square is 4 times the length of one of its sides, or $4s$.

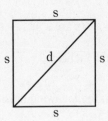

**Square**

| quantity | formula |
|---|---|
| area | $A = s^2$<br>$A = \frac{1}{2}d^2$ |
| perimeter | $P = 4s$ |

**304.** *Rectangle.* Let $a$ and $b$ represent the length of two adjacent sides of a rectangle, and let $A$ represent the area. Then the area of a rectangle is the product of the two adjacent sides. $A = ab$. The perimeter, $P$, is the sum of twice one side and twice the adjacent side. $P = 2a + 2b$.

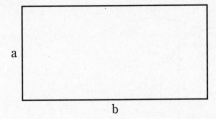

**Rectangle**

| quantity | formula |
|---|---|
| area | $A = ab$ |
| perimeter | $P = 2a + 2b$ |

**305.** *Parallelogram.* The area of a parallelogram is the product of a side and the altitude, $h$, to that side. $A = bh$ (in this case the altitude to side $b$). The area can also be expressed as the product of two adjacent sides and the sine of the included angle: $A = ab \sin c$, where $c$ is the angle included between side $a$ and side $b$. The perimeter is the sum of twice one side and twice the adjacent side. $P = 2a + 2b$. Let $a$ and $b$ represent the length of 2 adjacent sides of a parallelogram. Then, $c$ is the included angle. But $A$ represents its area, $P$ its perimeter, and $h$ the altitude to one of its sides.

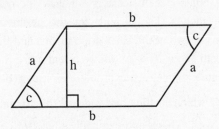

**Parallelogram**

| quantity | formula |
|---|---|
| area | $A = bh$<br>$A = ab \sin C$ |
| perimeter | $P = 2a + 2b$ |

**306.** *Triangle.* The area of any triangle is one-half of the product of any side and the altitude to that side. $A = \frac{1}{2}bh$, where $b$ is a side, and $h$ the altitude to that side. The area may be written also as one-half of the product of any two adjacent sides and the sine of the included angle. $A = \frac{1}{2}ab \sin C$, where $A$ is the area, $a$ and $b$ are two adjacent sides, and $C$ is the included angle. The perimeter of a triangle is the sum of the sides of the triangle. $P = a + b + c$, where $P$ is the perimeter, and $c$ is the third side.

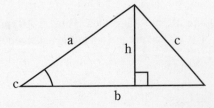

**Triangle**

| quantity | formula |
|---|---|
| area | $A = \frac{1}{2}bh$<br>$A = \frac{1}{2}ab \sin C$ |
| perimeter | $P = a + b + c$ |

**307.** *Right triangle.* The area of a right triangle is one-half of the product of the two sides adjacent to the right angle. $A = \frac{1}{2}ab$, where $A$ is the area, and $a$ and $b$ are the adjacent sides. The perimeter is the sum of the sides. $P = a + b + c$, where $c$ is the third side, or hypotenuse.

### Right Triangle

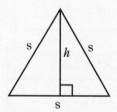

| quantity | formula |
|---|---|
| area | $A = \frac{1}{2}ab$ |
| perimeter | $P = a + b + c$ |
| hypotenuse | $c^2 = a^2 + b^2$ |

**308.** *Equilateral triangle.* The area of an equilateral triangle is one-fourth the product of a side squared and $\sqrt{3}$. $A = \frac{1}{4}s^2\sqrt{3}$, where $A$ is the area, and $s$ is one of the equal sides. The perimeter of an equilateral triangle is 3 times one side. $P = 3s$, where $P$ is the perimeter.

### Equilateral Triangle

| quantity | formula |
|---|---|
| area | $A = \frac{1}{4}s^2\sqrt{3}$ |
| perimeter | $P = 3s$ |
| altitude | $h = \frac{1}{2}s\sqrt{3}$ |

> **NOTE: The equilateral triangle and the right triangle are special cases of the triangle, and any law that applies to the triangle applies to both the right triangle and to the equilateral triangle.**

**309.** *Trapezoid.* The area of a trapezoid is one-half of the product of the altitude and the sum of the bases. $A = \frac{1}{2}h(B + b)$, where $A$ is the area, $B$ and $b$ are the bases, and $h$ is their altitude. The perimeter is the sum of the 4 sides. $P = B + b + c + d$, where $P$ is the perimeter, and $c$ and $d$ are the other 2 sides.

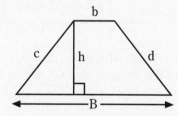

### Trapezoid

| quantity | formula |
|---|---|
| area | $A = \frac{1}{2}h(B + b)$ |
| perimeter | $P = B + b + c + d$ |

**310.** *Circle*. The area of a circle is $\pi$ (pi) times the square of the radius. $A = \pi r^2$, where $A$ is the area, and $r$ is the radius. The circumference is pi times the diameter or pi times twice the radius. $C = \pi d = 2\pi r$, where $C$ is the circumference, $d$ the diameter, and $r$ the radius.

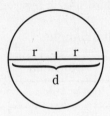

### Circle

| quantity | formula |
|---|---|
| area | $A = \pi r^2$ |
| circumference | $C = \pi d = 2\pi r$ |

**311.** *Semicircle*. The area of a semicircle is one-half pi times the square of the radius.

$A = \frac{1}{2}\pi r^2$, where $A$ is the area, and $r$ is the radius. The length of the curved portion of the semicircle is one-half pi times the diameter or pi times the radius. $C = \frac{1}{2}\pi d = \pi r$, where $C$ is the circumference, $d$ is the diameter, and $r$ is the radius. The perimeter of a semicircle is equal to the circumference plus the length of the diameter. $P = C + d = \frac{1}{2}\pi d + d$, where $P$ is the perimeter.

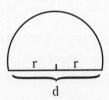

### Semicircle

| quantity | formula |
|---|---|
| area | $A = \frac{1}{2}\pi r^2$ |
| length | $L = \frac{1}{2}\pi d = \pi r$ |
| perimeter | $P = d(\frac{1}{2}\pi + 1)$ |

**312.** *Rectangular solid*. The volume of a rectangular solid is the product of the length, width, and height. $V = lwh$, where $V$ is the volume, $l$ is the length, $w$ is the width, and $h$ is the height. The volume is also the product of the area of one side and the altitude to that side. $V = Bh$, where $B$ is the area of its base and $h$ the altitude to that side. The surface area is the sum of the area of the six faces. $S = 2wh + 2hl + 2wl$, where $S$ is the surface area.

### Rectangular Solid

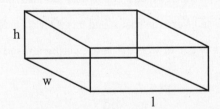

| quantity | formula |
|---|---|
| volume | $V = lwh$ <br> $V = Bh$ |
| surface area | $S = 2wh + 2hl + 2lw$ |

**313.** *Cube*. The volume of a cube is its edge cubed. $V = e^3$, where $V$ is the volume and $e$ is an edge. The surface area is the sum of the areas of the six faces. $S = 6e^2$, where $S$ is the surface area.

### Cube

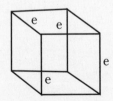

| quantity | formula |
|---|---|
| volume | $V = e^2$ |
| surface area | $S = 6e^2$ |

**314.** *Cylinder.* The volume of a cylinder is the area of the base times the height. $V = Bh$, where $V$ is the volume, $B$ is the area of the base, and $h$ is the height. Note that the area of the base is the area of the circle $= \pi r^2$, where $r$ is the radius of a base. The surface area not including the bases is the circumference of the base times the height. $S_1 = Ch = 2\pi rh$, where $S_1$ is the surface area without the bases, $C$ the circumference, and $h$ the height. The area of the bases $= 2\pi r^2$. Thus, the area of the cylinder, including the bases, $S_2 = 2\pi rh + 2\pi r^2 = 2\pi r(h + r)$.

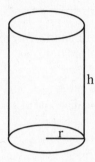

### Cylinder

| quantity | formula |
|---|---|
| volume | $V = Bh$ <br> $V = \pi r^2 h$ |
| surface area | $S_1 = 2\pi rh$ (without bases) <br> $S_2 = 2\pi r\,(h + r)$ (with bases) |

**315.** *Sphere.* The volume of a sphere is four-thirds $\pi$ times the cube of the radius. $V = \frac{4}{3}\pi r^3$, where $V$ is the volume and $r$ is the radius. The surface area is $4\pi$ times the square of the radius. $S = 4\pi r^2$, where $S$ is the surface area.

### Sphere

| quantity | formula |
|---|---|
| volume | $V = \frac{4}{3}\pi r^3$ |
| surface area | $S = 4\pi r^2$ |

**316.** *Hemisphere.* The volume of a hemisphere is two-thirds $\pi$ times the cube of the radius. $V = \frac{2}{3}\pi r^3$ where $V$ is the volume and $r$ is the radius. The surface area not including the area of the base is $2\pi$ times the square of the radius. $S_1 = 2\pi r^2$, where $S_1$ is the surface area without the base. The total surface area, including the base, is equal to the surface area without the base plus the area of the base. $S_2 = 2\pi r^2 + \pi r^2 = 3\pi r^2$, where $S_2$ is the surface area including the base.

### Hemisphere

| quantity | formula |
|---|---|
| volume | $V = \frac{2}{3}\pi r^3$ |
| surface area | $S_1 = 2\pi r^2$ (without bases) <br> $S_2 = 3\pi r^2$ (with bases) |

**317.** *Pythagorean Theorem.* The Pythagorean Theorem states a very important geometrical relationship. It states that in a right triangle, if $c$ is the hypotenuse (side opposite the right angle), and $a$ and $b$ are sides adjacent to the right angle, then $c^2 = a^2 + b^2$.

## Pythagorean Theorem

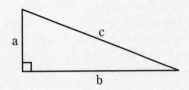

| quantity | formula |
|---|---|
| square of hypotenuse | $c^2 = a^2 + b^2$ |
| length of hypotenuse | $c = \sqrt{a^2 + b}$ |

Examples of right triangles are triangles with sides of 3, 4, and 5, or 5, 12, and 13. Any multiples of these numbers also form right triangles—for example, 6, 8, and 10, or 30, 40, 50.

Using the Pythagorean Theorem to find the diagonal of a square we get $d^2 = s^2 + s^2$ or $d^2 = 2s^2$, where $d$ is the diagonal and $s$ is a side. Therefore, $d = s\sqrt{2}$, or the diagonal of a square is $\sqrt{2}$ times the side.

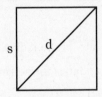

### Square

| quantity | formula |
|---|---|
| diagonal | $d = s\sqrt{2}$ |

**318.** Another important fact to remember in doing area problems is that areas of two similar (having the same shape) figures are in the same ratio as the squares of corresponding parts of the figures.

**Example:** Triangles $P$ and $Q$ are similar. Side $p$ of triangle $P$ is 2 inches, the area of triangle $P$ is 3 square inches, and corresponding side $q$ of triangle $Q$ is 4 inches. What is the area of triangle $Q$?

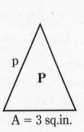

A = 3 sq.in.

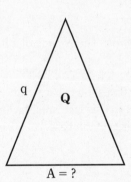

A = ?

*Solution:* The square of side $p$ is to the square of side $q$ as the area of $P$ is to the area of $Q$. If we call $x$ the area of triangle $Q$, then we get the following relationship: The square of side $p$ is to the square of side $q$ as the area of $P$ is to the area of $Q$, or

$$\frac{2^2}{4^2} = \frac{3}{x} \text{ or } \frac{4}{16} = \frac{3}{x}$$

Therefore, $x = 12$ square inches.

# Practice Test 3

## Area, Perimeter, and Volume Problems

Correct answers and solutions follow each test.

A B C D E
1.

1. Which of the following figures has the largest area?

   (A) a square with a perimeter of 12 inches
   (B) a circle with a radius of 3 inches
   (C) a right triangle with sides of 3, 4, and 5 inches
   (D) a rectangle with a diagonal of 5 inches
   (E) a regular hexagon with a perimeter of 18 inches

A B C D E
2.

2. If the area of the base of a rectangular solid is tripled, what is the percent increase in its volume?

   (A) 200%
   (B) 300%
   (C) 600%
   (D) 800%
   (E) 900%

A B C D E
3.

3. How many yards of a carpeting that is 26 inches wide will be needed to cover a floor that is 12′ by 13?

   (A) 22 yards
   (B) 24 yards
   (C) 27 yards
   (D) 36 yards
   (E) 46 yards

A B C D E
4.

4. If water flows into a rectangular tank at the rate of 6 cubic feet per minute, how long will it take to fill the tank, which measures $18'' \times 32'' \times 27''$?

   (A) less than one minute
   (B) less than two minutes, but not less than one minute
   (C) less than three minutes, but not less than two minutes
   (D) less than four minutes, but not less than three minutes
   (E) four minutes or more

A B C D E
5.

5. The ratio of the area of a circle to the radius of the circle is

   (A) $\pi$
   (B) $2\pi$
   (C) $\pi^2$
   (D) $4\pi^2$
   (E) not determinable

A B C D E
6.

6. Which of the following figures has the smallest perimeter or circumference?

   (A) a circle with a diameter of 2 feet
   (B) a square with a diagonal of 2 feet
   (C) a rectangle with sides of 6 inches and 4 feet
   (D) a pentagon with each side equal to 16 inches
   (E) a hexagon with each side equal to 14 inches

**7.**  A B C D E

7. In the figure shown, *DE* is parallel to *BC*. If the area of triangle *ADE* is half that of trapezoid *DECB*, what is the ratio of *AE* to *AC*?

(A) $1 : 2$
(B) $1 : \sqrt{2}$
(C) $1 : 3$
(D) $1 : \sqrt{3}$
(E) $1 : \sqrt{3} - 1$

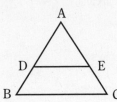

**8.**  A B C D E

8. At a speed of 22 revolutions per minute, how long will it take a wheel of radius 10″, rolling on its edge, to travel 10 feet? (Assume $\pi$ equals $\frac{22}{7}$, and express answer to nearest 0.1 second.)

(A) 0.2 seconds
(B) 0.4 seconds
(C) 5.2 seconds
(D) 6.3 seconds
(E) 7.4 seconds

**9.**  A B C D E

9. If the diagonal of a square is 16″ long, what is the area of the square?

(A) 64 square inches
(B) $64 \sqrt{2}$ square inches
(C) 128 square inches
(D) $128 \sqrt{2}$ square inches
(E) 256 square inches

**10.**  A B C D E

10. In the diagram shown, *ACDF* is a rectangle, and *GBHE* is a circle. If *CD* = 4 inches, and *AC* = 6 inches, what is the number of square inches in the shaded area?

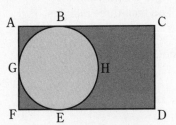

(A) $16 - 4\pi$ square inches
(B) $24 - 4\pi$ square inches
(C) $24 - 16\pi$ square inches
(D) $16 - 2\pi$ square inches
(E) $24 - 2\pi$ square inches

**11.** A B C D E

11. What is the area of an equilateral triangle with a side of 1 inch?

(A) 1 square inch

(B) $\frac{\sqrt{3}}{2}$ square inch

(C) $\frac{1}{2}$ square inch

(D) $\frac{\sqrt{3}}{4}$ square inch

(E) $\frac{1}{3}$ square inch

**12.** A B C D E

12. The measurements of a rectangle are 12 feet by 16 feet. What is the area of the smallest *circle* that can cover this rectangle entirely (so that no part of the rectangle is outside the circle)?

(A) 192 square feet
(B) 384 square feet
(C) $100\pi$ square feet
(D) $128\pi$ square feet
(E) $400\pi$ square feet

**13.** A B C D E

13. A man wishes to cover his floor with tiles, each one measuring $\frac{3}{4}$ inch by 2 inches. If his room is a rectangle, measuring 12 feet by 18 feet, how many such tiles will he need?

(A) 144
(B) 1,152
(C) 1,728
(D) 9,216
(E) 20,736

**14.** A B C D E

14. The volume of a sphere is equal to the volume of a cylinder. If the radius of the sphere is 4 miles and the radius of the cylinder is 8 miles, what is the height of the cylinder?

(A) 8 miles

(B) $\frac{4}{3}$ miles

(C) 4 miles

(D) $\frac{16}{3}$ miles

(E) 1 mile

**15.** A B C D E

15. A wheel travels 33 yards in 15 revolutions. What is its diameter? (Assume $\pi = \frac{22}{7}$.)

(A) 0.35 feet
(B) 0.70 feet
(C) 1.05 feet
(D) 1.40 feet
(E) 2.10 feet

**16.** A B C D E

16. If a rectangle with a perimeter of 48 inches is equal in area to a right triangle with legs of 12 inches and 24 inches, what is the rectangle's diagonal?

(A) 12 inches

(B) $12\sqrt{2}$ inches

(C) $12\sqrt{3}$ inches

(D) 24 inches

(E) The answer cannot be determined from the given information.

17.  A B C D E

17. What is the approximate area that remains after a circle $3\frac{1}{2}''$ in diameter is cut from a square piece of cloth with a side of 8″ ? (Use $\pi = \frac{22}{7}$ .)

(A) 25.5 square inches
(B) 54.4 square inches
(C) 56.8 square inches
(D) 142.1 square inches
(E) 284.2 square inches

18.  A B C D E

18. A container is shaped like a rectangular solid with sides of 3 inches, 3 inches, and 11 inches. What is its approximate capacity, if 1 gallon equals 231 cubic inches?

(A) 14 ounces
(B) 27 ounces
(C) 55 ounces
(D) 110 ounces
(E) 219 ounces

19.  A B C D E

19. The 20-inch-diameter wheels of one car travel at a rate of 24 revolutions per minute, while the 30-inch-diameter wheels of another car travel at a rate of 18 revolutions per minute. What is the ratio of the speed of the second car to that of the first?

(A) 1 : 1
(B) 3 : 2
(C) 4 : 3
(D) 6 : 5
(E) 9 : 8

20.  A B C D E

20. A circular garden twenty feet in diameter is surrounded by a path three feet wide. What is the area of the path?

(A) $9\pi$ square feet
(B) $51\pi$ square feet
(C) $60\pi$ square feet
(D) $69\pi$ square feet
(E) $90\pi$ square feet

21.  A B C D E

21. What is the area of a semicircle with a diameter of 16 inches?

(A) $32\pi$ square inches
(B) $64\pi$ square inches
(C) $128\pi$ square inches
(D) $256\pi$ square inches
(E) $512\pi$ square inches

22.  A B C D E

22. If the edges of a cube add up to 4 feet in length, what is the volume of the cube?

(A) 64 cubic inches
(B) 125 cubic inches
(C) 216 cubic inches
(D) 512 cubic inches
(E) None of these.

23.  A B C D E

23. The inside of a trough is shaped like a rectangular solid, 25 feet long, 6 inches wide, and filled with water to a depth of 35 inches. If we wish to raise the depth of the water to 38 inches, how much water must be let into the tank?

(A) $\frac{25}{96}$ cubic feet

(B) $\frac{25}{8}$ cubic feet

(C) $\frac{75}{2}$ cubic feet

(D) 225 cubic feet
(E) 450 cubic feet

**24.** A B C D E

**24.** If one gallon of water equals 231 cubic inches, approximately how much water will fill a cylindrical vase 7 inches in diameter and 10 inches high? (Assume $\pi = \frac{22}{7}$.)

(A) 1.7 gallons
(B) 2.1 gallons
(C) 3.3 gallons
(D) 5.3 gallons
(E) 6.7 gallons

**25.** A B C D E

**25.** Tiles of linoleum, measuring 8 inches × 8 inches, cost 9¢ apiece. At this rate, what will it cost a man to cover a floor with these tiles, if his floor measures 10 feet by 16 feet?

(A) $22.50
(B) $25.00
(C) $28.00
(D) $32.40
(E) $36.00

**26.** A B C D E

**26.** Which of the following figures has the largest area?

(A) a 3 : 4 : 5 triangle with a hypotenuse of 25 inches
(B) a circle with a diameter of 20 inches
(C) a square with a 20-inch diagonal
(D) a regular hexagon with a side equal to 10 inches
(E) a rectangle with sides of 10 inches and 30 inches

**27.** A B C D E

**27.** If the radius of the base of a cylinder is tripled, and its height is divided by three, what is the ratio of the volume of the new cylinder to the volume of the original cylinder?

(A) 1 : 9
(B) 1 : 3
(C) 1 : 1
(D) 3 : 1
(E) 9 : 1

**28.** A B C D E

**28.** If one cubic foot of water equals 7.5 gallons, how long will it take for a faucet that flows at a rate of 10 gal/min to fill a cube 2 feet on each side (to the nearest minute)?

(A) 4 minutes
(B) 5 minutes
(C) 6 minutes
(D) 7 minutes
(E) 8 minutes

**29.** A B C D E

**29.** The ratio of the area of a square to the *square of its diagonal* is which of the following?

(A) 2 : 1
(B) $\sqrt{2}$ : 1
(C) 1 : 1
(D) 1 : $\sqrt{2}$
(E) 1 : 2

**30.** A B C D E

**30.** If *ABCD* is a square, with side *AB* = 4 inches, and *AEB* and *CED* are semicircles, what is the area of the shaded portion of the diagram below?

(A) $8 - \pi$ square inches
(B) $8 - 2\pi$ square inches
(C) $16 - 2\pi$ square inches
(D) $16 - 4\pi$ square inches
(E) $16 - 8\pi$ square inches

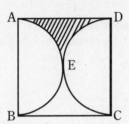

**31.** A B C D E

**31.** If the area of a circle is equal to the area of a rectangle, one of whose sides is equal to $\pi$, express the other side of the rectangle, *x*, in terms of the radius of the circle, *r*.

(A) $x = r$

(B) $x = \pi r$

(C) $x = r^2$

(D) $x = \sqrt{r}$

(E) $x = \dfrac{1}{r}$

**32.** A B C D E

**32.** If the volume of a cube is 27 cubic meters, find the surface area of the cube.

(A) 9 square meters
(B) 18 square meters
(C) 54 square meters
(D) 3 square meters
(E) 1 square meter

**33.** A B C D E

**33.** What is the area of a regular hexagon one of whose sides is 1 inch?

(A) $\dfrac{3\sqrt{3}}{4}$

(B) $\sqrt{3}$

(C) $\dfrac{3\sqrt{3}}{2}$

(D) 3

(E) 6

**34.** A B C D E

**34.** What is the area of the triangle pictured below?

(A) 18 square units
(B) 32 square units
(C) 24 square units
(D) 12 square units
(E) 124 square units

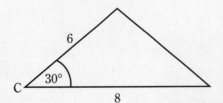

**35.** A B C D E  **35.** If a wheel travels 1 mile in 1 minute, at a rate of 600 revolutions per minute, what is the diameter of the wheel, in feet? (Use $\pi = \frac{22}{7}$.)

    (A) 2.2 feet
    (B) 2.4 feet
    (C) 2.6 feet
    (D) 2.8 feet
    (E) 3.0 feet

**36.** A B C D E  **36.** Which of the following figures has the largest perimeter?

    (A) a square with a diagonal of 5 feet
    (B) a rectangle with sides of 3 feet and 4 feet
    (C) an equilateral triangle with a side equal to 48 inches
    (D) a regular hexagon whose longest diagonal is 6 feet
    (E) a parallelogram with sides of 6 inches and 7 feet

**37.** A B C D E  **37.** A man has two containers: The first is a rectangular solid, measuring 3 inches × 4 inches × 10 inches; the second is a cylinder having a base with a radius of 2 inches and a height of 10 inches. If the first container is filled with water, and then this water is poured into the second container, which of the following occurs?

    (A) There is room for more water in the second container.
    (B) The second container is completely filled, without overflowing.
    (C) The second container overflows by less than 1 cubic inch.
    (D) The second container overflows by less than 2 (but not less than 1) cubic inches.
    (E) The second container overflows by 2 or more cubic inches.

**38.** A B C D E  **38.** If, in this diagram, $A$ represents a square with a side of $4''$, and $B$, $C$, $D$, and $E$ are semicircles, what is the area of the entire figure?

    (A) $16 + 4\pi$ square inches
    (B) $16 + 8\pi$ square inches
    (C) $16 + 16\pi$ square inches
    (D) $16 + 32\pi$ square inches
    (E) $16 + 64\pi$ square inches

**39.** A B C D E  **39.** The area of a square is $81p^2$. What is the length of the square's diagonal?

    (A) $9p$
    (B) $9p\sqrt{2}$
    (C) $18p$
    (D) $9p^2$
    (E) $18p^2$

**40.** A B C D E  **40.** The following diagram represents the floor of a room that is to be covered with carpeting at a price of $2.50 a square yard. What will be the cost of the carpeting?

    (A) $70
    (B) $125
    (C) $480
    (D) $630
    (E) None of these.

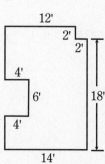

**41.** A B C D E

**41.** Which of the following has the largest perimeter?

(A) a square with a diagonal of 10 inches
(B) a 3-4-5 right triangle with a hypotenuse of 15 inches
(C) a pentagon, each of whose sides is 5 inches
(D) a right isosceles triangle with an area of 72 square inches
(E) a regular hexagon with a radius of 5 inches

**42.** A B C D E

**42.** If you double the area of the base of a rectangular solid, and also triple the solid's height, what is the ratio of the new volume to the old volume?

(A) 2 : 3
(B) 3 : 2
(C) 1 : 6
(D) 6 : 1
(E) None of these.

**43.** A B C D E

**43.** A certain type of linoleum costs $1.50 per square yard. If a room measures 27 feet by 14 feet, what will be the cost of covering it with linoleum?

(A) $44.10
(B) $51.60
(C) $63.00
(D) $132.30
(E) $189.00

**44.** A B C D E

**44.** How many circles, each with a 4-inch radius, can be cut from a rectangular sheet of paper, measuring 16 inches × 24 inches?

(A) 6
(B) 7
(C) 8
(D) 12
(E) 24

**45.** A B C D E

**45.** The ratio of the area of an equilateral triangle, in square inches, to its perimeter, in inches, is

(A) 3 : 4
(B) 4 : 3
(C) $\sqrt{3}$ : 4
(D) 4 : $\sqrt{3}$
(E) The answer cannot be determined from the given information.

**46.** A B C D E

**46.** What is the volume of a cylinder whose radius is 4 inches, and whose height is 10 inches? (Assume that $\pi = 3.14$.)

(A) 125.6 cubic inches
(B) 134.4 cubic inches
(C) 144.0 cubic inches
(D) 201.2 cubic inches
(E) 502.4 cubic inches

**47.** A B C D E

**47.** The area of a square is $144s^2$. What is the square's diagonal?

(A) 12s
(B) $12s\sqrt{2}$
(C) 24s
(D) 144s
(E) $144s^2$

48.  A B C D E

**48.** A circular pool is ten feet in diameter and five feet deep. What is its volume, in cubic feet?

(A)  50 cubic feet
(B)  $50\pi$ cubic feet
(C)  $125\pi$ cubic feet
(D)  $250\pi$ cubic feet
(E)  $500\pi$ cubic feet

49.  A B C D E

**49.** A certain type of carpeting is 30 inches wide. How many yards of this carpet will be needed to cover a floor that measures 20 feet by 24 feet?

(A)  48
(B)  64
(C)  144
(D)  192
(E)  None of these.

50.  A B C D E

**50.** Two wheels have diameters of 12 inches and 18 inches, respectively. Both wheels roll along parallel straight lines at the same linear speed until the large wheel has revolved 72 times. At this point, how many times has the small wheel revolved?

(A)  32
(B)  48
(C)  72
(D)  108
(E)  162

# Answer Key for Practice Test 3

| | | | |
|---|---|---|---|
| 1. B | 14. B | 27. D | 39. B |
| 2. A | 15. E | 28. C | 40. A |
| 3. B | 16. B | 29. E | 41. D |
| 4. B | 17. B | 30. B | 42. D |
| 5. E | 18. C | 31. C | 43. C |
| 6. B | 19. E | 32. C | 44. A |
| 7. D | 20. D | 33. C | 45. E |
| 8. C | 21. A | 34. D | 46. E |
| 9. C | 22. A | 35. D | 47. B |
| 10. B | 23. B | 36. D | 48. C |
| 11. D | 24. A | 37. A | 49. B |
| 12. C | 25. D | 38. B | 50. D |
| 13. E | 26. B | | |

# Answers and Solutions for Practice Test 3

1. Choice B is correct. This is a fairly difficult comparison problem, but the use of diagrams simplifies it considerably.

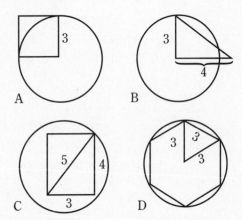

From diagram A it is apparent that the circle is larger than the square. Diagram B shows that the circle is larger than the right triangle. And, since a rectangle with a diagonal of 5 inches is made up of two right triangles, as shown in diagram C, the circle is larger than the rectangle. Finally, as shown in diagram D, the circle is larger than the hexagon. Thus, the circle is the largest of the five figures described. (302)

2. Choice A is correct. This is a formula problem: letting $V_o$ represent the original volume, $B_o$ represent the original area of the base, and $h_o$ represent the original height of the figure, we have the formula $V_o = h_o B_o$. The new volume, $V$ is equal to $3h_o B_o$. Thus, the new volume is three times the original volume—an *increase* of 200%. (301)

3. Choice B is correct. Here, we must find the length of carpeting needed to cover an area of 12′ × 13′, or 156 square feet. The formula needed is: $A = lw$, where $l$ = length and $w$ = width, both expressed in *feet*. Now, since we know that $A = 156$ square feet, and $w = 26$ inches, or $\frac{26}{12}$ feet, we can calculate $l$ as $156 \div \left(\frac{26}{12}\right)$, or 72 feet. But since the answer must be expressed in yards, we express 72 feet as 24 yards. (304)

4. Choice B is correct. First we must calculate the volume of the tank in cubic feet. Converting the dimensions of the box to feet, we get $1\frac{1}{2}$ feet × $2\frac{2}{3}$ feet × $2\frac{1}{4}$ feet, so the total volume is $\frac{3}{2} \times \frac{8}{3} \times \frac{9}{4}$, or 9, cubic feet. Thus, at a rate of 6 cubic feet per minute, it would take $\frac{9}{6}$, or $1\frac{1}{2}$ minutes to fill the tank. (312, 201)

5. Choice E is correct. Here, we use the formula $A = \pi r^2$, where $A$ = area, and $r$ = radius. Thus, the ratio of $A$ to $r$ is just $\frac{A}{r} = \pi r$. Since $r$ is not a constant, the ratio cannot be determined. (310)

6. Choice B is correct. First, we diagram the circle and the square and see that the square has a smaller perimeter. Next, we notice that the circle, which has a larger circumference than the square, has circumference $2\pi$, or about 6.3 feet. But the perimeters of the rectangle (9 feet), of the pentagon (5 × 16 inches = 80 inches = 6 feet, 8 inches), and of the hexagon (6 × 14 inches = 84 inches = 7 feet) are all greater than the circumference of the circle, and therefore also greater than the perimeter of the square. Thus, the square has the smallest perimeter. (302)

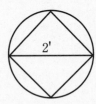

7. Choice D is correct. The formula involved here is $A_1 : A_2 = s_1^2 : s_2^2$, where $A_1$ represents the area of the triangle with one side of length $s_1$, and $A_2$ represents the area of the triangle corresponding to $s_2$. If we let $s_1$ represent $AE$, and $s_2$ represent $AC$, so that $A_1$ is the area of $ADE$ and $A_2$ is the area of $ABC$, then we have the resulting formula $\frac{AE}{AC} = \frac{s_1}{s_2} = \sqrt{\frac{A_1}{A_2}}$. The area of the trapezoid $DEBC$ is twice the area of $ADE$, or $2A_1$, so the area of $ABC$ is equal to the sum of the area of $ADE$ and $DECB$, which equal $A_1$ and

$2A_1$, respectively; thus, the area of $ABC$ is $3A_1$. So, $A_1 : A_2 = 1 : 3$. Thus, $s_1 : s_2 = \sqrt{\frac{1}{3}} = 1 : \sqrt{3}$.　(318)

8. Choice C is correct. Since the radius of the circle is 10 inches, its circumference is $2\pi$ (10 inches), or $2\left(\frac{22}{7}\right)$ (10 inches), which equals $\frac{440}{7}$ inches. This is the distance the wheel will travel in one revolution. To travel 10 feet, or 120 inches, it must travel $120 \div \frac{440}{7}$, or $\frac{21}{11}$ revolutions. At a speed of 22 revolutions per minute, or $\frac{11}{30}$ revolutions per second, it will take $\frac{21}{11} \div \frac{11}{30}$ or $\frac{630}{121}$ seconds. Carrying the division to the nearest tenth of a second, we get 5.2 seconds.　(310)

9. Choice C is correct. If we let $d$ represent the diagonal of a square, $s$ represent the length of one side, and $A$ represent its area, then we have two formulas: $d = s\sqrt{2}$, and $A = s^2$, relating the three quantities. However, from the first equation, we can see that $s^2 = \frac{d^2}{2}$, so we can derive a third formula, $A = \frac{d^2}{2}$, relating $A$ and $d$. We are given that $d$ equals 16″, so we can calculate the value of $A$ as $\frac{(16 \text{ inches})^2}{2}$, or 128 square inches.　(303)

10. Choice B is correct. The area of the shaded figure is equal to the difference between the areas of the rectangle and the circle. The area of the rectangle is defined by the formula $A = bh$, where $b$ and $h$ are the two adjacent sides of the rectangle. In this case, $A$ is equal to 4 inches × 6 inches, or 24 square inches. The area of the circle is defined by the formula $A = \pi r^2$, where $r$ is the radius. Since $BE$ equals the diameter of the circle and is equal to 4 inches, then the radius must be 2 inches. Thus, the area of the circle is $\pi(2 \text{ inches})^2$, or $4\pi$ square inches. Subtracting, we obtain the area of the shaded portion: $24 - 4\pi$ square inches.　(304, 310)

11. Choice D is correct. We use the formula for the area of an equilateral triangle, $\frac{\sqrt{3s^2}}{4}$, where $s$ is a side. If $s = 1$, then the area of the triangle is $\frac{\sqrt{3}}{4}$.　(308)

12. Choice C is correct. An angle, which is inscribed in a circle, whose sides cut off an arc of 180° (that is, intersects the ends of a diameter) is a right angle. According to the Pythagorean Theorem, the diameter $AC$, being the hypotenuse of a triangle with sides of 12 feet and 16 feet, has a length of $\sqrt{12^2 + 16^2} = \sqrt{400} = 20$ feet. Therefore, if we call $d$ the diameter, the area of the circle is $A = \pi\left(\frac{d}{2}\right)^2 = \pi\left(\frac{20}{2}\right)^2 = 100\pi$ square feet.

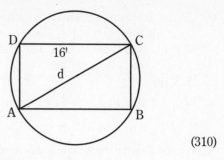

(310)

13. Choice E is correct. The area of the room = 12 feet × 18 feet = 216 square feet. The area of one tile = $\frac{3}{4}$ inches × 2 inches = $\frac{3}{2}$ square inches. The number of tiles = area of the room ÷ area of one tile

$$= \frac{216 \text{ square feet}}{\frac{3}{2} \text{ square inch}} = \frac{216 \times 144 \text{ square inches}}{\frac{3}{2} \text{ square inch}}$$

$$= 216 \times \overset{48}{\cancel{144}} \times \frac{2}{3} = 20{,}736 \text{ tiles.}$$　(304)

14. Choice B is correct. The volume of a sphere is found by using the formula $\frac{4}{3}\pi r^3$ where $r$ is the radius. In this case, the radius is 4 miles, so the volume is $\frac{256}{3}\pi$ cubic miles. This is equal to the volume of a cylinder of radius 8 miles so $\frac{256}{3}\pi = \pi 8^2 h$, since the volume of a cylinder is $\pi r^2 h$, where $h$ is the height, and $r$ is the radius of the base. Solving $\frac{256\pi}{3} = \pi 8^2 h$; $\frac{\frac{256\pi}{3}}{\pi 64} = \frac{\overset{16}{\cancel{256}}}{3} \times \frac{1}{\underset{4}{\cancel{\pi 64}}} = \frac{16}{12} = \frac{4}{3}$ miles.　(314, 315)

15. Choice E is correct. 33 yards = 99 feet = 15 revolutions. Thus, 1 revolution = $\frac{99}{15}$ feet = $\frac{33}{5}$ feet = 6.6 feet. Since 1 revolution = the circumference of the wheel, the wheel's diameter = circumference ÷ $\pi$. 6.6 feet ÷ $\frac{22}{7}$ = 2.10 feet.　(310)

16. Choice B is correct. The area of the right triangle is equal to $\frac{1}{2}ab$ where $a$ and $b$ are the legs of the triangle. In this case, the area is $\frac{1}{2} \times 12 \times 24$, or 144 square inches. If we call the sides of the rectangle $x$ and $y$ we get $2x + 2y = 48$, or $y = 24 - x$. The area of the rectangle is $xy$, or $x(24 - x)$. This must be equal to 144, so we get the equation $24x - x^2 = 144$. Rearranging the terms gives us $x^2 - 24x + 144 = 0$, or $(x - 12)^2$. Since $y = 24 - x$, $y = 24 - 12$, or $y = 12$. This is satisfied only by $x = 12$. By the Pythagorean Theorem we get: diagonal $= \sqrt{12^2 + 12^2} \sqrt{144 + 144} = \sqrt{2(144)} = 12\sqrt{2}$.　(304, 306, 317)

17. Choice B is correct. The area of the square is 64 square inches, since $A = s^2$ where $s$ is the length of a side, and $A$ is the area. The area of the circle is $\pi\left(\frac{7}{4}\right)^2 = \frac{22}{7} \times \frac{49}{16} = \frac{77}{8} = 9.625$. Subtracting, $64 - 9.625 = 54.375 = 54.4$ (approximately). (304, 310)

18. Choice C is correct. The capacity of the volume ($V = lwh$, where $l$, $w$, $h$, are the adjacent sides of the solid) of the container = (3 inches) (3 inches) (11 inches) = 99 cubic inches; since 1 gallon equals 231 cubic inches, 99 cubic inches equal $\frac{99}{231}$ gallons (the fraction reduces to $\frac{3}{7}$. One gallon equals 128 ounces (1 gallon = 4 quarts, 1 quart = 2 pints, 1 pint = 16 ounces), so the container holds $\frac{384}{7}$ ounces = 55 ounces (approximately). (312)

19. Choice E is correct. The speed of the first wheel is equal to its rate of revolution multiplied by its circumference, which equals $24 \times 20$ inches $\times \pi = 480\pi$ inches per minute. The speed of the second is $18 \times 30$ inches $\times \pi = 540\pi$ inches per minute. Thus, their ratio is $540\pi : 480\pi = 9 : 8$. (310)

20. Choice D is correct. The area of the path is equal to the area of the ring between two concentric circles of radii 10 feet and 13 feet. This area is obtained by subtracting the area of the smaller circle from the area of the larger circle. The area of the larger circle is equal to $\pi \times$ its radius squared = $\pi(13)^2$ feet$^2$ = $169\pi$ square feet. By the same process, the area of the smaller circle = $100\pi$ square feet. The area of the shaded part = $169\pi - 100\pi = 69\pi$ square feet. (310)

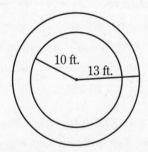

21. Choice A is correct. The diameter = 16 inches, so the radius = 8 inches. Thus, the area of the whole circle = $\pi(8 \text{ inches})^2 = 64\pi$ square inches. The area of the semicircle is one-half of the area of the whole circle, or $32\pi$ square inches. (311)

22. Choice A is correct. A cube has twelve equal edges, so the length of one side of the cube is $\frac{1}{12}$ of 4 feet, or 4 inches. Thus, its volume is 4 inches $\times$ 4 inches $\times$ 4 inches = 64 cubic inches. (313)

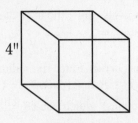

23. Choice B is correct. The additional water will take the shape of a rectangular solid measuring 25 feet $\times$ 6 inches $\times$ 3 inches (3″ = the added depth) $= 25 \times \frac{1}{2} \times \frac{1}{4}$ cubic feet $= \frac{25}{8}$ cubic feet. (312)

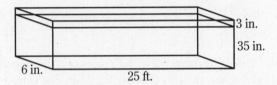

24. Choice A is correct. The volume of the cylinder $= \pi r^2 h = \left(\frac{22}{7}\right)\left(\frac{7}{2}\right)^2 (10)$ cubic inches = 385 cubic inches. 231 cubic inches = 1 gallon, so 385 cubic inches $= \frac{385}{231}$ gallons $= \frac{5}{3}$ gallons = 1.7 gallons (approximately). (314)

25. Choice D is correct. The area of floor = 10 feet $\times$ 16 feet = 160 square feet. Area of one tile = 8 inches $\times$ 8 inches = 64 square inches $= \frac{64}{144}$ square feet = $\frac{4}{9}$ square feet. Thus, the number of tiles = area of floor ÷ area of tile $= 160 \div \frac{4}{9} = 360$. At 9¢ apiece, the tiles will cost $32.40. (304)

26. Choice B is correct. Looking at the following three diagrams, we can observe that the triangle, square, and hexagon are all smaller than the circle.

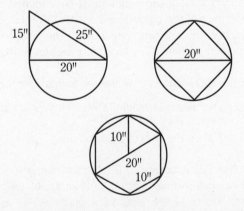

Comparing the areas of the circle and the rectangle, we notice that the area of the circle is $\pi (10 \text{ inches})^2 = 100\pi$ square inches, which is greater than (10 inches) (30 inches) = 300 square inches, the area of the rectangle. ($\pi$ is approximately 3.14.) (302)

27. Choice D is correct. In a cylinder, $V = \pi r^2 h$, where $r$ is the radius of the base, and $h$ is the height. The new volume, $V' = \pi(3r)^2 \left(\dfrac{h}{3}\right) = 3\pi r^2 h = 2V$. Thus, the ratio of the new volume to the old volume is 3 : 1.  (314)

28. Choice C is correct. A cube 2 feet on each side has a volume of $2 \times 2 \times 2 = 8$ cubic feet. Since 1 cubic foot equals 7.5 gallons, 8 cubic feet equals 60 gallons. If the faucet flows at the rate of 10 gallons/minute it will take 6 minutes to fill the cube.  (313)

29. Choice E is correct. Let $s$ = the side of the square. Then, the area of the square is equal to $s^2$. The diagonal of the square is $s\sqrt{2}$, so the square of the diagonal is $2s^2$. Thus, the ratio of the area of the square to the square of the diagonal is $s^2 : 2s^2$ or 1 : 2.  (303)

30. Choice B is correct. The area of the square $ABCD$ is equal to 4 inches $\times$ 4 inches = 16 square inches. The two semicircles can be placed together diameter-to-diameter to form a circle with a radius of 2 inches, and thus, an area of $4\pi$. Subtracting the area of the circle from the area of the square, we obtain the combined areas of $AED$ and $BEC$. But, since the figure is symmetrical, $AED$ and $BEC$ must be equal, so the area of $AED$ is one-half of this remainder, which equals $16 - 4\pi$, or $8 - 2\pi$ square inches.  (303, 310)

31. Choice C is correct. The area of the circle is equal to $\pi r^2$, and the area of the rectangle is equal to $\pi x$. Since these areas are equal, $\pi r^2 = \pi x$, and $x = r^2$.  (304, 310)

32. Choice C is correct. The volume of a cube is $e^3$ where $e$ is the length of an edge. If the volume is 27 cubic meters, then $e^3 = 27$ and $e = 3$ meters. The surface area of a cube is $6e^2$, and if $e = 3$ meters, then the surface area is 54 square meters.  (313)

33. Choice C is correct. The area of a regular hexagon, one of whose sides is 1 inch, is equal to the sum of the areas of 6 equilateral triangles, each with a side of 1 inch. The area of an equilateral triangle with a side of 1 inch is equal to $\dfrac{\sqrt{3}}{4}$ square inches. (The formula for the area of an equilateral triangle with a side of $s$ is $A = s^2\dfrac{\sqrt{3}}{4}$.) The sum of 6 such triangles is $\dfrac{6\sqrt{3}}{4}$, or $\dfrac{3\sqrt{3}}{2}$.  (308)

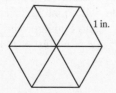

1 in.

34. Choice D is correct. The area of a triangle can be expressed as $\dfrac{1}{2}ab \sin C$ where $a$ and $b$ are any two sides and $C$ is the angle between them. In this case $a = 6$, $b = 8$, and $< C = 30°$. You should remember that the sine of 30° is $\dfrac{1}{2}$ so the area is $\dfrac{1}{2}(6)(8)\left(\dfrac{1}{2}\right)$ $= 12$.  (307)

35. Choice D is correct. Since the wheel takes 1 minute to make 600 revolutions and travels 1 mile in that time, we have the relation 1 mile = 5,280 feet = 600 revolutions. Thus, 1 revolution $\dfrac{5,280}{600}$ feet = 8.8 feet = circumference = $\pi$(diameter) = $\left(\dfrac{22}{7}\right)$ (diameter). Therefore, the diameter = 8.8 feet $\div \left(\dfrac{22}{7}\right) =$ 2.8 feet.  (310)

36. Choice D is correct. In this case, it is easiest to calculate the perimeters of the 5 figures. According to the Pythagorean Theorem, a square with a diagonal of 5 feet has a side of $\dfrac{5}{\sqrt{2}}$, which is equal to $\dfrac{5\sqrt{2}}{2}$. (This is found by multiplying the numerator and denominator of $\dfrac{5}{\sqrt{2}}$ by $\sqrt{2}$.) If each side of the square is $\dfrac{5\sqrt{2}}{2}$, then the perimeter is $4 \times \dfrac{5\sqrt{2}}{2} =$ $10\sqrt{2}$ feet. A rectangle with sides of 3 feet and 4 feet has a perimeter of $2(3) + 2(4)$, or 14 feet. An equilateral triangle with a side of 48 inches, or 4 feet, has a perimeter of 12 feet. A regular hexagon whose longest diagonal is 6 feet has a side of 3 feet and, therefore, a perimeter of 18 feet. (See the diagram for Solution 33.) Finally, a parallelogram with sides of 6 inches, or $\dfrac{1}{2}$ foot, and 7 feet has a perimeter of 15 feet. Therefore, the hexagon has the largest perimeter.  (302, 317)

37. Choice A is correct. The volume of the first container is equal to 3 inches $\times$ 4 inches $\times$ 10 inches, or 120 cubic inches. The volume of the second container, the cylinder, is equal to $\pi r^2 h = \pi(2 \text{ inches})^2$ (10 inches), or $40\pi$ cubic inches, which is greater than 120 cubic inches ($\pi$ is greater than 3). So the second container can hold more than the first. If the first container is filled and the contents poured into the second, there will be room for more water in the second.  (312, 314)

38. Choice B is correct. The area of the square is 16 square inches. The four semicircles can be added to form two circles, each of radius 2 inches, so the area of each circle is $4\pi$ square inches, and the two circles add up to $8\pi$ square inches. Thus, the total area is $16 + 8\pi$ square inches.  (303, 311)

**39.** Choice B is correct. Since the area of the square is $81p^2$, one side of the square will equal $9p$. According to the Pythagorean Theorem, the diagonal will equal $\sqrt{81p^2 + 81p^2} = 9p\sqrt{2}$.　　　(303, 317)

**40.** Choice A is correct. We can regard the area as a rectangle, 20 ft × 14 ft, with two rectangles, measuring 4 ft × 6 ft and 2 ft × 2 ft, cut out. Thus, the area is equal to 280 sq ft − 24 sq ft − 4 sq ft = 252 sq ft = $\frac{252}{9}$ sq yd = 28 sq yds. (Remember, 1 square yard equals 9 square feet.) At $2.50 a square yard, 28 square yards will cost $70.　　(304)

**41.** Choice D is correct. The perimeter of the square is equal to four times its side; since a side is $\frac{1}{\sqrt{2}}$, or $\frac{\sqrt{2}}{2}$ times the diagonal, the perimeter of the square in question is $4 \times 5\sqrt{2} = 20\sqrt{2}$, which is approximately equal to 28.28 inches. The perimeter of a right triangle with sides that are in a 3−4−5 ratio, i.e., 9 inches, 12 inches, and 15 inches, is 9 + 12 + 15 = 36 inches. The perimeter of the pentagon is 5 × 5 inches, or 25 inches. The perimeter of the right isosceles triangle (with sides of 12 inches, 12 inches, and $12\sqrt{2}$ inches) is 24 + $12\sqrt{2}$ inches, which is approximately equal to 40.968 inches. The perimeter of the hexagon is 6 × 5 inches, or 30 inches. Thus, the isosceles right triangle has the largest perimeter of those figures mentioned. You should become familiar with the approximate value of $\sqrt{2}$, which is 1.414.　　(302)

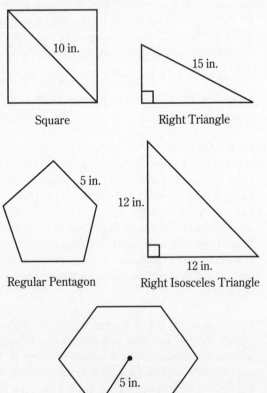

Square

Right Triangle

Regular Pentagon

Right Isosceles Triangle

Regular Hexagon

**42.** Choice D is correct. For rectangular solids, the following formula holds:

$$V = Ah, \text{ where } A \text{ is the area of the base, and } h \text{ is the height.}$$

If we replace $A$ by $2A$, and $h$ by $3h$, we get $V' = (2A)(3h) = 6V$. Thus, $V' : V = 6:1$. (312)

**43.** Choice C is correct. The area of the room is 27 feet × 14 feet = 378 square feet. 9 square feet = 1 square yard, so the area of the room is 42 square yards. At $1.50 per square yard the linoleum to cover the floor will cost $63.00.　　(304)

**44.** Choice A is correct. A circle with a 4-inch radius has an 8-inch diameter, so there can be only 2 rows of 3 circles each, or 6 circles.　　(310)

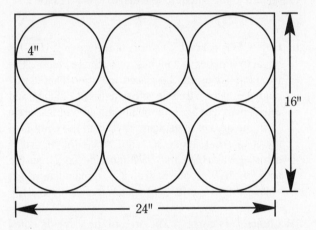

**45.** Choice E is correct. Let one side of the triangle be $s$. Then the area of the triangle is $\frac{s^2\sqrt{3}}{4}$. (Either memorize this formula or remember that it is derived by drawing an altitude to divide the triangle into two congruent 30°: 60°: 90° right triangles.) The perimeter of the equilateral triangle is $3s$, so the ratio of the area to the perimeter is $\frac{s^2\sqrt{3}}{4} : 3s$, or $s : 4\sqrt{3}$, which cannot be determined unless we know the value of $s$.　　(308)

**46.** Choice E is correct. The formula for volume of a cylinder is $V = r^2h$, where $r$ is the radius of the base, and $h$ is the height. Here, $r = 4$ inches, and $h = 10$ inches, while $\pi \approx 3.14$. (The symbol $\approx$ means "approximately equal to.") Thus $V \approx (4)^2(10)(3.14) = 160(3.14) = 502.4$ cubic inches.　　(314)

**47.** Choice B is correct. If the area of a square is $144s^2$, then one side will equal $12s$, so the diagonal will equal $12s\sqrt{2}$. (The Pythagorean Theorem may be used here to get $d = \sqrt{144s^2 + 144s^2}$, where $d$ is the diagonal.)　　(303, 317)

**48.** Choice C is correct. The inside of the pool forms a cylinder of radius 5 feet, and height 5 feet. The volume is $\pi r^2 h$, or $\pi \times 5 \times 5 \times 5 = 125\pi$ cubic feet. (314)

**49.** Choice B is correct. The area of the floor is 20 feet $\times$ 24 feet = 480 square feet. 30 inches is equal to $2\frac{1}{2}$ feet, and we must find the length which, when multiplied by $2\frac{1}{2}$ feet, will yield 480 square feet. This length is 192 feet, which equals 64 yards (3 feet = 1 yard). (304)

**50.** Choice D is correct. The circumference of the larger wheel is $18\pi$ inches ($C = \pi d$). After 72 revolutions, the larger wheel will have gone a distance of $72(18\pi)$ inches. Since the smaller wheel moves at the same linear speed, it will also have gone $72(18\pi)$ inches. The circumference of the smaller wheel is $12\pi$ inches, and if we call the number of revolutions that the smaller wheel makes, $r$, then we know that $12\pi r = 72(18\pi)$. Dividing both sides by $12\pi$ gives us $r = 6(18)$ or 108 revolutions. Note that in this problem we have used the relation, distance = rate $\times$ time, where the time for both wheels is a fixed quantity. (310)

# MATH REFRESHER
## SESSION 4

# Algebra Problems

## Algebraic Properties

Algebra is the branch of mathematics that applies the laws of arithmetic to symbols that represent unknown quantities. The most commonly used symbols are the letters of the alphabet such as $A, B, C, x, y, z$, etc. These symbols can be added, subtracted, multiplied, and divided like numbers. For example, $3a + 2a = 5a$, $2x - x = x$, $3(5b) = 15b$, $\frac{6x}{3x} = 2$. These symbols can be raised to powers like $a^3$ or $y^2$. Remember that raising a number to a power means multiplying the number by itself a number of times. For example, $a^3 = a \cdot a \cdot a$. The power is 3, and $a$ is multiplied by itself 3 times.

Generally, in algebra, a variable (an unknown represented by a symbol) appears in an *equation* (a statement that defines the relationship between certain quantities), and values of the variable that *satisfy* the equation must be found. For example, the equation $6a = 12$ is satisfied when the variable, $a$, is equal to 2. This section is a discussion on how to solve complicated algebraic equations and other related topics.

## Fundamental Laws of Our Number System

Following is a list of laws that apply to all the numbers necessary to work with when doing arithmetic and algebra problems. Remember these laws and use them in doing problems.

**401.** If $x = y$ and $y = z$, then $x = z$. This is called *transitivity*. For example, if $a = 3$ and $b = 3$, then $a = b$.

**402.** If $x = y$, then $x + z = y + z$, and $x - z = y - z$. This means that the same quantity can be added to or subtracted from both sides of an equation. For example, if $a = b$, then add any number to both sides, say 3, and $a + 3 = b + 3$. Or if $a = b$, then $a - 3 = b - 3$.

**403.** If $x = y$, then $x \cdot z = y \cdot z$ and $x \div z = y \div z$, unless $z = 0$ (see Section 404). This means that both sides of an equation can be multiplied by the same number. For example, if $a = n$, then $5a = 5n$. It also means that both sides of an equation can be divided by the same nonzero number. If $a = b$, then $\frac{a}{3} = \frac{b}{3}$.

**404.** *Never divide by zero.* This is a very important fact that must be remembered. The quotient of *any* quantity (except zero) divided by zero is infinity.

**405.** $x + y = y + x$, and $x \cdot y = y \cdot x$. Therefore, $2 + 3 = 3 + 2$, and $2 \cdot 3 = 3 \cdot 2$. Remember that this does not work for division and subtraction. $3 \div 2$ does not equal $2 \div 3$; and $3 - 2$ does not equal $2 - 3$. The property described above is called *commutativity*.

# Algebraic Expressions

**405a.** Since the letters in an algebraic expression stand for numbers, and since we add, subtract, multiply, or divide them to get the algebraic expression, the algebraic expression itself stands for a number. When we are told what value each of the letters in the expression has, we can evaluate the expression. Note that $(+a) \times (+b) = +ab; (+a) \times (-b) = -ab; (-a) \times (+b) = -ab$ and $-a \times -b = +ab$.

In evaluating algebraic expressions, place the value you are substituting for a letter in parentheses. (This is important when a letter has a negative value.)

**For example:** What is the value of the expression $a^2 - b^3$ when $a = -2$, and $b = -1$?
$a^2 - b^3 = (-2)^2 - (-1)^3 = 4 - (-1) = 5$.

If you can, simplify the algebraic expression before you evaluate it.

**For example:** Evaluate $\dfrac{32a^6b^2}{8a^4b^3}$ if $a = 4$, and $b = -2$.

First we divide:

$\dfrac{32a^6b^2}{8a^4b^3} = \dfrac{4a^2}{b}$. Then $\dfrac{4a^2}{b} = \dfrac{4(+4)^2}{-2} = -32$.

# Equations

**406.** *Linear equation in one unknown.* An equation of this type has only one variable and that variable is always in the first power, i.e., $x$ or $y$ or $a$, but never in a higher or fractional power, i.e., $x^2$, $y^3$, or $a^{1/2}$. Examples of linear equations in one unknown are $x + 5 = 7, 3a - 2 = 7a + 1, 2x - 7x = 8 + x, 8 = -4y$, etc. To solve these equations, follow these steps:

**STEP 1.** Combine the terms on the left and right sides of the equality. That is, (1) add all of the numerical terms on each side, and (2) add all of the terms with variables on each side. For example, if you have $7 + 2x + 9 = 4x - 3 - 2x + 7 + 6x$, combining terms on the left gives you $16 + 2x$, because $7 + 9 = 16$, and $2x$ is the only variable term on that side. On the right we get $8x + 4$, since $4x - 2x + 6x = 8x$ and $-3 + 7 = 4$. Therefore the new equation is $16 + 2x = 8x + 4$.

**STEP 2.** Put all of the numerical terms on the right side of the equation and all of the variable terms on the left side. This is done by subtracting the numerical term on the left from both sides of the equation and by subtracting the variable term on the right side from both sides of the equation. In the example $16 + 2x = 8x + 4$, subtract 16 from both sides and obtain $2x = 8x - 12$; then subtracting $8x$ from both sides gives $-6x = -12$.

**STEP 3.** Divide both sides by the coefficient of the variable. In this case, where $-6x = -12$, dividing by 6 gives 2. This is the final solution to the problem.

**Example:** Solve for $a$ in the equation $7a + 4 - 2a = 18 + 17a + 10$.

*Solution:* From Step 1, we combine terms on both sides to get $5a + 4 = 28 + 17a$. As in Step 2, we then subtract 4 and $17a$ from both sides to give $-12a = 24$. By Step 3, we then divide both sides of the equation by the coefficient of $a$, which is $-12$, to get $a = -2$.

**Example:** Solve for $x$ in $2x + 6 = 0$.

*Solution:* Here Step 1 is eliminated because there are no terms to combine on either side. Step 2 requires that 6 be subtracted from both sides to get $2x = -6$. Then dividing by 2 gives $x = -3$.

**407.** *Simultaneous equations in two unknowns.* These are problems in which two equations, each with two unknowns, are given. These equations must be solved together (simultaneously) in order to arrive at the solution.

**STEP 1.** Rearrange each equation so that both are in the form that has the $x$ term on the left side and the $y$ term and the constant on the right side. In other words, put the equations in the form $Ax = By + C$ where $A$, $B$, and $C$ are numerical constants. For example, if one of the equations is $9x - 10y + 30 = 11y + 3x - 6$, then subtract $-10y$ and 30 from both sides to get $9x = 21y + 3x - 36$. Subtracting $3x$ from both sides gives $6x = 21y - 36$, which is in the form of $Ax = By + C$.

The first equation should be in the form $Ax = By + C$, and the second equation should be in the form $Dx = Ey + F$ where $A$, $B$, $C$, $D$, $E$, and $F$ are numerical constants.

**STEP 2.** Multiply the first equation by the coefficient of $x$ in the second equation ($D$). Multiply the second equation by the coefficient of $x$ in the first equation ($A$). Now the equations are in the form $ADx = BDy + CD$ and $ADx = AEy + AF$. For example, in the two equations $2x = 7y - 12$ and $3x = y + 1$, multiply the first by 3 and the second by 2 to get $6x = 21y - 36$ and $6x = 2y + 2$.

**STEP 3.** Equate the right sides of both equations. This can be done because both sides are equal to $ADx$. (See Section 401 on transitivity.) Thus, $BDy + CD = AEy + AF$. So $21y - 36$ and $2y + 2$ are both equal to $6x$ and are equal to each other: $21y - 36 = 2y + 2$.

**STEP 4.** Solve for $y$. This is done in the manner outlined in Section 406. In the equation $21y - 36 = 2y + 2$, $y = 2$. By this method $y = \dfrac{AF - CD}{BD - AE}$.

**STEP 5.** Substitute the value of $y$ into either of the original equations and solve for $x$. In the general equations we would then have either $x = \dfrac{B}{A}\left[\dfrac{AF - CD}{BD - AE}\right] + \dfrac{C}{A}$, or $x = \dfrac{E}{D}\left[\dfrac{AF - CD}{BD - AE}\right] + \dfrac{E}{D}$. In the example, if $y = 2$ is substituted into either $2x = 7y - 12$ or $3x = y + 1$, then $2x = 14 - 12$ or $3x = 3$ can be solved to get $x = 1$.

**Example:** Solve for $a$ and $b$ in the equation $3a + 4b = 24$ and $2a + b = 11$.

*Solution:* First note that it makes no difference in these two equations whether the variables are $a$ and $b$ instead of $x$ and $y$. Subtract $4b$ from the first equation and $b$ from the second equation to get the equations $3a = 24 - 4b$ and $2a = 11 - b$. Multiply the first by 2 and the second by 3. Thus, $6a = 48 - 8b$ and $6a = 33 - 3b$. Equate $48 - 8b$ and $33 - 3b$ to get $48 - 8b = 33 - 3b$. Solving for $b$ in the usual manner gives us $b = 3$. Substituting the value of $b = 3$ into the equation $3a + 4b = 24$ obtains $3a + 12 = 24$. Solving for $a$ gives $a = 4$. Thus the complete solution is $a = 4$ and $b = 3$.

**408.** *Quadratic equations.* Quadratic equations are expressed in the form $ax^2 + bx + c = 0$; where $a$, $b$, and $c$ are constant numbers (for example, $\frac{1}{2}$, 4, $-2$, etc.) and $x$ is a variable. An equation of this form may be satisfied by two values of $x$, one value of $x$, or no values of $x$. Actually when there are no values of $x$ that satisfy the equation, there are only *imaginary* solutions. These will not be dealt with. To determine the number of solutions, find the value of the expression $b^2 - 4ac$ where $a$, $b$, and $c$ are the constant coefficients of the equation $ax^2 + bx + c = 0$.

---

If $b^2 - 4ac$ is **greater** than 0, there are two solutions.

If $b^2 - 4ac$ is **less** than 0, there are no solutions.

If $b^2 - 4ac$ is **equal** to 0, there is one solution.

---

If solutions exist, they can be found by using the formulas:

$$x = \frac{-b + \sqrt{b^2 - 4ac}}{2a} \text{ and } x = \frac{-b - \sqrt{b^2 - 4ac}}{2a}$$

Note that if $b^2 - 4ac = 0$, the two above solutions will be the same and there will be one solution.

**Example:** Determine the solutions, if they exist, to the equation $x^2 + 6x + 5 = 0$.

*Solution:* First, noting $a = 1$, $b = 6$, and $c = 5$, calculate $b^2 - 4ac$, or $6^2 - 4(1)(5)$. Thus, $b^2 - 4ac = 16$. Since this is greater than 0, there are two solutions. They are, from the formulas:

$$x = \frac{-6 + \sqrt{6^2 - 4 \cdot 1 \cdot 5}}{2 \cdot 1} \text{ and } x = \frac{-6 - \sqrt{6^2 - 4 \cdot 1 \cdot 5}}{2 \cdot 1}$$

Simplify these to:

$$x = \frac{-6 + \sqrt{16}}{2} \text{ and } x = \frac{-6 - \sqrt{16}}{2}$$

As $\sqrt{16} = 4$, $x = \frac{-6 + 4}{2} = \frac{-2}{2}$ and $x = \frac{-6 - 4}{2} = \frac{-10}{2}$. Thus, the two solutions are $x = -1$ and $x = -5$.

Another method of solving quadratic equations is to *factor* the $ax^2 + bx + c$ into two expressions. This will be explained in the next section.

**409.** *Factoring.* Factoring is breaking down an expression into two or more expressions, the product of which is the original expression. For example, 6 can be factored into 2 and 3 because $2 \cdot 3 = 6$. $x^2 - x$ can be factored into $x$ and $(x - 1)$ because $x^2 - x = x(x - 1)$. Then, if $x^2 + bx + c$ is factorable, it will be factored into two expressions in the form $(x + d)$ and $(x + e)$. If the expression $(x + d)$ is multiplied by the expression $(x + e)$, their product is $x^2 + (d + e)x + de$. For example, $(x + 3) \cdot (x + 2)$ equals $x^2 + 5x + 6$. To factor an expression such as $x^2 + 6x + 8$, find a $d$ and $e$ such that $d + e = 6$ and $de = 8$. Of the various factors of 8, we find that $d = 4$ and $e = 2$. Thus $x^2 + 6x + 8$ can be factored into the expressions $(x + 4)$ and $(x + 2)$. Below are factored expressions.

$$x^2 + 2x + 1 = (x + 1)(x + 1) \qquad x^2 + 3x + 2 = (x + 2)(x + 1)$$

$$x^2 + 4x + 4 = (x + 2)(x + 2) \qquad x^2 + 5x + 6 = (x + 3)(x + 2)$$

$$x^2 - 4x + 3 = (x - 3)(x - 1) \qquad x^2 - 4x - 5 = (x - 5)(x + 1)$$

$$x^2 + 10x + 16 = (x + 8)(x + 2) \qquad x^2 + 4x - 5 = (x + 5)(x - 1)$$

$$x^2 - 5x + 6 = (x - 2)(x - 3) \qquad x^2 - x - 6 = (x - 3)(x + 2)$$

An important rule to remember in factoring is that $a^2 - b^2 = (a + b)(a - b)$. For example, $x^2 - 9 = (x + 3)(x - 3)$. To apply factoring in solving quadratic equations, factor the quadratic expression into two terms and set each term equal to zero. Then, solve the two resulting equations.

**Example:** Solve $x^2 - x - 6 = 0$.

*Solution:* First factor the expression $x^2 - x - 6$ into $x - 3$ and $x + 2$. Setting each of these equal to 0 gives $x - 3 = 0$ and $x + 2 = 0$. Solving these equations gives us $x = 3$ and $x = -2$.

# Algebra of Graphs

**410a.** *Number Lines.* Numbers, positive and negative, can be represented as points on a straight line. Conversely, points on a line can also be represented by numbers. This is done by use of the number line.

The diagram above is an example of a number line. On a number line, a point is chosen to represent the number zero. Then a point that is 1 unit to the right of 0 represents $+1$; a point that is $\frac{1}{2}$ unit to the right of 0 is $+\frac{1}{2}$; a point that is 2 units to the right of 0 is $+2$; and so on. A point that is 1 unit to the left of 0 is $-1$; a point that is $\frac{1}{2}$ unit to the left of 0 is $-\frac{1}{2}$; a point that is 2 units to the left of 0 is $-2$; and so on. As you can see, all points to the right of the 0 point represent positive numbers, and all those to the left of the 0 point represent negative numbers.

<u>To find the distance between two points on the line:</u>

1. Find the numbers that represent the points.
2. The distance is the smaller number subtracted from the larger.

For example: Find the distance between point $A$ and point $B$ on the number line.

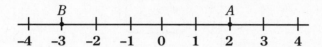

Point $A$ is $+2$ on the number line and point $B$ is $-3$. $+2$ is larger than $-3$, so the distance is $+2-(-3)$ or $+2+3=5$. By counting the number of units between $A$ and $B$, the distance is also found to be 5.

**410b.** *Coordinate geometry.* These problems deal with the algebra of graphs. A graph consists of a set of points whose position is determined with respect to a set of axes usually labeled the *X*-axis and the *Y*-axis and divided into appropriate units. Locate a point on the graph with an "*x* coordinate" of *a* units and a "*y* coordinate" of *b* units. First move *a* units along the *X*-axis (either to the left or right depending on whether *a* is positive or negative). Then move *b* units along the *Y*-axis (either up or down depending on the sign of *b*). A point with an *x* coordinate of *a*, and a *y* coordinate of *b*, is represented by $(a,b)$. The points $(2,3)$, $(-1,4)$, $(-2,-3)$, and $(4,-2)$ are shown on the following graph.

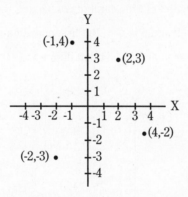

**411.** *Distance between two points.* If the coordinates of point $A$ are $(x_1,y_1)$ and the coordinates of point $B$ are $(x_2,y_2)$, then the distance on the graph between the two points is $d = \sqrt{(x_2\ x_1)^2 + (y_2-y_1)^2}$.

**Example:** Find the distance between the point $(2,-3)$ and the point $(5,1)$.

*Solution:* In this case $x_1 = 2$, $x_2 = 5$, $y_1 = -3$, and $y_2 = 1$. Substituting into the above formula gives us

$$d = \sqrt{(5-2)^2 + [1-(-3)]^2} = \sqrt{3^2 + 4^2} = \sqrt{25} = 5$$

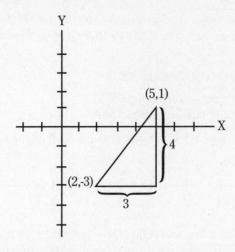

*Note:* This formula is a consequence of the Pythagorean Theorem. Pythagoras, an ancient Greek mathematician, discovered that the square of the length of the hypotenuse (longest side) of a right triangle is equal to the sum of the square of the lengths of the other two sides. See Sections 317 and 509.

**412.**  *Midpoint of the line segment joining two points.* If the coordinates of the first point are $(x_1, y_1)$ and the coordinates of the second point are $(x_2, y_2)$, then the coordinates of the midpoint will be $\left(\dfrac{x_1 + x_2}{2}, \dfrac{y_1 + y_2}{2}\right)$. In other words, each coordinate of the midpoint is equal to the *average* of the corresponding coordinates of the endpoints.

**Example:** Find the midpoint of the segment connecting the points (2,4) and (6,2).

*Solution:* The average of 2 and 6 is 4 so the first coordinate is 4. The average of 4 and 2 is 3; thus the second coordinate is 3. The midpoint is (4,3). $\left[\dfrac{2+6}{2} = 4, \dfrac{4+2}{2} = 3\right]$

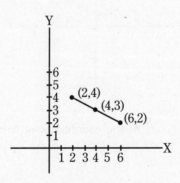

**413.**  *Plotting the graph of a line.* An equation that can be put in the form of $y = mx + b$, where $m$ and $b$ are numerical constants, can be represented as a line on a graph. This means that all of the points on the graph that the line passes through will satisfy the equation. Remember that each point has an $x$ and a $y$ value that can be substituted into the equation. To plot a line, follow the steps below:

**STEP 1.**  Select two values of $x$ and two values of $y$ that will satisfy the equation. For example, in the equation $y = 2x + 4$, the point ($x = 1, y = 6$) will satisfy the equation as will the point ($x = -2, y = 0$). There are an infinite number of such points on a line.

**STEP 2.**  Plot these two points on the graph. In this case, the two points are (1,6) and (−2,0). These points are represented below.

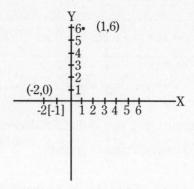

**STEP 3.** Draw a line connecting the two points. This is the line representing the equation.

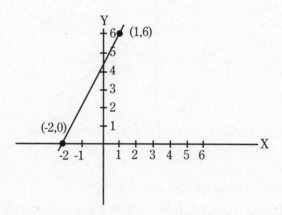

(Note: A straight line is completely specified by two points.)

**Example:** Graph the equation $2y + 3x = 12$.

*Solution:* Two points that satisfy this equation are (2,3) and (0,6). Plotting these points and drawing a line between them gives:

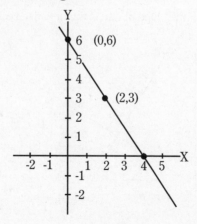

**414.** *Y-intercept.* The *Y*-intercept of a line is the point where the line crosses the *Y*-axis. At any point where a line, crosses the *Y*-axis, $x = 0$. To find the *Y*-intercept of a line, simply substitute $x = 0$ into the equation of the line, and solve for *y*.

**Example:** Find the *Y*-intercept of the equation $2x + 3y = 6$.

*Solution:* If $x = 0$ is substituted into the equation, it simplifies to $3y = 6$. Solving for *y* gives $y = 2$. Thus, 2 is the *Y*-intercept.

> **If an equation can be put into the form of $y = mx + b$ then $b$ is the Y-intercept.**

**415.**  *X-intercept.* The point where a line intersects the *X*-axis is called the *X*-intercept. At this point $y = 0$. To find the *X*-intercept of a line, substitute $y = 0$ into the equation and solve for *x*.

**Example:** Given the equation $2x + 3y = 6$, find the *X*-intercept.

*Solution:* Substitute $y = 0$ into the equation getting $2x = 6$. Solving for *x*, find $x = 3$. Thus the *X*-intercept is 3.

In the diagram below, the *Y*- and *X*-intercepts of the equation $2x + 3y = 6$ are illustrated.

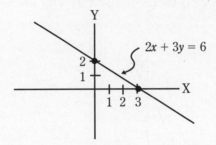

**416.**  *Slope.* The slope of a line is the change in *y* caused by a 1 unit increase in *x*. If an equation is in the form of $y = mx + b$, then as *x* increases 1 unit, *y* will increase *m* units. Therefore the slope is *m*.

**Example:** Find the slope of the line $2x + 3y = 6$.

*Solution:* First put the equation into the form of $y = mx + b$. Subtract $2x$ from both sides and divide by 3. The equation becomes $y = -\dfrac{2}{3}x + 2$. Therefore the slope is $-\dfrac{2}{3}$.

The slope of the line joining two points, $(x_1, y_1)$ and $(x_2, y_2)$, is given by the expression $m_{12} = \dfrac{y_2 - y}{x_2 - x}$.

**Example:** Find the slope of the line joining the points $(3,2)$ and $(4,-1)$.

*Solution:* Substituting into the above formula gives us $m = \dfrac{-3}{1} = -3$ where $x_1 = 3$, $x_2 = 4$, $y_1 = 2$, $y_2 = -1$.

If two lines are perpendicular, the slope of one is the negative reciprocal of the other.

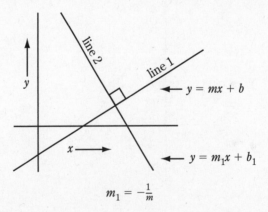

**Example:** What is the slope of a line perpendicular to the line $y = -3x + 4$?

*Solution:* Since the slope of the line $y = -3x + 4$ is $-3$, the slope of the line perpendicular to that line is the negative reciprocal, or $\dfrac{-1}{-3} = \dfrac{+1}{3}$.

**417.** *Graphing simultaneous equations.* Recall that simultaneous equations are a pair of equations in two unknowns. Each of these equations is graphed separately, and each is represented by a straight line. The solution of the simultaneous equations (i.e., the pair of values that satisfies *both* at the same time) is represented by the intersection of two lines. Now, for any pair of lines, there are three possible relationships:

1. The lines intersect at one and only one point; in this case, this point represents the unique solution to the pair of equations. This is most often the case. Such lines are called *consistent*.

2. The lines coincide exactly; this represents the case where the two equations are equivalent (just different forms of the same mathematical relation). Any point that satisfies *either* of the two equations automatically satisfies *both*.

3. The lines are parallel and never intersect. In this case the equations are called *inconsistent*, and they have *no* solution at all. Two lines that are parallel will have the same slope.

**Example:** Solve graphically the equations $4x - y = 5$ and $2x + 4y = 16$.

*Solution:* Plot the two lines represented by the two equations. (See Section 413.) The graph is shown below.

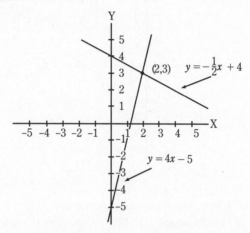

The two lines intersect in the point (2,3), which represents the solution $x = 2$ and $y = 3$. This can be checked by solving the equations as is done in Section 407.

**Example:** Solve $x + 2y = 6$ and $2x + 4y = 8$.

*Solution:* Find two points that satisfy each equation. Draw a line connecting these two points. The two graphs will look like this:

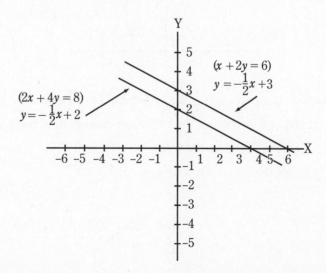

These lines will never intersect, and these equations are termed inconsistent. There is no solution.

Remember that two parallel lines have the same slope. This is an easy way to see whether two lines are consistent or inconsistent.

**Example:** Find the solution to $2x - 3y = 8$ and $4x = 6y + 16$.

*Solution:* On the graph these two lines are identical. This means that there are an infinite set of points that satisfy both equations.

Equations of identical lines are multiples of each other and can be reduced to a single equation.

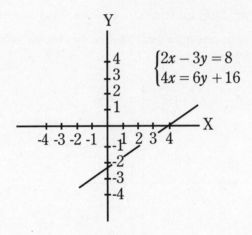

$$\begin{cases} 2x - 3y = 8 \\ 4x = 6y + 16 \end{cases}$$

**418.** *Areas of polygons.* Often, an elementary geometric figure is placed on a graph to calculate its area. This is usually simple for figures such as triangles, rectangles, squares, parallelograms, etc.

**Example:** Calculate the area of the triangle in the figure below.

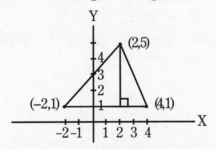

*Solution:* The area of a triangle is $\frac{1}{2}$ (base) (height). On the graph the length of the line joining $(-2,1)$ and $(4,1)$ is 6 units. The height, which goes from point $(2,5)$ to the base, has a length of 4 units. Therefore the area is $\frac{1}{2}$ (6) (4) = 12.

**Example:** Calculate the area of the square pictured below.

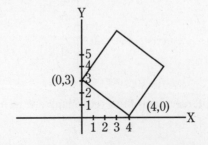

*Solution:* The area of a square is given by the square of the side. To find this area first find the length of one side. The length of a segment whose endpoints are $(x_1, y_1)$ and $(x_2, y_2)$ is given by the formula $\sqrt{(x_2-x_1)^2 + (y_2-y_1)^2}$. Substituting in (0,3) and (4,0) gives a length of 5 units. Thus the length of one side of the square is 5. Using the formula area = (side)$^2$ gives an area of 5$^2$ or 25 square units.

To find the area of more complicated polygons, divide the polygon into simple figures whose areas can be calculated. Add these areas to find the total area.

**Example:** Find the area of the figure below:

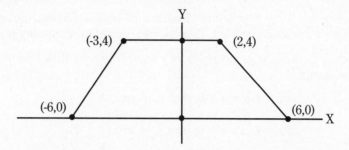

*Solution:* Divide the figure into two triangles and a rectangle by drawing vertical lines at $(-3,4)$ and $(2,4)$. Thus the polygon is now two triangles and a rectangle.

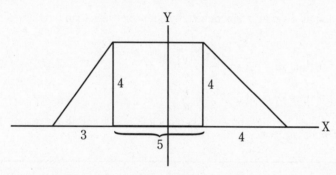

The height of the left triangle is 4 units, and the base is 3. Using $A = \frac{1}{2}bh$ gives the area as 6.

The height of the right triangle is 4, and the base is 4. The area is 8. The length of one side of the rectangle is 4, and the other side is 5. Using the formula, area = base · height, gives the area as 20. Thus the total area is 6 + 8 + 20 = 34.

## Inequalities

**419.** *Inequalities.* These problems deal with numbers that are less than, greater than, or equal to other numbers. The following laws apply to all inequalities:

< means less than, thus $3 < 4$

> means greater than, thus $5 > 2$

≤ means less than or equal to, thus $x \leq y$ means $x < y$ or $x = y$

≥ means greater than or equal to, thus $x \geq y$ means $x > y$ or $x = y$

**420.** If equal quantities are added to both sides of an inequality, the direction of the inequality does *not* change.

$$\text{If } x < y, \text{ then } x + z < y + z \text{ and } x - z < y - z.$$

$$\text{If } x > y, \text{ then } x + z > y + z \text{ and } x - z > y - z.$$

For example, given the inequality, $4 > 2$, with 1 added to or subtracted from both sides, the results, $5 > 3$ and $3 > 1$, have the same inequality sign as the original. If the problem is algebraic, i.e., $x + 3 < 6$, it is possible to subtract 3 from both sides to get this simple inequality $x < 3$.

**421.** Subtracting parts of an inequality from an equation *reverses* the order of the inequality.

$$\text{If } x < y, \text{ then } z - x > z - y.$$

$$\text{If } x > y, \text{ then } z - x < z - y.$$

For example, given that $3 < 5$, subtracting 3 from the left-hand and 5 from the right-hand sides of the equation $10 = 10$ results in $7 > 5$. Thus the direction of the inequality is reversed.

**422.** Multiplying or dividing an inequality by a number greater than zero does not change the order of the inequality.

$$\text{If } x > y, \text{ and } a > 0, \text{ then } xa > ya \text{ and } \frac{x}{a} > \frac{y}{a}.$$

$$\text{If } x < y, \text{ and } a > 0, \text{ then } xa < ya \text{ and } \frac{x}{a} < \frac{y}{a}.$$

For example, if $4 > 2$, multiplying both sides by any arbitrary number (for instance, 5) gives $20 > 10$, which is still true. Or, if algebraically $6h < 3$, dividing both sides by 6 gives $h < \frac{1}{2}$, which is true.

**423.** Multiplying or dividing an inequality by a number less than 0 reverses the order of the inequality.

$$\text{If } x > y, \text{ and } a < 0, \text{ then } xa < ya \text{ and } \frac{x}{a} < \frac{y}{a}.$$

$$\text{If } x < y, \text{ and } a < 0, \text{ then } xa > ya \text{ and } \frac{x}{a} > \frac{y}{a}.$$

If $-3 < 2$ is multiplied through by $-2$ it becomes $6 > -4$, and the order of the inequality is reversed.

---

> **Note that negative numbers are always less than positive numbers. Note also that the greater the absolute value of a negative number, the smaller it actually is. Thus, $-10 < -9$, $-8 < -7$, etc.**

---

**424.** The product of two numbers with like signs is positive.

$$\text{If } x > 0 \text{ and } y > 0, \text{ then } xy > 0.$$

$$\text{If } x < 0 \text{ and } y < 0, \text{ then } xy > 0.$$

For example, $-3$ times $-2$ is 6.

**425.** The product of two numbers with unlike signs is negative.

$$\text{If } x < 0 \text{ and } y > 0, \text{ then } xy < 0.$$

$$\text{If } x > 0 \text{ and } y < 0, \text{ then } xy < 0.$$

For example, $-2$ times 3 is $-6$. 8 times $-1$ is $-8$, etc.

**426.** *Linear inequalities in one unknown.* In these problems a first power variable is given in an inequality, and this variable must be solved for in terms of the inequality. Examples of linear inequalities in one unknown are: $2x + 7 > 4 + x$, $8y - 3 \leq 2y$, etc.

**STEP 1.** By ordinary algebraic addition and subtraction (as if it were an equality) get all of the constant terms on one side of the inequality and all of the variable terms on the other side. In the inequality $2x + 4 < 8x + 16$ subtract 4 and $8x$ from both sides and get $-6x < 12$.

**STEP 2.** Divide both sides by the coefficient of the variable. Important: If the coefficient of the variable is negative, you must reverse the inequality sign. For example, in $-6x < 12$, dividing by $-6$ gives $x > 2$. (The inequality is reversed.) In $3x < 12$ dividing by 3 gives $x < 4$.

**Example:** Solve for $y$ in the inequality $4y + 7 \geq 9 - 2y$.

*Solution:* Subtracting $-2y$ and 7 from both sides gives $6y \geq 2$. Dividing both sides by 6 gives $y \geq \frac{1}{3}$.

**Example:** Solve for $a$ in the inequality $10 - 2a < 0$.

*Solution:* Subtracting 10 from both sides gives $-2a < -10$. Dividing both sides by $-2$ gives $a > \frac{-10}{-2}$ or $a > 5$. Note that the inequality sign has been reversed because of the division by a negative number.

**427.** *Simultaneous linear inequalities in two unknowns.* These are two inequalities, each one in two unknowns. The same two unknowns are to be solved for in each equation. This means the equations must be solved simultaneously.

**STEP 1.** Plot both inequalities on the same graph. Replace the inequality sign with an equality sign and plot the resulting line. The side of the line that makes the inequality true is then shaded in. For example, graph the inequality $(2x - y > 4)$. First replace the inequality sign getting $2x - y = 4$; then, plot the line. The $X$-intercept is 2. The $Y$-intercept is $-4$.

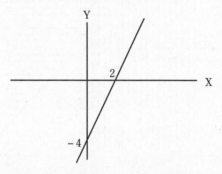

To decide which side of the line satisfies the inequality, choose a convenient point on each side and determine which point satisfies the inequality. Shade in that side of the line. In this case, choose the point (0,0). With this point the equation becomes $2(0) - 0 > 4$ or $0 > 4$. This is not true. Thus, shade in the other side of the line.

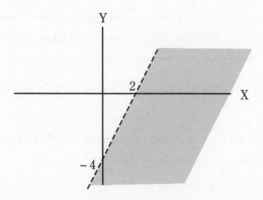

**STEP 2.** After both inequalities have been solved, the area that is common to both shaded portions is the solution to the problem.

**Example:** Solve $x + y > 2$ and $3x < 6$.

*Solution:* First graph $x + y > 2$ by plotting $x + y = 2$ and using the point (4,0) to determine the region where the inequality is satisfied:

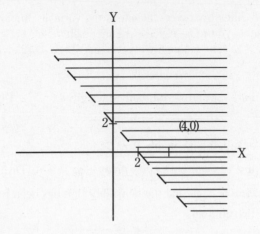

Graph the inequality $3x < 6$ on the same axes and get:

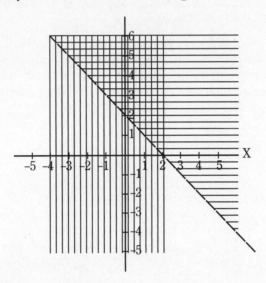

The solution is the double shaded area.

**428.** *Higher order inequalities in one unknown.* These are inequalities that deal with variables multiplied by themselves. For example, $x^2 + 3 \geq 0$, $(x - 1)(x + 2) < 4$ and $x^3 - 7x > 0$ are such inequalities. The basic rules to remember in doing such problems are:

> **1. The product of any number of positive numbers is positive.**

For example, $2 \times 3 \times 4 \times 5 = 120$, which is positive, or $\frac{1}{2} \times \frac{1}{2} = \frac{1}{4}$, which is positive.

> **2. The product of an even number of negative numbers is positive.**

For example, $(-3)(-2) = 6$ or $(-3)(-1)(-9)(-2) = 54$, which is positive.

> **3. The product of an odd number of negative numbers is negative.**

For example, $(-1)(-2)(-3) = -6$ or $(-\frac{1}{2})(-2)(-3)(-6)(-1) = -18$.

---

**4. Any number squared or raised to an even power is always positive or zero.**

---

For example, $x^2 \geq 0$ or $a^4 \geq 0$ for all $x$ and for all $a$.

Often these basic rules will make the solution to an inequality problem obvious.

**Example:** Which of the following values can $x^2$ not have?

(A) 5     (B) $-2$     (C) 0     (D) 144     (E) 9

*Solution:* We know that $x^2 \geq 0$ for all $x$ so $x^2$ cannot be negative. $-2$ is negative, so $x^2$ cannot equal $-2$.

The steps in solving a higher order inequality are:

**STEP 1.**   Bring all of the terms to one side of the inequality, making the other side zero. For example, in the inequality $x^2 > 3x - 2$, subtract $3x - 2$ from both sides to get $x^2 - 3x + 2 > 0$.

**STEP 2.**   Factor the resulting expression. To factor a quadratic expression means to write the original expression as the product of two terms in the 1st power, i.e., $x^2 = x \cdot x$. $x$ is a factor of $x^2$. (See Section 409 for a detailed explanation of factoring.) The quadratic expression $x^2 - 3x + 2$ when factored is $(x - 2)(x - 1)$. Note that $x \cdot x = x^2$, $- 2x - x = - 3x$ and $(-1)(-2) = 2$. Most quadratic expressions can easily be factored by taking factors of the last term (in this case 2 and 1) and adding or subtracting them to $x$. Through trial and error the right combination is found. An important fact to remember when factoring is: $(a + b)(c + d) = ac + ad + bc + bd$. Example: $(x + 4)(x + 2) = x^2 + 4x + 2x + 8 = x^2 + 6x + 8$. Another is that $a^2 - b^2 = (a + b)(a - b)$. Example: $x^2 - 16 = (x + 4)(x - 4)$.

**STEP 3.**   Investigate which terms are positive and which terms are negative. For example, in $(x - 3)(x + 2) > 0$, either $(x - 3)$ and $(x + 2)$ are both positive or $(x - 3)$ and $(x + 2)$ are both negative. If one were positive and the other were negative, the product would be negative and would not satisfy the inequality. If the factors are positive, then $x - 3 > 0$ and $x + 2 > 0$, which yields $x > 3$ and $x > -2$. For $x$ to be greater than 3 and to be greater than $-2$, it must be greater than 3. If it is greater than 3 it is automatically greater than $-2$. Thus, with positive factors $x > 3$ is the answer. If the factors are negative, $x - 3 < 0$ and $x + 2 < 0$, or $x < -2$. For $x$ to be less than 3 and less than $-2$ it must be less than $-2$. Thus, with negative factors $x < -2$ is the answer. As both answers are possible from the original equation, the solution to the original problem is $x > 3$ or $x < -2$.

**Example:** For which values of $x$ is $x^2 + 5 < 6x$?

*Solution:* First subtract $6x$ from both sides to get $x^2 - 6x + 5 < 0$. The left side factors into $(x - 5)(x - 1) < 0$. Now for this to be true one factor must be positive and one must be negative, i.e., their product is less than zero. Thus, $x - 5 > 0$ and $x - 1 < 0$ or $x - 5 < 0$ and $x - 1 > 0$. If $x - 5 < 0$ and $x - 1 > 0$ then $x < 5$ and $x > 1$, or $1 < x < 5$. If $x - 5 > 0$ and $x - 1 < 0$ then $x > 5$ and $x < 1$, which is impossible because $x$ cannot be less than 1 and greater than 5. Therefore, the solution is $1 < x < 5$.

**Example:** For what values of $x$ is $x^2 < 4$?

*Solution:* Subtract 4 from both sides to get $x^2 - 4 < 0$. Remember that $a^2 - b^2 = (a + b)(a - b)$; thus $x^2 - 4 = (x + 2)(x - 2)$. Hence, $(x + 2)(x - 2) < 0$. For this to be true $x + 2 > 0$ and $x - 2 < 0$ or $x + 2 < 0$ and $x - 2 > 0$. In the first case $x > -2$ and $x < + 2$ or $-2 < x < 2$. The second case is $x < -2$ and $x > + 2$ is impossible because $x$ cannot be less than $-2$ *and* greater than 2. Thus, the solution is $-2 < x < 2$.

**Example:** When is $(x^2 + 1)(x - 2)^2(x - 3)$ greater than or equal to zero?

*Solution:* This can be written as $(x^2 + 1)(x - 2)^2(x - 3) \geq 0$. This is already in factors. The individual terms must be investigated. $x^2 + 1$ is always positive because $x^2 \geq 0$ so $x^2 + 1$ must be greater than 0. $(x - 2)^2$ is a number squared so this is always greater than or equal to zero. Therefore, the product of the first two terms is positive or equal to zero for all values of $x$. The third term $x - 3$ is positive when $x > 3$, and negative when $x < 3$. For the entire expression to be positive, $x - 3$ must be positive, i.e., $x > 3$. For the expression to be equal to zero, $x - 3 = 0$, i.e., $x = 3$, or $(x - 2)^2 = 0$, i.e., $x = 2$. Thus, the entire expression is positive when $x > 3$ and zero when $x = 2$ or $x = 3$.

# Exponents and Roots

**429.** *Exponents.* An exponent is an easy way to express repeated multiplication. For example, $5 \times 5 \times 5 \times 5 = 5^4$. The 4 is the exponent. In the expression $7^3 = 7 \times 7 \times 7$, 3 is the exponent. $7^3$ means 7 is multiplied by itself three times. If the exponent is 0, the expression always has a value of 1. Thus, $6^0 = 15^0 = 1$, etc. If the exponent is 1, the value of the expression is the number base. Thus, $4^1 = 4$ and $9^1 = 9$.

In the problem $5^3 \times 5^4$, we can simplify by counting the factors of 5. Thus $5^3 \times 5^4 = 5^{3+4} = 5^7$. When we multiply and the base number is the same, we keep the base number and add the exponents. For example, $7^4 \times 7^8 = 7^{12}$.

For division, we keep the same base number and subtract exponents. Thus, $8^8 \div 8^2 = 8^{8-2} = 8^6$.

A negative exponent indicates the reciprocal of the expression with a positive exponent, thus $3^{-2} = \dfrac{1}{3^2}$.

**430.** *Roots.* The square root of a number is a number whose square is the original number. for example, $\sqrt{16} = 4$, since $4 \times 4 = 16$. (The $\sqrt{\phantom{x}}$ symbol always means a positive number.)

To simplify a square root, we factor the number.

$$\sqrt{32} = \sqrt{16 \cdot 2} = \sqrt{16} \cdot \sqrt{2} = 4\sqrt{2}$$
$$\sqrt{72} = \sqrt{36 \cdot 2} = \sqrt{36} \cdot \sqrt{2} = 6\sqrt{2}$$
$$\sqrt{300} = \sqrt{25 \cdot 12} = \sqrt{25} \cdot \sqrt{12}$$
$$= 5 \cdot \sqrt{12}$$
$$= 5 \cdot \sqrt{4 \cdot 3}$$
$$= 5\sqrt{4}\,\sqrt{3}$$
$$= 5 \cdot 2\sqrt{3}$$
$$= 10\sqrt{3}$$

We can add expressions with the square roots only if the numbers inside the square root sign are the same. For example,

$$3\sqrt{7} + 2\sqrt{7} = 5\sqrt{7}$$
$$\sqrt{18} + \sqrt{2} = \sqrt{9 \cdot 2} + \sqrt{2} = \sqrt{9}\,\sqrt{2} + \sqrt{2} = 3\sqrt{2} + \sqrt{2} = 4\sqrt{2}.$$

**431.** *Evaluation of expressions.* To evaluate an expression means to substitute a value in place of a letter. For example: Evaluate $3a^2 - c^3$; if $a = -2$, $c = -3$.

$$3a^2 - c^3 = 3(-2)^2 - (-3)^3 = 3(4) - (-27) = 12 + 27 = 39$$

Given: $a \nabla b = ab + b^2$. Find: $-2\nabla 3$.

Using the definition, w e get

$$-2\nabla 3 = (-2)(3) + (3)^2$$
$$= -6 + 9$$
$$-2\nabla 3 = 3$$

# Practice Test 4

## Algebra Problems

Correct answers and solutions follow each test.

1.  A B C D E

1. For what values of $x$ is the following equation satisfied: $3x + 9 = 21 + 7x$?

   (A) $-3$ only
   (B) $3$ only
   (C) $3$ or $-3$ only
   (D) no values
   (E) an infinite number of values

2.  A B C D E

2. What values may $z$ have if $2z + 4$ is greater than $z - 6$?

   (A) any values greater than $-10$
   (B) any values greater than $-2$
   (C) any values less than $2$
   (D) any values less than $10$
   (E) None of these.

3.  A B C D E

3. If $ax^2 + 2x - 3 = 0$ when $x = -3$, what value(s) can $a$ have?

   (A) $-3$ only
   (B) $-1$ only
   (C) $1$ only
   (D) $-1$ and $1$ only
   (E) $-3$, $-1$, and $1$ only

4.  A B C D E

4. If the coordinates of point $P$ are $(0,8)$, and the coordinates of point $Q$ are $(4,2)$, which of the following points represents the midpoint of $PQ$?

   (A) $(0,2)$
   (B) $(2,4)$
   (C) $(2,5)$
   (D) $(4,8)$
   (E) $(4,10)$

5.  A B C D E

5. In the formula $V = \pi r^2 h$, what is the value of $r$, in terms of $V$ and $h$?

   (A) $\dfrac{\sqrt{V}}{\pi h}$

   (B) $\pi\sqrt{\dfrac{V}{h}}$

   (C) $\sqrt{\pi V h}$

   (D) $\dfrac{\pi h}{\sqrt{V}}$

   (E) $\sqrt{\dfrac{V}{\pi h}}$

6.  A B C D E

6. Solve the inequality $x^2 - 3x < 0$.

   (A) $x < -3$
   (B) $-3 < x < 0$
   (C) $x < 3$
   (D) $0 < x < 3$
   (E) $3 < x$

7. **A B C D E**

7. Which of the following lines is parallel to the line represented by $2y = 8x + 32$?

$$\frac{2y}{2} = \frac{8x}{2} + \frac{32}{2}$$
$$y = 4x + 8$$

(A) $y = 8x + 32$
(B) $y = 8x + 16$
(C) $y = 16x + 32$
(D) $y = 4x + 32$
(E) $y = 2x + 16$

8. **A B C D E**

8. In the equation $4.04x + 1.01 = 9.09$, what value of $x$ is necessary to make the equation true?

$$\begin{array}{r} -1.01 \quad -1.01 \\ 4.04 = 8.08 \end{array}$$

(A) $-1.5$
(B) $0$
(C) $1$
(D) $2$
(E) $2.5$

9. **A B C D E**

9. What values of $x$ satisfy the equation $(x + 1)(x - 2) = 0$?

(A) $1$ only
(B) $-2$ only
(C) $1$ and $-2$ only
(D) $-1$ and $2$ only
(E) any values between $-1$ and $2$

10. **A B C D E**

10. What is the largest possible value of the following expression:
$$(x + 2)(3 - x)(2 + x)^2(2x - 6)(2x + 4)?$$

(A) $-576$
(B) $-24$
(C) $0$
(D) $12$
(E) Cannot be determined.

11. **A B C D E**

11. For what value(s) of $k$ is the following equation satisfied:
$$2k - 9 - k = 4k + 6 - 3k?$$
(A) $-5$ only
(B) $0$
(C) $\dfrac{5}{2}$ only
(D) no values
(E) more than one value

12. **A B C D E**

12. In the equation $p = aq^2 + bq + c$, if $a = 1$, $b = -2$, and $c = 1$, which of the following expresses $p$ in terms of $q$?

$$p = q^2 - 2q + 1$$
$$p = (q - 1)^2$$

(A) $p = (q - 2)^2$
(B) $p = (q - 1)^2$
(C) $p = q^2$
(D) $p = (q + 1)^2$
(E) $p = (q + 2)^2$

13. **A B C D E**

13. If $A + B + C = 10$, $A + B = 7$, and $A - B = 5$, what is the value of $C$?

(A) $1$
(B) $3$
(C) $6$
(D) $7$
(E) The answer cannot be determined from the given information.

**14.**  A B C D E

**14.** If $5x + 15$ is greater than 20, which of the following best describes the possible values of $x$?

(A) $x$ must be greater than 5
(B) $x$ must be greater than 3
(C) $x$ must be greater than 1
(D) $x$ must be less than 5
(E) $x$ must be less than 1

$5x + 15 > 20$
$-15 \qquad -15$
$\dfrac{5x}{5} = \dfrac{5}{5}$
$x > 1$

**15.**  A B C D E

**15.** If $\dfrac{t^2 - 1}{t - 1} = 2$, then what value(s) may $t$ have?

(A) 1 only
(B) $-1$ only
(C) 1 or $-1$
(D) no values
(E) an infinite number of values

**16.**  A B C D E

**16.** If $4m = 9n$, what is the value of $7m$, in terms of $n$?

(A) $\dfrac{63n}{4}$
(B) $\dfrac{9n}{28}$
(C) $\dfrac{7n}{9}$
(D) $\dfrac{28n}{9}$
(E) $\dfrac{7n}{4}$

$\dfrac{4m = 9n}{7m}$  $15\frac{3}{4}n$

$M = \dfrac{9n}{4}$

$7m = \dfrac{63n}{4}$

**17.**  A B C D E

**17.** The coordinates of a triangle are $(0,2)$, $(2,4)$, and $(1,6)$. What is the area of the triangle in square units (to the nearest unit)?

(A) 2 square units
(B) 3 square units
(C) 4 square units
(D) 5 square units
(E) 6 square units

**18.**  A B C D E

**18.** In the formula $s = \frac{1}{2} gt^2$, what is the value of $t$, in terms of $s$ and $g$?

(A) $\dfrac{2s}{g}$
(B) $2\sqrt{\dfrac{s}{g}}$
(C) $\dfrac{s}{2g}$
(D) $\sqrt{\dfrac{s}{2g}}$
(E) $\sqrt{\dfrac{2s}{g}}$

$2(s) = \left(\frac{1}{2}gt^2\right)^2$

$\sqrt{\dfrac{2s}{g}} = \sqrt{\dfrac{gt^2}{g}}$

$@ \; 2\sqrt{\dfrac{s}{g}}$

**19.**  A B C D E

**19.** In the triangle $ABC$, angle $A$ is a $30°$ angle, and angle $B$ is obtuse. If $x$ represents the number of degrees in angle $C$, which of the following best represents the possible values of $x$?

(A) $0 < x < 60$
(B) $0 < x < 150$
(C) $60 < x < 180$
(D) $120 < x < 180$
(E) $120 < x < 150$

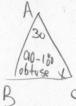

**20.** A B C D E

**20.** Which of the following sets of coordinates does *not* represent the vertices of an isosceles triangle?

    (A) (0,2), (0, −2), (2,0)
    (B) (1,3), (1,5), (3,4)
    (C) (1,3), (1,7), (4,5)
    (D) (2,2), (2,0), (1,1)
    (E) (2,3), (2,5), (3,3)

**21.** A B C D E

**21.** If $2 < a < 5$, and $6 > b > 3$, what are the possible values of $a + b$?

$a = 3, 4$     $4, 5$

    (A) $a + b$ must equal 8.
    (B) $a + b$ must be between 2 and 6.
    (C) $a + b$ must be between 3 and 5.
    (D) $a + b$ must be between 5 and 8.
    (E) $a + b$ must be between 5 and 11.

$7, 8, 9$

**22.** A B C D E

**22.** The area of a square will be doubled if:

    (A) The length of the diagonal is divided by 2.
    (B) The length of the diagonal is divided by $\sqrt{2}$.
    (C) The length of the diagonal is multiplied by 2.
    (D) The length of the diagonal is multiplied by $\sqrt{2}$.
    (E) None of the above.

**23.** A B C D E

**23.** Find the value of $y$ that satisfies the equation $8.8y − 4 = 7.7y + 7$.

$+4 \qquad +4$

    (A) 1.1
    (B) 7.7
    (C) 8.0
    (D) 10.0
    (E) 11.0

$8.8y = 7.7y + 11$
$-7.7y \quad -7.7y$
$1.1y = 11$

**24.** A B C D E

**24.** Which of the following is a factor of the expression $2x^2 + 1$?

    (A) $x + 2$
    (B) $x − 2$
    (C) $x + \sqrt{2}$
    (D) $x − \sqrt{2}$
    (E) None of these.

**25.** A B C D E

**25.** A businessman has ten employees; his salary is equal to six times the *average* of the employees' salaries. If the eleven of them received a total of $64,000 in one year, what was the businessman's salary that year?

$10$

    (A) $4,000
    (B) $6,000
    (C) $24,000
    (D) $40,000
    (E) $44,000

$6,400$    $\sqrt{64,000}$

$4000$

**26.** A B C D E

**26.** If $6x + 3$ equals 15, what is the value of $12x − 3$?

    (A) 21
    (B) 24
    (C) 28
    (D) 33
    (E) 36

$6x + 3 = 15$
$\quad -3 \quad -3$
$6x = 12$
$\frac{6x}{6} = \frac{12}{6}$
$x = 2$

**27.** A B C D E  **27.** If $2p + 7$ is greater than $3p - 5$, which of the following best describes the possible values of $p$?

     (A) $p$ must be greater than 2.
     (B) $p$ must be greater than 12.
     (C) $p$ must be less than 2.
     (D) $p$ must be less than 12.
     (E) $p$ must be greater than 2, but less than 12.

**28.** A B C D E  **28.** What is the value of $q$ if $x^2 + qx + 1 = 0$, if $x = 1$?

     (A) $-2$
     (B) $-1$
     (C) $0$
     (D) $1$
     (E) $2$

**29.** A B C D E  **29.** What is the area (to the nearest unit) of the shaded figure in the diagram below, assuming that each of the squares has an area of 1?

     (A) 12
     (B) 13
     (C) 14
     (D) 15
     (E) 16

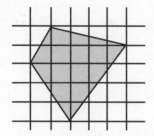

**30.** A B C D E  **30.** Which of the following statements is *false*?

     (A) Any two numbers, $a$ and $b$, have a sum equal to $a + b$.
     (B) Any two numbers, $a$ and $b$, have a product equal to $a \cdot b$.
     (C) Any two numbers, $a$ and $b$, have a difference equal to $a - b$.

     (D) Any two numbers, $a$ and $b$, have a quotient equal to $\dfrac{a}{b}$.

     (E) Any two numbers, $a$ and $b$, have an average equal to $\dfrac{(a + b)}{2}$.

**31.** A B C D E  **31.** If $(x - 1)(x - 2)(x^2 - 4) = 0$, what are the possible values of $x$?

     (A) $-2$ only
     (B) $+2$ only
     (C) $-1, -2$, or $-4$ only
     (D) $+1, +2$, or $+4$ only
     (E) $+1, -2$, or $+2$ only

**32.** A B C D E  **32.** If $P + Q = R$, and $P + R = 2Q$, what is the ratio of $P$ to $R$?

     (A) $1 : 1$
     (B) $1 : 2$
     (C) $2 : 1$
     (D) $1 : 3$
     (E) $3 : 1$

33.  A B C D E

**33.** For what value(s) of $r$ is $\dfrac{r^2 + 5r + 6}{r + 2}$ equal to 0?

(A) $-2$ only
(B) $-3$ only
(C) $+3$ only
(D) $-2$ or $-3$
(E) $+2$ or $+3$

34.  A B C D E

**34.** What is the value of $a^2b + 4ab^2 + 4b^3$, if $a = 15$ and $b = 5$?

(A) 1,625
(B) 2,125
(C) 2,425
(D) 2,725
(E) 3,125

35.  A B C D E

**35.** If $m + 4n = 2n + 8m$, what is the ratio of $n$ to $m$?

(A) $1:4$
(B) $1:-4$
(C) $-4:1$
(D) $2:7$
(E) $7:2$

36.  A B C D E

**36.** If the value of $a$ lies between $-5$ and $+2$, and the value of $b$ lies between $-7$ and $+1$, what are the possible values for the product, $a \cdot b$?

(A) between $-14$ and $+2$
(B) between $-35$ and $+2$
(C) between $+2$ and $+35$
(D) between $-12$ and $+3$
(E) between $-14$ and $+35$

37.  A B C D E

**37.** What is the area, in square units, of a triangle whose vertices lie on points $(-5,1)$, $(-5,4)$, and $(2,4)$?

(A) 10.5 square units
(B) 12.5 square units
(C) 15.0 square units
(D) 20.0 square units
(E) 21.0 square units

38.  A B C D E

**38.** If $A + B = 12$, and $B + C = 16$, what is the value of $A + C$?

(A) $-4$
(B) $-28$
(C) $+4$
(D) $+28$
(E) The answer cannot be determined from the given information.

39.  A B C D E

**39.** What is the solution to the equation $x^2 + x + 1 = 0$?

(A) $-\dfrac{1}{2} + \dfrac{\sqrt{3}}{2}$ and $-\dfrac{1}{2} - \dfrac{\sqrt{3}}{2}$

(B) $-\dfrac{1}{2} + \dfrac{\sqrt{3}}{2}$ only

(C) $-\dfrac{1}{2} - \dfrac{\sqrt{3}}{2}$ only

(D) no real solutions

(E) 0

**40.** A B C D E

**40.** Which of the following equations will have a vertical line as its graph?

(A) $x + y = 1$
(B) $x - y = 1$
(C) $x = 1$
(D) $y = 1$
(E) $xy = 1$

**41.** A B C D E

**41.** For what values of $x$ does $x^2 + 3x + 2$ equal zero?

(A) $-1$ only
(B) $+2$ only
(C) $-1$ or $-2$ only
(D) $1$ or $2$ only
(E) None of these.

**42.** A B C D E

**42.** If $a + b$ equals 12, and $a - b$ equals 6, what is the value of $b$?

(A) 0
(B) 3
(C) 6
(D) 9
(E) The answer cannot be determined from the given information.

**43.** A B C D E

**43.** For what values of $m$ is $m^2 + 4$ equal to $4m$?

(A) $-2$ only
(B) 0 only
(C) $+2$ only
(D) $+4$ only
(E) more than one value

**44.** A B C D E

**44.** If $x = 0$, and $y = 2$, and $x^2yz + 3xz^2 + y^2z + 3y + 4x = 0$, what is the value of $z$?

(A) $-\dfrac{4}{3}$

(B) $-\dfrac{3}{2}$

(C) $+\dfrac{3}{4}$

(D) $+\dfrac{4}{3}$

(E) The answer cannot be determined from the given information.

**45.** A B C D E

**45.** If $c + 4d = 3c - 2d$, what is the ratio of $c$ to $d$?

(A) $1 : 3$
(B) $1 : -3$
(C) $3 : 1$
(D) $2 : 3$
(E) $2 : -3$

**46.** A B C D E

**46.** If $3 < x < 7$, and $6 > x > 2$, which of the following best describes $x$?

(A) $2 < x < 6$
(B) $2 < x < 7$
(C) $3 < x < 6$
(D) $3 < x < 7$
(E) No value of $x$ can satisfy both of these conditions.

**47.**  A B C D E

**47.** What are the coordinates of the midpoint of the line segment whose endpoints are (4,9) and (5,15)?

    (A) (4,5)
    (B) (5,9)
    (C) (4,15)
    (D) (4.5,12)
    (E) (9,24)

**48.**  A B C D E

**48.** If $\dfrac{t^2 + 2t}{2t + 4} = \dfrac{t}{2}$, what does $t$ equal?

    (A) $-2$ only
    (B) $+2$ only
    (C) any value except $+2$
    (D) any value except $-2$
    (E) any value

**49.**  A B C D E

**49.** If $x + y = 4$, and $x + z = 9$, what is the value of $(y - z)$?

    (A) $-5$
    (B) $+5$
    (C) $-13$
    (D) $+13$
    (E) The answer cannot be determined from the given information.

**50.**  A B C D E

**50.** Of the following statements, which are equivalent?

    I. $-3 < x < 3$
    II. $x^2 < 9$
    III. $\dfrac{1}{x} < \dfrac{1}{3}$

    (A) I and II only
    (B) I and III only
    (C) II and III only
    (D) I, II, and III
    (E) None of the above.

# Answer Key for Practice Test 4

| | | | |
|---|---|---|---|
| **1.** A | **14.** C | **27.** D | **39.** D |
| **2.** A | **15.** D | **28.** A | **40.** C |
| **3.** C | **16.** A | **29.** B | **41.** C |
| **4.** C | **17.** B | **30.** D | **42.** B |
| **5.** E | **18.** E | **31.** E | **43.** C |
| **6.** D | **19.** A | **32.** D | **44.** B |
| **7.** D | **20.** E | **33.** B | **45.** C |
| **8.** D | **21.** E | **34.** E | **46.** C |
| **9.** D | **22.** D | **35.** E | **47.** D |
| **10.** C | **23.** D | **36.** E | **48.** D |
| **11.** D | **24.** E | **37.** A | **49.** A |
| **12.** B | **25.** C | **38.** E | **50.** A |
| **13.** B | **26.** A | | |

# Answers and Solutions for Practice Test 4

1. Choice A is correct. The original equation is $3x + 9 = 21 + 7x$. First subtract 9 and $7x$ from both sides to get: $-4x = 12$. Now divide both sides by the coefficient of $x$, $-4$, obtaining the solution, $x = -3$. (406)

2. Choice A is correct. Given $2z + 4 > x - 6$. Subtracting equal quantities from both sides of an inequality does not change the order of the inequality. Therefore, subtracting $z$ and 4 from both sides gives a solution of $z > -10$. (419, 420)

3. Choice C is correct. Substitute $-3$ for $x$ in the original equation to get the following:

$$a(-3)^2 + 2(-3) - 3 = 0$$
$$9a - 6 - 3 = 0$$
$$9a - 9 = 0$$
$$a = 1 \qquad (406)$$

4. Choice C is correct. To find the midpoint of the line segment connecting two points, find the point whose $x$-coordinate is the average of the two given $x$-coordinates, and whose $y$-coordinate is the average of the two given $y$-coordinates. The midpoint here will be $\left(\frac{0+4}{2}, \frac{8+2}{2}\right)$, or (2,5). (412)

5. Choice E is correct. Divide both sides of the equation by $\pi h$:

$$\frac{V}{\pi h} = r^2$$

Take the square root of both sides:

$$r \text{ equals } \sqrt{\frac{V}{\pi h}}. \qquad (408)$$

6. Choice D is correct. Factor the original expression into $x(x - 3) < 0$. In order for the product of two expressions to be less than 0 (negative), one must be positive and the other must be negative. Thus, $x < 0$ and $x - 3 > 0$; or $x > 0$ and $x - 3 < 0$. In the first case, $x < 0$ and $x > 3$. This is impossible because $x$ cannot be less than 0 and greater than 3 at the same time. In the second case $x > 0$ and $x < 3$ which can be rewritten as $0 < x < 3$. (428)

7. Choice D is correct. Divide both sides of the equation $2y = 8x + 32$ by 2 to get $y = 4x + 16$. Now it is in the form of $y = mx + b$, where $m$ is the slope of the line and $b$ is the $Y$ intercept. Thus the slope of the line is 4. Any line parallel to this line must have the same slope. The answer must have a slope of 4. This is the line $y = 4x + 32$. Note that all of the choices are already in the form of $y = mx + b$. (416)

8. Choice D is correct. Subtract 1.01 from both sides to give: $4.04x = 8.08$. Dividing both sides by 4.04 gives a solution of $x = 2$. (406)

9. Choice D is correct. If a product is equal to zero, then one of the factors must equal zero. If $(x + 1)(x - 2) = 0$, either $x + 1 = 0$, or $x - 2 = 0$. Solving these two equations, we see that either $x = -1$ or $x = 2$. (408, 409)

10. Choice C is correct. It is possible, but time-consuming, to examine the various ranges of $x$, but it will be quicker if you realize that the same factors appear, with numerical multiples, more than once in the expression. Properly factored, the expression becomes:

$$-4(x + 2)^4(3 - x)^2 = (x + 2)(2 + x)^2(2)(x + 2)(3 - x)(-2)(3 - x)$$

Since squares of real numbers can never be negative, the whole product has only one negative term and is therefore negative, except when one of the terms is zero, in which case the product is also zero. Thus, the product cannot be larger than zero for any $x$. (428)

11. Choice D is correct. Combine like terms on both sides of the given equations and obtain the equivalent form: $k - 9 = k + 6$. This is true for no values of $k$. If $k$ is subtracted from both sides, $-9$ will equal 6, which is impossible. (406)

12. Choice B is correct. Substitute for the given values of $a$, $b$, and $c$, and obtain $p = q^2 - 2q + 1$; or, rearranging terms, $p = (q - 1)^2$. (409)

13. Choice B is correct. $A + B + C = 10$. Also, $A + B = 7$. Substitute the value 7 for the quantity $(A + B)$ in the first equation and obtain the new equation: $7 + C = 10$ or $C = 3$. $A - B = 5$ could be used with the other two equations to find the values of $A$ and $B$. (406)

**14.** Choice C is correct. If $5x + 15 > 20$, then subtract 15 from both sides to get $5x > 5$. Now divide both sides by 5. This does not change the order of the inequality because 5 is a positive number. The solution is $x > 1$. (419, 426)

**15.** Choice D is correct. Factor $(t^2 - 1)$ to obtain the product $(t + 1)(t - 1)$. For any value of $t$, except 1, the equation is equivalent to $(t + 1) = 2$, or $t = 1$. One is the only possible value of $t$. However this value is not possible as $t - 1$ would equal 0, and the quotient $\dfrac{t^2 - 1}{t - 1}$ would not be defined. (404, 409)

**16.** Choice A is correct. If $4m = 9n$, then $m = \dfrac{9n}{4}$. Multiplying both sides of the equation by 7, we obtain: $7m = \dfrac{63n}{4}$. (403)

**17.** Choice B is correct. As the diagram shows, the easiest way to calculate the area of this triangle is to start with the area of the enclosing rectangle and subtract the three shaded triangles.

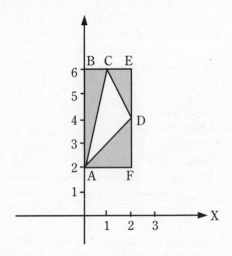

The area of the rectangle $ABEF = (2)(4) = 8$ square units.

The area of the triangle $ABC = \dfrac{1}{2}(1)(4) = 2$ square units.

The area of the triangle $CDE = \dfrac{1}{2}(1)(2) = 1$ square unit.

The area of the triangle $ADF = \dfrac{1}{2}(2)(2) = 2$ square units.

Thus the area of the triangle $ACD = 8 - 5 = 3$ square units. (418)

**18.** Choice E is correct. Since $s = \dfrac{1}{2}gt^2$, divide both sides of the equation by $\dfrac{1}{2}g$ to obtain the form, $\dfrac{2s}{g} = t^2$.
Then, after taking the square roots, $t = \sqrt{\dfrac{2s}{g}}$. (403)

**19.** Choice A is correct. The sum of the three angles of a triangle must be 180°. Since angle $A$ is 30°, and angle $B$ is between 90° and 180° (it is obtuse), their sum is greater than 120° and less than 180° (the sum of all three angles is 180°). Their sum subtracted from the total of 180° gives a third angle greater than zero, but less than 60°. (419)

**20.** Choice E is correct. An isosceles triangle has two equal sides. To find the length of the sides, we use the distance formula, $\sqrt{(x_2 - x_1)^2 + (y_2 - y_1)^2}$. In the first case the lengths of the sides are 4, $2\sqrt{2}$ and $2\sqrt{2}$. Thus two sides have the same length, and it is an isosceles triangle. The only set of points that is not an isosceles triangle is the last one. (411)

**21.** Choice E is correct. The smallest possible value of $a$ is greater than 2, and the smallest possible value of $b$ is greater than 3, so the smallest possible value of $a + b$ must be greater than $2 + 3 = 5$. Similarly, the largest values of $a$ and $b$ are less than 5 and 6, respectively, so the largest possible of $a + b$ is less than 11. Thus, the sum must be between 5 and 11. (419)

**22.** Choice D is correct. If the sides of the original square are each equal to $s$, then the area of the square is $s^2$, and the diagonal is $s\sqrt{2}$. Now, a new square, with an area of $2s^2$, must have a side of $s\sqrt{2}$. Thus, the diagonal is $2s$, which is $\sqrt{2}$ times the original length of the diagonal. (302, 303)

**23.** Choice D is correct. First place all of the variable terms on one side and all of the numerical terms on the other side. Subtracting $7.7y$ and adding 4 to both sides of the equation gives $1.1y = 11$. Now divide both sides by 1.1 to solve for $y = 10$. (406)

**24.** Choice E is correct. To determine whether an expression is a factor of another expression, give the variable a specific value in both expressions. An expression divided by its factor will be a whole number. If we give $x$ the value 0, then the expression $2x^2 + 1$ has the value of 1. $x + 2$ then has the value of 2. 1 is not divisible by 2, so the first choice is not a factor. The next choice has the value of $-2$, also not a factor of 1. Similarly $x + \sqrt{2}$ and $x - \sqrt{2}$ take on the values of $\sqrt{2}$ and $-\sqrt{2}$, respectively, when $x = 0$ and are not factors of $2x^2 + 1$. Therefore, the correct choice is (E). (409)

**25.** Choice C is correct. Let $x$ equal the average salary of the employees. Then the employees receive a total of $10x$ dollars, and the businessman receives six times the average, or $6x$. Together, the eleven of them receive a total of $10x + 6x = 16x$, which equals $64,000. Thus, $x$ equals $4,000, and the businessman's salary is $6x$, or $24,000. (406)

26. Choice A is correct. $6x + 3 = 15$, therefore $6x = 12$ and $x = 2$. Substituting $x = 2$ into the expression $12x - 3$, gives $24 - 3$ which equals 21.　　(406)

27. Choice D is correct. $2p + 7 > 3p - 5$. To both sides of the equation add 5 and subtract $2p$, obtaining $12 > p$. Thus, $p$ is less than 12.　　(419, 426)

28. Choice A is correct. Substituting 1 for $x$ in the given equation obtains $1 + q + 1 = 0$, or $q + 2 = 0$. This is solved only for $q = -2$.　　(406)

29. Choice B is correct.

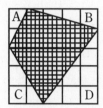

The area of the shaded figure can most easily be found by taking the area of the square surrounding it (25), and subtracting the areas of the four triangles marked A (1), B (2), C (3), and D (6), leaving an area of $25 - (1 + 2 + 3 + 6) = 13$ square units.　　(418)

30. Choice D is correct. If the number $b$ is equal to zero, the quotient $\frac{a}{b}$ is not defined. For all other pairs, all five statements are true.　　(401–405)

31. Choice E is correct. If a product equals zero, one of the factors must be equal to zero also. Thus, either $x - 1 = 0$, or $x - 2 = 0$, or $x^2 - 4 = 0$. The possible solutions, therefore, are $x = 1$, $x = 2$, and $x = -2$.　　(408)

32. Choice D is correct. Solve the equation $P + Q = R$, for $Q$ (the variable we wish to eliminate), to get $Q = R - P$. Substituting this for $Q$ in the second equation yields $P + R = 2(R - P) = 2R - 2P$, or $3P = R$. Therefore, the ratio of $P$ to $R$ is $\frac{P}{R}$, or $\frac{1}{3}$.　　(406)

33. Choice B is correct. The fraction in question will equal zero if the numerator equals zero, and the denominator is nonzero. The expression $r^2 + 5r + 6$ can be factored into $(r + 2)(r + 3)$. As long as $r$ is not equal to $-2$ the equation is defined, and $r + 2$ can be canceled in the original equation to yield $r + 3 = 0$, or $r = -3$. For $r$ equals $-2$ the denominator is equal to zero, and the fraction in the original equation is not defined.　　(404, 409)

34. Choice E is correct. This problem can be shortened considerably by factoring the expression $a^2b + 4ab^2 + 4b^3$ into the product $(b)(a + 2b)^2$. Now, since $b = 5$, and $(a + 2b) = 25$, our product equals $5 \times 25 \times 25$, or 3,125.　　(409)

35. Choice E is correct. Subtract $m + 2n$ from both sides of the given equation and obtain the equivalent form, $2n = 7m$. Dividing this equation by $2m$ gives $\frac{n}{m} = \frac{7}{2}$, the ratio of $n$ to $m$.　　(406)

36. Choice E is correct. The product will be positive in the case: $a$ positive and $b$ positive, or $a$ negative and $b$ negative; and negative in the case: $a$ positive and $b$ negative, or $a$ negative and $b$ positive. Thus, the positive products must be $(+2)(+1)$ and $(-5)(-7)$. The largest positive value is 35. Similarly, the negative products are $(-5)(+1)$ and $(+2)(-7)$; and the most negative value that can be obtained is $-14$. Thus, the product falls between $-14$ and $+35$.　　(419)

37. Choice A is correct. As can be seen from a diagram, this triangle must be a right triangle, since the line from $(-5,1)$ to $(-5,4)$ is vertical, and the line from $(-5,4)$ to $(2,4)$ is horizontal. The lengths of these two perpendicular sides are 3 and 7, respectively. Since the area of a right triangle is half the product of the perpendicular sides, the area is equal to $\frac{1}{2} \times 3 \times 7$, or 10.5.　　(410, 418)

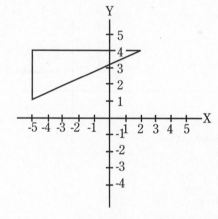

38. Choice E is correct. Solving the first equation for $A$ gives $A = 12 - B$. Solving the second equation for $C$ gives $C = 16 - B$. Thus, the sum $A + C$ is equal to $28 - 2B$. There is nothing to determine the value of $B$, so the sum of $A$ and $C$ is not determined from the information given.　　(406)

39. Choice D is correct. The value of $b^2 - 4ac$ determines the nature of the roots. From the equation substitute $a = 1$, $b = 1$, and $c = 1$ into the expression. $b^2 - 4ac = 1 - 4 = -3$. As $b^2 - 4ac$ is negative, there are no real solutions to the equation.　　(408)

**40.** Choice C is correct. If we graph the five choices we will get:

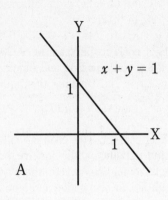

A

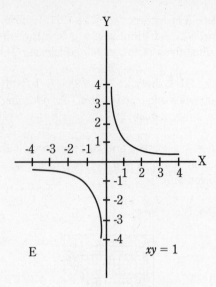

E

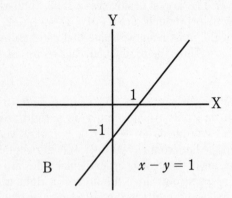

B

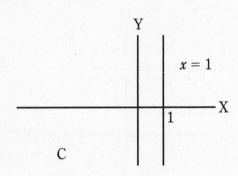

C

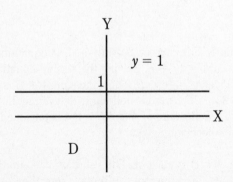

D

The only choice that is a vertical line is $x = 1$.

(413)

**41.** Choice C is correct. The factors of $x^2 + 3x + 2$ are $(x + 1)$ and $(x + 2)$. Either $x + 1 = 0$, or $x + 2 = 0$. $x$ may equal either $-1$ or $-2$. (408)

**42.** Choice B is correct. $a + b = 12$ and $a - b = 6$. Rewrite these equations as $a = 12 - b$ and $a = 6 + b$. $12 - b$ and $6 + b$ are both equal to $a$. Or, $12 - b = 6 + b$. Thus, $6 = 2b$ and $b = 3$. (407)

**43.** Choice C is correct. Let $m^2 + 4 = 4m$. Subtracting $4m$ from both sides yields $m^2 - 4m + 4 = 0$. Factor to get the following equation: $(m - 2)^2 = 0$. Thus, $m = 2$ is the only solution. (408)

**44.** Choice B is correct. Substitute for the given values of $x$ and $y$, obtaining: $(0)^2(2)(z) + (3)(0)(z)^2 + (2)^2(z) + (3)(2) + (4)(0) = 0$. Perform the indicated multiplications, and combine terms. $0(z) + 0(z^2) + 4z + 6 + 0 = 4z + 6 = 0$. This equation has $z = -\frac{3}{2}$ as its only solution. (406)

**45.** Choice C is correct. $c + 4d = 3c - 2d$. Add $2d - c$ to each side and get $6d = 2c$. (Be especially careful about your signs here.) Dividing by $2d$: $\frac{c}{d} = \frac{6}{2} = \frac{3}{1}$. Thus, $c : d = 3 : 1$. (406)

**46.** Choice C is correct. $x$ must be greater than 3, less than 7, greater than 2, and less than 6. These conditions can be reduced as follows: If $x$ is less than 6 it is also less than 7. Similarly, $x$ must be greater than 3, which automatically makes it greater than 2. Thus, $x$ must be greater than 3 and less than 6. (419)

**47.** Choice D is correct. To obtain the coordinates of the midpoint of a line segment, average the corresponding coordinates of the endpoints. Thus, the midpoint will be $\left(\dfrac{4+5}{2}, \dfrac{9+15}{2}\right)$ or $(4.5, 12)$. (412)

**48.** Choice D is correct. If both sides of the equation are multiplied by $2t + 4$, we obtain: $t^2 + 2t = t^2 + 2t$, which is true for every value of $t$. However, when $t = -2$, the denominator of the fraction on the left side of the original equation is equal to zero. Since division by zero is not a permissible operation, this fraction will not be defined for $t = -2$. The equation cannot be satisfied for $t = -2$. (404, 406, 409)

**49.** Choice A is correct. If we subtract the second of our equations from the first, we will be left with the following: $(x + y) - (x + z) = 4 - 9$, or $y - z = -5$. (402)

**50.** Choice A is correct. If $x^2$ is less than 9, then $x$ may take on any value greater than $-3$ and less than $+3$; other values will produce squares greater than or equal to 9. If $\dfrac{1}{x}$ is less than $\dfrac{1}{3}$, $x$ is restricted to positive values greater than 3, and all negative values. For example, if $x = 1$, then conditions I and II are satisfied, but $\dfrac{1}{x}$ equals 1, which is greater than $\dfrac{1}{3}$. (419)

# MATH REFRESHER
## SESSION 5

# Geometry Problems

## Basic Definitions

**500.** *Plane geometry* deals with points and lines. A point has no dimensions and is generally represented by a dot (.). A line has no thickness, but it does have length. Lines can be straight or curved, but here it will be assumed that a line is straight unless otherwise indicated. All lines have infinite length. Part of a line that has a finite length is called a line segment.

> Remember that the *distance* between two lines or from a point to a line always means the perpendicular distance. Thus, the distance between two lines pictured below is line *A* as this is the only perpendicular line. Also, the distance from a line to a point is the perpendicular from the point to the line. Thus, *AB* is the distance from point *A* to the line segment *CBD*.

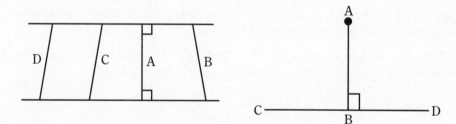

**501.** *Angles.* An angle is formed when two lines intersect at a point.

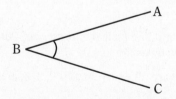

Angle *B*, angle *ABC*, ∠*B*, ∠*ABC* are all possible names for the angle shown.

The measure of the angle is given in degrees. If the sides of the angle form a straight line, then the angle is said to be a straight angle and has 180°. A circle has 360°, and a straight angle is a turning through a half circle. All other angles are either greater or less than 180°.

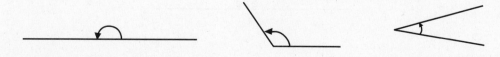

Angles are classified in different ways:
An *acute* angle has less than 90°.

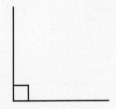

A *right* angle has exactly 90°.

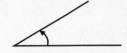

In the diagram, the small square in the corner of the angle indicates a right angle (90°).

An *obtuse* angle has between 90° and 180°.

A *straight* angle has exactly 180°.

A *reflex* angle has between 180° and 360°.

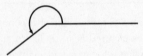

**502.** Two angles are *complementary* if their sum is 90°. For example, an angle of 30° and an angle of 60° are complementary. Two angles are *supplementary* if their sum is 180°. If one angle is 82°, then its supplement is 98°.

**503.** *Vertical angles.* These are pairs of opposite angles formed by the intersection of two straight lines. Vertical angles are always equal to each other.

   **Example:** In the diagram shown, angles *AEC* and *BED* are equal because they are vertical angles. For the same reason, angles *AED* and *BEC* are equal.

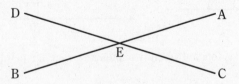

**504.** When two parallel lines are crossed by a third straight line (called a *transversal*), then all the acute angles formed are equal, and all of the obtuse angles are equal.

   **Example:** In the diagram below, angles 1, 4, 5, and 8 are all equal. Angles 2, 3, 6, and 7 are also equal.

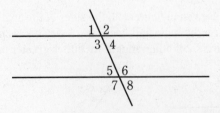

# Triangles

**505.** *Triangles.* A triangle is a closed figure with three sides, each side being a line segment. The sum of the angles of a triangle is *always* 180°.

**506.** *Scalene triangles* are triangles with no two sides equal. Scalene triangles also have no two angles equal.

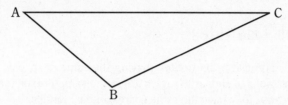

**507.** *Isosceles triangles* have two equal sides and two equal angles formed by the equal sides and the unequal side. See the figure below.

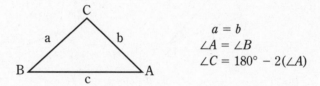

$$a = b$$
$$\angle A = \angle B$$
$$\angle C = 180° - 2(\angle A)$$

**508.** *Equilateral triangles* have all three sides and all three angles equal. Since the sum of the three angles of a triangle is 180°, each angle of an equilateral triangle is 60°.

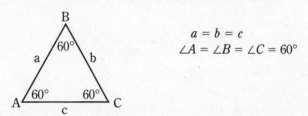

$$a = b = c$$
$$\angle A = \angle B = \angle C = 60°$$

**509.** A *right triangle* has one angle equal to a right angle (90°). The sum of the other two angles of a right triangle is, therefore, 90°. The most important relationship in a right triangle is the Pythagorean Theorem. It states that $c^2 = a^2 + b^2$, where $c$ is the length of the side opposite the right angle, and $a$ and $b$ are the lengths of the other two sides. Recall that this was discussed in Section 317.

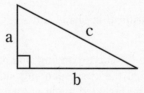

**Example:** If the two sides of a right triangle adjacent to the right angle are 3 inches and 4 inches respectively, find the length of the side opposite the right angle.

*Solution:*

Use the Pythagorean Theorem, $c^2 = a^2 + b^2$, where $a = 3$ and $b = 4$. Then, $c = 3^2 + 4^2$ or $c^2 = 9 + 16 = 25$. Thus $c = 5$.

Certain sets of integers will always fit the formula $c^2 = a^2 + b^2$. These integers can always represent the lengths of the sides of a right triangle. For example, a triangle whose sides are 3, 4, and 5 will always be a right triangle. Further examples are 5, 12, and 13; 8, 15, and 17. Any multiples of these numbers also satisfy the formula. For example, 6, 8, and 10; 9, 12, and 15; 10, 24, and 26; 24, 45, and 51; etc.

# Properties of Triangles

**510.** Two triangles are said to be *similar* (having the same shape) if their corresponding angles are equal. The sides of similar triangles are in the same proportion. The two triangles below are similar because they have the same corresponding angles.

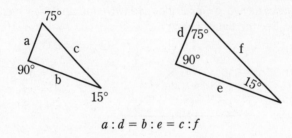

$$a : d = b : e = c : f$$

**Example:** Two triangles both have angles of 30°, 70°, and 80°. If the sides of the triangles are as indicated below, find the length of side $x$.

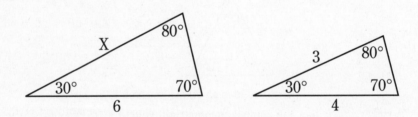

*Solution:* The two triangles are similar because they have the same corresponding angles. The corresponding sides of similar triangles are in proportion, so $x : 3 = 6 : 4$. This can be rewritten as $\frac{x}{3} = \frac{6}{4}$. Multiplying both sides by 3 gives $x = \frac{18}{4}$, or $x = 4\frac{1}{2}$.

**511.** Two triangles are *congruent* (*identical* in shape and size) if any one of the following conditions is met:

1. Each side of the first triangle equals the corresponding side of the second triangle.
2. Two sides of the first triangle equal the corresponding sides of the second triangle, and their included angles are equal. The included angle is formed by the two sides of the triangle.
3. Two angles of the first triangle equal the corresponding angles of the second triangle, and any pair of corresponding sides are equal.

**Example:** Triangles *ABC* and *DEF* in the diagram below are congruent if any one of the following conditions can be met:

1. The three sides are equal
   (*sss*) = (*sss*).

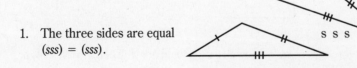

s s s

2. Two sides and the included angle are equal (*sas*) = (*sas*).

s a s

3. Two angles and any one side are equal (*aas*) = (*aas*) or (*asa*) = (*asa*).

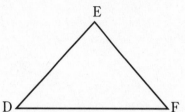

a s a

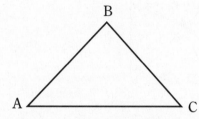

**Example:** In the equilateral triangle below, line *AD* is perpendicular (forms a right angle) to side *BC*. If the length of *BD* is 5 feet, what is the length of *DC*?

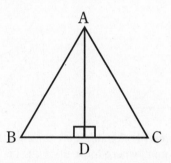

*Solution:* Since the large triangle is an equilateral triangle, each ∠ is 60°. Therefore ∠*B* is 60° and ∠*C* is 60°. Thus, ∠*B* = ∠*C*. *ADB* and *ADC* are both right angles and are equal. Two angles of each triangle are equal to the corresponding two angles of the other triangle. Side *AD* is shared by both triangles and side *AB* = side *AC*. Thus, according to condition 3 in Section 511, the two triangles are congruent. Then *BD* = *DC* and, since *BD* is 5 feet, *DC* is 5 feet.

**512.** The *medians* of a triangle are the lines drawn from each vertex to the midpoint of its opposite side. The medians of a triangle cross at a point that divides each median into two parts: one part of one-third the length of the median and the other part of two-thirds the length.

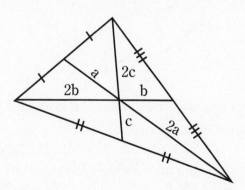

**513.** The *angle bisectors* of a triangle are the lines that divide each angle of the triangle into two equal parts. These lines meet in a point that is the center of a circle inscribed in the triangle.

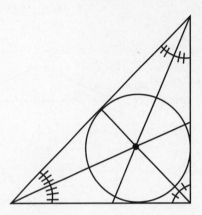

**514.** The *altitudes* of the triangle are lines drawn from the vertices perpendicular to the opposite sides. The lengths of these lines are useful in calculating the area of the triangle since the area of the triangle is $\frac{1}{2}$ (base)(height) and the height is identical to the altitude.

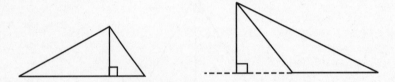

**515.** The *perpendicular bisectors* of the triangle are the lines that bisect and are perpendicular to each of the three sides. The point where these lines meet is the center of the circumscribed circle.

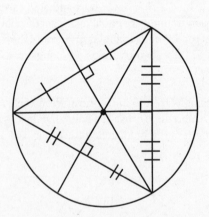

**516.** The sum of any two sides of a triangle is greater than the third side.

**Example:** If the three sides of a triangle are 4, 2, and $x$, then what is known about the value of $x$?

*Solution:* Since the sum of two sides of a triangle is always greater than the third side, then $4 + 2 > x$, $4 + x > 2$, and $2 + x > 4$. These three inequalities can be rewritten as $6 > x$, $x > -2$, and $x > 2$. For $x$ to be greater than $-2$ and 2, it must be greater than 2. Thus, the values of $x$ are $2 < x < 6$.

# Four-Sided Figures

**517.** A *parallelogram* is a four-sided figure with each pair of opposite sides parallel.

A parallelogram has the following properties:

1. Each pair of opposite sides are equal. ($AD = BC$, $AB = DC$)
2. The diagonals bisect each other. ($AF = FC$, $DF = FB$)
3. The opposite angles are equal. ($\angle A = \angle C$, $\angle D = B$)
4. One diagonal divides the parallelogram into two congruent triangles. Two diagonals divide the parallelogram into two pairs of congruent triangles.

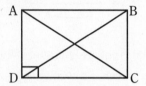

**518.** A *rectangle* is a parallelogram in which all the angles are right angles. Since a rectangle is a parallelogram, all of the laws that apply to a parallelogram apply to a rectangle. In addition, the diagonals of a rectangle are equal.

$AC = BD$

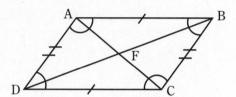

**519.** A *rhombus* is a parallelogram with four equal sides. Since a rhombus is a parallelogram, all of the laws that apply to a parallelogram apply to a rhombus. In addition, the diagonals of a rhombus are perpendicular to each other and bisect the vertex angles.

$\angle DAC = \angle BAC = \angle DCA = \angle BCA$
$\angle ADB = \angle CDB = \angle ABD = \angle CBD$
$AC$ is perpendicular to $DB$

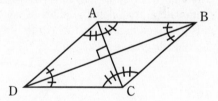

**520.** A *square* is a rectangular rhombus. Thus the square has the following properties:

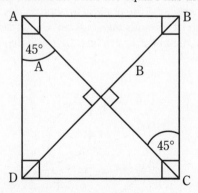

1. All four sides are equal. ($AB = BC = CD = DA$)
2. Opposite pairs of sides are parallel. ($AD \parallel BC$, $AB \parallel DC$)
3. Diagonals are equal, are perpendicular to each other, and bisect each other. ($AC = BD$, $AC \perp BD$, $AE = EC = DE = EB$)
4. All the angles are right angles (90°). ($\angle A = \angle B = \angle C = \angle D = 90°$)
5. Diagonals intersect the vertices at 45°. ($\angle DAC = \angle BAC = 45°$, and similarly for the other 3 vertices.)

# Many-Sided Figures

**521.** A *polygon* is a closed plane figure whose sides are straight lines. The sum of the angles in any polygon is equal to $180(n - 2)°$, where $n$ is the number of sides. Thus, in a polygon of 3 sides (a triangle), the sum of the angles is $180(3 - 2)°$ or $180°$.

**522.** A *regular polygon* is a polygon all of whose sides are equal and all of whose angles are equal. These polygons have special properties:

1.   A regular polygon can be inscribed in a circle and can be circumscribed about another circle. For example, a hexagon is inscribed in a circle in the diagram below.

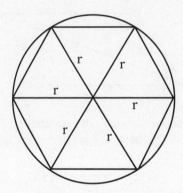

2.   Each angle of a regular polygon is equal to the sum of the angles divided by the number of sides, $\dfrac{180(n-2)°}{n}$. Thus, a square, which is a regular polygon of 4 sides, has each angle equal to $\dfrac{180(4-2)°}{4}$ or $90°$.

**523.** An important regular polygon is the *hexagon*. The diagonals of a regular hexagon divide it into 6 equilateral triangles, the sides of which are equal to the sides of the hexagon. If a hexagon is inscribed in a circle, the length of each side is equal to the length of the radius of the circle. (See diagram of hexagon.)

# Circles

**524.** A *circle* (also see Section 310) is a set of points equidistant from a given point, the *center*. The distance from the center to the circle is the *radius*. Any line that connects two points on the circle is a *chord*. A chord through the center of the circle is a *diameter*. On the circle below $O$ is the center, line segment $OF$ is a radius, $DOE$ is a diameter, and $AC$ is a chord.

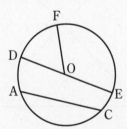

The length of the diameter of a circle is twice the length of the radius. The circumference (length of the curve) is $2\pi$ times the length of the radius. $\pi$ is a constant approximately equal to $\dfrac{22}{7}$ or 3.14. The formula for the circumference of a circle is, $C = 2\pi r$ where $C$ = circumference and $r$ = radius.

**525.** A *tangent* to a circle is a line that is perpendicular to a radius and that passes through only one point of the circle. In the diagram *AB* is a tangent.

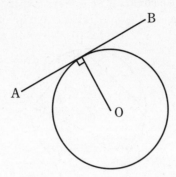

**526.** A *central angle* is an angle whose sides are two radii of the circle. The vertex of this angle is the center of the circle. The number of degrees in a central angle is equal to the amount of arc length that the radii intercept. As the complete circumference has 360°, any other arc lengths are less than 360°.

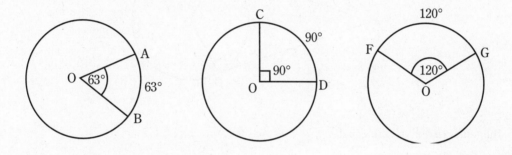

Angles *AOB*, *COD*, and *FOG* are all central angles.

**527.** An *inscribed angle* of a circle is an angle whose sides are two chords. The vertex of the angle lies on the circumference of the circle. The number of degrees in the inscribed angle is equal to one-half the intercepted arc.

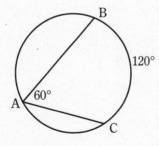

∠*BAC* is an inscribed angle.

**528.**  An angle inscribed in a semicircle is always a right angle. $\angle ABC$ and $\angle ADC$ are inscribed in semicircles *AOCB* and *AOCD*, respectively, and are thus right angles.

*Note:* A semicircle is one-half of a circle.

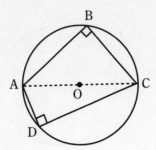

**529.**  Two tangents to a circle from a point outside of the circle are always equal.

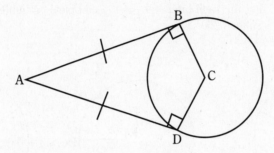

Tangents *AB* and *AD* are equal.

# Practice Test 5

## Geometry Problems

Correct answers and solutions follow each test.

1. In the following diagram, angle 1 is equal to 40°, and angle 2 is equal to 150°. What is the number of degrees in angle 3?

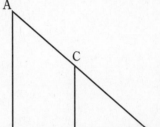

(A) 70°
(B) 90°
(C) 110°
(D) 190°
(E) The answer cannot be determined from the given information.

2. In this diagram, *AB* and *CD* are both perpendicular to *BE*. If *EC* = 5, and *CD* = 4, what is the ratio of *AB* to *BE*?

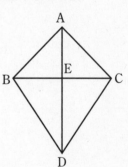

(A) 1 : 1
(B) 4 : 3
(C) 5 : 4
(D) 5 : 3
(E) None of these.

3. In triangle *PQR*, *PR* = 7.0, and *PQ* = 4.5. Which of the following cannot possibly represent the length of *QR*?

(A) 2.0
(B) 3.0
(C) 3.5
(D) 4.5
(E) 5.0

4. In this diagram, *AB* = *AC*, and *BD* = *CD*. Which of the following statements is true?

(A) *BE* = *EC*.
(B) *AD* is perpendicular to *BC*.
(C) Triangles *BDE* and *CDE* are congruent.
(D) Angle *ABD* equals angle *ACD*.
(E) All of these.

5. In the following diagram, if *BC* = *CD* = *BD* = 1, and angle *ADC* is a right angle, what is the perimeter of triangle *ABD*?

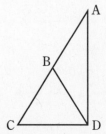

(A) 3
(B) $2 + \sqrt{2}$
(C) $2 + \sqrt{3}$
(D) $3 + \sqrt{3}$
(E) 4

**6.** A B C D E

6. In this diagram, if *PQRS* is a parallelogram, which of the following can be deduced:

   I.  $QT + PT = RT + ST$
   II.  *QS* is perpendicular to *PR*
   III.  The area of the shaded portion is exactly three times the area of triangle *QRT*.

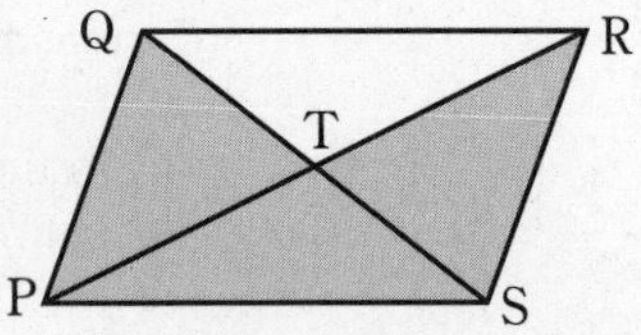

   (A) I only
   (B) I and II only
   (C) II only
   (D) I and III only
   (E) I, II, and III

**7.** A B C D E

7. James lives on the corner of a rectangular field that measures 120 yards by 160 yards. If he wants to walk to the opposite corner, he can either travel along the perimeter of the field or cut directly across in a straight line. How many yards does he save by taking the direct route? (Express to the nearest ten yards.)

   (A) 40 yards
   (B) 60 yards
   (C) 80 yards
   (D) 100 yards
   (E) 110 yards

**8.** A B C D E

8. In a square, the perimeter is how many times the length of the diagonal?

   (A) $\dfrac{\sqrt{2}}{2}$

   (B) $\sqrt{2}$

   (C) 2

   (D) $2\sqrt{2}$

   (E) 4

**9.** A B C D E

9. How many degrees are there in the angle formed by two adjacent sides of a regular nonagon (nine-sided polygon)?

   (A) 40°
   (B) 70°
   (C) 105°
   (D) 120°
   (E) 140°

**10.** A B C D E

10. In the diagram below, $AB = CD$. From this we can deduce that:

   (A) *AB* is parallel to *CD*.
   (B) *AB* is perpendicular to *BD*.
   (C) $AC = BD$
   (D) Angle *ABD* equals angle *BDC*.
   (E) Triangle *ABD* is congruent to triangle *ACD*.

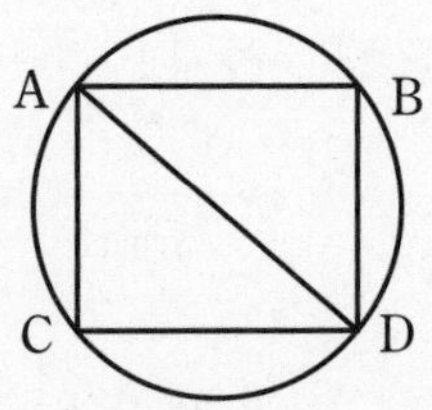

   (Note: Figure is not drawn to scale.)

**11.** A B C D E

11. If two lines, *AB* and *CD*, intersect at a point *E*, which of the following statements is *not* true?

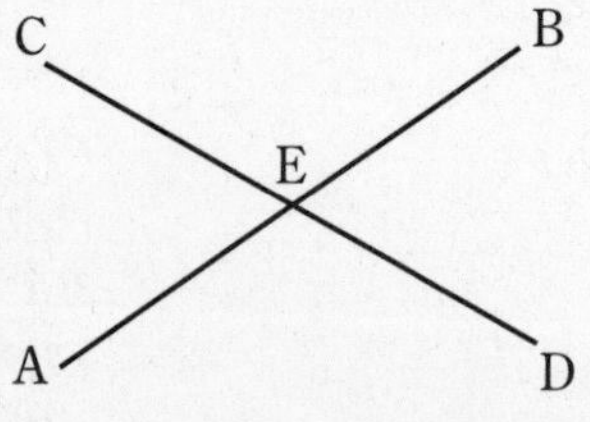

   (A) Angle *AEB* equals angle *CED*.
   (B) Angles *AEC* and *BEC* are complementary.
   (C) Angle *CED* is a straight angle.
   (D) Angle *AEC* equals angle *BED*.
   (E) Angle *BED* plus angle *AED* equals 180 degrees.

**A B C D E**
**12.**

12. In the following diagram, $AC = CE$ and $BD = DE$. Which of these statements is (are) true?

    I.   $AB$ is twice as long as $CD$.
    II.  $AB$ is parallel to $CD$.
    III. Triangle $AEB$ is similar to triangle $CED$.

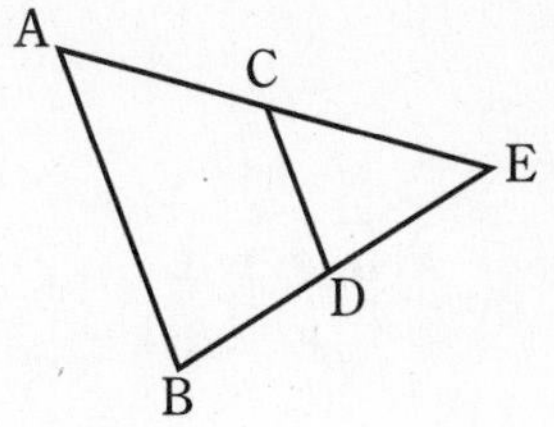

  (A) I only
  (B) II and III only
  (C) I and III only
  (D) I, II, and III
  (E) None of these.

**A B C D E**
**13.**

13. In triangle $ABC$, angle $A$ is obtuse, and angle $B$ equals $30°$. Which of the following statements *best* describes angle $C$?

  (A) Angle $C$ must be less than $60°$.
  (B) Angle $C$ must be less than or equal to $60°$.
  (C) Angle $C$ must be equal to $60°$.
  (D) Angle $C$ must be greater than or equal to $60°$.
  (E) Angle $C$ must be greater than $60°$.

**A B C D E**
**14.**

14. In this diagram, $ABCD$ is a parallelogram, and $BFDE$ is a square. If $AB = 20$ and $CF = 16$, what is the perimeter of the parallelogram $ABCD$?

  (A) 72
  (B) 78
  (C) 86
  (D) 92
  (E) 96

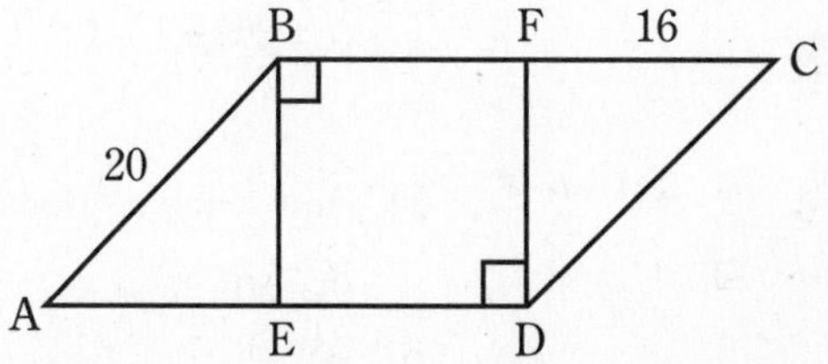

**A B C D E**
**15.**

15. The hypotenuse of a right triangle is exactly twice as long as the shorter leg. What is the number of degrees in the smallest angle of the triangle?

  (A) $30°$
  (B) $45°$
  (C) $60°$
  (D) $90°$
  (E) The answer cannot be determined from the given information.

**A B C D E**
**16.**

16. The legs of an isosceles triangle are equal to 17 inches each. If the altitude to the base is 8 inches long, how long is the base of the triangle?

  (A) 15 inches
  (B) 20 inches
  (C) 24 inches
  (D) 25 inches
  (E) 30 inches

**A B C D E**
**17.**

17. The perimeter of a right triangle is 18 inches. If the midpoints of the three sides are joined by line segments, they form another triangle. What is the perimeter of this new triangle?

  (A) 3 inches
  (B) 6 inches
  (C) 9 inches
  (D) 12 inches
  (E) The answer cannot be determined from the given information.

**18.** A B C D E

**18.** If the diagonals of a square divide it into four triangles, the triangles *cannot* be

(A) right triangles
(B) isosceles triangles
(C) similar triangles
(D) equilateral triangles
(E) equal in area

**19.** A B C D E

**19.** In the diagram below, *ABCDEF* is a regular hexagon. How many degrees are there in angle *ADC*?

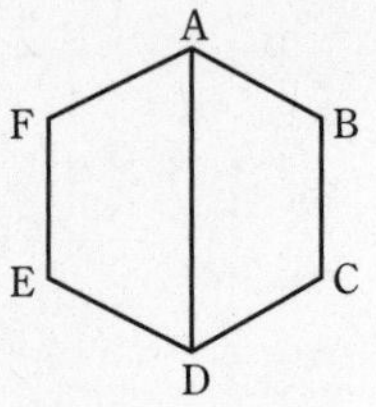

(A) 45°
(B) 60°
(C) 75°
(D) 90°
(E) None of these.

**20.** A B C D E

**20.** This diagram depicts a rectangle inscribed in a circle. If the measurements of the rectangle are 10″ × 14″, what is the area of the circle?

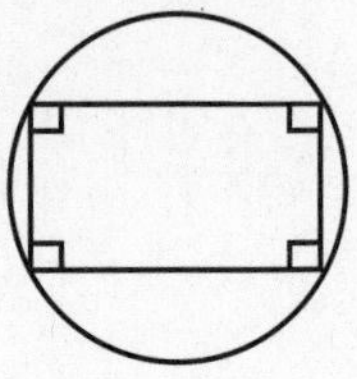

(A) $74\pi$
(B) $92\pi$
(C) $144\pi$
(D) $196\pi$
(E) $296\pi$

**21.** A B C D E

**21.** How many degrees are included between the hands of a clock at 5:00?

(A) 50°
(B) 60°
(C) 75°
(D) 120°
(E) 150°

**22.** A B C D E

**22.** *ABCD* is a square. If the midpoints of the four sides are joined to form a new square, the perimeter of the old square is how many times the perimeter of the new square?

(A) 1
(B) $\sqrt{2}$
(C) 2
(D) $2\sqrt{2}$
(E) 4

**23.** A B C D E

**23.** Angles *A* and *B* of triangle *ABC* are both acute angles. Which of the following *best* describes angle *C*?

(A) Angle *C* is between 0° and 180°.
(B) Angle *C* is between 0° and 90°.
(C) Angle *C* is between 60° and 180°.
(D) Angle *C* is between 60° and 120°.
(E) Angle *C* is between 60° and 90°.

**24.** A B C D E

**24.** The angles of a quadrilateral are in the ratio 1 : 2 : 3 : 4. What is the number of degrees in the largest angle?

(A) 72
(B) 96
(C) 120
(D) 144
(E) 150

25.  A B C D E

**25.** *ABCD* is a rectangle; the diagonals *AC* and *BD* intersect at *E*. Which of the following statements is *not necessarily true*?

(A) *AE* = *BE*
(B) Angle *AEB* equals angle *CED*.
(C) *AE* is perpendicular to *BD*.
(D) Triangles *AED* and *AEB* are equal in area.
(E) Angle *BAC* equals angle *BDC*.

26.  A B C D E

**26.** City A is 200 miles from City B, and City B is 400 miles from City C. Which of the following best describes the distance between City A and City C? (Note: The cities A, B, C do *not* all lie on a straight line.)

(A) It must be greater than zero.
(B) It must be greater than 200 miles.
(C) It must be less than 600 miles and greater than zero.
(D) It must be less than 600 miles and greater than 200.
(E) It must be exactly 400 miles.

27.  A B C D E

**27.** At 7:30, how many degrees are included between the hands of a clock?

(A) 15°
(B) 30°
(C) 45°
(D) 60°
(E) 75°

28.  A B C D E

**28.** If a ship is sailing in a northerly direction and then turns to the right until it is sailing in a southwesterly direction, it has gone through a rotation of:

(A) 45°
(B) 90°
(C) 135°
(D) 180°
(E) 225°

29.  A B C D E

**29.** $x$, $y$, and $z$ are the angles of a triangle. If $x = 2y$, and $y = z + 30°$, how many degrees are there in angle $x$?

(A) 22.5°
(B) 37.5°
(C) 52.5°
(D) 90.0°
(E) 105.0°

30.  A B C D E

**30.** In the diagram shown, *AB* is parallel to *CD*. Which of the following statements is *not necessarily true*?

(A) $\angle 1 + \angle 2 = 180°$
(B) $\angle 4 = \angle 7$
(C) $\angle 5 + \angle 8 + \angle 2 + \angle 4 = 360°$
(D) $\angle 2 + \angle 3 = 180°$
(E) $\angle 2 = \angle 6$

31.  A B C D E

**31.** What is the ratio of the diagonal of a square to the hypotenuse of the isosceles right triangle having the same area?

(A) $1 : 2$
(B) $1 : \sqrt{2}$
(C) $1 : 1$
(D) $\sqrt{2} : 1$
(E) $2 : 1$

**32.** A B C D E

**32.** How many degrees are there between two adjacent sides of a regular ten-sided figure?

(A) 36°
(B) 72°
(C) 120°
(D) 144°
(E) 154°

**33.** A B C D E

**33.** Which of the following sets of numbers *cannot* represent the lengths of the sides of a right triangle?

(A) 5, 12, 13
(B) 4.2, 5.6, 7.0
(C) 9, 28, 35
(D) 16, 30, 34
(E) 7.5, 18, 19.5

**34.** A B C D E

**34.** How many degrees are there in the angle that is its own supplement?

(A) 30°
(B) 45°
(C) 60°
(D) 90°
(E) 180°

**35.** A B C D E

**35.** If a central angle of 45° intersects an arc 6 inches long on the circumference of a circle, what is the radius of the circle?

(A) $\frac{24}{\pi}$ inches

(B) $\frac{48}{\pi}$ inches

(C) $6\pi$ inches
(D) 24 inches
(E) 48 inches

**36.** A B C D E

**36.** What is the length of the line segment connecting the two most distant vertices of a 1-inch cube?

(A) 1 inch
(B) $\sqrt{2}$ inches
(C) $\sqrt{3}$ inches
(D) $\sqrt{5}$ inches
(E) $\sqrt{6}$ inches

**37.** A B C D E

**37.** Through how many degrees does the hour hand of a clock move in 70 minutes?

(A) 35°
(B) 60°
(C) 80°
(D) 90°
(E) 120°

**38.** A B C D E

**38.** In the diagram pictured below, *BA* is tangent to circle *O* at point *A*. *CD* is perpendicular to *OA* at *C*. Which of the following statements is (are) true?

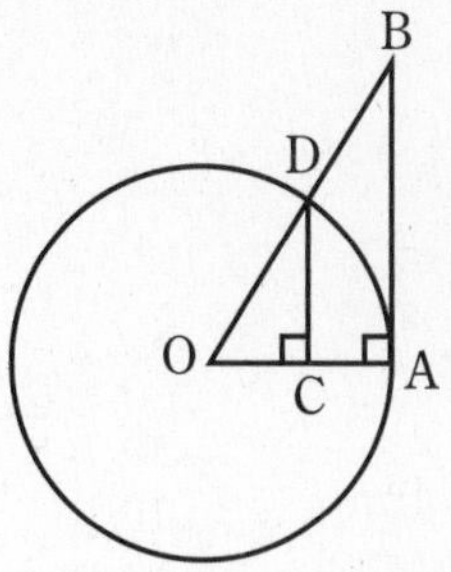

    I. Triangles *ODC* and *OBA* are similar.
    II. *OA* : *DC* = *OB* : *AB*
    III. *AB* is twice as long as *CD*.

    (A) I only
    (B) III only
    (C) I and II only
    (D) II and III only
    (E) None of the above combinations.

**39.** A B C D E

**39.** The three angles of triangle *ABC* are in the ratio $1:2:6$. How many degrees are in the largest angle?

    (A) $45°$
    (B) $90°$
    (C) $120°$
    (D) $135°$
    (E) $160°$

**40.** A B C D E

**40.** In this diagram, *AB* = *AC*, angle *A* = $40°$, and *BD* is perpendicular to *AC* at *D*. How many degrees are there in angle *DBC* ?

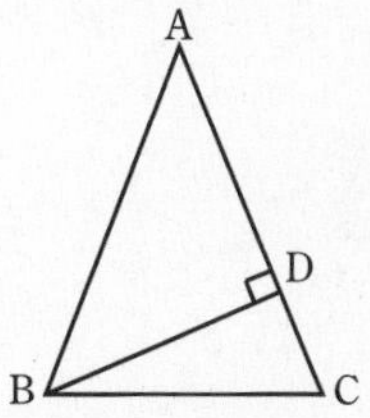

    (A) $20°$
    (B) $40°$
    (C) $50°$
    (D) $70°$
    (E) None of these.

**41.** A B C D E

**41.** If the line *AB* intersects the line *CD* at point *E*, which of the following pairs of angles need *not* be equal?

    (A) $\angle AEB$ and $\angle CED$
    (B) $\angle AEC$ and $\angle BED$
    (C) $\angle AED$ and $\angle CEA$
    (D) $\angle BEC$ and $\angle DEA$
    (E) $\angle DEC$ and $\angle BEA$

**42.** A B C D E

**42.** All right isosceles triangles must be

    (A) similar
    (B) congruent
    (C) equilateral
    (D) equal in area
    (E) None of these.

**43.** A B C D E

**43.** What is the area of a triangle whose sides are 10 inches, 13 inches, and 13 inches?

    (A) 39 square inches
    (B) 52 square inches
    (C) 60 square inches
    (D) 65 square inches
    (E) The answer cannot be determined from the given information.

**44.** A B C D E

**44.** If each side of an equilateral triangle is 2 inches long, what is the triangle's altitude?

    (A) 1 inch
    (B) $\sqrt{2}$ inches
    (C) $\sqrt{3}$ inches
    (D) 2 inches
    (E) $\sqrt{5}$ inches

**45.**  A B C D E

**45.** In the parallelogram *ABCD*, diagonals *AC* and *BD* intersect at *E*. Which of the following must be true?

(A) ∠*AED* = ∠*BEC*
(B) ∠*AE* = *EC*
(C) ∠*BDC* = ∠*DBA*
(D) Two of the above must be true.
(E) All three of the statements must be true.

**46.**  A B C D E

**46.** If *ABCD* is a square, and diagonals *AC* and *BD* intersect at point *E*, how many isosceles right triangles are there in the figure?

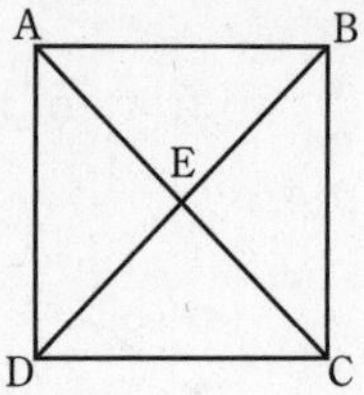

(A) 4
(B) 5
(C) 6
(D) 7
(E) 8

**47.**  A B C D E

**47.** How many degrees are there in each angle of a regular hexagon?

(A) 60°
(B) 90°
(C) 108°
(D) 120°
(E) 144°

**48.**  A B C D E

**48.** The radius of a circle is 1 inch. If an equilateral triangle is inscribed in the circle, what will be the length of one of the triangle's sides?

(A) 1 inch
(B) $\frac{\sqrt{2}}{2}$ inches
(C) $\sqrt{2}$ inches
(D) $\frac{\sqrt{3}}{2}$ inches
(E) $\sqrt{3}$ inches

**49.**  A B C D E

**49.** If the angles of a triangle are in the ratio 2 : 3 : 4, how many degrees are there in the largest angle?

(A) 20°
(B) 40°
(C) 60°
(D) 80°
(E) 120°

**50.**  A B C D E

**50.** Which of the following combinations may represent the lengths of the sides of a right triangle?

(A) 4, 6, 8
(B) 12, 16, 20
(C) 7, 17, 23
(D) 9, 20, 27
(E) None of these.

## Answer Key for Practice Test 5

| | | | | | | | |
|---|---|---|---|---|---|---|---|
| **1.** C | | **14.** E | | **27.** C | | **39.** C |
| **2.** B | | **15.** A | | **28.** E | | **40.** A |
| **3.** A | | **16.** E | | **29.** E | | **41.** C |
| **4.** E | | **17.** C | | **30.** D | | **42.** A |
| **5.** C | | **18.** D | | **31.** B | | **43.** C |
| **6.** D | | **19.** B | | **32.** D | | **44.** C |
| **7.** C | | **20.** A | | **33.** C | | **45.** E |
| **8.** D | | **21.** E | | **34.** D | | **46.** E |
| **9.** E | | **22.** B | | **35.** A | | **47.** D |
| **10.** D | | **23.** A | | **36.** C | | **48.** E |
| **11.** B | | **24.** D | | **37.** A | | **49.** D |
| **12.** D | | **25.** C | | **38.** C | | **50.** B |
| **13.** A | | **26.** D | | | | |

## Answers and Solutions for Practice Test 5

1. Choice C is correct. In the problem it is given that $\angle 1 = 40°$ and $\angle 2 = 150°$. The diagram below makes it apparent that: (1) $\angle 1 = \angle 4$ and $\angle 3 = \angle 5$ (vertical angles); (2) $\angle 6 + \angle 2 = 180°$ (straight angle); (3) $\angle 4 + \angle 5 + \angle 6 = 180°$ (sum of angles in a triangle). To solve the problem, $\angle 3$ must be related through the above information to the known quantities in $\angle 1$ and $\angle 2$. Proceed as follows: $\angle 3 = \angle 5$, but $\angle 5 = 180° - \angle 4 - \angle 6$. $\angle 4 = \angle 1 = 40°$ and $\angle 6 = 180° - \angle 2 = 180° - 150° = 30°$. Therefore, $\angle 3 = 180° - 40° - 30° = 110°$.

(501, 503, 505)

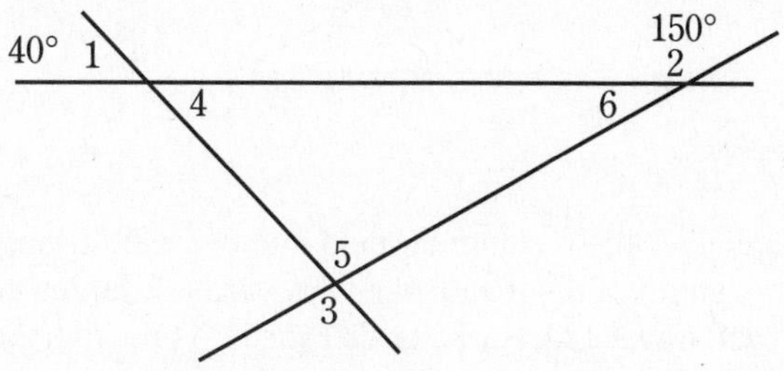

2. Choice B is correct. Since $CD$ is perpendicular to $DE$, $CDE$ is a right triangle, and using the Pythagorean Theorem yields $DE = 3$. Thus, the ratio of $CD$ to $DE$ is $4 : 3$. But triangle $ABE$ is similar to triangle $CDE$. Therefore, $AB : BE = CD : DE = 4 : 3$. (509, 510)

3. Choice A is correct. In a triangle, it is impossible for one side to be longer than the sum of the other two (a straight line is the shortest distance between two points). Thus 2.0, 4.5, and 7.0 cannot be three sides of a triangle. (516)

4. Choice E is correct. $AB = AC$, $BD = CD$, and $AD$ equal to itself is sufficient information (three sides) to prove triangles $ABD$ and $ACD$ congruent. Also, since $AB = AC$, $AE = AE$, and $\angle BAE = \angle CAE$ (by the previous congruence), triangles $ABE$ and $ACE$ are congruent. Since $BD = CD$, $ED = ED$, and angle $BDE$ equals angle $CDE$ (by initial congruence), triangles $BDE$ and $CDE$ are congruent. Through congruence of triangle $ABE$ and triangle $ACE$, angles $BEA$ and $CEA$ are equal, and their sum is a straight angle (180°). They must both be right angles. Thus, from the given information, we can deduce all the properties given as choices. (511)

**5.** Choice C is correct. The perimeter of triangle $ABD$ is $AB + BD + AD$. The length of $BD$ is 1. Since $BC = CD = BD$, triangle $BCD$ is an equilateral triangle. Therefore, angle $C = 60°$ and angle $BDC = 60°$. Angle $A$ + angle $C = 90°$ (the sum of two acute angles in a right triangle is 90°) and angle $BDC$ + angle $BDA = 90°$ (these two angles form a right angle). Since angle $C$ and angle $BDC$ both equal 60°, angle $A$ = angle $BDA = 30°$. Now two angles of triangle $ADB$ are equal. Therefore, triangle $ADB$ is an isosceles triangle with side $BD$ = side $AB$. Since $BD = 1$, then $AB = 1$. $AD$ is a leg of the right triangle, with side $CD = 1$ and hypotenuse $AC = 2$. ($AC = AB + BC = 1 + 1$.) Using the relationship $c^2 = a^2 + b^2$ gives us the length of $AD$ as $\sqrt{3}$. Thus the perimeter is $1 + 1 + \sqrt{3}$ or $2 + \sqrt{3}$. (505, 507, 509)

**6.** Choice D is correct. (I) must be true, since the diagonals of a parallelogram bisect each other, so $QT = ST$, and $PT = RT$. Thus, since the sums of equals are equal, $QT + PT = RT + ST$.

(II) is not necessarily true and, in fact, can be true only if the parallelogram is also a rhombus (all four sides equal).

(III) is true, since the four small triangles each have the same area. The shaded portion contains three such triangles. This can be seen by noting that the altitudes from point $P$ to the bases of triangles $PQT$ and $PTS$ are identical. We have already seen from part (I) that these bases ($QT$ and $TS$) are also equal. Therefore, only I and III can be deduced from the given information. (514, 517)

**7.** Choice C is correct.

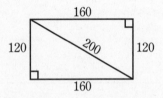

The diagonal path divides the rectangular field into two right triangles. The Pythagorean Theorem gives the length of the diagonal as 200 yards. If James takes the route around the perimeter, he will travel 120 + 160, or 280 yards. Thus, the shorter route saves him 80 yards. (509, 518)

**8.** Choice D is correct. Let one side of a square be $s$. Then the perimeter must be $4s$. The diagonal of a square with side $s$ is equal to $s\sqrt{2}$. Dividing the perimeter by the diagonal produces $2\sqrt{2}$. The perimeter is $2\sqrt{2}$ times the diagonal. (509, 520)

**9.** Choice E is correct. The sum of the angles of any polygon is equal to $180° (n - 2)$, where $n$ is the number of sides. Thus the total number of degrees in a nonagon = $180° (9 - 2)$ = $180° \times 7 = 1,260°$. The number of degrees in each angle is $\dfrac{1,260°}{n} = \dfrac{1,260°}{9} = 140°$. (521, 522)

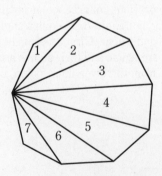

**10.** Choice D is correct. Since chord *AB* equals chord *CD*, it must be true that arc *AB* equals arc *CD*. By adding arc *AC* to arc *CD* and to arc *AB* it is apparent that arc *ACD* is equal to arc *CAB*. These arcs are intersected by inscribed angles *ABD* and *BDC*. Therefore, the two inscribed angles must be equal. If we redraw the figure as shown below, the falseness of statements (A), (B), (C), and (E) becomes readily apparent. (527)

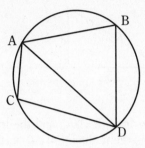

**11.** Choice B is correct. $\angle AEC + \angle BEC = \angle AEB$, a straight angle (180°). Thus, angles *AEC* and *BEC* are *supplementary*. (Complementary means that the two angles add up to a *right* angle, or 90°.) (501, 502)

**12.** Choice D is correct. Since $AC = CE$ and $BD = DE$, triangles *AEB* and *CED* are similar, and *AE* is twice as long as *CE*, since by proportionality, $AB : CD = AE : CE = 2 : 1$. From the similarity it is found that angle *ABE* equals angle *CDE*, and, therefore, that *AB* is parallel to *CD*. Thus, all three statements are true. (504, 510)

**13.** Choice A is correct. Angle *A* must be greater than 90°; angle *B* equals 30°. Thus, the sum of angles *A* and *B* must be greater than 120°. Since the sum of the three angles *A*, *B*, and *C* must be 180°, angle *C* must be *less than* 60°. (It cannot equal 60°, because then angle *A* would be a right angle instead of an obtuse angle.) (501, 505)

**14.** Choice E is correct. *CDF* is a right triangle with one side of 16 and a hypotenuse of 20. Thus, the third side, *DF*, equals 12. Since *BFDE* is a square, *BF* and *ED* are also equal to 12. Thus, $BC = 12 + 16 = 28$, and $CD = 20$. *ABCD* is a parallelogram, so $AB = CD$, $AD = BC$. The perimeter is $28 + 20 + 28 + 20 = 96$. (509, 517, 520)

**15.** Choice A is correct. Either recognize immediately that the sides of a $30° - 60° - 90°$ triangle are in the proportion $1 : \sqrt{3} : 2$, and the problem is solved, or construct an isosceles triangle by placing two of the right triangles so that the unknown sides touch (see diagram). This isosceles triangle is equilateral with angles of 60°. Therefore, the smallest angle in the right triangle is equal to angle *BAC*, or 30°. (509)

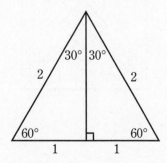

**16.** Choice E is correct. The altitude to the base of an isosceles triangle divides it into two congruent right triangles, each with one leg of 8 inches, and a hypotenuse of 17 inches. By the Pythagorean Theorem, the third side of each right triangle must be 15 inches long. The base of the isosceles triangle is the sum of two such sides, totaling 30 inches.

(507, 509, 514)

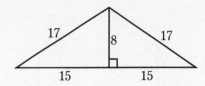

**17.** Choice C is correct. Call the triangle *ABC*, and the triangle of midpoints *PQR*, where *P* is the midpoint of *BC*, *Q* is the midpoint of *AC*, and *R* is the midpoint of *AB*. Then, *PQ* is equal to half the length of *AB*, $QR = \frac{1}{2} BC$, and $PR = \frac{1}{2} AC$. This has nothing to do with the fact that *ABC* is a right triangle. Thus, the perimeter of the small triangle is equal to $PQ + QR + PR = \frac{1}{2} (AB + BC + AC)$. The new perimeter is half the old perimeter, or 9 inches.

(509, 510, 512)

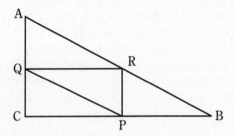

**18.** Choice D is correct. The diagonals of the square form four right triangles, each of which is isosceles because each has two 45° angles. The triangles are all identical in shape and size, so they all are similar and have the same area. The only choice left is equilateral, which cannot be true, since then the sum of the angles at the intersection of the diagonals must be 360°. The sum of four 60° angles would be only 240°.

(520)

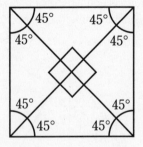

19. Choice B is correct. First, draw in the lines *CF* and *BE*. These intersect *AD* at its midpoint (also the midpoint of *CF* and *BE*) and divide the hexagon into six equilateral triangles. Since *ADC* is an angle of one of these equilateral triangles, it must be equal to 60°. (Another way to do this problem is to calculate the number of degrees in one angle of a regular hexagon and divide this by 2.) (508, 523)

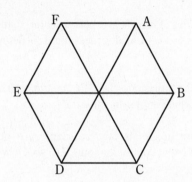

20. Choice A is correct. The diagonal of an inscribed rectangle is equal to the diameter of the circle. To find this length, use the Pythagorean Theorem on one of the two triangles formed by two of the sides of the rectangle and the diagonal. Thus, the square of the diagonal is equal to $10^2 + 14^2 + 100 + 196 = 296$. The area of the circle is equal to $\pi$ times the square of the radius. The square of the radius of the circle is one-fourth of the diameter squared (since $d = 2r$, $d^2 = 4r^2$) or 74. Thus, the area is $74\pi$. (509, 518, 524)

21. Choice E is correct. Each number on a clock (or hour marking) represents an angle of 30°, as 360° divided by 12 is 30° (a convenient fact to remember for other clock problems). Since the hands of the clock are on the 12 and the 5, there are five hour units between the hands; $5 \times 30° = 150°$. (501, 526)

22. Choice B is correct.

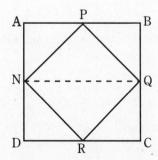

Let $S$ represent the side of the large square. Then the perimeter is $4S$. Let $s$ represent the side of the smaller square. Then the perimeter is $4s$. Line $NQ$ is the diagonal of the smaller square, so the length of $NQ$ is $\sqrt{2}s$. (The diagonal of a square is $\sqrt{2}$ times the side.) Now, $NQ$ is equal to $DC$, or $S$, which is the side of the larger square. So now $S = \sqrt{2}s$. The perimeter of the large square equals $4S = 4\sqrt{2}s = \sqrt{2}\,(4s) = \sqrt{2} \times$ perimeter of the small square. (520)

23. Choice A is correct. Angles $A$ and $B$ are both greater than 0 degrees and less than 90 degrees, so their sum is between 0 degrees and 180 degrees. Then angle $C$ must be between 0 and 180 degrees. (501, 505)

24. Choice D is correct. Let the four angles be $x$, $2x$, $3x$, and $4x$. The sum, $10x$, must equal $360°$. Thus, $x = 36°$, and the largest angle, $4x$, is $144°$. (505)

25. Choice C is correct. The diagonals of a rectangle are perpendicular only when the rectangle is a square. $AE$ is part of the diagonal $AC$, so $AE$ will not necessarily be perpendicular to $BD$. (518)

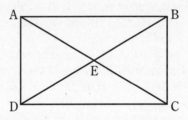

26. Choice D is correct.

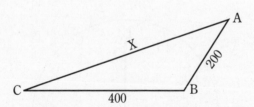

Draw the three cities as the vertices of a triangle. The length of side $CB$ is 400 miles, the length of side $AB$ is 200 miles, and $x$, the length of side $AC$, is unknown. The sum of any two sides of a triangle is greater than the third side, or in algebraic terms: $400 + 200 > x$, $400 + x > 200$ and $200 + x > 400$. These simplify to $600 > x$, $x > -200$, and $x > 200$. For $x$ to be greater than 200 and $-200$, it must be greater than 200. Thus, the values of $x$ are $200 < x < 600$. (506, 516)

27. Choice C is correct. At 7:30, the hour hand is *halfway between the 7 and the 8*, and the minute hand is on the 6. Thus, there are one and one-half "hour units," each equal to $30°$, so the whole angle is $45°$. (501, 526)

28. Choice E is correct. If a ship is facing north, a right turn of $90°$ will face it eastward. Another $90°$ turn will face it south, and an additional $45°$ turn will bring it to southwest. Thus, the total rotation is $90° + 90° + 45° = 225°$. (501)

29. Choice E is correct. Since $y = z + 30°$ and $x = 2y$, then $x = 2(z + 30°) = 2z + 60°$. Thus, $x + y + z$ equals $(2z + 60°) + (z + 30°) + z = 4z + 90°$. This must equal $180°$ (the sum of the angles of a triangle). So $4z + 90° = 180°$, and the solution is $z = 22\frac{1}{2}°$; $x = 2z + 60° = 45° + 60° = 105°$. (505)

30. Choice D is correct. Since $AB$ is parallel to $CD$, angle 2 = angle 6, and angle 3 + angle 7 = 180°. If angle 2 + angle 3 equals 180°, then angle 2 = angle 7 = angle 6. However, since there is no evidence that angles 6 and 7 are equal, angle 2 + angle 3 does not necessarily equal 180°. Therefore, the answer is (D). (504)

31. Choice B is correct. Call the side of the square, $s$. Then, the diagonal of the square is $\sqrt{2}s$ and the area is $s^2$. The area of an isosceles right triangle with leg $r$ is $\frac{1}{2}r^2$. Now, the area of the triangle is equal to the area of the square so $s^2 = \frac{1}{2}r^2$. Solving for $r$ gives $r = \sqrt{2}s$. The hypotenuse of the triangle is $\sqrt{r^2 + r^2}$. Substituting $r = \sqrt{2}s$, the hypotenuse is $\sqrt{2s^2 + 2s^2}$ $= \sqrt{4s^2} = 2s$. Therefore, the ratio of the diagonal to the hypotenuse is $\sqrt{2}s : 2s$, Since $\sqrt{2}s : 2s$ is $\frac{\sqrt{2}s}{2s}$ or $\frac{\sqrt{2}}{2}$, multiply by $\frac{\sqrt{2}}{\sqrt{2}}$ which has a value of 1. Thus $\frac{\sqrt{2}}{2} \cdot \frac{\sqrt{2}}{\sqrt{2}} = \frac{2}{2\sqrt{2}} = \frac{1}{\sqrt{2}}$ or $1 : \sqrt{2}$, which is the final result. (507, 509, 520)

32. Choice D is correct. The formula for the number of degrees in the angles of a polygon is $180(n-2)$, where $n$ is the number of sides. For a ten-sided figure this is $10(180°) - 360°$ $= (1800 - 360)° = 1440°$. Since the ten angles are equal, they must each equal 144°. (521, 522)

33. Choice C is correct. If three numbers represent the lengths of the sides of a right triangle, they must satisfy the Pythagorean Theorem: The squares of the smaller two must equal the square of the largest one. This condition is met in all the sets given except the set 9,28,35. There, $9^2 + 28^2 = 81 + 784 = 865$, but $35^2 = 1,225$. (509)

34. Choice D is correct. Let the angle be $x$. Since $x$ is its own supplement, then $x + x = 180°$, or, since $2x = 180°$, $x = 90°$. (502)

35. Choice A is correct. The length of the arc intersected by a central angle of a circle is proportional to the number of degrees in the angle. Thus, if a 45° angle cuts off a 6-inch arc, a 360° angle intersects an arc eight times as long, or 48 inches. This is equal to the circle's circumference, or $2\pi$ times the radius. Thus, to obtain the radius, divide 48 inches by $2\pi$. 48 inches $\div 2\pi = \frac{24}{\pi}$ inches. (524, 526)

36. Choice C is correct. Refer to the diagram pictured below. Calculate the distance from vertex 1 to vertex 2. This is simply the diagonal of a 1-inch square and equal to $\sqrt{2}$ inches. Now, vertices 1, 2, and 3 form a right triangle, with legs of 1 and $\sqrt{2}$. By the Pythagorean Theorem, the hypotenuse is $\sqrt{3}$. This is the distance from vertex 1 to vertex 3, the two most distant vertices. (509, 520)

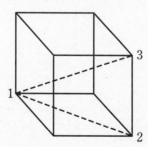

37. Choice A is correct. In one hour, the hour hand of a clock moves through an angle of 30° (one "hour unit"). 70 minutes equals $\frac{7}{6}$ hours, so during that time the hour hand will move through $\frac{7}{6} \times 30°$, or 35°. (501, 526)

**38.** Choice C is correct. In order to be similar, two triangles must have corresponding angles equal. This is true of triangles *ODC* and *OBA*, since angle *O* equals itself, and angles *OCD* and *OAB* are both right angles. (The third angles of these triangles must be equal, as the sum of the angles of a triangle is always 180°.) Since the triangles are similar, *OD* : *DC* = *OB* : *AB*. But, *OD* and *OA* are radii of the same circle and are equal. Therefore, substitute *OA* for *OD* in the above proportion. Hence, *OA* : *DC* = *OB* : *AB*. There is, however, no information given on the relative sizes of any of the line segments, so statement III may or may not be true.                                      (509, 510, 524)

**39.** Choice C is correct. Let the three angles equal *x*, 2*x*, and 6*x*. Then, *x* + 2*x* + 6*x* = 9*x* = 180°. Therefore, *x* = 20° and 6*x* = 120°.                                      (505)

**40.** Choice A is correct. Since *AB* = *AC*, angle *ABC* must equal angle *ACB*. (Base angles of an isosceles triangle are equal). As the sum of angles *BAC*, *ABC*, and *ACB* is 180°, and angle *BAC* equals 40°, angle *ABC* and angle *ACB* must each equal 70°. Now, *DBC* is a right triangle, with angle *BDC* = 90° and angle *DCB* = 70°. (The three angles must add up to 180°.) Angle *DBC* must equal 20°.                                      (507, 514)

**41.** Choice C is correct.

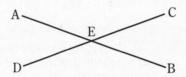

∠*AEB* and ∠*CED* are both straight angles, and are equal; similarly, ∠*DEC* and ∠*BEA* are both straight angles. ∠*AEC* and ∠*BED* are vertical angles, as are ∠*BEC* and ∠*DEA*, and are equal. ∠*AED* and ∠*CEA* are supplementary and need not be equal.                                      (501, 502, 503)

**42.** Choice A is correct. All right isosceles triangles have angles of 45°, 45°, and 90°. Since all triangles with the same angles are similar, all right isosceles triangles are similar.                                      (507, 509, 510)

**43.** Choice C is correct.

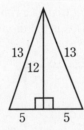

As the diagram shows, the altitude to the base of the isosceles triangle divides it into two congruent right triangles, each with 5 − 12 − 13 sides. Thus, the base is 10, height is 12 and the area is $\frac{1}{2}$(10)(12) = 60.                                      (505, 507, 509)

**44.** Choice C is correct. The altitude to any side divides the triangle into two congruent 30° − 60° −90° right triangles, each with a hypotenuse of 2 inches and a leg of 1 inch. The other leg equals the altitude. By the Pythagorean Theorem the altitude is equal to $\sqrt{3}$ inches. (The sides of a 30° −60° −90° right triangle are always in the proportion $1 : \sqrt{3} : 2$.)

(509, 514)

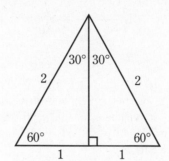

**45.** Choice E is correct.

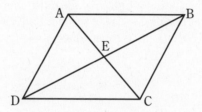

As the diagram illustrates, angles *AED* and *BEC* are vertical and, therefore, equal. *AE = EC*, because the diagonals of a parallelogram bisect each other. Angles *BDC* and *DBA* are equal because they are alternate interior angles of parallel lines (*AB∥CD*).  (503, 517)

**46.** Choice E is correct. There are eight isosceles right triangles: *ABE, BCE, CDE, ADE, ABC, BCD, CDA*, and *ABD*.  (520)

**47.** Choice D is correct. Recall that a regular hexagon may be broken up into six equilateral triangles.

Since the angles of each triangle are 60°, and two of these angles make up each angle of the hexagon, an angle of the hexagon must be 120°.  (523)

**48.** Choice E is correct.

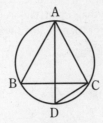

Since the radius equals 1″, $AD$, the diameter, must be 2″. Now, since $AD$ is a diameter, $ACD$ must be a right triangle, because an angle inscribed in a semicircle is a right angle. Thus, because $\angle DAC = 30°$, it must be a $30° - 60° - 90°$ right triangle. The sides will be in the proportion $1 : \sqrt{3} : 2$. As $AD : AC = 2 : \sqrt{3}$, so $AC$, one of the sides of the equilateral triangle, must be $\sqrt{3}$ inches long.                    (508, 524)

**49.** Choice D is correct. Let the angles be $2x$, $3x$, $4x$. Their sum, $9x = 180°$ and $x = 20°$. Thus, the largest angle, $4x$, is $80°$.                    (505)

**50.** Choice B is correct. The sides of a right triangle must obey the Pythagorean Theorem. The only group of choices that does so is the second: 12, 16, and 20 are in the $3 : 4 : 5$ ratio, and the relationship $12^2 + 16^2 = 20^2$ is satisfied.                    (509)

# MATH REFRESHER
## SESSION 6

# Miscellaneous Problems: Averages, Series, Properties of Integers, Approximations, Combinations, Probability, the Absolute Value Sign, and Functions

## Averages, Medians, and Modes

**601.** *Averages.* The average of $n$ numbers is merely their sum, divided by $n$.

**Example:** Find the average of: 20, 0, 80, and 12.

*Solution:* The average is the sum divided by the number of entries, or:

$$\frac{20 + 0 + 80 + 12}{4} = \frac{112}{4} = 28$$

A quick way of obtaining an average of a set of numbers that are close together is the following:

**STEP 1.** Choose any number that will approximately equal the average.

**STEP 2.** Subtract this approximate average from each of the numbers (this sum will give some positive and negative results). Add the results.

**STEP 3.** Divide this sum by the number of entries.

**STEP 4.** Add the result of Step 3 to the approximate average chosen in Step 1. This will be the true average.

**Example:** Find the average of 92, 93, 93, 96, and 97.

*Solution:* Choose 95 as an approximate average. Subtracting 95 from 92, 93, 93, 96, and 97 gives $-3$, $-2$, $-2$, 1, and 2. The sum is $-4$. Divide $-4$ by 5 (the number of entries) to obtain $-0.8$. Add $-0.8$ to the original approximation of 95 to get the true average, $95 - 0.8$ or 94.2.

**601a.** *Medians.* The median of a set of numbers is that number which is in the *middle* of all the numbers.

**Example:** Find the median of 20, 0, 80, 12, and 30.

*Solution:* Arrange the numbers in increasing order:

0
12
20
30
80

The *middle* number is 20, so 20 is the *median*.

Note: If there is an *even* number of items, such as

$$
\begin{array}{c}
0 \\
12 \\
20 \\
24 \\
30 \\
80
\end{array}
$$

there is no *middle* number.

So in this case we take the average of the two middle numbers, 20 and 24, to get 22, which is the *median*.

If there are numbers like 20 and 22, the median would be 21 (just the average of 20 and 22).

**601b.** *Modes.* The mode of a set of numbers is the number that occurs most frequently.

If we have numbers 0, 12, 20, 30, and 80 there is *no* mode, since no one number appears with the greatest frequency. But consider this:

**Example:** Find the mode of 0, 12, 12, 20, 30, 80.

*Solution:* 12 appears most frequently, so it is the mode.

**Example:** Find the mode of 0, 12, 12, 20, 30, 30, 80.

*Solution:* Here *both* 12 and 30 are modes.

## Properties of Integers

**603.** *Even-Odd.* These are problems that deal with even and odd numbers. An even number is divisible by 2, and an odd number is not divisible by 2. All even numbers end in the digits 0, 2, 4, 6, or 8; odd numbers end in the digits 1, 3, 5, 7, or 9. For example, the numbers 358, 90, 18, 9,874, and 46 are even numbers. The numbers 67, 871, 475, and 89 are odd numbers. It is important to remember the following facts:

**604.** The sum of *two* even numbers is *even*, and the sum of *two odd* numbers is *even*, but the sum of an *odd* number *and* an *even* number is *odd*. For example, $4 + 8 = 12$, $5 + 3 = 8$, and $7 + 2 = 9$.

**Example:** If $m$ is any integer, is the number $6m + 3$ an even or odd number?

*Solution:* $6m$ is even since 6 is a multiple of 2. 3 is odd. Therefore $6m + 3$ is odd since even + odd = odd.

**605.** The product of *two odd* numbers is *odd*, but the product of an even number and *any other* number is an *even* number. For example, $3 \times 5 = 15$ (odd); $4 \times 5 = 20$ (even); $4 \times 6 = 24$ (even).

**Example:** If $m$ is any integer, is the product $(2m + 3)(4m + 1)$ even or odd?

*Solution:* Since $2m$ is even and 3 is odd, $2m + 3$ is odd. Likewise, since $4m$ is even and 1 is odd, $4m + 1$ is odd. Thus $(2m + 3)(4m + 1)$ is (odd × odd) which is odd.

**606.** Even numbers are expressed in the form $2k$ where $k$ may be any integer. Odd numbers are expressed in the form of $2k + 1$ or $2k - 1$ where $k$ may be any integer. For example, if $k = 17$, then $2k = 34$ and $2k + 1 = 35$. If $k = 6$, then we have $2k = 12$ and $2k + 1 = 13$.

**Example:** Prove that the product of two odd numbers is odd.

*Solution:* Let one of the odd numbers be represented as $2x + 1$. Let the other number be represented as $2y + 1$. Now multiply $(2x + 1)(2y + 1)$. We get: $4xy + 2x + 2y + 1$. Since $4xy + 2x + 2y$ is even because it is a multiple of 2, that quantity is even. Since 1 is odd, we have $4xy + 2x + 2y + 1$ is odd, since even + odd = odd.

**607.** *Divisibility.* If an integer $P$ is divided by an integer $Q$, and an integer is obtained as the quotient, then $P$ is said to be divisible by $Q$. In other words, if $P$ can be expressed as an integral multiple of $Q$, then $P$ is said to be divisible by $Q$. For example, dividing 51 by 17 gives 3, an integer. 51 is divisible by 17, or 51 equals 17 times 3. On the other hand, dividing 8 by 3 gives $2\frac{2}{3}$, which is not an integer. 8 is not divisible by 3, and there is no way to express 8 as an integral multiple of 3. There are various tests to see whether an integer is divisible by certain numbers. These tests are listed below:

1. Any integer is divisible *by 2* if the last digit of the number is a 0, 2, 4, 6, or 8.

   **Example:** The numbers 98, 6,534, 70, and 32 are divisible by 2 because they end in 8, 4, 0, and 2, respectively.

2. Any integer is divisible *by 3* if the sum of its digits is divisible by 3.

   **Example:** Is the number 34,237,023 divisible by 3?

   *Solution:* Add the digits of the number. $3 + 4 + 2 + 3 + 7 + 0 + 2 + 3 = 24$. Now, 24 is divisible by $3 (24 \div 3 = 8)$ so the number 34,237,023 is also divisible by 3.

3. Any integer is divisible *by 4* if the last two digits of the number make a number that is divisible by 4.

   **Example:** Which of the following numbers is divisible by 4?
   3,456, 6,787,612, 67,408, 7,877, 345, 98.

   *Solution:* Look at the last two digits of the numbers, 56, 12, 08, 77, 45, 98. Only 56, 12, and 08 are divisible by 4, so only the numbers, 3,456, 6,787,612, and 67,408 are divisible by 4.

4. An integer is divisible *by 5* if the last digit is either a 0 or a 5.

   **Example:** The numbers 780, 675, 9,000, and 15 are divisible by 5, while the numbers 786, 5,509, and 87 are not divisible by 5.

5. Any integer is divisible *by 6* if it passes the divisibility tests for both 2 and 3.

   **Example:** Is the number 12,414 divisible by 6?

   *Solution:* Test whether 12,414 is divisible by 2 and 3. The last digit is a 4, so it is divisible by 2. Adding the digits yields $1 + 2 + 4 + 1 + 4 = 12$. 12 is divisible by 3 so the number 12,414 is divisible by 3. Since it is divisible by both 2 and 3, it is divisible by 6.

6. Any integer is divisible *by 8* if the last three digits are divisible by 8. (Since 1,000 is divisible by 8, you can ignore all multiples of 1,000.)

   **Example:** Is the number 342,169,424 divisible by 8?

   *Solution:* $424 \div 8 = 53$, so 342,169,424 is divisible by 8.

7. Any integer is divisible *by 9* if the sum of its digits is divisible by 9.

   **Example:** Is the number 243,091,863 divisible by 9?

   *Solution:* Adding the digits yields $2 + 4 + 3 + 0 + 9 + 1 + 8 + 6 + 3 = 36$. 36 is divisible by 9, so the number 243,091,863 is divisible by 9.

8. Any integer is divisible *by 10* if the last digit is a 0.

   **Example:** The numbers 60, 8,900, 5,640, and 34,000 are all divisible by 10 because the last digit in each is a 0.

---

Note that if a number $P$ is divisible by a number $Q$, then $P$ is also divisible by all the factors of $Q$. For example, 60 is divisible by 12, so 60 is also divisible by 2, 3, 4, and 6, which are all factors of 12.

**608.** *Prime numbers.* A prime number is one that is divisible only by 1 and itself. The first few prime numbers are 2, 3, 5, 7, 11, 13, 17, 19, 23, 29, 31, 37. . . . Note that the number 1 is not considered a prime number. To determine if a number is prime, follow these steps:

**STEP 1.** Determine a very rough approximate square root of the number. Remember that the square root of a number is that number which when multiplied by itself gives the original number. For example, the square root of 25 is 5 because $5 \times 5 = 25$.

**STEP 2.** Divide the number by all of the primes that are less than the approximate square root. If the number is not divisible by any of these primes, then it is prime. If it is divisible by one of the primes, then it is not prime.

**Example:** Is the number 97 prime?

*Solution:* An approximate square root of 97 is 10. All of the primes less than 10 are 2, 3, 5, and 7. Divide 97 by 2, 3, 5, and 7. No integer results, so 97 is prime.

**Example:** Is the number 161 prime?

*Solution:* An approximate square root of 161 is 13. The primes less than 13 are 2, 3, 5, 7, and 11. Divide 161 by 2, 3, 5, 7, and 11. 161 is divisible by 7 ($161 \div 7 = 23$), so 161 is not prime.

# Approximations

**609.** *Rounding off.* A number expressed to a certain number of places is rounded off when it is approximated as a number with fewer places of accuracy. For example, the number 8.987 is expressed more accurately than the number rounded off to 8.99. To round off to *n* places, look at the digit that is to the right of the *n*th digit. (The *n*th digit is found by counting *n* places to the right of the decimal point.) If this digit is less than 5, eliminate all of the digits to the right of the *n*th digit. If the digit to the right of the *n*th digit is 5 or more, then add 1 to the *n*th digit and eliminate all of the digits to the right of the *n*th digit.

**Example:** Round off 8.73 to the nearest tenth.

*Solution:* The digit to the right of the 7 (.7 is seven tenths) is 3. Since this is less than 5, eliminate it, and the rounded off answer is 8.7.

**Example:** Round off 986 to the nearest tens' place.

*Solution:* The number to the right of the tens' place is 6. Since this is 5 or more add 1 to the 8 and replace the 6 with a 0 to get 990.

**610.** *Approximating sums.* When adding a small (less than 10) set of numbers and when the answer must have a given number of places of accuracy, follow the steps below.

**STEP 1.** Round off each addend (number being added) to one more place than the number of places the answer is to have.

**STEP 2.** Add the rounded addends.

**STEP 3.** Round off the sum to the desired number of places of accuracy.

**Example:** What is the sum of 12.0775, 1.20163, and 121.303 correct to the nearest hundredth?

*Solution:* Round off the three numbers to the nearest thousandth (one more place than the accuracy of the sum): 12.078, 1.202, and 121.303. The sum of these is 134.583. Rounded off to the nearest hundredth, this is 134.58.

**611.** *Approximating products.* To multiply 2 or 3 numbers and have an answer to the desired number of places of accuracy, follow the steps below.

**STEP 1.** Round off the numbers being multiplied to one more place than the number of places of accuracy desired in the answer.

**STEP 2.** Multiply the rounded off factors (numbers being multiplied).

**STEP 3.** Round off the product to the desired number of places.

**Example:** Find the product of 3,316 and 1,432 to three places.

*Solution:* First, round off 3,316 to 3 places, to obtain 3,320. Round off 1,432 to 3 places to give 1,430. The product of these two numbers is 4,747,600. Rounded off to 3 places this is 4,750,000.

**612.** *Approximating square roots.* The square root of a number is that number which, when multiplied by itself, gives the original number. For example, 6 is the square root of 36. Often on tests a number with different choices for the square root is given. Follow this procedure to determine which is the best choice.

**STEP 1.** Square all of the choices given.

**STEP 2.** Select the closest choice that is too large and the closest choice that is too small (assuming that no choice is the exact square root). Find the average of these two *choices* (not of their squares).

**STEP 3.** Square this average; if the square is greater than the original number, choose the lower of the two choices; if its square is lower than the original number, choose the higher.

**Example:** Which of the following is closest to the square root of 86: 9.0, 9.2, 9.4, 9.6, or 9.8?

*Solution:* The squares of the five numbers are: 81, 84.64, 88.36, 92.16, and 96.04, respectively. (Actually it was not necessary to calculate the last two, since they are greater than the third square, which is already greater than 86.) The two closest choices are 9.2 and 9.4; their average is 9.3. The square of 9.3 is 86.49. Therefore, 9.3 is greater than the square root of 86. So, the square root must be closer to 9.2 than to 9.4.

# Combinations

**613.** Suppose that a job has 2 different parts. There are $m$ different ways of doing the first part, and there are $n$ different ways of doing the second part. The problem is to find the number of ways of doing the entire job. For each way of doing the first part of the job, there are $n$ ways of doing the second part. Since there are $m$ ways of doing the first part, the total number of ways of doing the entire job is $m \times n$. The formula that can be used is

$$\text{Number of ways} = m \times n$$

For any problem that involves 2 actions or 2 objects, each with a number of choices, and asks for the number of combinations, the formula can be used. For example: A man wants a sandwich and a drink for lunch. If a restaurant has 4 choices of sandwiches and 3 choices of drinks, how many different ways can he order his lunch?

Since there are 4 choices of sandwiches and 3 choices of drinks, using the formula

$$\text{Number of ways} = 4(3)$$
$$= 12$$

Therefore, the man can order his lunch 12 different ways.

If we have objects $a, b, c, d$, and want to arrange them two at a time—that is, like $ab, bc, cd$, etc.—we have four combinations taken two at a time. This is denoted as $_4C_2$. The rule is that $_4C_2 = \dfrac{(4)(3)}{(2)(1)}$. In general, $n$ combinations taken $r$ at a time is represented by the formula:

$$_nC_r = \frac{(n)(n-1)(n-2)...(n-r+1)}{(r)(r-1)(r-2)...(1)}$$

Examples: $_3C_2 = \dfrac{3 \times 2}{2 \times 1}$; $_8C_3 = \dfrac{8 \times 7 \times 6}{3 \times 2 \times 1}$

Suppose there are two groups, each with a certain number of members. It is known that some members of one group also belong to the other group. The problem is to find how many members there are in the 2 groups altogether. To find the numbers of members altogether, use the following formula:

Total number of members = Number of members in group I
+ Number of members in group II
− Number of members common to both groups

For example: In one class, 18 students received A's for English and 10 students received A's in math. If 5 students received A's in both English and math, how many students received at least one A?

In this case, let the students who received A's in English be in group I and let those who received A's in math be in group II.

Using the formula:

Number of students who received at least one A
= Number in group I + Number in group II − Number in both
= 18 + 10 − 5 = 23

Therefore, there are 23 students who received at least one A.

In combination problems such as these, the problems do not always ask for the total number. They may ask for any of the four numbers in the formula while the other three are given. In any case, to solve the problems, use the formula.

## Probability

**614.**   The probability that an event will occur equals the number of favorable ways divided by the total number of ways. If $P$ is the probability, $m$ is the number of favorable ways, and $n$ is the total number of ways, then

$$P = \frac{m}{n}$$

For example: What is the probability that a head will turn up on a single throw of a penny?

The favorable number of ways is 1 (a head).

The total number of ways is 2 (a head and a tail). Thus, the probability is $\frac{1}{2}$.

If $a$ and $b$ are two mutually exclusive events, then the probability that $a$ or $b$ will occur is the sum of the individual probabilities.

Suppose $P_a$ is the probability that an event $a$ occurs. Suppose that $P_b$ is the probability that a second independent event $b$ occurs. Then the probability that the first event $a$ occurs *and* the second event $b$ occurs subsequently is $P_a \times P_b$.

## The Absolute Value Sign

**615.**   The symbol | | denotes absolute value. The absolute value of a number is the numerical value of the number without the plus or minus sign in front of it. Thus all absolute values are positive. For example, $|+3|$ is 3, and $|-2|$ is 2. Here's another example:

If $x$ is positive and $y$ is negative $|x| + |y| = x - y$.

## Functions

**616.**   Suppose we have a function of $x$. This is denoted as $f(x)$ (or $g(y)$ or $h(z)$ etc.). As an example, if $f(x) = x$ then $f(3) = 3$.

In this example we substitute the value 3 wherever $x$ appears in the function. Similarly $f(-2) = -2$. Consider another example: If $f(y) = y^2 - y$, then $f(2) = 2^2 - 2 = 2. f(-2) = (-2)^2 - (-2) = 6. f(z) = z^2 - z. f(2z) = (2z)^2 - (2z) = 4z^2 - 2z$.

Let us consider still another example: Let $f(x) = x + 2$ and $g(y) = 2y$. What is $f[g(-2)]$? Now $g(-2) = 2^{-2} = \frac{1}{4}$. Thus $f[g(-2)] = f\left(\frac{1}{4}\right)$. Since $f(x) = x + 2, f\left(\frac{1}{4}\right) = \frac{1}{4} + 2 = 2\frac{1}{4}$.

# Practice Test 6

## Miscellaneous Problems Including Averages, Series, Properties of Integers, Approximations, Probability, the Absolute Value Sign, and Functions

Correct answers and solutions follow each test.

**1.** A B C D E

1. If $n$ is the first of five consecutive odd numbers, what is their average?

(A) $n$
(B) $n + 1$
(C) $n + 2$
(D) $n + 3$
(E) $n + 4$

**2.** A B C D E

2. What is the average of the following numbers: 35.5, 32.5, 34.0, 35.0, 34.5?

(A) 33.0
(B) 33.8
(C) 34.0
(D) 34.3
(E) 34.5

**3.** A B C D E

*3. What is the next number in the following series: 1, 5, 9, 13, . . . ?

(A) 11
(B) 15
(C) 17
(D) 19
(E) 21

**4.** A B C D E

*4. Which of the following is the next number in the series: 3, 6, 4, 9, 5, 12, 6, . . . ?

(A) 7
(B) 9
(C) 12
(D) 15
(E) 24

**5.** A B C D E

5. If $P$ is an even number, and $Q$ and $R$ are both odd, which of the following *must* be true?

(A) $P \cdot Q$ is an odd number
(B) $Q - R$ is an even number
(C) $PQ - PR$ is an odd number
(D) $Q + R$ cannot equal $P$
(E) $P + Q$ cannot equal $R$

**6.** A B C D E

6. If a number is divisible by 102, then it is also divisible by:

(A) 23
(B) 11
(C) 103
(D) 5
(E) 2

*Not tested on current SAT.

A B C D E
7. ‖ ‖ ‖ ‖ ‖

**7.** Which of the following numbers is divisible by 36?

(A) 35,924
(B) 64,530
(C) 74,098
(D) 152,640
(E) 192,042

A B C D E
8. ‖ ‖ ‖ ‖ ‖

**8.** How many prime numbers are there between 45 and 72?

(A) 4
(B) 5
(C) 6
(D) 7
(E) 8

A B C D E
9. ‖ ‖ ‖ ‖ ‖

**9.** Which of the following represents the smallest possible value of $(M - \frac{1}{2})^2$, if $M$ is an integer?

(A) 0.00
(B) 0.25
(C) 0.50
(D) 0.75
(E) 1.00

A B C D E
10. ‖ ‖ ‖ ‖ ‖

**10.** Which of the following best approximates $\dfrac{7.40096 \times 10.0342}{.2001355}$ ?

(A) 0.3700
(B) 3.700
(C) 37.00
(D) 370.0
(E) 3700

A B C D E
11. ‖ ‖ ‖ ‖ ‖

**11.** In a class with six boys and four girls, the students all took the same test. The boys' scores were 74, 82, 84, 84, 88, and 95 while the girls' scores were 80, 82, 86, and 86. Which of the following statements is true?

(A) The boys' average was 0.1 higher than the average for the whole class.
(B) The girls' average was 0.1 lower than the boys' average.
(C) The class average was 1.0 higher than the boys' average.
(D) The boys' average was 1.0 higher than the class average.
(E) The girls' average was 1.0 lower than the boys' average.

A B C D E
12. ‖ ‖ ‖ ‖ ‖

**\*12.** If the following series continues to follow the same pattern, what will be the next number: 2, 6, 3, 9, 6, . . . ?

(A) 3
(B) 6
(C) 12
(D) 14
(E) 18

\*Not tested on current SAT.

**13.** A B C D E

**13.** Which of the following numbers *must* be odd?

(A) The sum of an odd number and an odd number.
(B) The product of an odd number and an even number.
(C) The sum of an odd number and an even number.
(D) The product of two even numbers.
(E) The sum of two even numbers.

**14.** A B C D E

**14.** Which of the following numbers is the best approximation of the length of one side of a square with an area of 12 square inches?

(A) 3.2 inches
(B) 3.3 inches
(C) 3.4 inches
(D) 3.5 inches
(E) 3.6 inches

**15.** A B C D E

**15.** If $n$ is an odd number, then which of the following *best* describes the number represented by $n^2 + 2n + 1$?

(A) It can be odd or even.
(B) It must be odd.
(C) It must be divisible by four.
(D) It must be divisible by six.
(E) The answer cannot be determined from the given information.

**16.** A B C D E

*16. What is the next number in the series: 2, 5, 7, 8, . . . ?

(A) 8
(B) 9
(C) 10
(D) 11
(E) 12

**17.** A B C D E

**17.** What is the average of the following numbers: $3\frac{1}{2}, 4\frac{1}{4}, 2\frac{1}{4}, 3\frac{1}{4}, 4$?

(A) 3.25
(B) 3.35
(C) 3.45
(D) 3.50
(E) 3.60

**18.** A B C D E

**18.** Which of the following numbers is divisible by 24?

(A) 76,300
(B) 78,132
(C) 80,424
(D) 81,234
(E) 83,636

**19.** A B C D E

**19.** In order to graduate, a boy needs an average of 65 percent for his five major subjects. His first four grades were 55, 60, 65, and 65. What grade does he need in the fifth subject in order to graduate?

(A) 65
(B) 70
(C) 75
(D) 80
(E) 85

*Not tested on current SAT.

**20.**  A B C D E    **20.** If $t$ is any integer, which of the following represents an odd number?

(A) $2t$
(B) $2t + 3$
(C) $3t$
(D) $2t + 2$
(E) $t + 1$

**21.**  A B C D E    **21.** If the average of five whole numbers is an even number, which of the following statements is *not true*?

(A) The sum of the five numbers must be divisible by 2.
(B) The sum of the five numbers must be divisible by 5.
(C) The sum of the five numbers must be divisible by 10.
(D) At least one of the five numbers must be even.
(E) All of the five numbers must be odd.

**22.**  A B C D E    **22.** What is the product of 23 and 79 to one place of accuracy?

(A) 1,600
(B) 1,817
(C) 1,000
(D) 1,800
(E) 2,000

**23.**  A B C D E    *23. What is the next term in the series 1, 1, 2, 3, 5, 8, 13, . . . ?

(A) 18
(B) 21
(C) 13
(D) 9
(E) 20

**24.**  A B C D E    *24. What is the next number in the series 1, 4, 2, 8, 6, . . . ?

(A) 4
(B) 6
(C) 8
(D) 15
(E) 24

**25.**  A B C D E    **25.** Which of the following is closest to the square root of $\frac{1}{2}$ ?

(A) 0.25
(B) 0.5
(C) 0.6
(D) 0.7
(E) 0.8

**26.**  A B C D E    **26.** How many prime numbers are there between 56 and 100?

(A) 8
(B) 9
(C) 10
(D) 11
(E) None of the above.

*Not tested on current SAT.

27. | A B C D E

27. If you multiply one million, two hundred thousand, one hundred seventy-six by five hundred twenty thousand, two hundred four, and then divide the product by one billion, your result will be closest to:

(A) 0.6
(B) 6
(C) 600
(D) 6,000
(E) 6,000,000

28. | A B C D E

28. The number 89.999 rounded off to the nearest tenth is equal to which of the following?

(A) 90.0
(B) 89.0
(C) 89.9
(D) 89.99
(E) 89.90

29. | A B C D E

29. $a$, $b$, $c$, $d$, and $e$ are integers; $M$ is their average; and $S$ is their sum. What is the ratio of $S$ to $M$?

(A) 1 : 5
(B) 5 : 1
(C) 1 : 1
(D) 2 : 1
(E) depends on the values of $a$, $b$, $c$, $d$, and $e$

30. | A B C D E

*30. What is the next number in the series 1, 1, 2, 4, 5, 25, . . . ?

(A) 8
(B) 12
(C) 15
(D) 24
(E) 26

31. | A B C D E

31. The sum of five odd numbers is always:

(A) even
(B) divisible by three
(C) divisible by five
(D) a prime number
(E) None of the above.

32. | A B C D E

32. If $E$ is an even number, and $F$ is divisible by three, then what is the *largest* number by which $E^2F^3$ *must* be divisible?

(A) 6
(B) 12
(C) 54
(D) 108
(E) 144

33. | A B C D E

33. If the average of five consecutive even numbers is 8, which of the following is the smallest of the five numbers?

(A) 4
(B) 5
(C) 6
(D) 8
(E) None of the above.

*Not tested on current SAT.

**34.** A B C D E    *34. What is the next number in the sequence 1, 4, 7, 10, . . . ?

(A) 13
(B) 14
(C) 15
(D) 16
(E) 18

**35.** A B C D E    35. If a number is divisible by 23, then it is also divisible by which of the following?

(A) 7
(B) 24
(C) 9
(D) 3
(E) None of the above.

**36.** A B C D E    *36. What is the next term in the series 3, 6, 2, 7, 1, . . . ?

(A) 0
(B) 1
(C) 3
(D) 6
(E) 8

**37.** A B C D E    37. What is the average (to the nearest tenth) of the following numbers: 91.4, 91.5, 91.6, 91.7, 91.7, 92.0, 92.1, 92.3, 92.3, 92.4?

(A) 91.9
(B) 92.0
(C) 92.1
(D) 92.2
(E) 92.3

**38.** A B C D E    *38. What is the next term in the following series: 8, 3, 10, 9, 12, 27, . . . ?

(A) 8
(B) 14
(C) 18
(D) 36
(E) 81

**39.** A B C D E    39. Which of the following numbers is divisible by 11?

(A) 30,217
(B) 44,221
(C) 59,403
(D) 60,411
(E) None of the above.

**40.** A B C D E    *40. What is the next number in the series 1, 4, 9, 16, . . . ?

(A) 22
(B) 23
(C) 24
(D) 34
(E) 25

*Not tested on current SAT.

41.  A B C D E

**41.** Which of the following is the best approximation of the product (1.005)(20.0025)(0.0102)?

(A) 0.02
(B) 0.2
(C) 2.0
(D) 20
(E) 200

42.  A B C D E

**\*42.** What is the next number in the series 5, 2, 4, 2, 3, 2, . . . ?

(A) 1
(B) 2
(C) 3
(D) 4
(E) 5

43.  A B C D E

**43.** If $a$, $b$, and $c$ are all divisible by 8, then their average must be

(A) divisible by 8
(B) divisible by 4
(C) divisible by 2
(D) an integer
(E) None of the above.

44.  A B C D E

**44.** Which of the following numbers is divisible by 24?

(A) 13,944
(B) 15,746
(C) 15,966
(D) 16,012
(E) None of the above.

45.  A B C D E

**45.** Which of the following numbers is a prime?

(A) 147
(B) 149
(C) 153
(D) 155
(E) 161

46.  A B C D E

**\*46.** What is the next number in the following series: 4, 8, 2, 4, 1, . . . ?

(A) 1
(B) 2
(C) 4
(D) 8
(E) 16

47.  A B C D E

**47.** The sum of four consecutive odd integers must be:

(A) even, but not necessarily divisible by 4
(B) divisible by 4, but not necessarily by 8
(C) divisible by 8, but not necessarily by 16
(D) divisible by 16
(E) None of the above.

\*Not tested on current SAT.

48. A B C D E    **48.** Which of the following is closest to the square root of $\frac{3}{5}$?

(A) $\frac{1}{2}$

(B) $\frac{2}{3}$

(C) $\frac{3}{4}$

(D) $\frac{4}{5}$

(E) 1

49. A B C D E    ***49.** What is the next term in the series: 9, 8, 6, 3, . . . ?

(A) 0
(B) −2
(C) 1
(D) −3
(E) −1

50. A B C D E    **50.** The sum of an odd and an even number is

(A) a perfect square
(B) negative
(C) even
(D) odd
(E) None of the above.

*Not tested on current SAT.

## Answer Key for Practice Test 6

| | | | |
|---|---|---|---|
| 1. E | 14. D | 27. C | 39. A |
| 2. D | 15. C | 28. A | 40. E |
| 3. C | 16. A | 29. B | 41. B |
| 4. D | 17. C | 30. E | 42. B |
| 5. B | 18. C | 31. E | 43. E |
| 6. E | 19. D | 32. D | 44. A |
| 7. D | 20. B | 33. A | 45. B |
| 8. C | 21. E | 34. A | 46. B |
| 9. B | 22. E | 35. E | 47. C |
| 10. D | 23. B | 36. E | 48. C |
| 11. E | 24. E | 37. A | 49. E |
| 12. E | 25. D | 38. B | 50. D |
| 13. C | 26. B | | |

## Answers and Solutions for Practice Test 6

1. Choice E is correct. The five consecutive odd numbers must be $n, n + 2, n + 6$, and $n + 8$. Their average is equal to their sum, $5n + 20$, divided by the number of addends, 5, which yields $n + 4$ as the average. (601)

2. Choice D is correct. Choosing 34 as an approximate average results in the following addends: $+ 1.5, -1.5, 0, + 1.0$, and $+ 0.5$. Their sum is $+ 1.5$. Now, divide by 5 to get $+ 0.3$ and add this to 34 to get 34.3. (To check this, add the five original numbers and divide by 5.) (601)

3. Choice C is correct. This is an arithmetic sequence: Each term is 4 more than the preceding one. The next term is $13 + 4$ or 17. (602)

4. Choice D is correct. This series can be divided into two parts: the even-numbered terms: 6, 9, 12, . . . and the odd-numbered terms: 3, 4, 5, 6, . . . (Even- and odd-numbered terms refers to the terms' *place* in the series and not if the term itself is even or odd.) The next term in the series is even-numbered, so it will be formed by adding 3 to the 12 (the last of the even-numbered terms) to get 15. (602)

5. Choice B is correct. Since $Q$ is an odd number, it may be represented by $2m + 1$, where $m$ is an integer. Similarly, call $R, 2n + 1$ where $n$ is an integer. Thus, $Q - R$ is equal to $(2m + 1) - (2n + 1), 2m - 2n$, or $2(m - n)$. Now, since $m$ and $n$ are integers, $m - n$ will be some integer $p$. Thus, $Q - R = 5$ $2p$. Any number in the form of $2p$, where $p$ is any integer, is an even number. Therefore, $Q - R$ *must* be even. (A) and (C) are wrong, because an even number multiplied by an odd is always even. (D) and (E) are only true for specific values of $P, Q$, and $R$. (604)

6. Choice E is correct. If a number is divisible by 102 then it must be divisible by all of the factors of 102. The only choice that is a factor of 102 is 2. (607)

7. Choice D is correct. To be divisible by 36, a number must be divisible by both 4 and 9. Only (A) and (D) are divisible by 4. (Recall that only the last two digits must be examined.) Of these, only (D) is divisible by 9. (The sum of the digits of (A) is 23, which is not divisible by 9; the sum of the digits of (D) is 18.) (607)

8. Choice C is correct. The prime numbers between 45 and 72 are 47, 53, 59, 61, 67, and 71. All of the others have factors other than 1 and themselves. (608)

9. Choice B is correct. Since $M$ must be an *integer*, the closest value it can have to $\frac{1}{2}$ is either 1 or 0. In either case, $(M - \frac{1}{2})^2$ is equal to $\frac{1}{4}$, or 0.25. (409)

10. Choice D is correct. Approximate to only one place (this is permissible, because the choices are so far apart; if they had been closer together, two or three places would have been used). After this approximation, the expression is: $\frac{7 \times 10}{0.2}$, which is equal to 350. This is closest to 370. (609)

11. Choice E is correct. The average for the boys alone was $\frac{74 + 82 + 84 + 84 + 88 + 95}{6}$, or $507 \div 6 = 84.5$. The girls' average was $\frac{80 + 82 + 86 + 86}{4}$, or $334 \div 4 = 83.5$, which is 1.0 below the boys' average. (601)

12. Choice E is correct. To generate this series, start with 2; multiply by 3 to get 6; subtract 3 to get 3; multiply by 3; subtract 3; etc. Thus, the next term will be found by multiplying the previous term, 6, by 3 to get 18. (602)

13. Choice C is correct. The sum of an odd number and an even number can be expressed as $(2n + 1) + (2m)$, where $n$ and $m$ are integers. ($2n + 1$ must be odd, and $2m$ must be even.) Their sum is equal to $2n + 2m + 1$, or $2(m + n) + 1$. Since $(m + n)$ is an integer, the quantity $2(m + n) + 1$ *must* represent an odd integer. (604, 605)

14. Choice D is correct. The actual length of one of the sides would be the square root of 12. Square each of the five choices to find the square of 3.4 is 11.56, and the square of 3.5 is 12.25. The square root of 12 must lie between 3.4 and 3.5. Squaring 3.45 (halfway between the two choices) yields 11.9025, which is less than 12. Thus the square root of 12 must be greater than 3.45 and therefore closer to 3.5 than to 3.4. (612)

15. Choice C is correct. Factor $n^2 + 2n + 1$ to $(n + 1)(n + 1)$ or $(n + 1)^2$. Now, since $n$ is an odd number, $n + 1$ must be even (the number after every odd number is even). Thus, representing $n + 1$ as $2k$ where $k$ is an integer ($2k$ is the standard representation for an even number) yields the expression: $(n + 1)^2 = (2k)^2$ or $4k^2$. Thus, $(n + 1)^2$ is a multiple of 4, and it must be divisible by 4. A number divisible by 4 must also be even, so (C) is the best choice. (604–607)

16. Choice A is correct. The differences between terms are as follows: 3, 2, and 1. Thus, the next term should be found by adding 0, leaving a result of 8. (602)

17. Choice C is correct. Convert to decimals. Then calculate the value of: $\frac{3.50 + 4.25 + 2.25 + 3.25 + 4.00}{5}$. This equals $17.25 \div 5$, or 3.45. (601)

18. Choice C is correct. If a number is divisible by 24, it must be divisible by 3 and 8. Of the five choices given, only choice (C) is divisible by 8. Add the digits in 80,424 to get 18. As this is divisible by 3, the number is divisible by 3. The number, therefore, is divisible by 24. (607)

19. Choice D is correct. If the boy is to average 65 for five subjects, the total of his five grades must be five times 65 or 325. The sum of the first four grades is $55 + 60 + 65 + 65$, or 245. Therefore, the fifth mark must be $325 - 245$, or 80. (601)

20. Choice B is correct. If $t$ is any integer, then $2t$ is an even number. Adding 3 to an even number always produces an odd number. Thus, $2t + 3$ is always odd. (606)

21. Choice E is correct. Call the five numbers, $a$, $b$, $c$, $d$, and $e$. Then the average is $\frac{(a + b + c + d + e)}{5}$. Since this must be even, $\frac{(a + b + c + d + e)}{5} = 2k$, where $k$ is an integer. Thus $a + b + c + d + e = 10k$. Therefore, the sum of the 5 numbers is divisible by

10, 2, and 5. Thus the first three choices are eliminated. If the five numbers were 1, 1, 1, 1, and 6, then the average would be 2. Thus, the average is even, but not all of the numbers are even. Thus, choice (D) can be true. If all the numbers were odd, the sum would have to be odd. This contradicts the statement that the average is even. Thus, choice (E) is the answer. (601, 607)

22. Choice E is correct. First, round off 23 and 79 to one place of accuracy. The numbers become 20 and 80. The product of these two numbers is 1,600, which rounded off to one place is 2,000. (611)

23. Choice B is correct. Each term in this series is the sum of the two previous terms. Thus, the next term is 8 + 13 or 21. (602)

24. Choice E is correct. This series can be generated by the following steps: multiply by 4; subtract 2; multiply by 4; subtract 2; etc. Since the term "6" was obtained by subtracting 2, multiply by 4 to obtain $4 \times 6 = 24$, the next term. (602)

25. Choice D is correct. 0.7 squared is 0.49. Squaring 0.8 yields 0.64. Thus, the square root of $\frac{1}{2}$ must lie between 0.7 and 0.8. Take the number halfway between these two, 0.75, and square it. This number, 0.5625, is more than $\frac{1}{2}$, so the square root must be closer to 0.7 than to 0.8. An easier way to do problems concerning the square roots of 2 and 3 and their multiples is to memorize the values of these two square roots. The square root of 2 is about 1.414 (remember fourteen-fourteen), and the square root of three is about 1.732 (remember that 1732 was the year of George Washington's birth). Apply these as follows: $\frac{1}{2} = \frac{1}{4} \times 2$ Thus, $\sqrt{\frac{1}{2}} = \sqrt{\frac{1}{4}} \times \sqrt{2} = \frac{1}{2} \times 1.414 = 0.707$, which is very close to 0.7.

(612)

26. Choice B is correct. The prime numbers can be found by taking all the odd numbers between 56 and 100 (the even ones cannot be primes) and eliminating all the ones divisible by 3, by 5, and by 7. If a number under 100 is divisible by none of these, it must be prime. Thus, the only primes between 56 and 100 are 59, 61, 67, 71, 73, 79, 83, 89, and 97. (608)

27. Choice C is correct. Since all the answer requires is an order-of-ten approximation, do not calculate the exact answer. Approximate the answer in the following manner: $\frac{1,000,000 \times 500,000}{1,000,000,000} = 500$. The only choice on the same order of magnitude is 600. (609)

28. Choice A is correct. To round off 89.999, look at the number in the hundredths' place. 9 is more than 5, so add 1 to the number in the tenths' place and eliminate all of the digits to the right. Thus, we get 90.0. (609)

29. Choice B is correct. The average of five numbers is found by dividing their sum by five. Thus, the sum is five times the average, so $S : M = 5 : 1$. (601)

30. Choice E is correct. The series can be generated by the following steps: To get the second term, square the first term; to get the third, add 1 to the second; to get the fourth, square the third; to get the fifth, add 1 to the fourth; etc. The pattern can be written as: square; add 1; repeat the cycle. Following this pattern, the seventh term is found by adding one to the sixth term. Thus, the seventh term is 1 + 25, or 26. (602)

31. Choice E is correct. None of the first four choices is necessarily true. The sum, 5 + 7 + 9 + 13 + 15 = 49, is not even, divisible by 3, divisible by 5, nor prime. (604, 607, 608)

32. Choice D is correct. Any even number can be written as $2m$, and any number divisible by 3 can be written as $3n$, where $m$ and $n$ are integers. Thus, $E^2F^3$ equals $(2m)^2 (3n)^3 = (4m^2)(27n^3) = 108(m^2n^3)$, and 108 is the largest number by which $E^2F^3$ must be divisible. (607)

**33.** Choice A is correct. The five consecutive even numbers can be represented as $n$, $n + 2$, $n + 4$, $n + 6$, and $n + 8$. Taking the sum and dividing by five yields an average of $n + 4$. Thus, $n + 4 = 8$, the given average, and $n = 4$, the smallest number. (601)

**34.** Choice A is correct. To find the next number in this sequence, add 3 to the previous number. This is an arithmetic progression. The next term is $10 + 3$, or 13. (602)

**35.** Choice E is correct. If a number is divisible by 23, then it is divisible by all of the factors of 23. But 23 is a prime with no factors except 1 and itself. Therefore, the correct choice is (E). (607)

**36.** Choice E is correct. The steps generating the successive terms in this series are (to the previous term): add 3; subtract 4; add 5; subtract 6; add 7; etc. The next term is $1 + 7 = 8$. (602)

**37.** Choice A is correct. To find the average, it is convenient to choose 92.0 as an approximate average and then find the average of the differences between the actual numbers and 92.0. Thus, add up: $(-0.6) + (-0.5) + (-0.4) + (-0.3) + (-0.3) + (-0.0) + 0.1 + 0.3 + 0.3 + 0.4$, to $-1.0$; divide this by ten (the number of quantities to be averaged) to obtain $-0.1$. Finally, add this to the approximate average, 92.0, to obtain a final average of 91.9. (601)

**38.** Choice B is correct. This series is a combination of two sub-series: The odd-numbered terms, 3, 9, 27, etc., form a geometric series; the even-numbered terms, 8, 10, 12, 14, etc., form an arithmetic sequence. The next number in the sequence is from the arithmetic sequence and is 14. (Note that in the absence of any other indication, assume a series to be as simple as possible, i.e., arithmetic or geometric.) (602)

**39.** Choice A is correct. To determine if a number is divisible by 11, take each of the digits separately and, beginning with either end, subtract the second from the first, add the following digit, subtract the next one, add the one after that, etc. If this result is divisible by 11, the entire number is. Thus, because $3 - 0 + 2 - 1 + 7 = 11$, we know that 30,217 is divisible by 11. Using the same method, we find that the other four choices are not divisible by 11. (607)

**40.** Choice E is correct. This is the series of integers squared. $1^2, 2^2, 3^2, 4^2 \ldots$ the next term is $5^2$ or 25. (602)

**41.** Choice B is correct. This is simply an order-of-ten approximation, so round off the numbers and work the following problem. $(1.0)(20.0)(0.01) = 0.20$. The actual answer is closest to 0.2. (611)

**42.** Choice B is correct. The even-numbered terms of this series form the sub-series: 2, 2, 2, . . . The odd-numbered terms form the arithmetic series: 5, 4, 3, 2 , . . . The next term in the series is a 2. (602)

**43.** Choice E is correct. Represent the three numbers as $8p$, $8q$, and $8r$, respectively. Thus, their sum is $8p + 8q + 8r$, and their average is $\frac{(8p + 8q + 8r)}{3}$. This need not even be a whole number. For example, the average of 8, 16, and 32 is $\frac{56}{3}$, or $18\frac{2}{3}$. (601, 607)

**44.** Choice A is correct. To be divisible by 24, a number must be divisible by both 3 and 8. Only 13,944 and 15,966 are divisible by 3; of these, only 13,944 is divisible by 8 ($13,944 = 24 \times 581$). (607)

**45.** Choice B is correct. The approximate square root of each of these numbers is 13. Merely divide each of these numbers by the primes up to 13, which are 2, 3, 5, 7, and 11. The only number not divisible by any of these primes is 149. (608, 612)

**46.** Choice B is correct. The sequence is formed by the following operations: Multiply by 2, divide by 4, multiply by 2, divide by 4, etc. Accordingly, the next number is $1 \times 2$, or 2.

(602)

**47.** Choice C is correct. Call the first odd integer $2k + 1$. (This is the standard representation for a general odd integer.) Thus, the next 3 odd integers are $2k + 3$, $2k + 5$, and $2k + 7$. (Each one is 2 more than the previous one.) The sum of these integers is $(2k + 1) + (2k + 3) + (2k + 5) + (2k + 7) = 8k + 16$. This can be written as $8(k + 2)$, which is divisible by 8, but not necessarily by 16.

(606, 607)

**48.** Choice C is correct. By squaring the five choices, it is evident that the two closest choices are: $\left(\frac{3}{4}\right)^2 = 0.5625$ and $\left(\frac{4}{5}\right)^2 = 0.64$. Squaring the number halfway between $\frac{3}{4}$ and $\frac{4}{5}$ gives $(0.775)^2 = 0.600625$. This is greater than $\frac{3}{5}$, so the square root of $\frac{3}{5}$ must be closer to $\frac{3}{4}$ than to $\frac{4}{5}$.

(612)

**49.** Choice E is correct. The terms decrease by 1, then 2, then 3, so the next term is 4 less than 3, or $-1$.

(602)

**50.** Choice D is correct. Let the even number be $2k$, where $k$ is an integer, and let the odd number be $2m + 1$, where $m$ is an integer. Thus, the sum is $2k + (2m + 1)$, $2k + 2m + 1$, or $2(k + m) + 1$. Now $k + m$ is an integer since $k$ and $m$ are integers. Call $k + m$ by another name, $p$. Thus, $2(k + m) + 1$ is $2p + 1$, which is the representation of an odd number.

(604, 606)

# MATH REFRESHER
## SESSION 7

# Tables, Charts, and Graphs

## Charts and Graphs

**701.** Graphs and charts show the relationship of numbers and quantities in visual form. By looking at a graph, you can see at a glance the relationship between two or more sets of information. If such information were presented in written form, it would be hard to read and understand.

*Here are some things to remember when doing problems based on graphs or charts:*

1. Understand what you are being asked to do before you begin figuring.

2. Check the dates and types of information required. Be sure that you are looking in the proper columns, and on the proper lines, for the information you need.

3. Check the units required. Be sure that your answer is in thousands, millions, or whatever the question calls for.

4. In computing averages, be sure that you add the figures you need and no others, and that you divide by the correct number of years or other units.

5. Be careful in computing problems asking for percentages.
   (a) Remember that to convert a decimal into a percent you must multiply it by 100. For example, 0.04 is 4%.
   (b) Be sure that you can distinguish between such quantities as 1% (1 percent) and .01% (one one-hundredth of 1 percent), whether in numerals or in words.
   (c) Remember that if quantity X is greater than quantity Y, and the question asks what percent quantity X is of quantity Y, the answer must be greater than 100 percent.

## Tables and Charts

**702.** A table or chart shows data in the form of a box of numbers or chart of numbers. Each line describes how the numbers are connected.

**Example:**

| Test Score | Number of Students |
|:---:|:---:|
| 90 | 2 |
| 85 | 1 |
| 80 | 1 |
| 60 | 3 |

**Example:** How many students took the test?

*Solution:* To find out the number of students that took the test, just add up the numbers in the column marked "Number of Students." That is, add $2 + 1 + 1 + 3 = 7$.

**Example:** What was the difference in score between the highest and the lowest score?

*Solution:* First look at the highest score: 90. Then look at the lowest score: 60. Now calculate the difference: $90 - 60 = 30$.

**Example:** What was the <u>median</u> score?

*Solution:* The median score means the score that is in the *middle* of all the scores. That is, there are just as many scores above the median as below it. So in this example, the scores are 90, 90 (there are two 90's) 85, 80, and 60, 60, 60 (there are three 60's). So we have:

90
90
85
80
60
60
60

80 is right in the middle. That is, there are three scores above it and three scores below it. So 80 is the median.

**Example:** What was the <u>mean</u> score?

*Solution:* The mean score is defined as the *average* score. That is, it is the

$$\frac{\text{sum of the scores}}{\text{total number of scores}}$$

The sum of the scores is $90 + 90 + 85 + 80 + 60 + 60 + 60 = 525$. The total number of scores is $2 + 1 + 1 + 3 = 7$, so divide 7 into 525 to get the average: 75.

# Graphs

**703.** To read a graph, you must know what *scale* the graph has been drawn to. Somewhere on the face of the graph will be an explanation of what each division of the graph means. Sometimes the divisions will be labeled. At other times, this information will be given in a small box called a *scale* or *legend*. For instance, a map, which is a specialized kind of graph, will always carry a scale or legend on its face telling you such information as $1'' = 100$ miles or $\frac{1''}{4} = 2$ miles.

# Bar Graphs

**704.** The bar graph shows how the information is compared by using broad lines, called bars, of varying lengths. Sometimes single lines are used as well. Bar graphs are good for showing a quick comparison of the information involved, however, the bars are difficult to read accurately unless the end of the bar falls exactly on one of the divisions of the scale. If the end of the bar falls between divisions of the scale, it is not easy to arrive at the precise figure represented by the bar. In bar graphs, the bars can run either vertically or horizontally. The sample bar graph following is a horizontal graph.

EXPENDITURES PER PUPIL —1990

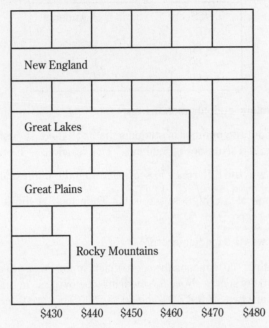

$430    $440    $450    $460    $470    $480

The individual bars in this kind of graph may carry a label within the bar, as in this example. The label may also appear alongside each bar. The scale used on the bars may appear along one axis, as in the example, or it may be noted somewhere on the face of the graph. Each numbered space on the *x*- (or horizontal) axis represents an expenditure of $10 per pupil. A wide variety of questions may be answered by a bar graph, such as:

(1) Which area of the country spends least per pupil? Rocky Mountains.

(2) How much does the New England area spend per pupil? $480.

(3) How much less does the Great Plains spend per pupil than the Great Lakes?
$464 − 447 = $17/pupil.

(4) How much more does New England spend on a pupil than the Rocky Mountain area?
$480 − 433 = $47/pupil.

# Circle Graphs

**705.**    A circle graph shows how an entire quantity has been divided or apportioned. The circle represents 100 percent of the quantity; the different parts into which the whole has been divided are shown by sections, or wedges, of the circle. Circle graphs are good for showing how money is distributed or collected, and for this reason they are widely used in financial graphing. The information is usually presented on the face of each section, telling you exactly what the section stands for and the value of that section in comparison to the other parts of the graph.

SOURCES OF INCOME—PUBLIC COLLEGES OF U.S.

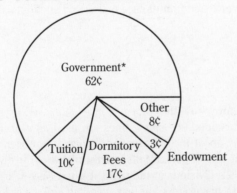

*Government refers to all levels of government—not exclusively the federal government.

The circle graph on the previous page indicates where the money originates that is used to maintain public colleges in the United States. The size of the sections tells you at a glance which source is most important (government) and which is least important (endowments). The sections total 100¢ or $1.00. This graph may be used to answer the following questions:

(1) What is the most important source of income to the public colleges? Government.

(2) What part of the revenue dollar comes from tuition? 10¢.

(3) Dormitory fees bring in how many times the money that endowments bring in? $5\frac{2}{3}$ times $\left(\frac{17}{3} = 5\frac{2}{3}\right)$.

(4) What is the least important source of revenue to public colleges? Endowments.

## Line Graphs

**706.** Graphs that have information running both across (horizontally) and up and down (vertically) can be considered to be laid out on a grid having a $y$-axis and an $x$-axis. One of the two quantities being compared will be placed along the $y$-axis, and the other quantity will be placed along the $x$-axis. When we are asked to compare two values, we subtract the smaller from the larger.

SHARES OF STOCK SOLD
NEW YORK STOCK EXCHANGE DURING ONE SIX-MONTH PERIOD

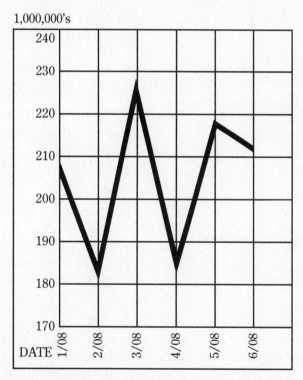

Our sample line graph represents the total shares of stock sold on the New York Stock Exchange between January and June. The months are placed along the $x$-axis, while the sales, in units of 1,000,000 shares, are placed along the $y$-axis.

(1) How many shares were sold in March? 225,000,000.

(2) What is the trend of stock sales between April and May? The volume of sales rose.

(3) Compare the share sales in January and February. 25,000,000 fewer shares were sold in February.

(4) During which months of the period was the increase in sales largest? February to March.

# Practice Test 7 and Solutions

## Tables, Charts, and Graphs

*Correct answers and solutions follow each test.*

## TABLE CHART TEST

*Questions 1–5 are based on this table chart.*

The following chart is a record of the performance of a baseball team for the first seven weeks of the season.

| | Games won | Games lost | Total No. of games played |
|---|---|---|---|
| First Week | 5 | 3 | 8 |
| Second Week | 4 | 4 | 16 |
| Third Week | 5 | 2 | 23 |
| Fourth Week | 6 | 3 | 32 |
| Fifth Week | 4 | 2 | 38 |
| Sixth Week | 3 | 3 | 44 |
| Seventh Week | 2 | 4 | 50 |

1. How many games did the team win during the first seven weeks?

   (A) 32
   (B) 29
   (C) 25
   (D) 21
   (E) 50

2. What percent of the games did the team win?

   (A) 75%
   (B) 60%
   (C) 58%
   (D) 29%
   (E) 80%

3. According to the chart, which week was the worst for the team?

   (A) second week
   (B) fourth week
   (C) fifth week
   (D) sixth week
   (E) seventh week

4. Which week was the best week for the team?

   (A) first week
   (B) third week
   (C) fourth week
   (D) fifth week
   (E) sixth week

5. If there are fifty more games to play in the season, how many more games must the team win to end up winning 70% of the games?

   (A) 39
   (B) 35
   (C) 41
   (D) 34
   (E) 32

## Solutions

1. Choice B is correct. To find the total number of games won, add the number of games won for all the weeks, $5 + 4 + 5 + 6 + 4 + 3 + 2 = 29$.
   (702)

2. Choice C is correct. The team won 29 out of 50 games or 58%.
   (702)

3. Choice E is correct. The seventh week was the only week that the team lost more games than it won.
   (702)

4. Choice B is correct. During the third week the team won 5 games and lost 2, or it won about 70% of the games that week. Compared with the winning percentages for other weeks, the third week's was the highest.
   (702)

5. Choice C is correct. To win 70% of all the games, the team must win 70 out of 100. Since it won 29 games out of the first 50 games, it must win $70 - 29$ or 41 games out of the next 50 games.
   (702)

## PIE CHART TEST

*Questions 1–5 are based on this pie chart.*

POPULATION BY REGION, 1964

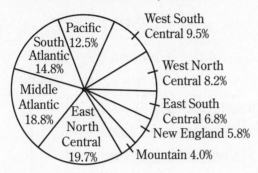

Total U.S. 191.3 million = 100%

1. Which region was the most populated region in 1964?

   (A) East North Central
   (B) Middle Atlantic
   (C) South Atlantic
   (D) Pacific
   (E) New England

2. What part of the entire population lived in the Mountain region?

   (A) $\frac{1}{10}$

   (B) $\frac{1}{30}$

   (C) $\frac{1}{50}$

   (D) $\frac{1}{25}$

   (E) $\frac{1}{8}$

3. What was the approximate population in the Pacific region?

   (A) 20 million
   (B) 24 million
   (C) 30 million
   (D) 28 million
   (E) 15 million

4. Approximately how many more people lived in the Middle Atlantic region than in the South Atlantic?

   (A) 4.0 million
   (B) 7.7 million
   (C) 5.2 million
   (D) 9.3 million
   (E) 8.5 million

5. What was the total population in all the regions combined?

   (A) 73.3 million
   (B) 100.0 million
   (C) 191.3 million
   (D) 126.8 million
   (E) 98.5 million

## Solutions

1. Choice A is correct. East North Central with 19.7% of the total population had the largest population. (705)

2. Choice D is correct. The Mountain region had 4.0% of the population. 4.0% is $\frac{1}{25}$. (705)

3. Choice B is correct. Pacific had 12.5% of the population. 12.5% of 191.3 million is .125 × 191.3 or about 24 million. (705)

4. Choice B is correct. Middle Atlantic had 18.8% and South Atlantic had 14.8% of the population. So, Middle Atlantic had 4.0% more. 4.0% of 191.3 million is .04 × 191.3 or about 7.7 million. (705)

5. Choice C is correct. All the regions combined had 100% of the population or 191.3 million. (705)

## LINE GRAPH TEST

*Questions 1–5 are based on this line graph.*

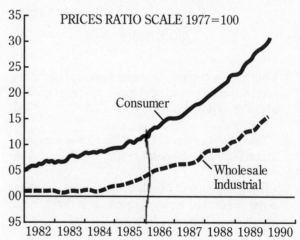

1. On the ratio scale what were consumer prices recorded as of the end of 1985?

   (A) 95
   (B) 100
   (C) 105
   (D) 110
   (E) 115

**2.** During what year did consumer prices rise fastest?

(A) 1983
(B) 1985
(C) 1987
(D) 1988
(E) 1989

**3.** When wholesale and industrial prices were recorded as 110, consumer prices were recorded as

(A) between 125 and 120
(B) between 120 and 115
(C) between 115 and 110
(D) between 110 and 105
(E) between 105 and 100

**4.** For the 8 years 1982–1989 inclusive, the average increase in consumer prices was

(A) 1 point
(B) 2 points
(C) 3 points
(D) 4 points
(E) 5 points

**5.** The percentage increase in wholesale and industrial prices between the beginning of 1982 and the end of 1989 was

(A) 1 percent
(B) 5 percent
(C) 10 percent
(D) 15 percent
(E) less than 1 percent

## Solutions

**1.** Choice D is correct. Drawing a vertical line at the end of 1985, we reach the consumer price graph at about the 110 level. (706)

**2.** Choice E is correct. The slope of the consumer graph is clearly steepest in 1989. (706)

**3.** Choice A is correct. Wholesale and industrial prices were about 110 at the beginning of 1989, when consumer prices were between 120 and 125. (706)

**4.** Choice C is correct. At the beginning of 1982 consumer prices were about 105; at the end of 1989 they were about 130. The average increase is $\frac{130-105}{8} = \frac{25}{8}$ or about 3. (706)

**5.** Choice D is correct. At the beginning of 1982 wholesale prices were about 100; at the end of 1989 they were about 115. The percent increase is about $\frac{115-100}{100} \times 100\%$ or 15%. (706)

## BAR GRAPH TEST

*Questions 1–3 are based on this bar graph.*

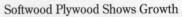

Softwood Plywood Shows Growth

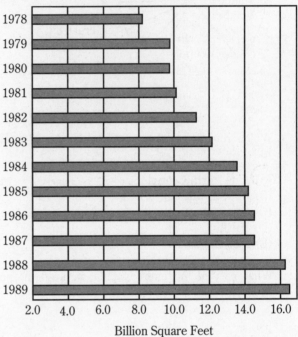

Billion Square Feet

**1.** What was the ratio of soft plywood produced in 1978 as compared with that produced in 1987?

(A) 1 : 1
(B) 2 : 3
(C) 1 : 2
(D) 3 : 4
(E) 1 : 3

**2.** For the years 1978 through 1983, excluding 1982, how many billion square feet of plywood were produced altogether?

(A) 23.2
(B) 29.7
(C) 34.1
(D) 40.7
(E) 50.5

3. Between which consecutive odd years and between which consecutive even years was the plywood production jump greatest?

(A) 1985 and 1987; 1978 and 1980
(B) 1983 and 1985; 1984 and 1986
(C) 1979 and 1981; 1980 and 1982
(D) 1981 and 1983; 1980 and 1982
(E) 1983 and 1985; 1982 and 1984

# Solutions

1. Choice C is correct. To answer this question, you will have to measure the bars. In 1978, 8 billion square feet of plywood were produced. In 1987, 14 billion square feet were produced. The ratio of 8 : 14 is the same as 4 : 7. (704)

2. Choice D is correct. All you have to do is to measure the bar for each year—of course, don't include the 1982 bar—and estimate the length of each bar. Then you add the five lengths. 1978 = 8, 1979 = 10, 1980 = 10, 1981 = 10, 1983 = 12. The total is 50. (704)

3. Choice E is correct. The jump from 1983 to 1985 was from 12 to 14 = 2 billion square feet. The jump from 1982 to 1984 was from 11 to 13.5 = 2.5 billion square feet. None of the other choices show such broad jumps. (704)

## CUMULATIVE GRAPH TEST

*Questions 1–5 are based on this cumulative graph.*

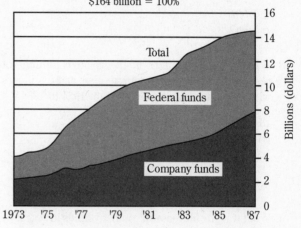

Spending for Research & Development by Type of Research, 1987
$164 billion = 100%

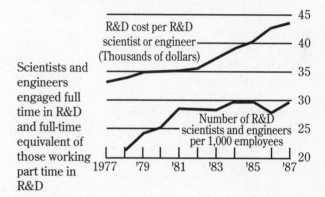

1. About how much in government funds was spent for research and development in 1987?

(A) $16 billion
(B) $8 billion
(C) $12 billion
(D) $24 billion
(E) $4 billion

2. In 1987, about what percent of the total spending in research and development were company funds?

(A) 40%
(B) 25%
(C) $33\frac{1}{2}$
(D) 50%
(E) 20%

3. What was the change in the relative number of research and development scientists and engineers with respect to all employees from 1984 to 1985?

(A) 10%
(B) 5%
(C) 2%
(D) 3%
(E) 0%

4. What was the increase in company funds in research and development from 1973 to 1987?

(A) $12 billion
(B) $6 billion
(C) $8 billion
(D) $4 billion
(E) $14 billion

5. What was the percent of increase of the company funds spent in research and development from 1973 to 1987?

(A) 100%
(B) 50%
(C) 300%
(D) 400%
(E) 1,000%

## Solutions

1. Choice B is correct. Total spending was about $16 billion, and company spending was $8 billion. So, government spending was about $8 billion.   (706)

2. Choice D is correct. Company funds totaled $8 billion, and the total funds were $16 billion. So, company funds were $\frac{1}{2}$ of total funds or 50%. (706)

3. Choice E is correct. The graph showing the relative employment of research and development scientists and engineers was horizontal between 1984 and 1985. This means no change.   (706)

4. Choice B is correct. Company funds totaled $8 billion in 1987 and $2 billion in 1973. The increase was $6 billion.   (706)

5. Choice C is correct. Company funds totaled $2 billion in 1973, and the increase from 1973 to 1987 was $6 billion or 300% of $2 billion.   (706)

# MATH REFRESHER
## SESSION 8

# Modern Math:
# Sets, Relations, Solution
# Sets, Closed Sets, and Axioms

## Sets

**801.** A set is a collection of anything: numbers, letters, objects, etc. The members, or elements, of the set are written between braces like this: {1, 2, 3, 4, 5}. The elements of this set are simply the numbers 1, 2, 3, 4, and 5. Another example of a set is {apples, peaches, pears}. Two sets are equal if they have the same elements. The order in which the elements of the set are listed does not matter. Thus {1, 2, 3, 4, 5} = {5, 4, 3, 2, 1}. We can use one letter to stand for a whole set; for example, $A$ = {1, 2, 3, 4, 5}.

**802.** To find the union of two sets:

Write down every member in one or both of the two sets. The union of two sets is a new set. The union of sets $A$ and $B$ is written $A \cup B$.

For example: If $A$ = {1, 2, 3, 4} and $B$ = {2, 4, 6} find $A \cup B$. All the elements in either $A$ or $B$ or both are 1, 2, 3, 4, and 6. Therefore $A \cup B$ = {1, 2, 3, 4, 6}.

**803.** To find the intersection of two sets:

Write down every member that the two sets have in common. The intersection of the sets $A$ and $B$ is a set written $A \cap B$.

For example: If $A$ = {1, 2, 3, 4} and $B$ = {2, 4, 6}, find $A \cap B$. The elements in both $A$ and $B$ are 2 and 4. Therefore $A \cap B$ ={2, 4}.

> If two sets have no elements in common, then their intersection is the null or empty set, written as $\varnothing$.

For example: The intersection of {1, 3, 5, 7} with {2, 4, 6, 8) is $\varnothing$ since they have no members in common.

**804.** To perform several union and intersection operations, first operate on sets within parentheses.

For example: If $A$ = {1, 2, 3} and $B$ = {2, 3, 4, 5, 6} and $C$ = {1, 4, 6} find $A \cup (B \cap C)$.
First we find $B \cap C$ by listing all the elements in both B and C. $B \cap C$ = {4, 6}.
Then $A \cup (B \cap C)$ is just the set of all members in at least one of the sets $A$ and {4, 6}.
Therefore, $A \cup (B \cap C)$ = {1, 2, 3, 4, 6}.

**805.** A subset of a set is a set, all of whose members are in the original set. Thus, {1, 2, 3} is a subset of the set {1, 2, 3, 4, 5}. Note that the null set is a subset of every set, and also that every set is a subset of itself. In general, a set with n elements has $2^n$ subsets. For example: How many subsets does {$x, y, z$} have? This set has 3 elements and therefore $2^3$ or 8 subsets.

# Relations

**806.** When the elements of a set are ordered pairs, then the set is called a relation. An ordered pair is written $(x, y)$. The order of the two components of the ordered pair matters. Therefore the ordered pairs $(x, y)$ and $(y, x)$ are not equal.

> The domain of a relation is the set of the first components of the ordered pairs. The range of a relation is the set of the second components of the ordered pairs. A relation is a function if each element of the domain occurs only once as a first component.

For example: $R = \{(a, b), (a, c), (b, c), (c, d)\}$. Find the domain and range of $R$. Is the relation $R$ a function?

The domain is the set of first components. These are $a, a, b$, and c, so that the domain is $\{a, b, c\}$. The range is the set of second components. These are $b, c, c$, and $d$. Thus the range is $\{b, c, d\}$. $R$ is not a function since the letter $a$ occurred twice as a first component.

**807.** The inverse of a relation is the relation with all the ordered pairs reversed. Thus, the inverse of $R = \{(1, 2), (3, 4), (5, 6)\}$ is $\{(2, 1), (4, 3), (6, 5)\}$.

For example: Find the domain of the inverse of $\{(m, n), (p, q), (r, s)\}$.

The domain of the inverse is simply the range of the original relation. So, the domain of the inverse is $\{n, q, s\}$. Similarly, the range of the inverse is the domain of the original relation.

# Solution Sets

**808.** Sets can be used to indicate solutions to equations or inequalities. These sets are called solution sets. A solution set is just the set of the solutions to an equation. We may also demand that the elements of the solution set meet another condition. Thus, the solution set for the equation $10x - 5 = 0$ is simply $\{\frac{1}{2}\}$, since only $x = \frac{1}{2}$ solves the equation. If we demanded that the solution set consists only of whole numbers, then the solution set would be $\varnothing$ since no whole number solves this equation.

The solution set in the positive integers (whole numbers) for the inequality $x < 4$ is $\{1, 2, 3\}$ since these are the only positive integers less than 4.

> When finding a solution set, first solve the equation or inequality and then use only the solutions which satisfy the condition required.

For example: Find the solution set in the positive integers for the inequality $4x < x + 13$.

First, $4x < x + 13$ means $3x < 13$ or $x < 4\frac{1}{3}$. Since $x$ must be a positive integer, the solution set is the set of positive integers less than $4\frac{1}{3}$, or $\{1, 2, 3, 4\}$. Sometimes we use the following notation:

$$R = \{x : x \geq 10\}$$

This would be read as "the set of all $x$ such that $x$ is greater than or equal to 10."

# Axioms

**809.** On your test, there may be a list of axioms, or rules, about arithmetical operations with numbers. The list will contain examples of the use of the axioms. Problems will then ask you to identify which axiom is used to make a specific statement. An example of these axioms is the distributive law. A problem may ask you: Which axiom is used to justify $3(4 + 1) = 3 \cdot 4 + 3 \cdot 1$? The distributive axiom is used to justify this statement.

Another axiom is the commutative axiom of addition and multiplication. The equations $5 + 3 = 3 + 5$ and $5 \cdot 3 = 3 \cdot 5$ illustrate these rules.

The last two rules are the associative axioms of addition and multiplication. Examples of these operations are the equations $(3 + 5) + 6 = 3 + (5 + 6)$ and $(3 \cdot 5) 6 = 3(5 \cdot 6)$.

# Closed Sets

**810.** A set is called "closed" under an operation if, under the operation, any two members of the set constitute an element of the set. Consider, for example, the set $\{0, 1\}$. This set is closed under the operation of multiplication because $0 \times 0 = 0$, $1 \times 1 = 1$, and $0 \times 1 = 0$. Note that in order for the set to be closed, the elements multiplied by themselves must also be an element of the set $\{0 \times 0 = 0$ and $1 \times 1 = 1\}$.

# Mathematical Symbols

- $\cdot$ multiplication dot; as in $x \cdot y$
- $(\,)$ parentheses; used to group expressions
- $\%$ percent
- $\div$ division symbol
- $:$ ratio symbol
- $=$ equals
- $\neq$ does not equal
- $<$ less than
- $>$ greater than
- $\leq$ less than or equal to
- $\geq$ greater than or equal to
- $\sqrt{\phantom{x}}$ square root symbol

- $\pi$ pi, the ratio between the circumference and diameter of a circle; approximately equal to $\frac{22}{7}$.
- $\angle$ angle
- $\parallel$ is parallel to
- $=$ is perpendicular to
- $\wedge$ and
- $\vee$ or
- $\sim$ not
- $\rightarrow$ implies
- $\in$ belongs to
- $\subset$ is a subset of

# Practice Test 8 and Solutions

## Modern Math

*Correct answers and solutions follow each test.*

### Sets Test

1. Which sets equals {1, 2, 3, 4}?

    (A) {a, b, c, d}
    (B) {4, 5, 6, 7}
    (C) {1, 3, 5, 7, 9}
    (D) {4, 3, 2, 1}
    (E) None of the above.

2. $A = \{1, 2, 3, 4, 5\}$ $B = \{2, 4, 6, 8\}$. $A \cap B$ equals

    (A) {1, 2, 3, 4, 5, 6, 7, 8}
    (B) {2, 4}
    (C) {1, 2, 3, 4, 5, 6, 8, 10}
    (D) {9}
    (E) {1, 2, 6, 8}

3. $C = \{a, b, c, d\}$. $D = \{3, 4, b\}$. $C \cup D$ equals

    (A) {a, b, c, d, 3, 4}
    (B) {b}
    (C) {3, 4}
    (D) {b, d, 4}
    (E) {a, c, 3, 4}

4. $A = \{1, 2, 3\}$. $B = \{2, 3, 4\}$. $C = \{3, 4, 5\}$. $(A \cap B) \cap C$ equals

    (A) {1, 2, 3, 4, 5}
    (B) {1, 3, 5}
    (C) {2, 3, 4}
    (D) {1}
    (E) {3}

5. How many elements are there in the set of even integers from 2 and 10 inclusive?

    (A) 3
    (B) 5
    (C) 7
    (D) 9
    (E) 10

6. How many subsets does {a, b, c} have?

    (A) 6
    (B) 7
    (C) 8
    (D) 9
    (E) 10

*Use the following information to answer Questions 7–10.*

$A = \{1, 3, 2, 5\}$.     $B = \{2, 4, 6\}$.     $C = \{1, 3, 5\}$.

7. $(A \cup B) \cap C$ equals

    (A) {1, 2, 3}
    (B) {2, 4, 5}
    (C) {1, 2, 5}
    (D) {1, 3, 5}
    (E) {3, 4, 5}

8. $(A \cap B) \cup C$ equals

    (A) {1, 2, 3, 5}
    (B) {4}
    (C) {2, 4}
    (D) {1, 3, 5}
    (E) {1, 2, 3, 4, 5}

9. How many subsets does $A \cup (B \cup C)$ have?

    (A) 2
    (B) 4
    (C) 16
    (D) 32
    (E) 64

10. Which set is not a subset of $A \cup C$?

    (A) $\varnothing$
    (B) $A$
    (C) $C$
    (D) {4}
    (E) {1, 2, 5}

# Answers and Solutions

1. **(D)** {4, 3, 2, 1} contains the same elements as {1, 2, 3, 4}. Since the order does not matter, the sets are equal. (801)

2. **(B)** $A \cap B$ means the set of elements in both $A$ and $B$ or {2, 4}. (803)

3. **(A)** $C \cup D$ means the set of elements in at least one of $C$ and $D$, or {$a, b, c, d$, 3, 4}. (802)

4. **(E)** $(A \cap B) \cap C$ is the set of elements in all three sets. Only 3 is a member of all three sets, so $(A \cap B) \cap C = \{3\}$. (803)

5. **(B)** The set of even integers from 2 and 10 inclusive is {2, 4, 6, 8, 10} which has 5 elements. (801)

6. **(C)** {$a, b, c$} has 3 elements and therefore $2^3$ or 8 subsets. (805)

7. **(D)** First $(A \cup B) = \{1, 2, 3, 4, 5, 6\}$
Then {1, 2, 3, 4, 5, 6} $\cap$ {1, 3, 5} = {1, 3, 5}. (804)

8. **(A)** First $(A \cap B) = \{2\}$
Then {2} $\cup$ {1, 3, 5} = {1, 2, 3, 5}. (804)

9. **(E)** $A \cup (B \cup C)$ is the set of elements in at least one of the three sets, or {1, 2, 3, 4, 5, 6}, which has $2^6$ or 64 subsets. (805)

10. **(D)** $A \cup C = \{1, 2, 3, 5\}$. Since 4 is not an element of this set, {4} is not a subset of $A \cup C$. (802, 805)

# Relations Test

1. Which of the following sets are relations?

   I. $\{(1, 2), (a, c)\}$
   II. $\{(3, 8), 8, 3\}$
   III. $\{(1, a), (2, c)\}$

   (A) I only
   (B) II only
   (C) III only
   (D) I and III only
   (E) II and III only

2. Which of the following relations equals the relation $\{(a, b), (1, 2), (x, y)\}$?

   (A) $\{(a, b), (1, x), (2, y)\}$
   (B) $\{(x, y), (a, b), (1, 2)\}$
   (C) $\{(12, xy), (a, b)\}$
   (D) $\{(b, a), (2, 1), (x, y)\}$
   (E) None of the above.

3. What is the range of $\{(1, 2), (3, 4), (5, 6)\}$?

   (A) $\{1, 2, 3, 4, 5, 6\}$
   (B) $\{(1, 2)\}$
   (C) $\{(1, 2), (3, 4), (5, 6)\}$
   (D) $\{1, 3, 5\}$
   (E) None of the above.

4. What is the domain of $\{(1, 2), (2, 1), (1, 5)\}$?

   (A) $\{1, 2\}$
   (B) $\{(1, 2)\}$
   (C) $\{1, 2, 5\}$
   (D) $\{8\}$
   (E) $\{3\}$

5. Which relation is a function?

   (A) $\{(1, 1), (2, 2), (3, 3)\}$
   (B) $\{(1, 1), (1, 2), (1, 3)\}$
   (C) $\{(a, b), (b, a), (b, b)\}$
   (D) $\{(1, 3), (1, 5), (1, 7)\}$
   (E) $\{(1, a), (2, b), (2, 1)\}$

6. What is the inverse of $\{(1, 2), (3, 6), (4, 2)\}$?

   (A) $\{1, 2, 3, 4, 5, 6\}$
   (B) $\{(1, 3), (1, 4), (1, 6)\}$
   (C) $\{(2, 1), (6, 3), (2, 4)\}$
   (D) $\{(3, 2), (6, 4), (4, 1)\}$
   (E) None of the above.

7. Which relation equals its inverse?

   (A) $\{(1, 2)\}$
   (B) $\{(1, 2), (3, 3)\}$
   (C) $\{(1, 2), (3, 3), (2, 1)\}$
   (D) $\{(4, 4), (2, 3), (3, 4)\}$
   (E) $\{(1, 2), (2, 3), (3, 1)\}$

8. What is the domain of the inverse of $\{(a, 1), (b, 3), (c, 5)\}$?

   (A) $\{a, b, c\}$
   (B) $\{1, 3, 5\}$
   (C) $\{1, a, 2, b, 3, c\}$
   (D) $\{a, 5\}$
   (E) $\{(a, 5)\}$

9. The inverse of which of the following is a function?

   (A) $\{(1, 1), (1, 2), (1, 3)\}$
   (B) $\{(a, 0), (b, 0), (c, 0)\}$
   (C) $\{(a, j), (r, j), (a, r)\}$
   (D) $\{(1, 2), (2, 3), (3, 2)\}$
   (E) $\{(u, v), (w, v), (y, x)\}$

10. What is the range of the inverse of $\{(P, Q), (R, S), (T, V)\}$?

    (A) $\{1, 2, 3\}$
    (B) $\{P, Q, R\}$
    (C) $\{Q, S, V\}$
    (D) $\{P, R, T\}$
    (E) $\{P, Q, R, S, T, V\}$

# Answers and Solutions

1. **(D)** A set is a relation if all its elements are ordered pairs; I and III meet this condition; II does not. (806)

2. **(B)** Two relations are equal if their elements are equal. Though it doesn't matter in what order the ordered pairs are listed, if the elements of the ordered pairs are switched the relation is changed. (806)

3. **(E)** The range of a relation is the set of second elements of the ordered pairs. The range of {(1, 2), (3, 4), (5, 6)} is {2, 4, 6}. (806)

4. **(A)** The domain is the set of first elements of the ordered pairs. The domain of {(1, 2), (2, 1), (1, 5)} is {1, 2}. (806)

5. **(A)** To be a function, a relation must not repeat any of the first elements of its ordered pairs. The first elements of {(1, 1), (2, 2), (3, 3)} are all distinct. (806)

6. **(C)** To find the inverse simply reverse all the ordered pairs. (807)

7. **(C)** Reversing (1, 2) we get (2, 1); reversing (3, 3) we get (3, 3); reversing (2, 1) we get (1, 2). Though they are in a different order, the ordered pairs of the inverse of (3) are the same as the ordered pairs of (3). (807)

8. **(B)** The domain of the inverse is the range of the relation, or {1, 3, 5}. (806, 807)

9. **(A)** If the inverse of the relation is to be a function, the second elements must be all distinct. The second elements of the ordered pairs of (1) are 1, 2, and 3, all distinct. (806, 807)

10. **(D)** The range of the inverse is the domain of the function, or {P, R, T}. (806, 807)

# Solution Sets Test

*Find the solution sets in Questions 1–3.*

**1.** $2x - 4 = 0$

(A) {2}
(B) {4}
(C) {−4}
(D) {0}
(E) {2, −4}

**2.** $x + 9 = 3 - x$

(A) {−3}
(B) {9}
(C) {3}
(D) {−3, 9}
(E) ∅

**3.** $(x + 2)(x - 1) = 0$

(A) {−1}
(B) {−2, −1}
(C) {1}
(D) {−2, 1}
(E) {2, 1}

*Find the solution sets in the positive integers for Questions 4–7.*

**4.** $x + 7 = 9$

(A) {7}
(B) {9}
(C) {16}
(D) {2}
(E) {9, 7}

**5.** $x - 3 = -4$

(A) {−3}
(B) {−4}
(C) {1}
(D) {−1}
(E) ∅

**6.** $x > 2x - 4$

(A) {1}
(B) {2, 3}
(C) {1, 2, 3}
(D) {1, 2, 3, 4}
(E) ∅

**7.** $(x + 1)(x - 4) = 0$

(A) {4}
(B) {1, 4}
(C) {−1, 1, 4}
(D) {0}
(E) {−4}

*Find the solution set in the negative integers for Questions 8–10.*

**8.** $(x + 3)(x + 6) = 0$

(A) {3, 6}
(B) {−3, −6}
(C) {−3}
(D) {−6}
(E) ∅

**9.** $(2x + 7)(x - 3) = 0$

(A) {2, 7, −3}
(B) {−3}
(C) {−3$\frac{1}{2}$}
(D) {2}
(E) ∅

**10.** $10 + 2x > 0$

(A) {−1, −2}
(B) {−10, −8, −6}
(C) {−1, −2, −3, −4, −5}
(D) {−1, −2, −3, −4}
(E) {1, 2, 3, 4}

# Answers and Solutions

1. **(A)** $2x - 4 = 0$. $x = 2$, so the solution set is $\{2\}$.
(808)

2. **(A)** $x + 9 = 3 - x$. $2x = -6$ or $x = -3$. The solution set is $\{-3\}$.
(808)

3. **(D)** $(x + 2)(x - 1) = 0$, so $x = -2$ or 1. The solution set is $\{-2, 1\}$.
(808)

4. **(D)** $x + 7 = 9$ or $x = 2$ which is a positive integer. The solution set is $\{2\}$.
(808)

5. **(E)** $x - 3 = -4$, or $x = -1$, which is not a positive integer. The solution set is $\varnothing$.
(808)

6. **(C)** $x > 2x - 4$, or $x < 4$. The positive integers less than 4 are 1, 2, and 3.
(808)

7. **(A)** $(x + 1)(x - 4) = 0$. $x = -1$ or 4. 4 is a positive integer but $-1$ is not, so the solution set is $\{4\}$.
(808)

8. **(B)** $(x + 3)(x + 6) = 0$. $x = -3$ or $-6$, both of which are negative integers, so the solution set is $\{-3, -6\}$.
(808)

9. **(E)** $(2x + 7)(x - 3) = 0$. $x = -3\frac{1}{2}$ or 3, neither of which is a negative integer. The solution set is $\varnothing$.
(808)

10. **(D)** $10 + 2x > 0$. $2x > -10$ or $x > -5$. The negative integers greater than $-5$ are $-1$, $-2$, $-3$, and $-4$.
(808)

# Axioms Test

*Use the following axioms to answer Questions 1–5.*

I. Commutative axiom for addition: $a + b = b + a$

II. Associative axiom for addition: $a + (b + c) = (a + b) + c$

III. Commutative axiom for multiplication: $ab = ba$

IV. Associative axiom for multiplication: $(ab)c = a(bc)$

V. Distributive axiom: $a(b + c) = ab + ac$

*In Questions 1–4, which axiom can be used to justify the given statements?*

1. $3 \cdot 5 = 5 \cdot 3$

   (A) I
   (B) II
   (C) III
   (D) IV
   (E) V

2. $(3 + 7) + 4 = 3 + (7 + 4)$

   (A) I
   (B) II
   (C) III
   (D) IV
   (E) V

3. $(2 \cdot 5) \cdot 3 = (5 \cdot 2) \cdot 3$

   (A) I
   (B) II
   (C) III
   (D) IV
   (E) V

4. $3(6 + 2) = 18 + 6$

   (A) I
   (B) II
   (C) III
   (D) IV
   (E) V

5. Which two axioms can be used to justify the following:
   $5(3 + 4) = 20 + 15$?

   (A) I and II
   (B) I and III
   (C) III and V
   (D) IV and V
   (E) V and I

# Answers and Solutions

1. **(C)** To go from $3 \cdot 5$ to $5 \cdot 3$ we switch the order of multiplication. The axiom that deals with order of multiplication is the commutative axiom for multiplication. (809)

2. **(B)** Switching parentheses in addition involves the associative axiom for addition, II. (809)

3. **(C)** To go from $(2 \cdot 5) \cdot 3$ to $(5 \cdot 2) \cdot 3$ we switch the order of multiplying inside the parentheses. This is justified by III. (809)

4. **(E)** To go from $3(6 + 2)$ to $3 \cdot 6 + 3 \cdot 2$ or $18 + 16$, we use the distributive axiom. (809)

5. **(E)** To go from $5(3 + 4)$ to $5 \cdot 3 + 5 \cdot 4$ or $15 + 20$ we use the distributive axiom. To go from $15 + 20$ to $20 + 15$ we use the commutative axiom of addition. (809)

# PART 6

# THE PSAT
# WRITING SKILLS TEST

# Types of Questions on the PSAT Writing Test

Following are some directions and samples of some of the question types on the PSAT Writing Test.

## Identifying Errors

**Directions:** The following sentences test your knowledge of grammar, usage, diction (choice of words), and idiom.

Some sentences are correct.
No sentence contains more than one error.

You will find that the error, if there is one, is underlined and lettered. Elements of the sentence that are not underlined will not be changed. In choosing answers, follow the requirements of standard written English.

If there is an error, select the <u>one underlined part</u> that must be changed to make the sentence correct and fill in the corresponding oval on your answer sheet.

If there is no error, fill in answer oval E.

**EXAMPLE:**

<u>The other</u> delegates and <u>him</u> <u>immediately</u>
   A                 B       C

accepted the resolution <u>drafted by</u> the
                            D

neutral states. <u>No error</u>
               E

**SAMPLE ANSWER**

Ⓐ ● Ⓒ Ⓓ Ⓔ

## Sample Questions with Answers

1. <u>Even before</u> he became the youngest player to win
   A
the Wimbledon men's <u>singles</u> championship, Boris
             B
Becker <u>had sensed</u> that his life would <u>no longer</u> be
      C                D
the same. <u>No error.</u>
       E

2. If any signer of the Constitution <u>was</u> to return to life
                          A
<u>for a day,</u> his opinion <u>of</u> our amendments <u>would be</u>
   B             C             D
interesting. <u>No error.</u>
        E

3. The dean <u>of the college</u>, together <u>with</u> some other
              A                 B
   faculty members, <u>are</u> planning a conference for
                     C
   the purpose of <u>laying</u> down certain regulations.
                  D
   <u>No error.</u>
      E

4. If one <u>lives</u> in Florida <u>one day</u> and in Iceland the
          A              B
   <u>next</u>, he is <u>certain</u> to feel the change in temperature.
   C         D
   <u>No error.</u>
      E

5. <u>Now</u> that the stress of examinations and interviews
   A
   <u>are</u> over, we can <u>all</u> <u>relax</u> for a while. <u>No error.</u>
   B            C  D           E

6. The industrial <u>trend</u> <u>is</u> in the direction of <u>more</u>
             A  B               C
   machines and <u>less</u> people. <u>No error.</u>
             D      E

7. The American standard of living <u>is</u> still <u>higher</u>
                         A      B
   <u>than most</u> of the <u>other countries</u> of the world.
   C            D
   <u>No error.</u>
      E

8. <u>At last</u>, <u>late</u> in the afternoon, a long line of flags and
   A    B
   colored umbrellas <u>were</u> seen moving <u>toward</u> the
                  C            D
   gate of the palace. <u>No error.</u>
                E

9. <u>Due to</u> the failure of the air-cooling system, many in
   A
   the audience <u>had left</u> the meeting <u>before</u> the principal
            B            C
   speaker <u>arrived</u>. <u>No error.</u>
         D    E

10. Psychologists and psychiatrists <u>will tell</u> us that it is
                       A
   of utmost importance that a <u>disturbed</u> child <u>receive</u>
                     B       C
   professional attention <u>as soon as</u> possible.
                 D
   <u>No error.</u>
      E

11. <u>After we were waiting</u> in line <u>for three hours</u>,
        A                      B
   <u>much to our disgust, the tickets had been</u> sold out
                      C
   <u>when</u> we reached the window. <u>No error.</u>
   D                        E

12. That angry outburst of <u>Father's</u> last night was so
                      A
   annoying that it resulted in our <u>guests</u> <u>packing up</u>
                          B    C
   and leaving <u>this</u> morning. <u>No error.</u>
            D          E

13. <u>Sharp</u> advances last week in the wholesale price of
   A
   beef <u>is</u> a strong indication of higher meat <u>costs</u> to
       B                        C
   come, but so far retail prices continue <u>favorable</u>.
                              D
   <u>No error.</u>
      E

14. An acquaintance with the memoirs of Elizabeth
   Barrett Browning and Robert Browning <u>enable</u> us
                                   A
   to appreciate the <u>depth of influence</u> that two people
                     B
   of talent can have <u>on</u> <u>each other</u>. <u>No error.</u>
                C      D        E

15. The supervisor <u>was advised</u> to give the assignment
                A
   to <u>whomever</u> <u>he believed</u> had a strong sense of
      B          C
   responsibility, and the courage <u>of</u> his conviction.
                            D
   <u>No error.</u>
      E

16. If he <u>would have</u> <u>lain</u> quietly as instructed by the
         A       B
   doctor, he <u>might not</u> <u>have had</u> a second heart attack.
             C       D
   <u>No error.</u>
      E

17. The founder and, <u>for many years</u>, the <u>guiding spirit</u>
                  A              B
   of the *Kenyon Review* is John Crowe Ransom, <u>who</u>
                                 C
   you must know <u>as</u> an outstanding American critic.
             D
   <u>No error.</u>
      E

18. <u>Though</u> you may not <u>agree with</u> the philosophy of
     A             B

   Malcolm X, you must admit that he <u>had</u> tremendous
                                    C

   influence <u>over</u> a great many followers. <u>No error.</u>
           D                             E

19. There is no objection to <u>him</u> joining the party
                        A

   <u>provided</u> he is willing to <u>fit in with</u> the plans of the
       B                      C

   group and is <u>ready and</u> able to do his share of the
                  D

   work. <u>No error.</u>
           E

20. <u>Ceremonies</u> <u>were opened</u> by a drum and bugle
        A           B

   corps of Chinese children parading <u>up</u> Mott Street
                                  C

   <u>in colorful uniforms.</u> <u>No error.</u>
           D        E

21. The reason <u>most</u> American <u>don't</u> pay much atten-
            A         B

   tion to <u>rising</u> African nationalism is <u>because</u> they
          C                   D

   really do not know modern Africa. <u>No error.</u>
                            E

22. There <u>remains</u> many reasons for the <u>animosity</u> that
          A                     B

   <u>exists</u> <u>between</u> the Arab countries and Israel.
    C     D

   <u>No error.</u>
     E

23. The Federal Aviation Administration <u>ordered</u> an
                                    A

   emergency inspection <u>of several</u> Pan American
                        B

   planes <u>on account of</u> a Pan American Boeing 707
             C

   <u>had crashed</u> on Bali, in Indonesia. <u>No error.</u>
       D                        E

24. A gang <u>of armed thieves</u>, directed by a young
              A

   woman, <u>has raided</u> the mansion of a <u>gold-mining</u>
           B                        C

   millionaire <u>near Dublin</u> late last night. <u>No error.</u>
             D                     E

25. I <u>had</u> a male <u>chauvinist pig dream</u> that the women
      A             B

   of the world <u>rose up</u> and denounced the <u>women's</u>
               C                   D

   liberation movement. <u>No error.</u>
                   E

# Improving Sentences

**Directions:** The following sentences test correctness and effectiveness of expression. In choosing answers, follow the requirements of standard written English; that is, pay attention to grammar, choice of words, sentence construction, and punctuation.

In each of the following sentences, part of the sentence or the entire sentence is underlined. Beneath each sentence you will find five ways of phrasing the underlined part. Choice A repeats the original; the other four are different.

Choose the answer that best expresses the meaning of the original sentence. If you think the original is better than any of the alternatives, choose it; otherwise choose one of the others. Your choice should produce the most effective sentence—clear and precise, without awkwardness or ambiguity.

EXAMPLE:

Laura Ingalls Wilder published her first book and she was sixty-five years old then.

SAMPLE ANSWER

(A) and she was sixty-five years old then
(B) when she was sixty-five
(C) being age sixty-five years old
(D) upon the reaching of sixty-five years
(E) at the time when she was sixty-five

## Sample Questions with Answers

26. Such of his novels as was humorous were successful.

    (A) Such of his novels as was humorous were successful.
    (B) Such of his novels as were humorous were successful.
    (C) His novels such as were humorous were successful.
    (D) His novels were successful and humorous.
    (E) Novels such as his humorous ones were successful.

27. Being that the plane was grounded, we stayed over until the next morning so that we could get the first flight out.

    (A) Being that the plane was grounded, we stayed over
    (B) In view of the fact that the plane was grounded, we stayed over
    (C) Since the plane was grounded, we stayed over
    (D) Because the plane was grounded, we stood over
    (E) On account of the plane being grounded, we stayed over

28. He never has and he never will keep his word.

    (A) He never has and he never will
    (B) He has never yet and never will
    (C) He has not ever and he will not
    (D) He never has or will
    (E) He never has kept and he never will

29. The teacher felt badly because she had scolded the bright child who was restless for want of something to do.

    (A) felt badly because she had scolded the bright child
    (B) felt badly why she had scolded the bright child
    (C) felt bad because she had scolded the bright child
    (D) felt bad by scolding the bright child
    (E) had felt badly because she had scolded the bright child

30. This book <u>does not describe the struggle of the blacks to win their voting rights that I bought</u>.

 (A) does not describe the struggle of the blacks to win their voting rights that I bought
 (B) does not describe the black struggle to win their voting rights that I bought
 (C) does not, although I bought it, describe the struggle of the blacks to win their voting rights
 (D) which I bought does not describe the struggle to win for blacks their voting rights
 (E) that I bought does not describe the struggle of the blacks to win their voting rights

31. <u>Barbara cannot help but think</u> that she will win a college scholarship.

 (A) Barbara cannot help but think
 (B) Barbara cannot help but to think
 (C) Barbara cannot help not to think
 (D) Barbara can help but think
 (E) Barbara cannot but help thinking

32. In spite of <u>Tom wanting to study</u>, his sister made him wash the dishes.

 (A) Tom wanting to study
 (B) the fact that Tom wanted to study
 (C) Tom's need to study
 (D) Tom's wanting to study
 (E) Tom studying

33. The old sea captain <u>told my wife and me</u> many interesting yarns about his many voyages.

 (A) my wife and me
 (B) me and my wife
 (C) my wife and I
 (D) I and my wife
 (E) my wife along with me

34. A great many students from several universities <u>are planning to, if the weather is favorable, attend next Saturday's mass rally in Washington</u>.

 (A) are planning to, if the weather is favorable, attend next Saturday's mass rally in Washington
 (B) are planning, if the weather is favorable, to attend next Saturday's mass rally in Washington
 (C) are planning to attend, if the weather is favorable, next Saturday's mass rally in Washington
 (D) are planning to attend next Saturday's mass rally in Washington, if the weather is favorable
 (E) are, if the weather is favorable, planning to attend next Saturday's mass rally in Washington

35. Jane's body movements are <u>like those of a dancer</u>.

 (A) like those of a dancer
 (B) the same as a dancer
 (C) like a dancer
 (D) a dancer's
 (E) like those of a dancer's

# Explanatory Answers

1. Choice E is correct. All underlined parts are correct.

2. Choice A is correct. "If any signer of the Constitution *were* to return to life..." The verb in the "if clause" of a present contrary-to-fact conditional statement must have a past subjunctive form (*were*).

3. Choice C is correct. "The dean of the college...*is* planning..." The subject of the sentence (*dean*) is singular. Therefore, the verb must be singular (*is planning*).

4. Choice E is correct. All underlined parts are correct.

5. Choice B is correct. "Now that the stress...*is* over..." The subject of the subordinate clause is singular (*stress*). Accordingly, the verb of the clause must be singular (*is*—not *are*). Incidentally, *examinations* and *interviews* are not subjects—they are objects of the preposition *of*.

6. Choice D is correct. "...of more machines and *fewer* people." We use *fewer* for persons and things that may be counted. We use *less* for bulk or mass.

7. Choice C or D is correct. "...than *that of most* of the other countries of the world." We must have parallelism so that the word *standard* in the main clause of the sentence acts as an antecedent for the pronoun *that* in the subordinate clause. As the original sentence reads, the American standard of living is still higher than the countries themselves. You could also have said, "The American standard of living is still higher than most of the other countries' of the world," making Choice D also correct.

8. Choice C is correct. "...a long line of flags...*was* seen..." The subject of the sentence is singular (*line*). Therefore, the verb must be singular (*was seen*).

9. Choice A is correct. "*Because of* the failure..." Never start a sentence with *Due to*.

10. Choice E is correct. All underlined parts are correct.

11. Choice C is correct. "After we were waiting in line for three hours, the tickets had, *much to our disgust*, been sold out when we reached the window." Avoid squinting constructions—that is, modifiers that are so placed that the reader cannot tell whether they are modifying the words immediately preceding the construction or the words immediately following the construction. As the sentence initially reads, we don't know whether *much to our disgust* modifies *after we were waiting in line for three hours* or *the tickets had been sold out when we reached the window*.

12. Choice B is correct. "...resulted in our *guests'* packing up..." A noun or pronoun immediately preceding a gerund is in the possessive case. Note that the noun *guests* followed by an apostrophe is possessive.

13. Choice B is correct. "Sharp advances...*are*..." Since the subject of the sentence is plural (*advances*), the verb must be plural (*are*).

14. Choice A is correct. "An acquaintance with the memoirs...*enables* us..." Since the subject of the sentence is singular (*acquaintance*), the verb must be singular (*enables*).

15. Choice B is correct. "...to *whoever*...had a strong sense..." The subject of the subordinate clause is *whoever*, and it takes a nominative form (*whoever*—not *whomever*) since it is a subject. Incidentally, the expression *he believed* is parenthetical, so it has no grammatical relationship with the rest of the sentence.

16. Choice A is correct. "If he *had lain*..." The verb in the "if clause" of a past contrary-to-fact conditional statement must take the *had lain* form—not the *would have lain* form.

17. Choice C is correct. "...John Crowe Ransom, *whom* you must know as an outstanding American critic." The direct object of the subordinate clause—or of any clause or sentence—must be in the objective case and, accordingly, must take the objective form (*whom*—not *who*).

18. Choice E is correct. All underlined parts are correct.

19. Choice A is correct. "There is no objection to *his* joining..." We have here a pronoun that is acting as the subject of the gerund *joining*. As a subject of the gerund, the pronoun must be in the possessive case (*his*).

20. Choice D is correct. "...of Chinese children parading *in colorful uniforms* up Mott Street." In the original sentence, *in colorful uniforms* was a misplaced modifier.

21. Choice D is correct. "The reason...is *that...*" We must say *the reason is that*—not *the reason is because.*

22. Choice A is correct. "There *remain* many reasons..." The word "There" in this sentence is an expletive or introductory adverb. The subject of the sentence ("reasons") must agree with the verb ("remain") in number.

23. Choice C is correct. "...*because* a Pan American Boeing 707 had crashed..." The word group *on account of* has the function of a preposition. We need a subordinate conjunction (*because*) here in order to introduce the clause.

24. Choice B is correct. "...*raided* the mansion..." The past tense (*raided*)—not the present perfect tense (*has raided*)—is necessary because the sentence has a specific past time reference (*last night*).

25. Choice E is correct. All underlined parts are correct.

26. Choice B is correct. Choice A is incorrect because the plural verb ("were") is necessary. The reason for the plural verb is that the subject "as" acts as a relative pronoun whose antecedent is the plural noun "novels." Choice B is correct. Choice C is awkward. Choice D changes the meaning of the original sentence—so does Choice E.

27. Choice C is correct. Choice A is incorrect— never start a sentence with "being that." Choice B is too wordy. Choice D is incorrect because we "stayed"—not "stood." Choice E is incorrect because "on account of" may never be used as a subordinate conjunction.

28. Choice E is correct. Avoid improper ellipsis. Choices A, B, C, and D are incorrect for this reason. The word "kept" must be included since the second part of the sentence uses another form of the verb ("keep").

29. Choice C is correct. Choice A is incorrect because the copulative verb "felt" takes a predicate adjective ("bad")—not an adverb ("badly"). Choice B is incorrect for the same reason. Moreover, we don't say "felt bad why." Choice D is incorrect because the verbal phrase "by scolding" is awkward in this context. Choice E is incorrect because of the use of "badly" and because the past perfect form of the verb ("had felt") is wrong in this time sequence.

30. Choice E is correct. Choices A, B, and C are incorrect because the part of the sentence that deals with the buying of the book is in the wrong position. Choice D is incorrect because the meaning of the original sentence has been changed. According to this choice, others besides blacks have been struggling.

31. Choice A is correct. The other choices are unidiomatic.

32. Choice D is correct. Choice A is incorrect because the possessive form of the noun ("Tom's") must be used to modify the gerund ("wanting"). Choice B is too wordy. Choice C changes the meaning of the original sentence. Choice E is incorrect for the same reason that Choice A is incorrect. Also, Choice E changes the meaning of the original sentence.

33. Choice A is correct. Choice B is incorrect because "wife" should precede "me." Choice C is incorrect because the object form "me" (not the nominative form "I") should be used as the indirect object. Choice D is incorrect for the reasons given above for Choices B and C. Choice E is too roundabout.

34. Choice D is correct. Choices A, B, C, and E are incorrect because of the misplacement of the subordinate clause ("if the weather is favorable").

35. Choice A is correct. Choices B and C are incorrect because of improper ellipsis. The words "those of" are necessary in these choices. Choice D is incorrect because the "body movements" are not "a dancer's." The possessive use of "dancer's" is incorrect in Choice E.

# Improving Paragraphs
## Revision-in Context
## Passage with Questions

One part of the Writing Test is the Improving Paragraphs section. This is by far the most difficult part of the Writing Test, and thus the reason I am including extensive instructional and practice material. Here are typical directions to that item-type on the test:

*Directions:* The following passage is an early draft of an essay. Some parts of the passage need to be rewritten. Read the passage and select the best answers for the questions that follow. Some questions are about particular sentences or parts of sentences and ask you to improve sentence structure and word choice. Other questions refer to parts of the essay or the entire essay and ask you to consider organization and development. In making your decisions, follow the conventions of standard written English.

Now in the passage you are given, the weaknesses in the passage may apply to the classifications listed below:

1. **Sentence Order.** The selection of the best order for the sentences in the passage.

2. **Diction.** The use of an appropriate word or words to express the meaning intended in a sentence, or to be consistent with the style of the passage.

3. **Sentence Relationship.** The use of a transitional word or words to establish the relationship between sentences.

4. **Irrelevancy.** A statement or part of a statement which is not related to the rest of the passage.

5. **Economy.** The combining of ideas by fusing two sentences into one. Also, the elimination of unnecessary words.

6. **Clarity.** The reconstruction of a sentence or the addition of an idea to make the sentence or the passage perfectly clear.

7. **Paragraphing.** The division of the passage into the logical number of paragraphs.

## Sentence Order

In order to bake a cake, a cook must take a certain number of steps in a certain order. To rearrange the order in which these steps are taken would be disastrous. No one would consider baking the ingredients before mixing them or buttering the pan.

Like baking a cake, writing a paragraph demands a certain kind of logic. The sentences must be arranged in an order which makes sense. When one writes a paragraph or a short selection, he must do so in an orderly manner. The sentences must appeal in the right order. They must fit together properly so that the whole passage is easy to understand and agreeable to read.

In the passages, your job will be to recognize when the order of a sentence in a passage is illogical. If your attention is directed to a particular sentence, determine whether that sentence logically follows the sentence that precedes it and logically leads into the sentence that follows it.

To answer a *sentence order* question correctly, you should be aware of certain clues:

1. The opening sentence should introduce the main idea of the passage or grab the reader's attention.

2. The closing sentence should sum up the information presented in the passage, draw a conclusion, or present the final step in a logically developed process.

3. Two sentences that are closely connected in meaning or closely related in some other way should be placed one after the other.

The following passage will illustrate the way in which poor sentence order can be recognized and corrected.

---

[1]John Joseph Haley, who played the Tin Man in the film version of *The Wizard of Oz*, began charming audiences as a 6-year-old singer in a church festival in Boston, where he was born in 1899. [2]He began in professional show business as a song-plugger in Philadelphia, then turned to song—comedy routines in vaudeville. [3]After graduating from high school, the youth bowed to his parents' wishes and began learning to be an electrician. [4]After saving up some of his earnings as an apprentice electrician, he ran away from home. [5]Moving to New York in the '20's, he finally began getting Broadway roles. [6]In the years that followed, Mr. Haley's bright blue eyes, his wavy hair, and his inexhaustible good humor made him sought after to fill some of the many light comic roles provided by the bountiful crops of musical comedies that Broadway produced.

## QUESTION

Sentence 2 should be

(A) left where it is
(B) moved to precede sentence 1
(C) moved to follow sentence 3
(D) moved to follow sentence 4
(E) omitted from the passage

## ANSWER

This passage, we should note as we read it, is organized on the principle of a chronology—that is, steps in time. The facts are presented in the order in which they occurred. The question directs our attention to sentence 2. Choice A suggests that sentence 2 is in the correct order as it stands. To check, reread sentence 1, then sentence 2, then sentence 3. Is this the logical order in which these sentences should be presented? No. Sentence 1 introduces the actor, his birth date, and his earliest experience as a performer. Sentence 2 jumps ahead to Mr. Haley's professional acting career in Philadelphia, while sentence 3 returns to his earlier days as a high school student. Such jumping around is not appropriate in a passage using a chronological time sequence. Accordingly, Choice A is incorrect.

Choice B suggests we move sentence 2 to precede sentence 1. We need not reread the sentences to check this. Sentence 1 begins the passage with the actor's earliest days and no sentence dealing with his later days should precede it. Choice B is incorrect and so we consider Choice C. Choice C would move sentence 2 to follow sentence 3. To check, we read sentence 3, then sentence 2, then sentence 4. Sentences 3 and 4 are closely related sentences, discussing Mr. Haley's early training after high school and his decision to leave Boston. These sentences should not be separated by sentence 2, which discusses a later event in Philadelphia. Having read sentence 4, we have already begun to check Choice D. The young man ran away from home. We are now ready for a sentence that shifts location. Reading sentence 4, then sentence 2, then sentence 5, we finally find the logical place for sentence 2. In chronological order, Mr. Haley ran away from home, began working as a performer in Philadelphia, then moved to New York and Broadway. Choice D is, therefore, the correct choice. Choice E, suggesting sentence 2 be omitted, is not correct as it would eliminate an important phase in Mr. Haley's life and career.

# Diction

Diction refers to the choice of words—their exact meanings, their overtones, their force.

A writer should, first and foremost, know the precise meanings of the words he uses. He should make every effort to use the best possible word in order to convey exactly what he wants to express. There are sometimes many words available from which a writer may choose that one word which best conveys the meaning he wishes to express.

In selecting the right word, a writer should take into account the intended tone of his writing. There are basically three tones a writer may use: a *formal* tone, a *semi-formal* tone, and an *informal* tone. A writer uses a formal tone when, for example, he is writing about a technical matter. Textbooks, legal documents, and instruction manuals are ordinarily written in a formal tone. The vocabulary tends to be formal or technical in nature. A semi-formal tone is used when a writer wants to express an idea in a way that will interest the average reader. The vocabulary will be less technical; certain informal or conversational expressions may be used occasionally. A writer uses an informal tone when his style is conversational throughout—when he writes as if he is talking to the reader. Colloquial expressions—and sometimes slang—are appropriate in an informally written passage.

In a passage, you should be aware of the tone in which the passage is written. Diction problems commonly arise when the writer is inconsistent, using words that are inappropriate to the overall tone of the passage.

Another type of diction problem occurs when a writer selects a word that does not accurately convey his intended meaning. You can judge the intended meaning from the context of a sentence or from the entire passage.

A third type of diction error may be the unintended use of an ungrammatical word or expression. Such nonstandard forms as "The boy *couldn't hardly* see in the fog," or "The teacher should *of knowed* I would be late to class" are hardly ever appropriate in conversation or writing.

Below you will find a passage, followed by a question which directs your attention to a diction problem in a sentence.

---

[1]In theory, bail is designed to ensure the presence of the defendant in court. [2]But a seemingly low bail—say $1000—for a person with fifty cents in his pocket is the same thing as preventive detention. [3]And although judges will deny in public that they do so, many admit in private that the real reason they set high bail is a deep feeling that the suspect is dangerous and guilty of a crime. [4]The alternative to bail is the clink. [5]It ensures that a defendant cannot flee the jurisdiction, tamper with the evidence, or threaten witnesses.

## QUESTION

In sentence 4, the clink should be

(A) left as it is
(B) the slammer
(C) entombment
(D) captivity
(E) incarceration

To answer a diction question like the one above, you are advised to use the substitution method. After having judged the general tone of the passage, substitute the possibly wrong word or expression given in the stem (beginning) of the question with the word or expression given in the choices.

## ANSWER

In the question given, our attention is directed to the expression <u>the clink</u>. Is <u>the clink</u> appropriate here? No. We are not dealing with a conversational passage so a slang expression is not appropriate. Therefore, Choice A is incorrect. Accordingly, Choice B (<u>the slammer</u>) is also incorrect since the expression is also slang.

 Consider Choice C. The word <u>entombment</u> does not provide the meaning needed to replace <u>the clink</u>. Therefore Choice C is incorrect.

 Consider Choice D. The word <u>captivity</u> does not provide the meaning needed to replace <u>the clink</u>. Therefore, Choice D is incorrect.

 Consider Choice E. The word <u>incarceration</u> is the appropriate replacement for <u>the clink</u>. Therefore, Choice E is correct.

# Sentence Relationship

When a writer makes use of a number of different thoughts to illustrate his point in writing, he must be sure to make the relationship between these ideas clear. A good writer should move from one idea to the next, or from one sentence to the next, logically and smoothly. He uses *transitional elements* to achieve *coherence* in his writing.

 **Transitional elements** make the relationship between ideas clear while at the same time they bring ideas together. Special *transitional words* are used to indicate the different types of relationships possible between ideas and sentences. Some examples are listed below.

### FOR COMPARING

similarly, likewise, in the same way, in a like manner

### FOR CONTRASTING

nevertheless, yet, but, still, however, on the other hand, after all, in spite of, although, on the contrary

### FOR GIVING AN EXAMPLE

that is, for example, as a matter of fact, for instance, in fact, specifically, in other words

### FOR GIVING A RESULT

consequently, therefore, accordingly, thus, as a result, hence

### FOR SHOWING A TIME RELATIONSHIP

afterward, since while, soon, finally, immediately, shortly, meanwhile, until

 *Transitional elements* are quite important in writing. They help us to understand what the writer is leading to. Connecting words and phrases act as signposts on a road. They direct us to our destination. To the traveler, his purpose is to get to a place. To the reader, his purpose is to understand what the writer is trying to convey. If traditional elements are misplaced or poorly placed, they cause the same problem that a misplaced or poorly placed road sign would cause—pointing us in the wrong direction. We, as a consequence, lose our sense of what the writer is trying to say, of where he is trying to lead us.

 In passages, you will have to be able to identify a misplaced or a poorly chosen transitional element. Watch out for such an element, be it a word or phrase which tends to confuse the reader by creating illogical relationships between sentences or within parts of a sentence. The transitional element should be clear and specific to do its job well.

Below you will find an example of a passage which contains a poor sentence relationship. The question following the passage will ask you to correct the error.

---

[1]Fine liquor was flowing in a foreign Embassy—down the drain. [2]Recently, the embassy dumped $22,000 worth of brand-name liquor found in its basement. [3]Under the embassy's last ambassador, the embassy entertained lavishly. [4]But the new government is strict and forbids drinking or selling liquor, so it directed the embassy to get rid of its stock. [5]Local dealers refused to buy the liquor back because the sales had been made more than three months before. [6]Next the embassy simply had eight to ten of its people methodically attack a huge stack of liquor cases. [7]They uncapped each bottle and poured its contents into a sewer.

## QUESTION

Sentence 6 should begin

(A) the way it begins now
(B) with Afterward
(C) with Presently
(D) with Finally
(E) with Consequently

## ANSWER

Consider Choice A. Next introduces sentence 6. Next is a transitional element which merely indicates a shift in time. First one thing happens. Next something else happens. The word Next is not a logical connective after sentence 5. Therefore, Choice A is wrong.

An appropriate transitional element would be one which indicated that sentence 6 was the result of or the consequence of sentence 5. Test the other choices by substituting a better connective for Next. Of the four choices remaining, only Choice E suggests an opening word which conveys not only a shift in time, but also a cause and effect relationship. Choice E, beginning sentence 6 with Consequently, is therefore the correct choice.

# Irrelevancy

Every time a person writes, he has a reason for writing. This reason may be to inform, entertain, or persuade the reader. The point that the author wants to make should be made clearly. To do this, he must stick to his point: Only sentences that are necessary to express an idea exactly belong in the passage. All other sentences are irrelevant; they should be omitted.

In the Improving Paragraphs section of the test, a question may direct your attention to a particular sentence in the passage. When you reread that sentence, test it for relevancy. Ask yourself, "Does this sentence belong in this passage? Does it add to the information offered in the passage or does it distract my attention from the point being made? Is the sentence relevant or irrelevant?"

Here is an example of a passage followed by one question:

---

[1]On May 6, 1954, Roger Bannister, an English medical student, became the first person to run a mile in under 4 minutes. [2]It was one of history's great sports achievements. [3]To some people of that era, breaking the 4-minute record for the mile was one of humanity's great feats. [4]Many people in the United States have taken up running, just for fun and recreation.

## QUESTION

What should be done with sentence 4?

(A) It should be left where it is.
(B) It should be moved to follow sentence 1.
(C) It should be moved to follow sentence 2.
(D) It should precede sentence 1.
(E) It should be omitted.

## ANSWER

Consider Choice A. Sentence 4 does not make much sense if it is placed after sentence 3. It is clearly irrelevant after sentence 3. Therefore, Choice A is incorrect.

Consider Choice B. Read sentence 1—then read sentence 4—then read sentence 2. These three sentences obviously do not belong together. Sentence 4 is out of place in this combination—it is an irrelevant sentence. Therefore, Choice B is incorrect.

Consider Choice C. Read sentence 2—then read sentence 4—then read sentence 3. Again, we find that sentence 4 is irrelevant. Therefore, Choice C is incorrect.

Consider Choice D. Read sentence 4—then read sentence 1. Once more we find that sentence 4 is irrelevant. Therefore, Choice D is incorrect.

Consider Choice E which tells us to omit sentence 4. Since we have placed sentence 4 in every possible position in the passage and found it irrelevant in every case, we can conclude that sentence 4 should be omitted from the passage. Therefore, Choice E is correct.

# Economy

A writer should include only those words or phrases necessary to make his point clear. He should avoid using words that add nothing to the meaning of his passage. Listed below, you will find examples of different kinds of wordiness, followed by sentences that correct the wordiness.

1. Sometimes, extra words can be replaced by appropriate punctuation.

    **Wordy:** Swimming and sailing and bicycling and tennis are summer sports.
    **Concise:** Swimming, sailing, bicycling, and tennis are summer sports.

2. Wordiness can be avoided by combining two sentences into one sentence.

    **Wordy:** We were hot and tired. We wanted to go home.
    **Concise:** Hot and tired, we wanted to go home.

Wordiness often stems from the careless or needless repetition of words or ideas. Such repetition may involve an entire sentence that needlessly repeats an idea already expressed in some other part of the passage. Unless words are used for emphasis or clarity, repetition is to be avoided. A good writer should practice economy with words as all of us practice economy with money.

In the Improving Paragraphs question-type, a passage may include words, phrases, or entire sentences that violate the *economy* of writing. When a question directs you to a certain sentence in the passage and asks you how that sentence would be best written, see whether part or all of that sentence could be omitted without changing the meaning of the passage. If such an omission is possible, you will know that the correct choice is the one which omits the unnecessary words. In this way, you will be correcting the lack of economy in the passage.

In the following passage, you will be given an opportunity to see how *economy* in writing works.

---

[1]They are in their thirties now, many of them married, the fathers of young children. [2]They have been home for ten or eleven years, having slipped back quietly into society without victory parades to welcome them, without brass bands or cheering crowds or even recognition.

[3]They are, in many ways, a perplexed and splintered generation. [4]They are a group of men, mostly blue-collar, who have, until recently, buried their experiences of the Vietnam War. [5]What has dominated the mood of Vietnam veterans has been a passion for isolation and anonymity. [6]What Vietnam veterans have felt most has been a desire to be left alone and unrecognized. [7]Only recently have the veterans begun to struggle to organize, to assert themselves, and to come to terms with an experience many of them sought to erase.

## QUESTION

Sentence 6 should be

(1) left as it is
(2) moved to follow sentence 1
(3) moved to follow sentence 2
(4) moved to follow sentence 3
(5) omitted

## ANSWER

Consider Choice A. Read sentence 5—then read sentence 6—then read sentence 7 (if necessary). Sentence 6 needlessly repeats the information which is already clearly stated in sentence 5. Accordingly, sentence 6 *violates the economy of writing*. Therefore, Choice A is incorrect. Since Choices B, C, and D would require the inclusion of sentence 6 in the passage, we know immediately that Choices B, C, and D are incorrect we must not include sentence 6 in the passage because it violates the economy principle. It follows that Choice E, which tells us to omit sentence 6 from the passage, is the correct choice.

# Clarity

Every sentence in a passage must be clear in its meaning. The writer should allow no doubt about what he wishes to convey in that sentence. Moreover, the entire passage must be clear as a whole to the reader. Lack of clarity in writing may be caused by any of the following weaknesses:

1. **Indefinite antecedent of a pronoun.** Ambiguity arises when the writer does not make clear just what the pronoun refers to.

NOT CLEAR: She took the delicious nuts out of the containers and hid them in the closet.

[Did she hide the nuts or the containers?]

CLEAR: She took the delicious nuts out of the containers and hid the nuts in the closet.

2. **Lack of parallelism.** The same grammatical construction should be used for ideas of equal importance.

NOT CLEAR: Jane helps her mother by cooking and making her own clothes.

[Does Jane cook her own clothes?]

CLEAR: Jane helps her mother by cooking and by making her own clothes.

3. **Incomplete comparison.** If a comparison is not complete, the sentence may have an ambiguous meaning.

NOT CLEAR: Ann loves Tony more than Dick.

[Does Ann love Tony more than Dick loves Tony?

*or*

Does Ann love Tony more than Ann loves Dick?]

CLEAR: Ann loves Tony more than she loves Dick.

4. **Misplaced modifier.** A modifier should be placed as close as possible to the word it modifies.

*Example 1*

NOT CLEAR: The restaurant only has fish on Wednesdays.

[Some restaurant! It serves only fish on Wednesdays?

No other food whatsoever on Wednesdays?]

CLEAR: The restaurant has fish only on Wednesdays.

*Example 2*

NOT CLEAR: Does a man live here with one eye named Smith?

[What's the name of his other eye—Jones?]

CLEAR: Does a one-eyed man named Smith live here?

*Example 3*

NOT CLEAR: The jeweler sold the watch to that attractive woman with the Swiss movement.

[The jeweler must have given her a bargain.]

CLEAR: The jeweler sold the watch with the Swiss movement to that attractive woman.

5. **Dangling construction.** A phrase or clause should be placed in the right position in order to avoid misunderstanding.

NOT CLEAR: While enjoying lunch, the fire alarm sounded.

[The fire alarm must have been hungry.]

CLEAR: While I was enjoying lunch, the fire alarm sounded.

6. **Omission of necessary words.** A word or phrase that is necessary for the full meaning of a sentence must not be omitted. Sometimes the addition of another sentence may be necessary to make the passage clear.

NOT CLEAR: Winning in Las Vegas is something I never thought would happen.

[Someone must win once in a while in Las Vegas.]

CLEAR: Winning in Las Vegas is something I never thought would happen to me.

7. **Awkwardness.** An awkward sentence stands in the way of clarity.

NOT CLEAR: A higher salary will provide me with a college degree with the money that I will get to take evening courses.

[Confusing!]

CLEAR: A higher salary will provide me with the money to take evening courses so that I can eventually get a college degree.

Now let us consider the following selection in which one of the sentences has a clarity problem.

---

[1]Outbreaks of recent deer killing have angered two Pennsylvania communities. [2]In both incidents, the deer were in captivity. [3]In Norristown, near Philadelphia, a 20-year-old man fatally shot a pregnant doe and a second deer in the Elmwood Park Zoo. [4]In Williamsport, a 20-year-old man stabbed a deer to death in a display pen. [5]The deer slayers were brought to trial on misdemeanor charges. [6]Each defendant told the judge that he had been drinking.

## QUESTION

Sentence 6 should be

(A) left as it is
(B) changed to <u>Appearing before the judge, both defendants said that they had been drinking.</u>
(C) omitted as of no importance
(D) changed to <u>Each defendant told the judge that they had been drinking.</u>
(E) changed to <u>Both defendants told the judge that drinking was what they had been doing.</u>

## ANSWER

Choice A is wrong because it lacks clarity. Who was drinking? Each defendant or the judge? Choice B is correct because it makes clear just who had been drinking. Choice C is incorrect because the sentence is quite relevant as it stands. Choice D is incorrect because there should be no switch from the singular subject (<u>Each</u>) of the main clause to the plural subject (<u>they</u>) of the dependent clause. Choice E is incorrect because it is awkward and verbose.

# Paragraphing

There are four important characteristics of a paragraph:

1. Every piece of prose of any length is divided into sections called paragraphs.

2. A paragraph may consist of a single sentence, but it usually consists of several sentences.

3. Each paragraph is a **complete unit**—that is, it deals with a particular thing, or idea, or division of the subject.

4. Each paragraph must be **well-arranged**. The sentences must come in the right order and fit together properly, so that the whole paragraph is easy to understand.

Occasionally, a Logic and Organization question may ask you to determine where a passage should be divided into two paragraphs. The four important characteristics of a paragraph listed above should be a helpful guide for you to answer a paragraph-type question correctly.

Following is a passage and then a question which asks you about paragraphing.

---

¹Stuart Gibbs was a 33-year-old history teacher at the high school in Mathews, Virginia. ²He asked his 11th-grade students to write reports on Aldous Huxley's *Brave New World*. ³This is a novel that depicts a world in which people are without traditional moral values. ⁴The school administration warned him that he would be fired if he went ahead with this assignment. ⁵He ignored the warning. ⁶Mr. Gibbs is out of a school job today. ⁷He has sued in Federal District Court for reinstatement. ⁸The principal of the high school gives no reason for the discharge except that of insubordination. ⁹The principal goes on to explain that, under the State of Virginia statute, a supervisor does not have to give a specific reason for discharging a teacher.

## QUESTION

If the passage were divided into two paragraphs, the second paragraph would best begin with which of the following?

(A) Sentence 2
(B) Sentence 3
(C) Sentence 6
(D) Sentence 7
(E) Sentence 9

# ANSWER

Consider Choice A. Sentence 2 cannot logically be separated from sentence 1. Therefore, Choice A is wrong.

Consider Choice B. Since sentence 3 explains sentence 2, Choice B is wrong.

Consider Choice C. Sentence 6 is a logical place for a new paragraph to start. The reason for this is that there is a definite time change between what has preceded sentence 6 and what begins with sentence 6. Therefore, Choice C is correct.

Consider Choice D. Sentence 7 indicates a direct follow-up of sentence 6: Mr. Gibbs was discharged so he sued. Therefore, Choice D is wrong.

Consider Choice E. The last sentence of the passage—sentence 9—"goes on to explain" what has been said in sentence 8. Therefore, Choice E is wrong.

# PART 7

# A BRIEF REVIEW OF ENGLISH GRAMMAR

# Frequent Grammatical Problems

**Split Infinitive.** By the 17th century English had developed a two-word infinitive—*to go, to run, to talk*, etc. The word *to* was coupled with the verb and stood next to it. Since the Latin infinitive was always treated as one word, scholars decided that the infinitive in English must also be treated as one word. It was considered an error to split these two words by inserting an adverb between them.

But English isn't Latin, so the people went on splitting the infinitive whenever it suited their purpose. And we've been doing it ever since.

It isn't necessary to split the infinitive deliberately, of course, but if it sounds better or seems more natural or will add emphasis, then do so. The following sentence is an example of a permissible split infinitive: "After they had won the baseball trophy, they went to the party *to proudly display* their prize." (*Proudly to display* or *to display proudly* makes the sentence stiff. And *they went proudly to the party to display their prize* changes the original meaning.)

**Ending a Sentence with a Preposition.** The old "rule" that you should never end a sentence with a preposition was another attempt to force Latin on English, and it also is fading out. Often, to avoid this "error," we have to write a much longer and more awkward sentence. Which sounds better?

> This is a rule up with which I will not put.
> This is a rule I won't put up with.

**Distinction between "Shall" and "Will."** Formal usage required *shall* in the first person and *will* in the second and third person when forming the simple future. For the emphatic future, these were reversed. Today most of us use *will* in all persons for both simple and emphatic future.

**"It Is I."** This question of which pronoun to use probably causes more uncertainty than any other problem in grammar. We do not change the form of a noun, whether we use it as a subject or as an object. But we do have different forms for our pronouns.

For example, *I, you, he, they, we, etc.,* are the nominative forms and are used as subjects. *Me, you, him, them, us,* etc., are the objective forms. Normally we use the objective form after a verb, but after the *be* verbs (am, is, are, was, will be, etc.) we have traditionally used the nominative form; thus, *it is I* rather than *it is me*.

Usage, however, is divided on this. In informal conversation we often say, "It's me," just as the French do—"C'est moi." The argument for this usage is pretty sound. The predicate is thought of as object territory, and it feels strange to us to use the nominative form here. Still, the traditional use of this form has come to be regarded as a sign of the well-educated man. So, until "it is me" has become more widely accepted, we should continue to use "it is I."

Examples of the nominative forms for other pronouns may prove helpful:

It was he (not *it was him*)
This is she (not *this is her*)
Had it been they (not *had it been them*)

There should be no question about using the objective case of the pronoun after other verbs. "The chairman appointed *him* and *me*," is considered correct, not "The chairman appointed *he* and *I*." But often in trying to avoid this decision we make an even worse error. Instead of the objective form we use the reflective—*myself, himself*, etc. "He appointed John and myself" is definitely wrong.

**"Who" versus "Whom."** The pronoun *who* is used for the subject and *whom* is used for the object.

Give the letter to *whoever* answers the door. (not to *whomever*...) The pronoun *whoever* is the subject of its clause.
Tell me *whom* you borrowed the money from. (not *who... from*)
The pronoun *whom* is the object of the preposition *from*.

The pronoun *who* used as the subject of a verb is not affected by a parenthetical expression such as *I think, he believes, they say* intervening between the subject and the verb.

He is the person *who* I think is best qualified.
Mr. Jameson is the attorney *who* we suppose will prepare the brief.

**Adverbs and Adjectives.** We seem to have more trouble with adverbs than with adjectives. A simple guide is this: An *adverb* may modify a verb, another adverb, or an adjective; an *adjective* may modify only a noun or a pronoun.

Our biggest problem comes in confusing adjectives and adverbs. For example, we may use the adjective *good* when we should use the adverb *well:*

*Poor:*    The engines are running *good*.
*Proper:*    The engines are running *well*.

*NOTE:* Both *good* and *well* may be used after a linking verb as predicate adjectives. For example: "I feel good" indicates a state of well-being; but "I feel well" indicates either that you are not sick or that your ability to use your sense of touch is above average.

## Common Errors in Grammar

Most of us do not have too much trouble writing grammatically acceptable sentences. We just habitually follow the basic word order. But sometimes we get careless or we fall into bad habits in our use of this important principle. When we do, we can interfere with the meaning and with the movement of our sentences.

Here are some common grammatical errors which may confuse our reader. They may be so simple that the reader quickly sees the error, revises the sentence in his mind, and gets the proper message. But this is your job, not his. Too often the reader won't catch the error and will get the wrong idea about what you are trying to say.

## Misplaced Modifiers

1. Avoid dangling modifiers. When a word or phrase seems to modify another word which it cannot logically modify, we say it has been left dangling. Usually it will be a phrase beginning the sentence. From its position we expect it to modify the subject. But the connection is illogical.

| | |
|---|---|
| *Confusing:* | Approaching the flight line from the east side, the operations building can be easily seen. (The operations building obviously does not approach the flight line.) |
| *Improved:* | A person approaching the flight line from the east side can easily see the operations building. |
| *Confusing:* | To make a climbing turn, the throttle is opened wider. |
| *Improved:* | To make a climbing turn, open the throttle wider. (The subject *you* is understood.) |

2. Keep your modifiers close to the words they modify. Sometimes we widely separate a modifier from its modified word and end up confusing the reader.

| | |
|---|---|
| *Confusing:* | It was impossible to find the book I had been reading in the dark. |
| *Improved:* | It was impossible in the dark to find the book I had been reading. |
| *Confusing:* | He had marked on the map the places where we were to watch for turns in red ink. |
| *Improved:* | He marked on the map in red ink the places where we were to watch for turns. |

3. Avoid using "squinting" modifiers that may refer to either of two parts of a sentence. A squinting modifier is so placed in a sentence that it could logically modify either the words that came before it or the words that follow it; it "squints" both ways. This may confuse the reader. He may not realize the ambiguity and misinterpret the intended meaning.

| | |
|---|---|
| *Confusing:* | Personnel who drive their cars to work *only occasionally* can count on finding a parking space. |
| *Improved:* | Only *occasionally* can personnel who drive their cars to work count on finding a parking space. |
| *Confusing:* | The electrician said Wednesday he would repair the light. (Did he make the statement on Wednesday, or did he say that he would repair the light on Wednesday?) |
| *Improved:* | Wednesday the electrician said he would repair the light. |

*or*

The electrician said that he would repair the light on Wednesday.

By misplacing modifiers we make it easy for the reader to misunderstand the meaning of our sentences, sometimes with dire results. We can eliminate such errors by reading and revising our writing before we release it. Don't confuse your reader or make him do your work. Keep your modifiers close to the words they modify.

# Confusing Pronouns and Other Reference Words

1. Make sure that a pronoun agrees in number with the noun it refers to.

| | |
|---|---|
| *Confusing:* | Though there may be different teacher unions, the policy of *its* delegates should be similar. |
| *Improved:* | Though there may be different teacher unions, the policy of *their* delegates should be similar. |

2. Make sure a pronoun or other reference word has a definite and clearly understood antecedent. We often use words or pronouns such as *which,* the *latter,* the *former, this, it,* etc., to refer to something we have previously mentioned. This reference must be clear to the reader.

| | |
|---|---|
| *Confusing:* | A piece of thread dangled over his belt which was at least 8 inches long. |
| *Improved:* | A piece of thread which was at least 8 inches long dangled over his belt. |
| *Confusing:* | The president told the executive he would handle all personnel assignments. |
| *Improved:* | The president told the executive to handle all personnel assignments. |

*or*

The president told the executive that he, the president, would handle all personnel assignments.

# Non-Parallel Structure

Express parallel ideas in words with the same grammatical construction. Nothing sounds quite so disorganized in writing as structure that is not parallel.

*Not Parallel:* Briefly, the functions of a staff are to advise the general manager, transmit his instructions, and the supervision of the execution of his decisions.

*Parallel:* Briefly, the functions of a staff are to advise the general manager, transmit his instructions, and supervise the execution of his decisions.

*Not Parallel:* I have learned three things: that one should not argue about legalisms, never expect miracles, and the impropriety of using a singular verb with a compound subject.

*Parallel:* I have learned three things: never argue about legalisms, never expect miracles, and never use a singular verb with a compound subject.

# Some Basic Grammatical Terms

## Parts of Speech

**Nouns:** names of people, things, qualities, acts, ideas, relationships: *General Smith, Texas, aircraft, confusion, running, predestination, grandfather.*

**Pronouns:** words that refer indirectly to people, places, things, etc.: *he, she, which, it, someone.*

**Adjectives:** words that point out or indicate a quality of nouns or pronouns: *big, lowest, cold, hard.*

**Prepositions:** words that link nouns and pronouns to other words by showing the relationship between them: *to, by, between, above, behind, about, of, in, on, from.*

**Conjunctions:** words used to join other words, phrases, and clauses: *and, but, however, because, although.*

**Verbs:** words that express action or indicate a state, feeling, or simply existence: go, hate, fly, feel, is.

**Adverbs:** words that tell how, where, when, or to what degree acts were performed, or indicate a degree of quality: *slowly, well, today, much, very.*

**Note:** Many of our words can serve as more than one part of speech. Some words may be used as nouns, adjectives, and verbs without any change in spelling: *Drinking* coffee is a popular pastime; He broke the *drinking* glass; The boy *is drinking* a glass of milk. Often they may be both adjectives and adverbs: *better, well, fast.* Ordinarily we add *-ly* to words to form adverbs, while adjectives may be formed by adding *-able, -ly, -ing, -al, -ese, -ful, -ish, -ous, -y,* etc. But these endings are not always necessary: *college* (noun); *college boy* (noun used as an adjective to modify the noun *boy*).

# Other Grammatical Terms

**Subject:** a noun or pronoun (or word or phrase used as a noun) which names the actor in a sentence. The term may be used in a broader sense to include all of the words that are related to the actor.

**Predicate:** the verb with its modifiers and its object or complement.

**Predicate complement:** a noun completing the meaning of a linking verb and modifying the subject.

    Jones is *chief* (noun). He was *pale* (adjective).

**Linking verb:** a verb with little or no meaning of its own that usually indicates a state of being or condition. It functions chiefly to connect the subject with an adjective or noun in the predicate. The most common linking verb is the verb *to be* (am, are, is, was, were, had been), but there are others.

> He *feels* nervous.
> He *acts* old.
> He *seems* tired.

**Clause:** an element which is part of a complex or compound sentence and has a subject, a verb, and often an object. "Nero killed Agrippina" is a clause but is not ordinarily called one because it is the complete sentence. In the compound sentence, *"Nero killed Agrippina,* but *he paid the penalty,"* each italicized group of words is an independent clause. In the complex sentence, "*Because he killed Agrippina,* Nero paid the penalty," the italicized clause is made dependent or subordinate by the word *because;* it depends upon the rest of the sentence for the complete meaning.

**Phrase:** two or more words without a subject and predicate that function as a grammatical unit in a clause or sentence. A phrase may modify another word or may be used as a noun or verb. For example: beside the radiator, approaching the pier, to fly a kite.

**Verbals:** words made from verbs but used as other parts of speech:

*Gerund:* a verb used as a noun:
> *Swimming* was his favorite sport.

*Participle:* a verb used as an adjective:
> The aircraft *piloted* by Colonel Jones has crashed.

*Infinitive:* a verb used as a noun, adjective, or adverb:
> *To travel* is my greatest pleasure. (infinitive used as a noun)
> We have four days *to spend* at home. (infinitive used as an adjective)
> Bruce was glad *to have joined.* (infinitive used as adverb)

# Common Grammar Errors Classified by Part of Speech

| I. NOUNS | CORRECTION |
|---|---|
| Incorrect form to express plural number:<br>*He shot two deers.* | He shot two *deer*. |
| Incorrect form to express masculine or feminine gender:<br>*She was a wizard.* | She was a *witch*. |
| Incorrect form of the possessive case:<br>*Two boy's heads and two sheeps' heads.* | Two *boys'* heads and two *sheep's* heads. |
| Use of the objective case for the possessive:<br>*I was sorry to hear of John doing wrong.* | I was sorry to hear of *John's* doing wrong. |

| II. PRONOUNS | |
|---|---|
| Pronoun *I* placed incorrectly:<br>*I and my sister will attend the concert.* | My *sister* and I will attend the concert. |
| Use of compound personal pronoun for simple personal pronoun:<br>*Sam and myself will do it.* | Sam and *I* will do it. |

Incorrect choice of relative pronoun:
> *I have a dog who barks at night. This is the person which did the wrong. This is the house what Jack built. Columbus, that discovered America, was an Italian.*

Lack of agreement between pronoun and antecedent:
> *Every one of the pupils lost their books.*

Incorrect case form:
> *The book is your's or his'. I recognize it's cover.*

Use of nominative case for objective:
> *Give it to Kate and I. I knew it to be she.*

Use of objective case for nominative:
> *Him and me are brothers. Whom do you suppose she is? It was her.*

Use of objective case for possessive:
> *There is no chance of me being chosen.*

Pleonastic use:
> *John, he tried, and then Mary, she tried.*

Ambiguous use:
> *The man told his son to take his coat to the tailor's.*

III. VERBS AND VERBALS.

Use of the indicative mood for the subjunctive:
> *I wish I was you.*

Use of the subjunctive mood for the indicative:
> *If the cavern were of artificial construction, considerable pains had been taken to make it look natural.*

Use of incorrect form to express tense:
> *I done it. He seen it. She come late yesterday. I see him last week. The boy has went home. My hands were froze. He teached me all I know. I ain't seen it.*

Error in sequence of tenses:
> *I meant, when first I came, to have bought all the parts. He did not know that mercury was a metal.*

Lack of agreement between verb and subject:
> *Was you glad to see us? Neither he nor she have ever been there. It don't cost much.*

Use of incorrect forms of principal parts of certain verbs; e.g., *sit* and *lie:*
> *The hen sets on the eggs. The book lays on the table. It laid there yesterday. It has laid there all week.*

## CORRECTION

I have a dog *which* barks at night. This is the person *who* did the wrong. This is the house *which* Jack built. Columbus, *who* discovered America, was an Italian.

Every one of the pupils lost *his* book.

The book is *yours* or *his*. I recognize *its* cover.

Give it to Kate and *me*. I knew it to be *her*.

*He* and *I* are brothers. *Who* do you suppose she is? It was *she*.

There is no chance of *my* being chosen.

John *tried* and then Mary *tried*.

The man told his son to take *his (the man's)* coat to the tailor's.

I wish I *were* you.

If the cavern *was* of artificial construction, considerable pains had been taken to make it look natural.

I *did* it. He *saw* it. She *came* late yesterday. I *saw* him last week. The boy *has gone* home. My hands were *frozen*. He *taught* me all I know. I *haven't seen* it.

I meant, when first I came, *to buy* all the parts. He did not know that mercury *is* metal.

*Were* you glad to see us? Neither he nor she *has* ever been there. It *doesn't* cost much.

The hen *sits* on the eggs. The book *lies* on the table. It *lay* there yesterday. It *has lain* there all week.

Use of adjective participle without modified word:

> *Coming into the room, a great noise was heard.*

> *Coming* into the room, *I* heard a great noise.

### IV. ADJECTIVES.

Omission of article:

> *The noun and pronoun are inflected.*

The noun and *the* pronoun are inflected.

Use of superfluous article:

> *I do not like this kind of a story.*

I do not like this *kind of* story.

Use of *a* for *an* and *an* for *a*:

> *This is an universal custom. I should like a apple.*

This is *a* universal custom. I should like *an* apple.

Use of adverb for predicate adjective:

> *She looks nicely.*

She looks *nice*.

Lack of concord between certain adjectives and the words they modify:

> *I do not like these kind of grapes.*

I do not like *this kind* of grapes.

Incorrect forms of comparison:

> *His ways have become eviler.*

His ways have become *more evil*.

Use of comparative form not accompanied by certain necessary words:

> *He is shorter than any boy in his class.*

He is shorter than any *other* boy in the class.

Use of superlative form accompanied by certain superfluous words:

> *This is of all others the most important.*

This is the most important.

Use of double comparative or superlative forms:

> *She is more kinder than you.*

She is *kinder* than you.

Incorrect placing of adjective phrases and clauses:

> *The mariner shot the bird with an unfeeling heart.*

*With an unfeeling heart,* the mariner shot the bird.

### V. ADVERBS.

Use of adjective for adverb:

> *She sings real well.*

She sings *really* well.

Incorrect use of double negatives:

> *I cannot go no faster.*

I cannot go *any* faster.

Incorrect placing of adverbs and of adverbial phrases and clauses:

> *I only came yesterday, and I go today.*

I came *only* yesterday, and I go today.

### VI. PREPOSITIONS.

Incorrect choice of prepositions:

> *I walked from the hall in the room.*
> *Divide this between the three boys.*
> *I was to New York today.*

I walked from the hall *into* the room.
Divide this *among* the three boys.
I was *in* New York today.

Omission of preposition:

> *She is an example of what a person in good health is capable.*

She is an example of what a person in good health is capable *of*.

Use of a superfluous preposition:
*The book in which the story appears in is mine.*

<u>CORRECTION</u>
The book in which the story appears is mine.

## VII. Conjunctions.

Incorrect choice of conjunctions, especially *like* for *as,* and *as* for *whether:*
    *I cannot write like you do. I don't know as I can go.*

I cannot write *as* you do. I don't know *whether* I can go.

Incorrect choice of correlatives:
    *Neither this or that will do.*

Neither this *nor* that will do.

Use of a superfluous conjunction:
    *I have no doubt but that he will come.*
    *This is a fine picture and which all will admire.*

I have no doubt *that* he will come.
This is a fine picture *which* all will admire.

Incorrect placing of correlatives:
    *He is neither disposed to sanction bloodshed nor deceit.* (Place *neither* before *bloodshed.*)

He is disposed to sanction *neither* bloodshed nor deceit.

# Correct Usage: Choosing the Right Word

*"The difference between the right word and the almost-right word is the difference between the lightning and the lightning-bug [firefly]."*

—Mark Twain

**A, an.**   The indefinite article *a* is used before a consonant sound; the indefinite article *an* is used before a vowel sound. Say *a plan, an idea.*

**Accept, except.**   *Accept* means *to receive; except* when used as a verb means *to leave out.* (We *accepted* the gift. Pedro's name was *excepted* from the honor roll.) The word *except* is used most often as a preposition. *Everyone went except me.*

**Affect, effect.**   *Affect* is a verb which means to *influence.* (Winning the sweepstakes will *affect* his attitude.) *Effect,* as a noun, means *an influence.* (Smoking has an *effect* on one's health.) *Effect,* as a verb, means to *bring about.* (The teacher's praise *effected* a change in the student.)

*Affected,* as an adjective, has the meaning of *false.* (She had an *affected* way of speaking.)

**Aggravate, irritate.**   *Aggravate* means to make worse. (Drinking iced water will *aggravate* your cold.) *Irritate* means to *annoy* or *exasperate.* (Mary's continuous chattering *irritated* me.)

**Ain't.**   Do not use this expression.

**Already, all ready.**   *Already* means *before* or *by a certain time.* (Mike said that he had *already* done the job.) *All ready* means *completely ready.* (When the buzzer sounded, the horses were *all ready* to start running.)

**All right, alright.**   The only correct spelling is *all right.*

**Altogether, all together.**   *Altogether* means *entirely, wholly.* (Jane is *altogether* too conceited to get along with people.) *All together* means *as a group.* (After the explosion, the boss was relieved to find his workers *all together* in front of the building.)

**Among, between.**   *Among* is used with more than two persons or things. (The manager distributed the gifts *among* all of the employees.) *Between* is used only with two persons or things. (The steak was divided *between* the two children.)

**Amount, number.**   *Amount* is used to refer to things in bulk. (The war costs a great *amount* of money.) *Number* is used to refer to things that can be counted. (A large *number* of pupils attend this school.)

**And etc.**   This is incorrect. The abbreviation *etc.* stands for the Latin *et cetera.* The *et* means *and;* the *cetera* means *other things.* It is wrong to say *and etc.* because the idea of *and* is already included in the *etc.*

**Anyways, anywheres, everywheres, somewheres.**   These expressions are not correct. Omit the final *s* after each.

**As, like.**   *As,* used as a conjunction, is followed by a verb. (Please do it *as* I told you to.) *Like* may not be used as a conjunction. If it is used as a preposition, it is not followed by a verb. (This ice cream looks *like* custard.)

**Awful.**   See **Terrific, terrible.**

**Being that.**   *Being that* is incorrect for *since* or *because.* (*Since* you are tired, you ought to rest.)

**Beside, besides.**   *Beside* means *alongside of; besides* means *in addition to.* (Nixon sat *beside* Autry at the baseball game.) (There is nobody *besides* her husband who understands Ann.)

**Between.**   See **Among.**

**Bring, take.**   Consider the speaker as a starting point. *Bring* is used for something carried in the direction of the speaker. (When you return from lunch, please *bring* me a ham sandwich.) *Take* is used for something carried away from the speaker. (If you are going downtown, please *take* this letter to the post office.)

**Bunch.**   *Bunch* means cluster. Do not use *bunch* for *group* or *crowd.* (This is a large *bunch* of grapes.) (A *crowd* of people was at the scene of the accident.)

**But that, but what.**   Do not use these expressions in place of *that* in structures like the following: I do not question *that* (not *but that*) you are richer than I am.

**Can't hardly.**   Don't use this double negative. Say *can hardly.*

**Continual, continuous.**   *Continual* means happening at intervals. (Salesmen are *continually* walking into this office.) *Continuous* means going on without interruption. (Without a moment of dry weather, it rained *continuously* for forty days and forty nights.)

**Could of.**   Do not use for *could have.*

**Data.**   Although *data* is the plural of *datum,* idiom permits the use of this word as a singular. Some authorities still insist on *Data are gathered* rather than *Data is gathered* or *these data* rather than *this data.* Most persons in computer programming now say *Data is gathered* or *this data.*

**Deal.**   Do not use this term for *arrangement* or *transaction.* (He has an *excellent arrangement* (not *deal*) with the manager.)

**Different from, different than.**   *Different from* is correct. *Different than* is incorrect. (His method of doing this is *different from* mine.)

**Discover, invent.**   *Discover* means to see or learn something that has not been previously known. (They say the Vikings, not Columbus, *discovered* America.) *Invent* means to create for the first time. (William S. Burroughs *invented* the adding machine.)

**Disinterested, uninterested.**   *Disinterested* means without bias. (An umpire must be *disinterested* to judge fairly in a baseball game.) *Uninterested* means not caring about a situation. (I am totally *uninterested* in your plan.)

**Doesn't, don't.**   *Doesn't* means *does not; don't* means *do not.* Do not say *He don't* (*do not*) when you mean *He doesn't* (*does not*).

**Due to.**   At the beginning of a sentence, *due to* is always incorrect. Use, instead, *on account of, because of,* or a similar expression. (*On account of* bad weather, the contest was postponed.) As a predicate adjective construction, *due to* is correct. His weakness was *due to* his hunger.

**Each other, one another.**   *Each other* is used for two persons. (The executive and his secretary antagonize *each other.*) *One another* is used for more than two persons. (The members of the large family love *one another.*)

**Effect.** See **Affect**.

**Enthuse.** Do not use this word. Say *enthusiastic*. (The art critic was *enthusiastic* about the painting.)

**Equally as good.** This expression is incorrect. Say, instead, *just as good*. (This car is *just as good* as that.)

**Farther, further.** *Farther* is used for a distance that is measurable. (The farmer's house is about 100 yards *farther* down the road.) *Further* is used to express the extension of an idea. (A *further* explanation may be necessary.)

**Fewer, less.** *Fewer* applies to what may be counted. (Greenwich Village has *fewer* conservatives than liberals.) *Less* refers to degree or amount. (*Less* rain fell this month than the month before.)

**Flout, flaunt.** *Flout* means to mock or insult. (The king *flouted* the wise man when the latter offered advice.) *Flaunt* means to make a pretentious display of. (The upstart *flaunted* his diamond ring.)

**Further.** See **Farther**.

**Get.** *Get* means *to obtain* or *receive*. Get should not be used in the sense of *to excite, to interest*, or *to understand*. Say: His guitar playing *fascinates* (not *gets*) me. Say: When you talk about lifestyles, I just don't *understand* (not *get*) *you*.

**Good, well.** Do not use the adjective *good* in place of the adverb *well* in structures like the following: John works *well* (not *good*) in the kitchen. Jim Palmer pitched *well* (not *good*) in last night's game.

**Graduate.** One *graduates from*, or *is graduated from*, a school. One does *not graduate a school*. (The student *graduated* [or was graduated] from high school.)

**Had of.** Avoid this for *had*. Say: My father always said that he wished he *had* (not *had of*) gone to college.

**Hanged, hung.** When a person is *executed*, he is *hanged*. When anything is *suspended* in space, it is *hung*.

**Hardly.** See **Can't hardly**.

**Healthful, healthy.** *Healthful* applies to *conditions that promote health*. *Healthy* applies to *a state of health*. Say: Stevenson found the climate of Saranac Lake very *healthful*. Say: Mary is a very *healthy* girl.

**If, whether.** Use *whether*—not *if*—in structures that follow verbs like *ask, doubt, know, learn, say*. Say: Hank Aaron didn't know *whether* (not *if*) he was going to break Babe Ruth's home-run record.

**Imply, infer.** The speaker *implies* when he suggests or hints at. (The owner of the store *implied* that the patron stole a box of toothpicks.) The listener *infers* when he draws a conclusion from facts or evidence. (From what you say, I *infer* that I am about to be discharged.)

**In, into.** *In* is used to express a location, without the involvement of motion. (The sugar is *in* the cupboard.) *Into* is used to express motion from one place to another. (The housekeeper put the sugar *into* the cupboard.)

**In regards to.** This is incorrect. Say *in regard to* or *with regard to*.

**Invent.** See **Discover**.

**Irregardless.** Do not use *irregardless*. It is incorrect for *regardless*. (You will not be able to go out tonight *regardless* of the fact that you have done all of your homework.)

**Its, it's.** *Its* is the possessive of *it; it's* is the contraction for *it is*.

**Kind of, sort of.** Do not use these expressions as adverbs. Say: Ali was *quite* (not *kind of* or *sort of*) witty in his post-fight interview.

**Kind of a, sort of a.** Omit the *a*. Say: What *kind of* (not *kind of a* or *sort of a*) game is lacrosse?

**Lay, lie.** *Lie* describes the subject. (The ball *lies* on the ground.) *Lay* describes the effect the subject has on the object. (I *lay* the ball on the ground.) However, the past tense of *lie*, an irregular verb, is also *lay*, which can cause confusion.

**Learn, teach.** *Learn* means *to gain knowledge*. *Teach* means *to impart knowledge*. Say: He *taught* (not *learned*) his brother how to swim.

**Leave, let.** The word *leave* means *to depart*. (I *leave* today for San Francisco.) The word *let* means to allow. (*Let* me take your place.)

**Less, fewer.** See **Fewer, less**.

**Liable, likely.** *Liable* means exposed to something unpleasant. (If you speed, you are *liable* to get a summons.) *Likely* means probable, with reference to either a pleasant or unpleasant happening. (It is *likely* to snow tomorrow.)

**Locate.** Do not use *locate* to mean *settle* or *move to*. Say: We will *move to* (not *locate in*) Florida next year.

**Might of, must of.** Omit the *of*.

**Myself, himself, yourself.** These pronouns are to be used as intensives. (The Chairman *himself* will open the meeting.) Do not use these pronouns when *me, him,* or *you* will serve. Say: We shall be happy if Joe and *you* (not *yourself*) join us for lunch at the Plaza.

**Nice.** See **Terrific, terrible**.

**Number, amount.** See **Amount, number**.

**Of, have.** Do not use *of* for *have* in structures like *could have*.

**Off of.** Omit the *of*. Say: The book fell *off* (not *off of*) the shelf.

**Pour, spill.** When one *pours,* he does it deliberately. (He carefully *poured* the wine into her glass.) When one *spills,* he does it accidentally. (I carelessly *spilled* some wine on her dress.)

**Practical, practicable.** *Practical* means *fitted for actual work*. *Practicable* means *feasible* or *possible*. Say: My business partner is a *practical man*. Say: The boss did not consider the plan *practicable* for this coming year.

**Principal, principle.** *Principal* applies to a *chief* or the *chief part* of something. *Principle* applies to a *basic law*. Say: Mr. Jones is the *principal* of the school. Professor White was the *principal* speaker. Honesty is a good *principle* to follow.

**Raise, rise.** *Rise* describes the subject. (The sun *rises* every morning.) *Raise* describes the effect the subject has on the object. (I *raise* my hand.)

**Reason is because.** Do not use the expression *reason is because*—it is always incorrect. Say the *reason is that*. (The *reason* Jack failed the course *is that* he didn't study.)

**Regardless.** See **Irregardless**.

**Respectfully, respectively.** *Respectfully* means *with respect*, as in the complimentary close of a letter, *respectfully yours*. *Respectively* means that each item will be considered *in the order given*. Say: This paper is *respectfully* submitted. Say: The hero, the heroine, and the villain will be played by Albert, Joan, and Harry *respectively*.

**Rise, raise.** See **Raise, rise**.

**Said.** Avoid the legalistic use of *said*, like *said letter, said plan, said program,* except in legal writing.

**Should of.** Do not use for *should have*.

**Sit, set.** *Sit* describes the subject. (I *sit* at my desk.) *Set* describes the effect the subject has on the object. (I *set* my notebook on the desk.)

**Some.**    Do not use *some* when you mean *somewhat.* Say: I'm confused *somewhat* (not *some*).

**Spill, pour.**    See **Pour, spill**.

**Suspicion.**    Do not use *suspicion* as a verb when you mean *suspect.*

**Take, bring.**    See **Bring, take**.

**Teach, learn.**    See **Learn, teach**.

**Terrific, terrible.**    Avoid "lazy words." Many people don't want to take the trouble to use the exact word. They will use words like *terrific, swell, great, beautiful,* etc., to describe anything and everything that is favorable. And they will use words like *terrible, awful, lousy, miserable,* etc., for whatever is unfavorable. Use the exact word. Say: We had a *delicious* (not terrific) meal. Say: We had a *boring* (not *terrible*) weekend.

**This kind, these kind.**    *This kind* is correct—as is *that kind, these kinds,* and *those kinds.* (My little brother likes *this kind* of pears.) *These kind* and *those kind* are incorrect.

**Try and.**    Do not say *try and.* Say *try to.* (*Try to* visit me while I am in Florida.)

**Uninterested.**    See **Disinterested**.

**Wait for, wait on.**    *Wait for* means *to await; wait on* means *to serve.* Say: I am waiting *for* (not *on*) Carter to call me on the telephone.

**Way, ways.**    Do not use *ways* for *way.* Say: It is a long *way* (not *ways*) to Japan.

**Where.**    Do not use *where* in place of *that* in expressions like the following: I see in the newspaper *that* (not *where*) a nuclear reactor may be built a mile away from our house.

**Would of.**    Do not use for *would have.*

# PART 8

# THREE
# PSAT PRACTICE
# TESTS

# Five Important Reasons for Taking These Practice Tests

Each of the three Practice PSATs in the final part of this book is modeled very closely after the actual PSAT. You will find that each of these Practice Tests has

a) the same level of difficulty as the actual PSAT

*and*

b) the same question formats that the actual PSAT questions have.

Accordingly, *taking each of the following tests is like taking the actual PSAT*. There are five important reasons for taking each of these Practice PSATs:

1. To find out in which areas of the PSAT you are still weak.

2. To know just where to concentrate your efforts to eliminate these weaknesses.

3. To reinforce the Critical-Thinking Skills—19 Math Strategies and 13 Verbal Strategies— that you learned in Part 3 of this book, "Strategy Section." As we advised you, at the beginning of Part 3, diligent study of these strategies will result in a sharp rise in your PSAT Math, Critical Reading, and Writing scores.

4. To strengthen your Basic Math skills that might still be a bit rusty. We hope that Part 5, "Complete PSAT Math Refresher," helped you substantially to scrape off some of this rust.

5. To strengthen your grammar and writing skills, look at Part 6, "The PSAT Writing Skills Test" and Part 7, "A Brief Review of English Grammar."

These five reasons for taking the three Practice Tests in this section of the book tie up closely with a very important educational principle:

## WE LEARN BY DOING!

# 10 Tips for Taking the Practice Tests

1. Observe the time limits exactly as given.

2. Allow no interruptions.

3. Permit no talking by anyone in the "test area."

4. Use the Answer Sheets provided at the beginning of each Practice Test. Don't make extra marks. Two answers for one question constitute an omitted question.

5. Use scratch paper to figure things out. (On your actual PSAT, you are permitted to use the testbook for scratchwork.)

6. Omit a question when you start "struggling" with it. Go back to that question later if you have time to do so.

7. Don't get upset if you can't answer several of the questions. You can still get a high score on the test. Even if only 40 to 60 percent of the questions you answer are correct, you will get an average or above-average score.

8. You get the same credit for answering an easy question correctly as you do for answering a tough question correctly.

9. It is advisable to guess if you are sure that at least one of the answer choices is wrong. If you are not sure whether one or more of the answer choices are wrong, statistically it will not make a difference to your total score if you guess or leave the answer blank.

10. *Your PSAT score increases by approximately 1 point for every answer you get correct.*

# PSAT PRACTICE TEST 1

## To See How You'd Do on a PSAT and What You Should Do to Improve

This PSAT test is very much like the actual PSAT. It follows the genuine PSAT very closely. Taking this test is like taking the actual PSAT. Following is the purpose of taking this test:

1. to find out what you are *weak* in and what you are *strong* in;

2. to know where to concentrate your efforts in order to be fully prepared for the actual test.

Taking this test will prove to be a very valuable TIME SAVER for you. Why waste time studying what you already know? Spend your time profitably by studying what you *don't* know. That is what this test will tell you.

In this book, we do not waste precious pages. We get right down to the business of helping you to increase your PSAT scores.

Other PSAT preparation books place their emphasis on drill, drill, drill. We do not believe that drill work is of primary importance in preparing for the PSAT exam. Drill has its place. In fact, this book contains a great variety of drill material—hundreds of PSAT-type multiple-choice questions (Critical Reading and Math and Writing), practically all of which have explanatory answers. But drill work must be coordinated with learning Critical-Thinking Skills. These skills will help you to think clearly and critically so that you will be able to answer many more PSAT questions correctly.

Ready? Start taking the test. It's just like the real thing.

Start at the beginning of each new section. If a section has fewer questions than answer spaces, leave the extra answer spaces blank. Be sure to erase any errors or stray marks completely.

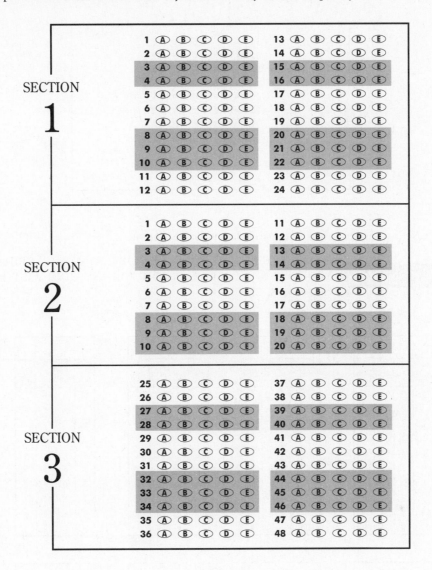

Start at the beginning of each new section. If a section has fewer questions than answer spaces, leave the extra answer spaces blank. Be sure to erase any errors or stray marks completely.

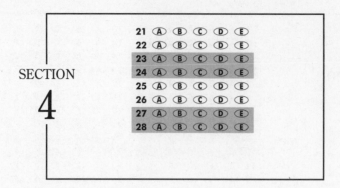

**CAUTION**    Use the answer spaces in the grids below for Section 4.

**Student-Produced Responses**    ONLY ANSWERS ENTERED IN THE CIRCLES IN EACH GRID WILL BE SCORED. YOU WILL NOT RECEIVE CREDIT FOR ANYTHING WRITTEN IN THE BOXES ABOVE THE CIRCLES.

Start at the beginning of each new section. If a section has fewer questions than answer spaces, leave the extra answer spaces blank. Be sure to erase any errors or stray marks completely.

SECTION

5

| 1 | Ⓐ Ⓑ Ⓒ Ⓓ Ⓔ | 11 | Ⓐ Ⓑ Ⓒ Ⓓ Ⓔ | 21 | Ⓐ Ⓑ Ⓒ Ⓓ Ⓔ | 31 | Ⓐ Ⓑ Ⓒ Ⓓ Ⓔ |
| 2 | Ⓐ Ⓑ Ⓒ Ⓓ Ⓔ | 12 | Ⓐ Ⓑ Ⓒ Ⓓ Ⓔ | 22 | Ⓐ Ⓑ Ⓒ Ⓓ Ⓔ | 32 | Ⓐ Ⓑ Ⓒ Ⓓ Ⓔ |
| 3 | Ⓐ Ⓑ Ⓒ Ⓓ Ⓔ | 13 | Ⓐ Ⓑ Ⓒ Ⓓ Ⓔ | 23 | Ⓐ Ⓑ Ⓒ Ⓓ Ⓔ | 33 | Ⓐ Ⓑ Ⓒ Ⓓ Ⓔ |
| 4 | Ⓐ Ⓑ Ⓒ Ⓓ Ⓔ | 14 | Ⓐ Ⓑ Ⓒ Ⓓ Ⓔ | 24 | Ⓐ Ⓑ Ⓒ Ⓓ Ⓔ | 34 | Ⓐ Ⓑ Ⓒ Ⓓ Ⓔ |
| 5 | Ⓐ Ⓑ Ⓒ Ⓓ Ⓔ | 15 | Ⓐ Ⓑ Ⓒ Ⓓ Ⓔ | 25 | Ⓐ Ⓑ Ⓒ Ⓓ Ⓔ | 35 | Ⓐ Ⓑ Ⓒ Ⓓ Ⓔ |
| 6 | Ⓐ Ⓑ Ⓒ Ⓓ Ⓔ | 16 | Ⓐ Ⓑ Ⓒ Ⓓ Ⓔ | 26 | Ⓐ Ⓑ Ⓒ Ⓓ Ⓔ | 36 | Ⓐ Ⓑ Ⓒ Ⓓ Ⓔ |
| 7 | Ⓐ Ⓑ Ⓒ Ⓓ Ⓔ | 17 | Ⓐ Ⓑ Ⓒ Ⓓ Ⓔ | 27 | Ⓐ Ⓑ Ⓒ Ⓓ Ⓔ | 37 | Ⓐ Ⓑ Ⓒ Ⓓ Ⓔ |
| 8 | Ⓐ Ⓑ Ⓒ Ⓓ Ⓔ | 18 | Ⓐ Ⓑ Ⓒ Ⓓ Ⓔ | 28 | Ⓐ Ⓑ Ⓒ Ⓓ Ⓔ | 38 | Ⓐ Ⓑ Ⓒ Ⓓ Ⓔ |
| 9 | Ⓐ Ⓑ Ⓒ Ⓓ Ⓔ | 19 | Ⓐ Ⓑ Ⓒ Ⓓ Ⓔ | 29 | Ⓐ Ⓑ Ⓒ Ⓓ Ⓔ | 39 | Ⓐ Ⓑ Ⓒ Ⓓ Ⓔ |
| 10 | Ⓐ Ⓑ Ⓒ Ⓓ Ⓔ | 20 | Ⓐ Ⓑ Ⓒ Ⓓ Ⓔ | 30 | Ⓐ Ⓑ Ⓒ Ⓓ Ⓔ | | |

# PSAT PRACTICE
# TEST 1

# SECTION 1

Time: 25 Minutes—Turn to Section 1 (page 339) of your answer sheet to answer the questions in this section.
   24 Questions

**Directions:** For each question in this section, select the best answer from among the choices given and fill in the corresponding circle on the answer sheet.

---

Each sentence below has one or two blanks, each blank indicating that something has been omitted. Beneath the sentence are five words or sets of words labeled A through E. Choose the word or set of words that, when inserted in the sentence, best fits the meaning of the sentence as a whole.

Example:

Hoping to _____ the dispute, negotiators proposed a compromise that they felt would be _____ to both labor and management.

(A) enforce...useful
(B) end...divisive
(C) overcome...unattractive
(D) extend...satisfactory
(E) resolve...acceptable

Ⓐ Ⓑ Ⓒ Ⓓ ●

---

1. Athens was ruled not by kings and emperors as was common among other _____ at the time, but by a citizenry, which _____ fully in the affairs of the city.

   (A) committees...cooperated
   (B) tribes...engaged
   (C) cities...revolutionized
   (D) populations...applied
   (E) societies...participated

2. Fossils are _____ in rock formations that were once soft and have _____ with the passage of time.

   (A) abolished...corresponded
   (B) interactive...communicated
   (C) preserved...hardened
   (D) created...revived
   (E) discounted...deteriorated

3. The social-cultural trends of the 1960s _____ not only the relative affluence of the postwar period but also the coming to maturity of a generation that was a product of that _____.

   (A) dominated...movement
   (B) reflected...prosperity
   (C) accentuated...depression
   (D) cautioned...decade
   (E) accepted...revolution

4. Rotation of crops helps to _____ soil fertility and soil usefulness for a long period of time.

   (A) conserve
   (B) disperse
   (C) employ
   (D) research
   (E) shorten

5. Some illnesses, such as malaria, which have been virtually eliminated in the United States, are still _____ in many places abroad.

   (A) discussed
   (B) prevalent
   (C) scarce
   (D) unknown
   (E) hospitalized

6. With lack of _____, almost anyone can develop the disease we call alcoholism, just as any of us can contract pneumonia by _____ exposing ourselves to its causes.

   (A) advice...carefully
   (B) control...foolishly
   (C) opportunity...knowingly
   (D) sympathy...fortunately
   (E) conscience...happily

GO ON TO THE NEXT PAGE

7. Use of air conditioners and other electrical apparatus had to be _____ that summer because of the _____ of the generating system.

    (A) postulated…reaction
    (B) curtailed…inefficiency
    (C) implemented…residuals
    (D) augmented…responsiveness
    (E) manipulated…intensity

8. The Bavarians consider beer their national beverage, yet at the same time they do not view it as a drink but rather as _____ bread—a staple food.

    (A) fresh
    (B) liquid
    (C) stale
    (D) bitter
    (E) costly

GO ON TO THE NEXT PAGE >

Each passage below is followed by questions based on its content. Answer the questions on the basis of what is stated or implied in each passage and in any introductory material that may be provided.

**Questions 9–10 are based on the following passage.**

1    Despite the many categories of the historian, there are only two ages of man. The first age, the age from the beginnings of recorded time to the present, is the age of the cave man. It is the age of war. It is today. The second age,
5 still only a prospect, is the age of civilized man. The test of civilized man will be represented by his ability to use his inventiveness for his own good by substituting world law for world anarchy. That second age is still within the reach of the individual in our time. It is not a part-time job, however.
10 It calls for total awareness, total commitment.

9. The title below that best expresses the ideas of this passage is:

(A) The Historian at Work
(B) The Dangers of All-out War
(C) The Power of World Anarchy
(D) Mankind on the Threshold
(E) The Decline of Civilization

10. The author's attitude toward the possibility of man's reaching an age of civilization is one of

(A) limited hope
(B) complete despair
(C) marked uncertainty
(D) complacency
(E) anger

**Questions 11–12 are based on the following passage.**

1    Readers in the past seem to have been more patient than the readers of today. There were few diversions, and they had more time to read novels of a length that seems to us now inordinate. It may be that they were not irritated
5 by the digressions and irrelevances that interrupted the narration. But some of the novels that suffer from these defects are among the greatest that have ever been written. It is deplorable that on this account they should be less and less read.

11. The title below that best expresses the ideas of this passage is:

(A) Defects of Today's Novels
(B) Novel Reading Then and Now
(C) The Great Novel
(D) The Impatient Reader of Novels
(E) Decline in Education

12. The author implies that

(A) authors of the past did not use narration to any extent
(B) great novels are usually long
(C) digressions and irrelevances are characteristic of modern novels
(D) readers of the past were more capable
(E) people today have more pastimes than formerly

GO ON TO THE NEXT PAGE

The two passages below are followed by questions based on their content and on the relationship between the two passages. Answer the questions on the basis of what is <u>stated</u> or <u>implied</u> in the passages and in any introductory material that may be provided.

## Questions 13–24 are based on the following passages.

*The following two passages are about science. The first describes science in general, and the second focuses on the subject of physics, one of the disciplines of science.*

### Passage 1

Science, like everything else that man has created, exists, of course, to gratify certain human needs and desires. The fact that it has been steadily pursued for so many centuries, that it has attracted an ever-wider extent of attention, and that it
5 is now the dominant intellectual interest of mankind, shows that it appeals to a very powerful and persistent group of appetites. It is not difficult to say what these appetites are, at least in their main divisions. Science is valued for its practical advantages, it is valued because it gratifies curiosity,
10 and it is valued because it provides the imagination with objects of great aesthetic charm. This last consideration is of the least importance, so far as the layman is concerned, although it is probably the most important consideration of all to scientific men. It is quite obvious, on the other
15 hand, that the bulk of mankind value science chiefly for the practical advantages it brings with it.

This conclusion is borne out by everything we know about the origin of science. Science seems to have come into existence merely for its bearings on practical life.
20 More than two thousand years before the beginning of the Christian era both the Babylonians and the Egyptians were in possession of systematic methods of measuring space and time. They had a rudimentary geometry and a rudimentary astronomy. This rudimentary science arose to
25 meet the practical needs of an agricultural population. Their geometry resulted from the measurements made necessary by the problems of land surveying. The cultivation of crops, dependent on the seasons, made a calendar almost a necessity. The day, as a unit of time, was, of course, imposed by
30 nature. The movement of the moon conveniently provided another unit, the month, which was reckoned from one new moon to the next. Twelve of these months were taken to constitute a year, and the necessary adjustments were made from time to time by putting in extra months.

### Passage 2

35 Let's be honest right at the start. Physics is neither particularly easy to comprehend nor easy to love, but then again, *what*—or for that matter, *who*—is? For most of us it is a new vision, a different way of understanding with its own scales, rhythms, and forms. And yet, as with *Macbeth, Mona Lisa*,
40 or *La Traviata*, physics has its rewards. Surely you have already somehow prejudged this science. It's all too easy to compartmentalize our human experience: science in one box, music, art, and literature in other boxes.

The Western mind delights in little boxes—life is
45 easier to analyze when it's presented in small pieces in small compartments (we call it specialization). It is our traditional way of seeing the trees and missing the forest. The label on the box for physics too often reads "Caution: Not for Common Consumption" or "Free from Sentiment."
50 If you can, please tear off that label and discard the box or we will certainly, sooner or later, bore each other to death. There is nothing more tedious than the endless debate between humanist and scientist on whose vision is truer; each of us is less for what we lack of the other.
55 It is pointless and even worse to separate physics from the body of all creative work, to pluck it out from history, to shear it from philosophy, and then to present it pristine pure, all-knowing, and infallible. We know nothing of what will be with absolute certainty. There is no scientific tome of unas-
60 sailable, immutable truth. Yet what little we do know about physics reveals an inspiring grandeur and intricate beauty.

13. The main idea of Passage 1 is that

(A) science originated and developed because of the practical advantages it offers
(B) the Egyptians and the Babylonians used scientific methods to meet the practical needs of feeding their people
(C) the use of geometry and astronomy are very important for agricultural development
(D) science has a different value for scientists than it does for the rest of the population
(E) science is valued not only for its practical contributions to mankind but also for its potential to stir the imagination

14. According to Passage 1,

(A) the Babylonians and the Egyptians were the first to use scientific methods
(B) the Christians were the first to have a calender
(C) a 12-month calendar was first used by the Egyptians or Babylonians
(D) the Christians preceded the Babylonians and Egyptians
(E) scientists are probably more attracted to the charm of science than to its practical benefits

15. The author of Passage 1 implies that scientists are generally

(A) sociable
(B) imaginative
(C) practical
(D) philosophical
(E) arrogant

GO ON TO THE NEXT PAGE

16. The word "rudimentary" in line 24 means

    (A) sophisticated
    (B) flawed
    (C) unworkable
    (D) basic
    (E) coarse

17. According to the author of Passage 2, what does the label on the box for physics suggest about physics?

    (A) It is a dangerous area of study.
    (B) It is a cause for great excitement.
    (C) It is uninteresting to the ordinary person.
    (D) It is difficult to understand because it is completely subjective.
    (E) It is a subject that should be elective but not required.

18. What statement does the author of Passage 2 make about physics?

    (A) It should be recognized for its unique beauty.
    (B) It is a boring course of study.
    (C) It appeals only to the Western mind.
    (D) It is superior to music, art, and literature.
    (E) It is unpopular with people who are romantic.

19. What is the main idea of Passage 2?

    (A) Scientists contribute more to mankind than do humanists.
    (B) The Western mind is more precise than other minds.
    (C) Complete vision needs both the scientist and the humanist.
    (D) Humanists and scientists share no common ground.
    (E) Physics is as important as other science.

20. In which manner does the author of Passage 2 address his audience?

    (A) affectionately
    (B) arrogantly
    (C) humorously
    (D) cynically
    (E) frankly

21. In line 47, the phrase "seeing the trees and missing the forest" means

    (A) putting experiences into categories
    (B) viewing the world too narrowly
    (C) analyzing scientific discoveries
    (D) making judgments too hastily
    (E) ignoring the beauty of natural surroundings

22. The author of Passage 2 leaves out an important aspect of the subject that, however, is contained in Passage 1. This aspect is the

    (A) reaction of laymen to physics
    (B) the specialization in science
    (C) the purity of physics
    (D) the practical applications of physics
    (E) the arguments between the humanists and scientists

23. Which device or method does the author of Passage 2 use that is not used by the author of Passage 1?

    (A) analogy through objects
    (B) critique
    (C) contrast with respect to perceived values
    (D) historical referencing
    (E) examples to support a claim

24. Which subject is not directly mentioned in either passage?

    (A) agriculture
    (B) astronomy
    (C) art
    (D) philosophy
    (E) chemistry

# STOP

If you finish before time is called, you may check your work on this section only.
Do not turn to any other section in the test.

# SECTION 2

Time: 25 Minutes—Turn to Section 2 (page 339) of your answer sheet to answer the questions in this section.
20 Questions

**Directions:** For this section, solve each problem and decide which is the best of the choices given. Fill in the corresponding circle on the answer sheet. You may use any available space for scratchwork.

**Notes:**

1. The use of a calculator is permitted.
2. All numbers used are real numbers.
3. Figures that accompany problems in this test are intended to provide information useful in solving the problems. They are drawn as accurately as possible EXCEPT when it is stated in a specific problem that the figure is not drawn to scale. All figures lie in a plane unless otherwise indicated.
4. Unless otherwise specified, the domain of any function $f$ is assumed to be the set of all real numbers $x$ for which $f(x)$ is a real number.

**REFERENCE INFORMATION**

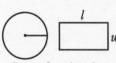  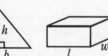  

$A = \pi r^2$    $A = lw$    $A = \frac{1}{2}bh$    $V = lwh$    $V = \pi r^2 h$    $c^2 = a^2 + b^2$    *Special Right Triangles*
$C = 2\pi r$

The number of degrees of arc in a circle is 360.
The sum of the measures in degrees of the angles of a triangle is 180.

$$\begin{array}{r} 59\Delta \\ -293 \\ \hline \square 97 \end{array}$$

1. In the subtraction problem above, what digit is represented by the □?

(A) 0
(B) 1
(C) 2
(D) 3
(E) 4

2. If $\dfrac{a-b}{b} = \dfrac{1}{2}$, find $\dfrac{a}{b}$

(A) $\dfrac{9}{2}$

(B) $\dfrac{7}{2}$

(C) $\dfrac{5}{2}$

(D) $\dfrac{1}{2}$

(E) $\dfrac{3}{2}$

GO ON TO THE NEXT PAGE

| Number of pounds of force | Height object is raised |
|---|---|
| 3 | 6 feet |
| 6 | 12 feet |
| 9 | 18 feet |

3. In a certain pulley system, the height an object is raised is equal to a constant $c$ times the number of pounds of force exerted. The table above shows some pounds of force and the corresponding height raised. If a particular object is raised 15 feet, how many pounds of force were exerted?

(A) $3\frac{3}{4}$

(B) 7

(C) $7\frac{1}{2}$

(D) 8

(E) 11

$P$

5. The above line is marked with 12 points. The distance between any 2 adjacent points is 3 units. Find the total number of points that are more than 19 units away from point $P$.

(A) 2
(B) 3
(C) 4
(D) 5
(E) 6

4. If $\frac{y}{3}$, $\frac{y}{4}$ and $\frac{y}{7}$ represent integers, then $y$ could be

(A) 42
(B) 56
(C) 70
(D) 84
(E) 126

6. Given $(a + 2, a - 2) = [a]$ for all integers $a$, $(6, 2) =$

(A) [3]
(B) [4]
(C) [5]
(D) [6]
(E) [8]

GO ON TO THE NEXT PAGE

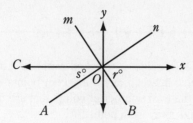

*Note:* Figure is not drawn to scale.

7. If $mB \perp nA$ in the figure above and $COx$ is a straight line, find the value of $r + s$.

(A) 180
(B) 135
(C) 110
(D) 90
(E) The answer cannot be determined from the information given.

9. One out of 4 students at Ridge High School studies German. If there are 2,800 students at the school, how many students do *not* study German?

(A) 2,500
(B) 2,100
(C) 1,800
(D) 1,000
(E) 700

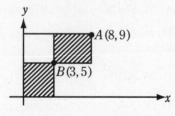

8. Points $A$ and $B$ have coordinates as shown in the figure above. Find the combined area of the two shaded rectangles.

(A) 20
(B) 26
(C) 32
(D) 35
(E) 87

10. The cost of a drive-in movie is \$$y$ per vehicle. A group of friends in a van shared the admission cost by paying \$0.40 each. If 6 more friends had gone along, everyone would have paid only \$0.25 each. What is the value of \$$y$?

(A) \$4
(B) \$6
(C) \$8
(D) \$10
(E) \$12

GO ON TO THE NEXT PAGE

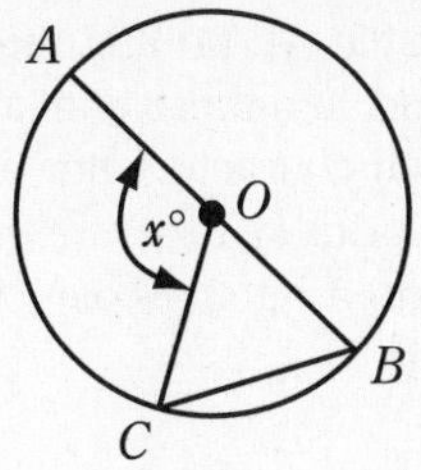

**11.** If $AB$ is a diameter of circle $O$ in the figure above, and $CB = OB$, then $\dfrac{x}{6} =$

(A) 60
(B) 30
(C) 20
(D) 10
(E) 5

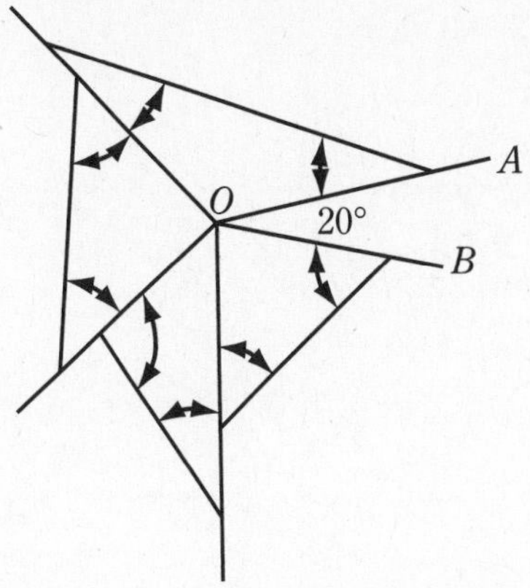

**13.** If $\angle AOB = 20°$ in the figure above and $O$ is a common vertex of the four triangles, find the sum of the measures of the marked angles in the triangles.

(A) 380
(B) 560
(C) 740
(D) 760
(E) 920

**12.** A certain store is selling an $80 radio for $64. If a different radio had a list price of $200 and was discounted at $1\frac{1}{2}$ times the percent discount on the $80 model, what would its selling price be?

(A) $90
(B) $105
(C) $120
(D) $140
(E) $160

**14.** Some integers in set X are odd.

If the statement above is true, which of the following must also be true?

(A) If an integer is odd, it is in set X.
(B) If an integer is even, it is in set X.
(C) All integers in set X are odd.
(D) All integers in set X are even.
(E) Not all integers in set X are even.

GO ON TO THE NEXT PAGE

**15.** If $|y+3| < 3$, then

(A) $0 > y > -6$
(B) $y > 3$
(C) $3 > y > 0$
(D) $y = -1$
(E) $y = -2$

**17.** A certain printer can print at the rate of 80 characters per second, and there is an average (arithmetic mean) of 2,400 characters per page. If the printer continued to print at this rate, how many *minutes* would it take to print an *M*-page report?

(A) $\dfrac{M}{30}$

(B) $\dfrac{M}{60}$

(C) $\dfrac{M}{2}$

(D) $\dfrac{2}{M}$

(E) $\dfrac{60}{M}$

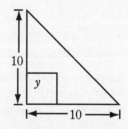

**16.** In the figure above, the area of the square is equal to $\frac{1}{5}$ the area of the triangle. Find the value of $y$, the side of the square.

(A) 2
(B) 4
(C) 5
(D) $2\sqrt{5}$
(E) $\sqrt{10}$

**18.** A certain satellite passed over Washington, D.C., at midnight on Friday. If the satellite completes an orbit every 5 hours, when is the next day that it will pass over Washington, D.C., at midnight?

(A) Monday
(B) Wednesday
(C) Friday
(D) Saturday
(E) Sunday

GO ON TO THE NEXT PAGE

**19.** The price of a car is reduced by 30 percent. The resulting price is reduced 40 percent. The two reductions are equal to one reduction of

(A) 28%
(B) 42%
(C) 50%
(D) 58%
(E) 70%

**20.** In the figure above, the circle is inscribed in the equilateral triangle. If the diameter of the circle is 2, what is the total shaded area?

(A) $3\sqrt{3} - \pi$
(B) $3\sqrt{3} - 4\pi$
(C) $3\sqrt{3} - \dfrac{3\pi}{2}$
(D) $6\sqrt{3} - \dfrac{3\pi}{2}$
(E) $108 - \pi$

# STOP
If you finish before time is called, you may check your work on this section only.
Do not turn to any other section in the test.

# SECTION 3

Time: 25 Minutes—Turn to Section 3 (page 339) of your answer sheet to answer the questions in this section.
   24 Questions

**Directions:** For each question in this section, select the best answer from among the choices given and fill in the corresponding circle on the answer sheet.

Each sentence below has one or two blanks, each blank indicating that something has been omitted. Beneath the sentence are five words or sets of words labeled A through E. Choose the word or set of words that, when inserted in the sentence, best fits the meaning of the sentence as a whole.

Example:

Hoping to _____ the dispute, negotiators proposed a compromise that they felt would be _____ to both labor and management.

(A) enforce...useful
(B) end...divisive
(C) overcome...unattractive
(D) extend...satisfactory
(E) resolve...acceptable

Ⓐ Ⓑ Ⓒ Ⓓ ●

25. The Forest Service warned that the spring forest fire season was in full swing and urged that _____ caution be exercised in wooded areas.

(A) moderate
(B) scant
(C) customary
(D) extreme
(E) reasonable

26. The Classical age of Greek art ended with the defeat of Athens by Sparta; the _____ effect of the long war was the weakening and _____ of the Greek spirit.

(A) cumulative...corrosion
(B) immediate...storing
(C) imagined...cooperation
(D) delayed...rebuilding
(E) intuitive...cancelation

27. Mary, bored by even the briefest periods of idleness, was _____ switching from one activity to another.

(A) hesitantly
(B) lazily
(C) slowly
(D) surprisingly
(E) continually

28. The bee _____ the nectar from the different flowers and then _____ the liquid into honey.

(A) consumes...conforms
(B) observes...pours
(C) rejects...solidifies
(D) crushes...injects
(E) extracts...converts

29. The plan turned out to be _____ because it would have required more financial backing than was available.

(A) intractable
(B) chaotic
(C) irreversible
(D) untenable
(E) superfluous

GO ON TO THE NEXT PAGE

The passages below are followed by questions based on their content; questions following a pair of related passages may also be based on the relationship between the paired passages. Answer the questions on the basis of what is <u>stated</u> or <u>implied</u> in the passages and in any introductory material that may be provided.

**Questions 30–33 are based on the following passages.**

**Passage 1**

1 All the arts contain some preposterous fiction, but the theatre is the most preposterous of all. Imagine asking us to believe that we are in Venice in the sixteenth century, and that Mr. Billington is a Moor, and that he is about to
5 stifle the much admired Miss Huckaby with a pillow; and imagine trying to make us believe that people ever talked in blank verse—more than that: that people were ever so marvelously articulate. The theatre is a lily that inexplicably arises from a jungle of weedy falsities. Yet it is precisely
10 from the tension produced by all this absurdity that it is able to create such poetry, power, enchantment and truth.

**Passage 2**

The theater is a venue for the most realistic and direct fiction ever imagined. So many of the contemporary plays make us realize how we are living our lives and perhaps
15 how we should change them. From these "reality shows" we can feel all the poverty, despair, and unfairness in our world which then affords us the opportunity for change for the better.

30. Which statement best illustrates the author's meaning when he says, "The theatre is a lily that inexplicably arises from a jungle of weedy falsities"?

(A) The theatre is the "flower" among the arts.
(B) The theatre helps to raise public taste to a higher level.
(C) The theatre can create an illusion of truth from improbable situations.
(D) The theatre has overcome the unsavory reputation of earlier periods.
(E) In the theatre, real acting talent can be developed from unpromising material.

31. The author's feeling toward contemporary plays is that they

(A) have no value for the spectator
(B) can be appreciated by everyone
(C) elicit the negative aspects of life
(D) have a long-lasting effect on us
(E) do not deal with poetry or truth

32. The two passages are similar in that

(A) both describe specific examples from specific plays
(B) both are completely objective in their respective arguments
(C) both authors of them believe that they depict the accuracy of the particular time
(D) both authors show the same intensity and passion in their argument
(E) both show that something positive can come out of something negative

33. Which of the following is true?

(A) One author would not disagree with the other's premise.
(B) The author of Paragraph 1 despises all characters in 16th century plays.
(C) The author of Paragraph 1 believes that people in the 16th century were very articulate.
(D) Analogies to objects and places is a literary device used in only one passage.
(E) The author of Paragraph 2 believes that the theater compromises reality.

GO ON TO THE NEXT PAGE

**Questions 34–38 are based on the following passage.**

*The following passage deals with adjustment to one's surroundings and the terms and theory associated with such adjustment.*

As in the case of so many words used by the biologist and physiologist, the word acclimatization is hard to define. With increase in knowledge and understanding, meanings of words change. Originally the term acclimatization was
5 taken to mean only the ability of human beings or animals or plants to accustom themselves to new and strange climatic conditions, primarily altered temperature. A person or a wolf moves to a hot climate and is uncomfortable there, but after a time is better able to withstand the heat. But
10 aside from temperature, there are other aspects of climate. A person or an animal may become adjusted to living at higher altitudes than those it was originally accustomed to. At really high altitudes, such as aviators may be exposed to, the low atmospheric pressure becomes a factor of
15 primary importance. In changing to a new environment, a person may, therefore, meet new conditions of temperature or pressure, and in addition may have to contend with different chemical surroundings. On high mountains, the amount of oxygen in the atmosphere may be relatively
20 small; in crowded cities, a person may become exposed to relatively high concentrations of carbon dioxide or even carbon monoxide, and in various areas may be exposed to conditions in which the water content of the atmosphere is extremely high or extremely low. Thus in the case of
25 humans, animals, and even plants, the concept of acclimatization includes the phenomena of increased toleration of high or low temperature, of altered pressure, and of changes in the chemical environment.
Let us define acclimatization, therefore, as the process
30 in which an organism or a part of an organism becomes inured to an environment which is normally unsuitable to it or lethal for it. By and large, acclimatization is a relatively slow process. The term should not be taken to include relatively rapid adjustments such as our sense organs are
35 constantly making. This type of adjustment is commonly referred to by physiologists as "adaptation." Thus our touch sense soon becomes accustomed to the pressure of our clothes and we do not feel them; we soon fail to hear the ticking of a clock; obnoxious orders after a time fail to make
40 much impression on us, and our eyes in strong light rapidly become insensitive.
The fundamental fact about acclimatization is that all animals and plants have some capacity to adjust themselves to changes in their environment. This is one of the most
45 remarkable characteristics of living organisms, a characteristic for which it is extremely difficult to find explanations.

34. It can be inferred from the reading selection that

(A) every change in the environment requires acclimatization by living things.
(B) plants and animals are more alike than they are different.
(C) biologists and physiologists study essentially the same things.
(D) the explanation of acclimatization is specific to each plant and animal.
(E) as science develops, the connotation of terms may change.

35. According to the reading selection, acclimatization

(A) is similar to adaptation.
(B) is more important today than it formerly was.
(C) involves positive as well as negative adjustment.
(D) may be involved with a part of an organism but not with the whole organism.
(E) is more difficult to explain with the more complex present-day environment than formerly.

36. By inference from the reading selection, which one of the following would *not* require the process of acclimatization?

(A) an ocean fish placed in a lake
(B) a skin diver making a deep dive
(C) an airplane pilot making a high-altitude flight
(D) a person going from daylight into a darkened room
(E) a businessman moving from Denver, Colorado, to New Orleans, Louisiana

37. The word "inured" in line 31 most likely means

(A) exposed
(B) accustomed
(C) attracted
(D) associated
(E) in love with

38. According to the passage, a major distinction between acclimatization and adaptation is that acclimatization

(A) is more important than adaptation.
(B) is relatively slow and adaptation is relatively rapid.
(C) applies to adjustments while adaptation does not apply to adjustments.
(D) applies to terrestrial animals and adaptation to aquatic animals.
(E) is applicable to all animals and plants and adaptation only to higher animals and man.

GO ON TO THE NEXT PAGE

**Questions 39–48 are based on the following passage.**

*The following passage is based on B. F. Skinner's book* About Behaviorism *and discusses the pros and cons of Skinner's work on behaviorism and the various points made by Skinner.*

In his compact and modestly titled book *About Behaviorism*, Dr. B.F. Skinner, the noted behavioral psychologist, lists the 20 most salient objections to "behaviorism or the science of behavior," and he has gone on to answer them both
5 implicitly and explicitly. He has answers and explanations for everyone.

For instance, to those who object "that behaviorists deny the existence of feelings, sensations, ideas, and other features of mental life," Dr. Skinner concedes that "a good
10 deal of clarification" is in order. What such people are really decrying is "methodological behaviorism," an earlier stage of the science whose goal was precisely to close off mentalistic explanations of behavior, if only to counteract the 2,500-year-old influence of mentalism. But Dr. Skinner
15 is a "radical behaviorist." "Radical behaviorism...takes a different line. It does not deny the possibility of self-observation or self-knowledge or its possible usefulness... It restores introspection...."

For instance, to those who object that behaviorism
20 "neglects innate endowment and argues that all behavior is acquired during the lifetime of the individual," Dr. Skinner expresses puzzlement. Granted, "A few behaviorists...have minimized if not denied a genetic contribution, and in their enthusiasm for what may be done through the environ-
25 ment, others have no doubt acted as if a genetic endowment were unimportant, but few would contend that behavior is 'endlessly malleable.' " And Dr. Skinner himself, sounding as often as not like some latter-day Social Darwinist, gives as much weight to the "contingencies of survival" in the
30 evolution of the human species as to the "contingencies of reinforcement" in the lifetime of the individual.

For instance, to those who claim that behaviorism "cannot explain creative achievements—in art, for example, or in music, literature, science, or mathematics"—Dr.
35 Skinner provides an intriguing ellipsis. "Contingencies of reinforcement also resemble contingencies of survival in the production of novelty....In both natural selection and operant conditioning the appearance of 'mutations' is crucial. Until recently, species evolved because of random changes
40 in genes or chromosomes, but the geneticist may arrange conditions under which mutations are particularly likely to occur. We can also discover some of the sources of new forms of behavior which undergo selection by prevailing contingencies or reinforcement, and fortunately the creative
45 artist or thinker has other ways of introducing novelties."

And so go Dr. Skinner's answers to the 20 questions he poses—questions that range all the way from asking if behaviorism fails "to account for cognitive processes" to wondering if behaviorism "is indifferent to the warmth and
50 richness of human life, and...is incompatible with the... enjoyment of art, music, and literature and with love for one's fellow men."

But will it wash? Will it serve to silence those critics who have characterized B. F. Skinner variously as a mad,
55 manipulative doctor, as a naive 19th-century positivist, as an unscientific technician, and as an arrogant social

engineer? There is no gainsaying that *About Behaviorism* is an unusually compact summary of both the history and "the philosophy of the science of human behavior" (as Dr.
60 Skinner insists on defining behaviorism). It is a veritable artwork of organization. And anyone who reads it will never again be able to think of behaviorism as a simplistic philosophy that reduces human beings to black boxes responding robotlike to external stimuli.

65 Still, there are certain quandaries that *About Behaviorism* does not quite dispel. For one thing, though Dr. Skinner makes countless references to the advances in experiments with human beings that behaviorism has made since it first began running rats through mazes many decades ago, he
70 fails to provide a single illustration of these advances. And though it may be true, as Dr. Skinner argues, that one can extrapolate from pigeons to people, it would be reassuring to be shown precisely how.

More important, he has not satisfactorily rebutted the
75 basic criticism that behaviorism "is scientistic rather than scientific. It merely emulates the sciences." A true science doesn't predict what it will accomplish when it is firmly established as a science, not even when it is posing as "the philosophy of that science." A true science simply advances
80 rules for testing hypotheses.

But Dr. Skinner predicts that behaviorism will produce the means to save human society from impending disaster. Two key concepts that keep accreting to that prediction are "manipulation" and "control." And so, while he reassures
85 us quite persuasively that his science would practice those concepts benignly, one can't shake off the suspicion that he was advancing a science just in order to save society by means of "manipulation" and "control." And that is not so reassuring.

39. According to the passage, Skinner would be most likely to agree that

(A) studies of animal behavior are applicable to human behavior
(B) introspection should be used widely to analyze conscious experience
(C) behaviorism is basically scientistic
(D) behavioristic principles and techniques will be of no use in preventing widespread disaster
(E) an individual can form an infinite number of sentences that he has never heard spoken

40. The reader may infer that

(A) Skinner's philosophy is completely democratic in its methodology
(B) behaviorism, in its early form, and mentalism were essentially the same
(C) the book *About Behaviorism* is difficult to understand because it is not well structured
(D) methodological behaviorism preceded both mentalism and radical behaviorism
(E) the author of the article has found glaring weaknesses in Skinner's defense of behaviorism

GO ON TO THE NEXT PAGE

**41.** When Skinner speaks of "contingencies of survival" (line 29) and "contingencies of reinforcement" (lines 30–31), the word "contingency" most accurately means

(A) frequency of occurrence
(B) something incidental
(C) a quota
(D) dependence on chance
(E) one of an assemblage

**42.** The author of the article says that Skinner sounds "like some latter-day Social Darwinist" (line 28) most probably because Skinner

(A) is a radical behaviorist who has differed from methodological behaviorists
(B) has predicted that human society faces disaster
(C) has been characterized as a 19th-century positivist
(D) has studied animal behavior as applicable to human behavior
(E) believes that the geneticist may arrange conditions for mutations to occur

**43.** It can be inferred from the passage that "extrapolate" (line 72) means

(A) to gather unknown information by extending known information
(B) to determine how one organism may be used to advantage by another organism
(C) to insert or introduce between other things or parts
(D) to change the form or the behavior of one thing to match the form or behavior of another thing
(E) to transfer an organ of a living thing into another living thing

**44.** One *cannot* conclude from the passage that

(A) Skinner is a radical behaviorist but not a methodological behaviorist
(B) *About Behavior* does not show how behaviorists have improved in experimentation with human beings
(C) only human beings are used in experiments conducted by behaviorists
(D) methodological behaviorism rejects the introspective approach
(E) the book being discussed is to the point and well organized

**45.** In Skinner's statement that "few would contend that behavior is 'endlessly malleable' " (lines 26–27), he means that

(A) genetic influences are of primary importance in shaping human behavior
(B) environmental influences may be frequently supplemented by genetic influences
(C) self-examination is the most effective way of improving a behavior pattern
(D) the learning process continues throughout life
(E) psychologists will never come to a common conclusion about the best procedure for studying and improving human behavior

**46.** According to the author, which of the following is true concerning *scientistic* and *scientific* disciplines?

I. The scientific one develops the rules for testing the theory; the scientistic one does not.
II. There is no element of prediction in scientistic disciplines.
III. Science never assumes a philosophical nature.

(A) I only
(B) I and III only
(C) I and II only
(D) II and III only
(E) I, II, and III

**47.** The word "veritable" (line 60) means

(A) abundant
(B) careful
(C) political
(D) true
(E) believable

**48.** The statement that best summarizes the author's attitude toward Skinner's prediction (lines 81–82) is that

(A) the consistency of Skinner's arguments lends credibility to his ideas
(B) manipulation and control are the only weak links in an otherwise solid theory
(C) Skinner's prediction lacks credibility because he has no supporting evidence
(D) scientists practicing manipulation and control misled Skinner about their true agenda
(E) Skinner's true agenda is unknown, which raises troubling questions about how manipulation and control might be applied in the future

# STOP

If you finish before time is called, you may check your work on this section only.
Do not turn to any other section in the test.

# SECTION 4

Time: 25 Minutes—Turn to Section 4 (page 340) of your answer sheet to answer the questions in this section.
18 Questions

**Directions:** This section contains two types of questions. You have 25 minutes to complete both types. For questions 21–28, solve each problem and decide which is the best of the choices given. Fill in the corresponding circle on the answer sheet. You may use any available space for scratchwork.

**Notes:**

1. The use of a calculator is permitted.
2. All numbers used are real numbers.
3. Figures that accompany problems in this test are intended to provide information useful in solving the problems. They are drawn as accurately as possible EXCEPT when it is stated in a specific problem that the figure is not drawn to scale. All figures lie in a plane unless otherwise indicated.
4. Unless otherwise specified, the domain of any function $f$ is assumed to be the set of all real numbers $x$ for which $f(x)$ is a real number.

**REFERENCE INFORMATION**

  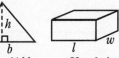 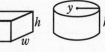   

$A = \pi r^2$   $A = lw$   $A = \frac{1}{2}bh$   $V = lwh$   $V = \pi r^2 h$   $c^2 = a^2 + b^2$   *Special Right Triangles*
$C = 2\pi r$

The number of degrees of arc in a circle is 360.
The sum of the measures in degrees of the angles of a triangle is 180.

---

21. In the equation $5\sqrt{x} + 14 = 20$, the value of $x$ is

    (A) $\sqrt{\dfrac{6}{5}}$

    (B) $\dfrac{34^2}{25^2}$

    (C) $6 - \sqrt{5}$

    (D) $\dfrac{6}{5}$

    (E) $\dfrac{36}{25}$

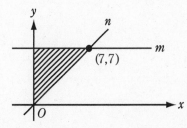

22. In the figure above, $m$ is parallel to the $x$-axis. All of the following points lie in the shaded area EXCEPT

    (A) (4,3)
    (B) (1,2)
    (C) (5,6)
    (D) (4,5)
    (E) (2,5)

GO ON TO THE NEXT PAGE

23. At Lincoln County High School, 36 students are taking either calculus or physics or both, and 10 students are taking both calculus and physics. If there are 31 students in the calculus class, how many students are in the physics class?

(A) 14
(B) 15
(C) 16
(D) 17
(E) 18

24. Mr. Simmons stated that if $a^2 > b^2$ where $a$ and $b$ are real, then it follows that $a > b$. Mr. Simmons', statement would be refuted if $(a, b) =$

(A) (2,3)
(B) (3,2)
(C) (4, −2)
(D) (−4, −2)
(E) (−2, −3)

25. Which of the following is always true for real numbers $a$, $b$, and $c$?

I. $\sqrt{a + b} = \sqrt{a} + \sqrt{b}$
II. $a^2 + b^2 = (a+b)^2$
III. $a^b + a^c = a^{(b+c)}$

(A) I only
(B) II only
(C) III only
(D) I, II, III
(E) neither I, II or III

*Question 6 refers to the following:*

$$R = \{x : 1 \geq x \geq -1\}$$
$$S = \{x : x \geq 1\}$$

26. The number of elements that is (are) common to both R and S is (are)

(A) 0
(B) 1
(C) 2
(D) 3
(E) infinite

GO ON TO THE NEXT PAGE

27. Two lines in a plane are represented by $y = x - 1$ and $2x + 5y = 9$. The coordinates of the point at which the lines intersect are

(A) (2,1)
(B) (1,2)
(C) (2,5)
(D) (5,2)
(E) (3,5)

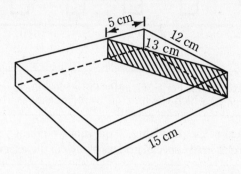

28. The rectangular box above has a rectangular dividing wall inside, as shown. The dividing wall has an area of 39 cm$^2$. What is the volume of the larger compartment?

(A) 90 cm$^3$
(B) 180 cm$^3$
(C) 360 cm$^3$
(D) 450 cm$^3$
(E) 540 cm$^3$

GO ON TO THE NEXT PAGE

**Directions:** For Student-Produced Response questions 29–38, use the grids at the bottom of the answer sheet page on which you have answered questions 21–28.

Each of the remaining 10 questions requires you to solve the problem and enter your answer by marking the circles in the special grid, as shown in the examples below. You may use any available space for scratchwork.

Answer: $\frac{7}{12}$ or 7/12      Answer: 2.5      Answer: 201
Either position is correct.

Write answer in boxes. →

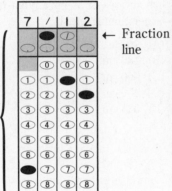

← Fraction line

← Decimal point

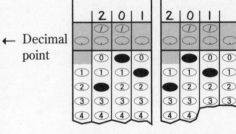

Grid in result. →

Note: You may start your answers in any column, space permitting. Columns not needed should be left blank.

- Mark no more than one oval in any column.

- Because the answer sheet will be machine-scored, **you will receive credit only if the ovals are filled in correctly.**

- Although not required, it is suggested that you write your answer in the boxes at the top of the columns to help you fill in the ovals accurately.

- Some problems may have more than one correct answer. In such cases, grid only one answer.

- No question has a negative answer.

- **Mixed numbers** such as $2\frac{1}{2}$ must be gridded as 2.5 or 5/2. (If ▢ is gridded, it will be interpreted as $\frac{21}{2}$, not $2\frac{1}{2}$.)

- <u>Decimal Accuracy</u>: If you obtain a decimal answer, **enter the most accurate value the grid will accommodate.** For example, if you obtain an answer such as 0.6666..., you should record the result as .666 or .667. **Less accurate values such as .66 or .67 are not acceptable.**

Acceptable ways to grid $\frac{2}{3}$ = .6666...

29. $\left(\frac{1}{2} - \frac{1}{3}\right) + \left(\frac{1}{3} - \frac{1}{4}\right) + \left(\frac{1}{4} - \frac{1}{5}\right) +$

$\left(\frac{1}{5} - \frac{1}{6}\right) + \left(\frac{1}{6} - \frac{1}{7}\right) + \left(\frac{1}{7} - \frac{1}{8}\right) +$

$\left(\frac{1}{8} - \frac{1}{9}\right)$ is equal to what value?

30. If the first two elements of a number series are 1 and 2, and if each succeeding term is found by multiplying the two terms immediately preceding it, what is the fifth element of the series?

GO ON TO THE NEXT PAGE ➡

**31.** If $p$ is $\frac{3}{5}$ of $m$ and if $q$ is $\frac{9}{10}$ of $m$, then, when $q \neq 0$, the ratio $\frac{p}{q}$ is equal to what value?

**32.** If the average (arithmetic mean) of 40, 40, 40, and $z$ is 45, then find the value of $z$.

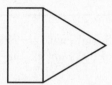

**33.** In the figure above, the perimeter of the equilateral triangle is 39 and the area of the rectangle is 65. What is the perimeter of the rectangle?

| Game | | Darrin | Tom |
|------|---|--------|-----|
| 1 | | 69 | 43 |
| 2 | | 59 | 60 |
| 3 | | 72 | 55 |
| 4 | | 70 | 68 |
| 5 | | 78 | 73 |
| Totals | | 348 | 299 |

**34.** Darrin and Tom played five games of darts. The table above lists the scores for each of the games. By how many points was Tom behind Darrin at the end of the first four games?

**35.** A box contains 17 slips of paper. Each is labeled with a different integer from 1 to 17 inclusive. If 5 even-numbered slips of paper are removed, what fraction of the remaining slips of paper are even numbered?

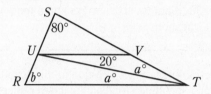

*Note:* Figure is not drawn to scale.

**36.** ∠In *RST* above *UV* ∥ *RT*. Find $b$.

**37.** Rose has earned $44 in 8 days. If she continues to earn at the same daily rate, in how many *more* days will her total earnings be $99?

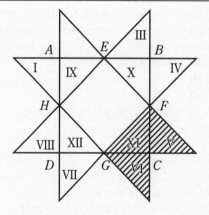

**38.** The areas of triangles I, II, III, IV, V, VI, VII, VIII, IX, X, XI, XII are the same. If the region outlined by the heavy line has area = 256 and the area of square *ABCD* is 128, determine the shaded area.

# STOP

**If you finish before time is called, you may check your work on this section only.
Do not turn to any other section in the test.**

# SECTION 5

Time: 30 Minutes—Turn to Section 5 (page 341) of your answer sheet to answer the questions in this section.
39 Questions

**Directions:** For each question in this section, select the best answer from among the choices given and fill in the corresponding circle on the answer sheet.

The following sentences test correctness and effectiveness of expression. Part of each sentence or the entire sentence is underlined; beneath each sentence are five ways of phrasing the underlined material. Choice A repeats the original phrasing; the other four choices are different. If you think the original phrasing produces a better sentence than any of the alternatives, select choice A; if not, select one of the other choices.

In making your selection, follow the requirements of standard written English; that is, pay attention to grammar, choice of words, sentence construction, and punctuation. Your selection should result in the most effective sentence—clear and precise, without awkwardness or ambiguity.

EXAMPLE:

Laura Ingalls Wilder published her first book and she was sixty-five years old then.

(A) and she was sixty-five years old then
(B) when she was sixty-five
(C) at age sixty-five years old
(D) upon the reaching of sixty-five years
(E) at the time when she was sixty-five

1. Joe couldn't wait for his return to his home after being in the army for two years.

(A) Joe couldn't wait for his return to his home
(B) There was a strong desire on Joe's part to return home
(C) Joe was eager to return home
(D) Joe wanted home badly
(E) Joe arranged to return home

2. Trash, filth, and muck are clogging the streets of the city and that's not all, the sidewalks are full of garbage.

(A) that's not all, the sidewalks are full of garbage
(B) another thing: garbage is all over the sidewalks
(C) the garbage cans haven't been emptied for days
(D) in addition, garbage is lying all over the sidewalks
(E) what's more, the sidewalks have garbage that is lying all over them

3. Tired and discouraged by the problems of the day, Myra decided to have a good dinner, and then lie down for an hour, and then go dancing.

(A) Myra decided to have a good dinner, and then lie down for an hour, and then go dancing.
(B) Myra decided to have a good dinner, lying down for an hour, and then dancing.
(C) Myra decided to have a good dinner, lie down for an hour, and then dancing.
(D) Myra decided to have a good dinner, lay down for an hour, and then dance.
(E) Myra decided to have a good dinner, lie down for an hour, and then go dancing.

4. I am not certain in respect to which courses to take.

(A) in respect to which courses
(B) about which courses
(C) which courses
(D) as to the choice of which courses
(E) for which courses I am

GO ON TO THE NEXT PAGE

5. The people of the besieged village had no doubt that the end was drawing near.

    (A) that the end was drawing near
    (B) about the nearness of the end
    (C) it was clear that the end was near
    (D) concerning the end's being near
    (E) that all would die

6. There isn't a single man among us who is skilled in the art of administering first-aid.

    (A) who is skilled in the art of administering first-aid
    (B) who knows how to administer first-aid
    (C) who knows the administration of first-aid
    (D) who is a first-aid man
    (E) who administers first-aid

7. This is the hole that was squeezed through by the mouse.

    (A) that was squeezed through by the mouse
    (B) that the mouse was seen to squeeze through
    (C) the mouse squeezed through it
    (D) that the mouse squeezed through
    (E) like what the mouse squeezed through

8. She soundly fell asleep after having finished the novel.

    (A) She soundly fell asleep
    (B) She decided to sleep
    (C) She went on to her sleep
    (D) She fell to sleep
    (E) She fell fast asleep

9. This is one restaurant I won't patronize because I was served a fried egg by the waitress that was rotten.

    (A) I was served a fried egg by the waitress that was rotten
    (B) I was served by the waitress a fried egg that was rotten
    (C) a fried egg was served to me by the waitress that was rotten
    (D) the waitress served me a fried egg that was rotten
    (E) a rotten fried egg was served to me by the waitress

10. Watching the familiar story unfold on the screen, he was glad that he read the book with such painstaking attention to detail.

    (A) that he read the book with such painstaking attention to detail
    (B) that he had read the book with such painstaking attention to detail
    (C) that he read the book with such attention to particulars
    (D) that he read the book with such intense effort
    (E) that he paid so much attention to the plot of the book

11. If anyone requested tea instead of coffee, it was a simple matter to serve it to them from the teapot at the rear of the table.

    (A) it was a simple matter to serve it to them
    (B) it was easy to serve them
    (C) it was a simple matter to serve them
    (D) it was a simple matter to serve it to him or to her
    (E) that person could serve himself or herself

12. He bought some bread, butter, cheese and decided not to eat them until the evening.

    (A) some bread, butter, cheese and decided
    (B) some bread, butter, cheese and then decided
    (C) a little bread, butter, cheese and decided
    (D) some bread, butter, cheese, deciding
    (E) some bread, butter, and cheese and decided

13. The things the children liked best were swimming in the river and to watch the horses being groomed by the trainer.

    (A) swimming in the river and to watch the horses being groomed by the trainer
    (B) swimming in the river and to watch the trainer grooming the horses
    (C) that they liked to swim in the river and watch the horses being groomed by the trainer
    (D) swimming in the river and watching the horses being groomed by the trainer
    (E) to swim in the river and watching the horses being groomed by the trainer

GO ON TO THE NEXT PAGE

14. If an individual wishes to specialize in electrical engineering, <u>they should take courses in trigonometry and calculus</u>.

   (A) they should take courses in trigonometry and calculus

   (B) trigonometry and calculus is what he should take courses in

   (C) trigonometry and calculus are what they should take courses in

   (D) he or she should take courses in trigonometry and calculus

   (E) take courses in trigonometry and calculus

15. If the dog will not <u>eat its food, put it through</u> the meat grinder once more.

   (A) eat its food, put it through

   (B) eat it's food, put it through

   (C) eat its food, you should put it through

   (D) eat food, put it through

   (E) eat its food, put the food through

16. The bank agreed to lend <u>Garcia the money, which made</u> him very happy.

   (A) Garcia the money, which made

   (B) Garcia the money, a decision which made

   (C) Garcia the money; this made

   (D) Garcia the money, this making

   (E) the money to Garcia and found

17. Miami's daytime attire is <u>less formal than New York</u>.

   (A) less formal than New York

   (B) less formal then that in New York

   (C) less formal than that in New York

   (D) less formal than in New York

   (E) less formal than the daytime attire we see in New York

18. <u>As the fisherman explained that he wanted to hire a guide and row</u> upstream in order to catch game fish.

   (A) As the fisherman explained that he wanted to hire a guide and row

   (B) The reason was as the fisherman explained that he wanted to hire a guide and row

   (C) As the fisherman explained that he wanted to hire a guide and to row

   (D) The fisherman explained that he wanted to hire a guide and row

   (E) The fisherman explaining that he wanted to hire a guide and row

19. The speaker was praised <u>for his organization, choice of subject, and because he was brief</u>.

   (A) for his organization, choice of subject, and because he was brief

   (B) for his organization, his choice of subject and the speech having brevity

   (C) on account of his organization and his choice of subject and the brevity of his speech

   (D) for the organization of his speech, for his choice of subject, and because he was brief

   (E) for his organization, his choice of subject, and his brevity

20. <u>The fact that Charles did not receive a college scholarship</u> disappointed his parents.

   (A) The fact that Charles did not receive a college scholarship

   (B) Because Charles did not receive a college scholarship was the reason he

   (C) Being that Charles did not receive a college scholarship

   (D) Charles not receiving a college scholarship

   (E) Charles did not receive a college scholarship

GO ON TO THE NEXT PAGE

The following sentences test your ability to recognize grammar and usage errors. Each sentence contains either a single error or no error at all. No sentence contains more than one error. The error, if there is one, is underlined and lettered. If the sentence contains an error, select the one underlined part that must be changed to make the sentence correct. If the sentence is correct, select choice E. In choosing answers, follow the requirements of standard written English.

EXAMPLE:

The other delegates and him immediately
  A                          B       C
accepted the resolution drafted by
                                  D
the neutral states. No error.
                        E

Ⓐ ● Ⓒ Ⓓ Ⓔ

21. Since we first started high school, there has been
    A                                            B
    great competition for grades between him and I.
                                       C            D
    No error.
    E

22. Many people in the suburbs scarcely know about
                                A            B
    the transportation problems that city dwellers
                                  C
    experience every day. No Error.
                  D            E

23. The subject of the evening editorial was us
                                            A
    instructors who have refused to cross the picket
                B    C
    lines of the striking food service workers.
                    D
    No error.
    E

24. After the contestants had completed their speeches,
                          A
    I knew that the prize would go to he whom
                                     B   C
    the audience had given a standing ovation.
                              D
    No error.
    E

25. Falsely accused of a triple-murder and imprisoned
                        A              B
    for 19 years, Ruben (Hurricane) Carter, a former
    boxer, was freed when a Federal judge declared
               C
    him guiltless. No error.
    D            E

26. Your math instructor would have been happy to
                                          A
    give you a makeup examination if you would have
                                          B
    gone to him and explained that your parents were
                    C
    hospitalized. No error.
    D            E

27. The child asking a difficult question was perhaps
        A    B
    more shocking to the speaker than to the child's
                                  C          D
    parents. No error.
             E

28. Now that the pressure of selling the house and
    A                       B
    packing our belongings is over, we can look forward
                               C            D
    to moving to our new home in California.
    No error.
    E

29. My grandmother leads a more active life than
                   A                          B
    many other retirees who are younger than her.
                         C                      D
    No error.
    E

30. I appreciate your offering to change my flat tire,
                  A          B
    but I would rather have you drive me to my meeting
                C
    so that I will be on time. No error.
    D                          E

31. The novelists who readers choose as their
                   A            B      C
    favorites are not always the most skilled writers.
                                 D
    No error.
    E

GO ON TO THE NEXT PAGE

32. The problem of <u>how to deal</u> with all the
                         A
<u>mosquitoes</u> <u>disturb</u> many <u>residents</u> of the Tropics.
       B            C              D
<u>No error</u>.
     E

33. The <u>family's</u> only son <u>could of</u> <u>gone</u> to college, but
          A                  B        C
he decided to join the army after he graduated

<u>from</u> high school. <u>No error</u>.
   D                    E

34. <u>Yesterday</u> at the race track many <u>persons</u> were
       A                                    B
<u>fearful of</u> betting on the horse <u>who</u> had fallen in the
       C                               D
last race. <u>No error</u>.
              E

GO ON TO THE NEXT PAGE

**Directions:** The following passage is an early draft of an essay. Some parts of the passage need to be rewritten.

Read the passage and select the best answers for the questions that follow. Some questions are about particular sentences or parts of sentences and ask you to improve sentence structure or word choice. Other questions ask you to consider organization and development. In choosing answers, follow the requirements of standard written English.

**Questions 35–39 refer to the following passage.**

[1]Lampe-Pigeon is the charming name for a tall kerosene lamp, over nine and one-half inches in height, created more than 100 years ago for use in the wine caves of France. [2]Its diminutive size makes it suitable for being used on a mantel, as a centerpiece in lieu of candles, or even bracketed as a wall sconce. [3]The brass lamp, which contains within it a glass globe, is still being handmade by the same company, though one is more likely to see it in a French home these days than in a cave. [4]And, of course, it would be a handy source of light in the event of a power failure. [5]Other antique-type lamps have been manufactured and they do not have the elegance or simplicity of the Lampe-Pigeon. [6]Many people prefer more modern lamps especially those of the halogen variety.

35. What should be done with sentence 3?

(A) It should end after the word <u>company</u>.
(B) It should remain as it is.
(C) It should be placed after sentence 4.
(D) It should follow sentence 1.
(E) It should introduce the passage.

36. Sentence 1 would be more logical if it read, Lampe-Pigeon is the charming name for

(A) <u>a tall kerosene lamp, measuring nine and one-half inches, created....</u>
(B) <u>a kerosene lamp, although nine and one-half inches tall, created....</u>
(C) <u>a nine-and-one-half-inch-tall kerosene lamp, created....</u>
(D) <u>a tall nine-and-one-half inch kerosene lamp, created....</u>
(E) <u>a kerosene lamp, of a height of nine and one-half inches, created....</u>

37. The phrase <u>for being used</u> in sentence 2 should be

(A) changed to <u>for use</u>.
(B) left as it is.
(C) changed to <u>for one to use it</u>.
(D) changed to <u>to being used</u>.
(E) changed to <u>as a piece used on a mantel</u>.

38. Sentence 3 would read more smoothly were it to begin

(A) <u>The glass globed brass lamp....</u>
(B) <u>The brass lamp with a glass globe....</u>
(C) <u>The glass globe, found in the brass lamp....</u>
(D) <u>as it does now.</u>
(E) <u>The brass lamp, inside of which is a glass globe....</u>

39. What should be done with sentence 6?

(A) It should be left as it is.
(B) It should be deleted from the paragraph.
(C) It should be placed before sentence 5.
(D) It should be placed before sentence 4.
(E) It should be placed before sentence 3.

# STOP

If you finish before time is called, you may check your work on this section only.
Do not turn to any other section in the test.

# How Did You Do on This Test?

Step 1.   Go to the Answer Key on pages 371–372.

Step 2.   For your "raw score," calculate it using the
          directions on pages 373–374.

Step 3.   Get your "scaled score" for the test by
          referring to the Raw Score/Scaled Score
          Conversion Table on page 375.

*THERE'S ALWAYS ROOM FOR
IMPROVEMENT!*

# Answer Key for Practice Test 1

## Critical Reading

### Section 1

| | Correct Answer |
|---|---|
| 1 | E |
| 2 | C |
| 3 | B |
| 4 | A |
| 5 | B |
| 6 | B |
| 7 | B |
| 8 | B |
| 9 | D |
| 10 | A |
| 11 | B |
| 12 | E |
| 13 | A |
| 14 | E |
| 15 | B |
| 16 | D |
| 17 | C |
| 18 | A |
| 19 | C |
| 20 | E |
| 21 | B |
| 22 | D |
| 23 | A |
| 24 | E |

Number correct

Number incorrect

### Section 3

| | Correct Answer |
|---|---|
| 25 | D |
| 26 | A |
| 27 | E |
| 28 | E |
| 29 | D |
| 30 | C |
| 31 | C |
| 32 | E |
| 33 | D |
| 34 | E |
| 35 | A |
| 36 | D |
| 37 | B |
| 38 | B |
| 39 | A |
| 40 | A |
| 41 | D |
| 42 | D |
| 43 | A |
| 44 | A |
| 45 | A |
| 46 | A |
| 47 | D |
| 48 | E |

Number correct

Number incorrect

## Math

### Section 2

| | Correct Answer |
|---|---|
| 1 | C |
| 2 | E |
| 3 | C |
| 4 | D |
| 5 | D |
| 6 | B |
| 7 | D |
| 8 | D |
| 9 | B |
| 10 | A |
| 11 | C |
| 12 | D |
| 13 | A |
| 14 | E |
| 15 | A |
| 16 | E |
| 17 | C |
| 18 | B |
| 19 | D |
| 20 | A |

Number correct

Number incorrect

### Section 4

| | Correct Answer |
|---|---|
| 21 | E |
| 22 | A |
| 23 | B |
| 24 | D |
| 25 | E |
| 26 | B |
| 27 | A |
| 28 | D |

Number correct

Number incorrect

**Student-Produced Response Questions**

| | |
|---|---|
| 29 | 7/18 or .388 or .389 |
| 30 | 8 |
| 31 | 2/3 or .667 or .666 |
| 32 | 60 |
| 33 | 36 |
| 34 | 44 |
| 35 | 1/4 or .25 |
| 36 | 60 |
| 37 | 10 |
| 38 | 48 |

Number correct

Number incorrect

# Writing Skills

Section 5

|  | Correct Answer |
|---|---|
| 1 | C |
| 2 | D |
| 3 | E |
| 4 | B |
| 5 | A |
| 6 | B |
| 7 | D |
| 8 | E |
| 9 | D |
| 10 | B |
| 11 | D |
| 12 | E |
| 13 | D |
| 14 | D |
| 15 | E |
| 16 | B |
| 17 | C |
| 18 | D |
| 19 | E |
| 20 | A |
| 21 | D |
| 22 | E |
| 23 | A |
| 24 | B |
| 25 | E |
| 26 | B |
| 27 | A |
| 28 | E |
| 29 | D |
| 30 | E |
| 31 | A |
| 32 | C |
| 33 | B |
| 34 | D |
| 35 | D |
| 36 | C |
| 37 | A |
| 38 | B |
| 39 | B |

Number correct

Number incorrect

## Scoring the PSAT Practice Test

Check your responses with the correct answers on the previous pages. Fill in the blanks below and do the calculations to get your math, critical reading, and writing raw scores. Use the table to find your math, critical reading, and writing scaled scores.

## Get Your Critical Reading Score

How many critical reading questions did you get **right?**

Section 1: Questions 1–24 _____

Section 3: Questions 25–48 + _____

Total = _____ **(A)**

How many critical reading questions did you get **wrong?**

Section 1: Questions 1–24 _____

Section 3: Questions 25–48 + _____

Total = _____

× 0.25 = _____ **(B)**

A – B = _____

Critical Reading Raw Score

Round critical reading raw score to the nearest whole number.

_____

Use the Score Conversion Table to find your critical reading scaled score.

_____

## Get Your Math Score

How many math questions did you get **right?**

Section 2: Questions 1–20 _____

Section 4: Questions 21–38 + _____

Total = _____ **(A)**

How many multiple-choice math questions did you get **wrong?**

Section 2: Questions 1–20 _____

Section 4: Questions 21–38 + _____

Total = _____

× 0.25 = _____ **(B)**

A – B = _____

Math Raw Score

Round math raw score to the nearest whole number.

_____

Use the Score Conversion Table to find your math scaled score.

_____

**Get Your Writing Skills Score**

How many multiple-choice writing questions did you get **right?**

Section 5: Questions 1–39 _____

Total = _____ **(A)**

How many multiple-choice writing questions did you get **wrong?**

Section 5: Questions 1–39 _____

Total = _____

$\times 0.25$ = _____ **(B)**

**A – B** = _____

Writing Raw Score

Round writing raw score to the nearest whole number.

_____

Use the Score Conversion Table to find your writing scaled score.

_____

# PSAT Score Conversion Table

| Raw Score | Scaled Scores | | | Raw Score | Scaled Scores | | |
|---|---|---|---|---|---|---|---|
| | Critical Reading | Math | Writing Skills | | Critical Reading | Math | Writing Skills |
| 48 | 80 | | | 15 | 43 | 45 | 44 |
| 47 | 80 | | | 14 | 42 | 44 | 43 |
| 46 | 77 | | | 13 | 41 | 43 | 42 |
| 45 | 75 | | | 12 | 40 | 42 | 41 |
| 44 | 74 | | | 11 | 38 | 42 | 40 |
| 43 | 72 | | | 10 | 38 | 40 | 39 |
| 42 | 70 | | | 9 | 37 | 39 | 38 |
| 41 | 68 | | | 8 | 35 | 38 | 37 |
| 40 | 67 | | | 7 | 34 | 37 | 36 |
| 39 | 66 | | 80 | 6 | 33 | 36 | 35 |
| 38 | 65 | 80 | 77 | 5 | 31 | 34 | 34 |
| 37 | 64 | 77 | 73 | 4 | 30 | 33 | 33 |
| 36 | 63 | 74 | 72 | 3 | 29 | 31 | 31 |
| 35 | 62 | 71 | 70 | 2 | 27 | 29 | 30 |
| 34 | 61 | 69 | 68 | 1 | 24 | 26 | 28 |
| 33 | 60 | 68 | 65 | 0 | 22 | 24 | 27 |
| 32 | 59 | 67 | 64 | −1 | 20 | 20 | 24 |
| 31 | 58 | 65 | 63 | −2 | 20 | 20 | 21 |
| 30 | 57 | 64 | 62 | −3 | 20 | 20 | 20 |
| 29 | 56 | 62 | 60 | −4 | 20 | 20 | 20 |
| 28 | 55 | 61 | 59 | −5 | 20 | 20 | 20 |
| 27 | 54 | 60 | 57 | −6 | 20 | 20 | 20 |
| 26 | 53 | 58 | 56 | −7 | 20 | 20 | 20 |
| 25 | 52 | 57 | 55 | −8 | 20 | | 20 |
| 24 | 51 | 56 | 54 | −9 | 20 | | 20 |
| 23 | 51 | 54 | 53 | −10 | 20 | | 20 |
| 22 | 50 | 53 | 52 | −11 | 20 | | |
| 21 | 49 | 52 | 51 | −12 | 20 | | |
| 20 | 48 | 51 | 50 | | | | |
| 19 | 47 | 50 | 49 | | | | |
| 18 | 46 | 49 | 48 | | | | |
| 17 | 45 | 48 | 46 | | | | |
| 16 | 44 | 47 | 45 | | | | |

# PSAT/NMSQT Percentiles and Mean Scores

*can be used to compare a student's performance with that of juniors and sophomores.*

| JUNIORS | | | | SOPHOMORES | | | |
|---|---|---|---|---|---|---|---|
| | Percentiles | | | | Percentiles | | |
| Score | Critical Reading | Math | Writing Skills | Score | Critical Reading | Math | Writing Skills |
| 80 | 99+ | 99+ | 99+ | 80 | 99+ | 99+ | 99+ |
| 79 | 99+ | 99+ | 99+ | 79 | 99+ | 99+ | 99+ |
| 78 | 99+ | 99+ | 99+ | 78 | 99+ | 99+ | 99+ |
| 77 | 99 | 99 | 99 | 77 | 99+ | 99+ | 99+ |
| 76 | 99 | 99 | 99 | 76 | 99+ | 99+ | 99+ |
| 75 | 99 | 99 | 99 | 75 | 99+ | 99+ | 99+ |
| 74 | 99 | 98 | 99 | 74 | 99+ | 99 | 99+ |
| 73 | 99 | 98 | 98 | 73 | 99+ | 99 | 99+ |
| 72 | 98 | 98 | 98 | 72 | 99 | 99 | 99+ |
| 71 | 98 | 97 | 98 | 71 | 99 | 99 | 99+ |
| 70 | 97 | 97 | 98 | 70 | 99 | 99 | 99 |
| 69 | 97 | 96 | 97 | 69 | 99 | 98 | 99 |
| 68 | 96 | 94 | 96 | 68 | 99 | 98 | 99 |
| 67 | 96 | 92 | 96 | 67 | 98 | 97 | 99 |
| 66 | 95 | 92 | 96 | 66 | 98 | 97 | 99 |
| 65 | 93 | 90 | 94 | 65 | 97 | 96 | 98 |
| 64 | 92 | 88 | 93 | 64 | 97 | 95 | 97 |
| 63 | 91 | 87 | 92 | 63 | 96 | 94 | 97 |
| 62 | 90 | 85 | 90 | 62 | 96 | 93 | 96 |
| 61 | 88 | 83 | 90 | 61 | 95 | 92 | 96 |
| 60 | 86 | 80 | 88 | 60 | 94 | 90 | 95 |
| 59 | 85 | 79 | 85 | 59 | 93 | 89 | 93 |
| 58 | 82 | 76 | 85 | 58 | 91 | 87 | 93 |
| 57 | 80 | 73 | 83 | 57 | 90 | 85 | 92 |
| 56 | 78 | 71 | 81 | 56 | 89 | 83 | 91 |
| 55 | 76 | 70 | 79 | 55 | 87 | 83 | 89 |
| 54 | 74 | 66 | 75 | 54 | 85 | 80 | 87 |
| 53 | 71 | 63 | 72 | 53 | 83 | 77 | 84 |
| 52 | 68 | 59 | 68 | 52 | 81 | 74 | 82 |
| 51 | 62 | 56 | 66 | 51 | 77 | 71 | 80 |
| 50 | 59 | 52 | 63 | 50 | 74 | 68 | 78 |
| 49 | 55 | 49 | 59 | 49 | 71 | 65 | 74 |
| 48 | 52 | 45 | 55 | 48 | 69 | 61 | 71 |
| 47 | 49 | 42 | 54 | 47 | 65 | 58 | 70 |
| 46 | 45 | 41 | 50 | 46 | 62 | 58 | 67 |
| 45 | 41 | 38 | 48 | 45 | 58 | 54 | 65 |
| 44 | 37 | 34 | 44 | 44 | 54 | 50 | 62 |
| 43 | 35 | 31 | 40 | 43 | 52 | 47 | 58 |
| 42 | 32 | 26 | 36 | 42 | 48 | 40 | 53 |
| 41 | 28 | 25 | 33 | 41 | 44 | 39 | 49 |
| 40 | 25 | 22 | 31 | 40 | 40 | 36 | 48 |
| 39 | 24 | 19 | 28 | 39 | 40 | 31 | 44 |
| 38 | 20 | 16 | 24 | 38 | 34 | 27 | 39 |
| 37 | 18 | 14 | 21 | 37 | 31 | 23 | 35 |
| 36 | 17 | 11 | 17 | 36 | 31 | 20 | 30 |
| 35 | 15 | 11 | 16 | 35 | 27 | 20 | 28 |
| 34 | 13 | 9 | 13 | 34 | 23 | 17 | 24 |
| 33 | 10 | 7 | 11 | 33 | 20 | 13 | 20 |
| 32 | 10 | 7 | 10 | 32 | 20 | 13 | 19 |
| 31 | 9 | 5 | 8 | 31 | 18 | 9 | 15 |
| 30 | 7 | 5 | 6 | 30 | 15 | 9 | 11 |
| 29 | 6 | 3 | 5 | 29 | 12 | 6 | 11 |
| 28 | 6 | 3 | 5 | 28 | 12 | 6 | 9 |
| 27 | 4 | 3 | 3 | 27 | 9 | 6 | 6 |
| 26 | 4 | 2 | 3 | 26 | 9 | 4 | 6 |
| 25 | 4 | 2 | 3 | 25 | 9 | 4 | 6 |
| 24 | 3 | 1 | 2 | 24 | 6 | 3 | 4 |
| 23 | 3 | 1 | 2 | 23 | 6 | 3 | 4 |
| 22 | 2 | 1 | 2 | 22 | 5 | 3 | 4 |
| 21 | 2 | 1 | 1 | 21 | 5 | 3 | 2 |
| 20 | 1 | 1 | 1 | 20 | 1 | 1 | 1 |
| Mean Score | 46.8 | 48.9 | 45.9 | Mean Score | 41.9 | 44.3 | 41.3 |

## Points to Note

• Percentiles indicate the percentage of students whose scores fall below each specified score.

• On the score report, percentiles for juniors compare their performance with that of other juniors who took the test. For sophomores or younger students, percentiles compare their performance with that of sophomores.

• Percentiles are based on the critical reading, math, and writing skills scores earned by a sample of college-bound juniors or sophomores who took the PSAT/NMSQT.

• The *mean* score is the statistic that describes the *average* performance of a group.

# National Merit Scholarship Selection Index Percentiles and Mean Score

| JUNIORS | | | | | |
|---|---|---|---|---|---|
| Composite Score | Percentile | Composite Score | Percentile | Composite Score | Percentile |
| 240–223 | 99+ | 173 | 83 | 123 | 28 |
| 222 | 99 | 172 | 82 | 122 | 27 |
| 221 | 99 | 171 | 81 | 121 | 26 |
| | | | | | |
| 220 | 99 | 170 | 81 | 120 | 25 |
| 219 | 99 | 169 | 80 | 119 | 24 |
| 218 | 99 | 168 | 79 | 118 | 23 |
| 217 | 99 | 167 | 78 | 117 | 22 |
| 216 | 99 | 166 | 77 | 116 | 21 |
| 215 | 99 | 165 | 76 | 115 | 20 |
| 214 | 99 | 164 | 75 | 114 | 20 |
| 213 | 99 | 163 | 74 | 113 | 19 |
| 212 | 99 | 162 | 73 | 112 | 18 |
| 211 | 98 | 161 | 72 | 111 | 17 |
| | | | | | |
| 210 | 98 | 160 | 71 | 110 | 16 |
| 209 | 98 | 159 | 70 | 109 | 16 |
| 208 | 98 | 158 | 69 | 108 | 15 |
| 207 | 98 | 157 | 68 | 107 | 14 |
| 206 | 98 | 156 | 67 | 106 | 13 |
| 205 | 97 | 155 | 66 | 105 | 13 |
| 204 | 97 | 154 | 65 | 104 | 12 |
| 203 | 97 | 153 | 64 | 103 | 12 |
| 202 | 97 | 152 | 62 | 102 | 11 |
| 201 | 96 | 151 | 61 | 101 | 10 |
| | | | | | |
| 200 | 96 | 150 | 60 | 100 | 10 |
| 199 | 96 | 149 | 59 | 99 | 9 |
| 198 | 96 | 148 | 58 | 98 | 9 |
| 197 | 95 | 147 | 56 | 97 | 8 |
| 196 | 95 | 146 | 55 | 96 | 8 |
| 195 | 95 | 145 | 54 | 95 | 7 |
| 194 | 94 | 144 | 53 | 94 | 7 |
| 193 | 94 | 143 | 52 | 93 | 6 |
| 192 | 94 | 142 | 50 | 92 | 6 |
| 191 | 93 | 141 | 49 | 91 | 6 |
| | | | | | |
| 190 | 93 | 140 | 48 | 90 | 5 |
| 189 | 92 | 139 | 47 | 89 | 5 |
| 188 | 92 | 138 | 45 | 88 | 5 |
| 187 | 91 | 137 | 44 | 87 | 4 |
| 186 | 91 | 136 | 43 | 86 | 4 |
| 185 | 90 | 135 | 42 | 85 | 4 |
| 184 | 90 | 134 | 41 | 84 | 3 |
| 183 | 89 | 133 | 39 | 83 | 3 |
| 182 | 89 | 132 | 38 | 82 | 3 |
| 181 | 88 | 131 | 37 | 81 | 2 |
| | | | | | |
| 180 | 88 | 130 | 36 | 80 | 2 |
| 179 | 87 | 129 | 35 | 79 | 2 |
| 178 | 86 | 128 | 34 | 78 | 2 |
| 177 | 86 | 127 | 32 | 77–60 | 1 |
| 176 | 85 | 126 | 31 | | |
| 175 | 84 | 125 | 30 | | |
| 174 | 84 | 124 | 29 | | |
| Mean Score | | | | | 141.6 |

## Points to Note

Reported on a sliding scale from 60 to 240, the Selection Index is the sum of the Critical Reading, Math, and Writing Skills scores. For example, a Critical Reading score of 56, a Math score of 62, and a Writing Skills score of 59 would result in a composite Selection Index of 177 (56 + 62 + 59).

Percentiles are based on the Selection Index earned by a sample of college-bound juniors who took the PSAT/NMSQT.

## How NMSC Uses the Selection Index

National Merit Scholarship Corporation (NMSC) uses the Selection Index score to designate groups of students to receive recognition in the programs it conducts. Entry to NMSC's competitions for scholarships is determined by students' responses to program entry questions on the PSAT/NMSQT answer sheet. Currently, more than 1.5 million test-takers meet requirements to enter NMSC's competitions each year.

Of the more than 1.5 million NMSC program entrants, about 55,000 will earn PSAT/NMSQT scores high enough to qualify them for recognition. These students will be notified of their standing through their high schools in September. Students who qualify to continue in the competitions for scholarships must then meet academic and other requirements specified by NMSC to be considered for awards.

Inquiries about any aspect of the National Merit Program or National Achievement Program—including entry requirements, the selection process, and awards to be offered—should be sent to:
National Merit Scholarship Corporation
1560 Sherman Avenue, Suite 200
Evanston, IL 60201-4897
Telephone: (847) 866-5100

# Explanatory Answers for PSAT Practice Test 1

## Section 1: Critical Reading

As you read these Explanatory Answers, refer to "Critical Reading Strategies" (beginning on page 80) whenever a specific Strategy is referred to in the answer. Of particular importance are the following Master Critical Reading Strategies:

Sentence Completion Master Strategy 1—page 81.
Sentence Completion Master Strategy 2—page 82.
Reading Comprehension Master Strategy 2—page 98.

*Note:* All Reading questions use Reading Comprehension Strategies 1, 2, and 3 (pp. 95–100) as well as other strategies indicated.

1. Choice E is correct. See **Sentence Completion Strategy 2.** Examine the first word of each choice. Choice (A) committees and Choice (B) tribes are incorrect because it is clear that committees and tribes cannot be equated with cities such as Athens. Now consider the other choices. Choice (E) societies...participated is the only choice which has a word pair that makes sentence sense.

2. Choice C is correct. See **Sentence Completion Strategy 2.** Examine the first word of each choice. Choice (A) abolished and Choice (E) discounted do not make sense because we cannot say that fossils are abolished or discounted in rock formations. Now consider the other choices. Choice (C) preserved...hardened is the only choice which has a word pair that makes sentence sense.

3. Choice B is correct. See **Sentence Completion Strategy 2.** Examine the first word of each choice. We eliminate Choice (A) dominated and Choice (D) cautioned because the trends do *not* dominate or caution affluence. Now consider the other choices.

Choice (C) accentuated...depression and Choice (E) accepted...revolution do *not* make sentence sense. Choice (B) reflected...prosperity *does* make sentence sense.

4. Choice A is correct. See **Sentence Completion Strategy 1.** The word "conserve" (meaning to "protect from loss") completes the sentence so that it makes good sense. The other choices don't do that.

5. Choice B is correct. See **Sentence Completion Strategy 1.** The word "prevalent" (meaning widely or commonly occurring) completed the sentence so that it makes good sense. The other choices don't do that.

6. Choice B is correct. Since this question has the two-blank choices, let us use **Sentence Completion Strategy 2.** When we use Step 1 of Strategy 2, we find a very unusual situation in this question—the first words in all five choices make sense: "With lack of" *advice* or *control* or *opportunity* or *sympathy* or *conscience*, "anyone can develop the disease of

alcoholism…" Accordingly, we must go to Step 2 of Strategy 2 and consider *both* words of each choice. When we do so, we find that only Choice (B) control…foolishly makes good sentence sense.

7. Choice B is correct. See **Sentence Completion Strategy 4.** "Because" is a *result indicator*. Since the generating system was not functioning efficiently, the use of electricity had to be *diminished* or *curtailed*.

8. Choice B is correct. See **Sentence Completion Strategy 1.** Something staple, such as bread, is in constant supply and demand. Beer, then, is considered a liquid bread by the Bavarians. Choices A, C, D, and E do not make good sense in the sentence.

9. Choice D is correct. One can see from the gist of the whole passage that the author is warning the reader of the dangers of anarchy and war. See line 4: "It is the age of war" and the need for "the age of civilized man" (line 5). Thus Choice D would be best.

10. Choice A is correct. See lines 8–10 where the author says that "It calls for total awareness, total commitment" indicating limited hope.

11. Choice B is correct. It can be seen that the author contrasts novel reading in the past with novel reading in the present throughout the passage. Although the author does mention a "defect in today's novels" (choice A), that is not the main consideration in the passage.

12. Choice E is correct. See lines 2–6: "there were few diversions…not irritated by the digressions and irrelevances…" Do not be lured into Choice B: Although some great novels are long, not all are.

13. Choice A is correct. The main idea of the passage is expressed in lines 18–19: "Science seems to have come into existence merely for its bearings on practical life." This main idea is also expressed in other parts of the passage. For example— lines 1–2: "Science, like everything else…needs and desires." Also lines 15–16: "…the bulk of mankind…advantages it brings with it." Finally, all through the last paragraph of the passage we learn how the Babylonians and the Egyptians reaped practical benefits with the help of science. Choices B, C, D, and E are true, but they are too confining to be considered the main idea of the passage. Therefore, these choices are incorrect.

14. Choice E is correct. See lines 8–14: "Science is valued…most important consideration of all to scientific men." Choice A is incorrect. The passage does not indicate that this choice is true. Furthermore, others *before* the Babylonians and the Egyptians

also used scientific methods. Choice B is incorrect. See lines 27–29: "The cultivation of crops…made a calendar almost a necessity [for the Babylonians and Egyptians]." Choice C is incorrect. First see lines 20–23: "More than two thousand years before… measuring space and time." Now see lines 32–34: "Twelve of these months…putting in extra months." Choice D is incorrect. See lines 20–23 again.

15. Choice B is correct. See lines 8–14: "Science is valued…provides the imagination…most important consideration of all to scientific men." Choices A, C, D, and E are incorrect because the author does not imply in any way that scientists are sociable, practical, philosophical, or arrogant people.

16. Choice D is correct. You can see from lines 20–25 that "rudimentary" must be related to something fundamental or basic. In fact in lines 24–25, this rudimentary science met the practical needs of the population, so choices B, C, and E would have been ruled out anyway. See also **Reading Comprehension Strategy 4.**

17. Choice C is correct. The two labels (lines 48–49) obviously have negative implications about the value of physics and thus indicate that physics is uninteresting and pointless to the ordinary person. Accordingly, Choice C is correct. It follows, then, that Choice B—which states that physics "is a cause for great excitement"—is incorrect. Choices A, D, and E are incorrect because none of these choices is stated or implied in the passage.

18. Choice A is correct. See lines 60–62: "Yet what little we do know…grandeur and intricate beauty." Choices B, C, D, and E are incorrect because none of these choices is brought out in the passage.

19. Choice C is correct. See lines 51–54: "There is nothing…what we lack of the other." Also see lines 55–58: "It is pointless…all-knowing, and infallible." None of the other choices is indicated in the passage. Accordingly, choices A, B, D, and E are incorrect.

20. Choice E is correct. See the very first sentence of the passage: "Let's be honest right at the start." This frankness on the part of the author pervades the entire passage. Choices A, B, C, and D are, therefore, incorrect.

21. Choice B is correct. The author is, in effect, saying that one must appreciate the forest as a whole—not merely certain individual trees. He therefore implies that we should not separate physics from the body of all creative work. See lines 55–56: "It is pointless…all creative work…" Choices A, C, D, and E are incorrect because they are not justified by the content of the passage.

22. Choice D is correct. The practical use of science is discussed in lines 20–34 of Passage 1 but not in Passage 2. Choice A is incorrect: lines 44–51 imply the way laymen view physics. Choice B is incorrect: Specialization in science is mentioned in lines 44–47 of Passage 2. Choice C is incorrect: Purity of physics is mentioned in line 57 of Passage 2. Choice E is incorrect: Lines 51–54 address the arguments between humanists and scientists.

23. Choice A is correct. See lines 44–51 of Passage 2: "boxes." Choices B, C, D, and E are incorrect: Critique is certainly used by both authors. The author in Passage 1 contrasts with respect to perceived values in lines 8–16. Historical referencing and examples to support a claim are used in Passage 1 in lines 20–34.

24. Choice E is correct. Choice A, agriculture, is mentioned in line 25. Choice B, astronomy, is mentioned in line 24. Choice C, art, is mentioned in line 43. Choice D, philosophy, is mentioned in line 57. However, Choice A, chemistry, is not directly mentioned.

# Explanatory Answers for Practice Test 1 (continued)

## Section 2: Math

As you read these solutions, you are advised to do two things if you answered the Math question incorrectly:

1. When a specific Strategy is referred to in the solution, study that strategy, which you will find in "19 Math Strategies" (beginning on page 51).

2. When the solution directs you to the "Math Refresher" (beginning on page 129)—for example, Math Refresher #305—study the 305 Math principle to get a clear idea of the Math operation that was necessary for you to know in order to answer the question correctly.

1. Choice C is correct.

$$\begin{array}{r} \text{Given:} \quad 59\Delta \\ -293 \\ \hline \square 97 \end{array} \quad \boxed{1}$$

**(Use Strategy 17: Use the given information effectively.)**

From $\boxed{1}$ we see that $\Delta - 3 = 7$ $\boxed{2}$

From $\boxed{2}$ we get $\Delta = 10$ $\boxed{3}$

From $\boxed{1}$ and $\boxed{3}$ we get $\Delta = 0$ in $\boxed{1}$ and we had to borrow to get 10. Thus, we have

$$\begin{array}{r} 8 \\ 5\cancel{9}0 \\ -293 \\ \hline \square 97 \end{array} \quad \boxed{4}$$

Calculating $\boxed{4}$, we get

$$\begin{array}{r} 8 \\ 5\cancel{9}0 \\ -293 \\ \hline 297 \end{array}$$

We see that the digit represented by the $\square$ is 2.

**(Logical Reasoning and Subtraction)**

2. Choice E is correct.

$$\text{Given:} \quad \frac{a-b}{b} = \frac{1}{2} \quad \boxed{1}$$

**(Use Strategy 13: Find unknowns by multiplication.)**

Multiply $\boxed{1}$ by $2b$. We have

$$2\cancel{b}\left(\frac{a-b}{\cancel{b}}\right) = \left(\frac{1}{\cancel{2}}\right)\cancel{2}b$$
$$2(a-b) = b$$
$$2a - 2b = b$$
$$2a = 3b \quad \boxed{2}$$

**(Use Strategy 13: Find unknowns by division.)**

Dividing $\boxed{2}$ by $2b$, we get

$$\frac{\cancel{2}a}{2b} = \frac{3\cancel{b}}{2\cancel{b}}$$

$$\frac{a}{b} = \frac{3}{2}$$

**(Math Refresher 406)**

3. Choice C is correct.

| Number of pounds of force | Height object is raised |
|:---:|:---:|
| 3 | 6 feet |
| 6 | 12 feet |
| 9 | 18 feet |

$\boxed{1}$

**(Use Strategy 2: Translate from words to algebra.)**

We are given that:

$$\text{height raised} = c \text{ (force exerted)} \quad \boxed{2}$$

Substituting $\boxed{1}$ into $\boxed{2}$, we get

$$6 = c(3)$$
$$2 = c \quad \boxed{3}$$

Given: Height object is raised = 15 feet $\boxed{4}$

Substituting $\boxed{3}$ and $\boxed{4}$ into $\boxed{2}$, we have

$$15 = 2 \text{ (force exerted)}$$
$$7\frac{1}{2} = \text{force exerted}$$

**(Math Refresher 200 and 406)**

4. Choice D is correct.

Given: $\frac{y}{3}, \frac{y}{4}, \frac{y}{7}$ are integers. $\boxed{1}$

**(Use Strategy 17: Use the given information effectively.)**

If all items in $\boxed{1}$ are integers, then 3, 4, and 7 divide $y$ evenly (zero remainder). $y$ must be a common multiple of 3, 4, and 7. Multiplying 3, 4, and 7 we get 84.

**(Math Refresher 607)**

5. Choice D is correct. **(Use Strategy 11: Use new definitions carefully.)**

We are told that the points are each 3 units apart, as indicated above. We are looking for all those points that are more than 19 units away from point $P$. By checking the diagram we find 5 such points (marked with arrow in diagram).

**(Logical Reasoning)**

6. Choice B is correct.

Given: $\boxed{1}$

$(a + 2, a - 2) = [a]$ for all integers $a$. $\boxed{2}$

We need to find $(6,2)$

**(Use Strategy 11: Use new definitions carefully.)** Using $\boxed{1}$ and $\boxed{2}$ we have

$$a + 2 = 6 \quad \text{and} \quad a - 2 = 2$$
$$a = 4 \qquad\qquad a = 4 \quad \boxed{3}$$

Using $\boxed{1}$, $\boxed{2}$, and $\boxed{3}$, we get

$$(6,2) = [4]$$

**(Math Refresher 431 and 406)**

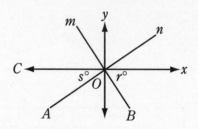

7. Choice D is correct.

Given: $m \perp n$ $\boxed{1}$

From $\boxed{1}$ we know that $\angle AOB$ is a right angle. Thus $\angle AOB = 90°$ $\boxed{2}$

From the diagram, we see that $\angle COx$ is a straight angle.

Thus $\angle COx = 180°$ $\boxed{3}$

**(Use Strategy 3: The whole equals the sum of its parts.)**

We know that $\angle COA + \angle AOB + \angle BOx = \angle COx$ $\boxed{4}$

Given: $\angle COA = s°$ $\boxed{5}$

$\angle BOx = r°$ $\boxed{6}$

Substituting $\boxed{2}$, $\boxed{3}$, $\boxed{5}$, and $\boxed{6}$ into $\boxed{4}$, we get

$$s + 90 + r = 180$$
$$s + r = 90$$
$$r + s = 90$$

**(Math Refresher 501, 511, and 406)**

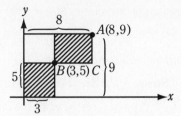

**8. Choice D is correct. (Use Strategy 17: Use the given information effectively.)**

From the given coordinates, we can find certain distances, as marked above.

Using these distances we find:

$$BC = 8 - 3 = 5 \qquad \boxed{1}$$
$$AC = 9 - 5 = 4 \qquad \boxed{2}$$

We know that Area of a rectangle = length × width $\qquad \boxed{3}$

Using the diagram and $\boxed{3}$ we have

Area of lower rectangle = $5 \times 3 = 15 \qquad \boxed{4}$

Substituting $\boxed{1}$ and $\boxed{2}$ into $\boxed{3}$, we get

Area of upper rectangle = $5 \times 4 = 20 \qquad \boxed{5}$

**(Use Strategy 13: Find unknowns by addition.)**

Adding $\boxed{4}$ and $\boxed{5}$ together, we get

Total area = $15 + 20 = 35$

**(Math Refresher 410 and 304)**

**9. Choice B is correct.**

Given: Total number of students = 2,800 $\quad \boxed{1}$

**(Use Strategy 2: Translate from words to algebra.)**

Number of German students = $\frac{1}{2} \times 2,800$

$$= \frac{2,800}{4}$$

$$= 700 \qquad \boxed{2}$$

**(Use Strategy 13: Find unknown by subtraction.)**

Subtracting $\boxed{2}$ from $\boxed{1}$ we get

Number of students
not studying German =
$2,800 - 700 = 2,100$

**(Math Refresher 200 and 111)**

**10. Choice A is correct. (Use Strategy 2: Translate from words to algebra.)**

Given:
cost per vehicle = $\$y$ $\qquad \boxed{1}$
Let $x$ = number of students paying \$0.40 $\quad \boxed{2}$

Then $x + 6$ = number of students paying \$0.25
$\qquad \boxed{3}$

Using $\boxed{1}$, $\boxed{2}$, and 3,

We are told that: $x(\$0.40) = \$y$ $\qquad \boxed{4}$
$$(x + 6)(\$0.25) = \$y \qquad \boxed{5}$$

From $\boxed{4}$ and $\boxed{5}$ we get

$$x(\$0.40) = (x + 6)(\$0.25)$$
$$.40x = .25x + 1.50$$
$$.15x = 1.50$$
$$x = 10 \qquad \boxed{6}$$

Substitute $\boxed{6}$ into $\boxed{4}$. We have

$$10(\$0.40) = \$y$$
$$\$4.00 = y$$
$$\$4 = y$$

**(Math Refresher 200, 406, and 431)**

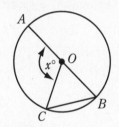

**11. Choice C is correct.**

Given: $AB$ is a diameter $\qquad \boxed{1}$
$O$ is the center of the circle $\qquad \boxed{2}$
$CB = OB$ $\qquad \boxed{3}$

Using $\boxed{2}$, we know that $OB$ and $OC$ are radii $\quad \boxed{4}$
From $\boxed{4}$ we get that $OB = OC$. $\qquad \boxed{5}$
Using $\boxed{3}$ and $\boxed{5}$ together, we have
$$OB = OC = CB \qquad \boxed{6}$$

**(Use Strategy 18: Remember the equilateral triangle.)**

From $\boxed{6}$, we have $\angle OBC$ is equilateral $\qquad \boxed{7}$

From $\boxed{7}$, we get that $\angle B = \angle C = \angle COB = 60° \qquad \boxed{8}$

From $\boxed{1}$, we get $\angle AOB$ is straight angle. $\qquad \boxed{9}$

From $\boxed{9}$, we have $\angle AOB = 180° \qquad \boxed{10}$

**(Use Strategy 3: The whole equals the sum of its parts.)**

From the diagram we see that:

$$\angle AOC + \angle COB = \angle AOB \qquad \boxed{11}$$

Given: $\quad \angle AOC = x° \qquad\qquad\qquad \boxed{12}$

Substituting $\boxed{8}$, $\boxed{10}$, and $\boxed{12}$ into $\boxed{11}$, we get

$$x + 60 = 180$$
$$x = 120 \qquad\qquad \boxed{13}$$

**(Use Strategy 13: Find unknowns by division.)**
Divide $\boxed{13}$ by 6. We have

$$\frac{x}{6} = \frac{120}{6}$$

$$\frac{x}{6} = 20$$

**(Math Refresher 501, 508, 524, and 406)**

12. Choice D is correct.

Given:    Selling price of radio = \$64    $\boxed{1}$
         Regular price of radio = \$80    $\boxed{2}$

**(Use Strategy 2: Remember how to find percent discount.)**

$$\text{Percent discount} = \frac{\text{Amount off}}{\text{original price}} \times 100 \quad \boxed{3}$$

Subtracting $\boxed{1}$ from $\boxed{2}$, we get

$$\text{Amount off} = \$80 - \$64 = \$16 \qquad \boxed{4}$$

Substituting $\boxed{2}$ and $\boxed{4}$ into $\boxed{3}$, we have

$$\text{Percent discount} = \frac{\$16}{\$80} \times 100$$

$$= \frac{\$16 \times 100}{\$80} \qquad \boxed{5}$$

**(Use Strategy 19: Factor and reduce.)**

$$\text{Percent discount} = \frac{\$\cancel{16} \times \cancel{5} \times 20}{\$\cancel{16} \times \cancel{5}}$$

$$\text{Percent discount} = 20 \qquad \boxed{6}$$

Given: Regular price of different radio = \$200   $\boxed{7}$

New percent discount

$$= 1\frac{1}{2} \times \text{Other radio's percent discount} \qquad \boxed{8}$$

Using $\boxed{6}$ and $\boxed{8}$, we have

$$\text{New percent discount} = 1\frac{1}{2} \times 20 =$$

$$= \frac{3}{2} \times 20$$

$$= 30 \qquad \boxed{9}$$

**(Use Strategy 2: Remember how to find percent of a number.)**

We know percent of a number

percent $\times$ number.        $\boxed{10}$

Substituting $\boxed{7}$ and $\boxed{9}$ into $\boxed{10}$, we have

Amount of discount = 30% $\times$ \$200

$$= \frac{30}{100} \times \$200$$

Amount of discount = \$60      $\boxed{11}$

**(Use Strategy 13: Find unknowns by subtraction.)**

Subtracting $\boxed{11}$ from $\boxed{7}$, we have

Selling price of different radio

= \$200 − \$60
= \$140

**(Math Refresher 200 and 114)**

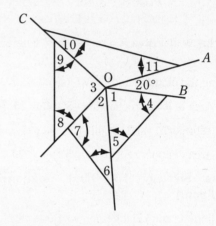

13. Choice A is correct.

Given: $\angle AOB = 20°$      $\boxed{1}$

**(Use Strategy 3: The whole equals the sum of its parts.)**

We know that the sum of the angles
of a triangle = 180°      $\boxed{2}$

For each of the four triangles, applying $\boxed{2}$ yields:

$$\angle 8 + \angle 9 + \angle 3 = 180 \qquad \boxed{3}$$
$$\angle 6 + \angle 7 + \angle 2 = 180 \qquad \boxed{4}$$
$$\angle 4 + \angle 5 + \angle 1 = 180 \qquad \boxed{5}$$
$$\angle 10 + \angle 11 + \angle COA = 180 \qquad \boxed{6}$$

We know that the sum of all the angles about a
point = 360°      $\boxed{7}$

Applying $\boxed{7}$ to point $O$, we have

$$\angle 1 + \angle 2 + \angle 3 + \angle COA + \angle AOB = 360° \qquad \boxed{8}$$

Substituting $\boxed{1}$ into $\boxed{8}$, we get

$$\angle 1 + \angle 2 + \angle 3 + \angle COA + 20 = 360$$
$$\angle 1 + \angle 2 + \angle 3 + \angle COA = 340 \qquad \boxed{9}$$

**(Use Strategy 13: Find unknowns by addition.)**

Adding ③, ④, ⑤, and ⑥, we have

$$\angle 4 + \angle 5 + \angle 6 + \angle 7 + \angle 8 + \angle 9 + \angle 10 + \angle 11 + \angle 1 + \angle 2 + \angle 3 + \angle COA = 720° \quad \boxed{10}$$

**(Use Strategy 13: Find unknowns by subtraction.)**

Subtracting ⑨ from ⑩, we get

$$\angle 4 + \angle 5 + \angle 6 + \angle 7 + \angle 8 + \angle 9 + \angle 10 + \angle 11 = 380° \quad \boxed{11}$$

Thus, the sum of the marked angles = 380°

**(Math Refresher 505 and 406)**

14. Choice E is correct. **(Use Strategy 8: When all choices must be tested, start with choice E.)** If some of the integers in the set are odd, then not all are even. Note the other choices are not correct. For (D), all integers cannot be even since some are odd. For (C), since *some* integers are odd we cannot imply that all integers are odd. For (B), if an integer is even, it may not be in set X. Similarly for (A) if an integer is odd, it may not be in set X.

**(Math Refresher 801 and 603)**

15. Choice A is correct. Since the absolute value of $y + 3$ must be less than 3, $y$ must be less than 0 but greater than −6.

**(Math Refresher 615)**

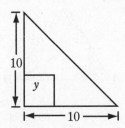

16. Choice E is correct.

We know that Area of a triangle

$$= \frac{1}{2} \times \text{base} \times \text{height} \quad \boxed{1}$$

Use the diagram, and substituting into ①, we get

$$\text{Area of triangle} = \frac{1}{2} \times 10 \times 10$$

$$= 50 \quad \boxed{2}$$

**(Use Strategy 2: Translate from words to algebra.)**

We are told:

$$\text{Area of square} = \frac{1}{5} \times \text{Area of triangle} \quad \boxed{3}$$

We know that

$$\text{Area of a square} = (\text{side})^2 \quad \boxed{4}$$

Using the diagram, and substituting into ④, we get

$$\text{Area of square} = y^2 \quad \boxed{5}$$

Substituting ② and ⑤ into ③, we have

$$y^2 = \frac{1}{5} \times 50$$

$$y^2 = 10 \quad \boxed{6}$$

Take the square root of both sides of ⑥. We get

$$y = \sqrt{10}$$

**(Math Refresher 200, 303, 307, and 430)**

17. Choice C is correct.

Given:   Print rate $= \dfrac{80 \text{ characters}}{\text{second}}$   $\boxed{1}$

$$\frac{\text{Number of characters}}{\text{Page}} = 2400 \quad \boxed{2}$$

**(Use Strategy 13: Find unknowns by division.)**

Dividing ② by ①, we have

$$\frac{2{,}400 \text{ characters}}{\text{page}} \div \frac{80 \text{ characters}}{\text{second}} =$$

$$\frac{2{,}400 \text{ characters}}{\text{page}} \times \frac{\text{second}}{80 \text{ characters}} =$$

$$\frac{2{,}400 \text{ second}}{80 \text{ page}}$$

$$= \frac{30 \text{ seconds}}{\text{page}} \quad \boxed{3}$$

The time for an $M$-page report will be

$$\frac{30 \text{ seconds}}{\text{page}} \times M \text{ pages} =$$

$$\text{Time for } M\text{-page report} = 30 \, M \text{ seconds} \quad \boxed{4}$$

**(Use Strategy 10: Know how to use units.)**

To change time from seconds to minutes we multiply

$$\text{by } \frac{1 \text{ minute}}{60 \text{ seconds}}. \quad \boxed{5}$$

Applying ⑤ to ④, we get

$$\text{Time for } M\text{-page report, in minutes} = 30M \text{ seconds} \times \frac{1 \text{ minute}}{60 \text{ seconds}}$$

$$= \frac{30 \, M \text{ minutes}}{60}$$

$$= \frac{M}{2} \text{ minutes}$$

**(Math Refresher 201 and 121)**

18. Choice B is correct.

Given: On Friday, the satellite passed over
Washington, D.C., at midnight $\boxed{1}$
Complete orbit 5 hours $\boxed{2}$

**(Use Strategy 17: Use the given information effectively.)**

Using $\boxed{2}$, we see that five complete

orbits = $5 \times 5 = 25$ hours = 1 day + 1 hour $\boxed{3}$

From $\boxed{1}$ and $\boxed{2}$ we know that

| DAY | TIME PASSING OVER D.C. | |
|---|---|---|
| Friday | 7:00 P.M., midnight | $\boxed{4}$ |

Applying $\boxed{3}$ to $\boxed{4}$, and continuing this chart, we have

| Saturday | 8:00 P.M., 1:00 A.M. |
|---|---|
| Sunday | 9:00 P.M., 2:00 A.M. |
| Monday | 10:00 P.M., 3:00 A.M. |
| Tuesday | 11:00 P.M., 4:00 A.M. |
| Wednesday | midnight, 5:00 A.M. |

**(Logical Reasoning)**

19. Choice D is correct. **(Use Strategy 2: Know how to find percent of a number.)**

Let $x$ = price of car $\boxed{1}$

Given: 1st reduction = 30% $\boxed{2}$

2nd reduction = 40% $\boxed{3}$

We know amount of discount
= percent × price $\boxed{4}$

Using $\boxed{1}$, $\boxed{2}$, and $\boxed{4}$, we get

Amount of 1st discount = 30% × $x$
= $.30x$ $\boxed{5}$

**(Use Strategy 13: Find unknowns by subtraction.)** Subtracting $\boxed{5}$ from $\boxed{1}$, we have

Reduced price = $x - .30x$
= $.70x$ $\boxed{6}$

Using $\boxed{3}$, $\boxed{6}$, and $\boxed{4}$, we get

Amount of 2nd discount = 40% × $.70x$
= $.40 \times .70x$
= $.28x$ $\boxed{7}$

Subtracting $\boxed{7}$ from $\boxed{6}$, we have

Price after 2nd reduction = $.70x \times .28x$
= $.42x$ $\boxed{8}$

**(Use Strategy 16: The obvious may be tricky!)**

Since $\boxed{8}$ = $.42x$, it is 42% of the original price of $x$. This is *not* the answer to the question.

Since $\boxed{8}$ is 42% of the original it is the result of a 58% discount.

The answer is 58%.

**(Math Refresher 200 and 114)**

20. Choice A is correct.

**(Use Strategy 3: Know how to find unknown quantities from known quantities.)**

The total shaded area = area of triangle − area of the circle

Given: Diameter of circle = 2

The radius, $r$, of the circle = 1 $\boxed{1}$

Thus, the area of the circle is $\pi r^2 = \pi(1) = \pi$ $\boxed{2}$

Now we have to find the area of the equilateral triangle. First, we need to find the length of the base.

**(Use Strategy 14: Draw lines to help find the answer.)**

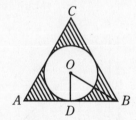

Draw radius $OD$, with $D$ the point of tangency, and $OB$ as shown above. $\boxed{3}$

**(Use Strategy 18: Remember the equilateral triangle.)**

Given: Triangle $ACB$ is equilateral $\boxed{4}$

From $\boxed{3}$ we get $OD \perp AB$, since radius $\perp$ tangent at point of tangency. $\boxed{5}$

From $\boxed{5}$, we get $\angle ODB = 90°$ $\boxed{6}$

From $\boxed{4}$, we get $\angle ABC = 60°$ $\boxed{7}$

From the geometry of regular polygons, we know that $OB$ bisects $\angle ABC$. $\boxed{8}$

From $\boxed{7}$ and $\boxed{8}$ we get $\angle DBO = 30°$ $\boxed{9}$

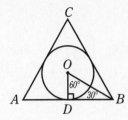

From $\boxed{6}$ and $\boxed{9}$ we see $\angle OBD$ is a 30–60–90 triangle

From $\boxed{1}$, we get $OD = 1$ $\qquad\qquad\boxed{10}$

**(Use Strategy 18: Remember the special right triangles.)**

Using $\boxed{10}$ and the properties of the 30–60–90 triangle, we get $OB = 2$, $DB = 1\sqrt{3} = \sqrt{3}$ $\quad\boxed{11}$

We know $AB = 2 \times DB$ $\qquad\qquad\qquad\boxed{12}$

Substituting $\boxed{11}$ into $\boxed{12}$, we get $AB = 2\sqrt{3}$ $\quad\boxed{13}$

Now that we know the length of the base ($AB$) we need to find the height of the triangle.

**(Use Strategy 14: Draw lines to help find the answer.)**

Where $h$ is the altitude of the triangle, the area is $(h \times 2\sqrt{3})/2 = h\sqrt{3}$

By the Pythagorean Theorem,

$$(2\sqrt{3})^2 - (\sqrt{3})^2 = h^2$$
$$4 \times 3 - 3 = h^2$$
$$9 = h^2$$
$$3 = h$$

So the area of the triangle =

$$(3 \times 2\sqrt{3})/2 = 3\sqrt{3} \qquad\boxed{14}$$

**(Use Strategy 13: Find unknowns by subtraction.)**

From $\boxed{2}$ we know the area of the circle is $\pi$

Subtracting $\boxed{2}$ from $\boxed{14}$, we get

Shaded area = $3\sqrt{3} - \pi$

**(Math Refresher 308, 310, 508, 524, 525, and 509)**

# Explanatory Answers for Practice Test 1 (continued)

## Section 3: Critical Reading

As you read these Explanatory Answers, refer to "Critical Reading Strategies" (beginning on page 80) whenever a specific Strategy is referred to in the answer. Of particular importance are the following Master Critical Reading Strategies:

Sentence Completion Master Strategy 1—page 81.
Sentence Completion Master Strategy 2—page 82.
Reading Comprehension Master Strategy 2—page 98.

*Note:* All Reading questions use Reading Comprehension Strategies 1, 2, and 3 (pp. 95–100) as well as other strategies indicated.

**25.** Choice D is correct. See **Sentence Completion Strategy 1.** The word "extreme" is the most appropriate among the five choices because the forest fire season is in *full swing*. The other choices are, therefore, not appropriate.

**26.** Choice A is correct. See **Sentence Completion Strategy 2.** Examine the first words of each choice. We eliminate Choice (C) imagined and Choice (E) intuitive. Reason: The effect of the long war was *not* imagined or intuitive (meaning knowing by a hidden sense). Now we consider Choice (B) immediate…staring and Choice (D) delayed…rebuilding. Neither word pair makes sense in the sentence. Choice (A) cumulative…corrosion *does* make sense in the sentence.

**27.** Choice E is correct. See **Sentence Completion Strategy 3.** If you had tried to complete the sentence *before* looking at the five choices, you might have come up with any of the following words meaning "continually" or "regularly":

constantly     always
perpetually    persistently
     habitually

The other choices are, therefore, incorrect.

**28.** Choice E is correct. See **Sentence Completion Strategy 2.** Examine the first word of each choice. Choice (D) crushes is eliminated because it is not likely that the bee will crush the nectar from different flowers. Now consider each pair of words in the other choices. We find that Choice (E) extracts…converts has the only word pair that makes sense in the sentence.

**29.** Choice D is correct. See **Sentence Completion Strategies 1 and 4.** The plan turned out to be impractical, unable to be logically supported. Note the root "ten" *to hold*, so "untenable" means *not holding*. Also note that the word "since" in the sentence is a *result indicator*.

30. Choice C is correct. In lines 8–11, the author is showing that through the "weedy falsities," truth can be created.

31. Choice C is correct. See the last lines 16–18…"we can feel all the poverty, despair, and unfairness in our world…" For choice A, there may be value for the spectator: see lines 14–15 "and perhaps how we should change them."

32. Choice E is correct. See lines 8–11, 13–15, and 15–18. This describes how something positive can come out from something negative. In Choice A, although specific references (lines 4 and 5) are made, there are no specific references in Paragraph 2. In Choice B, there is no indication of both being completely objective, especially in Passage 1 line 2 where the author states that the theater is the "most preposterous of all." Choice C is incorrect in that in Passage 1, the author certainly does not believe in the accuracy of the time (16th century) whereas in Passage 2, the author does believe in the accuracy of the time. Choice D is incorrect in that it appears that the intensity and passion of the author's arguments in Passage 1 is far greater than that of the author's in Passage 2.

33. Choice D is correct. In lines 8–9 note the words "lily" (a flower) and "jungle" (a place) which are used as analogies. We do not see such analogies in Passage 2. In Choice A, both authors would disagree as the author in Passage 1 states that theater is fiction, not reality and the author in Passage 2 states that the theater is real. In Choice B, see line 5: "the much admired Miss Huckaby." In Choice C, in lines 7–8, the author is sarcastic when he says that "people were ever so marvelously articulate." In Choice E, see lines 13–14: the author believes the contrary, that the theater is quite realistic.

34. Choice E is correct. See lines 4–7: "Originally the term acclimatization…altered temperature." Also see lines 9–12: "But aside from temperature… originally accustomed to." Choices A, B, C, and D are incorrect because one *cannot* infer from the passage what any of these choices state.

35. Choice A is correct. Acclimatization and adaptation are both forms of adjustment. Accordingly, these two processes are similar. The difference between the two terms, however, is brought out in lines 32–36: "By and large…as 'adaptation.'" Choice D is incorrect because the passage does not indicate what is expressed in Choice D. See lines 29–32: "Let us define acclimatization…lethal for it." Choices B, C, and E are incorrect because the passage does not indicate that any of these choices are true.

36. Choice D is correct. A person going from daylight into a darkened room is an example of adaptation—not acclimatization. See lines 32–36: "By and large…as 'adaptation.'" Choices A, B, C, and E all require the process of acclimatization. Therefore, they are incorrect choices. An ocean fish placed in a lake (Choice A) is a chemical change. Choices B, C, and E are all pressure changes. Acclimatization, by definition, deals with chemical and pressure changes.

37. Choice B is correct. Given the context in the sentence, Choice B is the best. See also **Reading Comprehension Strategy 4**.

38. Choice B is correct. See lines 33–36: "The term [acclimatization] should not be taken…as 'adaptation.'" Choices A, D, and E are incorrect because the passage does not indicate that these choices are true. Choice C is partially correct in that acclimatization does apply to adjustments, but the choice is incorrect because adaptation also applies to adjustments. See lines 35–36: "This type of adjustment… as 'adaptation.'"

39. Choice A is correct. See lines 71–72: "…as Dr. Skinner argues, that one can extrapolate from pigeons to people…" Choice B is incorrect because, though Skinner agrees that introspection may be of some use (lines 14–18), nowhere does the article indicate that he suggests wide use of the introspective method. Choice C is incorrect since Skinner, so the author says (lines 74–76), "has not satisfactorily rebutted…rather than scientific." Choice D is incorrect because lines 81–82 state that "…Skinner predicts…impending disaster." Choice E is incorrect because there is nothing in the passage to indicate this statement. Incidentally, this point of view (Choice E) is held by Noam Chomsky of linguistics fame.

40. Choice A is incorrect. See lines 83–89 to the end of the passage: "Two key concepts…not so reassuring." Choice B is incorrect. See lines 11–14: "…an earlier stage of…influence of mentalism." Choice C is incorrect. See lines 60–64: "It is a veritable…to external stimuli." Choice D is incorrect since mentalism evolved before methodological and radical behaviorism. See lines 10–17: "What such people…its possible usefulness." Choice E is correct. The passage, from line 63 to the end, brings out weaknesses in Skinner's presentation.

41. Choice D is correct. Skinner, in lines 26–27, says "…few would contend that behavior is 'endlessly malleable.'" Also, see lines 35–42: "Contingencies of reinforcement…likely to occur." In effect, Skinner is saying that behavior cannot always, by plan or design, be altered or influenced; behavior must depend, to some extent, on the element of chance.

42. Choice D is correct. Skinner is known for his experiments with pigeons. Also, rats have been used frequently by behaviorists in experimentation. See lines 65–73. In addition, see lines 37–38: "In both natural…is crucial." The other choices are not relevant to Darwin or his work.

43. Choice A is correct. From the context in the rest of the sentence where "extrapolate" appears, choice A fits best. Note, the word "extrapolate" is derived from the Latin "extra" (outside) and "polire" (to polish). See also **Reading Comprehension Strategy 5**.

44. Choice A is incorrect because Choice A is true according to lines 14–15. Choice B is incorrect because Choice B is true according to lines 65–70. Choice C is correct because Choice C is *not* true according to lines 68–72. Choice D is incorrect because Choice D is true according to lines 10–18. Choice E is incorrect because Choice E is true according to lines 57–61.

45. Choice A is incorrect. See lines 19–22: "…to those who object…Skinner expresses puzzlement." Choice B is correct because Skinner, a radical behaviorist, though believing that environmental influences are highly important in shaping human behavior, nevertheless states in lines 35–38: "Contingencies of reinforcement…is crucial." Operant conditioning is, according to behaviorists, a vital aspect of learning. Choice C is incorrect. Although Skinner accepts introspection (lines 16–18) as part of his system, nowhere does he place primary importance on introspection. Choice D is incorrect. Though Skinner may agree with this choice, nowhere in the passage does he state or imply this opinion. Choice E is incorrect. The word "malleable" means capable of being shaped or formed—from the Latin "malleare," meaning "to hammer." The quote in the stem of the question says, in effect, that few people would say that behavior can always be shaped.

46. Choice A is correct. I is correct; see the eighth paragraph, last sentence. II is incorrect; don't be fooled by what is in the third sentence of the eighth paragraph. It does not refer to *scientistic* areas. III is incorrect; see the third sentence in the eighth paragraph.

47. Choice D is correct. Given the context of the sentence and the sentences preceding and succeeding it, "veritable" means "true." One may also note the "ver" in "veritable" and may associate that with the word "verify," which also means true. This is the association strategy, which can be used to figure out clues to meanings of words. See also **Reading Comprehension Strategy 4**.

48. Choice E is correct. The phrases "one can't shake off the suspicion" (line 86) and "that is not so reassuring" (lines 88–89) reveal the author's position. Choice A is incorrect; in evaluating Skinner's work, the author makes no stated judgment of its *credibility,* only the possible moral implications. Choices B, C, and D are incorrect because none of these ideas is stated or implied in the paragraph.

# Explanatory Answers for Practice Test 1 (continued)

## Section 4: Math

As you read these solutions, do two things if you answered the Math question incorrectly:

1. When a specific Strategy is referred to in the solution, study that strategy, which you will find in "19 Math Strategies" (beginning on page 51).

2. When the solution directs you to the "Math Refresher" (beginning on page 129)—for example, Math Refresher #305—study the 305 Math principle to get a clear idea of the Math operation that was necessary for you to know in order to answer the question correctly.

21. Choice E is correct. Subtract 14 from both sides of the equation:

$$5\sqrt{x} + 14 = 20$$

$$5\sqrt{x} = 6$$

Divide by 5:

$$\sqrt{x} = 6/5$$

Square both sides:

$$x = 36/25$$

**(Math Refresher 430)**

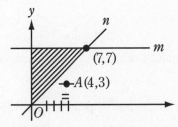

22. Choice A is correct. **(Use Strategy 17: Use the given information effectively.)** Since *n* goes through point *O*, the origin, whose coordinates are (0,0), and through (7,7), all of the points on *n* have the same *x* and *y* coordinates. Choice A, (4,3), is 4 units to the right of *O* but only 3 units up. It is below *n* and not in the shaded area.

**(Math Refresher 410)**

23. Choice B is correct. **(Use Strategy 2: Translate from words to algebra.)** This problem tests the concepts of set union and set intersection. We can solve these types of problems with a diagram. Let

$c$ = set of all calculus students

$p$ = set of all physics students

Thus, draw the diagram:

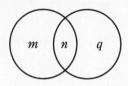

Where

$m$ = number of students taking *only* calculus

$q$ = number of students taking *only* physics

$n$ = number of students taking *both* calculus and physics

Thus,

$m + n$ = number of students in calculus class

$n + q$ = number of students in physics class

$m + n + q$ = number of students taking either calculus or physics or both

We are given that

$$m + n + q = 36 \qquad \boxed{1}$$
$$n = 10 \qquad \boxed{2}$$
$$m + n = 31 \qquad \boxed{3}$$

We want to find

$$n + q \qquad \boxed{4}$$

**(Use Strategy 13: Find unknowns by subtracting equations.)** Subtract equation $\boxed{2}$ from equation $\boxed{3}$ to get

$$m = 21 \qquad \boxed{5}$$

Now subtract equation $\boxed{5}$ from equation $\boxed{1}$ to get

$$n + q = 15$$

**(Math Refresher 406 and Logical Reasoning)**

24. Choice D is correct. In order to show a counterexample to refute Mr. Simmons' argument, we must come up with two numbers $a$ and $b$ such that $a^2 > b^2$ but that $a$ is not greater than $b$. Choice A is incorrect since it is not true that $a^2 > b^2$ in this case. Choice B is incorrect since it is true that $a^2 > b^2$ and that $a > b$. Choice C is incorrect because $a^2 > b^2$ and $a > b$. Choice D is correct: $a^2$ is greater than $b^2$ since $(-4)^2 > (-2)^2$. But it is not true that $a > b$ since $-4$ is *not* greater than $-2$.

**(Math Refresher 429, 424)**

25. Choice E is correct. **(Use Strategy 7: Use specific numerical examples to prove or disprove your guess.)**

$$\sqrt{2 + 2} \neq \sqrt{2} + \sqrt{2}$$
$$2^2 + 2^2 \neq (2 + 2)^2$$
$$2^1 + 2^2 \neq 2^{1+2}$$

Therefore, neither (I) nor (II) nor (III) is generally true.

**(Math Refresher 429, 430)**

26. Choice B is correct. The only element common to $R$ and $S$ is $x = 1$.

**(Math Refresher 803)**

27. Choice A is correct. To find the coordinates of the intersection point, we must first solve the equations $y = x - 1$ and $2x + 5y = 9$. In the equation $2x + 5y = 9$, we substitute $y = x - 1$. We obtain

$$2x + 5(x - 1) = 9$$

Thus

$$2x + 5x - 5 = 9$$

and

$$7x = 14$$
$$x = 2$$

From the first equation, $y = x - 1$, so $y = 2 - 1 = 1$. Thus $x = 2$ and $y = 1$ so the coordinates of the point are (2,1).

**(Math Refresher 417)**

28. Choice D is correct. **(Use Strategy 3: The whole equals the sum of its parts.)**

Volume of rectangular solid
= Volume of small compartment
+ Volume of larger compartment $\qquad \boxed{1}$
Area of rectangular dividing wall
$= l \times w$
$39\text{cm}^2 = 13\text{cm} \times w$
$3\text{cm} = w \qquad \boxed{2}$

$\boxed{2}$ is the height of the rectangular solid as well.

Volume of rectangular solid $= l \times w \times h$
$= 15\text{cm} \times 12\text{cm} \times h \qquad \boxed{3}$

Substituting $\boxed{2}$ into $\boxed{3}$, we get

Volume of rectangular solid =
$15\text{cm} \times 12\text{cm} \times 3\text{cm}$
Volume of rectangular solid = $540\text{cm}^3 \qquad \boxed{4}$

Volume of small compartment

$= $ Area of base height

$= \dfrac{1}{2} \times 12\text{cm} \times 5\text{cm} \times 3\text{cm} \qquad \boxed{5}$

Volume of small compartment = 90cm$^3$

Substitute $\boxed{4}$ and $\boxed{5}$ into $\boxed{1}$. We get

540cm$^3$ = 90cm$^3$ + Volume of larger compartment
450cm$^3$ = Volume of larger compartment

**(Math Refresher 312 and 306)**

29. $\dfrac{7}{18}$ or .388 or .389

**(Use Strategy 1: Simplify by cancelling.)**

$$\left(\frac{1}{2}-\frac{1}{3}\right)+\left(\frac{1}{3}-\frac{1}{4}\right)+\left(\frac{1}{4}-\frac{1}{5}\right)+$$

$$\left(\frac{1}{5}-\frac{1}{6}\right)+\left(\frac{1}{6}-\frac{1}{7}\right)+\left(\frac{1}{7}-\frac{1}{8}\right)+$$

$$\left(\frac{1}{8}-\frac{1}{9}\right)=$$

$$\frac{1}{2}+\left(-\frac{1}{3}+\frac{1}{3}\right)+\left(-\frac{1}{4}+\frac{1}{4}\right)+$$

$$\left(-\frac{1}{5}+\frac{1}{5}\right)+\left(-\frac{1}{6}+\frac{1}{6}\right)+\left(-\frac{1}{7}+\frac{1}{7}\right)+$$

$$\left(-\frac{1}{8}+\frac{1}{8}\right)-\frac{1}{9}=$$

$$\frac{1}{2}+0+0+0+0+0+0-\frac{1}{9}=$$

$$\frac{1}{2}-\frac{1}{9}=$$

$$\frac{9}{18}-\frac{2}{18}=$$

$$\frac{7}{18}$$

**(Math Refresher 110 and Logical Reasoning)**

30. **8**

**(Use Strategy 11: Use new definitions carefully.)** The first five elements of the series, calculated by the definition, are

$$1, 2, 2, 4, 8$$

**(Logical Reasoning)**

31. $\dfrac{2}{3}$ or .667 or .666

**(Use Strategy 2: Translate from words to algebra.)**

$$p = \frac{3}{5}m \qquad\qquad \boxed{1}$$

$$q = \frac{9}{10}m \qquad\qquad \boxed{2}$$

**(Use Strategy 13: Find unknowns by division of equations.)**

Thus, $\dfrac{p}{q} = \dfrac{\frac{3}{5}m}{\frac{9}{10}m}$

$$= \dfrac{\frac{3}{5}}{\frac{9}{10}}$$

$$= \frac{3}{5} \times \frac{10}{9} = \frac{\overset{1}{\cancel{3}}}{5} \times \frac{\overset{2}{\cancel{10}}}{\underset{3}{\cancel{9}}}$$

$$\frac{p}{q} = \frac{2}{3}$$

**(Math Refresher 200 and 112)**

33. **60**

$\Big($**Use Strategy 5:**

$$\textbf{Average} = \frac{\textbf{Sum of values}}{\textbf{Total number of values}}\Big)$$

Given: $\dfrac{40 + 40 + 40 + z}{4}$ $\qquad \boxed{1}$

Multiplying $\boxed{1}$ by 4,

$$40 + 40 + 40 + z = 180$$
$$120 + z = 180$$
$$z = 60$$

**(Math Refresher 601 and 406)**

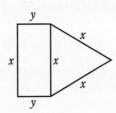

34. **36**

**(Use Strategy 2: Translate from words to algebra.)** When the given diagram has been labeled as above, then we know

$$3x = 39 \qquad\qquad \boxed{1}$$
$$xy = 65 \qquad\qquad \boxed{2}$$

From $\boxed{1}$ we have

$$x = 13 \qquad\qquad \boxed{3}$$

Substituting $\boxed{3}$ into $\boxed{2}$, we have

$$13y = 65$$
$$\text{or} \quad y = 5 \qquad\qquad \boxed{4}$$

The perimeter of the rectangle

$$= 2x + 2y$$
$$= 2(13) + 2(5)$$
$$= 36$$

**(Math Refresher 200, 304, 308, and 431)**

**35. 44**

**(Use Strategy 17: Use the given information effectively.)**

| Game | | Darrin | Tom |
|------|---|--------|-----|
| 1 | | 69 | 43 |
| 2 | | 59 | 60 |
| 3 | | 72 | 55 |
| 4 | | 70 | 68 |
| 5 | | 78 | 73 |
| Totals | | 348 | 299 |

We need the scores at the end of the first four games. We have been given the totals for all five games.

**(Use Strategy 13: Find unknowns by subtraction.)**

$$\text{Darrin's Total} = 348 \qquad \boxed{1}$$
$$\text{Darrin's Game 5} = 78 \qquad \boxed{2}$$
$$\text{Tom's Total} = 299 \qquad \boxed{3}$$
$$\text{Tom's Game 5} = 73 \qquad \boxed{4}$$

Subtract $\boxed{2}$ from $\boxed{1}$. We get

$$\text{Darrin's Total for 1st four games} = 348 - 78$$
$$= 270 \qquad \boxed{5}$$

Subtract $\boxed{4}$ from $\boxed{3}$. We get

$$\text{Tom's total for 1st four games} = 299 - 73$$
$$= 226 \qquad \boxed{6}$$

Subtracting $\boxed{6}$ from $\boxed{5}$, we have

Number of points Tom was behind Darrin after the first four games $= 270 - 226$
$$= 44$$

**(Subtraction and Logical Reasoning)**

**36. Choice $\frac{1}{4}$ or .25**

**(Use Strategy 17: Use the given information effectively.)**

The 17 slips, numbered from 1 to 17, consist of $\boxed{1}$
8 even numbers (2,4,6, . . . 16) and $\boxed{2}$
9 odd numbers (1,3,5, . . . 17). $\boxed{3}$

Subtracting 5 even-numbered slips from $\boxed{2}$ leaves

$8 - 5 = 3$ even-numbered slips. $\boxed{4}$

Adding $\boxed{3}$ and $\boxed{4}$ we have

$$9 + 3 = 12 \text{ slips remaining} \qquad \boxed{5}$$

We need $\dfrac{\text{even - numbered slips}}{\text{total numbered slips}}$ $\boxed{6}$

Substituting $\boxed{4}$ and $\boxed{5}$ into $\boxed{6}$, we have

$$\frac{3}{12} = \frac{1}{4}$$

**(Math Refresher 603 and Logical Reasoning)**

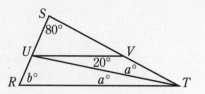

**37. 60**

Given:  $UV \parallel RT$ $\boxed{1}$

From $\boxed{1}$ we get $a = 20$, since alternate interior angles are equal $\boxed{2}$

**(Use Strategy 3: The whole equals the sum of its parts.)** From the diagram we see that

$$\angle STR = a + a \qquad \boxed{3}$$

Substituting $\boxed{2}$ into $\boxed{3}$, we have

$$\angle STR = 20 + 20 = 40 \qquad \boxed{4}$$

We know that the sum of the angles in a triangle $= 180$, thus

$$\angle R + \angle S + \angle STR = 180 \qquad \boxed{5}$$

We are given, in the diagram, that

$$\angle R = b \qquad \boxed{6}$$
$$\angle S = 80 \qquad \boxed{7}$$

Substituting $\boxed{6}$, $\boxed{7}$ and $\boxed{4}$ into $\boxed{5}$, we get

$$b + 80 + 40 = 180$$
$$b + 120 = 180$$
$$b = 60$$

**(Math Refresher 504, 505, and 406)**

**38. 10**

**(Use Strategy 2: Translate from words to algebra.)**

Given:  Rose's earnings $= \$44$ $\boxed{1}$

Rose's time worked $= 8$ days $\boxed{2}$

**(Use Strategy 13: Find unknowns by division.)**

Dividing $\boxed{1}$ by $\boxed{2}$, we have

$$\text{Rose's daily rate} = \frac{\$44}{8 \text{ days}}$$

$$\text{Rose's daily rate} = \frac{\$11}{2 \text{ days}} \qquad \boxed{3}$$

Given: Total earnings to equal $\$99$ $\boxed{4}$

Substituting $\boxed{1}$ from $\boxed{4}$, we get

Amount left to be earned $= \$55$ $\boxed{5}$
We know
(daily rate) (days worked) = money earned $\boxed{6}$

Substituting $\boxed{3}$ and $\boxed{5}$ into $\boxed{6}$, we get

$$\left(\frac{\$11}{2\text{ days}}\right)(\text{days worked}) = \$55 \qquad \boxed{7}$$

Multiplying $\boxed{7}$ by $\frac{2}{11}$ days, we have

$$\frac{2\text{ days}}{11}\left(\frac{11}{2\text{ days}}\right)(\text{days worked}) = (\overset{5}{\cancel{55}}\ \frac{2}{11}\text{ days}$$

$$\text{days worked} = 10\text{ days}$$

**(Math Refresher 200, 406, and 121)**

39. **48**

Given:  Areas of all 12 triangles are the same  $\boxed{1}$
        Area of outlined region = 256  $\boxed{2}$
        Area of square $ABCD$ = 128  $\boxed{3}$

**(Use Strategy 3: The whole equals the sum of the parts.)**

By looking at the diagram, we observe

Area of 8 triangles (I, II, . . . . , VIII) = Area of Outlined Region − Area of Square $ABCD$.

Substituting $\boxed{2}$ and $\boxed{3}$ into the above, we get

Area of 8 triangles (I, . . . . , VIII)
$$= 256 - 128$$
$$= 128 \qquad \boxed{4}$$

Using $\boxed{1}$, we get

Area of each of the 12 triangles =
$$\frac{\text{Area of 8 triangles}}{8}$$

Substituting $\boxed{4}$ into the above, we get

Area of each of the 12 triangles = $\frac{128}{8}$

Area of each of the 12 triangles = 16  $\boxed{5}$

**(Use Strategy 3: The whole equals the sum of its parts.)**

Shaded Area = Area $\Delta$V + Area $\Delta$VI + Area $\Delta$XI  $\boxed{6}$

Substituting $\boxed{1}$ and $\boxed{5}$ into $\boxed{6}$, we get

Shaded Area = 16 + 16 + 16 = 48

**(Logical Reasoning)**

# Explanatory Answers for Practice Test 1 (continued)

## Section 5: Writing Skills

For further practice and information, please refer to "A Brief Review of English Grammar" starting on page 321.

1. **(C)** Choice A is awkward and wordy. Choice B is indirect. Choice C is correct. Choice D is unacceptable idiomatically even though the meaning intended is there. Choice E changes the meaning of the original sentence.

2. **(D)** Choice A has incorrect punctuation. A dash (not a comma) is required after "that's not all." In Choice B, the expression "another thing" is too general. Choice C changes the meaning of the original sentence. Choice D is correct. Choice E is too indirectly expressed.

3. **(E)** Choice A suffers from too many "ands" (and-itis). Choice B and C are incorrect because they lack parallel construction. In Choice D, the correct form of the infinitive meaning "to rest" is "(to) lie"—not "(to) lay." Choice E is correct.

4. **(B)** Choice A is awkward. Choice B is correct. Choice C is ungrammatical—"courses" cannot act as a direct object after the copulative construction "am not certain." Choice D is too wordy. Choice E does not make sense.

5. **(A)** Choice A is correct. Choice B is too indirectly stated. Choice C is verbose—since the people "had no doubt," there is no need to use the expression "it was clear." Choice D is indirect and awkward. Choice E changes the meaning of the original sentence.

6. **(B)** Choice A is too wordy. Choice B is correct. Choice C is indirectly stated. Choices D and E change the meaning of the original sentence.

7. **(D)** Choice A is indirectly stated. Choice B deviates from the original statement. Choice C makes the whole sentence run-on. Choice D is correct. Choice E changes the meaning of the original sentence.

8. **(E)** Choice A is awkward. Choice B has a meaning which differs from that of the original sentence. Choices C and D are unidiomatic. Choice E is correct.

9. **(D)** The clause "that was rotten" is misplaced in Choices A, B, and C. Choice D is correct. Choice E is incorrect because the passive use of the verb is not as effective as the active use, in this context.

10. **(B)** Choice A uses wrong tense sequence. Since the reading of the book took place before the watching of the picture, the reading should be expressed in the past perfect tense, which shows action prior to the simple past tense. Choice B corrects the error with the use of the past perfect tense, "had read," instead of the past tense, "read." Choices C, D, and E do not correct the mistake, and Choice E in addition changes the meaning.

11. **(D)** Choice A is wrong because the word "them," being plural, cannot properly take the singular antecedent, "anyone." Choices B and C do not correct this error. Choice D corrects it by substituting "him" for "them." Choice E, while correcting the error, changes the meaning of the sentence.

12. **(E)** Choice A contains a "false series," meaning that the word "and" connects the three words in the series—bread, butter, cheese—with a wholly different clause, instead of with a similar fourth word. The series, therefore, needs its own "and" to complete it. Only Choice E furnishes this additional "and."

13. **(D)** Choice A violates the principle of parallel structure. If the first thing the children liked was "swimming" (a gerund), then the second thing they liked should be, not "to watch" (an infinitive), but "watching" (the gerund). Choice B does not improve the sentence. Choice C repeats the beginning of the sentence with the repetitious words "that they liked." Choice D is correct. Choice E simply reverses the gerund and the infinitive without correcting the error.

14. **(D)** Choice A is incorrect because the pronoun must be singular ("he or she"—not "they") since the antecedent ("individual") is singular. Choice C is incorrect for the same reason. Moreover, this choice is roundabout. Choice B is incorrect because it is roundabout. Choice D is correct for the reason that Choice A is incorrect. Choice C is incorrect because its subject is "you" (understood). A third person subject is required to coincide with the third person of the antecedent "individual."

15. **(E)** Choices A, B, C, and D are incorrect because these choices do not make it clear whether the dog or the food ought to be put through the meat grinder. Moreover, "it's" in Choice B is wrong. Choice 5 is correct because it makes clear that the food—not the dog—is to be put through the meat grinder.

16. **(B)** Choices A, C, and D are incorrect because the word "money" is incorrectly the antecedent in these three choices. Choice B is correct because "a decision" correctly refers to the whole idea—"The bank agreed to lend Garcia the money." Choice E is incorrect because it does not retain the complete meaning of the original sentence.

17. **(C)** Choices A and D are incorrect because the expression "that in" is required to complete the comparison. Choice C is correct because it includes the required expression "that in." Choice B is incorrect because "then" is incorrect here for "than." Choice E is incorrect because it changes the meaning of the original sentence.

18. **(D)** Choices A, C, and E are incorrect because they do not fulfill the requirement of contributing to the composition of a complete sentence. Choice D is correct because it does complete that requirement. Choice B is incorrect because it is awkward.

19. **(E)** Choices A, B, and D are incorrect because they lack balance of grammatical structure. Choice C is incorrect because the "and-and" construction is frowned upon by grammarians. Choice E is correct because the grammatical structure is balanced. This choice consists of three well-formed prepositional phrases.

20. **(A)** Choice A is correct. The words which make up the choice act as the subject of the sentence. Choice B is incorrect because it is awkward. Choice C is incorrect because one should never begin a sentence with "Being that." Choice D is incorrect as it stands. If "Charles" were changed to the possessive "Charles' " or "Charles's" the choice would be correct. Choice E is incorrect because it, in itself, is a complete sentence which, as it stands, cannot act as the grammatical subject of the verb "disappointed."

21. **(D)** "...between *him* and *me*."
The object of the preposition *between* must be an objective case form (*me*—not *I*).

22. **(E)** All underlined parts are correct.

23. **(A)** "The subject...was *we*..."
The predicate nominative form is *we*—not *us*.

24. **(B)** "...the prize would go to him..."
The object of the preposition *to* must be an objective case form (*him*—not he).

25. **(E)** All underlined parts are correct.

26. **(B)** "...if you *had gone to him*..."
In the "if clause" of a past contrary-to-fact condition, one must use the past perfect subjunctive form *had gone*—not the future perfect subjunctive form *would have gone*.

27. **(A)** "The *child's* asking..."
The subject of a gerund is in the possessive case. We, therefore, say *child's asking*—not *child asking*.

28. **(E)** All underlined parts are correct.

29. **(D)** "...who are younger than *she*."
The nominative case (*she*—not *her*) must be used after the conjunction *than* when the pronoun is the subject of an elliptical clause ("than she is").

30. **(E)** All underlined parts are correct.

31. **(A)** "The novelists *whom* readers choose…"
The direct object of the verb (choose) must be the objective case form (*whom*—not *who*).

32. **(C)** "The problem…disturbs…"
The subject (*problem*) is singular. Therefore the verb (*disturbs*) must be singular.

33. **(B)** "…son *could have* gone…"
The phrase *could of* is always considered substandard. Do not use *of* for *have*.

34. **(D)** "…. the horse *which* had fallen…."
The pronoun *which* should be used to refer to animals and things; *who* should be used to refer only to people.

35. **(D)** Choice A is incorrect because ending the sentence after company would destroy the charming contrasting idea which follows. Choice B is incorrect because sentence 3 clearly interrupts the flow of thought between sentences 2 and 4. Choice C is incorrect because sentence 3 relates closely in structure and content to sentence 1, especially in the reference to the caves of France, and should follow sentence 1. Choice D is correct. Choice E is incorrect because the explanation for Lampe-Pigeon which now introduces the passage is the best opening sentence. Sentence 3 clearly needs prior information to explain its references to the lamp and to the caves of France.

36. **(C)** Choices A and D are incorrect because they create a contradictory impression by equating tall

with nine and one-half inches, even though Choice D is preferable because it is more concise. Choice B is incorrect because it conveys an unwarranted apologetic note for the height of the lamp by using the conjunction although. Choice C is correct because it concisely and clearly describes the height and type of lamp being described. Choice E is incorrect because it is wordy and therefore awkward.

37. **(A)** Choice A is correct because the simple prepositional phrase is preferable to the more awkward gerund form of the incorrect Choice B. Choice C is incorrect because it is too wordy and awkward. Choice D, in addition to being the above-mentioned more awkward gerund form, is incorrect also because of the inappropriate use of the preposition to after the adjective suitable. Choice E is incorrect because it is overly long and also would create an inappropriate repetition with the word centerpiece which is used in the next phrase.

38. **(B)** Choice A is incorrect because glass globed is an awkward descriptive phrase. Choice B is correct because it is more concise than the repetitive clause which contains within it a glass globe. Choice C is incorrect and completely changes the focus of the sentence from the lamp to the globe. Choice D is incorrect because it is wordy and repetitive, Choice C is incorrect because it is too verbose.

39. **(B)** Sentence 6 contradicts and is not consistent with the paragraph and should be deleted. It would also make no sense to include that sentence in any other part of the paragraph.

# What You Must Do Now to Raise Your PSAT Score

1. Follow the directions on pages 373–375 to determine your scaled score for the PSAT Test you've just taken. These results will give you a good idea about whether or not you ought to study hard in order to achieve a certain score on the actual PSAT.

2. Eliminate your weaknesses in each of the PSAT test areas by taking the following Giant Steps toward SAT success:

## Critical Reading Part

### Giant Step 1

Take advantage of the Critical Reading Strategies that begin on page 80. Read again the Explanatory Answer for each of the Critical Reading questions that you got wrong. Refer to the Critical Reading Strategy that applies to each of your incorrect answers. Learn each of these Critical Reading Strategies thoroughly. These strategies are crucial if you want to raise your PSAT score substantially.

### Giant Step 2

You can improve your vocabulary by doing the following:

1) Learn the Hot Prefixes and Roots beginning on page 108.

2) Learn the 3 Vocabulary Strategies beginning on page 105.

3) Read as widely as possible—not only novels. Nonfiction is important too...and don't forget to read newspapers and magazines.

4) Listen to people who speak well. Tune in to worthwhile TV programs also.

5) Use the dictionary frequently and extensively—at home, on the bus, at work, etc.

6) Play word games—for example, crossword puzzles, anagrams, and Scrabble. Another game is to compose your own Sentence Completion questions. Try them on your friends.

## Math Part

### Giant Step 3

Make good use of the Math Strategies that begin on page 51. Read again the solutions for each Math question that you answered incorrectly. Refer to the Math Strategy that applies to each of your incorrect answers. Learn each of these Math Strategies thoroughly. We repeat that these strategies are crucial if you want to raise your PSAT Math score substantially.

### Giant Step 4

You may want to take **The 101 Most Important Math Questions You Need to Know How to Solve** test on page 13 and follow the directions after the test for a basic math skills diagnosis.

For each Math question that you got wrong in the test, note the reference to the Math Refresher section on page 129. This reference will explain clearly the mathematical principle involved in the solution of the question you answered incorrectly. Learn that particular mathematical principle thoroughly.

## For Both the Math and Critical Reading Parts

### Giant Step 5

You may want to take the **National Merit Scholarship Diagnostic Test** on page 1 to assess whether you're using the best strategies for the questions.

## For the Writing Part

### Giant Step 6

Take a look at Part 6—The PSAT Writing Skills Test, which describes the various item types in the Writing Section and includes sample questions with answers and explanations. Also make use of Part 7—A Brief Review of English Grammar.

3. After you have done some of the tasks you have been advised to do in the suggestions above, proceed to Practice Test 2, beginning on page 404.

 After taking Practice Test 2, concentrate on the weaknesses that still remain.

4. Continue the aforementioned procedures for Practice Test 3.

 If you do the job *right* and follow the steps listed above, you are likely to raise your PSAT score on each of the Critical Reading, Math, and Writing parts of the test 15 points—maybe 20 points—and even more.

I am the master of my fate;
I am the captain of my soul.

—From the poem "Invictus"
 by William Ernest Henley

Start at the beginning of each new section. If a section has fewer questions than answer spaces, leave the extra answer spaces blank. Be sure to erase any errors or stray marks completely.

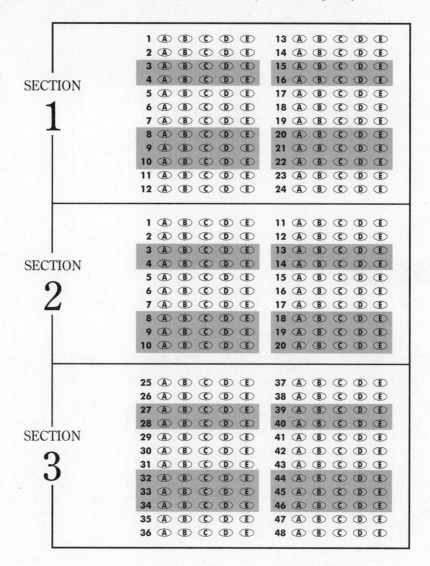

Start at the beginning of each new section. If a section has fewer questions than answer spaces, leave the extra answer spaces blank. Be sure to erase any errors or stray marks completely.

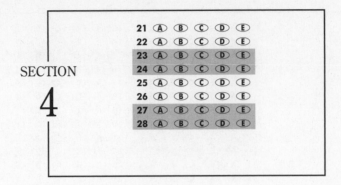

SECTION

4

CAUTION    Use the answer spaces in the grids below for Section 4.

Student-Produced Responses    ONLY ANSWERS ENTERED IN THE CIRCLES IN EACH GRID WILL BE SCORED. YOU WILL NOT RECEIVE CREDIT FOR ANYTHING WRITTEN IN THE BOXES ABOVE THE CIRCLES.

Start at the beginning of each new section. If a section has fewer questions than answer spaces, leave the extra answer spaces blank. Be sure to erase any errors or stray marks completely.

SECTION
5

| 1 | Ⓐ Ⓑ Ⓒ Ⓓ Ⓔ | 11 | Ⓐ Ⓑ Ⓒ Ⓓ Ⓔ | 21 | Ⓐ Ⓑ Ⓒ Ⓓ Ⓔ | 31 | Ⓐ Ⓑ Ⓒ Ⓓ Ⓔ |
| 2 | Ⓐ Ⓑ Ⓒ Ⓓ Ⓔ | 12 | Ⓐ Ⓑ Ⓒ Ⓓ Ⓔ | 22 | Ⓐ Ⓑ Ⓒ Ⓓ Ⓔ | 32 | Ⓐ Ⓑ Ⓒ Ⓓ Ⓔ |
| 3 | Ⓐ Ⓑ Ⓒ Ⓓ Ⓔ | 13 | Ⓐ Ⓑ Ⓒ Ⓓ Ⓔ | 23 | Ⓐ Ⓑ Ⓒ Ⓓ Ⓔ | 33 | Ⓐ Ⓑ Ⓒ Ⓓ Ⓔ |
| 4 | Ⓐ Ⓑ Ⓒ Ⓓ Ⓔ | 14 | Ⓐ Ⓑ Ⓒ Ⓓ Ⓔ | 24 | Ⓐ Ⓑ Ⓒ Ⓓ Ⓔ | 34 | Ⓐ Ⓑ Ⓒ Ⓓ Ⓔ |
| 5 | Ⓐ Ⓑ Ⓒ Ⓓ Ⓔ | 15 | Ⓐ Ⓑ Ⓒ Ⓓ Ⓔ | 25 | Ⓐ Ⓑ Ⓒ Ⓓ Ⓔ | 35 | Ⓐ Ⓑ Ⓒ Ⓓ Ⓔ |
| 6 | Ⓐ Ⓑ Ⓒ Ⓓ Ⓔ | 16 | Ⓐ Ⓑ Ⓒ Ⓓ Ⓔ | 26 | Ⓐ Ⓑ Ⓒ Ⓓ Ⓔ | 36 | Ⓐ Ⓑ Ⓒ Ⓓ Ⓔ |
| 7 | Ⓐ Ⓑ Ⓒ Ⓓ Ⓔ | 17 | Ⓐ Ⓑ Ⓒ Ⓓ Ⓔ | 27 | Ⓐ Ⓑ Ⓒ Ⓓ Ⓔ | 37 | Ⓐ Ⓑ Ⓒ Ⓓ Ⓔ |
| 8 | Ⓐ Ⓑ Ⓒ Ⓓ Ⓔ | 18 | Ⓐ Ⓑ Ⓒ Ⓓ Ⓔ | 28 | Ⓐ Ⓑ Ⓒ Ⓓ Ⓔ | 38 | Ⓐ Ⓑ Ⓒ Ⓓ Ⓔ |
| 9 | Ⓐ Ⓑ Ⓒ Ⓓ Ⓔ | 19 | Ⓐ Ⓑ Ⓒ Ⓓ Ⓔ | 29 | Ⓐ Ⓑ Ⓒ Ⓓ Ⓔ | 39 | Ⓐ Ⓑ Ⓒ Ⓓ Ⓔ |
| 10 | Ⓐ Ⓑ Ⓒ Ⓓ Ⓔ | 20 | Ⓐ Ⓑ Ⓒ Ⓓ Ⓔ | 30 | Ⓐ Ⓑ Ⓒ Ⓓ Ⓔ | | |

# PSAT PRACTICE
# TEST 2

# SECTION 1

Time: 25 Minutes—Turn to Section 1 (page 401) of your answer sheet to answer the questions in this section.
   24 Questions

**Directions:** For each question in this section, select the best answer from among the choices given and fill in the corresponding circle on the answer sheet.

---

Each sentence below has one or two blanks, each blank indicating that something has been omitted. Beneath the sentence are five words or sets of words labeled A through E. Choose the word or set of words that, when inserted in the sentence, best fits the meaning of the sentence as a whole.

Example:

Hoping to _____ the dispute, negotiators proposed a compromise that they felt would be _____ to both labor and management.

(A) enforce...useful
(B) end...divisive
(C) overcome...unattractive
(D) extend...satisfactory
(E) resolve...acceptable

Ⓐ Ⓑ Ⓒ Ⓓ ●

---

1. Joining _____ momentum for reform in intercollegiate sports, university presidents have called for swift steps to correct imbalances between classwork and _____ .

   (A) a maximum...studies
   (B) a rational...awards
   (C) an increasing...athletics
   (D) an exceptional...professors
   (E) a futile...contests

2. Thinking nothing can be done, many victims of arthritis ignore or delay _____ countermeasures, thus aggravating the problem.

   (A) tardy
   (B) injurious
   (C) characteristic
   (D) weird
   (E) effective

3. A strange and _____ fate seemed to keep him helpless and unhappy, despite occasional interludes of _____ .

   (A) malevolent...conflict
   (B) bizarre...disenchantment
   (C) virulent...tension
   (D) ineluctable...serenity
   (E) intriguing...inactivity

4. Samuel Clemens chose the _____ Mark Twain as a result of his knowledge of riverboat piloting.

   (A) protagonist
   (B) pseudonym
   (C) mountebank
   (D) hallucination
   (E) misanthrope

5. For years a vocalist of spirituals, Marian Anderson was finally recognized as _____ singer when the Metropolitan Opera House engaged her.

   (A) a versatile
   (B) an unusual
   (C) an attractive
   (D) a cooperative
   (E) a mediocre

6. Leonardo da Vinci _____ the law of gravity two centuries before Newton and also made the first complete _____ charts of the human body.

   (A) examined...colorful
   (B) anticipated...anatomical
   (C) avoided...meaningful
   (D) realized...explanatory
   (E) suspected...mural

GO ON TO THE NEXT PAGE ⟹

**7.** In a rising tide of _____ in public education, Miss Anderson was an example of an informed and _____ teacher—a blessing to children and an asset to the nation.

(A) compromise...inept
(B) pacifism...inspiring
(C) ambiguity...average
(D) mediocrity...dedicated
(E) oblivion...typical

**8.** By _____ the conversation, the girl had once again proved that she had overcome her shyness.

(A) appreciating
(B) recognizing
(C) hearing
(D) initiating
(E) considering

GO ON TO THE NEXT PAGE

The passages below are followed by questions based on their content; questions following a pair of related passages may also be based on the relationship between the paired passages. Answer the questions on the basis of what is <u>stated</u> or <u>implied</u> in the passages and in any introductory material that may be provided.

**Questions 9–12 are based on the following passages.**

### Passage 1

1 Home schooling is becoming more and more desirable because children do not have the burden of traveling to school and becoming exposed to other children's sickness and everything else that goes with being in a crowded
5 room. There is also the individual attention that the parent or tutor can give the student creating a better and more efficient learning environment. As standards become more and more flexible, home schooling may in fact be the norm of the future.

### Passage 2

10 In many studies, it was shown that students benefit in a classroom setting since the interaction and dialogue with other students creates a stimulating learning environment. The more students that are in a class, the more diversity of the group and the more varied the feedback. With a good
15 teacher and facilitator, a classroom can be very beneficial for the student's cognitive development.

9. In Passage 1, the author's condition for an effective learning condition is based on

   (A) flexible standards
   (B) the closeness of a parent and a child
   (C) the reduction of travel time
   (D) a one-on-one learning experience
   (E) the sanitary conditions in the learning environment

10. Which of the following is *not* addressed in Passage 2?

    (A) The advantage of classroom learning with the student interacting and sharing ideas with other students.
    (B) The student exposed to multicultural ways in approaching the learning experience.
    (C) The teacher playing an active role in the learning experience.
    (D) The more students in the classroom leading to the more feedback each student can receive.
    (E) The positive relationship between the different types of students and learning.

11. Which criterion is the same in home schooling and regular classroom schooling?

    (A) the health condition
    (B) the burden of travelling
    (C) the feedback with other students
    (D) the diversity of the students
    (E) the learning experience

12. How would one create a much more ideal environment for learning in either situation according to what is addressed in both passages?

    (A) In home schooling, the student could travel on weekends to cultural areas.
    (B) In school, the teacher could occasionally work with the student on an individual basis.
    (C) In home schooling, the student could be exposed to and interact with other students on a regular basis.
    (D) The student can spend one-half of his educational time in school and one-half of his educational time at home.
    (E) The student could learn at home and go to school to socialize.

GO ON TO THE NEXT PAGE

The passage below is followed by questions based on its content. Answer the questions on the basis of what is stated or implied in the passage and in any introductory material that may be provided.

## Questions 13–24 are based on the following passage.

*This passage describes the relationship between age and income throughout various periods of American history and the effects this trend will have on the various population groups in the future.*

The relationship between age and income is only casually appreciated by recent theories on the purported redistribution of income. It is known, of course, that the average person's income begins to decline after he is fifty-five years
5 of age, and that it declines sharply after sixty-five. For example as early as in 1957, 58 percent of the spending units headed by persons sixty-five years and older earned less than $2,000. The relationship between old age and low income has often been considered a reflection of
10 sociological rather than economic factors—and therefore not to be included in any study of the economy. Actually, the character of the relationship is too integrated to be dissected. However, its significance is mounting with the increase in the number of older persons. The lowest-income
15 groups include a heavy concentration of older persons—in 1957, one-third of all spending units in the $0–$2,000 class were headed by persons sixty-five years and older; in 1948, it was 28 percent.

But in economic planning and social policy, it must be
20 remembered that, with the same income, the sixty-five-or-more spending unit will not spend less or need less than the younger spending unit, even though the pressure to save is greater than on the young. The functional ethos of our economy dictates that the comparatively unproductive
25 old-age population should consume in accordance with their output rather than their requirements. Most social scientists have accepted these values; they have assumed that the minimum economic needs of the aged should be lower than those of the younger family. But it is precisely at retire-
30 ment that personal requirements and the new demands of leisure call for an even larger income if this period is to be something more enjoyable than a wait for death.

The relationship between age and income is seen most clearly in the unionized blue-collar worker. Except
35 for lay-offs, which his seniority minimizes, and wage incre-ments for higher productivity, awarded in many industries, his income range is determined by his occupation. But within that income range, the deciding factor is the man's age. After forty-five, the average worker who loses his
40 job has more difficulty in finding a new one. Despite his seniority, the older worker is likely to be downgraded to a lower-paying job when he can no longer maintain the pace set by younger men. This is especially true of unskilled and semi-skilled workers.
45 The early and lower income period of a person's working life, during which he acquires his basic vocational skills, is most pronounced for the skilled, managerial, or professional worker. Then, between the ages of twenty-five and fifty, the average worker receives his peak earnings.
50 Meanwhile, his family expenses rise, there are children to support and basic household durables to obtain. Although his family's income may rise substantially until he is somewhere between thirty-five and forty-five, per capita consumption may drop at the same time. For the growing,
55 working-class family, limited in income by the very nature of the breadwinner's occupation, the economic conse-quences of this parallel rise in age, income, and obligations are especially pressing. Many in the low-income classes are just as vulnerable to poverty during middle age, when they
60 have a substantially larger income, as in old age. As family obligations finally do begin declining, so does income. Consequently, most members of these classes never have an adequate income.

Thus we see that, for a time, increasing age means
65 increasing income, and therefore a probable boost in income-tenth position. Although there are no extensive data in the matter, it can be confidently asserted that the higher income-tenths have a much greater representation of spending units headed by persons aged thirty-five to fifty-
70 five than do the lower income-tenths. This is demonstrably the case among the richest 5 percent of the consumer units. The real question is: To what extent does distribution of income-tenths within a certain age group deviate from distribution of income-tenths generally? Although informa-
75 tion is not as complete as might be desired, there is more than enough to make contingent generalizations. Detailed data exist on income distribution by tenths and by age for 1935–36 and 1948, and on income-size distribution by age for the postwar years. They disclose sharp income inequali-
80 ties within every age group (although more moderate in the eighteen-to-twenty-five category)—inequalities that closely parallel the overall national income pattern. The implication is clear: A spending unit's income-tenth position *within his age category* varies much less, if at all, and is determined
85 primarily by his occupation.

In other words, in America, the legendary land of economic opportunity where any man can work his way to the top, there is only slight income mobility outside the natural age cycle of rising, then falling income. Since most
90 of the sixty-five-and-over age group falls into the low-income brackets and constitutes the largest segment of the $0–$2,000 income class, it is of obvious importance in analyzing future poverty in the United States to examine the growth trends of his group. The sixty-five-and-over population composed 4.0
95 percent of the total population in 1900, 5.3 percent in 1930, 8.4 percent in 1955, and will reach an estimated 10.8 percent in 2010. Between 1900 and 2010, the total national population is expected to increase 276 percent, but those from ages forty-five through sixty-four are expected to increase 416 percent,
100 and those sixty-five and over are expected to increase 672 percent. Between 1990 and 2010, the population aged eighteen to twenty-five is also expected to grow far more rapidly than the middle-aged population. With the more rapid expansion of these two low-income groups, the young and
105 the old, in the years immediately ahead, an increase in the extent of poverty is probable.

GO ON TO THE NEXT PAGE

13. According to the passage, most social scientists erroneously assume that

 (A) personal expenses increase with the age of the spending unit
 (B) the needs of the younger spending unit are greater than those of the aged
 (C) the relationship between old age and low income is an economic and not a sociological problem
 (D) members of the old-age population should consume in accordance with their requirements
 (E) leisure living requires increased income

14. The word "appreciated" in line 2 most nearly means

 (A) had artistic interest
 (B) increased in value
 (C) had curiosity
 (D) had gratitude
 (E) understood

15. It can be inferred that in the 35–55 age category

 (A) income-tenth positions vary greatly
 (B) income-tenth positions vary very little
 (C) earning potential does not resemble the overall national income pattern
 (D) occupations have little bearing on the income-tenth position
 (E) there is great mobility between income-tenth positions

16. The author believes which of the following?

 I. The aged will continue to increase as a percentage of the total population.
 II. Income inequalities decrease with increasing age.
 III. Managerial and professional workers have greater income mobility than blue-collar workers.

 (A) I only
 (B) II only
 (C) III only
 (D) I and II only
 (E) I and III only

17. In the passage the term "functional ethos" in line 23 means

 (A) national group
 (B) ethnic influence
 (C) prevailing ideology
 (D) biased opinion
 (E) practical ethics

18. The article states that the old-age population

 (A) has increased because of longer life expectancy
 (B) exceeds all but the 18–25 age group in growth rate
 (C) is well represented among the higher income-tenths
 (D) is increasing as a percentage of the low income-tenths
 (E) has its greatest numbers among the middle income group

19. According to the author, aside from the natural age cycle, economic opportunity in America is greatly limited by

 I. occupation
 II. income inequality within every group
 III. class

 (A) I only
 (B) II only
 (C) III only
 (D) I and III only
 (E) I and II only

20. The word "ethos" in line 23 most nearly means

 (A) the character of a group of people
 (B) economic–sociological ramifications
 (C) the productivity of all age groups
 (D) the management of large corporations
 (E) the social scientists who deal with the economy

21. According to the passage, the older, unionized blue-collar workers are

 (A) assured constant salary until retirement
 (B) given preference over new workers because of seniority
 (C) likely to receive downgraded salary
 (D) more susceptible to layoff after 40
 (E) encouraged to move to slower-paced but equal-paying jobs

GO ON TO THE NEXT PAGE

22. The article states that the average worker finds that

   (A) as family obligations begin escalating, income begins to decline
   (B) he reaches economic stability at middle age because of the parallel rise in age, obligations, and income
   (C) he earns least while he is acquiring vocational skills
   (D) he reaches peak earning power between the ages of 40 and 65
   (E) his wage gains coincide with the decline of family needs

23. It can be inferred that one could most accurately predict a person's income from

   (A) his age
   (B) his natural age cycle
   (C) his occupation
   (D) his occupation and age
   (E) his seniority position

24. Which lines in the passage illustrate the author's sarcasm?

   (A) lines 19–23
   (B) lines 45–48
   (C) lines 64–66
   (D) lines 86–89
   (E) lines 104–107

# STOP

If you finish before time is called, you may check your work on this section only.
Do not turn to any other section in the test.

# SECTION 2

Time: 25 Minutes—Turn to Section 2 (page 401) of your answer sheet to answer the questions in this section.
20 Questions

**Directions:** For this section, solve each problem and decide which is the best of the choices given. Fill in the corresponding circle on the answer sheet. You may use any available space for scratchwork.

## Notes:

1. The use of a calculator is permitted.
2. All numbers used are real numbers.
3. Figures that accompany problems in this test are intended to provide information useful in solving the problems. They are drawn as accurately as possible EXCEPT when it is stated in a specific problem that the figure is not drawn to scale. All figures lie in a plane unless otherwise indicated.
4. Unless otherwise specified, the domain of any function $f$ is assumed to be the set of all real numbers $x$ for which $f(x)$ is a real number.

**REFERENCE INFORMATION**

 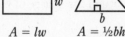    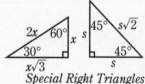

$A = \pi r^2$   $A = lw$   $A = \frac{1}{2}bh$   $V = lwh$   $V = \pi r^2 h$   $c^2 = a^2 + b^2$   *Special Right Triangles*
$C = 2\pi r$

The number of degrees of arc in a circle is 360.
The sum of the measures in degrees of the angles of a triangle is 180.

1. After giving $5 to Greg, David has $25. Greg now has $\frac{1}{5}$ as much as David does. How much did Greg start with?

(A) $0
(B) $5
(C) $7
(D) $10
(E) $15

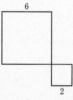

2. The figure above shows two squares with sides as shown. What is the ratio of the perimeter of the larger square to that of the smaller?

(A) 3 : 2
(B) 2 : 1
(C) 3 : 1
(D) 6 : 1
(E) 9 : 1

GO ON TO THE NEXT PAGE

3. A car travels 1,056 feet in 12 seconds. In feet per second, what is the average speed of the car?

(A) 98.0
(B) 78.8
(C) 85.8
(D) 84.0
(E) 88.0

5. $2(w)(x)(-y) - 2(-w)(-x)(y) =$

(A) 0
(B) $-4wxy$
(C) $4wxy$
(D) $-4w^2x^2y^2$
(E) $2w^2x^2y^2$

4. If $2z + 1 + 2 + 2z + 3 + 2z = 3 + 1 + 2$, then $z + 4 =$

(A) 1
(B) 4
(C) 5
(D) 6
(E) 10

6. What is an expression for 5 times the sum of the square of $x$ and the square of $y$?

(A) $5(x^2 + y^2)$
(B) $5x^2 + y^2$
(C) $5(x + y)^2$
(D) $5x^2 + y$
(E) $5(2x + 2y)$

GO ON TO THE NEXT PAGE

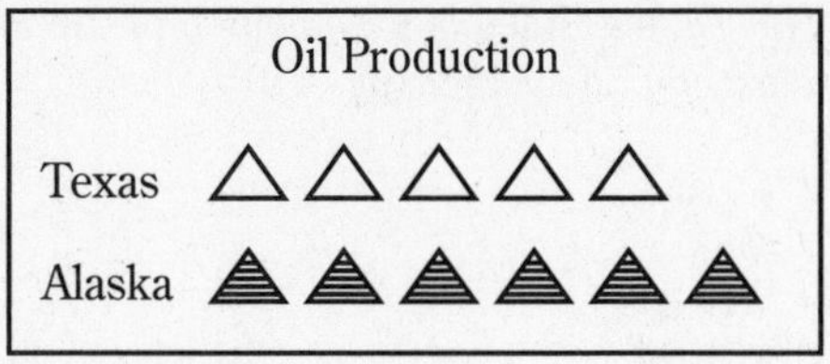

Oil Production

Texas △ △ △ △ △

Alaska ▲ ▲ ▲ ▲ ▲ ▲

**7.** In the chart above, the amount represented by each shaded triangle is three times that represented by each unshaded triangle. What fraction of the total production represented by the chart was produced in Alaska?

(A) $\dfrac{6}{11}$

(B) $\dfrac{18}{5}$

(C) $\dfrac{18}{23}$

(D) $\dfrac{12}{17}$

(E) $\dfrac{23}{17}$

**8.** If $a = 1$, $b = -2$ and $c = -2$, find the value of $\dfrac{b^2 c}{(a - c)^2}$

(A) $-\dfrac{8}{9}$

(B) $-\dfrac{2}{3}$

(C) $\dfrac{8}{9}$

(D) 8

(E) 9

**9.** If $y = 28j$, where $j$ is any integer, then $\dfrac{y}{2}$ will always be

(A) even
(B) odd
(C) positive
(D) negative
(E) less than $\dfrac{y}{3}$

**10.** If $3a + 4b = 4a - 4b = 21$, find the value of $a$.

(A) 3
(B) 6
(C) 21
(D) 42
(E) The answer cannot be determined from the information given.

GO ON TO THE NEXT PAGE

11. If $N$ is a positive integer, which of the following does *not* have to be a divisor of the sum of $N$, $6N$, and $9N$?

    (A)  1
    (B)  2
    (C)  4
    (D)  9
    (E)  16

13. If $p + pq$ is 4 times $p - pq$, which of the following has exactly one value? ($pq \neq 0$)

    (A)  $p$
    (B)  $q$
    (C)  $pq$
    (D)  $p + pq$
    (E)  $p - pq$

12. If $x = 3a - 18$ and $5y = 3a + 7$, then find $5y - x$.

    (A)  $-11$
    (B)  11
    (C)  18
    (D)  25
    (E)  $6a - 11$

14. If $2 + \dfrac{1}{z} = 0$, then what is the value of $9 + 9z$?

    (A)  $-\dfrac{9}{2}$
    (B)  $-\dfrac{1}{2}$
    (C)  0
    (D)  $\dfrac{9}{2}$
    (E)  The answer cannot be determined from the information given.

GO ON TO THE NEXT PAGE

**15.** How many times does the graph of $y = x^2$ intersect the graph of $y = x$?

(A) 0
(B) 1
(C) 2
(D) 3
(E) 4

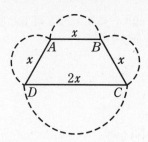

**17.** The quadrilateral $ABCD$ is a trapezoid with $x = 4$. The diameter of each semicircle is a side of the trapezoid. What is the sum of the lengths of the 4 dotted semicircles?

(A) $8\pi$
(B) $10\pi$
(C) $12\pi$
(D) $14\pi$
(E) $20\pi$

**16.** Let $wx = y$, where $wxy \neq 0$.

If both $x$ and $y$ are multiplied by 6, then $w$ is

(A) multiplied by $\frac{1}{36}$

(B) multiplied by $\frac{1}{6}$

(C) multiplied by 1
(D) multiplied by 6
(E) multiplied by 36

**18.** $\frac{7x}{144}$ yards and $\frac{5y}{12}$ feet together equal how many inches?

(A) $\frac{7x}{12} + \frac{5y}{4}$

(B) $\frac{7x}{12} + 5y$

(C) $\frac{7x}{4} + 5y$

(D) $\frac{7x}{4} + 60y$

(E) $7x + \frac{5}{4}y$

GO ON TO THE NEXT PAGE

19. If $x < 0$ and $y < 0$, which of the following must always be positive?

    I.  $x \times y$
   II.  $x + y$
  III.  $x - y$

  (A)  I only
  (B)  I and II only
  (C)  I and III only
  (D)  II and III only
  (E)  I, II, and III

20. Given that $a + 3b = 11$ and $a$ and $b$ are positive integers. What is the largest possible value of $a$?

  (A)  4
  (B)  6
  (C)  7
  (D)  8
  (E)  10

# STOP

If you finish before time is called, you may check your work on this section only.
Do not turn to any other section in the test.

# SECTION 3

Time: 25 Minutes—Turn to Section 3 (page 401) of your answer sheet to answer the questions in this section.
  24 Questions

**Directions:** For each question in this section, select the best answer from among the choices given and fill in the corresponding circle on the answer sheet.

Each sentence below has one or two blanks, each blank indicating that something has been omitted. Beneath the sentence are five words or sets of words labeled A through E. Choose the word or set of words that, when inserted in the sentence, best fits the meaning of the sentence as a whole.

Example:

Hoping to _____ the dispute, negotiators proposed a compromise that they felt would be _____ to both labor and management.

(A) enforce...useful
(B) end...divisive
(C) overcome...unattractive
(D) extend...satisfactory
(E) resolve...acceptable

Ⓐ Ⓑ Ⓒ Ⓓ ●

25. It is _____ that primitive man considered eclipses to be _____ .

(A) foretold...spectacular
(B) impossible...ominous
(C) understandable...magical
(D) true...rational
(E) glaring...desirable

26. Only an authority in that area would be able to _____ such highly _____ subject matter included in the book.

(A) understand...general
(B) confuse...simple
(C) read...useless
(D) comprehend...complex
(E) misconstrue...sophisticated

27. The professor displayed extreme stubbornness; not only did he _____ the logic of the student's argument, but he _____ to acknowledge that the textbook conclusion was correct.

(A) amplify...hesitated
(B) reject...refused
(C) clarify...consented
(D) justify...expected
(E) ridicule...proposed

28. The _____ of the explorers was reflected in their refusal to give up.

(A) tenacity
(B) degradation
(C) greed
(D) harassment
(E) sociability

29. Ironically, the protest held in order to strengthen the labor movement served to _____ it.

(A) justify
(B) coddle
(C) weaken
(D) invigorate
(E) appease

GO ON TO THE NEXT PAGE

Each passage below is followed by questions based on its content. Answer the questions on the basis of what is stated or implied in each passage and in any introductory material that may be provided.

**Questions 30–31 are based on the following passage.**

1    In the South American rain forest abide the greatest acrobats on earth. The monkeys of the Old World, agile as they are, cannot hang by their tails. It is only the monkeys of America that possess this skill. They are called ceboids
5  and their unique group includes marmosets, owl monkeys, sakis, spider monkeys, squirrel monkeys and howlers. Among these the star gymnast is the skinny, intelligent spider monkey. Hanging head down like a trapeze artist from the loop of a liana, he may suddenly give a short
10 swing, launch himself into space and, soaring outward and downward across a 50-foot void of air, lightly catch a bough on which he spied a shining berry. No owl monkey can match his leap, for their arms are shorter, their tails untalented. The marmosets, smallest of the tribe, tough noisy
15 hoodlums that travel in gangs, are also capable of leaps into space, but their landings are rough: smack against a tree trunk with arms and legs spread wide.

30. The title below that best expresses the ideas of this selection is:

(A)  The Star Gymnast
(B)  Monkeys and Trees
(C)  Travelers in Space
(D)  The Uniqueness of Monkeys
(E)  Ceboid Acrobats

31. Compared to monkeys of the Old World, American monkeys are

(A)  smaller
(B)  more quiet
(C)  more dexterous
(D)  more protective of their young
(E)  less at home in their surroundings

**Questions 32–33 are based on the following passage.**

1    A critic of politics finds himself driven to deprecate the power of words, while using them copiously in warning against their influence. It is indeed in politics that their influence is most dangerous, so that one is almost tempted
5  to wish that they did not exist, and that society might be managed silently, by instinct, habit and ocular perception, without this supervening Babel of reports, arguments and slogans.

32. The author implies that critics of misused language

(A)  become fanatical on this subject
(B)  are guilty of what they criticize in others
(C)  are clever in contriving slogans
(D)  tell the story of the Tower of Babel
(E)  rely too strongly on instincts

33. Which statement is true according to the passage?

(A)  Critics of politics are often driven to take desperate measures.
(B)  Words, when used by politicians, have the greatest capacity for harm.
(C)  Politicians talk more than other people.
(D)  Society would be better managed if mutes were in charge.
(E)  Reports and slogans are not to be trusted.

GO ON TO THE NEXT PAGE

The two passages below are followed by questions based on their content and on the relationship between the two passages. Answer the questions on the basis of what is <u>stated</u> or <u>implied</u> in the passages and in any introductory material that may be provided.

## Questions 34–42 are based on the following passages.

*The following two passages are about violence. The first discusses televised violence; the second attempts to address the history of violence in general.*

## Passage 1

Violence is alive and well on television. Yet there appears to be a difference in the quality, variety and pervasiveness of today's televised violence. Some observers believe that, as a result of more than three decades of television, viewers have

5 developed a kind of immunity to the horror of violence. By the age of 16, for example, the average young person will have seen some 18,000 murders on television. One extension of this phenomenon may be an appetite for more varied kinds of violence. On the basis of the amount of exposure,

10 certain things that initially would have been beyond the pale have become more readily accepted.

Violence on TV has been more prevalent than in recent years, in large measure because there are fewer situation comedies and more action series. But also because some 25

15 million of the nation's 85 million homes with television now receive one of the pay cable services which routinely show uncut feature films containing graphic violence as early as 8 in the evening.

The evidence is becoming overwhelming that just as

20 witnessing violence in the home may contribute to children learning and acting out violent behavior, violence on TV and in the movies may lead to the same result. Studies have shown that a steady diet of watching graphic violence or sexually violent films such as those shown on cable TV

25 has caused some men to be more willing to accept violence against women such as rape and wife-beating. Not only actual violence, but the kind of violence coming through the television screen is causing concern. One of the principal developments is the increasing sophistication of the weaponry. The

30 simple gunfight of the past has been augmented by high-tech crimes like terrorist bombings. A gunfighter shooting down a sheriff is one thing. When you have terrorist bombs, the potential is there for hundreds to die. Programs in the past used the occasional machine gun, but such weapons as the

35 M-60 machine gun and Uzi semi-automatic have become commonplace today on network shows.

Many people are no longer concerned about televised violence because they feel it is the way of the world. It is high time that broadcasters provide public messages on

40 TV screens that would warn viewers about the potentially harmful effects of viewing televised violence.

## Passage 2

We have always been a lawless and a violent people. Thus, our almost unbroken record of violence against the Indians and all others who got in our way—the Spaniards

45 in the Floridas, the Mexicans in Texas; the violence of the vigilantes on a hundred frontiers; the pervasive violence of slavery (a "perpetual exercise," Jefferson called it, "of the most boisterous passions"); the lawlessness of the Ku Klux Klan during Reconstruction and after; and of scores of

50 race riots from those of New Orleans in the 1960s to those of Chicago in 1919. Yet, all this violence, shocking as it doubtless was, no more threatened the fabric of our society or the integrity of the Union than did the lawlessness of Prohibition back in the Twenties. The explanation for this

55 is to be found in the embarrassing fact that most of it was official, quasi-official, or countenanced by public opinion: exterminating the Indian; flogging the slave; lynching the outlaw; exploiting women and children in textile mills and sweatshops; hiring Pinkertons to shoot down strikers;

60 condemning immigrants to fetid ghettos; punishing [Blacks] who tried to exercise their civil or political rights. Most of this was socially acceptable—or at least not wholly unacceptable—just as so much of our current violence is socially acceptable: the many thousands of automobile

65 deaths every year; the mortality rate for black babies twice that for white; the deaths from cancer induced by cigarettes or by air pollution; the sadism of our penal system and the horrors of our prisons; the violence of some police against the so-called "dangerous classes of society."

70 What we have now is the emergence of violence that is not acceptable either to the Establishment, which is frightened and alarmed, or to the victims of the Establishment, who are no longer submissive and who are numerous and powerful. This is now familiar "crime in the streets," or it

75 is the revolt of the young against the economy, the politics, and the wars of the established order, or it is the convulsive reaction of the blacks to a century of injustice. But now, too, official violence is no longer acceptable to its victims—or to their ever more numerous sympathizers: the violence

80 of great corporations and of government itself against the natural resources of the nation; the long drawn-out violence of the white majority against Blacks and other minorities; the violence of the police and the National Guard against the young; the massive violence of the military against the

85 peoples of other countries. These acts can no longer be absorbed by large segments of our society. It is this new polarization that threatens the body politic and the social fabric much as religious dissent threatened them in the Europe of the sixteenth and seventeenth centuries.

GO ON TO THE NEXT PAGE

34. The title that best summarizes the content of Passage 1 is

(A) TV's Role in the Rising Crime Rate
(B) Violence on TV—Past and Present
(C) TV Won't Let Up on Violence
(D) Violence Raises the TV Ratings
(E) Violence Galore on Cable TV

35. Which of the following types of TV programs would the author of Passage 1 be *least* likely to approve of?

(A) A cowboy Western called "Have Gun, Will Travel"
(B) A talk show dealing with teenage pregnancy caused by a rape
(C) A documentary dealing with Vietnam veterans suffering from the after-effects of herbicide spraying during the war
(D) A movie showing a bomb exploding in a bus carrying civilians on their way to work
(E) A soap opera in which a jealous husband is shown murdering his wife's lover, then his own wife

36. As an illustration of current "socially acceptable" violence, the author of Passage 2 would probably include

(A) National Guard violence at Kent, Ohio, during the Vietnam War
(B) the Vietnam War
(C) the cruelties of our prison system
(D) the police behavior in Chicago at the 1968 Democratic Convention
(E) "crime in the streets"

37. It can be inferred that the author's definition of violence (Passage 2)

(A) includes the social infliction of harm
(B) is limited to nongovernmental acts of force
(C) is confined to governmental acts of illegal force
(D) is synonymous with illegal conduct by either government or citizen
(E) is shared by the FBI

38. Which action or activity would the author of Passage 2 be most likely to disapprove of?

(A) trying to prevent a mugging
(B) reading a science fiction story
(C) watching a rock music TV performance
(D) attending a Super Bowl football game
(E) participating in a country square dance

39. The word "pervasiveness" in line 2 of Passage 1 (also note "pervasive" in line 46 of Passage 2) means

(A) variety
(B) televised
(C) seeping through
(D) quality
(E) terribleness

40. The author of Passage 2 would probably argue with the author of Passage 1 in the resolution of violence (lines 37–41) that

(A) if violence were curtailed on television, it would pop up elsewhere.
(B) television does not show a significant amount of violence to warrant warnings against such programs.
(C) television can also influence the public toward non-violence.
(D) there are more dangers to television than the portrayal of violence.
(E) violence is inbred in television.

41. From the passages, which can we assume to be *false*?

(A) Unlike the author of Passage 1, the author of Passage 2 believes that society is disgusted with violence.
(B) The author of Passage 1 believes that sophisticated weaponry causes increased violence, whereas the author of Passage 2 believes that violence is inherent in society.
(C) The type of violence discussed by the author of Passage 2 is much more encompassing than the type of violence discussed by the author of Passage 1.
(D) Both authors propose a direct resolution for at least a start to the end of violence.
(E) Both authors believe either that violence is a part of daily living or at least that many feel that violence is a part of daily living.

42. The word "polarization" in line 87 means

(A) electrical tendencies
(B) governments in different parts of the world
(C) completely opposing viewpoints
(D) extreme religious differences
(E) cold climatic conditions

GO ON TO THE NEXT PAGE →

**Questions 43–48 are based on the following passage.**

*The following passage is about the literature of the African-American culture and its impact on society.*

The literature of an oppressed people is the conscience of man, and nowhere is this seen with more intense clarity than in the literature of African-Americans. An essential element of African-American literature is that the literature as a
5 whole—not the work of occasional authors—is a movement against concrete wickedness. In African-American literature, accordingly, there is a grief rarely to be found elsewhere in American literature, and frequently a rage rarely to be found in American letters: a rage different in quality, profounder,
10 more towering, more intense—the rage of the oppressed. Whenever an African-American artist picks up pen or horn, his target is likely to be American racism, his subject the suffering of his people, and the core element his own grief and the grief of his people. Almost all of African-American
15 literature carries the burden of this protest.
 The cry for freedom and the protest against injustice indicate a desire for the birth of the New Man, a testament to the New Unknown World to be discovered, to be created by man. African-American literature is, as a body, a declara-
20 tion that despite the perversion and cruelty that cling like swamproots to the flesh of man's feet, man has options for freedom, for cleanliness, for wholeness, for human harmony, for goodness: for a human world. Like the spirituals that are a part of it, African-American literature is a passionate asser-
25 tion that man will win freedom. Thus, African-American literature rejects despair and cynicism; it is a literature of realistic hope and life-affirmation. This is not to say that no African-American literary work reflects cynicism or despair, but rather that the basic theme of African-American
30 literature is that man's goodness will prevail.
 African-American literature is a statement against death, a statement as to what life should be: life should be vivacious, exuberant, wholesomely uninhibited, sensual, sensuous, constructively antirespectable, life should
35 abound and flourish and laugh, life should be passionately lived and man should be loving: life should be not a sedate waltz or foxtrot but a vigorous breakdance; thus, when the African-American writer criticizes America for its cruelty, the criticism implies that America is drawn to death and
40 repelled by what should be the human style of life, the human way of living.
 Black literature in America is, then, a setting-forth of man's identity and destiny; an investigation of man's iniquity and a statement of belief in his potential godliness;
45 a prodding of man toward exploring and finding deep joy in his humanity.

43. The author states or implies that

 (A) a separate-but-equal doctrine is the answer to American racism
 (B) African-American literature is superior to American literature
 (C) hopelessness and lack of trust are the key-notes of African-American literature
 (D) standing up for one's rights and protesting about unfairness are vital
 (E) traditional forms of American-type dancing should be engaged in

44. When the author, in referring to African-American literature, states that "life should be...constructively antirespectable" (lines 32–34), it can be inferred that people ought to

 (A) do their own thing provided what they do is worthwhile
 (B) show disrespect for others when they have the desire to do so
 (C) be passionate in public whenever the urge is there
 (D) shun a person because he is of another race or color
 (E) be enraged if their ancestors have been unjustly treated

45. With reference to the passage, which of the following statements is true about African-American literature?

 I. It expresses the need for nonviolent opposition to antiracism.
 II. It urges a person to have respect for himself and for others.
 III. It voices the need for an active, productive, and satisfying life.

 (A) I only
 (B) II only
 (C) I and III only
 (D) II and III only
 (E) I, II, and III

46. The tone of the passage is one of

 (A) anger and vindictiveness
 (B) hope and affirmation
 (C) forgiveness and charity
 (D) doubt and despair
 (E) grief and cruelty

GO ON TO THE NEXT PAGE

**47.** Which of the following constitute(s) the author's view of a "human world?"

   I. harmony
  II. cleanliness
 III. wholeness

(A) I only
(B) I and II only
(C) II and III only
(D) I and III only
(E) I, II, and III

**48.** The word "iniquity" (line 44) means

(A) potential
(B) creation
(C) wickedness
(D) cleverness
(E) greatness

# STOP

If you finish before time is called, you may check your work on this section only.
Do not turn to any other section in the test.

# SECTION 4

Time: 25 Minutes—Turn to Section 4 (page 402) of your answer sheet to answer the questions in this section.
  18 Questions

**Directions:** For this section, solve each problem and decide which is the best of the choices given. Fill in the corresponding circle on the answer sheet. You may use any available space for scratchwork.

## Notes:

1. The use of a calculator is permitted.
2. All numbers used are real numbers.
3. Figures that accompany problems in this test are intended to provide information useful in solving the problems. They are drawn as accurately as possible EXCEPT when it is stated in a specific problem that the figure is not drawn to scale. All figures lie in a plane unless otherwise indicated.
4. Unless otherwise specified, the domain of any function $f$ is assumed to be the set of all real numbers $x$ for which $f(x)$ is a real number.

REFERENCE INFORMATION

      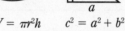 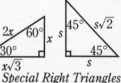

$A = \pi r^2$   $A = lw$   $A = \frac{1}{2}bh$   $V = lwh$   $V = \pi r^2h$   $c^2 = a^2 + b^2$   *Special Right Triangles*
$C = 2\pi r$

The number of degrees of arc in a circle is 360.
The sum of the measures in degrees of the angles of a triangle is 180.

---

21. Johnny buys a frying pan and two coffee mugs for $27. Joanna buys the same-priced frying pan and one of the same-priced coffee mugs for $23. How much does one of those frying pans cost?

    (A) $4
    (B) $7
    (C) $19
    (D) $20
    (E) $21

22. A rectangular floor 8 feet long and 6 feet wide is to be completely covered with tiles. Each tile is a square with a perimeter of 2 feet. What is the least number of such tiles necessary to cover the floor?

    (A) 7
    (B) 12
    (C) 24
    (D) 48
    (E) 192

GO ON TO THE NEXT PAGE

**23.** If 9 and 12 each divide $Q$ without remainder, which of the following must $Q$ divide without remainder?

(A) 1
(B) 3
(C) 36
(D) 72
(E) The answer cannot be determined from the given information.

**25.** Given three segments of length $x$, $11 - x$, and $x - 4$, respectively. Which of the following indicates the set of all numbers $x$ such that the 3 segments could be the lengths of the sides of a triangle?

(A) $x > 4$
(B) $x < 11$
(C) $0 < x < 7$
(D) $5 < x < 15$
(E) $5 < x < 7$

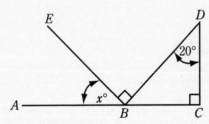

**24.** In the figure above, $DC \perp AC$, $EB \perp DB$, and $AC$ is a line segment. What is the value of $x$?

(A) 15
(B) 20
(C) 30
(D) 80
(E) 160

**26.** Given three integers $a$, $b$, and 4. If their average (arithmetic mean) is 6, which of the following could *not* be the value of the product $ab$?

(A) 13
(B) 14
(C) 40
(D) 48
(E) 49

GO ON TO THE NEXT PAGE

27. If $mn \neq 0$, then $\dfrac{1}{n^2}\left(\dfrac{m^5 n^3}{m^3}\right)^2 =$

(A) $mn^4$

(B) $m^4 n^2$

(C) $m^4 n^3$

(D) $m^4 n^4$

(E) $m^4 n^5$

28. Out of a group of 3 females and 3 males, 3 people at random enter a room. What is the probability that there are exactly 2 males in the room?

(A) $\dfrac{1}{4}$

(B) $\dfrac{3}{8}$

(C) $\dfrac{9}{20}$

(D) $\dfrac{2}{3}$

(E) $\dfrac{5}{6}$

GO ON TO THE NEXT PAGE

**Directions:** For Student-Produced Response questions 29–38, use the grids at the bottom of the answer sheet page on which you have answered questions 21–28.

Each of the remaining 10 questions requires you to solve the problem and enter your answer by marking the circles in the special grid, as shown in the examples below. You may use any available space for scratchwork.

Answer: $\frac{7}{12}$ or 7/12          Answer: 2.5          Answer: 201
Either position is correct.

Write answer in boxes. →          ← Fraction line          ← Decimal point

Grid in result. →

<u>Note</u>: You may start your answers in any column, space permitting. Columns not needed should be left blank.

- Mark no more than one oval in any column.

- Because the answer sheet will be machine-scored, **you will receive credit only if the ovals are filled in correctly.**

- Although not required, it is suggested that you write your answer in the boxes at the top of the columns to help you fill in the ovals accurately.

- Some problems may have more than one correct answer. In such cases, grid only one answer.

- No question has a negative answer.

- **Mixed numbers** such as $2\frac{1}{2}$ must be gridded as 2.5 or 5/2. (If [2 1/2] is gridded, it will be interpreted as $\frac{21}{2}$, not $2\frac{1}{2}$.)

- <u>Decimal Accuracy:</u> If you obtain a decimal answer, **enter the most accurate value the grid will accommodate.** For example, if you obtain an answer such as 0.6666..., you should record the result as .666 or .667. **Less accurate values such as .66 or .67 are not acceptable.**

Acceptable ways to grid $\frac{2}{3}$ = .6666...

29. If $\frac{5}{8}$ of $x$ is 40, then find the value of $\frac{3}{8}$ of $x$.

30. A piece of wire is bent to form a circle of radius 3 feet. How many pieces of wire, each 2 feet long, can be made from the wire?

31. Dick spent $7 in order to buy baseballs and tennis balls. If baseballs are 70¢ each and tennis balls are 60¢ each, what is the greatest possible number of tennis balls that Dick could have bought?

GO ON TO THE NEXT PAGE ⟹

**32.** Let $f(x)$ be defined for all $x$ by the equation $f(x) = 12x + 8$. Thus, $f(2) = 32$. If $f(x) \div f(0) = 2x$, then find the value of $x$.

|      |      |      |      |
|------|------|------|------|
| ABA  | BBB  | CBA  | BBA  |
| ACC  | CBC  | CCC  | ACA  |
| BAC  | ABC  | BCA  | CAB  |
| CBB  | BCA  | AAB  | ACC  |

**33.** In the triple arrangement of letters above, a triple has a value of 1 if exactly 2 of the letters in the triple are the same. Any other combination has a value of 0. The value of the entire arrangement is the sum of the values of each of the triples. What is the value of the above arrangement?

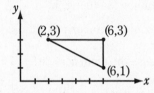

**34.** In the figure above, what is the area of the triangle?

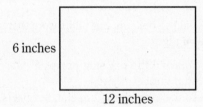

6 inches

12 inches

**35.** How many squares 2 inches on an edge can be placed, without overlapping, into the rectangle shown above?

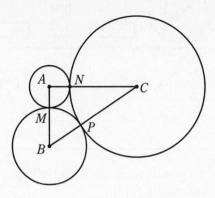

**36.** The circles having their centers at $A$, $B$, and $C$ have radii of 1, 2, and 3, respectively. The circles are tangent at points $M$, $N$, and $P$ as shown above. What is the product of the lengths of the sides of the triangle?

**37.** If the average (arithmetic mean) of 4 numbers is 8000 and the average (arithmetic mean) of 3 of the 4 numbers is 7500, then what must the fourth number be?

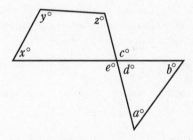

**38.** Five line segments intersect to form the figure above. What is the value of $x + y + z$ if $c = 100$?

# STOP

If you finish before time is called, you may check your work on this section only.
Do not turn to any other section in the test.

# SECTION 5

Time: 30 Minutes—Turn to Section 5 (page 403) of your answer sheet to answer the questions in this section.
    39 Questions

**Directions:** For each question in this section, select the best answer from among the choices given and fill in the corresponding circle on the answer sheet.

The following sentences test correctness and effectiveness of expression. Part of each sentence or the entire sentence is underlined; beneath each sentence are five ways of phrasing the underlined material. Choice A repeats the original phrasing; the other four choices are different. If you think the original phrasing produces a better sentence than any of the alternatives, select choice A; if not, select one of the other choices.

In making your selection, follow the requirements of standard written English; that is, pay attention to grammar, choice of words, sentence construction, and punctuation. Your selection should result in the most effective sentence—clear and precise, without awkwardness or ambiguity.

EXAMPLE:

Laura Ingalls Wilder published her first book and she was sixty-five years old then.

(A) and she was sixty-five years old then
(B) when she was sixty-five
(C) at age sixty-five years old
(D) upon the reaching of sixty-five years
(E) at the time when she was sixty-five

1. After the defendant charged him with being prejudiced, the judge withdrew from the case.

    (A) After the defendant charged him with being prejudiced
    (B) On account of the defendant charged him with being prejudiced
    (C) Charging the defendant with being prejudiced
    (D) Upon the defendant charging him with being prejudiced
    (E) The defendant charged him with being prejudiced

2. Although the mourners differed in color and in dress, they all sat silently together for an hour to honor Whitney M. Young, Jr.

    (A) Although the mourners differed in color and in dress
    (B) Because the mourners differed in color and in dress
    (C) The mourners having differed in color and in dress
    (D) When the mourners differed in color and in dress
    (E) The mourners differed in color and in dress

3. To avoid the hot sun, our plans were that we would travel at night.

    (A) To avoid the hot sun, our plans were that we would travel at night.
    (B) To try to avoid the hot sun, our plans were for travel at night.
    (C) Our plans were night travel so that we could avoid the hot sun.
    (D) We planned to travel at night, that's how we would avoid the hot sun.
    (E) To avoid the hot sun, we made plans to travel at night.

4. Whatever she had any thoughts about, they were interrupted as the hotel lobby door opened.

    (A) Whatever she had any thoughts about
    (B) Whatever her thoughts
    (C) Whatever be her thoughts
    (D) What her thoughts were
    (E) What thoughts

GO ON TO THE NEXT PAGE

5. The use of radar, as well as the two-way radio, <u>make it possible</u> for state troopers to intercept most speeders.

    (A) make it possible
    (B) makes it possible
    (C) allows the possibility
    (D) makes possible
    (E) make it a possibility

6. <u>Irregardless what reasons or excuses are offered</u>, there is only one word for his behavior: cowardice.

    (A) Irregardless what reasons or excuses are offered
    (B) Regardless about what reasons or excuses he may offer
    (C) Since he offered reasons and excuses
    (D) Nevertheless he offered reasons and excuses
    (E) No matter what reasons and excuses are offered

7. <u>What a man cannot state, he does not perfectly know.</u>

    (A) What a man cannot state, he does not perfectly know.
    (B) A man cannot state if he does not perfectly know.
    (C) A man cannot perfectly know if he does not state.
    (D) That which a man cannot state is that which he cannot perfectly know.
    (E) What a man cannot state is the reason he does not perfectly know.

8. Professional writers realize that <u>they cannot hope to effect</u> the reader precisely as they wish without care and practice in the use of words.

    (A) they cannot hope to effect
    (B) they cannot hope to have an effect on
    (C) they cannot hope to affect
    (D) they cannot hope effecting
    (E) they cannot try to affect

9. I've met two men <u>whom, I believe</u>, were policemen.

    (A) whom, I believe
    (B) who, I believe
    (C) each, I believe
    (D) and I believe they
    (E) who

10. Such people <u>never have and never will be trusted</u>.

    (A) never have and never will be trusted
    (B) never have and will be trusted
    (C) never have trusted and never will trust
    (D) never have been trusted and never will be trusted
    (E) never have had anyone trust them and never will have anyone trust them

11. Your employer would have been inclined to favor your request <u>if you would have waited for an occasion</u> when he was less busy.

    (A) if you would have waited for an occasion
    (B) if you would only have waited for an occasion
    (C) if you were to have waited for an occasion
    (D) if you waited for an occasion
    (E) if you had waited for an occasion

12. The porch of a famous home collapsed during a party last week, <u>which injured 23 people</u>.

    (A) which injured 23 people
    (B) causing 23 people to be injured
    (C) injuring 23 people
    (D) damaging 23 people
    (E) resulting in 23 people being injured

13. Jack's favorite summer supper includes barbecued chicken, grilled corn on the cob, sliced tomatoes, <u>and he likes green salad</u>.

    (A) and he likes green salad
    (B) in addition to green salad
    (C) adding green salad
    (D) including green salad
    (E) and green salad

14. I want the <u>best price</u> I can get for my car.

    (A) best price
    (B) most highest price
    (C) price which is the best
    (D) most best price
    (E) premium price

GO ON TO THE NEXT PAGE

15. The injured man was taken to the hospital, <u>where he was treated for facial lacerations and released</u>.

   (A) where he was treated for facial lacerations and released

   (B) where he was treated and released for facial lacerations

   (C) where his facial lacerations were treated and he was released from the hospital

   (D) where his treatment was for facial lacerations and he was released from the hospital

   (E) where he received facial lacerations treatment and was released

16. The wife of the new leader is tough, single-minded, and <u>tries to be independent</u>.

   (A) tries to be independent

   (B) acting in dependent

   (C) independent

   (D) an independent person

   (E) an independent

17. <u>I find Henry James' prose style more difficult to read than James Joyce</u>.

   (A) I find Henry James' prose style more difficult to read than James Joyce.

   (B) I find Henry Jame's prose style more difficult to read than James Joyce'.

   (C) I find Henry James's prose style more difficult to read than James Joyce's.

   (D) I find the prose style of Henry James more difficult to read than James Joyce.

   (E) Henry James' prose style I find more difficult to read than I find James Joyce.

18. <u>Neither Dr. Conant nor his followers knows what to do about the problem</u>.

   (A) Neither Dr. Conant nor his followers knows what to do about the problem.

   (B) Neither Dr. Conant or his followers knows what to do about the problem.

   (C) Neither Dr. Conant nor his followers know what to do about the problem.

   (D) Neither Dr. Conant nor his followers know what to do as far as the problem goes.

   (E) As to the problem, neither Dr. Conant nor his followers know what to do.

19. <u>The students requested a meeting with the chancellor</u> since they desired a greater voice in university policy.

   (A) The students requested a meeting with the chancellor

   (B) A meeting with the chancellor was requested by the students

   (C) It occurred to the students to request a meeting with the chancellor

   (D) The chancellor was the one with whom the students requested a meeting

   (E) The students insisted upon a meeting with the chancellor

20. Three American scientists were jointly awarded the Nobel Prize in Medicine <u>for their study of viruses which led to discoveries</u>.

   (A) for their study of viruses which led to discoveries

   (B) for their discoveries concerning viruses

   (C) as a prize for their discoveries about viruses

   (D) the discovery into viruses being the reason

   (E) for their virus discoveries

GO ON TO THE NEXT PAGE

The following sentences test your ability to recognize grammar and usage errors. Each sentence contains either a single error or no error at all. No sentence contains more than one error. The error, if there is one, is underlined and lettered. If the sentence contains an error, select the one underlined part that must be changed to make the sentence correct. If the sentence is correct, select choice E. In choosing answers, follow the requirements of standard written English.

EXAMPLE:

The other delegates and him immediately
    A                    B      C
accepted the resolution drafted by
                         D
the neutral states. No error.
                    E

21. Because of the bomb threat everyone was asked
    A                                     B
to evacuate the bank but a security guard,
                     C
a fireman, and I. No error.
              D    E

22. Having drank almost all the lemonade which his
    A                                   B
wife had made for the picnic, Dick could not face
     C                              D
her. No error.
     E

23. The wealthy socialite decided that her fortune

would be left to whomever of her relatives
    A            B
could present her with the best plan for dispensing
    C
part of the money to deserving charities. No error.
                     D                    E

24. Shortly after arriving at the amusement park with
                 A
the eager third-graders, the parents realized that
                                      B
they had brought nowhere near the number of
                 C              D
chaperones required to control the children.

No error.
    E

25. The board members along with the chairman were
                     A                        B
planning a series of speakers to lecture on different
    B     C
dividend plans for their employees. No error.
                   D                E

26. Due to his not studying and not attending review
    A    B
sessions, Paul got a failing mark in his bar exam,
                C
resulting in a retraction of the job offer from the
    D
law firm. No error.
          E

27. When I was in high school, I worked hard to buy
           A                          B
the kind of a car that most of my friends were
    C              D
also driving. No error.
              E

28. The literature professor has complained that many
                          A
student poets are so conceited that they compare
                   B
their poems with Robert Frost. No error.
C                 D            E

29. I appreciate you offering to help me with my
                A          B
research project, but the honor system prevents
                                       C
students from giving and receiving assistance.
                                    D
No error.
E

30. In the final heat of the mile race, only two runners
                                       A
finished the race, but even the slowest of the
                               B
two was able to break the school record that
    C
had been set a decade earlier. No error.
D                             E

GO ON TO THE NEXT PAGE

31. Passing the <u>written</u> test <u>that</u> is required for a
                A         B
    driver's license is usually <u>easier</u> than <u>to pass</u> the
                       C          D
    driving test. <u>No error</u>.
                 E

32. All the <u>aspiring</u> young writers submitted their
              A
    <u>stories</u>, each <u>hoping</u> that <u>they</u> would win first prize.
          B       C       D
    <u>No error</u>.
         E

33. Her answer <u>to</u> the essay question on the test was
               A
    <u>all together</u> incorrect, but because it was very
          B
    <u>well written</u> she received <u>partial</u> credit for her work.
            C             D
    <u>No error</u>.
         E

34. When I introduced Scott and Wilma, <u>they</u> acted
                               A
    <u>as if</u> they never <u>met</u> before <u>even though</u> they had
         B        C       D
    gone to the same high school. <u>No error</u>.
                          E

GO ON TO THE NEXT PAGE

**Directions:** The following passage is an early draft of an essay. Some parts of the passage need to be rewritten.

Read the passage and select the best answers for the questions that follow. Some questions are about particular sentences or parts of sentences and ask you to improve sentence structure or word choice. Other questions ask you to consider organization and development. In choosing answers, follow the requirements of standard written English.

**Questions 35–39 refer to the following passage.**

¹It has been proved beyond doubt that using seat belts in automobiles and wearing helmets while riding motorcycles can save lives. ²The federal government has passed laws requiring the installation of seat belts in all new cars. ³Still, there are people who argue that government has no right to interfere with individual comfort and freedom by mandating the installation and use of these safety devices. ⁴In many states, laws prohibit motorcyclists from riding without helmets. ⁵What these people fail to realize is that, although wearing a seat belt may be somewhat uncomfortable or confining, it is not as uncomfortable as broken bones nor as confining as a wheelchair or a coffin. ⁶Motorcyclists who refuse to wear helmets may enjoy a degree of pleasure in feeling the free wind blow through their hair, but, if thrown in an accident, their heads can be as easily squashed as "free and natural" cantaloupes. ⁷These safety devices may limit pleasure and freedom in small ways because they greatly increase the opportunity to live pleasant and free lives in more important ways.

35. What should be done with sentence four?

 (A) It should be placed before sentence one.
 (B) It should be attached to sentence three with and.
 (C) Nothing should be done with it.
 (D) It should be placed after sentence two.
 (E) It should be attached to sentence five with a semicolon.

36. In sentence six what change is needed?

 (A) These riders are should be inserted before thrown.
 (B) Cantaloupes should be changed to balloons.
 (C) They should be substituted for their heads.
 (D) Commas should be placed around who refuse to wear helmets.
 (E) Degree should be changed to measure.

37. Sentence seven would be improved by

 (A) turning it into two sentences, the first to end after small ways
 (B) putting a comma after devices
 (C) beginning the sentence with while
 (D) omitting in more important ways
 (E) changing because to but

38. Which would get the author's point across more effectively?

 (A) Inserting a sentence that would describe statistics about the danger of not wearing seat belts or helmets.
 (B) Describing the mechanics of how a seat belt works and how a helmet protects the head.
 (C) Describing the governmental agency that enforced the laws.
 (D) Pinpointing the states that enforce the helmet law.
 (E) Citing the safest cars and motorcycles.

39. To begin the author's paragraph,

 (A) sentence 2 should be placed first.
 (B) sentence 4 should be placed first.
 (C) sentence 6 should be placed first.
 (D) sentence 7 should be placed first deleting the first word, "These" in that sentence.
 (E) sentence 1 should remain as the introductory sentence.

# STOP

If you finish before time is called, you may check your work on this section only.
Do not turn to any other section in the test.

# How Did You Do on This Test?

Step 1. Go to the Answer Key on pages 435–436.

Step 2. For your "raw score," calculate it using the directions on pages 437–438.

Step 3. Get your "scaled score" for the test by referring to the Raw Score/Scaled Score Conversion Table on page 439.

*THERE'S ALWAYS ROOM FOR IMPROVEMENT!*

# Answer Key for Practice Test 2

## Critical Reading

### Section 1

| | Correct Answer |
|---|---|
| 1 | C |
| 2 | E |
| 3 | D |
| 4 | B |
| 5 | A |
| 6 | B |
| 7 | D |
| 8 | D |
| 9 | D |
| 10 | B |
| 11 | E |
| 12 | C |
| 13 | B |
| 14 | E |
| 15 | A |
| 16 | E |
| 17 | C |
| 18 | D |
| 19 | D |
| 20 | A |
| 21 | C |
| 22 | C |
| 23 | C |
| 24 | D |

Number correct

Number incorrect

### Section 3

| | Correct Answer |
|---|---|
| 25 | C |
| 26 | D |
| 27 | B |
| 28 | A |
| 29 | C |
| 30 | E |
| 31 | C |
| 32 | B |
| 33 | B |
| 34 | C |
| 35 | D |
| 36 | C |
| 37 | A |
| 38 | D |
| 39 | C |
| 40 | A |
| 41 | D |
| 42 | C |
| 43 | D |
| 44 | A |
| 45 | D |
| 46 | B |
| 47 | E |
| 48 | C |

Number correct

Number incorrect

## Math

### Section 2

| | Correct Answer |
|---|---|
| 1 | A |
| 2 | C |
| 3 | E |
| 4 | B |
| 5 | B |
| 6 | A |
| 7 | C |
| 8 | A |
| 9 | A |
| 10 | B |
| 11 | D |
| 12 | D |
| 13 | B |
| 14 | D |
| 15 | C |
| 16 | C |
| 17 | B |
| 18 | C |
| 19 | A |
| 20 | D |

Number correct

Number incorrect

### Section 4

| | Correct Answer |
|---|---|
| 21 | C |
| 22 | E |
| 23 | E |
| 24 | B |
| 25 | E |
| 26 | B |
| 27 | D |
| 28 | C |

Number correct

Number incorrect

**Student-Produced Response Questions**

| | |
|---|---|
| 29 | 24 |
| 30 | 9 |
| 31 | 7 |
| 32 | 2 |
| 33 | 8 |
| 34 | 4 |
| 35 | 18 |
| 36 | 60 |
| 37 | 9500 |
| 38 | 280 |

Number correct

Number incorrect

# Writing Skills

## Section 5

| | Correct Answer |
|---|---|
| 1 | A |
| 2 | A |
| 3 | E |
| 4 | B |
| 5 | B |
| 6 | E |
| 7 | A |
| 8 | C |
| 9 | B |
| 10 | D |
| 11 | E |
| 12 | C |
| 13 | E |
| 14 | A |
| 15 | A |
| 16 | C |
| 17 | C |
| 18 | C |
| 19 | A |
| 20 | B |
| 21 | D |
| 22 | A |
| 23 | B |
| 24 | C |
| 25 | E |
| 26 | A |
| 27 | C |
| 28 | D |
| 29 | A |
| 30 | B |
| 31 | D |
| 32 | D |
| 33 | B |
| 34 | C |
| 35 | A |
| 36 | A |
| 37 | E |
| 38 | A |
| 39 | E |

Number correct

Number incorrect

## Scoring the PSAT Practice Test

Check your responses with the correct answers on the previous pages. Fill in the blanks below and do the calculations to get your math, critical reading, and writing raw scores. Use the table to find your math, critical reading, and writing scaled scores.

## Get Your Critical Reading Score

How many critical reading questions did you get **right?**

Section 1: Questions 1–24 _____

Section 3: Questions 25–48 + _____

Total = _____ **(A)**

How many critical reading questions did you get **wrong?**

Section 1: Questions 1–24 _____

Section 3: Questions 25–48 + _____

Total = _____

× 0.25 = _____ **(B)**

**A – B** = _____

Critical Reading Raw Score

Round critical reading raw score to the nearest whole number.

_____

Use the Score Conversion Table to find your critical reading scaled score.

_____

## Get Your Math Score

How many math questions did you get **right?**

Section 2: Questions 1–20 _____

Section 4: Questions 21–38 + _____

Total = _____ **(A)**

How many multiple-choice math questions did you get **wrong?**

Section 2: Questions 1–20 _____

Section 4: Questions 21–38 + _____

Total = _____

× 0.25 = _____ **(B)**

**A – B** = _____

Math Raw Score

Round math raw score to the nearest whole number.

_____

Use the Score Conversion Table to find your math scaled score.

_____

## Get Your Writing Skills Score

How many multiple-choice writing questions did you get **right?**

Section 5: Questions 1–39 _____

Total = _____ **(A)**

How many multiple-choice writing questions did you get **wrong?**

Section 5: Questions 1–39 _____

Total = _____

$\times$ 0.25 = _____ **(B)**

**A – B** = _____

Writing Raw Score

Round writing raw score to the nearest whole number.

_____

Use the Score Conversion Table to find your writing scaled score.

_____

# PSAT Score Conversion Table

| Raw Score | Scaled Scores | | | Raw Score | Scaled Scores | | |
|---|---|---|---|---|---|---|---|
| | Critical Reading | Math | Writing Skills | | Critical Reading | Math | Writing Skills |
| 48 | 80 | | | 15 | 43 | 45 | 44 |
| 47 | 80 | | | 14 | 42 | 44 | 43 |
| 46 | 77 | | | 13 | 41 | 43 | 42 |
| | | | | | | | |
| 45 | 75 | | | 12 | 40 | 42 | 41 |
| 44 | 74 | | | 11 | 38 | 42 | 40 |
| 43 | 72 | | | 10 | 38 | 40 | 39 |
| 42 | 70 | | | 9 | 37 | 39 | 38 |
| 41 | 68 | | | 8 | 35 | 38 | 37 |
| | | | | | | | |
| 40 | 67 | | | 7 | 34 | 37 | 36 |
| 39 | 66 | | 80 | 6 | 33 | 36 | 35 |
| 38 | 65 | 80 | 77 | 5 | 31 | 34 | 34 |
| 37 | 64 | 77 | 73 | 4 | 30 | 33 | 33 |
| 36 | 63 | 74 | 72 | 3 | 29 | 31 | 31 |
| | | | | | | | |
| 35 | 62 | 71 | 70 | 2 | 27 | 29 | 30 |
| 34 | 61 | 69 | 68 | 1 | 24 | 26 | 28 |
| 33 | 60 | 68 | 65 | 0 | 22 | 24 | 27 |
| 32 | 59 | 67 | 64 | −1 | 20 | 20 | 24 |
| 31 | 58 | 65 | 63 | −2 | 20 | 20 | 21 |
| | | | | | | | |
| 30 | 57 | 64 | 62 | −3 | 20 | 20 | 20 |
| 29 | 56 | 62 | 60 | −4 | 20 | 20 | 20 |
| 28 | 55 | 61 | 59 | −5 | 20 | 20 | 20 |
| 27 | 54 | 60 | 57 | −6 | 20 | 20 | 20 |
| 26 | 53 | 58 | 56 | −7 | 20 | 20 | 20 |
| | | | | | | | |
| 25 | 52 | 57 | 55 | −8 | 20 | | 20 |
| 24 | 51 | 56 | 54 | −9 | 20 | | 20 |
| 23 | 51 | 54 | 53 | −10 | 20 | | 20 |
| 22 | 50 | 53 | 52 | −11 | 20 | | |
| 21 | 49 | 52 | 51 | −12 | 20 | | |
| | | | | | | | |
| 20 | 48 | 51 | 50 | | | | |
| 19 | 47 | 50 | 49 | | | | |
| 18 | 46 | 49 | 48 | | | | |
| 17 | 45 | 48 | 46 | | | | |
| 16 | 44 | 47 | 45 | | | | |

# PSAT/NMSQT Percentiles and Mean Scores

*can be used to compare a student's performance with that of juniors and sophomores.*

| JUNIORS | | | | SOPHOMORES | | | |
|---|---|---|---|---|---|---|---|
| | Percentiles | | | | Percentiles | | |
| Score | Critical Reading | Math | Writing Skills | Score | Critical Reading | Math | Writing Skills |
| 80 | 99+ | 99+ | 99+ | 80 | 99+ | 99+ | 99+ |
| 79 | 99+ | 99+ | 99+ | 79 | 99+ | 99+ | 99+ |
| 78 | 99+ | 99+ | 99+ | 78 | 99+ | 99+ | 99+ |
| 77 | 99 | 99 | 99 | 77 | 99+ | 99+ | 99+ |
| 76 | 99 | 99 | 99 | 76 | 99+ | 99+ | 99+ |
| 75 | 99 | 99 | 99 | 75 | 99+ | 99+ | 99+ |
| 74 | 99 | 98 | 99 | 74 | 99+ | 99 | 99+ |
| 73 | 99 | 98 | 98 | 73 | 99+ | 99 | 99+ |
| 72 | 98 | 98 | 98 | 72 | 99 | 99 | 99+ |
| 71 | 98 | 97 | 98 | 71 | 99 | 99 | 99+ |
| 70 | 97 | 97 | 98 | 70 | 99 | 99 | 99 |
| 69 | 97 | 96 | 97 | 69 | 99 | 98 | 99 |
| 68 | 96 | 94 | 96 | 68 | 99 | 98 | 99 |
| 67 | 96 | 92 | 96 | 67 | 98 | 97 | 99 |
| 66 | 95 | 92 | 96 | 66 | 98 | 97 | 99 |
| 65 | 93 | 90 | 94 | 65 | 97 | 96 | 98 |
| 64 | 92 | 88 | 93 | 64 | 97 | 95 | 97 |
| 63 | 91 | 87 | 92 | 63 | 96 | 94 | 97 |
| 62 | 90 | 85 | 90 | 62 | 96 | 93 | 96 |
| 61 | 88 | 83 | 90 | 61 | 95 | 92 | 96 |
| 60 | 86 | 80 | 88 | 60 | 94 | 90 | 95 |
| 59 | 85 | 79 | 85 | 59 | 93 | 89 | 93 |
| 58 | 82 | 76 | 85 | 58 | 91 | 87 | 93 |
| 57 | 80 | 73 | 83 | 57 | 90 | 85 | 92 |
| 56 | 78 | 71 | 81 | 56 | 89 | 83 | 91 |
| 55 | 76 | 70 | 79 | 55 | 87 | 83 | 89 |
| 54 | 74 | 66 | 75 | 54 | 85 | 80 | 87 |
| 53 | 71 | 63 | 72 | 53 | 83 | 77 | 84 |
| 52 | 68 | 59 | 68 | 52 | 81 | 74 | 82 |
| 51 | 62 | 56 | 66 | 51 | 77 | 71 | 80 |
| 50 | 59 | 52 | 63 | 50 | 74 | 68 | 78 |
| 49 | 55 | 49 | 59 | 49 | 71 | 65 | 74 |
| 48 | 52 | 45 | 55 | 48 | 69 | 61 | 71 |
| 47 | 49 | 42 | 54 | 47 | 65 | 58 | 70 |
| 46 | 45 | 41 | 50 | 46 | 62 | 58 | 67 |
| 45 | 41 | 38 | 48 | 45 | 58 | 54 | 65 |
| 44 | 37 | 34 | 44 | 44 | 54 | 50 | 62 |
| 43 | 35 | 31 | 40 | 43 | 52 | 47 | 58 |
| 42 | 32 | 26 | 36 | 42 | 48 | 40 | 53 |
| 41 | 28 | 25 | 33 | 41 | 44 | 39 | 49 |
| 40 | 25 | 22 | 31 | 40 | 40 | 36 | 48 |
| 39 | 24 | 19 | 28 | 39 | 40 | 31 | 44 |
| 38 | 20 | 16 | 24 | 38 | 34 | 27 | 39 |
| 37 | 18 | 14 | 21 | 37 | 31 | 23 | 35 |
| 36 | 17 | 11 | 17 | 36 | 31 | 20 | 30 |
| 35 | 15 | 11 | 16 | 35 | 27 | 20 | 28 |
| 34 | 13 | 9 | 13 | 34 | 23 | 17 | 24 |
| 33 | 10 | 7 | 11 | 33 | 20 | 13 | 20 |
| 32 | 10 | 7 | 10 | 32 | 20 | 13 | 19 |
| 31 | 9 | 5 | 8 | 31 | 18 | 9 | 15 |
| 30 | 7 | 5 | 6 | 30 | 15 | 9 | 11 |
| 29 | 6 | 3 | 5 | 29 | 12 | 6 | 11 |
| 28 | 6 | 3 | 5 | 28 | 12 | 6 | 9 |
| 27 | 4 | 3 | 3 | 27 | 9 | 6 | 6 |
| 26 | 4 | 2 | 3 | 26 | 9 | 4 | 6 |
| 25 | 4 | 2 | 3 | 25 | 9 | 4 | 6 |
| 24 | 3 | 1 | 2 | 24 | 6 | 3 | 4 |
| 23 | 3 | 1 | 2 | 23 | 6 | 3 | 4 |
| 22 | 2 | 1 | 2 | 22 | 5 | 3 | 4 |
| 21 | 2 | 1 | 1 | 21 | 5 | 3 | 2 |
| 20 | 1 | 1 | 1 | 20 | 1 | 1 | 1 |
| Mean Score | 46.8 | 48.9 | 45.9 | Mean Score | 41.9 | 44.3 | 41.3 |

## Points to Note

- Percentiles indicate the percentage of students whose scores fall below each specified score.

- On the score report, percentiles for juniors compare their performance with that of other juniors who took the test. For sophomores or younger students, percentiles compare their performance with that of sophomores.

- Percentiles are based on the critical reading, math, and writing skills scores earned by a sample of college-bound juniors or sophomores who took the PSAT/NMSQT.

- The *mean* score is the statistic that describes the *average* performance of a group.

# National Merit Scholarship Selection Index Percentiles and Mean Score

| JUNIORS | | | | | |
|---|---|---|---|---|---|
| Composite Score | Percentile | Composite Score | Percentile | Composite Score | Percentile |
| 240–223 | 99+ | 173 | 83 | 123 | 28 |
| 222 | 99 | 172 | 82 | 122 | 27 |
| 221 | 99 | 171 | 81 | 121 | 26 |
| 220 | 99 | 170 | 81 | 120 | 25 |
| 219 | 99 | 169 | 80 | 119 | 24 |
| 218 | 99 | 168 | 79 | 118 | 23 |
| 217 | 99 | 167 | 78 | 117 | 22 |
| 216 | 99 | 166 | 77 | 116 | 21 |
| 215 | 99 | 165 | 76 | 115 | 20 |
| 214 | 99 | 164 | 75 | 114 | 20 |
| 213 | 99 | 163 | 74 | 113 | 19 |
| 212 | 99 | 162 | 73 | 112 | 18 |
| 211 | 98 | 161 | 72 | 111 | 17 |
| 210 | 98 | 160 | 71 | 110 | 16 |
| 209 | 98 | 159 | 70 | 109 | 16 |
| 208 | 98 | 158 | 69 | 108 | 15 |
| 207 | 98 | 157 | 68 | 107 | 14 |
| 206 | 98 | 156 | 67 | 106 | 13 |
| 205 | 97 | 155 | 66 | 105 | 13 |
| 204 | 97 | 154 | 65 | 104 | 12 |
| 203 | 97 | 153 | 64 | 103 | 12 |
| 202 | 97 | 152 | 62 | 102 | 11 |
| 201 | 96 | 151 | 61 | 101 | 10 |
| 200 | 96 | 150 | 60 | 100 | 10 |
| 199 | 96 | 149 | 59 | 99 | 9 |
| 198 | 96 | 148 | 58 | 98 | 9 |
| 197 | 95 | 147 | 56 | 97 | 8 |
| 196 | 95 | 146 | 55 | 96 | 8 |
| 195 | 95 | 145 | 54 | 95 | 7 |
| 194 | 94 | 144 | 53 | 94 | 7 |
| 193 | 94 | 143 | 52 | 93 | 6 |
| 192 | 94 | 142 | 50 | 92 | 6 |
| 191 | 93 | 141 | 49 | 91 | 6 |
| 190 | 93 | 140 | 48 | 90 | 5 |
| 189 | 92 | 139 | 47 | 89 | 5 |
| 188 | 92 | 138 | 45 | 88 | 5 |
| 187 | 91 | 137 | 44 | 87 | 4 |
| 186 | 91 | 136 | 43 | 86 | 4 |
| 185 | 90 | 135 | 42 | 85 | 4 |
| 184 | 90 | 134 | 41 | 84 | 3 |
| 183 | 89 | 133 | 39 | 83 | 3 |
| 182 | 89 | 132 | 38 | 82 | 3 |
| 181 | 88 | 131 | 37 | 81 | 2 |
| 180 | 88 | 130 | 36 | 80 | 2 |
| 179 | 87 | 129 | 35 | 79 | 2 |
| 178 | 86 | 128 | 34 | 78 | 2 |
| 177 | 86 | 127 | 32 | 77–60 | 1 |
| 176 | 85 | 126 | 31 | | |
| 175 | 84 | 125 | 30 | | |
| 174 | 84 | 124 | 29 | | |
| Mean Score | | | | | 141.6 |

## Points to Note

Reported on a sliding scale from 60 to 240, the Selection Index is the sum of the Critical Reading, Math, and Writing Skills scores. For example, a Critical Reading score of 56, a Math score of 62, and a Writing Skills score of 59 would result in a composite Selection Index of 177 (56 + 62 + 59).

Percentiles are based on the Selection Index earned by a sample of college-bound juniors who took the PSAT/NMSQT.

## How NMSC Uses the Selection Index

National Merit Scholarship Corporation (NMSC) uses the Selection Index score to designate groups of students to receive recognition in the programs it conducts. Entry to NMSC's competitions for scholarships is determined by students' responses to program entry questions on the PSAT/NMSQT answer sheet. Currently, more than 1.5 million test-takers meet requirements to enter NMSC's competitions each year.

Of the more than 1.5 million NMSC program entrants, about 55,000 will earn PSAT/NMSQT scores high enough to qualify them for recognition. These students will be notified of their standing through their high schools in September. Students who qualify to continue in the competitions for scholarships must then meet academic and other requirements specified by NMSC to be considered for awards.

Inquiries about any aspect of the National Merit Program or National Achievement Program—including entry requirements, the selection process, and awards to be offered—should be sent to:
National Merit Scholarship Corporation
1560 Sherman Avenue, Suite 200
Evanston, IL 60201-4897
Telephone: (847) 866-5100

# Explanatory Answers for PSAT Practice Test 2

## Section 1: Critical Reading

> As you read these Explanatory Answers, refer to "Critical Reading Strategies" (beginning on page 80) whenever a specific Strategy is referred to in the answer. Of particular importance are the following Master Critical Reading Strategies:
>
> Sentence Completion Master Strategy 1—page 81.
> Sentence Completion Master Strategy 2—page 82.
> Reading Comprehension Master Strategy 2—page 98.

*Note:* All Reading questions use Reading Comprehension Strategies 1, 2, and 3 (pp. 95–100) as well as other strategies indicated.

1. Choice C is correct. See **Sentence Completion Strategy 2.** Examine the first word of each choice. Choice (E) a futile does *not* make good sense because we do not refer to momentum as futile. Now consider the other choices. Choice (C) an increasing…athletics is the only choice which has a word pair that makes sentence sense.

2. Choice E is correct. See **Sentence Completion Strategy 1.** The word "effective" (meaning "serving the purpose" or "producing a result") makes good sense in the sentence. The other choices don't do that.

3. Choice D is correct. See **Sentence Completion Strategy 4.** The word "despite" is an opposition indicator. A strange and inevitable or *ineluctable* fate seemed to keep him helpless and unhappy, despite occasional periods of calm, peacefulness, or *serenity*.

4. Choice B is correct. See **Sentence Completion Strategies 1 and 4.** Try each choice, being aware that "result" is, of course, a result indicator: Samuel Clemens chose the pen name Mark Twain.

5. Choice A is correct. See **Sentence Completion Strategy 1.** The word "versatile" means capable of turning competently from one task or occupation to another. Clearly, Choice (A) versatile is the only correct choice.

6. Choice B is correct. See **Sentence Completion Strategy 2.** Examine the first words of each choice. We eliminate Choice (C) avoided and Choice (D) realized because it does not make sense to say that Leonardo realized or avoided the Law of Gravity. Now we consider Choice (A) examined…colorful and Choice (E) suspected…mural, neither of which makes sentence sense. Choice (B) anticipated…anatomical is the only choice that makes sentence sense.

7. Choice D is correct. See **Sentence Completion Strategy 2**. Examine the first word of each choice. Choice (B) pacifism and Choice (E) oblivion are incorrect choices because a rising tide of pacifism or oblivion in public education does *not* make good sense. Now consider the other choices. Choice (A) compromise…inept and Choice (C) ambiguity…average do *not* make good sense in the sentence. Choice (D) mediocrity…dedicated *does* make good sense.

8. Choice D is correct. The fact that the girl had become more self-confident indicates that she would be more active in participating in a conversation. If you used **Sentence Completion Strategy 3**—trying to complete the sentence *before* looking at the five choices—you might have come up with any of the following appropriate words:

> starting     beginning
> launching    originating

The other choices are, therefore, incorrect.

9. (D) See lines 5–7: "…individual attention…creating a more efficient learning environment." Note that what is contained in Choice A (flexible standards), Choice B (parent and child), Choice C (travel time), and Choice E (conditions in learning environment) are all mentioned but an effective learning condition is not based upon them.

10. (B) Choice A is addressed in lines 10–12. Choice C is addressed in lines 14–16. Choice D is addressed in lines 13–14 (varied feedback). Choice E is addressed in lines 10–12 (diversity). For Choice B, multicultural ways are not mentioned in the passage and even though there may be many students, those students may all be of one culture.

11. (E) The criterion which appears in both passages is the learning experience. See lines 5–7 and lines 10–12.

12. (C) What is missing in home schooling is the interaction with other students as stated in lines 10–14. Thus interaction with students on a regular basis would fill the void. Note in Choice B, the "occasional" work may not be adequate. In Choice D, in spending one-half time at home and one-half time in school it may be difficult and awkward to coordinate or relate what is taught or developed at home and what is taught or developed at school.

13. Choice B is correct. See paragraph 2: "Most social scientists…have assumed that the minimum economic needs of the aged should be lower than those of the younger family."

14. Choice E is correct. Given the context of the sentence and the next sentence, Choice E is the best. See also **Reading Comprehension Strategy 4.**

15. Choice A is correct. See paragraph 5: "[The data] disclose sharp income inequalities within every age group…"

16. Choice E is correct. For I, see paragraph 6: "Those sixty-five and over are expected to increase 672 percent." For III, see paragraph 4: "For the growing working-class family, limited in income by the very nature of the breadwinner's occupation…"

17. Choice C is correct. See paragraph 2: The sentence after the "functional ethos" sentence refers to "these values." See also **Reading Comprehension Strategy 4.**

18. Choice D is correct. See paragraph 6: "With the more rapid expansion of these two low-income groups, the young and the old…"

19. Choice D is correct. For I, see paragraph 5: "A spending unit's income-tenth position *within his age category* varies much less, if at all, and is determined primarily by his occupation." For III, see paragraph 4: "For the growing working-class family, limited in income by the very nature of the breadwinner's occupation…"

20. Choice A is correct. From the context of the sentence, it can be seen that Choice A is the best. See also **Reading Comprehension Strategy 4.**

21. Choice C is correct. See paragraph 3: "Despite his seniority, the older worker is likely to be downgraded to a lower-paying job…"

22. Choice C is correct. See paragraph 4: "The early and lower income period of a person's working life, during which he acquires his basic vocational skills…"

23. Choice C is correct. See paragraph 5: "A spending unit's income-tenth position is…determined primarily by his occupation."

24. Choice D is correct. The phrase "the legendary land of economic opportunity where any man can work his way to the top" (lines 86–88), in contrast to what the author really believes, represents *sarcasm.*

# Explanatory Answers for Practice Test 2 (continued)

## Section 2: Math

As you read these solutions, do two things if you answered the Math question incorrectly:

1. When a specific Strategy is referred to in the solution, study that strategy, which you will find in "19 Math Strategies" (beginning on page 51).

2. When the solution directs you to the "Math Refresher" (beginning on page 129)—for example, Math Refresher #305—study the 305 Math principle to get a clear idea of the Math operation that was necessary for you to know in order to answer the question correctly.

1. Choice A is correct. **(Use Strategy 2: Translate from words to algebra.)**

   Let $x$ = Amount that Greg had to start.
   Then $x + 5$ = Amount that Greg has after receiving $5 from David.  $\boxed{1}$

   $$\$25 = \text{Amount David has.} \qquad \boxed{2}$$

   We are told that Greg now has $\frac{1}{5}$ as much as David does.

   This translates to:

   $$\text{Greg} = \frac{1}{5}(\text{David}) \qquad \boxed{3}$$

   Substituting $\boxed{1}$ and $\boxed{2}$ into $\boxed{3}$, we get

   $$x + 5 = \frac{1}{5}(25)$$
   $$x + 5 = \frac{1}{5} \times 5 \times 5$$
   $$x + 5 = 5$$
   $$x = 0$$

   **(Math Refresher 200 and 406)**

2. Choice C is correct.
   The ratio of the perimeter of the larger square to that of the smaller is

   $$\frac{6+6+6+6}{2+2+2+2} = \frac{24}{8} = \frac{3}{1} \text{ or } 3:1$$

   One can arrive at this result directly if one remembers that the ratio of the perimeters of two squares is the same as the ratio of the lengths of the sides of the two squares.

   **(Math Refresher 303)**

3. Choice E is correct. **(Use Strategy 9: Remember the rate, time, and distance relationship.)**
   Remember that rate × time = distance

   or     $\text{average rate} = \dfrac{\text{total distance}}{\text{total time}}$

   or     $\text{average rate} = \dfrac{1056 \text{ feet}}{12 \text{ seconds}}$

   $$= 88 \text{ feet/second}$$

   **(Math Refresher 201 and 202)**

4. Choice B is correct.

Given: $2z + 1 + 2 + 2z + 3 + 2z = 3 + 1 + 2$

**(Use Strategy 1: Cancel numbers from both sides of an equation.)**

We can immediately cancel the $+1$, $+2$, and $+3$ from each side.

We get $2z + 2z + 2z = 0$

$$6z = 0$$
$$z = 0$$

Thus, $z + 4 = 0 + 4 = 4$

**(Math Refresher 406 and 431)**

5. Choice B is correct.

$$2(w)(x)(-y) - 2(-w)(-x)(y) =$$
$$-2wxy - 2wxy$$
$$-4wxy$$

**(Math Refresher 406)**

6. Choice A is correct. **(Use Strategy 2: Translate from words to algebra.)**

The sum of <u>the square of $x$</u> and <u>the square of $y$</u>
$$\underbrace{\qquad}_{x^2} + \underbrace{\qquad}_{y^2}$$

So, five times that quantity is

$$5(x^2 + y^2)$$

**(Math Refresher 200)**

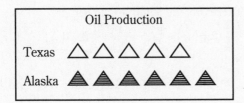

7. Choice C is correct. **(Use Strategy 2: Translate from words to algebra.)**

We are told ▲ $= 3\triangle$

**(Use Strategy 17: Use the given information effectively.)**

Texas total $= 5$
Alaska total $= 3(6) = 18$

**(Use Strategy 3: Know how to find unknown quantities from known quantities.)**

$$\frac{\text{Alaska production}}{\text{Total production}} = \frac{18}{5 + 18} =$$

$$\frac{18}{23} = \text{required ratio}$$

**(Math Refresher 200 and 431)**

8. Choice A is correct.

Given: $a = 1, b = -2, c = -2$ $\boxed{1}$

$$\frac{b^2 c}{(a-c)^2}$$ $\boxed{2}$

Substitute $\boxed{1}$ into $\boxed{2}$. We get

$$\frac{(-2)^2(-2)}{(1-(-2)^2} =$$

$$\frac{4(-2)}{(3)^2} =$$

$$\frac{-8}{9}$$

**(Math Refresher 429 and 431)**

9. Choice A is correct.

Given: $y = 28j$ $\boxed{1}$

$j$ is any integer $\boxed{2}$

**(Use Strategy 13: Find unknowns by division.)**

Divide $\boxed{1}$ by 2. We have

$$\frac{y}{2} = \frac{28j}{2}$$

$$\frac{y}{2} = 14j$$ $\boxed{3}$

**(Use Strategy 19: Factor.)**

Factor the 14 in $\boxed{3}$. We get

$$\frac{y}{2} = (2)(7)(j)$$ $\boxed{4}$

Using $\boxed{2}$ and $\boxed{4}$ we see that $\frac{y}{2}$ is an integer with a factor of 2.

Thus, $\frac{y}{2}$ is even.

**(Math Refresher 603 and 605)**

10. Choice B is correct.

Given: $3a + 4b = 4a - 4b = 21$ $\boxed{1}$

From $\boxed{1}$, we get

$$3a + 4b = 21$$ $\boxed{2}$
$$4a - 4b = 21$$ $\boxed{3}$

**(Use Strategy 13: Find unknowns by addition.)**

Add $\boxed{2}$ and $\boxed{3}$ together. We get

$$3a + \cancel{4b} = 21$$
$$+\;\underline{4a + \cancel{4b} = 21}$$
$$7a \qquad = 42$$
$$a \qquad = 6$$

**(Math Refresher 407)**

11. Choice D is correct. **(Use Strategy 2: Translate from words to algebra.)**

$$N + 6N + 9N = 16N$$

Any divisor of 16 or of $N$ will divide $16N$.

**(Use Strategy 8: When all choices must be tested, start with Choice E and work backward.)** Starting with Choice E, we see that 16 divides $16N$ evenly. Choice D, however, does *not* divide $16N$ evenly. Thus we have found the answer.

**(Math Refresher 200 and 431)**

12. Choice D is correct.

We are given: $x = 3a - 18$    $\boxed{1}$

$5y = 3a + 7$    $\boxed{2}$

We need $5y - x$.    $\boxed{3}$

**(Use Strategy 13: Find unknown expressions by subtracting equations.)** Subtracting $\boxed{1}$ from $\boxed{2}$, we get

$$5y - x = 3a + 7 - (3a - 18)$$
$$= 3a + 7 - 3a + 18$$
$$5y - x = 25$$

**(Math Refresher 406)**

13. Choice B is correct. **(Use Strategy 2: Translate from words to algebra.)**

Given:

$$p + pq = 4(p - pq)$$    $\boxed{1}$

**(Use Strategy 13: Find unknown expressions by division.)** Since $pq \neq 0$, divide 1 by $p$.

$1 + q = 4(1 - q)$    $\boxed{2}$

or   $1 + q = 4 - 4q$

or     $5q = 3$

or      $q = \dfrac{3}{5}$

Thus, $q$ has exactly one value.
Since $p$ cannot be determined from equation $\boxed{1}$, none of the other choices is correct.

**(Math Refresher 406)**

14. Choice D is correct. **(Use Strategy 17: Use the given information effectively.)**

Since $2 + \dfrac{1}{z} = 0$, we have

$$\frac{1}{z} = -2$$
$$z = -\frac{1}{2}$$    $\boxed{1}$

We need $9 + 9z$    $\boxed{2}$

Substituting $\boxed{1}$ into $\boxed{2}$, we get

$$9 + 9\left(-\frac{1}{2}\right) = 9 - 4\frac{1}{2} = 4\frac{1}{2} = \frac{9}{2}$$

**(Math Refresher 406 and 431)**

15. Choice C is correct. We set $y = x^2 = x$.
$x = 1$ or $x = 0$
Thus they intersect twice.

**(Math Refresher 417)**

16. Choice C is correct.

We are given: $wx = y$    $\boxed{1}$

or $w = \dfrac{y}{x}$    $\boxed{2}$

**(Use Strategy 2: Translate from words to algebra.)** If $x$ and $y$ are multiplied by 6, in $\boxed{1}$, we have

$$w(\cancel{6})(x) = (\cancel{6})(y)$$
$$wx = y$$
$$w = \frac{y}{x}$$    $\boxed{3}$

$\boxed{2}$ and $\boxed{3}$ are the same.

Therefore $\dfrac{y}{x} = 1\left(\dfrac{y}{x}\right)$

The answer is now clear.

**(Math Refresher 200 and 406)**

17. Choice B is correct. **(Use Strategy 3: The whole equals the sum of its parts.)** The path is made up of 4 semicircles, three of diameter 4 and one of diameter 8.

[Remember circumference is $2\pi r$. Thus,

$\dfrac{1}{2}$ circumference $= \dfrac{1}{2}(2\pi r)$.]

Therefore, the length of the path is

$$\frac{1}{2}(2\pi)\left(\frac{4}{2}\right) + \frac{1}{2}(2\pi)\left(\frac{4}{2}\right) + \frac{1}{2}(2\pi)\left(\frac{4}{2}\right) + \frac{1}{2}(2\pi)\left(\frac{8}{2}\right)$$
$$= 10\pi$$

**(Math Refresher 310 and 311)**

18. Choice C is correct. **(Use Strategy 10: Know how to use units.)**

$$\frac{7x}{144}\text{yards} = \left(\frac{7x}{144}\text{yards}\right)\left(\frac{36\,\text{inches}}{\text{yards}}\right) =$$

**(Use Strategy 19: Factor and reduce.)**

$$= \frac{7x}{\cancel{12} \times 12} \times \cancel{12} \times 3\,\text{inches}$$
$$= \frac{7x}{\cancel{3} \times 4} \times \cancel{3}\,\text{inches}$$

$$\frac{7x}{144}\text{yards} = \frac{7x}{4}\text{ inches}$$    $\boxed{1}$

$$\frac{5y}{12}\text{feet} = \left(\frac{5y}{\cancel{12}}\text{feet}\right)\left(\cancel{12}\frac{\text{inches}}{\text{foot}}\right) =$$

$$\frac{5y}{12}\text{feet} = 5y\text{ inches}$$    $\boxed{2}$

**(Use Strategy 13: Find unknown expressions by addition of equations.)** Adding $\boxed{1}$ and $\boxed{2}$, we have

$$\frac{7x}{144} \text{ yards} + \frac{5y}{12} \text{ feet} = \left(\frac{7x}{4} + 5y\right) \text{ inches}$$

**(Math Refresher 121 and 431)**

19. Choice A is correct.

$$\text{Given: } x < 0 \qquad \boxed{1}$$
$$y < 0 \qquad \boxed{2}$$

**(Use Strategy 6: Know how to manipulate inequalities.)**

Multiply $\boxed{1}$ by $\boxed{2}$, we get

$$x \cdot y > 0 \qquad \boxed{3}$$

Thus I is always positive

Adding $\boxed{1}$ and $\boxed{2}$ we get

$$x + y < 0 \qquad \boxed{4}$$

Thus II is not positive

**(Use Strategy 7: Use numerics to help find the answer.)**

$$\text{Let } x = -2, y = -3$$
$$\text{III becomes } x - y = -2 - (-3)$$
$$= -2 + 3$$
$$= 1 \qquad \boxed{5}$$

$$\text{Now let } x = -3, y = -2$$
$$\text{III becomes } x - y = -3 - (-2)$$
$$= -3 + 2$$
$$= -1 \qquad \boxed{6}$$

From $\boxed{5}$ and $\boxed{6}$ we see that III is not always positive.

Using $\boxed{3}$, $\boxed{4}$ and $\boxed{6}$, we find that only Choice A, I only, is correct.

**(Math Refresher 419, 420, and 424)**

20. Choice D is correct.

$$\text{Given: } a + 3b = 11 \qquad \boxed{1}$$
$$a \text{ and } b \text{ are positive integers} \qquad \boxed{2}$$

**(Use Strategy 17: Use the given information effectively.)**

From $\boxed{1}$, we get

$$a = 11 - 3b \qquad \boxed{3}$$

From $\boxed{3}$ we see that $a$ will be largest when $b$ is smallest. Using $\boxed{2}$, we get

$$b = 1 \text{ is its smallest value} \qquad \boxed{4}$$

Substituting $\boxed{4}$ into $\boxed{3}$, we have

$$a = 11 - 3(1)$$
$$a = 11 - 3$$
$$a = 8$$

**(Math Refresher 406 and Logical Reasoning)**

# Explanatory Answers for
# Practice Test 2
# (continued)

## Section 3: Critical Reading

As you read these Explanatory Answers, refer to "Critical Reading Strategies" (beginning on page 80) whenever a specific Strategy is referred to in the answer. Of particular importance are the following Master Critical Reading Strategies:

Sentence Completion Master Strategy 1—page 81.
Sentence Completion Master Strategy 2—page 82.
Reading Comprehension Master Strategy 2—page 98.

*Note:* All Reading questions use Reading Comprehension Strategies 1, 2, and 3 (pp. 95–100) as well as other strategies indicated.

**25.** Choice C is correct. See **Sentence Completion Strategy 2**. First we eliminate Choice (A) foretold, Choice (B) impossible, and Choice (E) glaring. Reason: These choices do not make sense in the sentence up to the word "eclipses." We further eliminate Choice (D) true...rational, because it does not make sense for anyone to consider an eclipse rational. Only Choice (C) understandable... magical makes sense.

**26.** Choice D is correct. See **Sentence Completion Strategy 2**.

### STEP 1

Let us first examine the first words of each choice. We can then eliminate Choice (B) confuse and Choice (E) misconstrue because it does *not* make sense to say that an authority would be able to "confuse" or "misconstrue" something in a book. So Choices B and E are incorrect.

### STEP 2

Let us now consider the remaining choices. Choice (A) understand...simple and Choice (C) read...useless do *not* make sense in the sentence. Therefore, these choices are incorrect. Choice (D) comprehend...complex *does* make sense.

**27.** Choice B is correct. See **Sentence Completion Strategy 4**. The words "not only" constitute a Support indicator. The second part of the sentence is, therefore, expected to reinforce the first part of the sentence. Choice (B) reject...refused supplies the two words that provide a sentence that makes sense. Choices A, C, D, and E are incorrect because their word pairs do not produce sentences that make sense.

**28.** Choice A is correct. See **Sentence Completion Strategy 3**. If you used this strategy of trying to complete the sentence *before* looking at the five choices, you might have come up with any of the following appropriate words:

persistence        perseverance
steadfastness      indefatigability

These words all mean the same as Choice (A) tenacity. Accordingly, Choices B, C, D, and E are incorrect.

29. Choice C is correct. See **Sentence Completion Strategy 4**. The adverb "ironically" means in a manner so that the opposite of what is expected takes place. So we have an Opposition indicator here. Choice (C) weaken is, of course, the opposite of strengthen. Accordingly, Choices A, B, D, and E are incorrect.

30. Choice E is correct. See the beginning sentence which states: "the greatest acrobats on earth" introducing the monkeys which in line 4 are called "ceboids." The whole passage is about the "ceboid acrobats."

31. Choice C is correct. See lines 12–17 where the comparisons are made.

32. Choice B is correct. See lines 1–3. Note that even if you didn't know the meaning of "deprecate," you could figure that the word imparted a negative connotation since the prefix "de" means away from and is negative. Also don't get lured into Choice D just because "Babel" was mentioned.

33. Choice B is correct. See line 4: "…influence is most dangerous…"

34. Choice C is correct. Throughout Passage 1, the author is bringing out the fact that violence is widely shown and well received on television. For example: Line 1: "Violence is alive and well on television." Lines 4–5: "…as a result of…the horror of violence." Lines 12–13: "Violence on TV…in recent years." Although Choices A, B, D, and E are discussed or implied in the passage, none of these choices summarizes the content of the passage as a whole. Therefore, these choices are incorrect.

35. Choice D is correct. See lines 29–33: "The simple gunfight…for hundreds to die." Accordingly, Choice A is incorrect. Choices B and C are incorrect because there is no violence shown on the screen in these choices. Choice E is incorrect because the violence of a double murder by a jealous husband hardly compares in intensity with the violence of a bomb exploding in a bus carrying a busload of innocent civilians.

36. Choice C is correct. The cruelties of our prison system are referred to in lines 63–69: "…just as so much of our current violence is socially acceptable…classes of society." The horrors of our prisons were current at the time the author wrote this article, and they are current today. The violence spoken about in Choices A, B, and D were socially acceptable at the time they occurred in the past. The question asks for an illustration of *current* "socially acceptable" violence. Accordingly, Choices A, B, and D are incorrect. Choice E, though it refers to current violence, is *not* socially acceptable. See lines 70–74: "What we have now…familiar 'crime in the streets.'" Therefore, Choice E is incorrect.

37. Choice A is correct. The author's definition of violence is extremely broad—including not only acts of force but also the social infliction of harm as in "exploiting women and children in textile mills and sweatshops" (lines 58–59). Passage 2 refers to acts of violence other than those expressed in Choices B and C. Therefore, these choices are incorrect. One could easily cite illegal conduct on the part of the government or a citizen that is *not* of a violent nature. Therefore, Choice D is incorrect. The FBI could conceivably commit an act of violence. The author would not condone this. See lines 77–79: "But now, too, official violence… numerous sympathizers." Therefore, Choice E is incorrect.

38. Choice D is correct. The author, throughout Passage 2, expresses opposition to any type of violence—whether one engages in violence or tolerates it. Therefore, Choice D is correct because the author would not approve of the violence practiced by football players. Accordingly, Choices A, B, C, and E are incorrect. Although Choice A involves violence, a person who tries to prevent a mugging is obviously opposed to the violence of the mugger.

39. Choice C is correct. In the context of the rest of the sentence in lines 2–3 and line 46, you can see that "pervasiveness" means "seeping through." Note that Choice A is incorrect because in lines 2–3, the word "variety" is used and would be redundant if repeated. This is also true for Choice B, "televised." See also **Reading Comprehension Strategy 4**.

40. Choice A is correct. The author's attitude in Passage 2 is that violence as shown historically is "a way of life." Thus if violence were curtailed on television, it would still exist elsewhere and continue to exist.

41. Choice D is correct. Only the author of Passage 1 proposes a direct resolution—lines 38–41. The statement in Choice A is *true*. See lines 70–89. The statement in Choice B is *true*. See lines 29–31 and 43–69. The statement in Choice C is *true*. The author of Passage 1 primarily talks only about televised violence, whereas the author of Passage 2 refers to corporate violence, air pollution, prison violence, and the like. The statement in Choice E is *true*. See lines 38–41 and lines 42–69.

**42.** Choice C is correct. It can be seen from what precedes in Passage 2 that "polarization" must mean some very great opposing viewpoints. Don't be lured into Choice A, thinking that polarization has to do with electrical current; or Choice B, that polarization has to do with governments, since society was discussed; or Choice D, that polarization has to do with religion because religious dissent was mentioned; or Choice E, that polarization has to do with climate because we have a north and south pole. See also **Reading Comprehension Strategy 4**.

**43.** Choice D is correct. See lines 16–17: "The cry for freedom...the birth of the New Man." Choice A is incorrect. Although the author may agree to what the choice says, he does not actually state or imply such. Choice B is incorrect because nowhere in the passage is Choice B stated or implied. Choice C is incorrect. See lines 25–27: "African-American literature rejects the despair and cynicism; it is a literature of realistic hope and life-affirmation." Choice E is incorrect. See lines 36–37: "...life should not be a sedate waltz or foxtrot..."

**44.** Choice A is correct. See lines 32–36: "...life should be vivacious, exuberant, wholesomely uninhibited...and man should be loving." Choice B is incorrect because nowhere does the passage indicate that Choice B is true. Choice C is incorrect. Although lines 35–36 state that "life should be passionately lived and man should be loving," these lines do not mean that people should demonstrate their passions in public whenever the urge is there. Choice D is incorrect. Nowhere does the passage recommend Choice D. Choice E is incorrect. Although lines 6–10 state "In African-American literature...the rage of the oppressed," the passage does not state or imply that the ancestors of those who have been oppressed should be enraged.

**45.** Choice D is correct. Let us consider each item. Item I is incorrect because the passage nowhere expresses the need for *nonviolent* opposition to racism. Item II is correct. See lines 42–46: "Black literature in America [African-American literature] is...finding deep joy in humanity," Item III is correct. See lines 31–36: "African-American literature is a statement...and man should be loving." Accordingly, only Choices II and III are correct. Therefore, Choice D is correct, and Choices A, B, C, and E are incorrect.

**46.** Choice B is correct. See lines 23–27: "Like the spirituals...realistic hope and life-affirmation." Choice A is incorrect. See lines 6–15: "In African-American literature...the burden of protest." Although an indication of anger is present in the passage, it is not dominant. Moreover, nowhere in the passage is there evidence of vindictiveness. Choice C is incorrect because forgiveness and charity are not referred to in the passage. Choice D is incorrect. See lines 23–30: "Like the spirituals...goodness will prevail." Choice E is incorrect. Although the passage refers to *grief* in line 14 and also *cruelty* in line 38, grief and cruelty do not represent the tone of the passage.

**47.** Choice E is correct. See lines 20–23: "...for a human world."

**48.** Choice C is correct. It can be seen from the context of the sentence that the word "iniquity" must mean something bad (the word is preceded by "investigation" and is in contrast to "an investigation...potential godliness," which appears in the same sentence). See also **Reading Comprehension Strategy 4**.

# Explanatory Answers for Practice Test 2 (continued)

## Section 4: Math

As you read these solutions, do two things if you answered the Math question incorrectly:

1. When a specific Strategy is referred to in the solution, study that strategy, which you will find in "19 Math Strategies" (beginning on page 51).

2. When the solution directs you to the "Math Refresher" (beginning on page 129)—for example, Math Refresher #305—study the 305 Math principle to get a clear idea of the Math operation that was necessary for you to know in order to answer the question correctly.

21. Choice C is correct. (**Use Strategy 2: Translate from words to algebra.**) The key is to be able to translate English sentences into mathematical equations.

Let $p$ = price of one frying pan
$m$ = price of one coffee mug
We are given

$$p + 2m = \$27 \qquad \boxed{1}$$
$$p + m = \$23 \qquad \boxed{2}$$

Subtract equation $\boxed{2}$ from equation $\boxed{1}$ to get

$$m = \$4 \qquad \boxed{3}$$

Substitute equation $\boxed{3}$ into equation $\boxed{2}$

$$p + \$4 = \$23$$

Subtract $4 from both sides of the above equation

$$p = \$19$$

(**Math Refresher 200, 406, and 407**)

22. Choice E is correct. (**Use Strategy 2: Translate from words to algebra.**)

Each tile is a square with perimeter = 2 feet

Each side of the tile is $\frac{1}{4}$ (2 feet) = $\frac{1}{2}$ foot $\boxed{1}$

The area of each tile is (Side)$^2$.

Using $\boxed{1}$, we get area of each tile

$$= \left(\frac{1}{2}\right)^2 = \frac{1}{4} \text{ square foot} \qquad \boxed{2}$$

The area of the floor is $b \times h =$
8 feet $\times$ 6 feet =
48 square feet $\qquad \boxed{3}$

(**Use Strategy 17: Use the given information effectively.**)

The number of tiles necessary, at minimum, to cover the floor

$$= \frac{\text{Area of floor}}{\text{Area of 1 tile}} \qquad \boxed{4}$$

Substituting $\boxed{2}$ and $\boxed{3}$ into $\boxed{4}$ we get:

The number of tiles necessary, at minimum, to cover the floor

$$= \frac{48}{\frac{1}{4}} = \$48 \times \frac{4}{1}$$

The number of tiles necessary, at minimum, to cover the floor

$$= 192$$

**(Math Refresher 200 and 303)**

23. Choice E is correct.

The only restriction is that 9 and 12 must each divide $Q$ without a remainder. $\boxed{1}$

**(Use Strategy 7: Use numerics to help find the answer.)**

Choose specific values for $Q$ that satisfy $\boxed{1}$.

EXAMPLE 1

$$Q = 36$$

Then, $Q$ will divide 36 and 72.

EXAMPLE 2

$$Q = 108$$

Then, $Q$ will divide neither 36 nor 72. Clearly, the answer to this question depends on the specific value of $Q$.

**(Math Refresher 431)**

24. Choice B is correct. Since $DC \perp AC$, $\angle DCB$ is a right angle and has a measure of 90°. **(Use Strategy 3: The whole equals the sum of its parts.)** Since the sum of the angles of a $\triangle$ is 180°, we have

$$\angle DBC + 90 + 20 = 180$$
$$\angle DBC = 70 \qquad \boxed{1}$$

Since $EB \perp BD$, $\angle DBE$ is a right angle and has a measure of 90° $\boxed{2}$

**(Use Strategy 3: The whole equals the sum of its parts.)** The whole straight $\angle ABC$ is = to the sum of its parts. Thus

$$\angle DBC + \angle DBE + x = 180 \qquad \boxed{3}$$

Substituting $\boxed{1}$ and $\boxed{2}$ into $\boxed{3}$ we have

$$70 + 90 + x = 180$$
$$x = 20$$

**(Math Refresher 501, 505, 406, and 431)**

25. Choice E is correct. **(Use Strategy 17: Use the given information effectively.)**

Given: $x$ $\boxed{1}$
$11 - x$ $\boxed{2}$
$x - 4$ $\boxed{3}$

as the lengths of the three sides of a triangle.

We know that the sum of any two sides of a triangle is greater than the third $\boxed{4}$

First, we use $\boxed{1} + \boxed{2} > \boxed{3}$. We have

$$x + 11 - x > x - 4$$
$$11 > x - 4$$
$$15 > x \qquad \boxed{5}$$

Next, we use $\boxed{2} + \boxed{3} > \boxed{1}$. We have

$$11 - x + x - 4 > x$$
$$7 > x \qquad \boxed{6}$$

To satisfy $\boxed{6}$ and $\boxed{5}$, we choose $\boxed{6}$.

$$7 > x, \text{ or } x < 7 \text{ satisfies both} \qquad \boxed{7}$$

Finally, we use $\boxed{1} + \boxed{3} > \boxed{2}$. We have

$$x + x - 4 > 11 - x$$
$$2x - 4 > 11 - x$$
$$3x > 15$$
$$x > 5, \text{ or, } 5 < x \qquad \boxed{8}$$

**(Use Strategy 6: Know how to manipulate inequalities.)** Combining $\boxed{7}$ and $\boxed{8}$, we get

$$5 < x < 7$$

**(Math Refresher 516, 419, and 420)**

26. Choice B is correct.

Given: $a, b$ are integers $\boxed{1}$
Average of $a, b$ and 4 is 6 $\boxed{2}$

**Use Strategy 5:**

$$\text{Average} = \frac{\text{Sum of values}}{\text{Total number of values}}$$

Using $\boxed{2}$, we have

$$\frac{a + b + 4}{3} = 6 \qquad \boxed{3}$$

**(Use Strategy 13: Find unknowns by multiplication.)**

Multiply $\boxed{3}$ by 3. We get

$$3\left(\frac{a + b + 4}{3}\right) = (6)3$$
$$a + b + 4 = 18$$
$$a + b = 14 \qquad \boxed{4}$$

Using $\boxed{1}$ and $\boxed{4}$, the possibilities are:

| $\frac{a + b}{1 + 13}$ | $\frac{ab}{13}$ | Choice A |
|---|---|---|
| 2 + 12 | 24 | |
| 3 + 11 | 33 | |
| 4 + 10 | 40 | Choice C |
| 5 + 9 | 45 | |
| 6 + 8 | 48 | Choice D |
| 7 + 7 | 49 | Choice E |

Checking all the choices, we find that only Choice B, 14, is not a possible value of *ab*.

**(Math Refresher 601, 406 and Logical Reasoning)**

27. Choice D is correct. **(Use Strategy 17: Use the given information effectively.)**

$$\frac{1}{n^2}\left(\frac{m^5 n^3}{m^3}\right)^2 = \frac{1}{n^2} = (m^2 n^3)^2 = \frac{m^4 n^6}{n^2} = m^4 n^4$$

**(Math Refresher 429)**

28. Choice C is correct. Label the females F1, F2, and F3 and the males M1, M2, and M3. The total number of possible combinations of three people (F1–F2–M1, F1–M2–M3, etc.) is 6 combinations taken 3 at a time, or $_6C_3$.

$$_6C_3 = \frac{(6\times5\times4)}{(3\times2\times1)} = 20$$

The number of favorable combinations is 9:

M1–M2–F1  M1–M3–F1  M2–M3–F1
M1–M2–F2  M1–M3–F2  M2–M3–F2
M1–M2–F3  M1–M3–F3  M2–M3–F3

Thus, the probability of only two males in the room is: $= \frac{9}{20}$

**(Math Refresher 613 and 614)**

29. 24 **(Use Strategy 2: Translate from words to algebra.)**

Given: $\frac{5}{8}$ of *x* is 40
↓ ↓↓↓↓
$\frac{5}{8} \times x = 40$ $\boxed{1}$

**(Use Strategy 13: Find unknowns by multiplication.)**

*Fast Method:* Multiply $\boxed{1}$ by $\frac{3}{5}$ to get

$$\frac{3}{5}\left(\frac{5}{8}x\right) = \frac{3}{5}(40)$$

$$\frac{3}{8}x = \frac{3}{5} \times 5 \times 8$$

$$\frac{3}{8}x = 24$$

*Slow Method:* Solve $\boxed{1}$ for *x* by multiplying $\boxed{1}$ by $\frac{8}{5}$:

$$x = 64 \qquad \boxed{2}$$

Now substitute $\boxed{2}$ into the unknown expression:

$$\frac{3}{8}x = \frac{3}{8}(64)$$
$$= \frac{3}{8} \times 8 \times 8$$
$$= 24$$

**(Math Refresher 200 and 406)**

30. 9 **(Use Strategy 2: Translate from words to algebra.)** We are given that the wire is bent to form a circle of radius 3 feet. This means that its length is equal to the circumference of the circle.

Thus, Length of wire $= 2\pi r = 2\pi(3)$ feet
$= 6\pi$ feet
$\approx 6(3.14)$ feet
Length of wire $\approx 18.84$ feet $\boxed{1}$

**(Use Strategy 3: Know how to find unknown quantities.)**

Number of pieces $= \dfrac{\text{Total length}}{2 \text{ feet}}$ $\boxed{2}$
2 feet long

Substituting $\boxed{1}$ into $\boxed{2}$, we have

Number of pieces $\approx \dfrac{18.84 \text{ feet}}{2 \text{ feet}}$
2 feet long

$\approx 9.42$
$= 9$ complete pieces

**(Math Refresher 310)**

31. 7 **(Use Strategy 2: Translate from words to algebra.)**

*Let* $b$ = number of baseballs that Dick bought
$t$ = number of tennis balls that Dick bought
$.70b$ = amount spent on baseballs
$.60t$ = amount spent on tennis balls

Thus, we are told

$.70b + .60t = 7.00$ $\boxed{1}$

Multiply $\boxed{1}$ by 10,

$7b + 6t = 70$ $\boxed{2}$

Solve $\boxed{2}$ for *t*,

$$t = \frac{70 - 7b}{6} = \frac{7(10-b)}{6} \qquad \boxed{3}$$

**(Use Strategy 17: Use the given information effectively.)** From $\boxed{3}$, we see that the maximum value of *t* occurs at the minimum value of *b*. Since *b* and *t* are numbers of balls, *b* and *t* must be non-negative integers. Thus, the minimum value of *b* is 0. When $b = 0$, $t = \frac{70}{6}$, which is not integral. For *t* to be an integer, $\boxed{3}$ tells us that $(10 - b)$ is a multiple of 6. The smallest value of *b* that makes $(10 - b)$ a multiple of 6 is $b = 4$. Thus, $t = 7$ is the maximum value of *t*, and 7 is the answer.

**(Math Refresher 200, 406, and 431 and Logical Reasoning)**

**32. 2 (Use Strategy 11: Use new definitions carefully.)**

Given:

$$f(x) = 12x + 8 \qquad \boxed{1}$$

$$\text{and } f(x) \div f(0) = 2x \qquad \boxed{2}$$

Calculate $f(0)$:

$$f(0) = 12(0) + 8 = 8 \qquad \boxed{3}$$

Substitute $\boxed{1}$ and $\boxed{3}$ into $\boxed{2}$:

$$\frac{12x + 8}{8} = 2x \qquad \boxed{4}$$

Multiply both sides of $\boxed{4}$ by 8:

$$12x + 8 = 16x$$
or $\qquad 8 = 4x$
or $\qquad x = 2$

**(Math Refresher 431 and 406)**

**33. 8 (Use Strategy 11: Use new definitions carefully.)**

In the given letter columns, only 8 triples have the property that exactly 2 of the letters in the triple are the same. Thus, 8 triples have a value of 1, and all the other triples have a value of 0. Hence, the value of the entire group of letter columns is 8.

**(Logical Reasoning)**

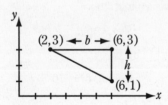

**34. 4 (Use Strategy 17: Use the given information effectively.)**

It is clear from the diagram above that the triangle is a right triangle whose area is

$$A = \frac{1}{2}bh \qquad \boxed{1}$$

From the given coordinates, we can also say that

$$b = 6 - 2 = 4 \qquad \boxed{2}$$
$$h = 3 - 1 = 2 \qquad \boxed{3}$$

Substituting $\boxed{2}$ and $\boxed{3}$ into $\boxed{1}$,

$$A = \frac{1}{2}(4)(2)$$

$$A = 4$$

**(Math Refresher 306 and 410)**

**35. 18 (Use Strategy 17: Use the given information effectively.)**

The area of a rectangle is length × width. The number of squares that can be packed into the rectangle

$$= \frac{\text{Area of entire rectangle}}{\text{Area of each square}}$$

$$= \frac{6 \times 12}{2 \times 2}$$

$$= \frac{72}{4}$$

$$= \frac{4 \times 18}{4}$$

$$= 18$$

**(Math Refresher 304 and 431)**

**36. 60** Since we are given the radii of the circles, we have

$$AN = AM = 1 \qquad \boxed{1}$$
$$BM = BP = 2 \qquad \boxed{2}$$
$$CN = CP = 3 \qquad \boxed{3}$$

We want to find

$$(AB)(BC)(AC) \qquad \boxed{4}$$

**(Use Strategy 3: The whole equals the sum of its parts.)** From the diagram, we see that

$$AB = AM + BM \qquad \boxed{5}$$
$$BC = BP + CP \qquad \boxed{6}$$
$$AC = AN + CN \qquad \boxed{7}$$

Substituting $\boxed{1}$, $\boxed{2}$, $\boxed{3}$ into $\boxed{5}$, $\boxed{6}$, $\boxed{7}$ we have

$$AB = 3$$
$$BC = 5$$
$$AC = 4$$

Thus,

$$(AB)(BC)(AC) = (3)(5)(4)$$
$$= 60$$

**(Math Refresher 524)**

**37. 9,500**

$\left(\text{**Use Strategy 5:**}\right.$

$$\left.\text{Average} = \frac{\text{Sum of values}}{\text{Total number of values}}\right)$$

We are given:

$$\frac{x + y + z + w}{4} = 8,000 \qquad \boxed{1}$$

**(Use Strategy 13: Find unknowns by multiplication.)** Multiplying $\boxed{1}$ by 4, we get

$$x + y + z + w = 32,000 \qquad \boxed{2}$$

We are given that any 3 have an average of 7,500, so using $x$, $y$ and $z$ as the 3, we get

$$\frac{x + y + z}{3} = 7,500 \qquad \boxed{3}$$

Multiplying $\boxed{3}$ by 3, we get

$$x + y + z = 22,500 \qquad \boxed{4}$$

Substituting $\boxed{4}$ into $\boxed{2}$, we get

$$22,500 + w = 32,000$$
or $\qquad w = 9,500$

**(Math Refresher 601 and 406)**

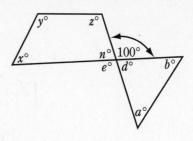

38. **280**

**(Use Strategy 17: Use the given information effectively.)**

From the diagram, $n = d$ (vertical angles) $\qquad \boxed{1}$

We know $x + y + z + n = 360$ $\qquad \boxed{2}$

Substituting $\boxed{1}$ into $\boxed{2}$, we get

$$x + y + z + d = 360 \qquad \boxed{3}$$

Subtracting $d$ from $\boxed{3}$, we have

$$x + y + z = 360 - d \qquad \boxed{4}$$

We know that $100 + d = 180$ from the diagram

So, $d = 180 - 100 = 80$ $\qquad \boxed{5}$

Substituting $\boxed{5}$ into $\boxed{4}$, we get

$$x + y + z = 360 - 80$$
$$x + y + z = 280$$

**(Math Refresher 521, 503, and 406)**

# Explanatory Answers for Practice Test 2 (continued)

## Section 5: Writing Skills

> For further practice and information, please refer to "A Brief Review of English Grammar" starting on page 321.

1. **(A)** Choice A is correct. Choice B is incorrect because "on account" may not be used as a subordinate conjunction. Choice C is incorrect because it gives the meaning that the judge is doing the charging. Choice D is incorrect because the possessive noun ("defendant") modifying the gerund ("charging") must take the form "defendant's." Choice E creates a run-on sentence.

2. **(A)** Choice A is correct. Choices B, C, and D are incorrect because they change the meaning of the original sentence. Choice E creates a run-on sentence.

3. **(E)** Choices A and B are incorrect because they give the idea that the plans are trying to avoid the hot sun. Choice C is awkward. Choice D is a run-on sentence. Choice E is correct.

4. **(B)** Choice A is too wordy. Choice B is correct. Choice C is incorrect because it changes the tense of the original sentence—"Whatever (may) be her thoughts" is in the present tense. Choice D does not retain the meaning of the original sentence. Choice E makes no sense.

5. **(B)** Choices A and E are incorrect because the subject word "use" requires a singular verb ("makes"). Choice B is correct. Choices C and D are awkward.

6. **(E)** "Irregardless" (Choice A) is incorrect. "Regardless about" (Choice B) is unidiomatic. Choices C and D change the meaning of the original sentence. Moreover, Choice D makes the sentence ungrammatical. Choice E is correct.

7. **(A)** Choice A is correct. Choices B, C, and E change the meaning of the original sentence. Choice D is too wordy.

8. **(C)** The infinitive "to effect" means "to bring about"—this is not the meaning intended in the original sentence. Therefore, Choices A, B, and D are incorrect. Choice C is correct. Choice E changes the meaning of the original sentence.

9. **(B)** In the original sentence, "who" should replace "whom" as the subject of the subordinate clause ("who were policemen"). "I believe" is simply a parenthetical expression. Therefore, Choice A is incorrect and Choice B is correct. Choice C creates a run-on sentence. Choice D improperly changes the sentence from a complex type to a compound type. Choice E does not retain the meaning of the original sentence.

10. **(D)** Choices A and B suffer from improper ellipsis. Choice C changes the meaning of the original sentence. Choice D is correct. Choice E is too wordy.

11. **(E)** Sequence of tenses in a past contrary-to-fact condition requires the "had waited" form in the "if" clause. Therefore Choices A, B, C, and D are incorrect and Choice E is correct.

12. **(C)** Choice A is incorrect because the pronoun *which* has an indefinite antecedent. Choices B and E are incorrect because they are too wordy. Choice C is correct. Choice D is incorrect because *damaging* is an inappropriate word choice.

13. **(E)** In this sentence we are looking for correct parallel structure in the last of a series of nouns. Choices A, B, C, and D are incorrect because they destroy the noun balance. Choice E is correct.

14. **(A)** Choice A is correct. Choices B and D are incorrect because the word *most* is unnecessary and incorrect here. Choice C is incorrect because it is wordy. Choice E is incorrect because *premium* is not the correct word for the meaning intended.

15. **(A)** Choice A is correct. Choice B is incorrect because the phrase *for facial lacerations* is misplaced. Choices C and D are incorrect because they are wordy. Choice C also contains the pronoun *it* which has an indefinite antecedent. Choice E is incorrect because of the awkward use of *facial lacerations* as an adjective modifying treatment.

16. **(C)** In this sentence we must have an adjective to balance with *tough* and *single-minded*. Choices A, B, D, and E are incorrect because they do not maintain the required parallel structure. Choice C is correct.

17. **(C)** We are concerned here with the apostrophe use with a singular name ending in "s." We are also concerned with improper ellipsis. In Choice A, "James'" is correct but we must either say "to read than *the prose style* of James Joyce" or "to read than James Joyce's." In Choice B, "Jame's" is incorrect—his name is not "Jame." Choice C is correct. Choices D and E are incorrect for the same reason that Choice A is incorrect—improper ellipsis.

18. **(C)** Choice A is incorrect because in a "neither... nor" construction, the number of the verb is determined by the "nor" subject noun ("followers"). Since "followers" is plural, the verb must be plural ("know"). Choices B, D, and E are incorrect for the same reason. Moreover, Choice B is incorrect for another reason: the correlative form is "neither... nor"—not "neither...or". Choice C is correct.

19. **(A)** Choice A is correct. Choice B's passive verb ("was requested") interferes with the flow of the sentence. "It occurred" in Choice C is unnecessary.

Choice D is too wordy for what has to be expressed. Choice E changes the meaning of the original sentence—the students did not "insist."

20. **(B)** Choice A is indirect. Choice B is correct. In Choice C, "as a prize" repeats unnecessarily the "Nobel Prize." Choice D is much too awkward. Choice E is incorrect—the scientists did not discover viruses.

21. **(D)** "...but a security guard, a fireman, and *me*." The preposition *but* is understood before *me*. Since *me* is the object of the preposition *but,* it has an objective form (*me*)—not a nominative form (*I* ).

22. **(A)** "Having drunk...the lemonade..." The past participle of *drink* is *having drunk*.

23. **(B)** "...to *whoever*...could present her..." The subject of the dependent clause must have a nominative case form (*whoever*)—not an objective case form (*whomever*).

24. **(C)** "...they had brought *not nearly* the number..." Do not use the expression *nowhere near* for *not nearly*.

25. **(E)** All underlined parts are correct.

26. **(A)** "*Because of* his not studying..." Do not begin a sentence with the words *due to. Due* is an adjective. As an adjective, it must have a noun to modify.

27. **(C)** "...to buy the *kind of* car..." Do not use the article *a* or *an* after *kind of, type of, sort of*, etc.

28. **(D)** "...compare their poems *with those of Robert Frost*." We have an improper ellipsis in the original sentence. The additional words (*those of*) are necessary to complete the meaning of the sentence.

29. **(A)** "I appreciate *your* offering..." The subject of a gerund is in the possessive case. We, therefore, say *your offering*—not *you offering*.

30. **(B)** "...the *slower* of the two..." Since we are here comparing two runners, we must use the comparative degree (*slower*)—not the superlative degree (*slowest*).

31. **(D)** "...is usually easier than passing the driving test." This sentence requires parallelism: *Passing the driving test*" should parallel "*Passing* the written test..."

32. **(D)** "...each hoping that *he* would win..." A pronoun should be in the same number as the noun or pronoun to which it refers. In the sentence, *he* refers to *each*, which is a singular pronoun.

**33.** **(B)** "Her answer…was *altogether* incorrect…" *Altogether* means *entirely, wholly. All together* means *as a group.*

**34.** **(C)** "…they acted as if they never *had met* before…" We must use the past perfect tense (*had met*) to indicate an action taking place before another past action (*acted*).

**35.** **(D)** Choice A is incorrect because sentence one is needed to open the paragraph in order to establish the fact that safety devices have been proven to save lives. If this information does not precede every other idea in the paragraph, the logical reasons for the laws and for obeying them are not clear. Therefore, sentence four should not be placed before sentence one. Choices B and C are incorrect in that sentence four is in an illogical position in the paragraph and should be moved rather than attached to sentence three (Choice B) or left in its present position (Choice C). Choice D is correct: The logical position for the idea about laws governing the use of motorcycle helmets is directly following the idea about laws governing the installation of seat belts. (The two ideas are so closely related that they might appropriately be joined in a complex sentence.) Additionally, in the present position of sentence four, "these safety devices" seem to apply only to "seat belts" in sentence two, whereas the clear intent of the paragraph as a whole is that "safety devices" refer to both seat belts and helmets. Choice E is incorrect because the present position of sentence four is not logical and creates the inaccurate reference to only one safety device.

**36.** **(A)** Choice A is correct: The insertion of "these riders are" is necessary to correct the existing situation in which the modifier "if thrown in an accident" incorrectly attaches itself to "their heads." Choice B is incorrect not only because the dangling modifier is not corrected but also because a cantaloupe, with its hard rind and juicy interior, is a better figure of speech for a human head than a flexible, partially transparent balloon filled with gas or air. Choice C is incorrect because replacing "their heads" with "they" would create a situation in which "if thrown in an accident" would modify a pronoun which might refer either to motorcyclists or to helmets. The rest of the sentence referring to cantaloupes would make a poor comparison if applied to the bodies of the motorcyclists and would convey no pertinent meaning if applied to helmets. Choice D is incorrect because "who refuse to wear helmets" is a restrictive clause defining particular motorcyclists and should not be made into a nonrestrictive clause by placing commas around it. Choice E is incorrect in that the dangling modifier would not be corrected and nothing would be gained in sense by creating the awkwardly repetitive sounds of "measure of pleasure."

**37.** **(E)** Choice A is incorrect: Turning sentence seven into two sentences with the first ending after "small ways" would leave the second sentence as a dependent clause fragment. Choice B is incorrect because the subject and its verb should not be separated with a comma. Choice C is incorrect: Beginning the sentence with "while" would be a good choice if "because" were removed; but Choice C does not specify this omission, and "because" is not an appropriate conjunction. Choice D is incorrect: While the phrase "in more important ways" could be omitted (even though it adds balance to the sentence in paralleling "in small ways"), the major problem in the sentence would be passed over in making only this deletion. Choice E is correct: The word "because" should be changed to "but." The second idea in the sentence is not "a reason for" or "the result of" the first idea, relationships indicated by "because." The two ideas in the sentence are contrasting (that devices may "limit" but also "greatly increase" comfort and freedom) and should be connected with a conjunction showing this contrast.

**38.** **(A)** Statistical backup would qualify the author's position and show the dangers more specifically and in a more documented fashion. Choices B, C, D are weak and choice E is irrelevant.

**39.** **(E)** Since the paragraph is pro wearing seat belts and helmets, the author must have a strong first introductory statement for why seat belts and helmets are warranted. Sentence 1 serves that purpose and should be kept as the first sentence.

# What You Must Do Now to Raise Your PSAT Score

1. Follow the directions on pages 437–439 to determine your scaled score for the PSAT Test you've just taken. These results will give you a good idea about whether or not you ought to study hard in order to achieve a certain score on the actual PSAT.

2. Eliminate your weaknesses in each of the PSAT test areas by taking the following Giant Steps toward PSAT success:

## Critical Reading Part

### Giant Step 1

Take advantage of the Critical Reading Strategies that begin on page 80. Read again the Explanatory Answer for each of the Critical Reading questions that you got wrong. Refer to the Critical Reading Strategy that applies to each of your incorrect answers. Learn each of these Critical Reading Strategies thoroughly. These strategies are crucial if you want to raise your PSAT score substantially.

### Giant Step 2

You can improve your vocabulary by doing the following:

1) Learn the Hot Prefixes and Roots beginning on page 108.

2) Learn the 3 Vocabulary Strategies beginning on page 105.

3) Read as widely as possible—not only novels. Nonfiction is important too...and don't forget to read newspapers and magazines.

4) Listen to people who speak well. Tune in to worthwhile TV programs also.

5) Use the dictionary frequently and extensively—at home, on the bus, at work, etc.

6) Play word games—for example, crossword puzzles, anagrams, and Scrabble. Another game is to compose your own Sentence Completion questions. Try them on your friends.

## Math Part

### Giant Step 3

Make good use of the Math Strategies that begin on page 51. Read again the solutions for each Math question that you answered incorrectly. Refer to the Math Strategy that applies to each of your incorrect answers. Learn each of these Math Strategies thoroughly. We repeat that these strategies are crucial if you want to raise your PSAT Math score substantially.

### Giant Step 4

You may want to take **The 101 Most Important Math Questions You Need to Know How to Solve** test on page 13 and follow the directions after the test for a basic math skills diagnosis.

For each Math question that you got wrong in the test, note the reference to the Math Refresher section on page 129. This reference will explain clearly the mathematical principle involved in the solution of the question you answered incorrectly. Learn that particular mathematical principle thoroughly.

## For Both the Math and Critical Reading Parts

### Giant Step 5

You may want to take the **National Merit Scholarship Diagnostic Test** on page 1 to assess whether you're using the best strategies for the questions.

## For the Writing Part

### Giant Step 6

Take a look at Part 6—The PSAT Writing Skills Test, which describes the various item types in the Writing Section and includes sample questions with answers and explanations. Also make use of Part 7—A Brief Review of English Grammar.

3. After you have done some of the tasks you have been advised to do in the suggestions above, proceed to Practice Test 3, beginning on page 464.

   After taking Practice Test 3, concentrate on the weaknesses that still remain.

   If you do the job *right* and follow the steps listed above, you are likely to raise your PSAT score on each of the Critical Reading, Math, and Writing parts of the test 15 points—maybe 20 points—and even more.

> I am the master of my fate;
> I am the captain of my soul.

—From the poem "Invictus"
   by William Ernest Henley

Start at the beginning of each new section. If a section has fewer questions than answer spaces, leave the extra answer spaces blank. Be sure to erase any errors or stray marks completely.

**SECTION 1**

1 Ⓐ Ⓑ Ⓒ Ⓓ Ⓔ    13 Ⓐ Ⓑ Ⓒ Ⓓ Ⓔ
2 Ⓐ Ⓑ Ⓒ Ⓓ Ⓔ    14 Ⓐ Ⓑ Ⓒ Ⓓ Ⓔ
3 Ⓐ Ⓑ Ⓒ Ⓓ Ⓔ    15 Ⓐ Ⓑ Ⓒ Ⓓ Ⓔ
4 Ⓐ Ⓑ Ⓒ Ⓓ Ⓔ    16 Ⓐ Ⓑ Ⓒ Ⓓ Ⓔ
5 Ⓐ Ⓑ Ⓒ Ⓓ Ⓔ    17 Ⓐ Ⓑ Ⓒ Ⓓ Ⓔ
6 Ⓐ Ⓑ Ⓒ Ⓓ Ⓔ    18 Ⓐ Ⓑ Ⓒ Ⓓ Ⓔ
7 Ⓐ Ⓑ Ⓒ Ⓓ Ⓔ    19 Ⓐ Ⓑ Ⓒ Ⓓ Ⓔ
8 Ⓐ Ⓑ Ⓒ Ⓓ Ⓔ    20 Ⓐ Ⓑ Ⓒ Ⓓ Ⓔ
9 Ⓐ Ⓑ Ⓒ Ⓓ Ⓔ    21 Ⓐ Ⓑ Ⓒ Ⓓ Ⓔ
10 Ⓐ Ⓑ Ⓒ Ⓓ Ⓔ   22 Ⓐ Ⓑ Ⓒ Ⓓ Ⓔ
11 Ⓐ Ⓑ Ⓒ Ⓓ Ⓔ   23 Ⓐ Ⓑ Ⓒ Ⓓ Ⓔ
12 Ⓐ Ⓑ Ⓒ Ⓓ Ⓔ   24 Ⓐ Ⓑ Ⓒ Ⓓ Ⓔ

**SECTION 2**

1 Ⓐ Ⓑ Ⓒ Ⓓ Ⓔ    11 Ⓐ Ⓑ Ⓒ Ⓓ Ⓔ
2 Ⓐ Ⓑ Ⓒ Ⓓ Ⓔ    12 Ⓐ Ⓑ Ⓒ Ⓓ Ⓔ
3 Ⓐ Ⓑ Ⓒ Ⓓ Ⓔ    13 Ⓐ Ⓑ Ⓒ Ⓓ Ⓔ
4 Ⓐ Ⓑ Ⓒ Ⓓ Ⓔ    14 Ⓐ Ⓑ Ⓒ Ⓓ Ⓔ
5 Ⓐ Ⓑ Ⓒ Ⓓ Ⓔ    15 Ⓐ Ⓑ Ⓒ Ⓓ Ⓔ
6 Ⓐ Ⓑ Ⓒ Ⓓ Ⓔ    16 Ⓐ Ⓑ Ⓒ Ⓓ Ⓔ
7 Ⓐ Ⓑ Ⓒ Ⓓ Ⓔ    17 Ⓐ Ⓑ Ⓒ Ⓓ Ⓔ
8 Ⓐ Ⓑ Ⓒ Ⓓ Ⓔ    18 Ⓐ Ⓑ Ⓒ Ⓓ Ⓔ
9 Ⓐ Ⓑ Ⓒ Ⓓ Ⓔ    19 Ⓐ Ⓑ Ⓒ Ⓓ Ⓔ
10 Ⓐ Ⓑ Ⓒ Ⓓ Ⓔ   20 Ⓐ Ⓑ Ⓒ Ⓓ Ⓔ

**SECTION 3**

25 Ⓐ Ⓑ Ⓒ Ⓓ Ⓔ   37 Ⓐ Ⓑ Ⓒ Ⓓ Ⓔ
26 Ⓐ Ⓑ Ⓒ Ⓓ Ⓔ   38 Ⓐ Ⓑ Ⓒ Ⓓ Ⓔ
27 Ⓐ Ⓑ Ⓒ Ⓓ Ⓔ   39 Ⓐ Ⓑ Ⓒ Ⓓ Ⓔ
28 Ⓐ Ⓑ Ⓒ Ⓓ Ⓔ   40 Ⓐ Ⓑ Ⓒ Ⓓ Ⓔ
29 Ⓐ Ⓑ Ⓒ Ⓓ Ⓔ   41 Ⓐ Ⓑ Ⓒ Ⓓ Ⓔ
30 Ⓐ Ⓑ Ⓒ Ⓓ Ⓔ   42 Ⓐ Ⓑ Ⓒ Ⓓ Ⓔ
31 Ⓐ Ⓑ Ⓒ Ⓓ Ⓔ   43 Ⓐ Ⓑ Ⓒ Ⓓ Ⓔ
32 Ⓐ Ⓑ Ⓒ Ⓓ Ⓔ   44 Ⓐ Ⓑ Ⓒ Ⓓ Ⓔ
33 Ⓐ Ⓑ Ⓒ Ⓓ Ⓔ   45 Ⓐ Ⓑ Ⓒ Ⓓ Ⓔ
34 Ⓐ Ⓑ Ⓒ Ⓓ Ⓔ   46 Ⓐ Ⓑ Ⓒ Ⓓ Ⓔ
35 Ⓐ Ⓑ Ⓒ Ⓓ Ⓔ   47 Ⓐ Ⓑ Ⓒ Ⓓ Ⓔ
36 Ⓐ Ⓑ Ⓒ Ⓓ Ⓔ   48 Ⓐ Ⓑ Ⓒ Ⓓ Ⓔ

Start at the beginning of each new section. If a section has fewer questions than answer spaces, leave the extra answer spaces blank. Be sure to erase any errors or stray marks completely.

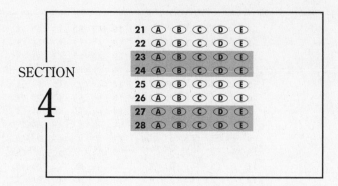

SECTION

4

CAUTION    Use the answer spaces in the grids below for Section 4.

Student-Produced Responses    ONLY ANSWERS ENTERED IN THE CIRCLES IN EACH GRID WILL BE SCORED. YOU WILL NOT RECEIVE CREDIT FOR ANYTHING WRITTEN IN THE BOXES ABOVE THE CIRCLES.

Start at the beginning of each new section. If a section has fewer questions than answer spaces, leave the extra answer spaces blank. Be sure to erase any errors or stray marks completely.

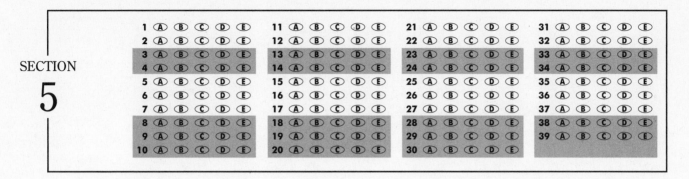

SECTION

5

# PSAT PRACTICE
# TEST 3

# SECTION 1

Time: 25 Minutes—Turn to Section 1 (page 461) of your answer sheet to answer the questions in this section.
24 Questions

**Directions:** For each question in this section, select the best answer from among the choices given and fill in the corresponding circle on the answer sheet.

---

Each sentence below has one or two blanks, each blank indicating that something has been omitted. Beneath the sentence are five words or sets of words labeled A through E. Choose the word or set of words that, when inserted in the sentence, best fits the meaning of the sentence as a whole.

Example:

Hoping to _____ the dispute, negotiators proposed a compromise that they felt would be _____ to both labor and management.

(A) enforce...useful
(B) end...divisive
(C) overcome...unattractive
(D) extend...satisfactory
(E) resolve...acceptable

Ⓐ Ⓑ Ⓒ Ⓓ ●

---

1. In spite of David's tremendous intelligence, he was frequently _____ when confronted with practical matters.

    (A) coherent
    (B) baffled
    (C) cautious
    (D) philosophical
    (E) pensive

2. Governor Edwards combined _____ politics with administrative skills to dominate the state; in addition to these assets, he was also _____.

    (A) corrupt...glum
    (B) inept...civil
    (C) incriminating...sincere
    (D) astute...dapper
    (E) trivial...lavish

3. After four years of _____ curbs designed to protect the American auto industry, the president cleared the way for Japan to _____ more cars to the United States.

    (A) profitable...drive
    (B) flexible...produce
    (C) motor...direct
    (D) import...ship
    (E) reciprocal...sell

4. The photographs of Ethiopia's starving children demonstrate the _____ of drought, poor land use, and overpopulation.

    (A) consequences
    (B) prejudices
    (C) inequities
    (D) indications
    (E) mortalities

5. There had been a yearning for an end to _____ with the Soviet Union, but little evidence had existed that nuclear-arms agreements had contributed to our _____.

    (A) treaties...silence
    (B) advantages...relations
    (C) differences...amity
    (D) tensions...security
    (E) commerce...decision

GO ON TO THE NEXT PAGE

6. The union struck shortly after midnight after its negotiating committee _____ a company offer of a 20% raise.

   (A) applauded
   (B) rejected
   (C) considered
   (D) postponed
   (E) accepted

7. Although our team was aware that the Raiders' attack power was _____ as compared with that of our players, we were stupid to be so _____.

   (A) calculated...alert
   (B) sluggish...easygoing
   (C) acceptable...serious
   (D) determined...detailed
   (E) premeditated...willing

8. The _____ prime minister caused the downfall of the once _____ country.

   (A) heroic...important
   (B) respected...rich
   (C) incompetent...powerful
   (D) vacillating...confidential
   (E) insightful...unconquerable

GO ON TO THE NEXT PAGE

Each passage below is followed by questions based on its content. Answer the questions on the basis of what is stated or implied in each passage and in any introductory material that may be provided.

**Questions 9–10 are based on the following passage.**

1　A cliché is made, not born. The process begins when someone hits upon a bright new way of stating a common experience. At that point, the remark is an epigram. But if it is particularly apt as well as catchy, the saying receives
5　wide circulation as verbal coin. Soon it is likely to be suffering from overwork. It has then arrived at cliché-hood. The dictionary records the doom of the successful epigram in defining a cliché: "A trite phrase; a hackneyed expression." For the epigrammatist, the only cheer in this
10　process is that it proves his expression was good. Even this situation is covered by a cliché: "Imitation is the sincerest form of flattery."

9. The writer suggests that an epigram is

(A) fresh
(B) trite
(C) ordinary
(D) cheerful
(E) noble

10. According to the author, the chief difference between an epigram and a cliché is in their

(A) origin
(B) length
(C) meaning
(D) use
(E) purpose

**Questions 11–12 are based on the following passage.**

1　In the ordinary course of nature, the great beneficent changes come slowly and silently. The noisy changes, for the most part, mean violence and disruption. The roar of storms and tornadoes, the explosions of volcanoes, the
5　crash of thunder, are the result of a sudden break in the equipoise of the elements; from a condition of comparative repose and silence they become fearfully swift and audible. The still small voice is the voice of life and growth and perpetuity…In the history of a nation it is the same.

11. As used in the passage, the word: "equipoise" (line 6) most nearly means

(A) stress
(B) balance
(C) course
(D) slowness
(E) condition

12. The author implies that growth and perpetuity in nature and in history are the result of

(A) quiet changes
(B) a period of silence
(C) undiscovered action
(D) storms and tornadoes
(E) violence and disruptions

GO ON TO THE NEXT PAGE

The two passages below are followed by questions based on their content and on the relationship between the two passages. Answer the questions on the basis of what is <u>stated</u> or <u>implied</u> in the passages and in any introductory material that may be provided.

## Questions 13–24 are based on the following passages.

*The following two passages describe two views of the makeup and character of an artist.*

### Passage 1

The special quality which makes an artist of any worth might be defined, indeed, as an extraordinary capacity for irritation, a pathological sensitiveness to environmental pricks and stings. He differs from the rest of us mainly
5 because he reacts sharply and in an uncommon manner to phenomena which leave the rest of us unmoved, or, at most, merely annoy us vaguely. He is, in brief, a more delicate fellow than we are, and hence less fitted to prosper and enjoy himself under the conditions of life which he and we must
10 face alike. Therefore, he takes to artistic endeavor, which is at once a criticism of life and an attempt to escape from life.

So much for the theory of it. The more the facts are studied, the more they bear it out. In those fields of art, at all events, which concern themselves with ideas as well as
15 with sensations it is almost impossible to find any trace of an artist who was not actively hostile to his environment, and thus an indifferent patriot. From Dante to Tolstoy and from Shakespeare to Mark Twain the story is ever the same. Names suggest themselves instantly: Goethe, Heine,
20 Shelley, Byron, Thackeray, Balzac, Rabelais, Cervantes, Swift, Dostoevsky, Carlyle, Moliere, Pope—all bitter critics of their time and nation, most of them piously hated by the contemporary 100 percenters, some of them actually fugitives from rage and reprisal.
25 Dante put all of the patriotic Italians of his day into Hell, and showed them boiling, roasting and writhing on hooks. Cervantes drew such a devastating picture of the Spain that he lived in that it ruined the Spaniards. Shakespeare made his heroes foreigners and his clowns Englishmen.
30 Goethe was in favor of Napoleon. Rabelais, a citizen of Christendom rather than of France, raised a cackle against it that Christendom is still trying in vain to suppress. Swift, having finished the Irish and then the English, proceeded to finish the whole human race. The exceptions are few and
35 far between, and not many of them will bear examination. So far as I know, the only eminent writer in English history who was also a 100% Englishman, absolutely beyond suspicion, was Samuel Johnson. But was Johnson actually an artist? If he was, then a kazoo-player is a musician. He
40 employed the materials of one of the arts, to wit, words, but his use of them was mechanical, not artistic. If Johnson were alive today, he would be a United States Senator, or a university president. He left such wounds upon English prose that it was a century recovering from them.

### Passage 2

45 For the ease and pleasure of treading the old road, accepting the fashions, the education, the religion of society, he takes the cross of making his own, and, of course, the self-accusation, the faint heart, the frequent uncertainty and loss of time, which are the nettles and tangling vines in
50 the way of the self-relying and self-directed, and the state of virtual hostility in which he seems to stand to society, and especially to educated society. For all this loss and scorn, what offset? The artist is to find consolation in exercising the highest functions of human nature. The artist is one
55 who raises himself from private consideration and breathes and lives on public and illustrious thoughts. The artist is the world's eye. He is the world's heart. He is to resist the vulgar prosperity that retrogrades ever to barbarism, by preserving and communicating heroic sentiments, noble
60 biographies, melodious verse, and the conclusions of history. Whatsoever oracles the human heart, in all emergencies, in all solemn hours, has uttered as its commentary on the world of actions—these he shall receive and impart. And whatsoever new verdict Reason from her inviolable
65 seat pronounces on the passing men and women and events of today—this he shall hear and promulgate.

These being his functions, it becomes the artist to feel all confidence in himself, and to defer never to the popular cry. He and he only knows the world. The world of any
70 moment is the merest appearance. Some great decorum, some fetish of a government, some ephemeral trade, or war, or man, is cried up by half mankind and cried down by the other half, as if all depended on this particular up or down. The odds are that the whole question is not worth
75 the poorest thought which the scholar has lost in listening to the controversy. Let her not quit her belief that a popgun is a popgun, though the ancient and honorable of the earth affirm it to be the crack of doom. In silence, in steadiness, in severe abstraction, let him hold by himself; add observation
80 to observation, patient of neglect, patient of reproach, and bide his own time—happy enough if he can satisfy himself alone that this day he has seen something truly. Success treads on every right step. For the instinct is sure, that prompts him to tell his brother what he thinks. The artist
85 then learns that in going down into the secrets of his own mind he has descended into the secrets of all minds. He learns that the artist who has mastered any law in his private thoughts is master to that extent of all translated. The poet, in utter solitude remembering his spontaneous thoughts
90 and recording them, is found to have recorded that which men in crowded cities find true for them also. The orator distrusts at first the fitness of his frank confessions, his want of knowledge of the persons he addresses, until he finds

GO ON TO THE NEXT PAGE

that he is the complement of his hearers—that they drink
95 his words because he fulfills for them their own nature; the
deeper he dives into his privatest, secretest presentiment, to
his wonder he finds this is the most acceptable, most public,
and universally true. The people delight in it; the better part
of every man feels. This is my music; this is myself.

13. Which of the following quotations is related most
closely to the principal idea of Passage 1?

(A) "All nature is but art unknown to thee, All
chance, direction which thou canst not see."
(B) "When to her share some human errors fall,
Look on her face and you'll forget them all."
(C) "All human things are subject to decay, "And,
when fate summons, monarchs must obey."
(D) "A little learning is a dangerous thing, Drink
deep or taste not the Pierian spring."
(E) "Great wits are sure to madness near allied,
And thin partitions do their bounds divide."

14. It can be inferred that the author of Passage 1
believes that United States Senators and university
presidents

(A) must be treated with respect because of their
position
(B) are to be held in low esteem
(C) are generally appreciative of the great literary
classics
(D) have native writing ability
(E) have the qualities of the artist

15. All of the following ideas about artists are mentioned
in Passage 1 *except* that

(A) they are irritated by their surroundings
(B) they are escapists from reality
(C) they are lovers of beauty
(D) they are hated by their contemporaries
(E) they are critical of their times

16. Which of the following best describes Passage 1
author's attitude toward artists?

(A) sharply critical
(B) sincerely sympathetic
(C) deeply resentful
(D) mildly annoyed
(E) completely delighted

17. It is a frequent criticism of the artist that he lives
by himself, in an "ivory tower," remote from the
problems and business of the world. Which of
these below constitutes the best refutation by the
writer of Passage 2 to the criticism here noted?

(A) The world's concerns being ephemeral, the artist does well to renounce them and the world.
(B) The artist lives in the past to interpret the present.
(C) The artist at his truest is the spokesman of the
people.
(D) The artist is not concerned with the world's
doings because he is not selfish and therefore
not engrossed in matters of importance to
himself and neighbors.
(E) The artist's academic researches of today are the
businessman's practical products of tomorrow.

18. The artist's road is rough, according to Passage 2.
Which of these is the artist's greatest difficulty?

(A) The artist must renounce religion.
(B) The artist must pioneer new approaches.
(C) The artist must express scorn for and hostility
to society.
(D) The artist is uncertain of his course.
(E) There is a pleasure in the main-traveled roads
in education, religion, and all social fashions.

19. When the writer of Passage 2 speaks of the "world's
eye" and the "world's heart" he means

(A) the same thing
(B) culture and conscience
(C) culture and wisdom
(D) a scanning of all the world's geography and a
deep sympathy for every living thing
(E) mind and love

20. By the phrase "nettles and tangling vines" (line 49)
the author probably refers to

(A) "self-accusation" and "loss of time"
(B) "faint heart" and "self-accusation"
(C) "the slings and arrows of outrageous fortune"
(D) a general term for the difficulties of a scholar's
life
(E) "self-accusation" and "uncertainty"

GO ON TO THE NEXT PAGE

21. The various ideas in Passage 2 are best summarized in which of these groups?

   I. truth versus society
     the artist and books
     the world and the artist
  II. the ease of living traditionally
     the glory of an artist's life
     true knowledge versus trivia
 III. the hardships of the scholar
     the artist's functions
     the artist's justifications for disregarding the world's business

   (A) I and III together
   (B) I only
   (C) III only
   (D) I, II, and III together
   (E) I and II together

22. "seems to stand" (line 51) means

   (A) is
   (B) ends probably in becoming
   (C) gives the false impression of being
   (D) is seen to be
   (E) the quicksands of time

23. The difference between the description of the artist in Passage 1 as compared with the artist in Passage 2 is that

   (A) one is loyal to his fellow men and women whereas the other is opposed to his or her environment
   (B) one is sensitive to his or her environment whereas the other is apathetic
   (C) one has political aspirations; the other does not
   (D) one has deep knowledge; the other has superficial knowledge
   (E) one could be proficient in a field other than art; the other could create only in his or her present field

24. Which of the following describes statements that refer to the *same* one artist (either the one in Passage 1 *or* the one in Passage 2)?

   I. This artist's thoughts are also the spectator's thoughts.
     This artist lives modestly and not luxuriously.
  II. This artist admires foreigners over his own countrymen.
     This artist reacts to many things that most people would be neutral to.
 III. This artist is happy to be at his best.
     This artist accepts society.

   (A) I only
   (B) II only
   (C) III only
   (D) I and III only
   (E) I, II, and III

# STOP

If you finish before time is called, you may check your work on this section only.
Do not turn to any other section in the test.

# SECTION 2

Time: 25 Minutes—Turn to Section 2 (page 461) of your answer sheet to answer the questions in this section.
   20 Questions

**Directions:** This section contains two types of question. You have 25 minutes to complete both types. For questions 1–8, solve each problem and decide which is the best of the choices given. Fill in the corresponding circle on the answer sheet. You may use any available space for scratchwork.

## Notes:

1. The use of a calculator is permitted.
2. All numbers used are real numbers.
3. Figures that accompany problems in this test are intended to provide information useful in solving the problems. They are drawn as accurately as possible EXCEPT when it is stated in a specific problem that the figure is not drawn to scale. All figures lie in a plane unless otherwise indicated.
4. Unless otherwise specified, the domain of any function $f$ is assumed to be the set of all real numbers $x$ for which $f(x)$ is a real number.

**REFERENCE INFORMATION**

$A = \pi r^2$   $A = lw$   $A = \frac{1}{2}bh$   $V = lwh$   $V = \pi r^2 h$   $c^2 = a^2 + b^2$   *Special Right Triangles*
$C = 2\pi r$

The number of degrees of arc in a circle is 360.
The sum of the measures in degrees of the angles of a triangle is 180.

1. If $x + by = 3x + y = 5$ and $y = 2$, then $b =$

   (A) 0
   (B) 1
   (C) 2
   (D) 3
   (E) 4

2. There are 2 boys and 3 girls in the class. The ratio of boys to girls in the class is equal to all of the following *except*

   (A) 4:6
   (B) 9:12
   (C) 6:9
   (D) 12:18
   (E) 18:27

GO ON TO THE NEXT PAGE

3. Which of the following is equal to $\left|\dfrac{x}{y}\right|$ for all real numbers $x$ and $y$?

(A) $\dfrac{x}{y}$

(B) $\dfrac{|x|}{y}$

(C) $\dfrac{x}{|y|}$

(D) $\left|\dfrac{x}{y}\right|$

(E) $-\left|\dfrac{x}{y}\right|$

$$C = md + t$$

5. The cost, $C$, of a business trip is represented by the equation above, where $m$ is a constant, $d$ is the number of days of the complete trip, and $t$ is the cost of transportation, which does not change. If the business trip was increased by 5 days, how much more did the business trip cost than the original planned trip?

(A) $5d$
(B) $5m$
(C) $5t$
(D) $d(m - 3)$
(E) $m(d - 3)$

4. If $(x + y)^2 = 9$, what is $x + y$?

(A) 0
(B) 3
(C) 9
(D) 27
(E) The answer cannot be determined from the information given.

6. Which of the following represents $x$ on a number line if $(x - 3) \leq 0$?

(A)

(B)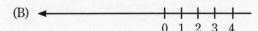

(C)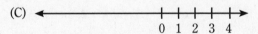

(D)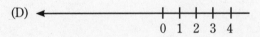

(E)

GO ON TO THE NEXT PAGE

$$4x - 3y = 9$$
$$8x + ky = 19$$

7. For which value of $k$ will the system of the equations above have *no* solution?

(A) $+6$

(B) $+3$

(C) $0$

(D) $-3$

(E) $-6$

9. A population that starts at 100 and doubles after eight years can be expressed as the following where $t$ stands for the number of years that have elapsed from the start:

(A) $100 \times 2^t$

(B) $100 \times 2^{t/7}$

(C) $100 \times 2^{t-8}$

(D) $100 \times 2^{t/8}$

(E) $100 \times 2^{16t}$

8. Given that $r \neq 0$ and $r = 5w = 7a$, find the value of $r - w$ in terms of $a$.

(A) $\dfrac{1a}{7}$

(B) $\dfrac{7a}{5}$

(C) $3a$

(D) $\dfrac{28a}{5}$

(E) $28a$

10. Find the solution set in positive integers of $2x + 5 < 5$.

(A) $\{1, 2, 3, 4\}$

(B) $\{1, 2\}$

(C) $\{0\}$

(D) $\varnothing$

(E) infinity

GO ON TO THE NEXT PAGE

11. If $a^b = x$ and $x^b = y$, then

   (A) $a^{2b} = y$
   (B) $a^{b^2} = y$
   (C) $b^a = y$
   (D) $(ax)^b = y$
   (E) $(ax)^b = x$

*Question 9* refers to the figure above, where $W$, $X$, $Y$, and $Z$ are four distinct digits from 0 to 9, inclusive, and $W + X + Y = 5Z$.

13. Under the given conditions, all of the following could be values of $Z$ EXCEPT

   (A) 1
   (B) 2
   (C) 3
   (D) 4
   (E) 5

12. Two lines in a plane are represented by $y = x - 1$ and $2x + 5y = 9$. The coordinates of the point at which the lines intersect are

   (A) (2,1)
   (B) (1,2)
   (C) (2,5)
   (D) (5,2)
   (E) (3,3)

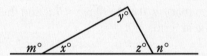

14. In the figure above, $m + n =$

   (A) 90
   (B) 180
   (C) $180 + y$
   (D) $90 + x + y + z$
   (E) $2(x + y + z)$

GO ON TO THE NEXT PAGE

15. A box contains exactly 24 coins—nickels, dimes, and quarters. The probability of selecting a nickel by reaching into the box without looking is $\frac{3}{8}$. The probability of selecting a dime by reaching into the box without looking is $\frac{1}{8}$. How many quarters are in the box?

(A) 6
(B) 8
(C) 12
(D) 14
(E) 16

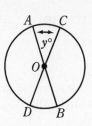

*Note:* Figure is not drawn to scale

17. In the figure above, $\overline{AB}$ and $\overline{CD}$ are diameters of the circle whose center is $O$. If the radius of the circle is 2 inches and the sum of the lengths of arcs $\overarc{AD}$ and $\overarc{BC}$ is $3\pi$ inches, then $y =$

(A) 45
(B) 60
(C) 75
(D) 90
(E) 120

16. Which of the following designs *can* be formed by combining rectangles with size and shading the same as that shown above if overlap is not permitted?

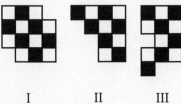

I  II  III

(A) I only
(B) II only
(C) III only
(D) I and II only
(E) II and III only

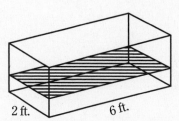

18. The figure above shows water in a tank whose base is 2 feet by 6 feet. If a rectangular solid whose dimensions are 1 foot by 1 foot by 2 feet is totally immersed in the water, how many *inches* will the water rise?

(A) $\frac{1}{6}$
(B) 1
(C) 2
(D) 3
(E) 12

**GO ON TO THE NEXT PAGE**

$$\begin{array}{r} AB \\ +BA \\ \hline CDC \end{array}$$

**19.** If each of the four letters in the sum above represents a *different* digit, which of the following *cannot* be a value of $A$?

(A) 6
(B) 5
(C) 4
(D) 3
(E) 2

**20.** If for real $x$, $y$, $f(x) = x^2 + x$ and $g(y) = y^2$, then $f[g(-1)] =$

(A) 2
(B) $-2$
(C) 4
(D) $-4$
(E) $-8$

# STOP
If you finish before time is called, you may check your work on this section only.
Do not turn to any other section in the test.

# SECTION 3

Time: 25 Minutes—Turn to Section 3 (page 461) of your answer sheet to answer the questions in this section.
24 Questions

**Directions:** For each question in this section, select the best answer from among the choices given and fill in the corresponding circle on the answer sheet.

Each sentence below has one or two blanks, each blank indicating that something has been omitted. Beneath the sentence are five words or sets of words labeled A through E. Choose the word or set of words that, when inserted in the sentence, best fits the meaning of the sentence as a whole.

Example:

Hoping to _____ the dispute, negotiators proposed a compromise that they felt would be _____ to both labor and management.

(A) enforce...useful
(B) end...divisive
(C) overcome...unattractive
(D) extend...satisfactory
(E) resolve...acceptable

Ⓐ Ⓑ Ⓒ Ⓓ ⬤

25. The girl's extreme state of _____ aroused in him a feeling of pity.

(A) disapproval
(B) exultation
(C) enthusiasm
(D) degradation
(E) jubilation

26. The main character in the novel was dignified and _____, a man of great reserve.

(A) garrulous
(B) aloof
(C) boring
(D) hypocritical
(E) interesting

27. The nonsmoker's blood contains _____ amounts of carbon monoxide; on the other hand, the smoker's blood contains _____ amounts.

(A) frequent...extensive
(B) heavy...adequate
(C) minute...excessive
(D) definite...puzzling
(E) bland...moderate

28. Violent crime has become so _____ in our cities that hardly a day goes by when we are not made aware of some _____ act on our local news broadcasts.

(A) scarce...momentous
(B) pervasive...benign
(C) conclusive...serious
(D) common...heinous
(E) ridiculous...unacceptable

29. Since he had not worked very hard on his project, the student was quite _____ upon learning that he had won the contest.

(A) annoyed
(B) apathetic
(C) rebuffed
(D) dismayed
(E) elated

GO ON TO THE NEXT PAGE ⟶

The passages below are followed by questions based on their content; questions following a pair of related passages may also be based on the relationship between the paired passages. Answer the questions on the basis of what is <u>stated</u> or <u>implied</u> in the passages and in any introductory material that may be provided.

**Questions 30–33 are based on the following passages.**

**Passage 1**

1 Classical music is termed "classical" because it can be heard over and over again without the listener tiring of the music. A symphony of Brahms can be heard and heard again with the same or even hightened enjoyment a few
5 months later. It is unfortunate that the Compact Disc (CD) sales of classical music is dismal compared to other types of music. Perhaps this is because many people in our generation were not exposed to classical music at an early age and therefore did not get to know the music.

**Passage 2**

10 Rock and contemporary music has a high impact on the listener but unfortunately is not evergreen. Its enjoyment lasts only as long as there is current interest in the topic or emotion that the music portrays and that only lasts for 3 months or so until other music replaces it, especially
15 when another best-selling song comes out. The reason why the impact of this type of music is not as great when it first comes out is thought to be because technically the intricacy of the music is not high and not sophisticated, although many critics believe it is because the music elicits
20 a particular emotional feeling which gradually becomes worn out in time.

30. According to the passage, it can be assumed that the majority of younger people do not like classical music because they

   (A) buy only the best-selling CDs
   (B) do not have the sophistication of a true music lover
   (C) grow tired of classical music
   (D) did not hear that type of music in their youth
   (E) are more restless than the older generation

31. The reason why the enjoyment of a particular piece of contemporary music may not last as long as a piece of classical music is due to the

   (A) emotion of a person, which is thought to change in time
   (B) high sophistication of the classical music and its technical intricacy
   (C) fact that there is always another piece of contemporary music that replaces the one before it
   (D) youth desiring something new
   (E) economy and marketing of the CDs

32. The term "evergreen" in line 11 most nearly means

   (A) colorful
   (B) lasting
   (C) current
   (D) likeable
   (E) encompassing

33. Which of the following is addressed in one passage but not the other?

   (A) The time period of enjoyment of the music
   (B) The type of music
   (C) A specific example illustrating a point
   (D) The instruments used in the music
   (E) The musicians playing the music

GO ON TO THE NEXT PAGE

**Questions 34–38 are based on the following passage.**

*The following passage is excerpted from the Brahmin's life, Siddhartha.*

Siddhartha was now pleased with himself. He could have dwelt for a long time yet in that soft, well-upholstered hell, if this had not happened, this moment of complete hopelessness and despair and the tense moment when he was ready
5 to commit suicide. Was it not his Self, his small, fearful and proud Self, with which he had wrestled for many years, which had always conquered him again and again, which robbed him of happiness and filled him with fear?
Siddhartha now realized why he had struggled in vain
10 with this Self when he was a Brahmin and an ascetic. Too much knowledge had hindered him; too many holy verses, too many sacrificial rites, too much mortification of the flesh, too much doing and striving. He had been full of arrogance; he had always been the cleverest, the most eager—always a
15 step ahead of the others, always the learned and intellectual one, always the priest or the sage. His Self had crawled into his priesthood, into this arrogance, into this intellectuality. It sat there tightly and grew, while he thought he was destroying it by fasting and penitence. Now he understood
20 it and realized that the inward voice had been right, that no teacher could have brought him salvation. That was why he had to go into the world, to lose himself in power, women and money; that was why he had to be a merchant, a dice player, a drinker and a man of property, until the priest and
25 Samana in him were dead. That was why he had to undergo those horrible years, suffer nausea, learn the lesson of the madness of an empty, futile life till the end, till he reached bitter despair, so that Siddhartha the pleasure-monger and Siddhartha the man of property could die. He had died
30 and a new Siddhartha had awakened from his sleep. He also would grow old and die. Siddhartha was transitory, all forms were transitory, but today he was young, he was a child—the new Siddhartha—and he was very happy.
These thoughts passed through his mind. Smiling, he
35 listened thankfully to a humming bee. Happily he looked into the flowing river. Never had a river attracted him as much as this one. Never had he found the voice and appearance of flowing water so beautiful. It seemed to him as if the river had something special to tell him, something
40 which he did not know, something which still awaited him. The new Siddhartha felt a deep love for this flowing water and decided that he would not leave it again so quickly.

34. The "soft, well-upholstered hell" (lines 2–3) is a reference by the speaker to

(A) an attractive yet uncomfortable dwelling where he resided
(B) his lifestyle, which made him an unhappy person
(C) a place to which he went when he wished to be completely by himself
(D) his abode in a previous life not referred to in the passage
(E) a figment of his imagination that used to haunt him

35. Which of the following best describes the relation between the second and third paragraphs?

(A) Paragraph 3 shows how much happier one can be by living alone than in living with others, as brought out in paragraph 2.
(B) Paragraph 3 discusses the advantages of a simple life as opposed to the more complicated lifestyle discussed in paragraph 2.
(C) Paragraph 3 contrasts the life of a person without wealth and a formal religion with a person who has wealth and a formal religion, as in paragraph 2.
(D) Paragraph 3 demonstrates the happiness that can come as a result of giving up the power and the worldly pleasures referred to in paragraph 2.
(E) Paragraph 3 generalizes about the specific points made in paragraph 2.

36. Which of the following questions does the passage answer?

(A) What is the meaning of a Brahmin?
(B) Why did Siddhartha decide to commit suicide?
(C) Where did Siddhartha own property?
(D) For how many years was Siddhartha a member of the priesthood?
(E) Where did Siddhartha go to school?

37. The word "transitory" in line 31 most likely means

(A) quick on one's feet
(B) invisible
(C) short-lived
(D) going from one place to another
(E) frozen

38. Which statement best expresses the main idea of this passage?

(A) Arrogance constitutes a great hindrance for one who seeks to lead a peaceful life.
(B) One has to discipline himself so that he will refrain from seeking pleasures that will prove harmful later.
(C) The quest for knowledge is commendable provided that search has its limitations.
(D) There is a voice within a person that can advise him how to attain contentment.
(E) Peace and quiet are more important than wealth and power in bringing happiness.

GO ON TO THE NEXT PAGE

**Questions 39–48 are based on the following passage.**

*The following passage explores how brilliant people think, how they may come up with their theories, and what motivates their thinking and creativity.*

The discoveries made by scientific geniuses, from Archimedes through Einstein, have repeatedly revolutionized both our world and the way we see it. Yet no one really knows how the mind of a genius works. Most people think
5 that a very high IQ sets the great scientist apart. They assume that flashes of profound insight like Einstein's are the product of mental processes, so arcane, that they must be inaccessible to more ordinary minds.

But a growing number of researchers in psychology,
10 psychiatry, and the history of science are investigating the way geniuses think. The researchers are beginning to give us tantalizing glimpses of the mental universe that can produce the discoveries of an Einstein, an Edison, a DaVinci—or any Nobel prizewinner.
15 Surprisingly, most researchers agree that the important variable in genius is not the IQ but creativity. Testers start with 135 as the beginning of the "genius" category, but the researchers seem to feel that, while an IQ above a certain point—about 120—is very helpful for a scientist,
20 having an IQ that goes much higher is not crucial for producing a work of genius. All human beings have at least four types of intelligence. The great scientist possesses the ability to move back and forth among them—the logical-mathematical, the spatial which includes visual perception,
25 the linguistic, and the bodily-kinesthetic.

Some corroboration of these categories comes from the reports of scientists who describe thought processes centered around images, sensations, or words. Einstein reported a special "feeling at the tips of the fingers" that
30 told him which path to take through a problem. The idea for a self-starting electric motor came to Nikola Tesla one evening as he was reciting a poem by Goethe and watching a sunset. Suddenly he imagined a magnetic field rapidly rotating inside a circle of electro-magnets.
35 Some IQ tests predict fairly accurately how well a person will do in school and how quickly he or she will master knowledge, but genius involves more than knowledge. The genius has the capacity to leap significantly beyond his present knowledge and produces something
40 new. To do this, he sees the relationship between facts or pieces of information in a new or unusual way.

The scientist solves a problem by shifting from one intelligence to another, although the logical-mathematical intelligence is dominant. Creative individuals seem to be
45 marked by a special fluidity of mind. They may be able to think of a problem verbally, logically, and also spatially.

Paradoxically, fluid thinking may be connected to another generally agreed upon trait of the scientific genius— persistence, or unusually strong motivation to work on a
50 problem. Persistence kept Einstein looking for the solution to the question of the relationship between the law of gravity and his special theory of relativity. Yet surely creative fluidity enabled him to come up with a whole new field that included both special relativity and gravitation.

55 Many scientists have the ability to stick with a problem even when they appear not to be working on it. Werner Heisenberg discovered quantum mechanics one night during a vacation he had taken to recuperate from the mental jumble he had fallen into trying to solve the atomic-
60 spectra problem.

39. Which statement is true, according to the passage?

   (A) The law of gravity followed the publication of Einstein's theory of relativity.
   (B) Nikola Tesla learned about magnets from his research of the works of Goethe.
   (C) Archimedes and Einstein lived in the same century.
   (D) Most scientists have IQ scores above 120.
   (E) We ought to refer to intelligences rather than to intelligence.

40. The author believes that, among the four intelligences he cites, the most important one is

   (A) spatial
   (B) bodily-kinesthetic
   (C) linguistic
   (D) logical-mathematical
   (E) not singled out

41. The author focuses on the circumstances surrounding the work of great scientists in order to show that

   (A) scientific geniuses are usually eccentric in their behavior
   (B) the various types of intelligence have come into play during their work
   (C) scientists often give the impression that they are relaxing when they are really working on a problem
   (D) scientists must be happy to do their best work
   (E) great scientific discoveries are almost always accidental

42. The passage can best be described as

   (A) a comparison of how the average individual and the great scientist think
   (B) an account of the unexpected things that led to great discoveries by scientists
   (C) an explanation of the way scientific geniuses really think
   (D) a criticism of intelligence tests as they are given today
   (E) a lesson clarifying scientific concepts such as quantum mechanics and relativity

GO ON TO THE NEXT PAGE →

43. The passage suggests that a college football star who is majoring in literature is quite likely to have which intelligences to a high degree?

    I. logical-mathematical
    II. spatial
    III. linguistic
    IV. bodily-kinesthetic

    (A) I only
    (B) II only
    (C) III only
    (D) I, II, and III only
    (E) II, III, and IV only

44. Which statement would the author most likely *not* agree with?

    (A) Most people believe that IQ is what makes the brilliant scientist.
    (B) Some scientists may come up with a solution to a problem when they are working on something else.
    (C) Creativity is much more important than basic intelligence in scientific discovery.
    (D) Scientists and artists may think alike in their creative mode.
    (E) Scientists usually get the answer to a problem fairly quickly, and if they get stuck they usually go on to another problem.

45. "Fluidity" as described in lines 52–53 can best be defined as

    (A) persistence when faced with a problem
    (B) having a flighty attitude in dealing with scientific problems
    (C) being able to move from one scientific area to another
    (D) having an open mind in dealing with scientific phenomena
    (E) being able to generate enormous excitement in the scientist's work

46. The word "paradoxically" in line 47 means

    (A) ironically
    (B) seemingly contradictory
    (C) in a manner of speaking
    (D) experimentally
    (E) conditionally

47. The author's attitude toward scientists in this passage can be seen as one of

    (A) objective intrigue
    (B) grudging admiration
    (C) subtle jealousy
    (D) growing impatience
    (E) boundless enthusiasm

48. According to the author, the best way to understand genius is as a combination of

    (A) high IQ, content knowledge, and ability to multi-task
    (B) creativity, persistence, and mental flexibility
    (C) relativity, creativity, and knowledge of quantum physics
    (D) revolutionary outlook, sensitivity, and desire for variety
    (E) qualities that no one has yet identified with a high degree of certainty

# STOP

If you finish before time is called, you may check your work on this section only.
Do not turn to any other section in the test.

# SECTION 4

Time: 25 Minutes—Turn to Section 4 (page 462) of your answer sheet to answer the questions in this section.
18 Questions

**Directions:** For this section, solve each problem and decide which is the best of the choices given. Fill in the corresponding circle on the answer sheet. You may use any available space for scratchwork.

**Notes:**

1. The use of a calculator is permitted.
2. All numbers used are real numbers.
3. Figures that accompany problems in this test are intended to provide information useful in solving the problems. They are drawn as accurately as possible EXCEPT when it is stated in a specific problem that the figure is not drawn to scale. All figures lie in a plane unless otherwise indicated.
4. Unless otherwise specified, the domain of any function $f$ is assumed to be the set of all real numbers $x$ for which $f(x)$ is a real number.

**REFERENCE INFORMATION**

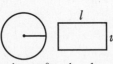 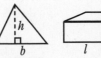 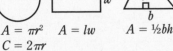    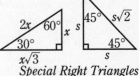

$A = \pi r^2$    $A = lw$    $A = \frac{1}{2}bh$    $V = lwh$    $V = \pi r^2 h$    $c^2 = a^2 + b^2$    *Special Right Triangles*
$C = 2\pi r$

The number of degrees of arc in a circle is 360.
The sum of the measures in degrees of the angles of a triangle is 180.

---

**21.** If $5x = 3$, then $(5x + 3)^2 =$

(A) 0
(B) 9
(C) 25
(D) 36
(E) 64

**22.** The ratio of girls to boys in a class is 8 : 7. The number of students in the class could be any of the following *except*

(A) 15
(B) 45
(C) 50
(D) 60
(E) 90

GO ON TO THE NEXT PAGE

**23.** The above figure is an equilateral triangle divided into four congruent, smaller, equilateral triangles. If the perimeter of a smaller triangle is 1, then the perimeter of the whole large triangle is

(A) 2
(B) 4
(C) 6
(D) 8
(E) 16

**25.** If $p$ and $q$ are positive integers, $x$ and $y$ are negative integers, and if $p > q$ and $x > y$, which of the following must be less than zero?

I. $q - p$
II. $qy$
III. $p + x$

(A) I only
(B) III only
(C) I and II only
(D) II and III only
(E) I, II, and III

**24.** Given $\dfrac{4^3 + 4^3 + 4^3 + 4^3}{4^y} = 4$, find $y$.

(A) 3
(B) 4
(C) 8
(D) 12
(E) 64

**26.** The average (arithmetic mean) of five numbers is 34. If three of the numbers are 28, 30, and 32, what is the sum of the other two?

(A) 40
(B) 50
(C) 60
(D) 70
(E) 80

GO ON TO THE NEXT PAGE

27. For any positive integer, $x$, $\circledx = \dfrac{x^2}{3}$ and $\boxed{x} = \dfrac{9}{x}$. What is an expression for $\circledx \times \boxed{x}$?

(A) $3x$

(B) $x$

(C) $1$

(D) $\dfrac{x^3}{64}$

(E) $27x^3$

28. Of the following four diagrams below, which diagram describes the dark region as the set of elements that belongs to all of the sets A, B, and C?

(A)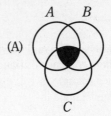

(B)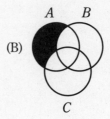

(C)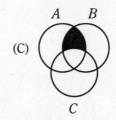

(D)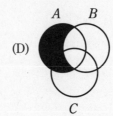

(E)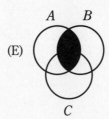

GO ON TO THE NEXT PAGE

**Directions:** For Student-Produced Response questions 29–38, use the grids at the bottom of the answer sheet page on which you have answered questions 21–28.

Each of the remaining 10 questions requires you to solve the problem and enter your answer by marking the circles in the special grid, as shown in the examples below. You may use any available space for scratchwork.

Answer: $\frac{7}{12}$ or 7/12

Write answer in boxes. →

← Fraction line

Grid in result. →

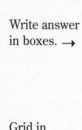
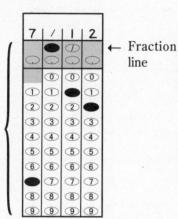

Answer: 2.5

← Decimal point

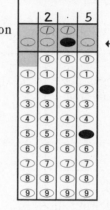

Answer: 201
Either position is correct.

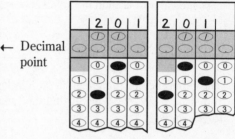

<u>Note:</u> You may start your answers in any column, space permitting. Columns not needed should be left blank.

- Mark no more than one oval in any column.

- Because the answer sheet will be machine-scored, **you will receive credit only if the ovals are filled in correctly.**

- Although not required, it is suggested that you write your answer in the boxes at the top of the columns to help you fill in the ovals accurately.

- Some problems may have more than one correct answer. In such cases, grid only one answer.

- No question has a negative answer.

- **Mixed numbers** such as $2\frac{1}{2}$ must be gridded as 2.5 or 5/2. (If [2|1|/|2] is gridded, it will be interpreted as $\frac{21}{2}$, not $2\frac{1}{2}$.)

- <u>Decimal Accuracy:</u> If you obtain a decimal answer, **enter the most accurate value the grid will accommodate.** For example, if you obtain an answer such as 0.6666..., you should record the result as .666 or .667. **Less accurate values such as .66 or .67 are not acceptable.**

Acceptable ways to grid $\frac{2}{3}$ = .6666...

29. If $ab = 40$, $\frac{a}{b} = \frac{5}{2}$, and $a$ and $b$ are positive numbers, find the value of $a$.

30. Stephanie earned $\$x$ while working 10 hours. Evelyn earned $\$y$ while working 20 hours. If they both earn the same hourly wage and $x + y = 60$, how many dollars did Stephanie earn?

GO ON TO THE NEXT PAGE ⟹

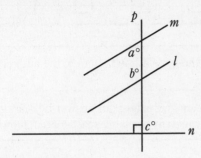

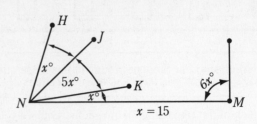

$x = 15$

*Note:* Figure is not drawn to scale.

**31.** In the figure above, *m* is parallel to *l* and *p* is perpendicular to *n*. Find the value of $a + b + c$.

**34.** If the figure above were drawn to scale and all line segments were extended indefinitely in *both directions*, how many intersection points would there be in addition to *N* and *M*?

**32.** The difference of the areas of two circles is $21\pi$. If their radii are $r + 3$ and $r$, find the radius of the *larger* circle.

**35.** If *a* is 10 percent greater than *b*, and *ac* is 32 percent greater than *bd*, then *c* is what percent greater than *d*?

**36.** Since one gross = 12 dozen, what fraction of a gross of eggs is 3 eggs?

|  | FIRST PLACE | SECOND PLACE | THIRD PLACE |
|---|---|---|---|
|  | (8 points) | (4 points) | (2 points) |
| EVENT ① | TEAM A | TEAM B | TEAM C |
| EVENT ② | TEAM B | TEAM A | TEAM C |

**33.** The results of two games involving 3 teams are shown above. Thus, we have the following standings: *A* and *B* both have 12 points, and *C* has 4 points. Assuming no ties, what is the least number of additional games that Team *C* will have to play in order to have the highest total score?

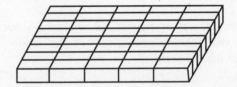

**37.** This figure above represents a layer of bricks, where each brick has a volume of 40 cubic inches. If all bricks are stacked in layers as shown, and the final pile of bricks occupies 8,000 cubic inches, how many layers are there in the final pile of bricks?

**38.** Let *x* be the smallest possible 3-digit number greater than or equal to 100 in which no digit is repeated. If *y* is the largest positive 3-digit number that can be made using all of the digits of *x*, which is the value of $y - x$?

# STOP

If you finish before time is called, you may check your work on this section only.
Do not turn to any other section in the test.

# SECTION 5

Time: 30 Minutes—Turn to Section 5 (page 463) of your answer sheet to answer the questions in this section.
39 Questions

**Directions:** For each question in this section, select the best answer from among the choices given and fill in the corresponding circle on the answer sheet.

The following sentences test correctness and effectiveness of expression. Part of each sentence or the entire sentence is underlined; beneath each sentence are five ways of phrasing the underlined material. Choice A repeats the original phrasing; the other four choices are different. If you think the original phrasing produces a better sentence than any of the alternatives, select choice A; if not, select one of the other choices.

In making your selection, follow the requirements of standard written English; that is, pay attention to grammar, choice of words, sentence construction, and punctuation. Your selection should result in the most effective sentence—clear and precise, without awkwardness or ambiguity.

EXAMPLE:

Laura Ingalls Wilder published her first book and she was sixty-five years old then.

(A) and she was sixty-five years old then
(B) when she was sixty-five
(C) at age sixty-five years old
(D) upon the reaching of sixty-five years
(E) at the time when she was sixty-five

1. In the next booklet, the sales manager and personnel director will tell you something about his work.

   (A) the sales manager and personnel director will tell you something about his work
   (B) the sales manager who is also director of personnel will tell you something about their work
   (C) the sales manager who is also personnel director will tell you something
   (D) the sales manager and personnel director will tell you something as it applies to his work
   (E) the sales manager and the personnel director will tell you something about what his work is

2. I have enjoyed the study of the Spanish language not only because of its beauty but also to make use of it in business.

   (A) to make use of it in business
   (B) because of its use in business
   (C) on account it is useful in business
   (D) one needs it in business
   (E) since all business people use it

3. Known to every man, woman, and child in the town, friends were never lacking to my grandfather.

   (A) friends were never lacking to my grandfather
   (B) my grandfather was not lacking to his friends
   (C) friends never lacked my grandfather
   (D) my grandfather never lacked no friends
   (E) my grandfather never lacked friends

4. No sooner had he entered the room when the lights went out and everyone began to scream.

   (A) when the lights went out
   (B) than the lights went out
   (C) and the lights went out
   (D) but the lights went out
   (E) the lights went out

5. John, whose mother is a teacher, is not so good a student as many other friends I have with no academic background in their families.

   (A) is not so good a student as many other friends
   (B) is not as good a student like many other friends
   (C) is not quite the student as are other friends
   (D) as a student is not a good as many other friends
   (E) does not have the studious qualities of many other friends

GO ON TO THE NEXT PAGE ⟹

6. After our waiting in line for three hours, <u>much to our disgust, the tickets had been sold out</u> when we reached the window.

    (A) much to our disgust, the tickets had been sold out
    (B) the tickets had been, much to our disgust, sold out
    (C) the tickets had been sold out, much to our disgust,
    (D) the sold-out tickets had, much to our disgust, been disposed of
    (E) and much to our disgust, the tickets had been sold out

7. When the members of the committee are at odds, <u>and when also, in addition, they are in the process</u> of offering their resignations, problems become indissoluble.

    (A) and when also, in addition, they are in the process
    (B) and also when they are in the process
    (C) and when, in addition, they are in the process
    (D) they are in the process
    (E) and when the members of the committee are in the process

8. <u>There is no objection to him joining the party</u> if he is willing to fit in with the plans of the group.

    (A) There is no objection to him joining the party
    (B) There is no objection on him joining the party
    (C) There is no objection to his joining the party
    (D) No objection will be raised upon him joining the party
    (E) If he decides to join the party, there will be no objection

9. As no one knows the truth <u>as fully as him, no one but him</u> can provide the testimony needed to clear the accused of the very serious charges.

    (A) as fully as him, no one but him
    (B) as fully as he, no one but him
    (C) as fully as he, no one but he
    (D) as fully as he does, no one but he
    (E) as fully as he does, no one but he alone

10. <u>After having completed his experiments on cancer,</u> the scientist tried to determine if his findings could be used to help prevent this dreaded disease.

    (A) After having completed his experiments on cancer
    (B) As soon as he completed his experiments on cancer
    (C) Having completed his experiments on cancer
    (D) After the experiments of the scientist on cancer were completed
    (E) When his experiments on cancer are completed

11. The principal, as well as the students and faculty, <u>is trying to affect</u> constructive changes in the school curriculum.

    (A) is trying to affect
    (B) try to affect
    (C) are trying to effect
    (D) is trying to effect
    (E) does try to encourage

12. Because of the recent General Motors strike, <u>less men will be hired in the coming year</u>.

    (A) less men will be hired in the coming year
    (B) not as many men will be hired in the coming year as before
    (C) in the coming year less men will be hired
    (D) few men will be hired in the coming year
    (E) fewer men will be hired in the coming year

13. <u>If the director would have changed</u> some of the dialogue in the script, the scene would have worked better.

    (A) If the director would have changed
    (B) If changes had been made in
    (C) If the director had changed
    (D) Had there been changes made in
    (E) If there would have been changes in

14. <u>Neither Bill nor Jack had their money with them.</u>

    (A) Neither Bill nor Jack had their money with them.
    (B) Neither of the boys had their money with them.
    (C) Neither Bill or Jack had his money with him.
    (D) Neither boy had his money with him.
    (E) Neither Bill nor Jack had his money with him.

15. <u>You must convince me of promptness in returning the money</u> before I can agree to lend you $100.

    (A) You must convince me of promptness in returning the money
    (B) The loan of the money must be returned promptly
    (C) You must understand that you will have to assure me of a prompt money return
    (D) You will have to convince me that you will return the money promptly
    (E) You will return the money promptly

GO ON TO THE NEXT PAGE

16. Because Bob was an outstanding athlete in high school, <u>in addition to a fine scholastic record</u>, he was awarded a scholarship at Harvard.

(A) in addition to a fine scholastic record
(B) also a student of excellence
(C) and had amassed an excellent scholastic record
(D) his scholastic record was also outstanding
(E) as well as a superior student

17. Although pre-season odds against the Mets had been 100 to 1, <u>the Orioles were trounced by them in the World Series.</u>

(A) the Orioles were trounced by them in the World Series
(B) the World Series victors were the Mets who trounced the Orioles
(C) they won the World Series by trouncing the Orioles
(D) which is hard to believe since the Orioles were trounced in the World Series
(E) it was the Mets who trounced the Orioles in the World Series

18. Before you can make a fresh fruit salad, <u>you must buy oranges, bananas, pineapples and peaches are necessary.</u>

(A) you must buy oranges, bananas, pineapples and peaches are necessary
(B) you must buy oranges and bananas and pineapples and peaches
(C) you must buy oranges and bananas. And other fruit such as pineapples and peaches
(D) you must buy oranges and bananas and other fruit. Such as pineapples and peaches
(E) you must buy oranges, bananas, pineapples, and peaches

19. The physical education department of the school offers instruction <u>to learn how to swim, how to play tennis, and how to defend oneself.</u>

(A) to learn how to swim, how to play tennis, and how to defend oneself
(B) in swimming, playing tennis, and protecting oneself
(C) in regard to how to swim, how to play tennis, and how to protect oneself
(D) for the purpose of swimming, playing tennis, and protecting oneself
(E) in swimming, playing tennis, and to protect oneself

20. <u>He is not only chairman of the Ways and Means Committee, but also of the Finance Committee.</u>

(A) He is not only chairman of the Ways and Means Committee, but also of the Finance Committee.
(B) He is the chairman not only of the Ways and Means Committee, but also of the Finance Committee.
(C) He is the chairman of the Ways and Means Committee and the chairman of the Finance Committee.
(D) Not only is he the chairman of the Ways and Means Committee, but also of the Finance Committee.
(E) Both the Finance Committee and the Ways and Means Committee are committees in which he is the chairman.

GO ON TO THE NEXT PAGE

The following sentences test your ability to recognize grammar and usage errors. Each sentence contains either a single error or no error at all. No sentence contains more than one error. The error, if there is one, is underlined and lettered. If the sentence contains an error, select the one underlined part that must be changed to make the sentence correct. If the sentence is correct, select choice E. In choosing answers, follow the requirements of standard written English.

EXAMPLE:

The other delegates and him immediately
    A            B    C
accepted the resolution drafted by
                       D
the neutral states. No error.
                E

Ⓐ ● Ⓒ Ⓓ Ⓔ

**21.** If someone wants to buy all the antiques that I have
                       A            B
for the rummage sale, then they should make me
                   C   D
a reasonable offer. No error.
               E

**22.** The man who Mexican authorities believe to be
         A                          B
the country's number 1 drug trafficker has been
                     C     D
arrested in a Pacific resort area. No error.
 D                       E

**23.** While her mother was inside the house talking on
 A                           B
the phone, the child fell off of the unscreened
                  C     D
porch. No error.

**24.** The racehorse ran swifter in today's race than he
              A     B
ran in his practice sessions last week. No error.
 C                 D      E

**25.** The realtor felt badly about not being able to sell
         A          B
their house because they were in a big hurry
 C
to move to their condominium. No error.
   D                E

**26.** The president of the newly formed nation took
                              A
steps to encourage several thousands of people to
     B      C
immigrate into the country. No error.
 D               E

**27.** The Governor asked the attorney to head the
                        A
committee because he was convinced that the
          B    C     D
committee needed to start work immediately.

No error.
 E

**28.** Both my sisters participate in sports, but my older
 A         B                  C
sister is the better athlete. No error.
        D          E

**29.** When the hurricane struck, the people who
                 A
had gone to the shelter found that there wasn't
 B                        C
scarcely enough food for everyone. No error.
               D     E

**30.** By the time I graduate from law school, my sister
           A   B
will have been practicing law for three years.
          C           D
No error.
 E

**31.** I had to borrow a book off of my English instructor
               A
since the campus bookstore had sold all the copies
 B              C   D
of the required text. No error.
            E

**32.** Neither the school board members or the city
                     A
council wanted to change the school boundaries
 B      C
in order to reduce the over enrollment. No error.
 D                   E

**33.** When my neighbor, who cannot swim, was a
            A      B
teenager, he had rescued a drowning swimmer by
          C    D
pulling him into his rowboat. No error.
                  E

**34.** As an incentive to attend the local college, our
 A         B
father told my brother and I that we could use his
                    C
company car for transportation. No error.
      D            E

GO ON TO THE NEXT PAGE

**Directions:** The following passage is an early draft of an essay. Some parts of the passage need to be rewritten.

Read the passage and select the best answers for the questions that follow. Some questions are about particular sentences or parts of sentences and ask you to improve sentence structure or word choice. Other questions ask you to consider organization and development. In choosing answers, follow the requirements of standard written English.

**Questions 35–39 refer to the following passage.**

[1]We know that a proportion of our sleeping time is spent dreaming. [2]This is true for everyone, whether you are the kind of person who ordinarily remembers your dreams or not. [3]Often our dreams show us "the other side of the picture," making us aware of things we have failed to take conscious note of during the day. [4]Moreover, if you dream that your new boss, who seems gruff and unfriendly during waking hours, is smiling at you and praising you for your work, perhaps you have subliminally picked up signals that day that his bark is worse than his bite.

[5]All of us need our dreams, and the younger we are, the more necessary they appear to be. [6]Babies spend nearly half their sleep in the dreaming phase. [7]When adult subjects in an experiment were given drugs that eliminated their dreaming for several nights, they became increasingly irritable and anxious, and often began having difficulty concentrating. [8]Too much dreaming appears to have its drawbacks too. [9]If you doze late on Sunday morning, you often wake up feeling tired. [10]The reason is that the longer you sleep, the longer your dreams become. [11](Dreaming periods are short during the first part of the night and lengthen as your sleep progresses.)

35. The word Moreover, in sentence 4 should be

(A) left as it is
(B) changed to However,
(C) changed to For instance,
(D) changed to In short,
(E) changed to Some people believe

36. Sentence 8 would be improved if

(A) it were joined to sentence 7 with a semicolon
(B) it were joined to sentence 7 with and
(C) it began with Although
(D) it began with Yet
(E) it were placed after sentence 9

37. Which of the following sentences would make the best introductory sentence to the passage?

(A) Dreams have fascinated man since ancient times.
(B) Many people dismiss dreams as unimportant.
(C) You do not need a psychoanalyst to learn something from your dreams.
(D) Socrates said dreams represented the voice of our consciences; Freud called them "the royal road to the unconscious."
(E) New research indicates that, night and day, dreams play an important part in all of our lives.

38. In sentence 7, the word When should be

(A) left as it is
(B) changed to If
(C) changed to Only
(D) changed to Before
(E) changed to Nevertheless

39. What should be done with sentence 11?

(A) The parentheses should be eliminated.
(B) An exclamation point should be used instead of a period.
(C) The sentence should be italicized.
(D) The sentence should be made into two sentences without the parentheses.
(E) It should be left as it is.

# STOP
If you finish before time is called, you may check your work on this section only.
Do not turn to any other section in the test.

# How Did You Do on This Test?

Step 1. Go to the Answer Key on pages 493–494.

Step 2. For your "raw score," calculate it using the directions on pages 495–496.

Step 3. Get your "scaled score" for the test by referring to the Raw Score/Scaled Score Conversion Table on page 497.

*THERE'S ALWAYS ROOM FOR IMPROVEMENT!*

# Answer Key for Practice Test 3

## Critical Reading

### Section 1

| | Correct Answer |
|---|---|
| 1 | B |
| 2 | D |
| 3 | D |
| 4 | A |
| 5 | D |
| 6 | B |
| 7 | B |
| 8 | C |
| 9 | A |
| 10 | D |
| 11 | B |
| 12 | A |
| 13 | E |
| 14 | B |
| 15 | C |
| 16 | B |
| 17 | C |
| 18 | B |
| 19 | C |
| 20 | E |
| 21 | C |
| 22 | C |
| 23 | A |
| 24 | E |

Number correct

Number incorrect

### Section 3

| | Correct Answer |
|---|---|
| 25 | D |
| 26 | B |
| 27 | C |
| 28 | D |
| 29 | E |
| 30 | D |
| 31 | A |
| 32 | B |
| 33 | C |
| 34 | B |
| 35 | D |
| 36 | B |
| 37 | C |
| 38 | E |
| 39 | E |
| 40 | D |
| 41 | B |
| 42 | C |
| 43 | E |
| 44 | E |
| 45 | C |
| 46 | B |
| 47 | A |
| 48 | B |

Number correct

Number incorrect

## Math

### Section 2

| | Correct Answer |
|---|---|
| 1 | C |
| 2 | B |
| 3 | D |
| 4 | E |
| 5 | B |
| 6 | D |
| 7 | E |
| 8 | D |
| 9 | D |
| 10 | D |
| 11 | B |
| 12 | A |
| 13 | E |
| 14 | C |
| 15 | C |
| 16 | C |
| 17 | A |
| 18 | C |
| 19 | E |
| 20 | A |

Number correct

Number incorrect

### Section 4

| | Correct Answer |
|---|---|
| 21 | D |
| 22 | C |
| 23 | A |
| 24 | A |
| 25 | C |
| 26 | E |
| 27 | A |
| 28 | A |

Number correct

Number incorrect

**Student-Produced Response Questions**

| | |
|---|---|
| 29 | 10 |
| 30 | 20 |
| 31 | 270 |
| 32 | 5 |
| 33 | 2 |
| 34 | 2 |
| 35 | 20 |
| 36 | 1/48 |
| 37 | 5 |
| 38 | 108 |

Number correct

Number incorrect

# Writing Skills

Section 5

| | Correct Answer |
|---|---|
| 1 | A |
| 2 | B |
| 3 | E |
| 4 | B |
| 5 | A |
| 6 | C |
| 7 | C |
| 8 | C |
| 9 | B |
| 10 | C |
| 11 | D |
| 12 | E |
| 13 | C |
| 14 | E |
| 15 | D |
| 16 | E |
| 17 | C |
| 18 | E |
| 19 | B |
| 20 | B |
| 21 | D |
| 22 | A |
| 23 | C |
| 24 | A |
| 25 | A |
| 26 | E |
| 27 | B |
| 28 | E |
| 29 | C |
| 30 | E |
| 31 | A |
| 32 | A |
| 33 | C |
| 34 | C |
| 35 | C |
| 36 | D |
| 37 | E |
| 38 | A |
| 39 | E |

Number correct

Number incorrect

## Scoring the PSAT Practice Test

Check your responses with the correct answers on the previous pages. Fill in the blanks below and do the calculations to get your math, critical reading, and writing raw scores. Use the table to find your math, critical reading, and writing scaled scores.

## Get Your Critical Reading Score

How many critical reading questions did you get **right**?

Section 1: Questions 1–24 _____

Section 3: Questions 25–48 + _____

Total = _____ **(A)**

How many critical reading questions did you get **wrong**?

Section 1: Questions 1–24 _____

Section 3: Questions 25–48 + _____

Total = _____

$\times 0.25$ = _____ **(B)**

$A - B$ = _____

Critical Reading Raw Score

Round critical reading raw score to the nearest whole number.

_____

Use the Score Conversion Table to find your critical reading scaled score.

_____

## Get Your Math Score

How many math questions did you get **right**?

Section 2: Questions 1–20 _____

Section 4: Questions 21–38 + _____

Total = _____ **(A)**

How many multiple-choice math questions did you get **wrong**?

Section 2: Questions 1–20 _____

Section 4: Questions 21–38 + _____

Total = _____

$\times 0.25$ = _____ **(B)**

$A - B$ = _____

Math Raw Score

Round math raw score to the nearest whole number.

_____

Use the Score Conversion Table to find your math scaled score.

_____

**Get Your Writing Skills Score**

How many multiple-choice writing questions did you get **right?**

Section 5: Questions 1–39 _____

Total = _____ **(A)**

How many multiple-choice writing questions did you get **wrong?**

Section 5: Questions 1–39 _____

Total = _____

× 0.25 = _____ **(B)**

**A – B** = _____

Writing Raw Score

Round writing raw score to the nearest whole number.

_____

Use the Score Conversion Table to find your writing scaled score.

_____

# PSAT Score Conversion Table

| Raw Score | Scaled Scores | | | Raw Score | Scaled Scores | | |
|---|---|---|---|---|---|---|---|
| | Critical Reading | Math | Writing Skills | | Critical Reading | Math | Writing Skills |
| 48 | 80 | | | 15 | 43 | 45 | 44 |
| 47 | 80 | | | 14 | 42 | 44 | 43 |
| 46 | 77 | | | 13 | 41 | 43 | 42 |
| 45 | 75 | | | 12 | 40 | 42 | 41 |
| 44 | 74 | | | 11 | 38 | 42 | 40 |
| 43 | 72 | | | 10 | 38 | 40 | 39 |
| 42 | 70 | | | 9 | 37 | 39 | 38 |
| 41 | 68 | | | 8 | 35 | 38 | 37 |
| 40 | 67 | | | 7 | 34 | 37 | 36 |
| 39 | 66 | | 80 | 6 | 33 | 36 | 35 |
| 38 | 65 | 80 | 77 | 5 | 31 | 34 | 34 |
| 37 | 64 | 77 | 73 | 4 | 30 | 33 | 33 |
| 36 | 63 | 74 | 72 | 3 | 29 | 31 | 31 |
| 35 | 62 | 71 | 70 | 2 | 27 | 29 | 30 |
| 34 | 61 | 69 | 68 | 1 | 24 | 26 | 28 |
| 33 | 60 | 68 | 65 | 0 | 22 | 24 | 27 |
| 32 | 59 | 67 | 64 | −1 | 20 | 20 | 24 |
| 31 | 58 | 65 | 63 | −2 | 20 | 20 | 21 |
| 30 | 57 | 64 | 62 | −3 | 20 | 20 | 20 |
| 29 | 56 | 62 | 60 | −4 | 20 | 20 | 20 |
| 28 | 55 | 61 | 59 | −5 | 20 | 20 | 20 |
| 27 | 54 | 60 | 57 | −6 | 20 | 20 | 20 |
| 26 | 53 | 58 | 56 | −7 | 20 | 20 | 20 |
| 25 | 52 | 57 | 55 | −8 | 20 | | 20 |
| 24 | 51 | 56 | 54 | −9 | 20 | | 20 |
| 23 | 51 | 54 | 53 | −10 | 20 | | 20 |
| 22 | 50 | 53 | 52 | −11 | 20 | | |
| 21 | 49 | 52 | 51 | −12 | 20 | | |
| 20 | 48 | 51 | 50 | | | | |
| 19 | 47 | 50 | 49 | | | | |
| 18 | 46 | 49 | 48 | | | | |
| 17 | 45 | 48 | 46 | | | | |
| 16 | 44 | 47 | 45 | | | | |

# PSAT/NMSQT Percentiles and Mean Scores

*can be used to compare a student's performance with that of juniors and sophomores.*

| JUNIORS | | | | SOPHOMORES | | | |
|---|---|---|---|---|---|---|---|
| | Percentiles | | | | Percentiles | | |
| Score | Critical Reading | Math | Writing Skills | Score | Critical Reading | Math | Writing Skills |
| 80 | 99+ | 99+ | 99+ | 80 | 99+ | 99+ | 99+ |
| 79 | 99+ | 99+ | 99+ | 79 | 99+ | 99+ | 99+ |
| 78 | 99+ | 99+ | 99+ | 78 | 99+ | 99+ | 99+ |
| 77 | 99 | 99 | 99 | 77 | 99+ | 99+ | 99+ |
| 76 | 99 | 99 | 99 | 76 | 99+ | 99+ | 99+ |
| 75 | 99 | 99 | 99 | 75 | 99+ | 99+ | 99+ |
| 74 | 99 | 98 | 99 | 74 | 99+ | 99 | 99+ |
| 73 | 99 | 98 | 98 | 73 | 99+ | 99 | 99+ |
| 72 | 98 | 98 | 98 | 72 | 99 | 99 | 99+ |
| 71 | 98 | 97 | 98 | 71 | 99 | 99 | 99+ |
| 70 | 97 | 97 | 98 | 70 | 99 | 99 | 99 |
| | | | | | | | |
| 69 | 97 | 96 | 97 | 69 | 99 | 98 | 99 |
| 68 | 96 | 94 | 96 | 68 | 99 | 98 | 99 |
| 67 | 96 | 92 | 96 | 67 | 98 | 97 | 99 |
| 66 | 95 | 92 | 96 | 66 | 98 | 97 | 99 |
| 65 | 93 | 90 | 94 | 65 | 97 | 96 | 98 |
| 64 | 92 | 88 | 93 | 64 | 97 | 95 | 97 |
| 63 | 91 | 87 | 92 | 63 | 96 | 94 | 97 |
| 62 | 90 | 85 | 90 | 62 | 96 | 93 | 96 |
| 61 | 88 | 83 | 90 | 61 | 95 | 92 | 96 |
| 60 | 86 | 80 | 88 | 60 | 94 | 90 | 95 |
| | | | | | | | |
| 59 | 85 | 79 | 85 | 59 | 93 | 89 | 93 |
| 58 | 82 | 76 | 85 | 58 | 91 | 87 | 93 |
| 57 | 80 | 73 | 83 | 57 | 90 | 85 | 92 |
| 56 | 78 | 71 | 81 | 56 | 89 | 83 | 91 |
| 55 | 76 | 70 | 79 | 55 | 87 | 83 | 89 |
| 54 | 74 | 66 | 75 | 54 | 85 | 80 | 87 |
| 53 | 71 | 63 | 72 | 53 | 83 | 77 | 84 |
| 52 | 68 | 59 | 68 | 52 | 81 | 74 | 82 |
| 51 | 62 | 56 | 66 | 51 | 77 | 71 | 80 |
| 50 | 59 | 52 | 63 | 50 | 74 | 68 | 78 |
| | | | | | | | |
| 49 | 55 | 49 | 59 | 49 | 71 | 65 | 74 |
| 48 | 52 | 45 | 55 | 48 | 69 | 61 | 71 |
| 47 | 49 | 42 | 54 | 47 | 65 | 58 | 70 |
| 46 | 45 | 41 | 50 | 46 | 62 | 58 | 67 |
| 45 | 41 | 38 | 48 | 45 | 58 | 54 | 65 |
| 44 | 37 | 34 | 44 | 44 | 54 | 50 | 62 |
| 43 | 35 | 31 | 40 | 43 | 52 | 47 | 58 |
| 42 | 32 | 26 | 36 | 42 | 48 | 40 | 53 |
| 41 | 28 | 25 | 33 | 41 | 44 | 39 | 49 |
| 40 | 25 | 22 | 31 | 40 | 40 | 36 | 48 |
| | | | | | | | |
| 39 | 24 | 19 | 28 | 39 | 40 | 31 | 44 |
| 38 | 20 | 16 | 24 | 38 | 34 | 27 | 39 |
| 37 | 18 | 14 | 21 | 37 | 31 | 23 | 35 |
| 36 | 17 | 11 | 17 | 36 | 31 | 20 | 30 |
| 35 | 15 | 11 | 16 | 35 | 27 | 20 | 28 |
| 34 | 13 | 9 | 13 | 34 | 23 | 17 | 24 |
| 33 | 10 | 7 | 11 | 33 | 20 | 13 | 20 |
| 32 | 10 | 7 | 10 | 32 | 20 | 13 | 19 |
| 31 | 9 | 5 | 8 | 31 | 18 | 9 | 15 |
| 30 | 7 | 5 | 6 | 30 | 15 | 9 | 11 |
| | | | | | | | |
| 29 | 6 | 3 | 5 | 29 | 12 | 6 | 11 |
| 28 | 6 | 3 | 5 | 28 | 12 | 6 | 9 |
| 27 | 4 | 3 | 3 | 27 | 9 | 6 | 6 |
| 26 | 4 | 2 | 3 | 26 | 9 | 4 | 6 |
| 25 | 4 | 2 | 3 | 25 | 9 | 4 | 6 |
| 24 | 3 | 1 | 2 | 24 | 6 | 3 | 4 |
| 23 | 3 | 1 | 2 | 23 | 6 | 3 | 4 |
| 22 | 2 | 1 | 2 | 22 | 5 | 3 | 4 |
| 21 | 2 | 1 | 1 | 21 | 5 | 3 | 2 |
| 20 | 1 | 1 | 1 | 20 | 1 | 1 | 1 |
| Mean Score | 46.8 | 48.9 | 45.9 | Mean Score | 41.9 | 44.3 | 41.3 |

## Points to Note

- Percentiles indicate the percentage of students whose scores fall below each specified score.

- On the score report, percentiles for juniors compare their performance with that of other juniors who took the test. For sophomores or younger students, percentiles compare their performance with that of sophomores.

- Percentiles are based on the critical reading, math, and writing skills scores earned by a sample of college-bound juniors or sophomores who took the PSAT/NMSQT.

- The *mean* score is the statistic that describes the *average* performance of a group.

# National Merit Scholarship Selection Index Percentiles and Mean Score

| JUNIORS | | | | | |
|---|---|---|---|---|---|
| Composite Score | Percentile | Composite Score | Percentile | Composite Score | Percentile |
| 240–223 | 99+ | 173 | 83 | 123 | 28 |
| 222 | 99 | 172 | 82 | 122 | 27 |
| 221 | 99 | 171 | 81 | 121 | 26 |
| 220 | 99 | 170 | 81 | 120 | 25 |
| 219 | 99 | 169 | 80 | 119 | 24 |
| 218 | 99 | 168 | 79 | 118 | 23 |
| 217 | 99 | 167 | 78 | 117 | 22 |
| 216 | 99 | 166 | 77 | 116 | 21 |
| 215 | 99 | 165 | 76 | 115 | 20 |
| 214 | 99 | 164 | 75 | 114 | 20 |
| 213 | 99 | 163 | 74 | 113 | 19 |
| 212 | 99 | 162 | 73 | 112 | 18 |
| 211 | 98 | 161 | 72 | 111 | 17 |
| 210 | 98 | 160 | 71 | 110 | 16 |
| 209 | 98 | 159 | 70 | 109 | 16 |
| 208 | 98 | 158 | 69 | 108 | 15 |
| 207 | 98 | 157 | 68 | 107 | 14 |
| 206 | 98 | 156 | 67 | 106 | 13 |
| 205 | 97 | 155 | 66 | 105 | 13 |
| 204 | 97 | 154 | 65 | 104 | 12 |
| 203 | 97 | 153 | 64 | 103 | 12 |
| 202 | 97 | 152 | 62 | 102 | 11 |
| 201 | 96 | 151 | 61 | 101 | 10 |
| 200 | 96 | 150 | 60 | 100 | 10 |
| 199 | 96 | 149 | 59 | 99 | 9 |
| 198 | 96 | 148 | 58 | 98 | 9 |
| 197 | 95 | 147 | 56 | 97 | 8 |
| 196 | 95 | 146 | 55 | 96 | 8 |
| 195 | 95 | 145 | 54 | 95 | 7 |
| 194 | 94 | 144 | 53 | 94 | 7 |
| 193 | 94 | 143 | 52 | 93 | 6 |
| 192 | 94 | 142 | 50 | 92 | 6 |
| 191 | 93 | 141 | 49 | 91 | 6 |
| 190 | 93 | 140 | 48 | 90 | 5 |
| 189 | 92 | 139 | 47 | 89 | 5 |
| 188 | 92 | 138 | 45 | 88 | 5 |
| 187 | 91 | 137 | 44 | 87 | 4 |
| 186 | 91 | 136 | 43 | 86 | 4 |
| 185 | 90 | 135 | 42 | 85 | 4 |
| 184 | 90 | 134 | 41 | 84 | 3 |
| 183 | 89 | 133 | 39 | 83 | 3 |
| 182 | 89 | 132 | 38 | 82 | 3 |
| 181 | 88 | 131 | 37 | 81 | 2 |
| 180 | 88 | 130 | 36 | 80 | 2 |
| 179 | 87 | 129 | 35 | 79 | 2 |
| 178 | 86 | 128 | 34 | 78 | 2 |
| 177 | 86 | 127 | 32 | 77–60 | 1 |
| 176 | 85 | 126 | 31 | | |
| 175 | 84 | 125 | 30 | | |
| 174 | 84 | 124 | 29 | | |
| Mean Score | | | | | 141.6 |

## Points to Note

Reported on a sliding scale from 60 to 240, the Selection Index is the sum of the Critical Reading, Math, and Writing Skills scores. For example, a Critical Reading score of 56, a Math score of 62, and a Writing Skills score of 59 would result in a composite Selection Index of 177 (56 + 62 + 59).

Percentiles are based on the Selection Index earned by a sample of college-bound juniors who took the PSAT/NMSQT.

## How NMSC Uses the Selection Index

National Merit Scholarship Corporation (NMSC) uses the Selection Index score to designate groups of students to receive recognition in the programs it conducts. Entry to NMSC's competitions for scholarships is determined by students' responses to program entry questions on the PSAT/NMSQT answer sheet. Currently, more than 1.5 million test-takers meet requirements to enter NMSC's competitions each year.

Of the more than 1.5 million NMSC program entrants, about 55,000 will earn PSAT/NMSQT scores high enough to qualify them for recognition. These students will be notified of their standing through their high schools in September. Students who qualify to continue in the competitions for scholarships must then meet academic and other requirements specified by NMSC to be considered for awards.

Inquiries about any aspect of the National Merit Program or National Achievement Program—including entry requirements, the selection process, and awards to be offered—should be sent to:
National Merit Scholarship Corporation
1560 Sherman Avenue, Suite 200
Evanston, IL 60201-4897
Telephone: (847) 866-5100

# Explanatory Answers for PSAT Practice Test 3

## Section 1: Critical Reading

As you read these Explanatory Answers, refer to "Critical Reading Strategies" (beginning on page 80) whenever a specific Strategy is referred to in the answer. Of particular importance are the following Master Critical Reading Strategies:

Sentence Completion Master Strategy 1—page 81.
Sentence Completion Master Strategy 2—page 82.
Reading Comprehension Master Strategy 2—page 98.

*Note:* All Reading questions use Reading Comprehension Strategies 1, 2, and 3 (pp. 95–100) as well as other strategies indicated.

1. Choice B is correct. See **Sentence Completion Strategy 4**. The words "in spite of" constitute an Opposition indicator. We can then expect an opposing idea to complete the sentence. The word "baffled" means "puzzled" or "unable to comprehend." Choice (B) baffled gives us the word that brings out the opposition thought we expect in the sentence. Choices A, C, D, and E do not give us a sentence that makes sense.

2. Choice D is correct. See **Sentence Completion Strategy 4**. The words "in addition to" constitute a Support indicator. We can then expect an additional favorable word to complete the sentence. That word is dapper (Choice D), meaning "neatly dressed." Choices A, B, C, and E are incorrect because they do not make good sense in the sentence.

3. Choice D is correct. See **Sentence Completion Strategy 2**. Examine the first word of each choice. We eliminate Choice (C) motor and Choice (E) reciprocal because motor curbs and reciprocal curbs do not make good sense in the

opening clause of the sentence. Now we consider Choice (A) profitable...drive, which does not make sentence sense; Choice (B) flexible...produce, which also does *not* make sentence sense; and Choice (D) export...ship, which *does* make sentence sense.

4. Choice A is correct. See **Sentence Completion Strategy 1**. Photographs of starving children demonstrate something. The logical choice among all the choices constitutes the results of consequences of drought, poor land, and overpopulation. The other choices are incorrect because they do not make sense in the sentence.

5. Choice D is correct. See **Sentence Completion Strategy 2**. Examine the first words of each choice. We can eliminate Choice (B) advantages... because it doesn't make sense in the sentence. The first words of the other four choices *do* make sense, so let us proceed to fill the two spaces for each of these remaining choices. Only Choice (D) tensions...security makes good sentence sense.

6. Choice B is correct. If you used **Sentence Completion Strategy 3**, you might have come up with any of the following words:

    refused        repudiated        shunned

    These words all mean about the same as the correct Choice (B) rejected.

7. Choice B is correct. See **Sentence Completion Strategy 4.** The key word "although" in this sentence indicates that there is opposition or difference between the first part of the sentence and the last part. Since our team knew that the opponents (the Raiders) were "sluggish," we were stupid—we should have pushed hard instead of being so "easygoing." The other four choices are incorrect because their word pairs do not make sense in the sentence.

8. Choice C is correct. See **Sentence Completion Strategy 2**.

### STEP 1

We first examine the first word of each choice. We then eliminate Choice (A) heroic, Choice (B) respected, and Choice (E) insightful because a prime minister with any of these positive qualities would hardly be expected to cause a downfall of his country. So Choices A, B, and E are incorrect.

### STEP 2

We now consider the remaining choices. Choice (D) vacillating…confidential does not make sense in the sentence because we cannot refer to a country as confidential. Therefore, Choice D is also incorrect. Choice (C) incompetent…powerful makes sense and *is* the correct choice.

9. Choice A is correct. See lines 2–3: "hits upon a bright new way…At that point, the remark is an epigram."

10. Choice D is correct. See lines 5–6: "Soon it is likely to be suffering from overwork. It has then arrived at clichéhood." This indicates how the epigram is used.

11. Choice B is correct. From the context in the sentence: "…the crash of thunder, are the result of a sudden break in the equipoise…" you can see that "equipoise" must relate to "status quo" or "balance."

12. Choice A is correct. See lines 8–9: "The still small voice…"

13. Choice E is correct. The author is stressing the point that the true artist—the person with rare creative ability and keen perception, or high intelligence—fails to communicate well with those about him—"differs from the rest of us" (line 4). He is likely to be considered a "nut" by many whom he comes in contact with. "Great wits" in the Choice E quotation refers to the true artist. The quotation states, in effect, that there is a thin line between the true artist and the "nut." Choices A, B, C, and D are incorrect because they have little, if anything, to do with the main idea of the passage.

[Note: Choices C and E were composed by John Dryden (1631–1700), and Choices A, B, and D by Alexander Pope (1688–1744).]

14. Choice B is correct. The author ridicules Samuel Johnson, saying that he is as much a true artist as a kazoo player is a musician. He then says that if Johnson were alive today, he would be a Senator or a university president. The author thus implies that these positions do not merit high respect. Choice A is the opposite of Choice B. Therefore, Choice A is incorrect. Choice C is incorrect because, although the statement may be true, the author neither states nor implies that senators and university presidents are generally appreciative of the great literary classics. Choice D is incorrect. The fact that the author lumps Johnson, senators, and university presidents together as non-artistic people indicates that senators and university presidents do not have native writing ability. Choice E is incorrect for this reason: The author believes that Johnson lacked the qualities of an artist. Johnson, if alive today, would be a senator or a university president. We may conclude, then, that Senators and university presidents lack the qualities of an artist.

15. Choice C is correct. Although a love of beauty is a quality we usually associate with artists, that idea about artists is never mentioned in the passage. All of the other characteristics are expressly mentioned in the first two paragraphs of the passage.

16. Choice B is correct. The author's sincere sympathy is shown toward artists in lines 17–24: "From Dante to Tolstoy…actually fugitives from range and reprisal." There is no evidence in the passage to indicate that the author's attitude toward artists is Choice A, C, D, or E. Therefore, these choices are incorrect.

17. Choice C is correct. See the sentence in the second paragraph of Passage 2: "He and only he knows the world."

18. Choice B is correct. See the first paragraph in Passage 2.

19. Choice C is correct. From the context in Passage 2, we see that "world's eye" and "world's heart" refer to culture and wisdom, respectively. See lines 56–60, "…public and illustrious thoughts…resist the vulgar prosperity…by preserving communicating…noble biographies…melodious verse…" This is all about *culture* and *wisdom*.

**20.** Choice E is correct. See the first sentence in Passage 2: "…the self-accusation, the faint heart, the frequent uncertainty and loss of time, which are the nettles and tangling vines…" Here "nettles and tangling vines" refers to "self-accusation" and "uncertainty." Nettles are plants covered with stinging hairs. Tangling vines give the impression of weaving all around in no particular or certain direction. So nettles can be thought of as "self-accusation"—something "stinging." And "tangling vines" can be thought of as "uncertainty." See also **Reading Comprehension Strategy 4**.

**21.** Choice C is correct. See Passage 2: The most appropriate groups are the hardships of the scholar, the scholar's functions, and the scholar's justifications for disregarding the world's business, as can be seen from the structure and content of the passage.

**22.** Choice C is correct. Given the context of the rest of the sentence, the author uses the phrase "seems to stand" as "giving the false impression of being." See also **Reading Comprehension Strategy 4.**

**23.** Choice A is correct. See lines 91–98 and 54–56 in Passage 2 and lines 13–17 and 25–34 in Passage 1.

**24.** Choice E is correct. The statements in I can be seen to be associated with the artist in Passage 2 from lines 85–86 and 57–58 respectively. The statements in II can be seen to be associated with the artist in Passage 1 from lines 27–33 and 5, respectively. The statements in III can be seen to be associated with the artist in Passage 2 from lines 53–54 and 45–52 respectively.

# Explanatory Answers for Practice Test 3 (continued)

## Section 2: Math

As you read these solutions, do two things if you answered the Math question incorrectly:

1. When a specific Strategy is referred to in the solution, study that strategy, which you will find in "19 Math Strategies" (beginning on page 51).

2. When the solution directs you to the "Math Refresher" (beginning on page 129)—for example, Math Refresher #305—study the 305 Math principle to get a clear idea of the Math operation that was necessary for you to know in order to answer the question correctly.

1. Choice C is correct. **(Use Strategy 17: Use the given information effectively.)**

Given:
$$x + by = 5 \qquad \boxed{1}$$
$$3x + y = 5 \qquad \boxed{2}$$
$$y = 2 \qquad \boxed{3}$$

We want to find $b$.

Substituting $\boxed{3}$ into $\boxed{2}$, we get

$$3x + 2 = 5$$
$$\text{or} \qquad x = 1 \qquad \boxed{4}$$

Substituting $\boxed{3}$ and $\boxed{4}$ into $\boxed{1}$, we have

$$1 + 2b = 5$$
$$\text{or} \qquad 2b = 4$$
$$\text{or} \qquad b = 2$$

**(Math Refresher 406 and 431)**

2. Choice B is correct.

The ratio of boys to girls in the class is $2 : 3$. Choice C is the answer because $9 : 12 = 3 : 4$, which does not equal $2 : 3$.

**(Math Refresher 108)**

3. Choice D is correct. It is easily seen that

$$\frac{|x|}{|y|} = \left|\frac{x}{y}\right|$$

For example: $\dfrac{|-2|}{|4|} = \left|\dfrac{-2}{4}\right| = \dfrac{1}{2}, \dfrac{|-3|}{|-6|} = \left|\dfrac{-3}{-6}\right| = \dfrac{1}{2}$

**(Math Refresher 615)**

4. Choice E is correct. **(Use Strategy 16: The obvious may be tricky!)**

Given:   $(x + y)^2 = 9$
So that   $x + y = 3$ or $-3$

From the information given, we cannot determine whether $x + y$ equals 3 or $-3$.

**(Logical Reasoning)**

5. Choice B is correct. Using $C = md + t$, if the business trip were increased by 5 days, $C' = m (d + 5) + t$. Subtracting equations, $C' - C = m(d + 5) + t - (md + t) = md + 5m + t - md - t = 5m$.

**(Math Strategy 13: Subtract Equations)**
**(Math Refresher 122)**

6. Choice D is correct. Since $x - 3 \leq 0, x \leq 3$. Choice D represents $x$ on the number line.

**(Math Refresher 129, 420)**

7. Choice E is correct. If we multiply the first equation by 2, we get: $8x - 6y = 18$. Subtract this equation from the second equation in the question:

$$8x + ky = 19$$
$$-[(8x - 6y) = 18]$$
$$\overline{ky + 6y = 1}$$

If $k = -6$, we would have: $-6y + 6y = 0 = 1$ which is not true. Thus if $k = -6$, there will be no solution to the equations.

**(Math Refresher 407)**

8. Choice D is correct.

Given:   $r = 7a$   $\boxed{1}$
     $5w = 7a$   $\boxed{2}$

From $\boxed{2}$ we get $w = \dfrac{7a}{5}$   $\boxed{3}$

**(Use Strategy 13: Find unknowns by subtracting.)**

Subtract $\boxed{3}$ from $\boxed{1}$. We get

$$r - w = 7a - \frac{7a}{5}$$
$$= \frac{35a}{5} - \frac{7a}{5}$$
$$r - w = \frac{28a}{5}$$

**(Math Refresher 406)**

9. Choice D is correct. Perhaps the best way to answer this type of question is to write a description of what occurs:

starting point   100   $t = 0$
after 8 yrs     200   $t = 8$
after $8 \times 2$ yrs   400   $t = 16$
after $8 \times 3$ yrs   800   $t = 24$

You can see that this is represented as population $100 \times 2^{t/8}$

**(Math Refresher 429)**

10. Choice D is correct. $2x + 5 < 5$

Subtracting 5 from both sides, $2x < 0$.
Dividing both sides by 2, $x < 0$.
Since $x$ must be positive integer, i.e., $x$ is greater than 0, the solution set is the empty set or $\varnothing$.

**(Math Refresher 803 and 808)**

11. Choice B is correct. $(a^b)^b = x^b = y$. $(a^b)^b = a^{b^2} = y$

**(Math Refresher 429)**

12. Choice A is correct. To find the coordinates of the intersection point, we must first solve the equations $y = x - 1$ and $2x + 5y = 9$. In the equation $2x + 5y = 9$, we substitute $y = x - 1$. We obtain

$$2x + 5(x - 1) = 9$$

Thus

$$2x + 5x - 5 = 9$$

and

$$7x = 14$$
$$x = 2$$

From the first equation, $y = x - 1$ so, $y = 2 - 1 = 1$. Thus $x = 2$ and $y = 1$ so the coordinates of the point are (2,1).

**(Math Refresher 417)**

13. Choice E is correct. **(Use Strategy 11: Use new definitions carefully.)**
Since $W, X, Y,$ and $Z$ are distinct digits from 0 to 9, the largest possible sum of $W + X + Y = 7 + 8 + 9 = 24$.   $\boxed{1}$

By definition, $W + X + Y = 5Z$   $\boxed{2}$

Substituting $\boxed{1}$ into $\boxed{2}$, we get

largest value of $5Z = 24$

**(Use Strategy 8: When all choices must be tested, start with Choice E and work backward.)** Look at the choices, starting with Choice E. If $Z = 5$, then $5Z = 25$, which is larger than 24. Thus, Choice E is correct.

**(Math Refresher 431 and Logical Reasoning)**

**14.** Choice C is correct. **(Use Strategy 3: The whole equals the sum of its parts.)** From the diagram, we see that each straight angle is equal to the sum of two smaller angles. Thus,

$$m = 180 - x \qquad \boxed{1}$$
$$n = 180 - z \qquad \boxed{2}$$

**(Use Strategy 13: Find unknown expressions by addition of equations.)** Adding $\boxed{1}$ and $\boxed{2}$ we have

$$m + n = 180 + 180 - x - z \qquad \boxed{3}$$

We know that the sum of the angles of a triangle = 180

Therefore, $y + x + z = 180$

or $y = 180 - x - z$

Substituting $\boxed{4}$ into $\boxed{3}$, we have

$$m + n = 180 + y$$

Accordingly, Choice C is the correct choice.

**(Math Refresher 406, 505, and 501)**

**15.** Choice C is correct. Probability is defined as

$$\frac{\text{number of favorable ways (coins)}}{\text{total number of ways (coins)}} = \frac{F}{N}.$$

If the probability of selecting a nickel is $\frac{3}{8}$, then for nickels, $\frac{F}{N} = \frac{3}{8}$. But N [the total number of ways (or coins)] is 24.

So $\frac{F}{N} = \frac{3}{8} = \frac{F}{24}$; F = 9 (nickels)

The probability of selecting a dime is $\frac{1}{8}$, so for a dime, $\frac{F}{N} = \frac{1}{8} = \frac{F}{24}$; F = 3 (dimes)

Since there are 24 coins and there are 9 nickels and 3 dimes, $24 - 3 - 9 = 12$ quarters. **(Use Strategy 3: Subtract whole from parts.)**

**(Math Refresher 614)**

**16.** Choice C is correct. **(Use Strategy 17: Use the given information effectively.)**

Given: ▢◼ $\qquad \boxed{1}$

In order for a given figure to have been formed from $\boxed{1}$, it must have the same number of shaded and unshaded squares.

Choice I has 8 unshaded and 6 shaded squares. Thus, it could *not* be formed from $\boxed{1}$.

Choice II has 5 unshaded and 6 shaded squares. Thus, it could *not* be formed from $\boxed{1}$.

Looking at Choices A through E, we see that the correct choice must be Choice C: III only.

**(Logical Reasoning)**

**17.** Choice A is correct.

Given

that the radius of the circle = 2, we have

Circumference $2\pi(\text{radius}) = 2\pi(2)$

$$= 4\pi \text{ inches} \qquad \boxed{1}$$

We are given that $\overarc{AD} + \overarc{BC} = 3\pi$ inches $\qquad \boxed{2}$

**(Use Strategy 3: The whole equals the sum of its parts.)**

We know that $\overarc{AD} + \overarc{BC} + \overarc{AC} + \overarc{DB}$ circumference of circle $\qquad \boxed{3}$

Substituting $\boxed{1}$ and $\boxed{2}$ into $\boxed{3}$, we have

$$3\pi \text{ inches} + \overarc{AC} + \overarc{DB} = 4\pi \text{ inches}$$
$$\overarc{AC} + \overarc{DB} = \pi \text{ inches} \qquad \boxed{4}$$

We know that the measure of an arc can be found by:

$$\text{measure of arc} = \left(\frac{\text{length of arc}}{\text{circumference}}\right) \times 360 \qquad \boxed{5}$$
$$\text{of circle}$$

Substituting $\boxed{1}$ and $\boxed{4}$ into $\boxed{5}$, we get

measure of $AC + DB$

$$= \left(\frac{\pi \text{ inch}}{4\pi \text{ inches}}\right) \times 360 = 90 \qquad \boxed{6}$$

**(Use Strategy 19: Factor and reduce.)**

From the diagram $m \angle AOC = m \angle DOB = y$

Therefore, $m \overarc{AC} = m \overarc{DB} = y \qquad \boxed{7}$

Substituting $\boxed{7}$ into $\boxed{6}$, we get

$$y + y = 90 \text{ or } 2y = 90$$
$$\text{or } y = 45$$

**(Math Refresher 310 and 524)**

**18.** Choice C is correct.

The volume of the rectangular solid to be immersed is:

$$V = (1 \text{ ft.})(1 \text{ ft.})(2 \text{ ft.}) = 2 \text{ cu. ft.} \qquad \boxed{1}$$

When the solid is immersed, the volume of the displaced water will be:

$$(2 \text{ ft.})(6 \text{ ft.})(x \text{ ft.}) = 12x \text{ cu. ft.} \qquad \boxed{2}$$

where $x$ represents the height of the displaced water. $\boxed{1}$ and $\boxed{2}$ must be equal. So

$$2 \text{ cu. ft.} = 12x \text{ cu. ft.}$$
$$\frac{1}{6} \text{ ft.} = x$$

**(Use Strategy 10: Know how to use units.)**

$$\left(\frac{1}{6} \text{ ft.}\right)\left(\frac{12 \text{ inches}}{\text{foot}}\right) =$$

$$\frac{12}{6} = 2 \text{ inches that the displaced water will rise.}$$

**(Math Refresher 312 and 121)**

**19.** Choice E is correct.

$$\begin{array}{r} AB \\ + \underline{BA} \\ CDC \end{array}$$

Given: *A, B, C,* and *D* are different digits.  $\boxed{1}$

Let's get a range of digits so we don't have to work with so many possibilities.

The largest possible *AB* is 98.

$$\begin{array}{r} 98 \\ + \underline{89} \\ 187 \end{array}$$

Thus, the only possible value for *C* is 1.

(*C* cannot be greater than 1 since we used the largest value of *AB*.)

Plugging in for *C*, the problem becomes

$$\begin{array}{r} AB \\ + \underline{BA} \\ 1D1 \end{array}$$

Which means the sum of *B* + *A* must end in a 1.  $\boxed{2}$

Using $\boxed{2}$ and $\boxed{1}$, we know *B* + *A* = 11

**(Use Strategy 8: When testing all of the choices, start with Choice E.)**

Suppose *A* = 2. If that were the case

$$B + 2 = 11$$
$$B = 9$$

Plugging in *A, B,* and *C,* we have

$$\begin{array}{r} 29 \\ + \underline{92} \\ 1D1 \end{array}$$

But this would mean *D* = 2, the same digit assigned to *A*.

The equation does not work when *A* = 2, so Choice E is correct.

**20.** Choice A is correct. $g(-1) = 1$, $f[g(-1)] = f(1) = 1^2 + 1 = 2$.

**(Math Refresher 616)**

# Explanatory Answers for Practice Test 3 (continued)

## Section 3: Critical Reading

As you read these Explanatory Answers, refer to "Critical Reading Strategies" (beginning on page 80) whenever a specific Strategy is referred to in the answer. Of particular importance are the following Master Critical Reading Strategies:

Sentence Completion Master Strategy 1—page 81.
Sentence Completion Master Strategy 2—page 82.
Reading Comprehension Master Strategy 2—page 98.

*Note:* All Reading questions use Reading Comprehension Strategies 1, 2, and 3 (pp. 95–100) as well as other strategies indicated.

25. Choice D is correct. The word "degradation" means deterioration, a lowering of position. The sight of a person in such a state would generally bring about a feeling of pity. Choices A, B, C, and E do *not* make good sense in the sentence. Therefore, these choices are incorrect. See **Sentence Completion Strategy 1.**

26. Choice B is correct. See **Sentence Completion Strategy 1.** The word "aloof " means withdrawn, distant, uninvolved. A character who is dignified and who is a man of reserve is likely to be aloof.

27. Choice C is correct. See **Sentence Completion Strategy 2.**

### STEP 1

Let us first examine the first words of each choice. We can then eliminate Choice (A) frequent, Choice (B) heavy, and Choice (E) bland because saying that blood contains frequent or heavy or bland amounts does not make sense. So Choices A, B, and E are incorrect.

### STEP 2

We now consider the remaining choices. Choice (D) definite . . puzzling does not make sense because blood does not contain puzzling amounts. Therefore, Choice D is also incorrect. Choice (C) minute (pronounced "mine-yute"—meaning exceptionally small) . . excessive makes sense and is the correct choice.

28. Choice D is correct. See **Sentence Completion Strategy 2.** We first examine the first words of each choice. We can then eliminate Choice C conclusive...and Choice E ridiculous...because violent crime does not become conclusive or ridiculous. Now we go on to the three remaining choices. When you fill in the two blanks of Choice A and of Choice B, the sentence does not make sense. So these two choices are also incorrect. Filling in the two blanks of Choice D makes the sentence acceptable.

29. Choice E is correct. See **Sentence Completion Strategy 4.** We have an opposition indicator here—the student's not working hard and his winning the contest. We, therefore, look for a definitely positive word as our choice to contrast with the negative thought embodied in his not working hard. That positive word is "elated" (Choice E), which means delighted beyond measure. Accordingly Choices A, B, C, and D are incorrect.

30. Choice D is correct. See lines 7–9 where it states that many people in our generation were not exposed to classical music. Don't be lured into the distractor choice A even though there was mention of sales.

31. Choice A is correct. See lines 19–21 where it mentions that the emotional feeling gradually wears out in time.

32. Choice B is correct. Since the next sentence after the word "evergreen" qualifies that enjoyment lasts only for a short time, "lasting" would be an appropriate definition of "evergreen" in this context. Be careful of the distractor choice "colorful."

33. Choice C is correct. Note that only in Passage 1 lines 3–5 is an example of a symphony of Brahms illustrating the point. No specific examples are presented in Passage 2. In Choice A, the time period is addressed in *both* passages. In Choice B the types of music are presented in *both* passages (classical in Passage 1 and rock and contemporary in Passage 2). In Choice D, no instrument is addressed in either passage and in Choice E, specific musicians are not mentioned in either passage.

34. Choice B is correct. See lines 25–29: "That was why...till he reached bitter despair...the man of property could die." The "well-upholstered hell" constituted the lifestyle that almost caused him to commit suicide. The passage shows no justification for Choices A, C, D, and E. Accordingly, these are incorrect choices.

35. Choice D is correct. Throughout paragraph 3 we see the evidences of the speaker's happiness as a result of his renouncing the "power, women and money" (lines 22–23) as well as the arrogance and intellectuality referred to in line 17. Choices A, B, and C are incorrect because, though the passage discusses these choices, they do not really *pinpoint* the relation between the third and fourth paragraphs. Choice E is incorrect because paragraph 3 does not generalize about the specific points made in paragraph 2.

36. Choice B is correct. His "complete hopelessness and despair" (lines 3–4) led to Siddhartha's decision to commit suicide. The passage does not answer the questions expressed in Choices A, C, D, and E. Therefore, these choices are incorrect.

37. Choice C is correct. From the context of the sentence and the one preceding it, we can see that the word "transitory" means short-lived. (We are dealing with time). See also **Reading Comprehension Strategy 4**.

38. Choice E is correct. The unhappiness that may result from wealth and power are brought out clearly throughout the second paragraph. In contrast, peace and quiet are likely to assure a happy life. The last paragraph demonstrates this conclusively. Although Choices A, B, C, and D are vital points, none of the choices is sufficiently inclusive to be considered the *main* idea of the passage. References to these choices follow. Choice A—lines 13–21: "He had been full of arrogance...brought him salvation." Choice B—lines 5–8: "Was it not his Self...filled him with fear?" Choice C—lines 10–11: "Too much knowledge had hindered him." Choice D—lines 19–21: "Now he understood...brought him salvation."

39. Choice E is correct. See lines 21–22: "All human beings have at least four types of intelligence." Choice A is incorrect. See lines 50–52: "Persistence kept Einstein looking for the solution to the question of the relationship between the law of gravity and his special theory of relativity." Isaac Newton (1642–1727) formulated the law of gravitation. Choice B is incorrect. The passage simply states: "The idea for a self-starting electric motor came to Nikola Tesla one evening as he was reciting a poem by Goethe and watching a sunset" (lines 30–33). Choice C is incorrect. The author indicates a span of time when he states: "The discoveries made by scientific geniuses, from Archimedes through Einstein..." (lines 1–2). Archimedes was an ancient Greek mathematician, physicist, and inventor (287–212 B.C.), whereas Einstein was, of course, a modern scientist (1879–1955). Choice D is incorrect. The passage states: "...while an IQ above a certain point—about 120—is very helpful for a scientist,...[it] is not crucial for producing a work of genius" (lines 18–21). The passage does not specifically say that most scientists have IQ scores above 120.

40. Choice D is correct. See lines 42–44: "The scientist solves a problem by shifting from one intelligence to another, although the logical-mathematical intelligence is dominant." Accordingly, Choices A, B, C, and E are incorrect.

41. Choice B is correct. When the author describes the work experiences of Einstein and Tesla, he refers to their use of one or more of the four types of intelligence. Moreover, lines 26–28 state: "Some corroboration of these [four intelligence] categories comes from the reports of scientists who describe thought processes centered around images, sensations, or words." Choices A, C, D, and E are incorrect because the author does not refer to these choices in the passage.

42. Choice C is correct. The author indicates that great scientists use to advantage four intelligences—logical-mathematical, spatial, linguistic, and bodily-kinesthetic. See lines 22–25: "The great scientist possesses the ability to move back and forth among them—the logical-mathematical, the spatial which includes visual perception, the linguistic, and the bodily-kinesthetic." Choices B and D are brought out in the passage but not at any length. Therefore, Choices B and D are incorrect. Choice A is incorrect because the author nowhere compares the thinking of the average individual and that of the great scientist. Choice E is incorrect because though the concepts are mentioned, they are certainly not clarified in the passage.

43. Choice E is correct. As a football star, he would certainly have to have a high level of (a) spatial intelligence [II], which involves space sensitivity as well as visual perception, and (b) bodily-kinesthetic intelligence [IV], which involves the movement of muscles, tendons, and joints. As a literature major, he would certainly have to have a high level of linguistic intelligence [III], which involves the ability to read, write, speak, and listen. Whether he would have logical-mathematical intelligence to a high degree is questionable. It follows that Choices A, B, C, and D are incorrect.

44. Choice E is correct. According to what is stated in lines 50–56, persistence is an important characteristic of the scientist. Thus the author would probably not agree with the statement in Choice E. The author would agree with the statement in Choice A: See lines 4–5. Note that although the author may not agree that IQ is what makes the scientist brilliant, he believes that *most* people feel that way. The author would agree with the statement in Choice B. See lines 30–32 and lines 56–60. The author would agree with the statement in Choice C. See lines 15–16 in the context with the rest of the passage. The author would probably not disagree with the statement in Choice D since the author does not appear to distinguish artists from scientists in their thinking process even though the passage is primarily about the scientists: See lines 9–14.

45. Choice C is correct. See lines 52–54. Note that although "persistence" is mentioned in lines 47–52, the passage states that fluid thinking may be connected to persistence, not defined as persistence. Thus Choice A is incorrect. See also **Reading Comprehension Strategy 4**.

46. Choice B is correct. Given the context in lines 47–54, the word "paradoxically" means seemingly contradictory. See also **Reading Comprehension Strategy 4**.

47. Choice A is correct. It can be seen in the passage that the author is intrigued by and interested in the way the scientist thinks but at the same time reports the findings very objectively.

48. Choice B is correct. See lines 16, 45, 50, 52, and 56. Choice A is incorrect because the author notes that IQ above a certain point does not contribute to the productivity of a genius (lines 20–21) and that content knowledge is not as important as how the genius connects pieces of information (lines 40–41). Choice C is incorrect because the theory of relativity is mentioned as one of Einstein's most worthy contributions, not as a quality of genius. Choice D is incorrect because none of the examples of genius have an explicitly "revolutionary" agenda. Although the essay begins by describing the difficulty of defining genius, Choice E is incorrect because the author gradually identifies criteria.

# Explanatory Answers for Practice Test 3 (continued)

## Section 4: Math

As you read these solutions, do two things if you answered the Math question incorrectly:

1. When a specific Strategy is referred to in the solution, study that strategy, which you will find in "19 Math Strategies" (beginning on page 51).

2. When the solution directs you to the "Math Refresher" (beginning on page 129)—for example, Math Refresher #305—study the 305 Math principle to get a clear idea of the Math operation that was necessary for you to know in order to answer the question correctly.

**21.** Choice D is correct.

Given:

$$5x = 3 \qquad \boxed{1}$$

**(Use Strategy 12: Try not to make tedious calculations.)**

*Method 1:* Add 3 to both sides of $\boxed{1}$

$$5x + 3 = 6 \qquad \boxed{2}$$

**(Use Strategy 13: Find unknown expressions by multiplication.)**

Square both sides of $\boxed{2}$

$$(5x + 3)^2 = 36 \qquad \boxed{3}$$

This method involves simpler arithmetic (no fractions) than the next method.

*Method 2:* This method is a bit slower. Solve $\boxed{1}$ for $x$ to get

$$x = \frac{3}{5} \qquad \boxed{4}$$

Using $\boxed{4}$, calculate the unknown expression.

$$(5x + 3)^2 =$$
$$\left[5\left(\frac{3}{5}\right) + 3\right]^2 =$$
$$(3 + 3)^2 =$$
$$6^2 = 36$$

**(Math Refresher 406 and 431)**

**22.** Choice C is correct. **(Use Strategy 2: Translate from words to algebra.)**

$$\text{Let } 8n = \text{number of boys} \qquad \boxed{1}$$
$$7n = \text{number of girls} \qquad \boxed{2}$$

The ratio of $\dfrac{\text{boys}}{\text{girls}} = \dfrac{8n}{7n} = \dfrac{8}{7}$ and the given condition is satisfied.

**(Use Strategy 3: The whole equals the sum of its parts.)**

Total number of students = Boys plus Girls   3

Substitute 1 and 2 into 3, we get

Total number of students = $8n + 7n = 15n$   4

4 is a multiple of 15

Choices A, B, D, and E are multiples of 15:

    Ⓐ $15 = 15 \times 1$
    Ⓑ $45 = 15 \times 3$
    Ⓒ $60 = 15 \times 4$
    Ⓓ $90 = 15 \times 6$

Only Choice C, 50, is *not* a multiple of 15.

**(Math Refresher 200 and 431)**

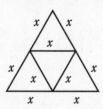

23. Choice A is correct. **(Use Strategy 2: Translate from words to algebra.)**

    Let $x$ = side of smaller triangles
Thus, $3x$ = perimeter of each smaller triangle
    $6x$ = perimeter of largest triangle

We are told

$$3x = 1$$
$$x = \frac{1}{3} \qquad \boxed{1}$$

**(Use Strategy 13: Find unknowns by multiplication.)**

Multiply 1 by 6, we get

    $6x = 2$ = perimeter of largest triangle

**(Math Refresher 200 and 306)**

24. Choice A is correct. **(Use Strategy 17: Use the given information effectively.)**

Given: $\dfrac{4^3 + 4^3 + 4^3 + 4^3}{4^y} = 4$

$$\frac{4(4^3)}{4^y} = 4$$
$$\frac{4^4}{4^y} = 4$$
$$4^{4-y} = 4^1 \qquad \boxed{1}$$

In 1 each expression has base 4. Since the expressions are equal, the exponents must also be equal. Thus,

$$4 - y = 1$$
$$-y = -3$$
$$y = 3$$

**(Math Refresher 429 and 406)**

25. Choice C is correct. **(Use Strategy 2: Translate from words to algebra.)** We are given

$$p > 0 \qquad \boxed{1}$$
$$q > 0 \qquad \boxed{2}$$
$$x < 0 \qquad \boxed{3}$$
$$y < 0 \qquad \boxed{4}$$

**(Use Strategy 6: Know how to manipulate inequalities.)**

$$p > q \text{ or } q < p \qquad \boxed{5}$$
$$x > y \text{ or } y < x \qquad \boxed{6}$$

For I: Add $-p$ to both sides of inequality 5:

$$q - p < 0$$

Thus, I is less than zero.

For II: From inequalities 2 and 4, $qy < 0$, and II is less than zero.

For III: The value of $p$ and $x$ depends on specific values of $p$ and $x$:

**(Use Strategy 7: Use numerics to help decide the answer.)**

EXAMPLE 1

$$p = 3 \text{ and } x = -5$$

Thus,      $p + x < 0$

EXAMPLE 2

$$p = 5 \text{ and } x = -3$$

Thus,      $p + x > 0$

Thus, II is not always less than zero. Choice C is correct.

**(Math Refresher 420, 421, and 431)**

26. Choice E is correct.

$\Big($ **Use Strategy 5: Average**

$$= \frac{\textbf{Sum of values}}{\textbf{Total number of values}}\Big)$$

Let $x, y$ = two unknown numbers.

Thus, $\dfrac{28 + 30 + 32 + x + y}{5} = 34$     $\boxed{1}$

Multiplying 1 by 5,

$$28 + 30 + 32 + x + y = 170$$
or $$90 + x + y = 170$$
or $$x + y = 80$$

**(Math Refresher 601 and 406)**

**27.** Choice A is correct. **(Use Strategy 11: Use new definitions carefully.)**

Given: $\textcircled{x} = \dfrac{x^2}{3}$ and $\boxed{x} = \dfrac{9}{x}$

Thus, $\textcircled{x} \times \boxed{x} = \dfrac{x^2}{3} \times \dfrac{9}{x} = 3x$

**(Math Refresher 431)**

**28.** Choice A is correct. It can be seen that the dark region in Choice A is common to sets A, B, and C. Thus the diagram in Choice A describes the dark region as the set of elements that belongs to all of the sets A, B, and C.

**(Math Refresher 803)**

**29. 10**

Given: $ab = 40$ $\boxed{1}$

$\dfrac{a}{b} = \dfrac{5}{2}$ $\boxed{2}$

**(Use Strategy 13: Find unknowns by multiplication.)**

Multiplying $\boxed{2}$ by $2b$, we get

$$2b\left(\dfrac{a}{b}\right) = \left(\dfrac{5}{2}\right)2b$$

$$2a = 5b$$

$$\dfrac{2a}{5} = b \qquad \boxed{3}$$

Substitute $\boxed{3}$ into $\boxed{1}$. We have

$$ab = 40$$

$$a\left(\dfrac{2a}{5}\right) = 40$$

$$\dfrac{2a^2}{5} = 40 \qquad \boxed{4}$$

Multiplying $\boxed{1}$ by $\dfrac{5}{2}$, we get

$$\dfrac{5}{2}\left(\dfrac{2a^2}{5}\right) = (40)\dfrac{5}{2}$$

$$a^2 = 100$$

$$\sqrt{a^2} = \sqrt{100}$$

$$a = \pm\,10$$

Since we were given that $a$ is positive, we have $a = 10$.

**(Math Refresher 406, 429, and 430)**

**30. 20**

**(Use Strategy 2: Translate from words to algebra.)**

Given: Stephanie's earnings = \$x $\boxed{1}$
Stephanie's time = 10 hours $\boxed{2}$
Evelyn's earnings = \$y $\boxed{3}$
Evelyn's time = 20 hours $\boxed{4}$
$x + y$ = 60 $\boxed{5}$

We know that hourly wage = $\dfrac{\text{Total Earnings}}{\text{Total Hours}}$ $\boxed{6}$

Substituting $\boxed{1}$ and $\boxed{2}$ into $\boxed{6}$, we get

Stephanie's hourly wage = $\dfrac{\$x}{10 \text{ hours}}$ $\boxed{7}$

Substituting $\boxed{3}$ and $\boxed{4}$ into $\boxed{6}$, we get

Evelyn's hourly wage = $\dfrac{\$y}{20 \text{ hours}}$ $\boxed{8}$

We are told that they have the same hourly wage. Using $\boxed{7}$ and $\boxed{8}$, we have

$$\dfrac{\$x}{10 \text{ hours}} = \dfrac{\$y}{20 \text{ hours}}$$

$$\dfrac{x}{10} = \dfrac{y}{20} \qquad \boxed{9}$$

$$\overset{2}{20}\left(\dfrac{x}{10}\right) = \left(\dfrac{y}{20}\right)\overset{}{20}$$

$$2x = y \qquad \boxed{10}$$

Substituting $\boxed{10}$ into $\boxed{5}$, we get

$$x + 2x = 60$$

$$3x = 60$$

$$x = 20$$

**(Math Refresher 200, 201, and 406)**

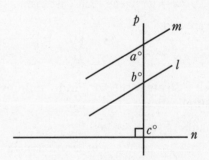

**31. 270**

Given: $m \parallel l$ $\boxed{1}$
$p \perp n$ $\boxed{2}$

From $\boxed{1}$ we get that $a + b = 180$, $\boxed{3}$ because when 2 lines are parallel, the interior angles on the same side of the transversal are supplementary.

From $\boxed{2}$ we get that $c = 90$ $\boxed{4}$ because perpendicular lines form right angles.

**(Use Strategy 13: Find unknowns by addition.)**

Add $\boxed{3}$ and $\boxed{4}$. We have

$$a + b + c = 180 + 90$$

$$= 270$$

**(Math Refresher 504, 501, and 511)**

**32. 5**

We know Area of circle = $\pi(\text{radius})^2$    □1

Given:  radius of larger circle = $r + 3$    □2

         radius of small circle = $r$    □3

Substitute □2 into □1. We have

$$\text{Area of larger circle} = \pi(r + 3)^2 \qquad □4$$

**(Use Strategy 4: Remember classic expressions.)**

$$(r + 3)^2 = r^2 + 6r + 9 \qquad □5$$

Substitute □5 into □4. We have

$$\text{Area of larger circle} = \pi(r^2 + 6r + 9) \qquad □6$$

Substituting □3 into □1, we get

$$\text{Area of small circle} = \pi r^2 \qquad □7$$

**(Use Strategy 13: Find unknowns by subtraction.)**

Subtract □7 from □6. We have

Difference of areas

$$= \pi(r^2 + 6r + 9) - \pi r^2 \qquad □8$$

Given:  Difference of areas = $21\pi$    □9

Substitute □9 into □8. We have

$$21\pi = \pi(r^2 + 6r + 9) - \pi r^2 \qquad □10$$

**(Use Strategy 13: Find unknowns by division.)**

$$\frac{21\pi}{\pi} = \frac{\pi(r^2 + 6r + 9)}{\pi} - \frac{\pi r^2}{\pi}$$
$$21 = r^2 + 6r + 9 - r^2$$
$$21 = 6r + 9$$
$$12 = 6r$$
$$2 = r \qquad □11$$

Substitute □11 into □2. We get

$$\text{radius of larger circle} = 2 + 3$$
$$= 5$$

**(Math Refresher 409, 310, and 406)**

**33. 2**

**(Use Strategy 17: Use the given information effectively.)**

The most favorable conditions for Team C would be the following:

|  | FIRST PLACE | SECOND PLACE | THIRD PLACE |
|---|---|---|---|
|  | (8 points) | (4 points) | (2 points) |
| EVENT ③ | TEAM C (4+5=12) | TEAM A (12+4=16) | TEAM B (12+2=14) |
| EVENT ④ | TEAM C (12+8=20) | TEAM B (14+4=18) | TEAM A (16+2=18) |

Thus, Team C has a total of $4 + 8 + 8 = 20$ points after 2 more games. Team A has $12 + 4 + 2 = 18$ points. Team B has $12 + 2 + 4 = 18$ points. Thus, Team C will have to play at least 2 more games.

**(Logical Reasoning)**

**34. 2**

**(Use Strategy 17: Use the given information effectively.)**

Since $x = 15$, then

$$\angle LMN = 90°$$
$$\angle JNK = 75°$$
$$\angle KNM = 15°$$
$$\angle JNM = 90°$$

Thus, the figure, with dashed line extensions, follows:

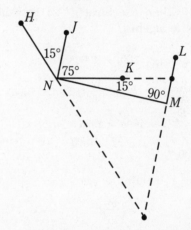

Clearly $\overleftrightarrow{JN} \parallel \overleftrightarrow{ML}$ and $\overleftrightarrow{JN}$ will not intersect $\overleftrightarrow{ML}$. $\overleftrightarrow{NK}$ and $\overleftrightarrow{NH}$ will each intersect $\overleftrightarrow{ML}$ exactly once. Thus, there will be exactly 2 more additional points of intersection.

**(Math Refresher 504 and Logical Reasoning)**

**35. 20**

**(Use Strategy 2: Translate from words to algebra.)**

We are told that

$$a = b + \frac{10}{100}\,b = \frac{11}{10}\,b \qquad □1$$

$$ac = bd + \frac{32}{100}\,bd = \frac{33}{25}\,bd \qquad □2$$

**(Use Strategy 13: Find unknowns by division.)**

We divide □2 by $a$

$$c = \frac{33}{25}\left(\frac{b}{a}\right)d \qquad □3$$

**(Use Strategy 13: Find unknowns by multiplication.)**

Multiply □1 by $\frac{1}{b}$, giving

$$\frac{a}{b} = \frac{11}{10}$$

or $\qquad \frac{b}{a} = \frac{10}{11}$ $\qquad$ $\boxed{4}$

Substituting $\boxed{4}$ into $\boxed{3}$, we get

$$c = \frac{6}{5}d$$

or $\qquad c = d + \frac{1}{5}d$

or $\qquad c = d + \frac{20}{100}d$

Thus, $c$ is 20 percent greater than $d$.

**(Math Refresher 200, 406, and 431)**

Alternate method:

**Use Strategy 7: Use numerics.** Let $b = 100$, $d = 10$. **Then use Strategy 2: Translate from words to algebra.**

Then $a = \frac{10}{100}(100) + 100 = 110$

$ac = \frac{32}{100}bd + bd = \frac{32}{100}(100)d + 100d$

$110c = 32d + 100d = 132d$ $\qquad$ $\boxed{1}$

$c = \frac{x}{100}d + d = \frac{xd + 100d}{100} = \frac{(x + 100)d}{100}$ $\qquad$ $\boxed{2}$

Divide $\boxed{1}$ by 110:

$$c = \frac{132}{110}d$$ $\qquad$ $\boxed{3}$

Compare $\boxed{3}$ with $\boxed{2}$:

$$\frac{132}{110} = \frac{x + 100}{100}$$

$$\frac{13200}{110} = x + 100$$

$$120 = x + 100$$

$$20 = x$$

36. $\frac{1}{48}$ **or .020 or .021**

**(Use Strategy 2: Translate from words to algebra.)**

Given: We know that $\qquad$ 1 gross = 12 dozen
$\qquad\qquad\qquad\qquad\qquad$ 1 dozen = 12 (eggs)

Thus,

1 gross of eggs = (12 dozens) (12 eggs/dozen)
$\qquad\qquad\qquad$ = 144 eggs

3 eggs, expressed as a fraction of a gross, $= \frac{3}{144}$

$$= \frac{1}{48}$$

**(Math Refresher 200 and 121)**

37. **5**

We are given that

$\qquad$ Volume of 1 brick = 40 cubic inches $\qquad$ $\boxed{1}$

Volume of the final pile

$\qquad\qquad$ of bricks = 8000 cubic inches $\qquad$ $\boxed{2}$

**(Use Strategy 3: The whole equals the sum of its parts.)** Logically, we know the number of layers in the final pile of bricks

$$= \frac{\text{Volume of the final pile of bricks}}{\text{Volume of each layer of bricks}}$$ $\qquad$ $\boxed{3}$

From the diagram in the question, we see that

$\qquad$ 1 layer of bricks = 40 bricks $\qquad$ $\boxed{4}$

Thus, by using $\boxed{1}$ and $\boxed{4}$, we know that the volume of each layer of bricks

= volume of 1 brick
$\qquad$ × number of bricks in 1 layer
= 40 cubic inches × 40
= 1600 cubic inches $\qquad$ $\boxed{5}$

Substituting $\boxed{2}$ and $\boxed{5}$ into $\boxed{3}$, the number of layers in the final pile of bricks

$$= \frac{8000 \text{ cubic inches}}{1600 \text{ cubic inches}}$$

**(Use Strategy 19: Factor and reduce.)**

$$= \frac{8 \times 1000}{16 \times 100}$$

$$= \frac{8 \times 10 \times 100}{8 \times 2 \times 100}$$

$$= \frac{10}{2} = 5$$

**(Math Refresher 200 and 601)**

38. **108**

**(Use Strategy 11: Use new definitions carefully.)**

The first few 3-digit numbers are 100, 101, 102, 103, 104, etc.

Clearly, the smallest possible 3-digit number in which no digit is repeated is $x = 102$.

From the definition of $y$, $y$ must be $y = 210$.

Thus, $y - x =$

$210 - 102 =$

$\qquad$ 108

**(Logical Reasoning)**

# Explanatory Answers for Practice Test 3 (continued)

## Section 5: Writing Skills

> For further practice and information, please refer to "A Brief Review of English Grammar" starting on page 321.

1. **(A)** Choice A is correct. If you are questioning the singularity of the possessive pronoun-adjective "his," it is correct. The subject of the sentence consists of a singular compound subject, "the sales manager and personnel director." If we wanted to indicate plurality here, we would have to insert the article "the" before the second member ("personnel director") of the compound subject. Choice B is incorrect because "their" must refer to a plural antecedent. Choice C is incorrect because it changes the meaning of the original sentence. Choice D is awkward. Choice E is too wordy.

2. **(B)** Choice A is incorrect because it does not parallel the structure of "not only because of its beauty." Choice B is correct. Choices C, D, and E are incorrect for the same reason that Choice A is incorrect—the lack of parallel structure. Moreover, Choice C is incorrect because "on account" cannot be used as a subordinate conjunction.

3. **(E)** The past participle "known" must modify the subject of the sentence. Choices A and C are, therefore, incorrect because the subject must be "grandfather"—he is the one (not "friends") that is "known to every man, woman, and child in the town." Choice B changes the meaning of the original sentence. Choice D has a double negative ("never...no..."). Choice E is correct.

4. **(B)** Choice A is incorrect since the correct expression is "no sooner...than..." Choice B is correct. Choices C, D, and E are incorrect because we must have the "no sooner...than" construction.

5. **(A)** Choice A is correct. Choice B is incorrect for two reasons: (1) We use the adverb "so" instead of "as" in a negative comparison; (2) "like" may not be used instead of "as" in this type of comparison. Choice C is awkward. Choice D is roundabout. Choice E changes the meaning of the original sentence.

6. **(C)** The problem in this question is the correct placement of the modifier. The preposition phrase "much to our disgust" is an adverbial phrase showing result. The phrase, therefore, modifies the verb "had been sold out." Accordingly, the phrase should, in this sentence, follow right after the verb it modifies. Choice C, therefore, is correct and the other choices are incorrect. Choice D, incidentally, is incorrect for another reason—it is illogical: the sold-out tickets are obviously disposed of when they are sold out.

7. **(C)** Choice A is incorrect because in this sentence "also" means the same as "in addition." Choice B is awkward. Choice C is correct as a subordinate clause which parallels the preceding subordinate clause. Choice D creates a run-on sentence. Choice E is too wordy.

8. **(C)** Choices A, B, and D are incorrect because of the use of "him joining." The word "joining" is a gerund in this sentence. Its possessive pronoun-adjective must be "his"—not "him." Choice B, moreover, has the unidiomatic expression "objection on." Choice C is correct. Choice E changes the meaning of the original sentence.

9. **(B)** Choice A is incorrect because the nominative form ("he") is required: "as fully as him" is wrong. Choice B is correct. Choices C, D, and E are incorrect because the object of the preposition must have an objective case form—the preposition "but" must be followed by the object case form "him."

10. **(C)** Choice A is incorrect because the verb should be the past perfect form ("had completed") to indicate an action that took place prior to "tried." Choice B changes the meaning of the original sentence. Choice C is correct. Choice D is awkward. Choice E changes the tense of the original sentence.

11. **(D)** Choice A uses the word "affect" incorrectly. It means "to influence" and in the original sentence it is incorrectly used to mean "to bring about." Choice B also uses the word "affect" incorrectly and in addition the verb needed is "is trying" as it refers to the principal *only*. Choice C is incorrect because the singular verb is required. Choice D is correct. Choice E is not correct because it changes the meaning of the original sentence.

12. **(E)** Choice A is incorrect because the word "fewer" should be used instead of "less" because "less" denotes amount or degree and "fewer" denotes number. Choice B is not correct because "as before" is superfluous. Choice C is incorrect for the same reason as Choice A (above). Choice D changes the meaning of the original sentence. Choice E is correct.

13. **(C)** Choice A is incorrect because in this past contrary-to-fact situation, the verb of the "if" clause should be expressed in the past perfect tense ("had changed"). Choice B does not include a reference to the director, which is necessary to the meaning of the original sentence. Choice C is correct. Choice D is incorrect because it does not include a reference to the director, which, as indicated previously, is necessary to the meaning of the original sentence. Choice E omits a reference to the director and also uses "would have been" incorrectly.

14. **(E)** Choices A and B are incorrect because when two singular antecedents are joined by "nor," they should be referred to by a singular pronoun. Also, Choice B does not include the names of the boys,

which were included in the original sentence. Choice C uses the word "or" incorrectly, rather than "nor." Choice D does not include the names of the boys and so it changes the meaning of the original sentence. Choice E is correct.

15. **(D)** The important thing is not "promptness"; accordingly, Choice A is wrong. Choice B is incorrect because it is not the "loan" that must be returned. In Choice C, "You must understand" is unnecessary. Choice D is correct. Choice E changes the meaning of the original sentence.

16. **(E)** Choice A, as a phrase, hangs without clearly modifying anything else in the sentence. Choice B would be correct if it were preceded and followed by a dash in order to set the choice off from what goes before and after. Choice C is wrong because one does not "amass a scholastic record." Choice D is a complete sentence within a sentence, thus creating a run-on sentence situation. Choice E is correct.

17. **(C)** In Choice A, the use of the passive verb ("were trounced") reduces the effectiveness of expression. Choice B is indirect. Choice C is correct. In Choice D, "which is hard to believe" is unnecessary. Choice E is indirect.

18. **(E)** In Choice A, "are necessary" is not only not necessary, but the expression makes the sentence ungrammatical with the additional complete predicate ("are necessary"). There are too many "ands" in Choice B. Some grammarians call this an "Andy" sentence. In Choice C, "And other fruit…peaches" is an incomplete sentence—also called a sentence fragment. Choice D also suffers from sentence fragmentation: "Such as pineapples and peaches." Choice E is correct.

19. **(B)** In Choice A, it is unidiomatic to say "instruction to learn." Choice B is correct. Choice C is too wordy. Choice D is not as direct as Choice B. Choice E suffers from lack of parallelism.

20. **(B)** Choice A is incorrect because the words "not only…but also" should be placed immediately before the parallel terms, which are "of the Ways and Means Committee" and "of the Finance Committee." Choice B is correct. Choice C is too wordy. Choice D is incorrect because it does not place the words "not only…but also" directly before the parallel terms. Choice E is awkward.

21. **(D)** "…then *he or she* should make…"
A pronoun must agree with its antecedent (*someone*) in number. Since *someone* is singular, the pronoun must be singular (*he or she*—not *they*).

22. **(A)** "The man *whom* Mexican authorities believe to be…"

    The subject of an infinitive must be in the objective case. The pronoun "whom" in the objective case—not "who" in the nominative case—is the subject of the verbal infinitive "to be."

23. **(C)** "…the child fell *off* the unscreened porch." The correct preposition is simply "off "—not "off of"—to introduce a noun or pronoun.

24. **(A)** "…ran *more swiftly*…"
    We must use an adverb—not an adjective—to modify a verb. Therefore, we use the adverbial comparative construction "more swiftly" instead of the comparative adjective "swifter" to modify the verb "ran."

25. **(A)** "The realtor felt *bad*…"
    After the copulative verb ( *felt*), the word referring to the subject should be a predicate adjective (*bad*)—not an adverb (*badly*).

26. **(E)** All underlined parts are correct.

27. **(B)** The pronoun *he* has an indefinite antecedent. We cannot tell whether *he* refers to the Governor or the attorney. Accordingly, we must be specific by using either *the Governor* or *the attorney*.

28. **(E)** All underlined parts are correct.

29. **(C)** "…there *was* scarcely enough food…" The word *scarcely* is considered a negative. Using *scarcely* with the word *not* (a double negative) is to be avoided.

30. **(E)** All underlined parts are correct.

31. **(A)** "…to borrow a book *from*…" One borrows *from* someone. The phrase *off of* is always incorrect.

32. **(A)** "Neither the school board members *nor* the city council…" Correlative conjunctions are always used in pairs. The correlative conjunction pair is *neither…nor*—not *neither…or*.

33. **(C)** We must preserve sequence of tenses. When two different parts of a sentence refer to the same period of time, the same tense must be used in each case. In this sentence, when the neighbor *was* (past tense) a teenager, he *rescued* (past tense) a swimmer.

34. **(C)** "…our father told my brother and *me*…" The indirect object of a clause or sentence must be in the objective case and, accordingly, must take the objective form (*me*—not *I* ).

35. **(C)** The word *Moreover* is misused in the sentence as it stands; it means "besides." Thus Choice A is incorrect. Choice B is wrong since far from showing contrast to sentence 3, sentence 4 gives a specific example to show what the previous sentence means. Therefore, Choice C is correct: It is the only suggestion that shows an example is coming up. Choice D is wrong since *In short* implies that a summary statement is to follow (nor is sentence 4 particularly brief!). Although it is the second best answer, Choice E is inappropriate since it suggests that there is doubt about sentence 4. The writer has stated sentence 3 as a fact (having qualified it with the word *often*); therefore, sentence 4 should be stated more definitely. Note too that sentence 4 is already qualified by the word *perhaps;* beginning the sentence *Some people believe* would water down the example to the point that it means almost nothing.

36. **(D)** Since sentence 8 has nothing to do with what has been said in sentence 7, it should not be joined to this sentence with either a semicolon or *and*. Therefore Choices A and B are both incorrect. Choice C is wrong as well, since if the sentence began with *Although,* it would be a fragment. Choice D is correct: *Yet* is a transitional word that sets up the contrast with sentence 7, but, unlike *Although,* leaves it a complete sentence. Choice E is incorrect—if the sentence were moved, sentence 9 would be a complete non-sequitur after sentence 7. Nor would the transition *The reason is* in sentence 10 follow logically after sentence 8.

37. **(E)** Although Choices A, B, C, and D would all make good introductory sentences for a general passage on dreams, Choice E is the only one that applies directly to this particular passage. Note how "New research indicates" leads smoothly into the beginning of the next sentence: "We know that…" The intention of the entire passage is to show us that dreams "play an important part in all of our lives." Choice C is probably the next best choice, but it would apply only to sentences 3 and 4.

38. **(A)** Since we are concerned with timing, that is, adults at a certain time are given drugs, we use the word, <u>When</u>. None of the other choices serve what the author is trying to get across.

39. **(E)** Sentence 11 further explains and clarifies the previous sentence and should therefore be in parentheses. None of the other choices describe anything that would be useful or better clarify the passage.

# What You Must Do Now to Raise Your PSAT Score

1. Follow the directions on pages 493–495 to determine your scaled score for the PSAT Test you've just taken. These results will give you a good idea about whether or not you ought to study hard in order to achieve a certain score on the actual PSAT.

2. Eliminate your weaknesses in each of the PSAT test areas by taking the following Giant Steps toward PSAT success:

## Critical Reading Part

### Giant Step 1

Take advantage of the Critical Reading Strategies that begin on page 80. Read again the Explanatory Answer for each of the Critical Reading questions that you got wrong. Refer to the Critical Reading Strategy that applies to each of your incorrect answers. Learn each of these Critical Reading Strategies thoroughly. These strategies are crucial if you want to raise your PSAT score substantially.

### Giant Step 2

You can improve your vocabulary by doing the following:

1) Learn the Hot Prefixes and Roots beginning on page 108.

2) Learn the 3 Vocabulary Strategies beginning on page 105.

3) Read as widely as possible—not only novels. Nonfiction is important too...and don't forget to read newspapers and magazines.

4) Listen to people who speak well. Tune in to worthwhile TV programs also.

5) Use the dictionary frequently and extensively—at home, on the bus, at work, etc.

6) Play word games—for example, crossword puzzles, anagrams, and Scrabble. Another game is to compose your own Sentence Completion questions. Try them on your friends.

## Math Part

### Giant Step 3

Make good use of the Math Strategies that begin on page 51. Read again the solutions for each Math question that you answered incorrectly. Refer to the Math Strategy that applies to each of your incorrect answers. Learn each of these Math Strategies thoroughly. We repeat that these strategies are crucial if you want to raise your PSAT Math score substantially.

### Giant Step 4

You may want to take **The 101 Most Important Math Questions You Need to Know How to Solve** test on page 13 and follow the directions after the test for a basic math skills diagnosis.

For each Math question that you got wrong in the test, note the reference to the Math Refresher section on page 129. This reference will explain clearly the mathematical principle involved in the solution of the question you answered incorrectly. Learn that particular mathematical principle thoroughly.

## For Both the Math and Critical Reading Parts

### Giant Step 5

You may want to take the **National Merit Scholarship Diagnostic Test** on page 1 to assess whether you're using the best strategies for the questions.

## For the Writing Part

### Giant Step 6

Take a look at Part 6—The PSAT Writing Skills Test, which describes the various item types in the Writing Section and includes sample questions with answers and explanations. Also make use of Part 7—A Brief Review of English Grammar.

If you do the job *right* and follow the steps listed above, you are likely to raise your PSAT score on each of the Critical Reading, Math, and Writing parts of the test 15 points—maybe 20 points—and even more.

I am the master of my fate;
I am the captain of my soul.

—From the poem "Invictus"
    by William Ernest Henley

# Notes

# Master the nation's most-feared test with the complete line of Gruber SAT books

978-1-4022-1846-0            978-1-4022-1847-7            978-1-4022-1848-4

$14.99 U.S./$15.99 CAN/£7.99 UK    $14.99 U.S./$15.99 CAN/£7.99 UK    $14.99 U.S./$15.99 CAN/£7.99 UK

## In-depth practice with the brand you trust

Are your practice test scores lopsided one way or another? Succeed across the test with the Gruber workbook series!

The name you trust in SAT prep focuses his unique test-taking strategies on each section of the SAT individually:

*Gruber's Complete SAT Math Workbook*
*Gruber's Complete SAT Reading Workbook*
*Gruber's Complete SAT Writing Workbook*

978-1-4022-1442-4

$16.95 U.S./$18.99 CAN/£9.99 UK

## Set your sights on a perfect score

If you're a top student aiming to achieve the perfect SAT score, here are the inside tips and exclusive strategies you'll need to beat the toughest questions and get into the best college! *Gruber's SAT 2400* will teach you how to think critically about what is being tested. Solve any math question in a minute or less, and learn how to locate answers in the critical readings based on how the questions are phrased. Save time, eliminate frustration, and earn your best score with Dr. Gruber's proven methods.

Sourcebooks brings you the complete line of Gruber test-taking books,
available at your local bookseller or online.
Visit www.sourcebookscollege.com for more information.